# TRIUMPH

# TRIUMPH

The Power and the Glory
of the Catholic Church—
A 2,000-Year History

H. W. CROCKER III

FORUM

*An Imprint of Prima Publishing*

Published by Prima Publishing, Roseville, California.
Member of the Crown Publishing Group, a division of Random House, Inc.

PRIMA PUBLISHING, FORUM, and colophons are trademarks of Random
House, Inc., registered with the United States Patent and Trademark Office.

**Library of Congress Cataloging-in-Publication Data**
Crocker, H. W.
Triumph : the power and the glory of the Catholic Church—
a 2,000-year history / H. W. Crocker III
p.    cm.
Includes bibliographical references and index.
ISBN 0-7615-2924-1
1. Catholic Church—History.  I. Title.
BX945.3 .C76 2001
282'.09—dc21                    2001038270

02  03  04  05  HH  10  9  8  7  6  5  4
Printed in the United States of America

First Edition

Visit us online at www.primapublishing.com

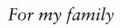

*For my family*

The principles are settled. Life is the pageant of men and women living up to them or failing to live up to them—and I think that to-day, if we are to save ourselves, we need to close our minds, to take honour's worth for granted and to escape back into certainty from the atmosphere of eternal questioning.

—CHRISTOPHER HOLLIS, *Death of a Gentleman*

# CONTENTS

# TRIUMPH

# IN HOC SIGNO VINCES

## A.D. 312

Perhaps the legions had grown overconfident.

Their Augustus, the swift-moving Constantine, had led them over the Alps and, as he had done against the Picts, the Franks, and other enemies of the empire, now led them to victory after victory in a civil war—civil war being practically a tradition these days—rolling up armies loyal to Maxentius, the young, decadent usurper in Rome.

Maxentius had risen to power by promising to keep Rome free of taxes and had kept power by seeing off the mightiest of armies—whether led by Caesar Severus or by the emperors Galerius and Domitius Alexander. He had even faced down his own father, the former emperor Maximian, and the greatest of recent emperors, Diocletian, who had divided the responsibilities of the empire, only to have Maxentius seize its capital city.

Yet now, on a path parallel to the River Po, Constantine's legions had thrown back Maxentius's armies again and again, smashing his shock troops, the heavily armored cavalry known as the *katafraktoi*. Constantine had a plan to neutralize them. His infantry trapped them in a pocket of legionnaires, where the horses could neither maneuver nor charge; then the foot soldiers, holding four-foot-high shields close to their helmets, slashed at the horses' unprotected fetlocks. The steel-encased cavalrymen were hurled to the ground, where Constantine's men butchered them.

But while he conquered, Constantine was forgiving to the civilians who lay in his path. Word of his generosity spread. Now, after a march down the Adriatic coast, he had camped at the gates of Rome, a short siege away from restoring the ancient seat of imperial grandeur to the Western Empire, *his* Western Empire.

Behind Rome's walls, an indifferent Maxentius awaited the defeat of yet another challenger. Protected by his Praetorian Guard, he serenely pursued his pastimes of drinking and sleeping with other men's wives, knowing (had not the auguries foretold it?) that Constantine was marching to his doom. The very words of the omen in the Sibylline books had stated it clearly: "Tomorrow the enemy of Rome will perish."

Maxentius was making sure of it. At the Circus Maximus, the people had publicly mocked him with jeers of "Are you a coward?" for relying on the strength of Rome's defenses and not taking the field against Constantine. While Maxentius was popular with the common people, he was resented by many of the aristocracy. They hated his demands for bribes, his importuning of their wives for his private sport. Some remembered the martyrdom of Sophronia, who had killed herself rather than obey Maxentius's summons to leave her husband's bed for his own.

The time would come when, with the marriage of soldiering and the Catholic Church, chivalry would be born and, in Edmund Burke's phrase, "ten thousand swords must have leaped from their scabbards to avenge even a look that threatened" a woman "with insult."[1]

But that time had not yet arrived. And if Constantine was the rescuer of Sophronia's metaphorical sisters, it was not for their sake that he acted, but for Rome's and his own.

Maxentius, stung by the mob's call of cowardice, decided to end Constantine's impertinence now. Early on the morning of October 28, A.D. 312, Rufius Volusanius, prefect of Maxentius's Praetorian Guard, led his crack troops across the river Tiber in a surprise attack on Constantine's encamped forces.

Constantine's men were sleeping when the Praetorians burst upon them, piercing their unprotected bellies with swords or *pilums*—six-foot lances tipped by eighteen inches of steel. While Constantine's vanguard struggled to protect itself, the legionnaires farther back hurriedly donned their breastplates and helmets, grabbed their arms, and ran to rescue their comrades. Constantine, to the shock of his own officers, swung aboard his horse and rode at the enemy, plunging into the blood-spattering scrimmage just as he had done in Verona. Too much was at stake—it was death or glory.

And there was something more. Constantine meant to deny fate—the fate prophesied by the Sibylline books, a prophecy that had been broadcast to his men by Maxentius's agents.

Constantine had a new symbol, a prophecy of his own. At Verona, he had called upon *Sol Invictus,* the invincible sun god. But here, before the gates of Rome, he had a dream, a vision that he would conquer under the sign of the cross—the cross of Christianity, an unpopular and persecuted minority religion.[2] Constantine himself had, as of yet, no belief in Christianity, but his mother and stepmother were Christians. His late father, Constantius, Augustus of the West, had been lax when ordered to persecute the sect. And earlier in his own career, as a young officer serving the emperor Diocletian, Constantine had seen Christians go to their death rather than accept other gods. Perhaps too he was encouraged in interpreting his dream by his stepmother's confessor Osius, the Catholic bishop of Cordova, who was traveling with him, an unofficial chaplain on the campaign.

As Constantine's men sprang to battle, it was with the Christian symbol marked on their shields in charcoal. Constantine and his officers also drew the cross on their helmets. With sanctified bucklers they parried blows; with swords they plunged at the enemy. The Praetorians were outnumbered, and the advantage they had gained by surprise was collapsing under Constantine's counterattack. Archers pummeled the Praetorians with arrows; cavalry crashed against their infantry. Constantine saw what needed to be done: Drive the Praetorians to the river at their backs, leaving them no escape save a jammed, panic-stricken flight across the Milvian Bridge—a bridge that he could turn into a slaughter pen.

Crossing the bridge on horseback was Maxentius, who was expecting the acclamation of his victorious soldiers; instead he saw their imminent collapse. He ordered their recall: in the open field they might be destroyed; behind Rome's walls they would be impregnable. But Praetorian discipline had snapped; the retreat was a mass stampede of fear-frenzied men, razor-sharp swords thrusting at their backs, cavalry horses pounding after them, arrows slashing down in unpredictable, deadly flurries. They turned as a mob against their own officers, who tried in vain to stop them. In their blood-pounding ears was the roar of Constantine's legions, roused as the Augustus of the West reared his horse and waved his bloody sword at the enemy.

Maxentius, trying to rally his men at the Milvian Bridge, was hurled into the rushing river as the brutal, blood-panicked mob tackled his horse. Shaken by the impact of his fall, and weighted by his heavy armor, he was swept helplessly along by the swift current. The emperor's lungs were punished by blow after blow of suffocating water until he sank to the weeds at river's bottom, eventually resurfacing, only to have his head severed by a soldier of the new emperor.

As Constantine rode victorious into the city, Maxentius's head, raised on spear point, followed him—a trophy for the conqueror, a warning to rivals, a target for the spit of the Roman mob, and something more than all this. For Constantine gave no thanks to the Roman gods. If Maxentius was their champion, here was his head.

Triumphant Constantine, Augustus Maximus of the empire, was about to inaugurate a revolution in the history of the world. Shortly after his victory, Constantine and his fellow Augustus, Licinius, met in Milan to discuss imperial problems. Constantine's priority was a guarantee of religious freedom, which became known as the Edict of Milan. It is the first legal affirmation of religious liberty, issued more than 1,400 years before a similar idea would be promulgated in America. But what is equally interesting about the Edict of Milan is that it mentions only one specific religion—Christianity—and mentions it repeatedly. Eusebius, who knew Constantine, reproduces the imperial edicts in his *The History of the Church*: "Christians and non-Christians alike should be allowed to keep the faith of their own religious beliefs and worship. . . . Christians and all others [should have] liberty. . . . [N]o one whatever was to be denied the right to follow and choose the Christian observance or form of worship. . . . [E]very individual still desirous of observing the Christian form of worship should without interference be allowed to do so. . . . [W]e have given the said Christians free and absolute permission to practice their own form of worship." In a follow-up document, the Augusti are more specific still: "Accordingly it is our wish that when you receive this letter you will see to it that any of the former property of the Catholic Church of the Christians . . . shall be restored forthwith."[3]

The Edict of Milan, issued by two professing pagans, was the first royal proclamation in a series that would establish Catholic Christianity as the religion of empire, an empire of which it remains the living embodiment, from a beginning that stretches before all time.

## CHAPTER ONE

# FONS ET ORIGO

————⟶⊷●⊷⟵————

P OMPEY'S SWORD WAS DRAWN as he entered the Holy of Holies. The great Roman general had already rid the Mediterranean of pirates; smashed the massive slave uprising of Spartacus (the consul Crassus assisted by crucifying 6,000 slave-rebels along the Via Appia); sent Mithradates VI of Asia Minor, Rome's great enemy to the east, fleeing behind the Crimea; and absorbed Syria. His latest conquest, Judea, seemed the least of his achievements. He had come to settle a dynastic dispute, and ended it by slaughtering 12,000 Jews and capturing their holy city of Jerusalem. Now, in the spirit of the adventurer Ulysses, he brushed aside the keepers of the sacred temple to see for himself where these people—so uniquely stubborn in their monotheistic religion—kept their earthly sanctuary of God. Tossing back the curtain and going where for any Gentile to go meant death, the general was dumbfounded. The room was bare. No grand statue, for graven images were forbidden. No ark of the covenant, for it had gone missing more than five hundred years before. No window for the sun. Nothing.

This was the house of God?

The Jews baffled Pompey, just as they had baffled previous conquerors. The books of the Maccabees—included in Catholic Bibles, which is one of their advantages—introduce Alexander the Great into the Old Testament. "Alexander son of Philip, the Macedonian . . . had smitten

7

Darius king of the Persians and the Medes . . . reigned in his stead, the
first over Greece, and made many wars, and won many strongholds, and
slew the kings of the earth . . . and took spoils of many nations."[1] The
Jews were among the conquered, and were submerged in Hellenism for
roughly two centuries before they rebelled. That rebellion is less important for our story than is recognizing that Judea, home of a religion of un-
traceable antiquity, bore the imprint of the two greatest civilizations of
the classical age: Greece and Rome.[2]

The Roman conqueror Pompey, with the blood stench of battle
behind him, greeted the Jews as a tribune of the *Pax Romana* and magnanimously allowed the ruling Hasmonean dynasty to remain. The Has-
moneans returned Pompey's trust by supporting his rival, Julius Caesar, in
the Roman civil war, and the grateful Caesar gave the Jews a protected
status within the empire. That status ended, however, in the subsequent
reign of Augustus, when Syria's Roman governor Publius Quintilius
Varus invaded Judea, putting down a nationalist uprising against the pro-
Roman Jewish ruling class. He laid waste to nationalist strongholds, executed 2,000 reported traitors, sold 30,000 rebellious Jews into slavery,
and annexed Judea as a province under a Roman governor, or procurator.
In the year A.D. 26—though it was not yet called that—a new procurator
was appointed. His name was Pontius Pilate.

At roughly the same time, a holy man named John the Baptist, a
"voice of one crying in the wilderness," was calling Jews to repent, "for
the kingdom of heaven is at hand. . . . Prepare ye the way of the Lord,
make his paths straight." John gathered flocks of Jews from "Jerusalem,
and all Judea, and all the region around about Jordan," where they "were
baptized of him in Jordan, confessing their sins."[3] Among those who
came to him was a young man named Jesus, the protagonist of the
Gospels of the New Testament, and the man of whom the Baptist said: "I
have need to be baptized of thee."[4]

The Gospels need to be read rather than reproduced in miniature
here, though we will touch on a few of their salient points. As for their
authenticity, nothing in serious Biblical scholarship has changed the commonsensical view of one Church historian of sixty years ago: "the New
Testament writings are what they propose themselves to be—authentic
records of trustworthy contemporary witnesses."[5]

# THE LAMB OF GOD

LITTLE IS KNOWN of Jesus' early years. But we do know from two of the Gospels—though they offer different genealogies—that Jesus is of the line of David, the royal house of Israel; or more accurately that Jesus' *foster father* and guardian, Joseph, was of the blood royal. Both Gospels proclaim Jesus as conceived of the "Holy Spirit" and the Virgin Mary, giving Him divine paternity within a family bosom of *nouveaux pauvres* blue bloods, who taught Him a trade, carpentry, and no doubt provided a proper Jewish home, instructing Him in the ways of religion, with Joseph, as a frayed aristocrat, perhaps also inculcating a sense of noblesse oblige.

In the year A.D. 31 or 32, Jesus began His mission, preaching, like John the Baptist, a message of repentance, forgiveness of sins, and the coming of the kingdom of God and attaching to Himself the men known as the Apostles to serve as His especial lieutenants. But it wasn't only Jesus' teaching that attracted followers to Him and that inspired the Apostles to abandon their lives in His service. Jesus worked miracles, healing the sick, turning water into wine, walking on the sea, commanding storms to be stilled, feeding the many with a few loaves and fishes. He was so well known for His miracles that, outside the Gospels, the prime Jewish historian of the period, Josephus, noted Him as a performer of "astonishing feats."[6]

For those with ears to hear, there were perhaps even more astonishing claims being made. For though Jesus preached a gospel of humility and forgiveness, He saw himself as one set apart. Throughout the Gospel of John, Jesus is depicted as the "light of the world"[7] and as "the way, the truth, and the life: no man shall come unto the Father, but by me."[8] When He "cleanses" the temple with His scourge of cords, it is to drive the moneychangers from "my Father's house."[9] He leaves His listeners "astonished at his doctrine: For he taught as one having authority, and not as the scribes."[10]

Jesus is a new lawgiver, a new Moses, but He claims an authority even greater than that of Moses and sets a standard that goes beyond Mosaic Law. Jesus proclaims, "Think not that I am come to destroy the law or the prophets. I am not come to destroy, but to fulfill."[11] He intensifies the strictures against divorce, adultery, swearing, and hate. He

chides the people to love their enemies, to avoid judging others, to pray
and give alms secretly rather than boastfully, and to exceed the scribes
and Pharisees in righteousness. He warns that it is impossible to "serve
God and mammon"[12] and cautions that "narrow is the way, which lead-
eth unto life, and few there be that find it."[13] His litany is as stunning—
and arresting—today as it was two thousand years ago.

The Gospels show Jesus doing things that no ordinary Jew would do.
He forgives sins—which the Jewish officials view as blasphemy, for only
God can forgive sins. He consorts with sinners, yet claims to be pure. He
breaks the Sabbath, saying, "For the Son of man is Lord even of the sabbath day."[14] He is not averse to the good things of life, drinking wine, ignoring the Jewish fasts when it suits Him, and rebuking His disciples for
their prudery. When a woman pours expensive ointment on Him, some of
the Apostles protest that the ointment should have been sold and the
money given to the poor, but Jesus says, "Let her alone; why trouble ye
her? . . . For ye have the poor with you always. . . . But me you have not
always. She hath done what she could. She has come aforehand to anoint
my body to the burying."[15] In both Matthew and Mark, it is immediately
after this incident that Judas betrays Jesus, as though he is scandalized by
what he has seen—thus establishing a continuing current of Christian history, the holier than thou apostate.

But Jesus knew that He would be betrayed, and the story of the
woman anointing Jesus is not the only time that He predicts His own
death. There is the drama of the last supper: "Verily I say unto you, I will
drink no more of the fruit of the vine, until that day that I drink it new in
the kingdom of God."[16] There is the parable of the wicked tenants that
foreshadows Jesus' death, sets forth His place in Jewish history, and, in
Matthew's rendition, foresees the coming break between Judaism and
Christianity.[17]

Judea was rife with expectations of the coming of the Messiah, but
the Messiah was, among other things, to be the *political* savior of Israel.
Jesus repudiated any interest in politics. Beyond his famous dictum "Render unto Caesar the things which are Caesar's; and unto God the things
that are God's,"[18] Jesus accepts the political and economic arrangements
of Roman Judea. He has no concern with changing the world; He looks
to change the hearts of individual men, starting with the lost sheep of

Israel. From His parables, it appears that He accepts private property and the right of a businessman to dispense wealth as he sees fit; though to be perfect, a man should give up all his wealth and serve God. He praises the faithful servant (or slave), and does not condemn slavery as ungodly, or service to a master as demeaning. On the contrary, He praises faithful service as ennobling, and Jesus himself washes His disciples' feet, a ceremony reenacted by Catholic priests on Maundy Thursday. Serving others is God's highest calling—especially helping the poor and the sick, for when one aids the least of men, one does the work of God. As Jesus says, "I am among you as he that serveth."[19] By word and deed, Jesus' ideal seems that of St. Francis of Assisi, who was often called *alter Christus:* celibate, totally devoting oneself to God, helping the unfortunate, living communally from charity.

When Jesus enters Jerusalem, it is not triumphantly on a white charger—and not on foot, the traditional sign of respect for the Holy City—but on an ass, in fulfillment of a prophecy more than five centuries old, from the Jewish prophet Zechariah, "Rejoice greatly, O daughter of Zion; shout, O daughter of Jerusalem: behold, thy King cometh unto thee: he is just, and having salvation; lowly and riding upon an ass . . . and his dominion shall be from sea even to sea, and from the river even to the ends of the earth."[20] But His reign is of a heavenly kingdom, not of an imperial court, a Roman senate, or a Jewish Sanhedrin. When Peter leaps, sword in hand, to Jesus' protection, slashing the ear of a slave sent to arrest Jesus, Jesus rebukes his leading disciple. Jesus has come not to lead an armed revolt, or to resist the principalities and powers, but to fulfill a God-sent mission. He has come to shed His blood for the sins of the world, to make God man in order to share in human suffering, and to offer redemption through His sacramental Church led by the Apostles, of whom Peter, the fisherman and impetuous sword-wielder, is to be the head. "Thou art Peter, and upon this rock I will build my church; and the gates of hell shall not prevail against it. And I will give unto thee the keys of the kingdom of heaven; and whatsoever thou shalt bind on earth shall be bound in heaven: and whatsoever thou shalt loose on earth shall be loosed in heaven."[21] With that proclamation of Jesus, the Catholic Church properly takes shape and begins.

# THE HISTORICAL TRUTH
# OF CHRISTIANITY

THE NEW TESTAMENT writings, however, are not the foundation of the Church, or even, in a manner of speaking, its operating manual. The Church *precedes* them. The New Testament consists of teaching tools about Jesus (the Gospels), a history (The Acts of the Apostles), letters of correction and instruction (such as Paul's epistles), and what some consider a symbolic condemnation of the Roman emperor Nero (Revelation), under whose persecution St. Peter and St. Paul were martyred. The New Testament was assembled to serve a Church already functioning and growing. Papias, the bishop of Hierapolis in the early second century, records that "Matthew compiled the *Sayings* in the Aramaic language, and everyone translated them as well as he could."[22]

The original gospel tradition was oral, though it is probable that some believers owned small chapbooks. At the earliest, the first written gospels date two decades after the death of Jesus. They had the dual challenge of capturing an oral tradition and accurately translating it from Aramaic or Hebrew to Greek, which is the language of the earliest gospels we have. There was also the difficulty of establishing the *canon*. The Gospels according to Mark, Matthew, Luke, and John were not the only sayings of Jesus circulating among believers. There were numerous apocryphal books—some merely fictionalized devotional literature, some outright forgeries, others representing contesting views.

The authority that sorted through this tangle was the Church, and while the New Testament it endorsed is apparently imperfect—with gospel accounts differing on points of detail and incident—it is nevertheless invaluable. By any objective standard it is also reliable *history*—that is, an account of actual fact. This is the summary judgment of the popular classical historian Michael Grant, who concludes in his own "historian's view of the gospels" that "the picture they present is largely authentic." It is a view widely shared.[23]

But the greatest historical "proof" of Christianity is found not in the Codex Vaticanus or the Codex Sinaiticus, the two oldest surviving, nearly complete Bibles, which approximate our own in content, dating from the mid-fourth century. The greatest proof of Christianity is the very fact of its existence. One can strain the New Testament through a colander of modern textual analysis, criticism, and subjective interpretation and be left, in the words of Paul Johnson, "with a phenomenon almost devoid of significance. This 'residual' Jesus told stories, uttered various wise sayings, was executed in circumstances which are not clear, and was then commemorated in a ceremony by his followers." But this won't do, as Johnson explains lapidarily:

> Such a version is incredible because it does not explain Christianity. And in order to explain Christianity we have to postulate an extraordinary Christ who did extraordinary things. . . . Men and women began frantically and frenetically to preach Jesus's gospel because they believed he had come back to them from the dead and given them authority and the power to do so. Naturally, their evangelical efforts were imperfect, for, despite Jesus's instructions, they could not always remember his teachings accurately or coherently and they were not trained divines, or orators, or indeed educated people. But, even more important, the teaching he had given them was itself difficult both to understand and convey. Both these factors left their mark on the gospels and explain their imperfections, for the gospels were a transcribed version of what the first and second generation of Christians believed and taught.[24]

Indeed, Jesus did not write a book. He taught the Apostles, infused them with the Holy Spirit, and told them to make converts of the world. His divine authority was given to men, not to a collated New Testament, and the message His disciples preached was startling.

Certainly, there have been other great religious movements in the world—but Christianity is unique in its historical claims. In no other religion has there been a man who claimed to be God, who rose from the dead and was witnessed and touched by others—these others then risking death to go forth as his missionaries. The Eastern mystery cults of the time were just that—mysteries. And no one claimed to have seen the gods that made up the theogonies of the Egyptians, Greeks, Romans, and Hindus—or, for that matter, of the Aztecs, Incas, or any other peoples. Buddha and, later, Mohammed were known, but Buddha and Mohammed never claimed to be divine or to rise from the dead. The God of the Old Testament spoke to such prophets as Abraham and Moses, but it is only in the New Testament that we have groups of individual men and women testifying to have seen, supped with, and been inspired by a risen God. This remarkable claim is not easily dismissed, nor has it been in two thousand years of history.

If we are to understand it, perhaps the best entrée is through a man like us—a man not chosen by Jesus during His lifetime, but a man who comes across the early Church as a fact, even a noisome fact, and yet becomes its greatest convert.

## PAUL, THE MISSIONARY SAINT

PAUL WAS A CHRISTIAN-HUNTER, a strict Jew, a Pharisee out to exterminate the early followers of Jesus, just as witch-finder generals would later flush out suspected witches for rough justice. "Many of the saints did I shut up in prison," says Paul, "having received authority from the chief priests; and when they were put to death, I gave my voice against them. And I punished them oft in every synagogue, and compelled them to blaspheme; and being exceedingly mad against them, I persecuted them even unto strange cities."[25]

It was on the road to Damascus, carrying "authority and commission from the chief priests" to continue his work of snuffing out the Jesus sect, that Paul suddenly "saw in the way of light from heaven, above the brightness of the sun, shining round about me and them which journeyed with me. And when we were all fallen to the earth, I heard a voice speaking unto me, and saying in the Hebrew tongue, 'Saul, Saul, why persecutest thou me? . . .' And then I said, 'Who art thou, Lord?' And he said, 'I am Jesus who thou persecutest.'"[26]

Jesus called Paul to "rise and stand upon thy feet: for I have appeared unto thee for this purpose, to make thee a minister and a witness both of these things which thou hast seen, and of those things in the which I will appear unto thee; delivering thee from the people, and from the Gentiles, unto whom now I send thee, to open their eyes, and to turn them from darkness to light, and from the power of Satan unto God, that they may have forgiveness of sins, and inheritance among them which are sanctified by faith that is in me."[27]

The story of Paul's conversion is so fantastic that it would be easy to dismiss save for this: According to the Book of Acts, Paul was present at the stoning, by a mob, of St. Stephen, the first Christian martyr.[28] He knew the penalty—indeed by his own confession he had often enforced it—for professing faith in Jesus. Yet it was in the effort of spreading such faith that Paul—the educated, comfortable, middle-class, Jewish Pharisee—devoted his life, becoming the "envoy extraordinary" of Christ. In that cause, he endured hardship, imprisonment, and martyrdom and fought, even amongst the other Apostles, for the validity of *his* vision, what *he* had seen, and the commission that Jesus had given *him*. For "these causes," Paul says, "the Jews caught me in the temple, and went about to kill me."[29] But they did not succeed—yet.

Thus Paul began the greatest early adventure of the Church, spreading the gospel to Cyprus, Asia Minor, and the Aegean, with plans to go to Spain and even distant Britain. His evangelical path was not an easy one. Though he generally began his missionary work in synagogues—or perhaps because of it—Paul recorded that

> Of the Jews five times I received forty stripes save one. Thrice I have been beaten with rods, once I was stoned, thrice I suffered shipwreck, and night and day I have been in the deep; in journeying often, in perils of waters, in perils of robbers, in perils of mine own countrymen, in perils of heathen, in perils in the city, in perils in the wilderness, in perils in the sea, in perils among false brethren; in weariness and painfulness, in watchings often, in hunger and thirst, in fastings often, in cold and nakedness. . . . In Damascus the governor . . . kept the city of the Damscenes with a garrison, desirous to apprehend me: And through a window in a basket I was let down by the wall and escaped his hands.[30]

It is surely hard for most readers of the New Testament to identify with Jesus' Twelve Apostles. Not only does the imagination stagger at such conceit, but we know so little about them. Only a few emerge as individuals, and even they are incomplete sketches—Thomas the doubter, Judas the betrayer, Peter the chief Apostle. We know more about Paul. He is the focal point of the Book of Acts. After the Gospels, his letters dominate the New Testament.

As is true with Peter and Jesus, we have no contemporary account of what Paul looked like, but his letters present us with a recognizable human personality—passionate, resolute, intellectually limber. In his mission to seek converts, Paul can sound like an early Jesuit. He tells us "though I be free from all men, yet have I made myself servant unto all, that I might gain the more. And unto the Jews I became as Jew, that I might gain the Jews. . . . To them that are without law, as without law . . . that I might gain them that are without the law. . . . Even as I please all men in all things, not seeking mine own profit, but the profit of many, that they may be saved."[31] Paul did not dilute his message—it was too powerful and important for that—but he spoke as a Greek to the Greeks, as a Jew to the Jews, and became the first theologian of the Church.

None of Paul's letters is a definitive statement of the faith, for none of them was written for that purpose. Instead, Paul's letters are the work of an itinerant doctor of the Church, traveling the Eastern half of the Roman empire, prescribing cures for the numerous controversies that were already causing confusion, discord, and fallings away among gatherings of converts.

There were two main strands to Paul's thought, and with them he would weave a tapestry of faith that would eventually focus the mind and capture the imagination of the Roman world. The first was that salvation was available to anyone—Jew or Gentile—who had faith in God's Son or who did His works. God had been born among the Jews, and to the Jews He had a special calling, but even Gentiles who never learned of Jesus could be saved through good works. As Paul says in his Epistle to the Romans, "For not the hearers of the law are just before God, but the doers of the law shall be justified. For when the Gentiles, which have not the law, do by nature the things contained in the law, these, having not the law, are a law unto themselves, which shew the work of the law written in their hearts, their conscience also bearing witness."[32]

The second was that the Jewish law, which Paul had so zealously upheld as a Pharisee, was no longer binding. Paul had kept the law and it had led him not to righteousness, but to persecuting the followers of Christ. So the law was not enough; the law could even blind one to the truth, and no law could rightly stand between man and the new covenant of Jesus. Indeed, *nothing* could separate the faithful from God. "Who shall separate us from the love of Christ?" Paul asked. "Shall tribulation, or distress, or persecution, or famine, or nakedness, or peril, or sword? . . . Nay, in all these things we are more than conquerors through him that loved us. For I am persuaded that neither death, nor life, nor angels, nor principalities, nor powers, nor things present, nor things to come, nor height, nor depth, nor any other creature, shall be able to separate us from the love of God, which is in Christ Jesus our Lord."[33]

These are brave, striking, inspiring words—and from a Pharisee, they were shocking words. But it was with words such as these that Paul confronted the apostle Peter and the head of the church in Jerusalem, James, and freed the Gentiles from the Jewish law on circumcision and from every other impediment to their full communion with the Church of Jesus. "For it seemed good to the Holy Ghost, and to us, to lay upon you no greater burden than these necessary things: That ye abstain from meats offered to idols, and from blood, and from things strangled, and from fornication; from which if ye keep yourselves, ye shall do well."[34]

But in doing this Paul was not bringing the moral standards of the Church into line with the moral standards of the pagan world, in which homosexuality, fornication, adultery, fertility fetishes, erotic images, and prostitution were commonplace. The traditional stoic virtues of Rome— the centrality of family, duty, hearthside piety, and household gods—were collapsing like an undermined cliff to popular ideas of self-fulfillment, circus entertainments, and the ways of the libertine.

Paul was loyal to the singular moral vision of the Jews, and of Jesus. Like Jesus, he believed in celibacy. "It is good for a man not to touch a woman," he said. If not all could manage this perfect imitation of Christ, then "to avoid fornication, let every man have his own wife, and let every woman have her own husband." He emphasized, however, that this was a concession to human weakness, not the standard of Christian perfection. "I speak this by permission, and not of commandment. For I would that all men were given as myself"—that is, completely devoted to God, setting the disciplinary standard that would eventually be adopted by the Catholic priesthood. As Paul wrote to the Corinthians, "I would have you without carefulness. He that is unmarried careth for the things that belong to the Lord, how he may please the Lord: But he that is married careth for the things that are of the world, how he may please his wife."[35]

Despite the prominence of women among the converts to Christianity—and despite the role that priestesses played in pagan religion—Paul no more raised the status of women than did Jesus who chose twelve male Apostles. On the contrary, Paul's message was one of submission. He told the Corinthians, "Let your women keep silence in the churches: for it is not permitted unto them to speak; but they are commanded to be under obedience. . . . And if they will learn any thing, let them ask their husbands at home: for it is a shame for women to speak in the church."[36]

Paul shared with the Jews, and with the early Church, a fear of women's erotic power, a fear that could trace its roots all the way to Eden. If "a woman have long hair, it is a glory to her," Paul wrote. But because of that, it should be kept under a shawl in church. "For a man indeed ought not to cover his head, foreasmuch as he is the image and glory of God: but the woman is the glory of the man."[37]

The attractiveness of women could lead men astray. It was for this very reason that Paul could not make celibacy binding on men unless they had a special calling to Christ. But Paul warned, as Jesus did, that the entrance gates to Heaven could be narrow.

If sexual desire could be tolerated within marriage, homosexuality, rampant in the pagan world, was an abomination to Paul, as it was to every Jew. "Know ye not that the unrighteous shall not inherit the kingdom of God? Be not deceived: neither fornicators, nor idolators, nor adulterers, nor effeminate, nor abusers of themselves with mankind, nor thieves, nor covetous, nor drunkards, nor revilers, nor extortioners, shall inherit the kingdom of God."[38]

Paul's famous strictures on the flesh scandalize moderns who would rather the Church adopt modern (that is, pagan) sexual mores and modern (that is, confused) attitudes about feminist equality. But Paul's words can no more be erased than can their historic influence in shaping the Church.

But their modern notoriety can also distort our impressions of Paul and only highlight how far modern man is removed from the moral sense of Jesus and the Apostles. For however justified, however true, and however necessary to maintain the right conduct of the scattered Christian churches, Paul's call to morality is the least of his messages. It merely recapitulates what abides from the Old Testament for the new faith.

If these laws come from the mind and heart of Paul the Pharisee, there is also Paul the poet, who reminded us that "the letter killeth, but the spirit giveth life"[39] and who in a letter to the Corinthians reached deeper into the heart of the Christian message than any academic theological speculation:

Though I speak with the tongues of men and of angels, and have not charity, I am become as a sounding brass, or a tinkling cymbal. And though I have the gift of prophecy, and understand all mysteries, and all knowledge; and though I have all faith, so that I can move mountains, and have not charity, I am nothing. And though I bestow all my goods to feed the poor, and though I give my body up to be burned, and have not charity, it profiteth me nothing. Charity suffereth long, and is kind; charity envieth not; charity vaunteth not itself; it is not puffed up, doth not behave itself unseemly, seeketh not her own, is not easily provoked, thinketh no evil; rejoiceth not in iniquity, but rejoiceth in the truth; beareth all things, believeth all things, hopeth all things, endureth all things. Charity never faileth: but whether there be prophecies, they shall fail; whether there be tongues, they shall cease; whether there be knowledge, it shall vanish away. For we know in part, and we prophesy in part. But when that which is perfect is come then that which is in part shall be done away. When I was a child, I thought as a child: but when I became a man, I put away childish things. For now we see through a glass, darkly; but then face to face: now I know in part; but then shall I know even also as I am known. And now abideth faith, hope, charity, these three; but the greatest of these is charity.[40]

With faith in Christ paramount, this is Paul's transcendent message—a message that was embodied in the participation of individual, community, and God, in a visible, tangible, and sacramental Church. It was a Church that left pagans remarking about the Christian spirit of love; and it represented a new thing in the world—a thing that would be both sheltered and persecuted by edicts from Rome.

CHAPTER TWO

# UNDER THE
# ROMAN IMPERIUM

⟶⟫⟶⟩⊙⟨⟵⟵

DESPITE HIS SHIPWRECKS, lashings, and beatings, Paul did not meet with consistent hostility from either the Jews of the Diaspora or the secular authorities. In the Greek city of Corinth, Paul even converted "Crispus, the chief ruler of the synagogue," and "many Corinthians hearing believed and were baptized." Such success, however, led numerous Corinthian Jews to despise him, and Paul was brought before the Roman governor Gallio on charges of persuading men "to worship God contrary to the law." The Roman dismissed the charges, telling the Jews that "if it be a question of words and names, and of your law, look ye to it; for I will be no judge of such matters."[1]

This was not the only time Paul received protection from Roman law. Roman soldiers would later protect him from a Jewish mob. It was Roman centurions who guarded the roads of his missionary journeys. And it was, of course, a Roman centurion who first recognized the divinity of Paul's Lord at the Crucifixion. Paul was proud of his Roman citizenship, and the New Testament in which he figures so prominently is a notably pro-Roman book (with the exception of The Revelation of St. John the Divine). At the day of Pentecost, when tongues of fire descend on the Apostles, giving them knowledge of foreign languages so that they can evangelize the world, among the witnesses are "strangers of Rome."[2] One of Peter's most important conversions in the Book of Acts is of the Gentile Cornelius, a Roman centurion. Even during the trial and crucifixion of Jesus, it is not the Roman governor of Judea, Pontius Pilate, who is the villain. Pilate says, "I find no fault in this man."[3] It is the Jewish mob that repeatedly rejects Pilate's offer of clemency for Jesus, demands His crucifixion, and insists that if there be clemency, it should go to Barabbas, the thief, and not to Jesus. "Why," asks Pilate, "what evil hath he [Jesus] done? I have found no cause of death in him: I will therefore chastise him, and let *him*," not Barabbas, go.[4]

When Pilate finally succumbs to the demands of the mob, we cannot help but compare the exasperated Roman governor's sense of tolerance and justice with the deadly demands of the Jewish crowd. Like many an imperial counsel, Pilate appeases the *vox populi* in order to keep the peace among a people he no doubt regards—and as the Jews must certainly regard him—as a "lesser breed without the law."[5] Roman and Jewish ears were, of course, attuned to different laws. How much more remarkable, then, that in the Gospels, imperial Roman jurisprudence is favorably contrasted to Jewish democracy.

Paul, like Jesus, preached submission to Rome's secular authority. "Let every soul be subject unto the higher powers. For there is no power but of God: the powers that be are ordained by God. Whosoever therefore resisteth the power, resisteth the ordinance of God: and they that resist further shall receive to themselves damnation. For rulers are not a terror to good works, but to evil. Wilt thou then be afraid of the power? Do that which is good, and thou shalt have praise of the same."[6] The very fact that Paul could write this—with its implication of the divine right of kings—shows how beneficent was Roman rule. No man who feared Roman injustice could write, "rulers are not a terror to good works, but to evil." Paul, in other words, like Jesus, had no truck with Jewish nationalism, or any other political agitation, but was a loyal subject of the Roman Empire.

Neither was Paul an abolitionist of what the American South would later call "the peculiar institution." Though many Christians were slaves, Paul accepted slavery as a given. In one of his letters, Paul returns a slave to his master, Philemon, while reminding Philemon that the slave is now a brother in Christ. For Paul, slavery is not an issue, because *status* is not an issue. Slave or free, circumcised or uncircumcised, male or female, in the world to come—that is, in Heaven—these things will not matter, and our status here on earth should not bother us. "For we brought nothing into this world, and it is certain that we can carry nothing out."[7] We should seek neither riches—"for the love of money is the root of all evil"[8]—nor disputation, nor self-advancement. We should instead seek to serve and love one another. Wives should submit to their husbands, and husbands should love their wives, "even as Christ also loved the church, and gave himself for it."[9] A slave should serve his master as best he can, with "singleness of your heart. . . . Not with eye service, as men pleasers; but as servants of Christ, doing the will of God from the heart . . . knowing that whatsoever good thing any man doeth, the same shall he receive from the Lord, whether he be bond or free. And ye masters, do the same things unto them, forbearing threatening: knowing that your Master also is in heaven; neither is there respect of persons with him."[10]

Far from being a social revolutionary, or an advocate of radical individualism, Paul writes that every man should "abide in the same calling wherein he was called."[11] Paul's is the religion of the Tory party, the rich man in his castle, the workman at his plow. And the reason for this is simple—it is contentment in our earthly position that gives us peace, encourages us to love and be forbearing, and turns our thoughts from gain in this world to gain in the next.

So while to Roman ears Christianity might sound odd, conflict between Romans and Christians during the Apostolic Age was not inevitable. The real danger lay in Christian-Jewish conflict. The Jews, alone among the peoples of the empire, refused to go along with Rome's tolerant, mix-and-match paganism, and had imperial concessions to their monotheistic belief. But if the Christians stirred up the contentious Jews—as Jesus had—Rome might be compelled to intervene for the sake of the *Pax Romana*.

The theologian Tertullian asserts that the Roman emperor Tiberius, "in whose time the name of Christian came into the world," actually regarded the new religion sympathetically. Tiberius, Tertullian writes, made "it clear to them that he favoured the doctrine. The senate however, because they had not examined the doctrine for themselves, rejected it; but Tiberius stuck to his own view, and threatened to execute any who accused the Christians."[12]

With Roman tolerance, or benign neglect, in "every town and village, like a well-filled threshing floor, churches shot up bursting with eager members,"[13] a miraculous testimony to the power of the Apostles' teaching, and of the readiness of the Greek-speaking world to accept Christianity as the answer to Greek philosophical questions.

# NERO, THE MARTYR-MAKER

THE INFAMOUS ROMAN PERSECUTIONS of Christianity began only when the emperor was a lunatic, who fancied himself an artist in the Greek mold and who needed a scapegoat for a disastrous piece of performance art.

The lunatic emperor was Nero, who served as the model for the Antichrist in the Book of Revelation. The historian Suetonius described him as having "light blond" hair, a "squat" neck, a "protuberant" stomach, "spindling" legs, and a "pustular and malodorous" body.[14] But these were the least of his faults, which included perpetrating history's most famous arson. Nero had stood by while Rome was consumed by fire for seven nights—a conflagration, says Suetonius, set by Nero himself, who wanted to destroy "drab old buildings," seize property, and enjoy the spectacle of "the beauty of the flames."[15] Now the Emperor needed someone to blame for the destruction.

Nero was not particular about whom he abused. He robbed the temples of the gods and urinated on an image of the pagan goddess Atargatis. His sole religious profession was for a "statuette of a girl sent him by an anonymous commoner as a charm against conspiracies."[16]

Nero might have felt the need to be particularly careful of conspiracies because he himself was a murderer. Indeed, "nothing could restrain Nero from murdering anyone he pleased, on whatever pretext," including his mother and his aunt, and "Nero was no less cruel to strangers than to members of his family."[17] He was also a rapist and a sodomite, not to mention quite mad, even going so far as to marry a boy he had castrated specially for the occasion. Actually, he had several wives, one of whom helped him invent bizarre sexual games; another he had executed, and a fourth he kicked to death.

Given that "Nero practiced every kind of obscenity,"[18] it is no surprise that the persecution of a little-known and little-respected religion went unnoticed in Suetonius's catalogue of Nero's villainy. But what might surprise is that Paul—facing the prospect of a trial in Jerusalem on charges of violating Jewish and, more ambiguously, Roman law—appealed, as was his right as a Roman citizen, to a trial before Caesar. For Paul to appeal to Nero betrayed either an ignorance of the emperor's character or the most colossal distrust of the authorities in Jerusalem.

His journey to Rome wasn't easy. A shipwreck left him tossed on the rocks of Malta, and it was three months before he made it to the imperial capital. There, once again, he seemed a beneficiary of Roman justice. He was free to live on his own, greet friends, and travel in the city. The emperor Nero had many more pressing duties—and depravities—than hearing the case of a Jewish preacher who had run afoul of his own people, and the case was left pending for at least two years. Paul, at this point, disappears from the written record of history. The Book of Acts does not record his death, but it has generally been held that Paul, like Peter, came to Nero's attention after the great Roman fire. We know from the Roman historian Tacitus that Christians became Nero's target. Tacitus wrote that Christian-killing "was made a matter of sport: some were sewn up in the skins of wild beasts and savaged to death by dogs; others were fastened to crosses as living torches, to serve as lights when daylight failed. Nero made his gardens available for the show and held games in the Circus, mingling with the crowd or standing in his chariot in charioteer's uniform."[19]

Paul did not fear suffering or death. He knew the call of the early Church had been to martyrdom. Before his conversion he had even enforced it. He knew the fate of Jesus, St. Stephen, and the early faithful. "There were two Jameses," writes Clement of Alexandria, by way of example, "one the Righteous, who was thrown down from a parapet and beaten to death with a fuller's club, the other the James who was beheaded."[20] Now it was by the blood of Paul, Peter, and the other martyrs in Rome that the Roman Church would be sanctified as the seat of the Christian faith. By early Christian tradition, it was during Nero's persecutions that Christ's chosen Apostle, St. Peter, the bishop or leader of the Church in Rome, was crucified, at his request upside down so as not to imitate the sacrificial crucifixion of his Lord. By the same tradition, it was in Nero's Rome that St. Paul was beheaded.[21]

But Roman violence against the Christians was sporadic. The first persecutions under the emperors Nero (who was emperor from A.D. 54 to 68) and Domitian (who was emperor from A.D. 81 to 96) were fierce, yet apparently short-lived. Domitian's persecutions were directed at Jews who owed taxes to support the Jewish temples. In Roman eyes the Christians were quasi-Jews and so were immediately suspect as tax dodgers. As with Nero, however, the list of Domitian's victims seems to have spilled over to cover anyone in disfavor. According to Eusebius, "Many were the victims of Domitian's appalling cruelty. At Rome great numbers of men distinguished by birth and attainments were for no reason at all banished from the country and their property confiscated. Finally he showed himself the successor of Nero in enmity and hostility to God. He was, in fact, the second to organize persecution against us."[22]

Domitian, like Nero, was a less than stellar representative of the Roman ruling class. In the early days of his reign "Domitian would spend hours alone every day catching flies . . . and stabbing them with a needle sharp pen,"[23] which was of a piece with his preference "to depilate his concubines himself."[24] He was also, however, a reformer. Among his other innovations, "Castration was now strictly prohibited, and the price of eunuchs remaining in slave-dealers' hands officially controlled."[25] When Domitian was assassinated, "the general public greeted the news . . . with indifference," but "it deeply affected the troops, who at once began to speak of Domitian the God."[26]

Domitian shows that the Romans were fully capable of accepting that a man could become a god. Indeed, Julius Caesar and several of his immediate successors—the late emperors Augustus, Claudius, Vespasian, and Titus—had already been deified. But Domitian's life also proves that the common Roman grunt had a different idea of what made for a divine personage than did the Christians.

What was crucially important about the persecutions that began under Nero and continued under Domitian was that they established the legal precedent that Christians could be singled out for punishment solely on the basis of their belief. But persecution was still irregular. Eusebius notes, for example, that Domitian's father, the emperor (and, after his death, the deity) Vespasian, "had had no mischievous designs against us."[27]

In fact, despite the abominations of monsters like Nero and Domitian, Christians in general had less to fear from the Roman rulers than from the masses who always liked a new round of expropriation and persecution. Roman governors had one overriding passion—to keep the peace. A good example is the correspondence between the emperor Trajan, who reigned from A.D. 98 to 117, and his imperial legate Pliny, which provides, in the words of Trajan's biographer Julian Bennett, "the earliest non-Semitic evidence for the Christian Church."[28] In a case likely revolving around the refusal of Christians to swear by the name of the emperor, Trajan counseled a moderate dose of moderation—enough, in any event, for the Christians to preserve his letter and to enshrine him in the Christian imagination. According to medieval legend, Pope Gregory offered a prayer—"Forgive, O dear and almighty God, the errors of Trajan, because he always maintained right and justice."—and God immediately, if exasperatedly, answered it. Dante, in his *Divine Comedy,* likewise placed Trajan in Heaven with the Just and Temperate Rulers.[29]

Failing to swear by the emperor was, strictly speaking, treason; and for the more mystical Eastern half of the empire where emperor worship was rife (Pliny was writing from the Eastern province of Bythnia), it was also blasphemy. But Trajan told Pliny that recanting Christians were to be pardoned. In addition, as Julian Bennett summarizes, "Anonymous charges were not to be entertained, nor should Christians be specifically sought out; but if publicly charged, and if they recanted after accusation, they should be pardoned; obstinacy in the face of the law, however, was to be severely punished."[30]

The documents of the Roman world are full of the testimonies of men like Pilate and Trajan, who were trying to find an excuse not to send Christians to a martyrdom they sometimes seemed to desire. This customary Roman forbearance was acknowledged not only by the Christian legends that grew up around Trajan, but by Pilate's being made a saint (his feast day is June 25) by the Ethiopian Coptic Christians, and by the Church father Tertullian proclaiming Pilate "a Christian in his conscience."[31]

The uneasy tolerance of Rome's ruling class was, of course, no guarantee of justice. It could be punctuated by bloodshed and persecution. As historian Robin Lane Fox notes, "until 180, no governor in Africa was known to have put a Christian to death," though the governors sometimes "banished Christians instead of killing them" or "sent them to work in mines and quarries, where they served, their heads half shaven, under constant threat of the lash."[32]

Moreover, the images we have of Christians being torn to pieces by wild animals or gladiators are true. These persecutions, in fact, made martyrdom—an idea Christians had adapted from the Jews—the most profound testament of the Christian faith to the pagans in Rome. While these slaughters were organized for the entertainment of the public, there were some spectators—more thoughtful than those joyfully shouting "well washed, well washed" at the blood-soaked martyrs—whose minds were indelibly marked by Christians calmly accepting, or even seeking out, their own deaths.[33] Christianity was set apart as a religion of self-sacrifice—even of a volunteer's eagerness to experience imprisonment, torture, or death to prove, and gain a heavenly reward for, his faith.

Jesus and Paul had taught submission to lawful authority, and submission in particular to the laws of Rome. But there were limits. Christians were perfectly willing to pray *for* the Roman emperor, but never *to* the emperor. They would offer thanks to God, but not the gods. Like the Jews, Christians refused to acknowledge pagan beliefs as anything other than false and malicious. This bloody-minded stubbornness is how the Church transformed the world.

## HOW THE CATHOLIC CHURCH SAVED CHRISTIANITY

WHILE THE NEW FAITH spread with remarkable rapidity, it faced two other enormous problems. First was resolving Christianity's relationship with Judaism, which confused both the faithful and the Romans.

Had Jerusalem become the center of Christianity, the faith would be different from what we know today. The head of the church in Jerusalem was James, a cousin of Jesus.[34] James was a doubter until he saw the risen Christ. Even then he continued to beat a different path from what would become the main current of the Catholic Church. James was the leader of the Jewish-Christian faction that thought Jesus' message was only for Jews, not Gentiles, and bore at least a passing resemblance to John the Baptist, minus the water. Eusebius quotes the Jewish-Christian writer Hegesippus, who "belonged to the first generation after the apostles," as testifying that James, unlike Jesus, "drank no wine or intoxicating liquor and ate no animal food; no razor came near his head; he did not smear himself with oil, and took no baths. . . . He used to enter the Sanctuary alone, and was often found on his knees beseeching forgiveness for the people, so that his knees grew hard like a camel's from his continually bending them in worship of God and beseeching forgiveness for the people."[35]

But James was martyred, and the Jewish-Christian sect was effectively destroyed when the Romans crushed the massive Jewish revolt of mid-century. The Church historian Eusebius sees Roman vengeance and the destruction of Jerusalem in A.D. 70 as divine retribution, payment for what the Jews had done to Jesus' disciples. First the Jews, he writes, "stoned Stephen to death; then James the son of Zebedee and brother of John was beheaded; and finally James, the first after our Saviour's Ascension to be raised to the bishop's throne there [in Jerusalem], lost his life . . . while the remaining apostles, in constant danger from murderous plots, were driven out of Judea."[36] Interestingly, the Jewish historian Josephus—a contemporary and a participant of the Jewish War—agrees, though on different grounds, that Jerusalem suffered divine wrath of which the Roman legions were the mere instrument.[37]

Whether it was with divine sanction or not, Roman swords forever severed any continuing Jewish influence over the development of the Christian Church. With Jerusalem and its temple destroyed, Christianity was now, more than ever, a missionary Church to the Gentiles, traveling on Roman roads, sailing in Roman waters made peaceful by Pompey's crushing of the Mediterranean pirates, and communicating in the language of the Greeks. There was no danger that Christianity would be a hermetic religion of a single people. Instead, it was a cosmopolitan religion spreading to all the lands covered by Roman law and garrisoned by Roman soldiers.

But while Christianity was charged with becoming a universal faith, there was still the fundamental challenge of defining what the faith actually was, and then ensuring that it was everywhere the same. This last challenge had been an especial interest of St. Paul, who knew that if the faith were to survive, if its truth were to be maintained, it had to be a uniform system of belief—from the Colossians, to the Ephesians, to the Romans, and all the rest. His letters are warnings against error. They are calls to the faithful to stay true to "one Lord, one faith, one baptism."[38] And staying true to the faith would be no simple thing. Christianity was born in a world of religious ferment, and, certainly within the Roman Empire, it was born in a syncretist tradition, where mystery cults and Greco-Roman paganism freely adopted and multiplied gods.

The first heroic chapter of the Catholic Church is written in its clinging fast to the traditional teachings of the Church and the Apostles

against a multitude of innovative heresies. Had these heresies succeeded—
and some were as popular as modern Protestantism—they would have
stripped away so many believers, would have so splintered the Church,
and so muddied and variously distorted the Christian message that, save
for Jesus' proclamation to Peter that "I will build my church; and the
gates of hell shall not prevail against it,"[39] there is no historical reason to
believe that the Church would not have sunk back to the obscurity into
which, among Roman historians of the period, it was born. Christianity
would have been just another mystery religion, giving birth to many variations, none of which would necessarily have survived antiquity.

The Church's role was thus as deceptively simple as it was heroic. As
the second-century theologian St. Irenaeus wrote in his book, *Against Heresies,* "We must obey the elders in the Church, who hold the succession from
the Apostles . . . who with the episcopal succession have received the sure
gift of truth. As for the rest, who are divorced from the principal succession
and gather where they will, they are to be held in suspicion, as heretics and
evil-thinkers, faction makers, swelled-headed, self-pleasing."[40] In other
words, Catholics—members of the universal church, which St. Ignatius,
writing in A.D. 110, called the *katholike ecclesia,* giving Catholics their
name—were to be submissive to Church authority, teaching, and tradition,
and be stubborn in defense of it.

But what was the early Church? It has left few records, yet certain
things about it can be said with certainty.

First, it was *apostolic.* Jesus had chosen and instructed his disciples to
spread the gospel to the ends of the earth. It was on the basis of the Apostles' authority, by their instruction, that the faith was passed on.

Second, the authority of the Apostles and of the Church came from a
*historical* event, witnessed, according to St. Paul, by many. Whatever
other justifications there might be for proclaiming the divinity of
Christ—as the fulfillment of Old Testament prophecies, or as the substance of the divine shadow chased by the best Greek philosophers, or
on the basis of the miracles He wrought—all ultimately, as St. Paul said,
comes down to the Resurrection, the historical fact of Jesus rising from
the dead and appearing before the Apostles. "For I delivered unto you
first of all that which I have received," said Paul, "how that Christ died
for our sins according to the scriptures; and that he was buried; and that
he rose again the third day according to the scriptures; and that he was

seen of Cephas [Peter], then of the twelve; after that, he was seen of above five hundred brethren at once; of whom the greater part remain unto this present, but some are fallen asleep. After that, he was seen by James; then of all the apostles. And last of all he was seen of me also, as of one born out of due time."[41]

Third, the Church was *hierarchical*. As Jesus had made the Apostles fishers of men, so too would the Apostles, in His name, have the authority to create bishops and deacons, who, in turn, gained their own handed-on apostolic authority

Fourth, the Church defined its doctrine by *tradition,* not *sola scriptura* (by Scripture alone)—to adopt the rallying cry of a controversy that would rend the Church a millennium and a half later. When Apostles like Paul—whose letters pre-date the written Gospels—refer to Scripture, they refer to what Christians now call the Old Testament. The early tradition of the Church was oral rather than written, and the New Testament writings are, as Father Philip Hughes notes, "supplementary to the basic knowledge which they presuppose."[42] The Biblical canon of what was true, valuable, binding, and instructive took centuries to compile and assess. The Bible as we have it today assumed its general form by the end of the second century. The canon of St. Athanasius was agreed upon by the end of the fourth century and became the definitive, authoritative canon for the Western Church with Pope Innocent I's approval of it in 405. Eleven hundred years later, this Bible would itself be re-edited by Protestants during the Reformation and made the foundation stone of Protestant Christian belief. For the first centuries of the Christian Church, however, it was *tradition* that was the Church's shield, not Scripture, and it was tradition-minded clerics who sifted through the competing documents to establish the Biblical canon that would be unchallenged for more than a thousand years.

Finally, we know that the Church was *Roman*—that it was born and grew within the confines of the Roman Empire. We also know that Rome was a focal point of early Church authority. By the stated directive of Jesus choosing Peter for a special mission—"I will give unto thee the keys of the kingdom of heaven"[43]—and by the martyrdom of the two foremost of the Apostles, Rome, capital of empire and bishopric of Peter, became Rome, capital of the faith, and was recognized as such by the early Church. One possible example of such recognition is one of the earliest surviving Christian documents, an epistle to the Church at Corinth by the bishop of Rome, St. Clement—third in succession after St. Peter—around the year 96, when at least one of the Apostles, St. John, was still alive. In his letter Clement describes the Church as an army. "[N]ot all are officers . . . each has his rank, carrying out the orders of the leader."[44] Clement goes on to instruct the church in Corinth on healing a rift among its members, his intervention justified, apparently, by the superior status of Rome as an arbiter of disputes in the early Church. Certainly by the second century, Rome was recognized as the plumb line to keep Christianity straight. "For with this Church," wrote St. Irenaeus of Lyons, "all other churches must bring themselves into line, on account of its superior authority."[45] In the third century, St. Cyprian affirmed, "To be in communion with the bishop of Rome is to be in communion with the Catholic Church."[46]

Without Rome's central authority, it might have been impossible for the Church to defeat the early heretics. One of the first organized assaults came from the Gnostics, who promised a specialized "higher" knowledge that would offer the elect—the few who could understand its mysteries— the promise of salvation. The secret knowledge held by the Gnostics was supposed to be the ultimate distillation of the truth of every religion, Christianity included.

The Church responded by dismissing Gnosticism for what it was—esoteric theorizing, appealing to human vanity—and by affirming, as Father Philip Hughes put it, "that the Faith is not a thing to be refashioned by any human intelligence, but something to be safeguarded by the Church's authority against any such refashioning."[47]

But especially in the East, where sophistry was rife, a faith refashioned by human intelligence was a continual threat to the faith of the Apostles. Among the early heretics were the Marcionites, who held that the God of the Old Testament was incompatible with the message of Jesus. Rejecting the Jewish Bible, Marcion compiled his own, consisting largely of Paul's letters, heavily edited. Marcionites had their own churches and many adherents, as did the Montanists, who believed in personal revelations equal in authority to the teachings of the Church and to Scripture. Both the Marcionites and the Montanists were ascetic sects, and there were plenty of these that condemned, variously, alcohol, meat, sex, and marriage.

But there was a quasi-Christian sect for every taste. There was a sect that believed that every sin had to be tried. There were those who denied that Jesus was a man (the Docetists) and those who denied that he was God (the Theodotians). To go through every heresy would be tedious and pointless. The important fact to grasp is that heresy has been a challenge to the Church from the beginning, and though these early heresies were defeated, they have never truly gone away. They are merely readapted to suit changing times. But certain themes are perennial. Many of the early heresies were what we would today call "holier than thou," enforcing a more rigorous moral discipline than the Roman Church. Common to every heresy is the assertion of private judgment, revelation, and choice against the Catholic Church's adherence to the authoritative tradition of Apostolic Christianity.

When in the twentieth century Joseph Cardinal Ratzinger wrote, "Meaning that is self-made is in the last analysis no meaning. Meaning, that is, the ground on which our existence as a totality can stand and live, cannot be made but only received,"[48] he was enunciating a truth as old as the Catholic faith. That belief in objective authority—based on the testimony of the Apostles and guarded by the veneration of tradition—has made the historic faith of the Catholic Church and kept it alive and triumphant through persecutions, schisms, wars, and rumors of war—outlasting every empire, constitution, and philosophy born of man. By its faith, it has provided "the substance of things hoped for, the evidence of things not seen."[49] It has provided the key that "fits the lock; because it is like life."[50] It is that faith whose history opens before us.

## CHAPTER THREE

# TRIAL BY FIRE

————➤●◄————

ORIGEN SEVERED HIS GENITALS, interpreting Jesus' words, as quoted in the Gospel of St. Matthew, as a command: "there be eunuchs, which have made themselves eunuchs for the kingdom of heaven's sake. He that is able to receive it, let him receive it."[1] This was odd, because Origen, the great reconciler of Christianity with Greek philosophy, was the prime exponent of a non-literalist interpretation of the Bible. Lest any Biblical literalists be tempted to follow Origen's example, perhaps it should be added that there is a good argument to be made that even in literalist terms, Origen was confused. Jesus says, "All men cannot receive this saying, save they to whom it is given. For there are some eunuchs, which were so from their mother's womb: and there are some eunuchs, which were made eunuchs of men: and there be eunuchs, which have made themselves eunuchs for the kingdom of heaven's sake." This would seem to imply a difference between those who were born eunuchs, those who were surgically "made eunuchs of men," and those who chose to become eunuchs for the kingdom of Heaven. In any event, there is no record of Jesus mutilating himself, or of any of the Apostles doing so. We know that far from ripping the genitals off converts, St. Paul ensured that they did not even have to undergo the Jewish rite of circumcision. While Paul preached celibacy as a means to better devote oneself to God, to him it was a matter of personal will and choice, not a matter to be resolved by a doctor's scalpel or a zealot's knife.

But if Origen got it wrong, it is a salutary reminder that even the greatest and most active intellects—Origen is said to have written 6,000 books or pamphlets—are not always the most balanced, commonsensical, or even sane. Origen, who lived from 185 to 254, was never validly ordained or made a saint, but so enormous and valuable was his work that he was the most frequently cited theological authority in the third century, even if the Church in Rome, to which he appealed when accused of heresy in Alexandria, corrected him, held him to be in error, and, after his death, ultimately condemned his teachings.

In its battle against heresy, the Church welcomed the works of men like Origen when they could be helpful but had no qualms about dismissing them when they were not. Christian doctrine was not—in contrast to paganism—willing to incorporate rival schools of thought. It would not accept philosophical theories that drifted into gnosticism or stoicism or Platonism. If these philosophies could be brought into accord with Catholic Christianity, fine—the greater the glory to God who made all things. Catholic Christianity itself, however, would not budge.

This stubbornness was partly a tradition of the Jews, who would acknowledge no God but Yahweh. But the Church, as it began a more thorough articulation of Christian doctrine, also became increasingly Roman in its mental outlook—Roman in the classical sense of being pragmatic, practical, and rooted in experience rather than in abstract philosophy; Roman in its eventual expropriation—not merging with, but taking—of pagan festivals and using them to mark Christian holy days; and Roman in thinking of itself as cosmopolitan, universal, and, as eschatological expectations faded, even worldly, in that it harbored no utopian illusions. The idea of building a shining city on the hill, that gleaming lodestar in the mental landscape of the puritan dissenters who settled early New England fourteen centuries after Origen's death, was not, and has never been, part of the mental outlook of the Catholic Church. If genius is, as F. Scott Fitzgerald claimed, the ability to hold two contradictory ideas in one's mind at once, the Catholic Church has accomplished that genius by propounding, on the one hand, a tangible, incarnational, divine history of extraordinary claims along with, on the other hand, the most tough-minded realism.

This realism was part of Christian teaching from the beginning: from the Gospel writers noting the faults of the Apostles, to Jesus warning his disciples that He was sending them "forth as sheep in the midst of wolves: be ye therefore wise as serpents, and harmless as doves. But beware of men: for they will deliver you up to the councils, and they will scourge you in their synagogues; and ye shall be brought before governors and kings for my sake . . . and you shall be hated of all men for my name's sake. . . . Think not that I am come to send peace on earth: I came not to send peace, but a sword."[2] Contrary to what some might think, such realism was endangered, rather than sharpened, by outbreaks of Roman persecution. Persecution bred martyrs; martyrs could breed fanaticism; fanaticism bred heresy.

Persecutions, like heresy, continued. The two great persecutions of the third century came under the emperors Decius (emperor from 249 to 251) and Diocletian (emperor from 284 to 305). Decius intended to stamp out Christianity as an assault on Roman traditions. Among his targets was Origen. The then elderly ascetic was kept in chains, tortured, and imprisoned. Pope Fabian of Rome—to whom Origen had appealed against charges of heresy—was himself jailed and beaten to death.

Again, however, Rome scourged the Christians only when they would not submit to Roman authority. Decius's persecution followed an edict that required all subjects of the empire—save for the Jews, who were exempted—to make sacrifices to Rome's pagan gods. Christians who complied would be spared, and compliance was easy. It generally meant sacrificing to Roman idols and eating sacrificial meat. Under lax enforcement, it was sufficient to offer the gods a pinch of incense. But those who would not comply would be charged with treason, punishable by imprisonment, torture, or death. Decius's persecution was unlike Nero's—it was not the work of a mad man. It was a matter of rationally considered state policy. Decius had inherited an empire under threat from barbarians and rivals. His predecessor, Philip the Arab, whom he had killed, was regarded as sympathetic to the Christians, having even (according to one story) attended Easter services as a penitent, taking orders from a bishop.[3]

Decius's objective was to shore up Roman discipline and patriotism, and he knew that persecuting Christians—something that had not been done on a major scale since the emperor Domitian, a century and a half earlier—was popular. Before the imperial edict, riots had already spontaneously erupted in Egypt and Rome against the ever more visible Church.

If the official persecutions were popular, they also highlighted the fact that, as the number of converts had grown, the heroic blood of the early martyrs had gone thin. Thousands of Christians lapsed. Bishops hid rather than face death. Rich Christians offered bribes that provided them with certificates of compliance or had slaves comply on their behalf. Even those Christians who went to prison sometimes thought their impending martyrdom would bring remission of sins and excuse drunkenness and debauchery in their prison cells. None of this would have surprised Christ. Had not the chosen people worshiped the golden calf? Had not Peter denied Him three times? Had not Thomas doubted His resurrection? Had not the entirety of human history been a testimony to original sin, of perpetual falling away from the truth? The spirit was willing, but the flesh was weak—and sometimes the spirit was not terribly strong either.

Nor did such weakness surprise the Catholic Church. The Church did not, of course, condone apostasy, but it did offer forgiveness to the sincerely penitent whose faith had failed the test of persecution. For a stern-minded presbyter named Novatian, such forgiveness was itself unforgivable, an intolerable falling away from Christian ideals. He thought it a weak-willed, weak-minded compromise with cowards who had proved they were not true Christians at all. Novatian was so angered by papal policy that he challenged the election of Pope Cornelius to the throne left vacant by the martyred Pope Fabian. But Novatian's attempt to harden Church discipline failed. It was for the pope to decide whether forgiveness was merited, not a presbyter. Novatian took his followers into schism and made himself an antipope, perhaps the first in history.[4]

The dispute erupted again, and more seriously, in the early fourth century, after the persecutions launched by the emperors Diocletian and Galerius. The hard-liners, the new Novatians, came from Africa and were known as the Donatists, after Donatus, their leader. The Donatists argued that clerics who betrayed the faith—the *Traditores*—could not be restored to holy office, were divorced from the apostolic succession, and that the congregants of churches where they held office were effectively denied the sacraments.

It would take a century for the Donatists to fade from history, but fade they eventually did, leaving behind this lesson: The Catholic Church is not a church reserved exclusively for latter-day saints. Nor is it a church that expects its ministers to be without fault. A universal church must expect trouble from universal sins. Catholics are not an elect, immune from temptation, but strivers after God who inevitably stumble and need forgiveness. The contretemps with Novatian and the Donatists highlights, again, the reality principle within the Church, and the Church's dismissal of those who would limit its benefactions to the holy few, rather than the unholy many. In Oscar Wilde's memorable phrase—and Wilde himself was a deathbed convert—"The Catholic Church is for saints and sinners alone. For respectable people the Anglican Church will do."[5]

Decius's persecution ended before his death on the battlefield in 251. Between Decius and Diocletian, there were eleven emperors—all of whom died violently—and the treatment of Christians, who would probably number around 10 percent of the population by the year 300,[6] was far from a major concern to soldier-emperors who were facing war at every extremity of the empire.

As usual, Christians were caught between the swinging doors of benign neglect and malign punishment. Under the emperor Valerian (253–260), nobles were forbidden to join the Church, Church leaders were compelled to acknowledge the pagan gods or face death, Pope Sixtus II was beheaded, and the great theologian St. Cyprian was martyred. Valerian himself, though in his sixties, led the imperial legions in the East, disgracing himself by incompetence and surrendering to the Persians. The Persian king Sapor kept him as a slave, using him as a step to mount his horse. When Valerian died, Sapor had him stuffed as a trophy. Such were the new challenges confronting Rome, challenges that fed Roman fears of losing favor with the gods who had kept Roman arms victorious and subdued the Mediterranean world to the *Pax Romana*.

Still, under Valerian's son Gallienus—and until Diocletian's persecutions four decades later—the Church regained its right to property and the free practice of the faith, enjoying relative peace. It was only late in Diocletian's reign that the peace ended, a sorry coda to the reign of one of Rome's great emperors, a man who reversed the empire's decline, rebuffed its enemies, and reformed its administration, giving the empire an order it would not enjoy again until it was united by Constantine.

Diocletian's most important reform was to divide the empire's administration between an Augustus of the West and one of the East, each supported by a Caesar. He also divided Rome's provinces into a system of dioceses, which would be inherited in the fullness of time, with the decline of the empire, by a governing Catholic Church. Moreover, it was in

Diocletian's court that Constantine, who would become the first Christian emperor, learned the craft of statesmanship.

Persecuting the Christians was not Diocletian's priority. But in his massive work of rebuilding the empire, he was wary of any crack that might undermine its new foundation. His Caesar, Galerius, disliked the Christians. So did many other Romans, who saw their rise in secular society, including the army, as a dangerous, potentially treasonous, faction within the state. Rome was used to its soldiers belonging to religious cults, especially the cult of Mithras, but Christianity was seen as radically different. The Greek philosopher Hierocles warned Diocletian that Christianity is not "like the cult of Mithras. The followers of Mithras never spoke against the gods. But the Christians consider our gods to be demons, unholy spirits, and claim that only the Hebrew rebel they worship is the one true god."[7]

The singularity of Christian belief made the Christians easy targets, and their well-organized episcopal hierarchy made it easy to find their leaders. All that was necessary was for suspicion to be ignited by evidence of criminal intent, or for an augury of the gods to accuse the Christians of bringing ill favor on Rome. Such an augury came from Apollo in the winter of 302. The temple oracle warned that its prophetic powers had been compromised by the presence of the Christians, and the implication was that something must be done against the usurpers to restore the pagan religion. Diocletian reluctantly agreed, but he wanted to avoid the bloodshed of previous anti-Christian measures. He did not want to create new martyrs. Nevertheless, Diocletian's edicts of "the great persecution"—issued in sharpening crescendo over the course of several months—became the most detailed, forcible, and coherent plan for the extermination of the Church. The edicts allowed for destroying churches, burning Scriptures, enforcing sacrifice to the pagan gods, executing clergy who refused to submit, and depriving noble Christians of their rights as Roman citizens and eventually outlawed Christianity entirely, under pain of death. As sweeping as these powers were, their enforcement was, again, often in the hands of reluctant executioners. In the East, always prone to extremism and emperor worship, the persecutions were much more severe than in the West.

Eusebius reports, "I saw with my own eyes the places of worship thrown down from top to bottom, to the very foundations, the inspired holy Scriptures committed to the flames in the middle of the public squares, and the pastors of the churches hiding disgracefully."[8] But not all behaved disgracefully. He testifies that Christians in the army resigned rather than carry out their orders, and some of them faced death for their refusal. Diocletian's naïve belief that he could unleash the sweeping, destructive powers of the state and cow Christians out of their faith without eventual bloodshed betrays that even the most hardened statesmen can harbor illusions about what is "reasonable." In Diocletian's case this was proven personally when two of his long-standing secretaries refused to offer a pinch of incense to the gods, even after the emperor pleaded with them. They said they remained faithful servants, but they could acknowledge no God but Christ; the emperor waved them away to be tortured and beheaded.

Tens of thousands suffered similarly. Under a benevolent governor, such as Constantine's father, Flavius Constantius, who governed Britain and Gaul, there was little to fear. But many were less fortunate, especially the clergy, for once the persecutions gained momentum, killing the officers of the Church was recognized as the most effective way of terminating the Christian religion. So many clergy were arrested that prisons burst their capacity. With the usual stupidity of the bureaucratic state, murderers were set free so that extra clergymen could be squeezed into filthy prison cells, where their only release—unless they agreed to sacrifice to the pagan gods—was for periods of torture or final execution.

Eusebius records a vast catalog of torture that was inflicted on Christians, whether men or women. "Some were scraped, racked, mercilessly flogged, subjected to countless other torments too terrible to describe in endless variety, and finally given to the flames; some were submerged in the sea; others cheerfully stretched out their necks to the headsman's axe; some died under torture; others were starved to death; others again were crucified, some as criminals usually are, some with still greater cruelty nailed the other way up, head down, and kept alive until starved to death on the very cross."[9] This is but a small part of Eusebius's list of the means of torture and execution used by the state against the Christians. He adds, "I was in these places, and saw many of the executions for myself. Some of the victims suffered death by beheading, others punishment by fire. So many were killed in a single day that the axe, blunted and worn out by the slaughter was broken in pieces, while the exhausted executioners had to be periodically relieved. All the time I observed a most wonderful eagerness and a truly divine power and enthusiasm in those who had put their trust in the Christ of God."[10] "Eagerness" and "enthusiasm" perhaps, but their sanguine facing down of death should not make it any less engraved on our imaginations. Rather it should make it more so—an example of calm in the midst of persecution, of refusal to panic before the flames, of hymn-singing while spear points probed. This is the Christian standard. This is what impressed Constantine. And while the Church would forgive those who failed, it cherishes those who did not.

## THE VISIBLE CHURCH

THE INSTITUTIONS OF THE CHURCH had taken definite form from at least the beginning of the second century. Bishops led individual churches and were assisted by presbyters, or elders; this was the caste that would eventually become "priests." There were also deacons, whose especial responsibility was to administer the social welfare programs—caring for widows, orphans, and the poor—that were a distinguishing characteristic of the Church. Pagans often remarked on the charity, compassion, and kindliness of Catholic Christians. Tertullian, writing at the end of the second century, noted that Christians share "all things in common except our wives," concluding, "at that point we dissolve our partnership, precisely where the rest of men make it effective."[11]

Tertullian's sarcasm highlights another important point. It is often said that early Christianity was merely another Eastern mystery religion full of adoptions from other cults, ranging from the ideas of an afterlife adapted from ancient Egypt to the ceremonies of the Mass being a variation of the secret ceremonies of Mithraism, and innumerable other presumed parallels and intersections. Most religions have commonalities—whether it is using candles and incense, or employing priests, or advising prayer—but what struck every pagan observer about Christianity was how different it was, and how different its believers were. It was for this very reason that it could be isolated and persecuted. It also gave birth to Tertullian's famous witticism about Christianity: "God's son died: it is believable precisely because it is absurd. He was buried and rose again: it is certain because it is impossible."[12] This is hardly something that could have been said if Christianity had been similar to every other cult.[13]

We must remember that the world was old before Christianity came into it, and man's innate religious instinct was well practiced. The Jewish religion from which it sprang was the most ancient religion known to the Romans. The classical world, in which Christianity was nourished, was more popularly devoted to and intellectually sophisticated in philosophical argument than our own world. We should not, therefore, think of the early Christians as primitives. Though theirs was an oral tradition, so was Homer's. Both the ancient Greeks and the early Christians came from cultures that nurtured memory. They were cultures that listened, cultures that debated, cultures that sought truth.

The difference was that the Christians believed they *had* truth in the deposit of faith. Argument was meant to lead—it was the road—to that truth. So while Christian argument could be wide-ranging, suited for any audience, Christian belief was settled. For intellectuals like Origen and Tertullian, who weren't bound to consistency or orthodoxy, this could prove a problem. Tertullian had once written that Christians "are always praying for all emperors, for . . . a safe dynasty, brave armies, a faithful Senate, and a quiet world,"[14] which would have put him in accord with St. Paul. But as he grew older, Tertullian became an extreme puritan—hating women, repudiating Christian service to the state, embracing pacifism, refusing forgiveness, and denying any wisdom outside of revelation. In technical terms, he went into schism as a Montanist, a proto-Protestant sect of ascetics who disliked the developing structure of the Church and preferred more ecstatic forms of worship (something that was anathema to the very proper St. Paul). Tertullian had his reasons, of course—well-argued ones—but they were his own, not consistent with Catholic dogma, not understanding that for Catholics the Christian faith is a marriage. As in a marriage, Catholics are not required to be brilliant, creative, or original—though these talents, in their own sphere, are to be welcomed. What they are charged with is *fidelity*.

The ethical and dogmatic—not to mention conjugal—fidelity of Catholic Christians raised their profile among intelligent men. In the second century, the great Greek physician Galen noted, even if backhandedly, that Christians were "so far advanced in self-discipline and . . . intense desire to attain moral excellence that they are in no way inferior to true philosophers."[15] Marcus Aurelius, the great philosopher-emperor who ruled Rome from 161 to 180, saw fit to include Abraham and Jesus in his pantheon of pagan gods. Such high-mindedness did not stop him, however, from presiding over an empire that tossed the Christian philosopher Justin to the lions, giving him his historical name of St. Justin Martyr.

Justin is an interesting case. A professional philosopher converted to Christianity at the age of thirty-eight, he was a precursor of Origen in seeing the philosophical reasonableness of Christianity. He believed that God had spoken through both the Jewish prophets *and* the Greek philosophers. While the Jews had received a more direct and fuller presentation of the *Logos,* the word of God, Jew, Greek, or anyone should be able to apprehend the philosophical truth of Christianity because it was the natural religion of mankind. As mankind's natural religion, it was right, Justin argued, to call great men of understanding, like Socrates, Christians—a humane idea of which Catholics, never severed from the classical world, have always been fond. Marcus Aurelius, too, believed in natural religion, but he would have held that Christianity was part of the truth, not the whole—in other words, the reverse of what Justin held. But the ideas of Justin Martyr and Marcus Aurelius, Stoic philosophers by training, show how pagan and Christian thought were on convergent paths, rather than the divergent ones they are on today (perhaps because today's pagans are too unphilosophical and ignoble to be Stoics).

But if their philosophies were coming together, in their social conventions Christians stood well outside the Roman mainstream. When it came to sex, for example, Christians, unlike the Romans, were officially against it. Christians, following the teachings of Jesus, St. Paul, and the Church Fathers, thought sex was a powerful distraction from serving God. Then, as now, sex was a major issue dividing contesting views of the world. The Church managed to strike the proper via media. It faced, on the one hand, heretical, puritanical sects—and also Platonist philosophical schools and other cults—that held that the material world was evil and inevitably corrupt. On the other hand, it confronted such practices as ritual prostitution and the usual fornications of the fallen. The Church endorsed neither the puritan nor the profligate. Instead, it upheld the strict moral teachings of Jesus and Paul but did not divorce these teachings from the full body of Christian philosophy or, for that matter, from a right reading of Jesus and Paul. All men were charged to put God first, and some men, like St. Paul, were called to celibacy so as to fully submit themselves to God's service.

Simultaneously, the Church taught that creation was good. It commemorated "the fruit of the vine, the work of human hands." It remembered Jesus' fondness for children. It fully embraced the Incarnation—of God becoming man through Mary. Unlike the ascetic sects and heresies, the Church sanctified the goodness of family life.

While officially illegal under Roman law, many Romans practiced abortion and infanticide. In the brave days of the Republic, children were regarded as sources of family pride and honor. Now they were seen as limits on one's freedom to enjoy the pleasures of the world. The Romans also practiced contraception, which could take a variety of forms, the most drastic of which was marriage to a eunuch. But contraception was denied to the Catholic Christian.[16] Life, he was taught, is God's gift. As Christians were to welcome life's entrance, so too were they not to trifle with its exit. To the Roman, suicide was a noble act to compensate for failure or dishonor. But the Christian, though he might embrace martyrdom as an imitation of Christ, was forbidden to take his own life because he did not own it; his life belonged to God.

Some put their lives totally in God's service. In the third century, the monastic tradition developed in the Church, with St. Anthony of Egypt. The monks responded to Christ's call to follow Him, forsaking all else—material possessions, family, personal ambition—in His service. They were a powerful testimony to the faith and would play an enormous role in saving civilization after the fall of Rome, developing the uniquely Christian culture of the Middle Ages. There were different varieties of monks, but in general they devoted their lives to solitary prayer and study of the Scriptures, gathering together for worship and work.

All Christians—priests, monks, and laypeople—were encouraged in their imitation of Christ by what Catholics call the Communion of Saints. The belief in sainthood goes back to Scripture and to the earliest foundations of the Church. The first saints were the Apostles and the early martyrs, such as St. Stephen. In their missionary work, the saintly Apostles performed miracles, and it was another practice of the early Church to venerate relics connected with the saints. These, too, were often held to have miraculous properties, but they were sometimes honored simply as the remains and effects of great Christians. The lives of the saints also inspired early Christian novels of moral instruction, and artwork that gave visual form—and encouragement—to the faith. But here, as in everything,

there were controversies. Was it appropriate to depict God in art, a practice that went against Jewish law? Were icons acceptable, or did they vio-
late the commandment against idolatry? In resolving these issues, the
Catholic Church consulted traditional practice and planted itself on the
side of art and popular devotion.

Among the bishops of the apostolic Church, there was a need for a
Solomon to resolve disputes about standards, practices, and doctrine. That
Solomon was Rome. Every non-schismatic Christian church—even the rigorist churches of Africa and the old churches of the East, at Antioch and
elsewhere—accepted the bishop of Rome as, at a minimum, primus inter
pares (first among equals), to be consulted and often deferred to in the establishment of Christian unity.

Fundamental to Rome's authority was the ability to document the
apostolic succession of the Roman See. Between the reign of Nero and the
rise of Constantine, the Roman Church was able to trace a line from St.
Peter to St. Eusebius—thirty-one bishops over the course of a quarter of a
millennium. At least three of the Roman bishops had been martyrs, quite
possibly more, because for many of them—given fires, persecutions, an
extremely limited written record, and the oral traditions of the Church—
we know little beyond their names and dates.

We do know, however, that the first clearly monarchical pope was
Anicetus, who held the See of St. Peter from 155 to 166. We know this
because we have records of Anicetus attempting to bring a uniform date
for the Christian celebration of Easter—something that divided the Eastern and Western churches. The Western churches celebrated Easter on
Sunday. The Eastern churches followed a Jewish system of dating and allowed Easter to fall on any day of the week, including what in the Western church might be marked as Holy Thursday, Good Friday, or Holy
Saturday. Though the issue was not resolved, it is interesting that the
Eastern bishop Polycarp of Smyrna came to Rome to discuss the matter,
rather than Anicetus traveling to Smyrna.

During the pontificate of St. Eleutherus (175–189), the Roman
church promulgated the Apostles' Creed, the earliest existing summary of
the essentials of Christian belief as transmitted by the Apostles.[17] The
creed is worth reprinting here as a reminder of what early Christians believed to be the basic truths of the faith.

I believe in God, the Father almighty, creator of heaven and earth. I believe in Jesus Christ, his only son, our Lord. He was conceived by the power of the Holy Spirit and born of the Virgin Mary. He suffered under Pontius Pilate, was crucified, died, and was buried. He descended to the dead. On the third day he rose again. He ascended into heaven, and is seated at the right hand of the Father. He will come again to judge the living and the dead. I believe in the Holy Spirit, the holy catholic Church, the communion of saints, the forgiveness of sins, the resurrection of the body, and the life everlasting. Amen.[18]

With the election of Pope Victor in 189, the Roman Church gained its first Latin-speaking, rather than Greek-speaking, bishop, marking the ascendancy of the language that would define the universal rite of the Catholic Church, with few exceptions, for nearly 1,800 years. To this day, Latin is the Catholic Church's lingua franca for official documents.

Victor was a strict disciplinarian. To resolve the Easter dispute, which remained unsettled after a series of synods called during his pontificate, he threatened to excommunicate the Eastern churches. Many bishops felt that Victor had gone too far, contrasting Victor in his tempestuousness with Anicetus, who had been a peacemaker and willing, at the end of the day, to settle for a twofold tradition as the price of unity. But Pope Victor's brinksmanship showed that Rome did not view itself as primus inter pares, but primus, period, with the right to compel conformity, at pain of labeling others schismatics.

More often than not, however, the bishop of Rome imitated the good shepherd in such interventions, tempering the rulings of the harsh and forgiving the weak. Pope Callistus, whose pontificate ran from 217 to 222, clashed with Tertullian over the readmittance of adulterers, fornicators, and other fallen-away Christians to the universal Church after a suitable penance. Pope Stephen, who reigned from 254 to 257, was a strong defender of papal monarchy and the first Roman bishop to cite St. Matthew's gospel as the source of his preeminent authority. He wanted repentant Novatians restored to the Church with a simple laying on of hands, rather than a rebaptism, as the more rigorist African bishops preferred. When Bishop Cyprian of Carthage rallied resistance to the

pope's ruling, Stephen threatened noncompliant churches with excommunication. Stephen's death and the flames of the Decian persecution that martyred both St. Cyprian and Stephen's successor, Pope Sixtus II, submerged
the controversy in ashes.[19] But again, the papacy had intervened on the side
of forgiveness, behaving like the father in the parable of the prodigal son,
but also asserting its authority as the paterfamilias of the Church.

As the Church entered the fourth century, persecuted and battered, it
would soon rejoice at the rise of another leader claiming universal authority—a son of the empire, a witness to Christian persecution, a soldier
whose legions robed him in the imperial purple. The emperor Constantine was not a pope, but he was as necessary as anyone to the triumph of
Christianity.

## CHAPTER FOUR

# CONSTANTINE

⎯⎯►◄⎯⎯

THE EASTERN ORTHODOX CHURCH calls Constantine a saint and "the Peer of the Apostles." Most saints don't order the extra-judicial execution of rivals, but then again most saints don't lead military empires. There is no denying that it was Constantine who raised Christianity from the catacombs, brought it to the imperial councils, and cracked—as was necessary—contentious bishops' heads together to resolve the unending and unedifying theological disputes that continually threatened to rend the Church asunder. Sometimes Christianity needs hard men, and it benefited greatly from Constantine.

His background was romantic. He was born from a one-night liaison between a young Roman officer, Flavius Constantius, and a peasant maid named Helena. Nine years later, Flavius Constantius became governor of Dalmatia, where, unknown to him, his son Constantine was growing up. When two Roman soldiers cuffed the young boy for annoying their horses, Helena rebuked them. They had struck the governor's son, she said, and as proof she produced Flavius Constantius's old military cloak. The soldiers reported the incident, and, as in a fairy tale, the governor married the peasant girl and was reunited with his son. By law, the differences in rank between Flavius Constantius and Helena made their marriage less than fully binding. It also limited Constantine's right to inherit from his father. The Romans termed such arrangements *matrimonium concubinatum*. The marriage nevertheless brought Helena and

Constantine from pig slops to a Roman court and a sudden immersion into learning how to behave as a Roman governor's wife and son.

While his father became Caesar of the West, Constantine rose in imperial service at the court of Diocletian. Later, as an experienced officer and gentleman—athletic, handsome, and clear-eyed—he joined his father in Britain. When his father died, Constantine's troops—as was the custom—proclaimed him Augustus. Imperial edict, however, forced Constantine to accept the lesser title and responsibilities of Caesar. He accepted this with a wisdom and good grace that was increasingly rare in Rome's ambitious, jostling ruling classes and took over his father's responsibilities, keeping the peace in Gaul, Spain, and Britain and eventually going up against the German tribes. Before he was forty, Constantine was officially recognized as Augustus of the West, and after the battle of the Milvian Bridge, he became senior Augustus, master of Rome and of every province from North Africa to Britain. The new Augustus proclaimed religious freedom and toleration for Christians under the Edict of Milan. By the age of forty-five, he was de facto ruler, the sole emperor, of all Rome's possessions.

Constantine had nothing to gain by embracing Christianity—a small, unpopular, and persecuted faith. His mother was a Christian,[1] and his father had been sympathetic to Christians, but their influence was secondary. It was battle that convinced him—the Christian God delivered him victory at the Milvian Bridge. The new emperor would repay that debt and honor the true God. One of Constantine's first official acts after the battle was to give the bishop of Rome the Lateran Palace as his official residence. He also created a new battle standard, the labarum, that made Christ's monogram the symbol of the legions. Constantine's Augustus of the East, Licinius, though himself a pagan, thought that if the Christian God worked for Constantine it might work for him, and had a quasi-Christian war prayer delivered to his commanders as he moved to crush an imperial rival—a rival who had renewed Christian persecutions.

Battlefield victories, however, were simple compared to resolving what Constantine called the "rabid and implacable hatreds of the obstinate bishops."[2] He viewed episcopal feuds as a disgrace, self-evidently displeasing to God and inviting judgment on the empire. So while he treated the bishops, especially the bishop of Rome, with deference, he trusted his own imperial power to achieve Christian unity. He poured money into the Catholic Church, assured Pope Miltiades that heresy and schism would not be tolerated, and put Caesar's sword at St. Peter's service. In a letter to his proconsul Aelianus, Constantine wrote that he would not rest easy until everyone worshipped "the most Holy God . . . in the rites of the Catholic religion."[3]

The Donatists were the immediate disciplinary problem. These hardline churchmen, who considered themselves the "pure," uncontaminated by the *"Traditores,"* were especially prominent in North Africa. They denied the authority of the pope and of the synods of Rome and of Arles because nothing would reconcile them to a Church that forgave apostasy. So Constantine resorted to force, with legionnaires transferring Donatist churches to Catholics.

He was harsher with schismatic Christians than he was with Rome's traditional pagans. As emperor, he was the Pontifex Maximus of state paganism and, as such, a possible future divinity, a status not to be surrendered lightly. While Constantine did not forbid pagan practices, he skirted public disfavor—and, more important, disfavor among the old Roman aristocracy—by making a show of not participating in pagan rituals. Just a few years earlier, he could have been executed on grounds of treason for such non-performance, or a rival with a following among the legions could have challenged him for the purple. But the people were happy and at peace, however shocking it was to have Christianity enshrined as the emperor's religion.

Christianity was increasingly manifest in Roman law. Constantine codified Christian practice from the time of the Apostles and made Sunday—the day Christ rose from the dead—the day of rest, appropriating the day from Roman sun worshipers, of whom he had been one. He took the pagan Saturnalia and made it the official date for the celebration of Christmas. He ordered returned all Christian property that had been confiscated during the persecutions, recalled Christians from exile and imprisonment, prohibited branding prisoners on the face on the grounds that man had been made in God's image, and legislated that slaves could no longer be killed at a master's whim. He increased public welfare spending, lavished money and property on the Church, and was an assiduous builder of basilicas—including St. Peter's, which he built over the grave of the Apostle, a site he believed he had found with certainty. Constantine's basilicas were enormous—capable of holding thousands of worshippers—and decked out in gold, silver, and marble. Such Christian splendor was a statement to the pagans. But Constantine found that he had less trouble from paganism than he had from a turbulent Libyan presbyter. His name was Arius, and he hammered a fissure into Christianity that would not be equaled until the Protestant Revolution, more than a thousand years later.

## THE ARIAN HERESY

ARIUS TAUGHT WHAT had been speculated for more than fifty years among Eastern thinkers—that Jesus could not have been fully God, for there was only one eternal God, and that was God the Father. For the faith, this idea had horrific consequences. If Jesus were of a different substance from God, he was like all creation, subject to change and decay, capable of committing sin, and perhaps better described as a prophet than as God. If Christ was not eternally divine, He was what Constantine took himself to be—God's tool.

Arius defended his position as scriptural and logical in a way that Catholic belief in the Holy Trinity was not. As Arius argued, how could a father not exist before his son? God, the Father, is eternal, with no beginning and no end, but Jesus, the Son, was obviously subordinate, created, and therefore different in kind from God. Arius had more than the presumption of logic on his side. He was an inspiring preacher, and the Arian heresy soon began packing the churches, sweeping up believers, and giving Catholicism its greatest heretical challenge yet—a Christian schism that denied the divinity of Christ on the basis of reason and the Bible.

The bishop of Alexandria tried to convince Arius—through private, personal appeals—to cease preaching what was obviously heresy.[4] Arius refused, and at a regional council of North African bishops, he was excommunicated. But Arius did not go quietly into the night. With so much popularity at his back, not only among laypeople—including seven hundred women, self-proclaimed holy virgins, who campaigned on his behalf—but among Eastern clerics, he knew that he could successfully mount a rhetorical army to challenge the supremacy of the Catholic Church. He was a clerical Caesar raising legions to overthrow the papal Augustus in Rome.

Before Protestants made schism and religious subjectivism acceptable, defining orthodoxy fired Christian passions. The Arian heresy ripped through the empire and tore individual families between fidelity to the Catholic Church and the attractions of a new, supposedly more rational doctrine. Soon there were riots among contending mobs—mobs that became gang armies. Penalties of exile and excommunication were inflicted on rival clerics. Under the Arian emperor Constantius II, ecclesiastical murder was sanctioned. The most famous case involved the Catholic bishop of Constantinople, Paul, who was repeatedly deposed and finally exiled, tortured, and then strangled to death, so that his Arian rival Macedonius could supersede him.

In resolving the Arian dispute, ecclesiastical councils were of no use because they could not agree. Some synods confirmed Arianism and others repudiated it. The only institution that stood firmly against Arianism was the papacy. Even after Arius's death in 336, and after the final defeat of his doctrine within the Roman Empire in 381 at the Second General Council of the Church, it returned in degraded form, because the barbarian tribes overrunning the Western Empire had been converted to Arian Christianity. Its heretical embers continued to glow for the next three hundred years, until completely quenched by the Church of the Middle Ages.

The great hero in the fight against Arianism was St. Athanasius, the doughtiest Catholic *fides defensor* of the age, gaining the title "Father of Orthodoxy." Even the historian Edward Gibbon, though himself a mocking skeptic, wrote that "Athanasius displayed a superiority of character and abilities which would have qualified him, far better than the degenerate sons of Constantine, for the government of a great monarchy."[5] Well educated in the most philosophically sophisticated of cities, Alexandria, Athanasius was a prodigy, ordained (according to his critics) before he was legally entitled to the honor. His liberal education and natural gifts made him confident, quick in argument, brilliant in rebuttal. Unlike so many of his contemporaries, he found Catholic dogma more intellectually compelling than Arian speculation. But this wasn't an issue of mere intellectual preference; if the deposit of faith were true, defending it was a sacred duty—a duty Athanasius freely accepted. The Arians diligently courted patrons to punish their enemies, and Athanasius suffered exile five times—once under sentence of death. But he never wavered.

He began his career as secretary to the bishop of Alexandria and wrote many books during the course of his life, including a biography of

St. Anthony, whom he apparently met. Throughout his exceedingly active career in combating Arianism, he dreamt of pursuing a monastic vocation. For one short period of exile, when he was under threat of execution, he temporarily achieved it. But his life was fulfilled not in the peace of the cloister, but in the battle against Arian heresy.

Constantine and Athanasius made natural early allies. Constantine, like the Church in Rome, scorned lucubrations that challenged Catholic unity. To a practical soldier like Constantine, the Arian controversy was the product of "misused leisure." He condemned "those who dared with senseless levity to rend the worship of the people into separate sects."[6] Such sectarianism was the temptation of the Devil, who knew as well as any soldier the strategy of "divide and conquer."

Politically, Constantine had only just forcibly united his empire. In 320, Licinius, the Augustus of the East, began stripping the Church of its rights. He purged believers from his government, demanded sacrifice to pagan gods, burned churches, and sent Christians to slave labor, torture, and death. Like so many rulers to come, Licinius saw the Church as a barrier to his absolute power. In 323, he found a more difficult barrier. Constantine's legions, flying their Christian battle standard, marched against Licinius, hurling back his soldiers, then crushing his fleet. Constantine advanced to the strategic point of Byzantium (Istanbul), while his son Crispus brought Rome's navy from the Aegean through the Dardanelles, which divides modern Turkey. Together, they seized the city. At the final showdown, in the battle of Chrysopolis, tens of thousands of Licinius's men fell before he surrendered to promises of mercy. Constantine held him for a year before ordering his execution, the execution of his wife (Constantine's half sister), and one of his sons; another son was eventually reduced to slavery. When it suited him in matters of state, Constantine could act without Christian compassion. He proved that most notoriously when he ordered the execution of his own golden son Crispus and his second wife, Fausta, in circumstances that remain unclear.

So Arius had no reason to expect mercy from Constantine. But in this case, the emperor acted through the Church, not via the legions. In 325 he called the Council at Nicea, over which he would preside, paying the costs of every representative coming to do the Lord's and Constantine's work. The task was to find agreement on Christian truth. Such agreement would prove elusive.

# THE NICENE COUNCIL

THOUGH IT WAS MEANT to be a universal meeting of the Church, the landmark Council at Nicea was dominated by Eastern bishops, for whom the Arian Crisis was a wild and raging tempest. In the West, clerics by and large remained lambs of the Good Shepherd, flicking their ears at the pesky flies of controversy, but not much troubled by them, content to follow their master's crook, and ignored the summons to Nicea for an argument that was of no parochial concern. The pope himself remained in Rome, sending as his representative two priests, one of whom was named Vito.[7]

As the Council began, Constantine made a dramatic gesture. He held up the many accusatory petitions that feuding clerics had submitted to him for arbitration: accusations of heresy; accusations of loyalty to the exiled—and soon to be executed—rival Licinius; accusations of all sorts of misdoing. Constantine announced that he had read none of them, and threw the petitions into a fire. As flames cut through the scrolls, he hoped that his magnanimous example would dissolve the dissensions between Arians, Catholics, and "the Church of the Martyrs," the last being another sect opposed to forgiving apostatized clerics. It was a nice try, but if he had been a more sophisticated man rather than a plain soldier-politician, he would have known that the Arians and the Church of the Martyrs would not be so easily humbled. And Catholics, of course, would never renounce the Trinity or Christ's call to forgive penitent sinners.

After heated conciliar arguments, the Arians were defeated by overwhelming vote and at Constantine's order were consigned to exile—where, however, they would continue their war against the Church. The Church also formally adopted what we know as the Nicene Creed as a definitive summary of Christian belief. The draft that emerged from the Council specifically and repeatedly condemned Arian assertions. But as the Arian threat became more shadowy, the Creed underwent minor changes and refinements. The Creed gained its final form at the Council of Constantinople in 381. Recited in churches around the world every Sunday, it reads:

> We believe in one God, the Father, the Almighty, maker of heaven and earth, of all that is, seen and unseen. We believe in one Lord,

Jesus Christ, the only Son of God, eternally begotten of the Father,
God from God, Light from Light, true God from true God, begotten,
not made, one in Being with the Father. Through whom all things
were made. For us men and for our salvation he came down from
heaven: by the power of the Holy Spirit he was born of the Virgin
Mary, and became man. For our sake he was crucified under Pontius
Pilate; he suffered, died, and was buried. On the third day he rose
again in fulfillment of the Scriptures; he ascended into heaven and is
seated at the right hand of the Father. He will come again in glory to
judge the living and the dead, and his kingdom will have no end. We
believe in the Holy Spirit, the Lord, the giver of life, who proceeds
from the Father and the Son. With the Father and the Son he is worshipped and glorified. He has spoken through the Prophets. We believe in one holy catholic and apostolic Church. We acknowledge
one baptism for the forgiveness of sins. We look for the resurrection
of the dead, and the life of the world to come. Amen.

A few things should be immediately noted about the Nicene Creed.
The first is its continuity with the old Roman baptismal rite of the Apostles' Creed. There is nothing in the Nicene Creed about which the Apostles would have any doubt. The Creed has merely been enlarged to
answer new challenges, misunderstandings, or ignorance—and indeed
this is the pattern followed by Catholic doctrinal development. Another
thing to be noted is that the Nicene Creed scandalized contemporary Biblical literalists by using a non-Biblical word—*homoousios* in the Greek—
to describe the consubstantiality of God the Father and God the Son. As a
result, some of the literalists became Arians. But the Nicene Church did
not limit its understanding of Christianity to Scripture alone.

On other matters, the Council of Nicea resolved the date of Easter by
adopting the Western model. This was the work of Constantine, who
pointedly broke with the traditional Roman indulgence of Judaism by
telling the Eastern churches that it was wrong to date a Christian celebration on the basis of Jewish customs—the customs of the very people who
had rejected Jesus. The Eastern churches found this argument impossible
to counter and succumbed.

With regard to the Church of the Martyrs, its founder and leader,
Bishop Miletius, was, with surprising leniency, allowed to keep his title

but was denied all episcopal powers. Those he had ordained were to be replaced on their death by orthodox Catholic clergy as appointed by the rightful Catholic bishop. In the meantime, if they wished to continue in their offices they were to be received back into the Church by the laying on of hands.

Miletius, consistent with his puritan beliefs, repudiated the Church's leniency and cast his lot with the Arians, who were gathering together every schism against the Catholic faith.

The Council also clarified various items of Church discipline, the most interesting of which, in the light of modern controversies, was the Church's strengthening of the practice of celibacy. The third canon of the Nicene Council prohibits all clergy from living with women unless they are blood relatives, such as a mother or a sister, who will not distract them from a celibate life. Thus the discipline of celibacy, which was in use, if not mandatory, from the days of the Apostles, entered canon law from at least the beginning of the fourth century, though it was not always enforced.

Constantine assumed that after the Council all would be well with the Church. But that was far from the case. Soldiers might accept the verdict of the battlefield—and rival Augusti and their families could be executed, exterminating their threat forever—but contumacious clerics refused to be bound by council, pope, or emperor. Persecution appeared futile, extermination impossible. Constantine cleaved to the Nicene Creed, hoping it would provide the basis for "mere Christianity," and for Catholics it does.

## THE IMPERIAL LEGACY

CONSTANTINE REMAINED LOYAL to the Church even when it cost him in popularity. After the Nicene Council, he traveled to Rome as part of his celebration of twenty years as emperor. There, when he refused to partake in pagan ceremonies, riots erupted and a statue of the emperor was literally defaced by mob-thrown rocks. But St. John Chrysostom reports that Constantine's response when told the news was to touch his face and say, "I am not able to see any wound inflicted on my face. Both the head and the face appear to be quite sound,"[8] an appropriately regal rejoinder. But the antipathy of the pagans in Rome was surely one factor among many in Constantine's decision to build his own capital, a New Rome, on the banks of the Bosporus, in Byzantium, the bridge between Europe and Asia, from which he had chased Licinius.

Constantine's decision to build Constantinople would have profound implications for the development of the Church, aside from the obvious one of underlining the divisions between the Greek-speaking East and the Latin West. Disturbing to Catholic sensibilities might have been Constantine's adopting the trappings of what to the Roman mind were signs of Eastern despotism—elaborate ceremonials, jewel-studded royal garments, flower-tongued courtiers, and other bows in the direction of the mystical Orient, away from the stoicism of Rome.

To Catholics in the Western Empire, such Eastern embellishments were more than mere Persian symbolism. The rise of Constantinople and the Eastern court would establish a rivalry between the secular and papal thrones. In the West, after the fall of the Western Roman Empire, the papacy would fill the void of secular leadership. It would assert papal supremacy—God's law—over secular law. It would proclaim the independence of Church from state. It would uphold the pope as the sanctifier and final check on the power of kings, his power resting on the deference of a uniformly Catholic culture.

In the East, the rise of Constantinople would inaugurate the beginnings of what has been called Caesaropapism, of imperial supremacy over the Church, which would be the rule in Orthodox Christianity from the New Rome's Eastern, or Byzantine, Empire—until it was overrun by Islam in the fifteenth century.[9] In the West, Caesaropapism would not develop until after the Reformation, and then in the more muted form of the Anglican church and the various Lutheran or Calvinist churches established as the state religion by European monarchs.

Some have argued that Constantine's legacy is mixed, that his support for Christianity came at the price of severely compromising the Church by making its operations part of imperial policy. But this seems carping. Without Constantine's defending sword, the Church faced the prospect of endless persecution. Without Constantine's taking a hand in Church affairs, providing common sense, the threat of force, munificent sums, and marvelous basilicas, the Arian controversy or any of the virtually innumerable other heresies might, in combination, have fractured the Church into near nonexistence.

Constantine began the creation of a Christian empire, furthering Christ's call to the Apostles to bring the faith to all the peoples of the world. It was to Constantine's great delight that even delegates from outside the empire attended the Nicene Council. The model for a Christian society was taking shape. For believers, it was now obvious that the best form of rule was when cross and sword, crozier and scepter, worked in unison. Constantine provided the starting point for the divine right of kings as the guardians of a Christian world until liberal, secular democracy altered the equation by making religious indifference the paramount value.

There are other aspects of Constantine's life important to the development of the Church. One was his attitude to pagan art. He was not an iconoclast. When he built his New Rome, he brought fantastic pagan statuary to his eponymous capital to give it grandeur. It was a typically Roman attitude—at variance, perhaps, with his religious profession—but it was a view largely accepted by the Catholic Church, which, though it preferred to co-opt pagan art for Christian purposes, never saw a conflict between truth and beauty. Constantine's enjoyment of sumptuous art certainly showed in the imperial accounts. His enormous building program of splendid churches, a new imperial city, and Christian-inspired welfare spending for widows, orphans, the sick, and the poor meant painfully high taxes.[10] But with high taxes came Christian-inspired law granting legal rights to slaves, abolishing gladiatorial exhibitions, prohibiting crucifixion, and closing down pagan temples that were hideaways of sexual immorality—immorality, that is, as defined by Christian terms. While pagans in general were tolerated, Christian heretics, at least those groups that were small in number, were not. Their writings were burned, their churches consecrated to the Catholic faith.

For Constantine, however, the issue was not necessarily doctrine—which he did not profess to understand beyond adherence to the Nicene Creed—but unity. The Arian-Catholic division within the Eastern half of the empire was so profound that even an apostolic city like Antioch had a Catholic *and* an Arian bishop. The Arians were strenuous lobbyists for Constantine's support, attempting to convince him that Arianism should be the unifying religious principle of his empire. As Arian influence flared—even within his own court—he felt pressured to appease it. The focus of Arian hostility became a single man: Athanasius. The Arians

believed that if the leading defender of Catholic orthodoxy could be discredited, they would finally win Constantine to their side. Among other
crimes, the Arians accused Athanasius of ordering the murder of Arsenius, a bishop from the schismatic Church of the Martyrs, which had become allied with the Arian insurgency. A synod was called to establish
Athanasius's guilt, and Constantine sent the Eastern Empire's highest-
ranking praetorian prefect, his half brother, Dalmatius, to observe and
investigate.

The chief piece of evidence at the trial was a shocker—the fire-
blackened hand of Arsenius, which was passed around for all to see and
touch. Athanasius stood before the synod knowing it was disposed
against him, but he had a masterstroke. He produced a witness whose
face and hands were hidden. He threw back the hood and lifted the
sleeves, shouting, "Has God given any man more than two hands?"[11] For
before the synod stood Arsenius.

While his opponents screamed witchcraft, Athanasius explained that
the Arians and their allies had sent Arsenius into hiding so that they could
launch these false and malicious charges. His truth telling was greeted in
the usual manner—by a riot. A Roman officer rescued him, just as a
Roman officer had rescued St. Paul at the Temple in Jerusalem.

The Catholic bishop made another extraordinary appearance, this
time before the emperor himself, surprising Constantine while he rode
from Constantinople. Athanasius demanded a hearing before the emperor—for his definitive judgment—where he could defend himself
against incessant Arian charges. His request was granted, but prior to the
trial Constantine received word that a gathering of Eastern bishops had
condemned Athanasius and pronounced the Church of the Martyrs and
the Arians in full communion.

Wanting no more trouble from his Eastern clerics, Constantine sent
Athanasius into exile—but it was a soft exile that put the brave defender
of the Catholic Church at the court of the Caesar of the West, Constantine's son, Constantine II. This exile would have long-lasting effects for
Church history, strengthening Catholic orthodoxy in the West and leaving
the East in contentious feuds and confusion about the divinity of Christ,
the nature of the trinity, and loyalty to the Apostolic See in Rome.

As a further sop to the Eastern bishops and to his pro-Arian court
advisers, Constantine agreed to interview Arius as a step toward lifting

his excommunication. The emperor demanded that Arius swear before the judgment of God that he was of the true faith, as written in the Nicene Creed. Arius did so, and Constantine ordered that he be accepted back into the Church. There was, however, a serious hitch. The aged bishop of Constantinople, Alexander, told the emperor that he could not offer communion to a man who was so obviously a heretic and had done so much to destroy the unity of the Catholic faith.

As ever, Constantine dismissed such scruples and ordered that on Sunday, Arius receive communion. Bishop Alexander secluded himself in prayer, begging God to preserve the sanctity of his church from the heretic and to bring His divine will down upon Arius. On Sunday, as Arius strolled happily toward the church, accompanied by friends, he was suddenly doubled over with pain. He died, on gore-slicked tiles, in a public restroom. His death was an immediate news sensation, with the city's churches rejoicing that the heresiarch was dead. No act could have done more to shore up Constantine's Catholic faith than this. To Constantine, God's hand was in everything. It had led him to victory at the Milvian Bridge. It had made him sole emperor and defender of the faith. Now it had struck down a religious troublemaker from whom he had explicitly required an oath of fidelity to the Creed, an oath that Arius had taken, apparently, without true belief.

Constantine died seven months later. He was officially received into the Church on his deathbed, an act of prudence from a man who feared he would be called to do unChristian things as emperor. With baptism a one-time sacrament to wash away sins, Constantine wanted to receive it after the danger of further sin had passed. He told his confessors that he originally hoped to be baptized in the River Jordan. But now it was too late. The bishop presiding at the baptism was Eusebius of Nicomedia. If the Arians had ultimately not won Constantine to their side, one of their supporters nevertheless was the bearer who brought him into communion with the faith.

With Constantine dead, the empire suffered from his crucial mistake of dividing the imperial realms among his family. It seems odd that one who so understood the need for religious and political unity should have willingly sown familial divisions over succession to the purple, but such was the case. In the West, the ruler of Britain, France, and Spain was Constantine II, friend of Athanasius and soon-to-be imperial defender of the Church. Young Constans was an obvious subordinate for Constantine II, as he held Italy and North Africa. In the East, Constantius II held sway, his domains stretching from Egypt to Iraq and swinging west to incorporate parts of Turkey, where he faced Dalmatius, who inherited Constantinople and Greece. Constantine's nephew, Hannibalianus, was given a portion of Asia Minor, which made him a tool to be used by either Dalmatius or Constantius II. All Roman history pointed to the impossibility of this arrangement ending in anything other than civil war. By dividing the empire into five parts, Constantine ensured that such a civil war would not be easily resolved. Perhaps he was hoping that its complexity would force a balance of power and a precarious peace. If so, this occasionally idealistic soldier-statesman betrayed a disconcerting innocence about the ways of men. It was not long before the legions began buckling on their shields.

## CHAPTER FIVE

# THE WAR FOR
# THE EMPIRE

⟹●⟸

AFTER THE AMERICAN CONSTITUTION was ratified, Benjamin Franklin said the American people had been given "A Republic, Madam, if you can keep it."[1] Similarly, Constantine had given the Catholic Church religious authority over an empire, if it could keep it.

The popes who paralleled Constantine's reign—St. Miltiades, who had received from him the gift of the Lateran Palace; St. Sylvester I, who was pope for more than twenty years; and the short-lived St. Marcus—had been pressed off the historical stage by the brilliant illumination of the emperor. For a quarter of a century, Constantine had been the real focal point of Christianity. There was, however, no one to take his place as the new imperial defender of the faith. Of the inheritors, Dalmatius and Hannibalianus were quickly seized and executed by their own legions at the instigation of Constantine's sons, who then re-divided the empire. The three Augusti were young, ranging in age from 18 to 22, but not callow. They had been born and trained to the purple. Religiously, there were strong grounds for hope. From his time with Athanasius, Constantine II was a firm Catholic, as was Constans, who held Italy and now also Constantinople, with secular authority over both the old and the new Rome. Even Constantius II, who was fashionably, after the manner of his father's court, pro-Arian, did not object when Constantine II restored Athanasius as bishop of Alexandria, which was officially in Constantius II's domain. With Constantine's passing, there also came a new pope,

St. Julius I, who was determined to stop any further slippage of the empire into Arianism.

The trouble began when Constans looked to Constantius II as his protector from the overweening ambitions of Constantine II. Though religious allies, the relationship between Constans and Constantine II was the first of many historical proofs that the religious professions of kings do not necessarily determine how they array their armies. Constantine II, as the eldest brother, decided that he should add Italy to his possessions while Constans was away fighting barbarians along the Danube. Returning to defend his third of the empire, Constans cleverly ambushed the self-styled senior Augustus, his archers cutting him down in a torrent of arrows.

From five original inheritors, now there were two. The empire was divided between Constans in the West and Constantius II in the East. Constans survived until the legions grew tired of his high-handedness and deposed him in favor of an officer named Magnetius, who himself survived only long enough for Constantius II to take his legions West and crush him. That accomplished, Constantius II returned to the Eastern Empire, executed the Caesar he had elevated to rule while he was gone, and pronounced himself sole emperor. With miserable luck, the one Augustus left standing after the near extinction of the male heirs of Constantine was the only pro-Arian among them. There was, however, one other with at least a partial claim to the blood royal, and that was Julian, the son of Constantine's half brother Julius Constantius, who had perished at the beginning of the familial bloodletting that followed Constantine's death. Julian was regarded as a gifted young man, and Constantius raised him to the rank of Caesar.

Julian, like Constantius, had been instructed by the Arian bishop Eusebius of Nicomedia, but his imagination wandered far from the dry philosophizing of Christian heresy to dreams of past Roman glory, of the gods who had elevated Rome to greatness, of the Greek mystery religions that were so much more creative and stimulating and self-affirming than Christianity, with its endless doctrinal squabbles. And there was a personal reason, too, for turning from Christianity. Constantine's sons were Christians. It was they, Christians, who had ordered his father's death for no reason other than a fear of future familial rivalry. Ironically, that rivalry would not have occurred had his pleasure-loving, unambitious father lived. But now revenge lurked in Julian's heart. As he made his way upward in Rome's ruling class, he nurtured a desire to restore the old gods, to honor the old ways of pagan Rome against the Church.

At Constantius's direction, Julian became Caesar of the West, leading campaigns against the barbarians, while the emperor returned to govern the Arian East and fight the Persians. Inevitably, the imperial forces of West and East clashed again, as the Western legions proclaimed Julian emperor. His elevation was secured when Constantius II—who demanded Julian's unconditional surrender—died on the march to destroy his upstart cousin in battle.

Julian was now the last descendant of Constantine Chlorus left standing, and the only pagan. His belief would not remain private. During the reign of Constantius II, in St. Jerome's famous formulation, "The whole world groaned when, to its astonishment, it discovered that it was Arian. . . . The little ship of the Apostles was in peril."[2] Now the whole world would awake to find the pagan gods returned to imperial favor and religious supremacy.

This period from Constantine to Julian covers nearly two and a half decades. For the near entirety of this time, Pope Julius held the See of Peter, focusing his attention on three main tasks—spreading the gospel, building churches, and fighting Arianism. It is also from his pontificate that we have the first written records of the feast days of the saints. Also surviving is a letter from Pope Julius that is of continuing relevance because of the claims it makes for the papacy. The letter concerns the charges of the Arians against Athanasius. Two years after Constantine II had restored him to his bishopric in Alexandria, Athanasius was again exiled by the conspiring, Arian-influenced bishops of the Eastern Church. Roused to Athanasius's defense, Pope Julius accuses the bishops of acting contrary to the Apostles, contrary to Church tradition, and, most of all, contrary to the ecclesiastical rights of the pontiff in Rome to whom the matter should have been referred for judgment. "Are you ignorant that the custom has been to write first to us, and then for a just decision to be passed from this place? . . . But now, after they have done as they pleased, they want to obtain our concurrence. . . . Not thus are the constitutions of Paul, not thus the traditions of the Fathers. This is another form of procedure, and a novel practice. I beseech you, bear with me willingly: what I write about is for the common good. For what we have received from the blessed Apostle Peter, these things I signify to you."[3] The protest about "another form of procedure, and a novel practice" perfectly captures the Roman spirit of fidelity, which was embodied and to be enforced by the papacy.

The Eastern bishops, however, refused to comply, calling their own synod and condemning Athanasius yet again. Like their father before them, the dual emperors Constans and Constantius II tried to bring peace to this endless dispute. In 343, they called for an episcopal council of the Eastern and Western Churches in what is now Sofia. The council was not a success from an imperial point of view. The Eastern bishops continued their litany of condemnation, including Athanasius, as was now traditional; the pope; and the council itself, which they abandoned in a huff. In their absence, the more orthodox Western bishops added to canon law the stipulation that any bishop condemned by his fellows had the right to appeal to Rome. Though the Eastern and Western Churches were still officially one, it was apparent that schism was virtually inevitable, the West accepting Catholic orthodoxy, the East drifting into Arian heresy.

Indeed, the immediate decades after the death of Constantine seemed to presage disaster for the faith. In the past, "slowly the cross followed the fasces, and the Roman eagles made straight the way for Christ."[4] But now, with the refusal of the Eastern bishops to accept the pope's authority and the empire finally reunited under the emperor Constantius II, a professed Arian, imperial Catholicism was like a shattered glass that only a miracle could reassemble. The ancient pagan historian Ammianus Marcellinus, a soldier and contemporary of Constantius II, wrote of the Arian emperor that the "Christian religion, which in itself is plain and simple, *he* confounded by the dotage of superstition. Instead of reconciling the parties by the weight of his authority, he cherished and propagated, by verbal disputes, the differences that his vain curiosity had excited. The highways were covered with troops of bishops galloping from every side to the assemblies, which they called synods; and . . . they laboured to reduce the whole sect to their own particular opinions."[5] Pagans and Catholics understood that clerical dissent discredited Christian claims to truth. Edward Gibbon, commenting on this passage, noted that it "justifies the rational apprehensions of Athanasius, that the restless activity of the clergy, who wandered round the empire in search of the true faith, would excite the contempt and laughter of the unbelieving world."[6]

There was a price to be paid for such chaos. In Gibbon's marvelous summation, the "divisions of Christianity suspended the ruin of Paganism" and the pagan "religion which had so long . . . been established in the Roman Empire was still revered by numerous people, less attached indeed to speculative opinion than to ancient custom."[7] It was the strength of the Catholic Church—however embattled it now was—that it recognized that "ancient custom" had a greater claim on men's hearts than did "speculative opinion," and that in Christian disputes was more likely to be true, untouched by Greek sophistry. But the heretical bishops who refused to bow to Rome and unity ensured that the whole edifice of a Christian empire collapsed. Julian, the pagan standard-bearer, came to the purple to liberate the Romans who were languishing "under the ignominious tyranny of eunuchs and bishops."[8]

## JULIAN THE APOSTATE, AND THE WAR OF THE GODS

BUT IF THE ROMANS expected that under Julian they would see a rebirth of "*laissez les bon temps rouler,*" they were mistaken, for the paganism Julian had developed in his study was of an idiosyncratic kind and likely held solely by himself. It was an admixture of pagan religion, Christian organization and morality, and classical philosophy. It was truly traditional only in the sense that it adapted Rome's traditional syncretism—and massively enlarged it. The new emperor was chaste, ascetic to the point of personal filth—including a beard that was infested with lice. Apparently this delighted him, for he wrote that the lice "run about in it like wild beasts in a thicket."[9] He was a vegetarian, shunned the imperial pomp of Constantine and his sons, and preferred sleeping on the ground to living in a palace. In an effort to reduce the enormous tax burden imposed by Constantine, Julian abolished the imperial court and its staff. The one luxury Julian indulged was his library and the consolations of philosophy. His Enlightenment votary Edward Gibbon muses that Julian "might perhaps sincerely have preferred the groves of the Academy and the society of Athens; but he was constrained . . . to expose his person and fame to the dangers of Imperial greatness; and to make himself accountable to the world and to posterity for the happiness of millions"[10]—a commentary proving that religious historians have no monopoly on hagiography.

Julian was brave and talented. He won the purple leading legions, and he was enormously capable in administration. It is claimed that he could write, listen, and dictate simultaneously. He had a reactionary attachment to Roman civic virtue, announcing that he would be bound by the laws of the Republic and could claim no legal advantages over any other citizen. As Constantine had endowed churches, Julian restored pagan temples and aided the ancient cities of Greece, the home of classical philosophy, his holy land. Constantine had treated the pagans with benign neglect, but his sons had made foolish, ineffectual, half hearted efforts to end paganism before succumbing to popular opinion. Julian enjoined popular pagan resentment to end Christianity's status as the official imperial religion and renewed, though in a comparatively mild way, anti-Christian persecutions. Christians were expelled from state schools and forbidden to read or teach anything but the Christian Scriptures. Modern Biblical fundamentalists might approve of that policy. Catholics at the time, being classical men, did not.

Constantine's policy of state support for Christian clerics was reversed so that Christians were now obliged to repay the state for previous benefactions. These financial reparations would be used to compensate paganism for its half-century of neglect. Worse, the new wall of separation dividing Christianity from the state meant that anti-Christian mobs could—and did—attack Christians with impunity, encouraged by the emperor, who reminded them that Christians were taught to endure suffering joyfully—so suffer they jolly well should.

Edward Gibbon, whose *History of the Decline and Fall of the Roman Empire* is the most influential history of the period, closes his portrait of Julian by asserting that the "generality of princes, if they were stripped of their purple and cast naked into the world, would immediately sink to the lowest rank of society, without a hope of emerging from their obscurity." Except of course for Julian, who, Gibbon says, would have risen to the highest rungs of any profession on sheer merit. We must "confess, with a sigh," writes Gibbon, "that the apostate Julian was a lover of his country, and that he deserved the empire of the world."[11]

Gibbon's infatuation aside, however, there is no reason why Julian "deserved the empire of the world." His reign lasted less than two years. His attempt at reviving paganism proved entirely misbegotten. His religious opinions were an adolescent mishmash of neo-Platonism, abject superstition of a sort Gibbon would have mocked in a Christian, and personal vendetta. In its totality, Julian's religion likely appealed to no one but himself. His ultimate legacy was to thoroughly discredit the paganism he hoped to restore. Nevertheless, he continues to act as a bug light down the ages, attracting secular intellectuals who yearn to restore a pre-Christian world. He is their model, their tragic and doomed Alexander the Great.

Like Alexander, Julian met his end in battle in the ever turbulent East. One accolade we cannot deny Julian is that of patriot. He died fighting the Persians. According to some sources—whom Gibbon of course discounts—his last words were "Galilean, Thou hast triumphed," though frankly there is little reason to doubt that these were indeed his last words, given that his imagination was so entirely given over to undoing the Christianization of Rome, and "Galileans" was his disparaging term for Christians. It is certainly easier to believe that than to believe that his last words, or actually his last speech—since he reportedly continued to converse on philosophy, the soul, and other matters before expiring— were as given by Gibbon, citing Ammianus Marcellinus. The emperor, though felled by a lance (or, in some sources, an arrow) that pierced his ribs and penetrated his liver, supposedly addressed his comrades thus:

Friends and fellow-soldiers, the seasonable period of my departure is now arrived, and I discharge, with the cheerfulness of a ready debtor, the demands of nature. I have learned from philosophy how much the soul is more excellent than the body; and that the separation of the nobler substance should be the subject of joy, rather than of affliction. I have learned from religion that an early death has often been the reward of piety; and I accept, as a favour of the gods, the mortal stroke that secures me from danger of disgracing a character which has hitherto been supported by virtue and fortitude. I die without remorse, as I have lived without guilt. I am pleased to reflect on the innocence of my private life; and I can affirm with confidence that the supreme authority, that emanation of the Divine Power, has been preserved in my hands pure and immaculate. Detesting the corrupt and destructive maxims of despotism, I have considered the happiness of the people as the end of government. Submitting my actions to the laws of prudence, of justice, and of moderation, I have

trusted the event to the care of Providence. Peace was the object of
my counsels, as long as peace was consistent with the public welfare;
but when the imperious voice of my country summoned me to arms,
I exposed my person to the dangers of war, with the clear fore-
knowledge (which I have acquired from the art of divination) that I
was destined to fall by the sword. I now offer my tribute of gratitude
to the Eternal Being, who has not suffered me to perish by the cruelty of a tyrant, by the secret dagger of conspiracy, or by the slow
tortures of lingering disease. He has given me, in the midst of an honourable career, a splendid and glorious departure from this world;
and I hold it equally absurd, equally base, to solicit, or to decline,
the stroke of fate—Thus much I have attempted to say; but my
strength fails me, and I feel the approach of death—I shall cautiously
refrain from any word that may tend to influence your suffrages in
the election of an emperor. My choice might be imprudent or injudi-
cious; and if it should be ratified by the consent of the army, it might
be fatal to the person whom I should recommend. I shall only, as a
good citizen, express my hopes that the Romans may be blessed with
the government of a virtuous sovereign.[12]

If these were Julian's last words, he was a noble soul indeed, and his
comrades-in-arms could only have responded by exclaiming, "Are you
quite sure you're dying?"

But we know, as an historical fact, that Julian did die on the field of
battle. The legions were so impressed by Julian's religious reforms that
they gave a blue-blooded captain named Jovian, a Catholic, a battlefield
promotion to emperor. His first military challenge was to extricate the legions from their failed campaign, which meant a disastrous surrender of
Armenia and other Eastern possessions to the Persians. More happily,
Jovian reinstated Constantine's Christian battle standard, the labarum, to
the legions. He restored Constantine's laws, including the Edict of Milan,
ensuring religious tolerance for pagan and Christian. Finally, he returned
the aged and exiled Athanasius to his bishopric in Alexandria, from
which the great man would not again be banished, and in which post he
would serve another ten years.

Jovian, however, served only nine months before dying in his sleep at
the age of thirty-three; whether by poison (unlikely), from too much drink

(Catholic soldiers were not teetotalers), or from some other cause remains a matter of dispute. The next emperor was another Catholic, Valentinian I, who would retain the purple for a decade, reigning from 364 to 375, and who, like Julian—and like Jovian during his brief reign—was a reactionary, though Valentinian's model was Constantine. Valentinian, though openly Catholic, was adamant about governing with religious impartiality, granting benefits equally to pagan and Catholic alike. The prototypical Valentinian statement was this one, on the Arian versus Catholic controversy, "I am a layman. It is no business of mine to scrutinize Christian dogma. That is the bishop's affair."[13] A sound view for a soldier-emperor to take—mixing appropriate Catholic humility before designated authority, a commonsensical practicality, and a Christ-sanctified division of labor, a division that did not prevent him from outlawing the practice of infanticide against the pagan adherents of familial "choice."

While some, such as Gibbon, see Julian as a paragon of Roman tolerance—tolerance then as now being defined as accepting of everything except Christianity—it is Valentinian who strikes the note of true tolerance, a tolerance that skeptics ignore and that Protestants suspect. Commenting on pagan auguries, Valentinian commented, "I do not consider this art to be criminal, nor indeed any of the religious observances established by our ancestors. The laws enacted at the beginning of my reign are proof of this. They grant to every man the right to follow whatever religion he prefers. I do not, therefore, condemn the auspices. I simply forbid them to be used for criminal purposes."[14]

Catholic Christianity, as reflected by the emperor Valentinian, did not oppose Roman patriotism; it could not find it in its heart to condemn those Romans who spake like "brave Horatius, the Captain of the Gate: 'To every man upon this earth / Death cometh soon or late. / And how can man die better / Than facing fearful odds, / For the ashes of his fathers, / And the temples of his Gods."[15] Rather than condemn such patriotism tied to Rome's pagan gods, Valentinian sought to absorb it, letting each man follow his conscience, confident that, over time, the cross of Catholicism, the labarum of the legions, would become the symbol of every Roman's God. In this, he would in large part be vindicated. The military historian Vegetius, writing little more than a decade after Valentinian's reign, records a Christianized *sacramentum,* the sacred oath taken by the legionnaires: "They swear by God, by Christ, and by the Holy

Spirit; and by the Majesty of the Emperor, which, next to God, should be loved and worshipped by the human race. . . . The soldiers swear to perform with enthusiasm whatever the Emperor commands, never to desert, and not to shrink from death itself on behalf of the Roman state."[16]

Valentinian was emperor of the West. He appointed his brother Valens as emperor of the East, an appointment that might have been wise on grounds of personal loyalty, but which furthered the cultural divide between East and West, for while the West remained Catholic and pagan, the East continued its course of being Arian and pagan. Valens was a patron of the Arian cause, and just as the Arians had joined forces with the Church of the Martyrs against Catholics, now they enlisted the pagans on the grounds of *pas des ennemis à gauche*.

Valens was a former pagan himself who, taking the Eastern-throne, had his rival, Procopius, an ally of Julian, literally torn asunder. He was baptized in 367 as an Arian and brought a pagan sense of justice to the Arian-Catholic war of words. His most famous atrocity was with eighty Catholic bishops and priests who were petitioning him for tolerance. He assembled them on a ship, sent it out to sea, and then set it aflame. He had a member of his court, Theodorus, murdered after it was predicted that the name of Valens's successor would begin with the letters THEOD. Though Theodorus died, the prophecy came true. The next emperor in the East, following Valens's death in a war against the barbarians in 378, was Theodosius.

In the West, Gratian succeeded Valentinian. With Theodosius in the East, he stamped the Christian religion firmly and forever on the empire. Though only sixteen when he gained the purple, he was a forceful presence, kicking the struts from beneath what was now a shriveled paganism. Rather than assume the title Pontifex Maximus, he abolished the office and eventually abolished all pagan privileges from the state. But there were no persecutions. Paganism was left to evaporate on its own. In this, Gratian was guided by St. Ambrose, the great doctor of the Church and bishop of Milan, in whom "the magnanimity of the Roman patrician was tempered by the meekness and charity of the Christian saint."[17] After Gratian was killed trying to put down rebellious legions in Gaul, Ambrose became the religious adviser to his eventual successor, Valentinian II. The new emperor dabbled with Arianism, the creed of his mother, but returned, under Ambrose's influence, to the Catholic faith. Ambrose also guided the thought of the greatest Roman emperor since Constantine, Theodosius, the Augustus of the East and finally of all the empire.

## THEODOSIUS, AMBROSE, AND A CHRISTIAN IMPERIUM

THE EMPEROR THEODOSIUS was the *Restitutor Reipublicae,* the last emperor to unite the Eastern and Western Empires. He also dealt the deathblow to paganism and the Arian heresy. A handsome, virile, clean-shaven Spaniard,[18] he was the first emperor to hail from the West in a century and a half. Raised as a soldier and a gentleman, when his father was unjustly disgraced and executed, he retired to private life. There, in Gibbon's words, he "displayed a firm and temperate character . . . and the diligence of the soldier was profitably converted to the improvement of his ample patrimony."[19] Theodosius's meritorious conduct—along with the memory of his previous battlefield exploits—won him elevation to the purple. He was also a Catholic and made sure when he was baptized, at the age of thirty-four, that the ceremony was performed by an orthodox Catholic bishop. That same year, 380, he issued a joint edict with the emperor Gratian, defining Christianity as "the religion which was taught by St. Peter to the Romans, which faithful tradition has preserved, and which is now professed by the pontiff Damasus,[20] and by Peter, bishop of Alexandria, a man of apostolic holiness. According to the discipline of the apostles, and the doctrine of the Gospel, let us believe the sole deity of the Father, the Son, and the Holy Ghost, under an equal majesty and a pious Trinity. We authorise the followers of this doctrine to assume the title of Catholic Christians; and as we judge that all others are extravagant madmen, we brand them with the infamous name of Heretics, and declare that all their conventicles shall no longer usurp the respectable appellation of churches."[21]

Theodosius took the same tough-minded approach to heretics as he had against the barbarians, whom he had defeated and then brought into the empire as allies. Heretical churches were restored to the Catholic faith. Pagan practices—including witchcraft—were officially outlawed, their performance designated as treason to the emperor. Theodosius's legions put Valentinian II on the Western throne. When the Western emperor was murdered, Theodosius avenged him in an Alpine battle that proved the last stand of Roman paganism. The murderer was a barbarian commander named Abrogastes, a supposed ally of Rome. He proclaimed Eugenius, a nominal Christian, Augustus; and to rally pagan support, Eugenius led his rebels with a banner proclaiming *Hercules Invictus.* Theodosius's legions marched under the labarum of Constantine. Again the Christian God triumphed as a God of battle. In 394, Catholic Christianity's every opponent within the empire had been subdued by the emperor's sword.

But there was another famous incident during the reign of Theodosius that presaged the beginnings of medieval Christendom. In 390, after a Roman general was killed by a mob in Thessalonica—the mob was incensed by the officer's jailing of their favorite charioteer—Theodosius ordered a swift and terrible punishment on the city. The Thessalonians were called, in the name of the emperor, to the circus where they had missed their hero. There a detachment of soldiers, recruited from barbarian tribes, plunged their swords into the unsuspecting crowd. At least seven thousand Thessalonians were slaughtered. It was a crime of revenge, a throwback to Neronian ideas of justice. St. Ambrose, the confessor of emperors, would not let Theodosius escape responsibility for it. In a letter, the saint told the emperor that his hands were stained with blood, that he had no place before Christ's altar, that he was unworthy, in his current state of sin, to receive the body of Christ in the Eucharist, and that he should commit himself to a regimen of prayer to mark the beginning of his penance.

Theodosius the sword-wielder now became Theodosius the penitent. He wrote to Ambrose, pleading in expiation that if he was guilty of murder, so was David of the Old Testament, and surely David was beloved of God. Ambrose responded, "You have imitated David in his crime, imitate then his repentance."[22] Theodosius appeared in Ambrose's church in Milan, stripped of all symbols of imperial power, begging forgiveness, which was granted him after a penitential period of eight months. In Ambrose's own words, "Stripping himself of every emblem of royalty he publicly in church bewailed his sin. That public penance, which private individuals shrink from, an Emperor was not ashamed to perform; nor was there afterwards a day on which he did not grieve for his mistake."[23]

This image—of the Imperial Augustus, master of all the legions, ruler of the entire Roman Empire, bowing before an unarmed cleric of the

Catholic Church—is surely one of the most shocking in the history of Rome. It shows not only the triumph of the Catholic Church, but the first, most dramatic instance of its supremacy over a king, with the laws of God, executed by His apostolic bishops, being the ultimate restraint on the fiery, tempestuous acts of Christian princes. Gibbon aptly cites the aphorism of Montesquieu: "The prince who is actuated by the hopes and fears of religion, may be compared to a lion, docile only to the voice, and tractable to the hand, of his keeper."[24] The fourth century, which opened with Decius's and Diocletian's anti-Christian persecutions, closed with their mighty, warlike successor to the imperial purple prostrating himself in penitence before a bishop and a saint.[25]

St. Ambrose came from a noble family. His father had governed, as a praetorian prefect, vast parts of the Western Empire, including Spain, France, and Britain. Imperial service was Ambrose's own first profession. Like Athanasius, he received a sterling liberal education, in Ambrose's case in Rome, and was fluent in Greek. He studied law and became a governor, domiciled in Milan. He was immensely popular, so popular that, when the oppressive Arian bishop of the city died, Ambrose was universally acclaimed as the heir apparent—the *vox populi* prompted, it is said, by a baby that cried, "Ambrose, bishop."[26] It was an honor he felt unqualified to accept, but to refuse was to risk inciting the mob to riot.

Ambrose was known as a Catholic, and to Catholics he represented relief. But Arians were willing to accept him as well, because as governor, he had carefully avoided theological controversies. Like the Catholic emperor Valentinian, he had seen to the secular law and left theology to the bishops, and it was Valentinian who approved him to the post and threatened penalties against any who would deny it to him. He was consecrated as bishop of Milan on December 7—what is now his feast day in the calendar of saints—374, and created, "the familiar role of the patriot prelate, statesman and diplomatist."[27]

As such, he resolved a dispute over the statue of Victory that had once decorated the chambers of the Senate. In the past, senators had made offerings of incense to the statue as they entered to perform their duties. Victory was a symbol of the Roman state religion and as such had been banished by Constantius II—though popular disapproval made him reverse his decision—and then by the firmer-minded Gratian. Gratian's successor was Valentinian II, but being just a boy, power lay with the

regent, the empress-mother Justina, who was an Arian. She wanted to restore Victory to its place, a symbol of pagan-Arian cooperation. But Ambrose's deft diplomacy kept that from happening. To Ambrose, it was not
an aesthetic matter, but a crucially important matter of symbols, of
whether the Roman Senate would be consecrated to paganism or whether
the new dispensation of a rising Catholic empire would be maintained.
Ambrose knew—as Catholics know—that symbolism is important, and
he asserted a vital Catholic principle: On issues of state that involve religion, the Church must be heard.

Ambrose continued to stake out the claims of Church power, of
which the dispute over Victory was a part. Ambrose routed the empress-
mother Justina on the appointment of bishops (she wanted Arians) and
over the assignment of churches (she wanted some designated for Arian
use). Churches, he said, were to be controlled by the bishops, not the emperor—and not the people. The Church was not a democracy, and if a
majority of parishioners wished to convert a church to Arianism, it was
the bishop's responsibility to stop them. Moreover, such laymen had no
right to appeal to the emperor. "In cases where matters of faith are in
question it is the custom for bishops to judge Emperors when the Emperors are Christians, and not for Emperors to judge bishops."[28] Ambrose's
great doctrine was that "The Emperor is within the Church, and not
above the Church."[29] Though he foiled the empress-mother's plans, he
was careful not to stir popular feeling—which he could easily have
done—against her. He was not a revolutionary. In his mind, her political
function was as necessary in its proper sphere as his ecclesiastical function
was in matters religious. It was a matter of checks and balances.

Ambrose was a practical man—a lawyer, let it be remembered, and a
governor—and he brought a Roman sense of statesmanship to the
Church. Like a Roman Senator, cast in the mold of Cicero, "He was,"
wrote St. Augustine, "one of those who speak the truth, and speak it well,
judiciously, pointedly, and with beauty and power of expression."[30] Like
many Romans—even with his liberal education—he had little time for the
abstruse theorizing of the Greeks. But he was devout and put himself
through an intense course of study on the Church fathers and the Scriptures. As bishop he showed himself a perfect follower of the Lord. He
made a gift of his land to the Church and donated his belongings to the
poor. Like Jesus and St. Paul, he preached the virtues of celibacy, perhaps

inspired on a personal level by the holy ideal of his sister, who was a nun. He led by example, devoting his evenings to long periods of prayer, and, like many a great man, was apparently too busy for any but the lightest fare. Indeed, it is said that he fasted from Monday through Friday, except on feast days of the saints. Such fasting did not make him impatient. He made time for anyone who came to see him or who wrote to him seeking instruction or advice. He carried on the daily responsibilities of a priest and focused, in his own preaching and writing, on the practical applications of Christian belief to leading a Christian life. He remained so beloved by the people—and so respected by the government that relied on his counsel—that, when he was nearing death in 397, a delegation of leading citizens was deputized to pray that he might live a bit longer. As the emperor Theodosius said of him, "I know of no bishop worthy of the name, except Ambrose."[31]

Though there were, of course, the bishops of Rome, who in the turbulent last half of the fourth century provided their own enduring witness to the faith and to the laying of the Catholic foundations of Western Europe. The popes of this period from 352 to 399 were Liberius, St. Damasus I, and St. Siricius. Their consistent theme was emphasizing the universal law-giving power of the papacy.

Liberius, the first pope not to be made a saint, spent his reign, from 352 to 366, defending Athanasius, combating the Arian treason of the bishops of the East, and withstanding pressure from the Arian emperor Constantius II, whose "burning desire" was that his condemnation of Athanasius "be confirmed by the higher authority of the bishop of the eternal city."[32] Unable to bribe him into compliance, Constantius II ordered the pope arrested. When the pope appeared before him, Constantius II demanded, "Who are you to stand up for Athanasius against the world?"[33] But stand he did, and Constantius II installed an Arian antipope, Felix, on the throne of St. Peter.

But even Constantius II was forced to confess the illegitimacy of this move, and its recognition as such by the people of Rome, whom he saw praying for Liberius's restoration. As a compromise, Constantius II had a proclamation read at the circus, which announced that Liberius and Felix would be joint bishops of the Eternal City. The people replied with a chant: "One God, One Christ, One Bishop."[34] Felix was driven out, and Liberius returned. Whether he returned in triumph is a matter of dispute.

Certainly the people of Rome greeted him with hosannas, and the pope himself appeared unbowed. St. Ambrose and Pope Anastasius I (399–401), among others, would testify to Liberius's holiness and courage. But some—including St. Athanasius—believed Liberius had been coerced into signing an imperial condemnation of the oft-exiled bishop in order to regain his throne. Athanasius said of Pope Liberius, "If he did not endure the tribulation to the end yet he remained in his exile for two years knowing the conspiracy against me."[35]

This shadow of doubt has been enough to permanently damage Liberius's reputation. While Athanasius might reasonably wonder why an Arian emperor would allow Liberius to return, it is equally reasonable to wonder why the emperor made no display of a document condemning Athanasius and signed by the legitimate pope, if he had one. What is beyond dispute is that once returned to his papal office, Liberius continued his defense of the orthodox Catholic faith. He annulled pro-Arian councils, ordered lapsed bishops to reaffirm their belief in the Nicene Creed, and, as the Church had always done, condemned as schismatics those who would force the rebaptism of believers who had been brought into the faith by Arian bishops.

Nevertheless, Liberius's reputation was further damaged, posthumously, when gang warfare, with one side invoking his name, decided the new pope. After weeks of street fighting and more than a hundred casualties, Pope Damasus I emerged victorious over Liberius's deacon Ursinus. Ursinus and his factionaries were exiled, where their bad behavior lost them any previous sympathy. Though the manner of his election—and the fact that he had served Constantius's antipope, Felix, when Liberius was held hostage—got Damasus off to an inauspicious start, he proved a worthy pope. He was as ardent against heresy as any, had no qualms ordering the state to do his bidding, restored the catacombs as a testimonial to Roman faith, built churches, and had the added advantage of seducing aristocratic women into thinking Catholicism the height of fashion—which of course it is.

His most lasting achievement, however, was arranging for St. Jerome, who worked as his secretary, to prepare a new Latin edition of the Bible, what we now know as the Vulgate. That was not St. Jerome's only contribution to Catholic letters. The ascetic scholar-saint was also a lively satirist of his time, with passages that read as much as satires of the Western world of the twentieth-first century as they do of the fading morality of Rome. "Some unmarried women prevent conception by the help of potions, murdering human beings before they are conceived; others, when they find themselves with child as the result of sin, secure abortions with drugs. . . . Yet there are women who say, 'To the pure all things are pure. . . . Why should I refrain from the food which God made for my enjoyment.'"[36] But it was not just members of the ancient Roman chapter of "Catholics for Choice" whom he mocked, but also professed Christians who did not accept that the monk and the virgin are the models of the Christian life. Celibacy was the proper discipline for the faithful—most especially for priests—and Jerome himself retired to monastic vows and lived in a cave while teaching classics to children and writing his translation of the Bible.

For a pope to employ such a brilliant wit, perfectionist, and idealist was undoubtedly dangerous, especially when Damasus was known as a smooth and worldly man. But, like many such men, Damasus had enough confidence not to worry about employing the sharpest tongue in the Catholic world. Damasus also proclaimed—and perhaps this was another source of his confidence—that the authority of the pope rested firmly on the words of Jesus to St. Peter and was therefore not subject to Church councils, whose authority and orthodoxy had been so discredited by the Arian schism.

The next pope, St. Siricius, whose pontificate covered 384 to 399, continued the promotion of papal supremacy. He quickly brushed aside a second challenge from Ursinus and, assembling a synod in Rome, reasserted the essentials of universal canon law for the Church. He joined forces with St. Ambrose to put down a variety of incipient heretical movements that included among their targets the virtues of celibacy and good works, as well as the perpetual virginity of Mary. Such debates, as important as they were in the defense of truth, were soon to be overshadowed by a Visigothic king named Alaric.

CHAPTER SIX

# A NEW BARBARIAN
# WORLD ORDER

———◦◦◦———

Aᴸɪᴛᴛʟᴇ ʟᴏᴏᴛɪɴɢ goes a long way. When the emperor Theodosius brought the Goths into the empire, it was with the promise of
the entertaining distraction of laying waste to Rome's enemies and the
pleasure of an annual subsidy.

But Theodosius's sons were unworthy successors who lacked their father's understanding of the barbarians. The new emperor of the West was
Honorius; in the East it was Arcadius. They were unworthy because they
were effete—a disability that was weakening the manly sinews that had
built the empire. The barbarians were impressed neither by their vigor,
nor by their plans to cut Theodosius's subsidy, nor by the once vaunted
legions of Rome. The mighty legions that had stamped the *Pax Romana*
on the world had degenerated into the Roman equivalent of the post-
Vietnam, pot-smoking, demoralized American army under President
Jimmy Carter. Gibbon, citing the military historian Vegetius, records that
the "relaxation of discipline and the disuse of exercise rendered the soldiers less able and less willing to support the fatigues of service; they complained of the weight of the armour, which they seldom wore; and they
successively obtained the permission of laying aside both their cuirasses
and their helmets. The heavy weapons of their ancestors, the short sword
and the formidable *pilum,* which had subdued the world, insensibly
dropped from their feeble hands. . . . [T]hey reluctantly marched into the
field, condemned to suffer either the pains of wounds or the ignominy of

flight, and always disposed to prefer the more shameful alternative. . . . The enervated soldiers abandoned their own and the public defense; and their pusillanimous indolence may be considered as the immediate cause of the downfall of the empire."[1]

Displacing them were the barbarians, as both the defenders and the assaulters of Rome. Real power in the West lay not with Honorius, but with his barbarian nobleman and adviser Stilicho, the Vandal who had married Theodosius's adopted daughter and whose own daughter married Honorius. Gibbon calls him "the sagacious and intrepid Stilicho"[2]— but the valiant Romanized barbarian would be undercut by political backbiting at home. In the East, power lay not with the pleasure-seeking Arcadius, but with his cruel and treacherous adviser Rufinus, who was eventually executed to popular applause.

Stilicho was the one man with any claim—on grounds of ability, valor, and battlefield success—to restore Rome against the barbarian threats that surrounded it. To the south, in North Africa, a rebellious Moorish kingdom had risen against the empire. To the north and west were the Goths, the most important being the ambitious Visigothic king Alaric. In the Eastern empire, a growing sense of estrangement and separate destiny was arising, by reason of differing languages, customs, ceremonies, and military challenges, and the great city, Constantinople, which had displaced the Greek-speakers' religious and secular attachment to Rome.

The East's sense of estrangement became mixed with a sense of self-preservation as Alaric's Visigoths first ravaged Greece, and then, in 410 sacked the greatest city of the ancient world, sending an earth-shattering shock wave throughout the empire.

During this period, Stilicho was the great military fixer. He stalled the Visigoths' advance in Greece, prevented self-destructive war between the two halves of the empire, and attempted to save Rome by successfully thwarting every move of the barbarian hordes. But the political intriguers of the Western Empire seemed intent on suicide, more concerned with eliminating talented, industrious men who by their courage might rise to the purple, than with fighting the enemy. Stilicho was too honorable a man—and too busy doing what needed to be done—to guard against the political conspirers who finally convinced Honorius to order his death, which Stilicho accepted with unresisting stoicism. His execution in 408 made Alaric's invasion possible, and the perfidy, corruption, and shortsightedness it revealed almost make the barbarian invasion a consummation devoutly to be wished.

In fact, at least in retrospect, something close to that pro-barbarian attitude became the position of many Christian intellectuals, who saw God's judgment in Rome's fall. A fifth-century Catholic priest of Marseilles named Salvianus saw the invading barbarians as noble savages—Arians for the most part, yes, but more Christian in their comradely behavior, their straightforwardness, and their manly devotion to chastity and monogamy than the weak, dissolute, and conniving Romans. It was the barbarians who were shocked by prostitution, not the Romans; it was the barbarians who could overwhelm cities because the Roman rabble was too busy sating its lust for blood and spectacle at the circus to think of dutiful self-defense; it was the barbarians who tempered violence with mercy, rather than with refined and cowardly cruelty.

Such was the argument of Salvianus's book *On the Government of God*. But the most famous Christian meditation on the fall of Rome came not from Salvianus, but from a saint.[3]

## THE BISHOP OF HIPPO

THE WAYWARD, sinful early life of St. Augustine—the pear-thieving boy; the scholar of restless mind who explores every philosophical school; the young man who finally hearkens to his mother's Christianity but finds he cannot embrace it as easily as a concubine, "Give me chastity, but not yet!"—is well known because his *Confessions* is one of the most famous books of Western literature, and one of the most profound and emotional examinations of conscience. It can even be shocking for modern readers who think of God as a smiling, yellow happy-face and who see Augustine's sins—if such they be—as venial at worst. But Augustine saw something much different. He saw himself blinded by the light of God, a small figure in his Father's hands, knowing, under His steady gaze, that he had lived wrongly, unjustly, unfaithfully to the One to Whom he owed everything. It was, he knew, the most important revelation a man could have. He resolved to live his life by this discovery and make right his failing before God.

Still, Augustine had to be dragged into the faith. As a classically trained intellectual, he was more interested in debate—and when it came

to personal behavior, finding individual loopholes—than he was in
dogma. He objected to the Bible. To read it was only to prove its absurdity. But the great St. Ambrose told him it was not to be read literally, but
symbolically. Ambrose recommended "most emphatically to his congregation this text as the rule to go by: 'The letter killeth, but the spirit
giveth life.' So he would draw aside the veil of mystery and explain in a
spiritual sense the meanings of things which, if understood literally, appeared to be teaching what was wrong."[4]

Reading the Bible under Ambrose's sophisticated guidance brought
Augustine closer to Christianity, but for a mind shot through with the ele-
gance of Platonism it was not enough. "I wanted to be just as certain
about things which I could not see as I was certain that seven and three
make ten."[5] He was cautious not only because he wanted to be certain,
but because he knew, painfully, that he had made philosophical errors before. He had once, and for nine years, accepted the religion of the
Manicheans—who saw a world starkly divided between good and evil,
who mixed Eastern and Western religion to find universal truth, and who
offered the promise, like the Gnostics, of secret knowledge—before he
recognized its faults. If common sense and a realization of the Manicheans' superficiality freed him from that error, it was recognizing the
limits of reason—something that is the mark of the truly reasonable
man—that helped incline him to the Catholic Church.

Ambrose directed him to St. Paul, a figure with whom the hot-
blooded Augustine could identify—a man who began violently opposed
to Christianity, but who was, against his will, shaken by revelation and a
concomitant sense of unshakable faith that Jesus was the Son of God.
Augustine would soon have his own revelation. One day he heard a
voice chanting in his ear, "Take it and read it." He opened the epistles of
St. Paul and his eyes fell upon "Not in rioting and drunkenness, not in
chambering and wantonness, not in strife and envying: but put ye on the
Lord Jesus Christ, and make not provision for the flesh in concupis-
cence." That had been his life; that was what he must change. He was already resolved to action before he showed the passage to his friend
Alypius. But Alypius pointed out a line that followed: "Him that is weak
in the faith, receive."[6]

Whatever weakness afflicted Augustine's faith did not last long. After
his reception into the Church by St. Ambrose, Augustine organized a

monastic community—what would become the Augustinian order, the oldest continuing monastic order in Christendom—intending to devote himself to chastity, poverty, prayer, and Christian scholarship. While Augustine remained true to his monastic vows, he did not live his life secluded from the tempests of his age. Instead, he would become a titanic public force and refuter of heresy, who died urging his fellow bishops to stand by their churches amidst the footfalls of the Vandal invasion of Roman North Africa.

Valerius, bishop of Hippo, importuned Augustine to become his assistant and, when Augustine assented, ordained him a priest. Augustine's burgeoning reputation as a homilist of extraordinary force, and as a debater who could see off all comers, led to his being elected successor bishop. Like Ambrose, Augustine tried to refuse the honor. He pleaded that he be allowed to return to the monastic vocation he had chosen. His entreaties were denied, and it was in this office that Augustine would become the Catholic thunderer of North Africa.

Decades of philosophical study—for he had been a teacher of rhetoric—now released itself in a flood of books, letters, and polemics on behalf of the Church. First, he battled the Donatists. For a hundred years in North Africa these churches had refused to accept repentant apostates, as ordered by forgiving Rome. Augustine became the leading Catholic spokesman in the rhetorical campaign against this pointless schism—a campaign that succeeded, by imperial decree, with the forcible return of Donatist churches to the Catholic faith.

Next, he wrestled with Pelagianism. Pelagius was a British monk of ascetic temperament and optimistic ideas. Like many moderns, Pelagius denied Original Sin, argued for a radical view of the freedom of man, and, like Luther, was an antinomian, believing that faith alone is sufficient for salvation. With these ideas the logic of Christianity began to unravel. By denying Original Sin, he necessarily cast doubt on the sacrament of baptism, on the practice of prayer, perhaps even on the role of the priesthood, and, most fundamentally, on the redemptive nature of Christ's sacrifice. In essence, to Pelagius, Jesus was a Stoic philosopher with a few enhancements.

No man was better placed by temperament and knowledge than Augustine to rebut the Pelagian heresy and discredit its philosophical shortcomings, for no man was more convinced of the truth of Original Sin, and man's continuing propensity to sin, than St. Augustine. The battle, however, was not easily won. Pelagius and his allies were clever and able to divide Christianity. Two councils of Eastern bishops had exonerated him, in the tradition of Greek openness to heretical ideas.[7] Two synods in North Africa rejected Pelagian doctrine, in the tradition of the strict African Church. A letter signed by five North African bishops, including Augustine, referred the matter to Pope Innocent I. Pope Innocent's response was that no ruling of a synod was binding until approved by the See of Rome. He wrote, "it has been decreed by a divine, not a human authority, that whatever action is taken in any of the provinces, however distant or remote, it should not be brought to a conclusion before it comes to the knowledge of this see, so that every decision may be affirmed by our authority."[8] The pope decreed Pelagianism heretical, prompting Augustine's famous affirmation of papal primacy: "Two synods having written to the Apostolic See about this matter; the replies have come back; the question is settled."[9]

Unfortunately, the question wasn't settled. Pelagianism was discredited, but a new pope, Zosimus, had ascended the throne, and he received an appeal from Pelagius and his ally Caelestius. In a spirit of fairness and mercy, the pope was loath to excommunicate the two men unless absolutely necessary. Pelagius in particular had been covering his tracks, trying to limit the distance between his beliefs and Augustine's. He offered to let any errors of his be corrected by the pope, who "holds the faith and see of Peter."[10] Caelestius, too, professed his loyalty to Catholic teaching.

Pope Zosimus was naturally inclined to leniency, and told the African bishops so, while also affirming that he wanted their help in fully investigating the matter. The Council of Carthage, which convened in 418, definitively condemned Pelagianism as heretical. It also affirmed as universal Church doctrine the practice of infant baptism, the belief that all men are sinners, and other points that had been called into question by Pelagius. The bishops received the assistance of the pope, who issued his own encyclical on the Pelagian heresy, and of the emperor Honorius, who, taking time from watching the barbarians overrun his domain, ordered that the Pelagians exile themselves from Italy.

As was so often the case with heresies, the battle continued even after the war was over. Pelagianism was beaten, but St. Augustine was soon pitted against a heretical bishop named Julian who had picked up the

Pelagian banner. While their dispute led to a battle of polemics, the heresy moved its officers and pitched its tents in the East, where heresies generally had an easier time of it. But here, too, they lost imperial favor and were banished by the emperor Theodosius II. The last remnants of the creed lay among believers in its birthplace, Britain, and in neighboring France, which finally sent bishops to correct "the Pelagian island."[11] The heresy petered out, in every realm, by the early sixth century.

The victories against the heretics proved Augustine's energy and rhetorical vigor and also provided the spark for many of his books defining various aspects of the faith. But in addition to his personal confessions, his polemics, and his encyclopedic theological writings, Augustine was called to speak out on history, to explain to Christians why the very Roman civilization they had conquered and transformed from within was now divided and being torn to shreds by the wild tribes of Germany. Were men like Julian the Apostate right? Had the old gods of Rome been the city's and the empire's protectors? Had turmoil struck because the Romans turned their backs on their ancestral gods? It seemed a compelling argument, one that was picked up by Gibbon thirteen hundred years later. But Augustine said no. His massive treatise *The City of God* argued that Rome was not punished because she was Christian, but because she had failed to right herself from a course of sin. One of the most important points Augustine made, which would reverberate down the history of Catholicism, was to cite the elements of Christian virtue in pre-Christian Rome. Augustine praised Rome's noble, pre-Christian Stoic philosophers. He condemned the corruption of the quasi-Christian empire. There was no comparison between the gallant legions of Trajan and the moral and physical weaklings with which Stilicho had to make do. God, said Augustine, had recognized pagan Rome's virtues and rewarded her.

This teaching—that Christians could learn from pagan Rome, from the Stoics and other virtuous Romans—ensured that Catholicism never narrowed itself intellectually, the way Protestantism later did by relying on the Bible and faith alone, never denied history or history's complexity or its relevance to the faith, never repudiated the wisdom and the talents of the ancients, never limited Christian salvation, as in the theology of Luther and Calvin. Here are the seeds of the high Middle Ages—of Dante touring the afterlife with the Roman poet Virgil, a virtuous pagan—and of the Renaissance.

Of course Augustine's praise for pre-Christian Rome had its limits. The pagan gods, being false, far from helping Rome, accelerated its fall. Paganism sowed sexual immorality and rampant license; it removed checks from every desire and subverted the Stoic virtues that had made Rome great. Christianity, had it been truly held by the people, could have reinforced the sources of Roman greatness by stiffening Roman morality. As for God's judgment, look, said Augustine, at how the barbarians did not single out Christians for destruction or level churches; but they were unforgiving with symbols of paganism.

Beyond this empirical observation, Augustine added a philosophical one that became another keynote of Catholic thinking: A Christian's ultimate faith cannot be in the City of Man, no matter how mighty its fortunes, for all that is built on dust will return to dust. A Christian's ultimate home is in the City of God, and that is where he should seek his salvation.

Augustine's trust in God was exemplified beyond the printed page, beyond his loyalty to his vows, to the spear point of the Vandal invasion of North Africa. It was Augustine who, recognizing the danger of his times, developed the Catholic theory of just war. He knew that, unlike the Visigoths who sacked Rome, the Vandals spared no one and nothing. As they lay siege to his city—a siege that would last eighteen months— Bishop Augustine used his rhetorical skills to rally his starving people and maintain the morale of refugees who had sought sanctuary within the walls of his city. He died three months into the siege, at the age of seventy-six. Hippo, his city of man, was annihilated.

Augustine's massive body of written work survived, remaining the central influence on Catholic thought for the next eight hundred years, until St. Thomas Aquinas wrote the *Summa Theologica*. As has been noted by many, St. Augustine, as a philosopher, presages the thinking not only of later theologians, but also of Descartes, Kant, Schopenauer, Bergson, and others.[12] Augustine developed a permanent philosophical treasury in Catholic theology that has kept it intellectually richer than any other Western faith. As the scholar William Jurgens writes in his third volume of *The Faith of the Early Fathers*, "If we were faced with the unlikely proposition of having to destroy completely either the works of Augustine or the works of all the other Fathers and Writers, I have little doubt that all the others would have to be sacrificed. Augustine must remain."[13] Such is his influence that even many Protestant thinkers feel compelled to make claims to him. But St. Augustine's relentless rhetoric against every heresy and schism—from the Manicheans, to the Donatists, to the Pelagians, to the Arians, to every other anti-Catholic faction—make his continually restated loyalty to Catholicism undeniable. As Augustine himself wrote in his book *The True Faith,* "We must hold to the Christian religion and to communication in her Church which is Catholic, and which is called Catholic not only by her own members but even by all her enemies."[14]

## THE CINDERS OF EMPIRE, THE CANDLE OF FAITH

THE MOST OBVIOUS ENEMIES of the Roman Empire and the Church—the barbarians—were out in force. With the Western Empire now swept by currents of Goths, Vandals, and Huns, with secular authority crumbling, it became the Church's duty to become the bearer and defender of Roman and Christian civilization and to stand opposed—both in government and religion—against all who would desecrate and defile this inheritance. As Philip Hughes writes, from "the fifth century, down to the time of the discovery of America in the fifteenth, Europe and the Catholic Church are two names for the one thing."[15] That one thing was the melding of the Catholic religion—which survived the torches, rapes, and pillages of the Vandals and others—with the memory of Roman grandeur and the virtues of the rough-hewn, honor-driven, warlike Germanic peoples. It was a combination that would eventually find itself immortalized in chivalry. Where once Christianity followed the march of the Roman eagle, now it would sanctify the warrior spirit in the cult of the knight, the protector of the faith. But it was a process of centuries, of bringing a light to the dark forests that overgrew the ruins of Rome, of restoring the world through the establishment of castles and monasteries, crusaders and cathedrals, the work of peasants, princes, and popes.

The short-lived capital of the crumbling Western Empire was Ravenna, in northeastern Italy. From there, Honorius still laid claim to every Roman province. But Britain had slipped entirely from Roman control, and Visigothic chieftains held Spain and France, doing more or less as they pleased while professing loyalty to the emperor. The truly remarkable thing was that the transfer of power was so surprisingly pacific. The Romans simply gave way—they could not resist—and the Visigoths knew enough of Roman ways to fill the breach or to employ their former masters. By the middle of the fifth century, the effective reach of the old Western empire, of Caesar's great conquests, was contained behind the borders of Italy.

In contrast to the Visigoths, the Vandals who ravaged North Africa hated Rome as much as Hannibal had. They were also vehemently—where the Goths were only tepidly—anti-Catholic in the name of Arianism, which like the stench from a reopened tomb re-infected the Western world. Before the century was over, even the last remnant of the Western Roman Empire was crushed, the Italian peninsula conquered by the Ostrogoths. The imperial insignia of Rome were packed off to Constantinople, where an Orientalized Roman court lived on for another thousand years.

In the West, we enter the Dark Ages. The great monuments were rubble. The great unifying government of Roman law was shattered. There was now only one universal institution—the Church—and it operated without the defense of the Roman legions, weaving between the authority of scores of barbarian kings and scores more subsidiary chieftains, in a Western world that was now either officially Arian or pagan with Norse, Germanic, Celtic, or Slavonic gods. It verges on the miraculous that from the wreckage of Rome a Catholic network of monastic scholars and saints preserved the memory of the imperial city—its language, its literature, and its former grandeur, a thing that would haunt the Western imagination. But they also, of course, as their primary task, preserved the wisdom of Christ's Church, a wisdom that the world, in its ignorance, would have chosen to extinguish had it not been for the heroic witness of a new generation of brave, evangelizing saints.

It is all the more amazing that even amidst this chaos and ruin, the Catholic Church calmly continued to proclaim its universality and the primacy of the See of St. Peter, even against the ambitious church patriarchs who lived in the safety of Constantinople. On a cultural level, the pagan aristocracy of Rome had been converted to the Church. The pope was now as much for them as he was for families with a longer Catholic tradition, a connection to past Roman glory, and they became, as a class,

eager servants of the Church and defenders of its prerogatives, prerogatives that, in an Augustinian sense, were greater than those of any Augustus because the Church was an intermediary with the City of God.

Pope Leo, who held St. Peter's throne from 440 to 461, preached
that Rome had become "a holy people, an elect nation, a priestly and
royal city; become, through the See of St. Peter established here, the head
of the world, ruling more widely now through divine religion than it ever
did by worldly dominion. Though enlarged by many victories, you have
spread the authority of your rule over land and sea. What your warlike
labours have obtained for you is less than what Christian peace has
brought you."[16] In secular fact, this was a terrific exaggeration. But it
also made this point: Through the See of St. Peter, Rome was the center
of God's kingdom on earth, a position from which Rome could not—in
its own theological opinion—be budged, even by the wealth and security
of Constantinople.

A prime example of papal supremacy in action was the great Pope
St. Leo. It was St. Leo who famously rode from the gates of Rome and
convinced Attila the Hun to turn away from the city, sparing it. The story
loses a bit of its glamour, however, because another invader—the Vandal
chief Gaiseric—could not be dissuaded by Leo, except that he agreed to
loot peaceably and not, as it were, like the Vandal that he was.

The prime theological event of St. Leo's pontificate was the Council
of Chalcedon in 451, the largest gathering of Christian bishops up to that
time. All the bishops came from the East, but it was two representatives
sent by the pope who governed the Council. The main business of Chalcedon was refuting the latest in the long string of heretical ideas from the
East. In this case, the disputes were about whether Christ could be considered to have two separate natures or was one undivided person. This
was a continuation of an earlier controversy, dealt with at the Council of
Ephesus in 431, about whether Mary had given birth to Christ in only his
human nature and therefore could not be called the Mother of God. In
both cases, the Church held that Jesus' two natures were indivisible. Leo
wrote as much, and when his epistle, known as the *Tome,* was read to the
Council at Chalcedon, the bishops agreed, saying, "This is the faith of the
Fathers and of the Apostles. This we all believe. Peter has spoken through
Leo."[17] Those who disagreed—and there were always, somewhere, those
who disagreed—protestantized themselves as either Nestorians, who

clung to the idea "that there were two separate Persons in the Incarnate Christ, the one Divine and the other human,"[18] or Monophysites, who denied—and continue to do so in the Coptic and Syrian churches—that Jesus had any but a divine nature.

Along with these theological issues came an administrative one that, ironically, given its purpose, underscored the legitimacy of papal power. Among the decisions made by the Council was "Canon III," which gave Constantinople a place of honorary precedence behind Rome. For the Eastern bishops, however, this wasn't enough; they tried to enlarge their claims in Canon XXVIII of the Council by asserting "the privileges of the most holy Church of Constantinople, which is New Rome. For the Fathers rightly granted privileges to the throne of Old Rome, because it was the imperial city." Now with the Senate and the emperor residing in Constantinople, enjoying "equal privileges with the old Rome," so should Constantinople "in ecclesiastical matters also be magnified," as Rome is, "and rank next to her." The bishops proclaimed that "the Pontic, the Asian, and the Thracian Dioceses" should be granted to Constantinople's control.[19] In fact, these were powers that Constantinople had claimed—and had at least partly enforced—since 381 when it appropriated them at the First Council of Constantinople with the approval of the Eastern emperor, but not the pope.

The Eastern bishops' attempt to ratify their power grab, however, only showed their faulty presumption. As in 381, Constantinople based its claim on being a city of wealth and power. But the pope ruled from the See of St. Peter, not the See of Caesar, and papal authority rested on scriptural and apostolic grounds, not on the fact that Rome was "the imperial city." The Caesaropapism of the Eastern Church is here undisguised. But it is also interesting to note that the real target of the Eastern bishops was not Rome, but Alexandria, traditionally second in precedence to Rome and with which Constantinople had been in long and continuing administrative controversies.[20] The papal legates protested against Canon XXVIII, and Pope Leo rejected it outright—a rejection that the Eastern Church accepted, with the patriarch of Constantinople agreeing that the canon would not be officially binding; but how unofficially binding it would be was left open, and would remain a matter of dispute.

Rebellion erupted immediately after the Council. The breach was not between Rome and Constantinople, but between the Council's reassertion of orthodox Catholic belief and the tumultuous churches of Egypt and the Middle East. Nationalism and political rivalry with Constantinople became conjoined with the Monophysite heresy in an émeute—led by mad monks who had spent too long in the desert—against the orthodox Catholic bishops. The patriarch of Jerusalem required an army to return to his See. In Egypt, the warfare exploded for five years, with the province's government nearly overthrown and a mob killing and desecrating the body of the Catholic bishop of Alexandria. With the bishop's death and Catholic bishops everywhere deposed, Egypt became officially Monophysite in religion.

It was Pope Leo who convinced the wavering government in Constantinople that Egypt's imperial garrisons had to be reinforced, the mob put down, and the Monophysites ejected. Victory was achieved—and then swiftly overturned. A change of government in Constantinople meant a change of policy, with the Monophysites gaining imperial favor. But within two years the imperial preference reverted to Catholicism. With singular exceptions, the bishops of the East bowed to imperial demands like reeds beaten by the wind, signing successive imperial edicts that tried to find a middle ground that would satisfy every Eastern faction. These edicts took an unintentional note of self-parody during the reign of the emperor Basiliscus when he not only first favored the Monophysites, and then the Catholics, but also issued both the *Encyclion* and later the *Anti-Encyclion*.

Recognizing popular feeling in Egypt and the Middle East—and recognizing also that the Monophysites could rally armies of tens of thousands of mad-eyed desert monks, a new imperial compromise was issued from Constantinople. It put a Monophysite bishop in Alexandria, but on condition that he keep Catholics in communion with his church. This was, from a theological point of view, patently absurd. It was therefore accepted in the East, along with an ambiguous statement of faith meant to reconcile Catholics and Monophysites. Even the bishop of Constantinople, who had been a lone and heroic voice of Catholicism in the wavering East, tried to consider it a victory. But Rome did not. The bishop of Constantinople was declared schismatic. The deposit of faith was not subject to deal-making with Monophysites or anyone else. The pope excommunicated him, and the patriarch, in pique, responded in kind. This was the so-called Acacian Schism of

484—named after Acacius, the patriarch of Constantinople—which left the East divided between Monophysites and schismatics. It lasted for thirty-five years, until Emperor Justin restored the Catholic religion as the faith of Byzantium.

## THE BARBARIAN CONVERSION AND THE MISSION OF ST. PATRICK

IT IS WITH RELIEF that one turns from the courtly intrigue and endless theological disputes in the East to the Western Church, where Roman practicality and Germanic bluntness—with arguments settled straightfor-wardly by fist or by the sword—refresh rather than horrify. The West in fact saw a renewal of the missionary spirit of St. Paul. Where once the faith had been virtually coterminous with the borders of Rome, now it brought light into darkness. One of the foremost among the new apostles was St. Patrick, patron saint of Ireland.

The outlines of Patrick's life are well known: his birth in Britain to a well-to-do Romanized family, capture by pirates at the age of sixteen, six years as a slave in Ireland; his escape, consecration, and extraordinary work in establishing the Catholic Church in the Emerald Isle; his survival of twelve kidnappings, an order of death, and the violent hatred of the Druidic priests. Perhaps less well remembered than Patrick's adventures—including the apocryphal legend of his ridding Ireland of snakes—is his striking orthodoxy. Patrick wrote rough Latin, but we should not under-estimate the intellectual and spiritual preparation he had for his task. Patrick entered a monastery in France in his early twenties, roundabout the time Rome fell to the Visigoths. He later accompanied St. Germain on his mission to Britain, rooting out the Pelagian heresy. It was not until his mid-forties that Patrick received his long-sought commission from Pope Celestine to return to Ireland as a missionary.

Like many of the missionary saints, Patrick won his converts by miraculous acts that are impossible to explain to the modern rationalist, but that have as their supporting testimony the fact that Irish chieftain after Irish chieftain—and their tribes—accepted the Catholic faith as de-livered by Patrick, rejecting their Druidic gods. One can only ask why, given that Patrick brought them no secular advantages. In their own minds, certainly, he was a man of miraculous power, a power captured in countless Irish legends.

He was also a man of monastic prayer and penance. The famous prayer "St. Patrick's Breastplate" offers an enlightening glimpse into the mind and heart of the saint, a man devoted to the Trinity, which legend has he taught the Irish by means of the shamrock, and to orthodox Catholicism:

> I bind to myself today
> The strong virtue of the Invocation of the Trinity:
> I believe the Trinity in the Unity
> The Creator of the Universe.
>
> I bind to myself today
> The virtue of the Incarnation of Christ with His Baptism,
> The virtue of His crucifixion with His burial,
> The virtue of His Resurrection with His Ascension,
> The virtue of His coming on the Judgement Day.
>
> I bind to myself today
> The virtue of the love of seraphim,
> In the obedience of angels,
> In the hope of resurrection unto reward,
> In prayers of Patriarchs,
> In predictions of Prophets,
> In preaching of Apostles,
> In faith of Confessors,
> In purity of holy Virgins,
> In deeds of righteous men.
>
> I bind to myself today
> The power of Heaven,
> The light of the sun,
> The brightness of the moon,
> The splendour of fire,
> The flashing of lightning,
> The swiftness of wind,
> The depth of sea,

The stability of earth,
The compactness of rocks.

I bind to myself today
God's Power to guide me,
God's Might to uphold me,
God's Wisdom to teach me,
God's Eye to watch over me,
God's Ear to hear me,
God's Word to give me speech,
God's Hand to guide me,
God's Way to lie before me,
God's Shield to shelter me,
God's Host to secure me,
Against the snares of demons,
Against the seductions of vices,
Against the lusts of nature,
Against everyone who meditates injury to me,
Whether far or near,
Whether few or with many.

I invoke today all these virtues
Against every hostile merciless power
Which may assail my body and my soul,
Against the incantations of false prophets,
Against the black laws of heathenism,
Against the false laws of heresy,
Against the deceits of idolatry,
Against the spells of women, and smiths, and druids,
Against every knowledge that binds the soul of man.

Christ, protect me today
Against every poison, against burning,
Against drowning, against death-wound,
That I may receive abundant reward.

Christ with me, Christ before me,
Christ behind me, Christ within me,
Christ beneath me, Christ above me,

Christ at my right, Christ at my left,
Christ in the fort,
Christ in the chariot seat,
Christ in the poop,
Christ in the heart of everyone who thinks of me,
Christ in the mouth of everyone who speaks to me,
Christ in every eye that sees me,
Christ in every ear that hears me.

I bind to myself today
The strong virtue of an invocation of the Trinity,
I believe the Trinity in the Unity
The Creator of the Universe.[21]

It is also said of St. Patrick that, in prayer, he wrestled with God in one particular terrific bout of fasting and exposure to the elements on Eagle Mountain—now known as Croagh Patrick—refusing to end his fast until he was promised, among other things, that penitents who recited this prayer before death would receive Heaven; that the barbarians would never overrun the Church; and that the Irish would be spared from the final temptations before Judgment Day and given to St. Patrick to judge.

When St. Patrick retired from the mountain, he was convinced his prayer had been answered.

As befitted one who had fought heresy, he made a point, in converting the Irish, of teaching them a pure Catholic doctrine that openly refuted the ideas of the Arians, the Monophysites, the Pelagians, and others—a sort of inoculation against heretics who might follow—preaching the indivisibility of the Trinity, baptism to wash away Original Sin, the sacrament of penance, and submission to the universal Church centered on the See of St. Peter.

Patrick established Church government in Ireland, receiving the pope's permission to create a bishopric in Armagh. He created a system of monasteries where the Irish were taught to write Latin, bringing the Celts into the universal culture of Rome and introducing the Roman alphabet. In this rough age, the Irish—learning Latin by the classics and, like St. Patrick, in deep and continual reading of the Bible—became masters of rhetoric and scholarship, which were elsewhere being trampled under barbarian heels. Irish monks would thus become the tutors of Europe.

Patrick not only Christianized Ireland, but inspired a missionary diaspora from the Emerald Isle to Europe, promoting a Catholicism that was
perfectionist in its monastic thrust (the Irish also established convents),
endowed with a love of nature and creation—as seen in "St. Patrick's
Breastplate," the sentiments of which prefigure the personality of Saint
Francis—and for nearly the first time since the life of Christ, gave Christianity assumptions and an evangelical mission that were rural rather
than urban.

Patrick died in the latter half of the fifth century, and if we compare
him and his monastic successors in the West to the febrile monks of the
East, we have a startling illustration of the ever-widening mental rift between the two halves of Christianity. In the West, we have the missionary
monks—prayerful, scholarly, obedient. In the East, from at least the fourth
century, we have extremists—hot to theological controversy and prone to
almost absurd acts of mortification and bizarre forms of hermeticism. The
most famous of these ascetics were the Stylites, men who mortified the
flesh and removed themselves from the world by standing on pillars for
years, even decades—something that to the practical and missionary Western mind served no purpose. Yet this practice lived on as a recognized
mode of life in branches of the Eastern Orthodox Church through at least
the fifteenth century, serving as a symbol of extreme penance.

In the West, though, two great men shaped the monastic tradition: St.
Martin of Tours and St. Benedict. Martin was a man of the fourth century, dying close to the year 400. A former legionnaire, a monk by vocation, then a missionary, and finally a bishop, he spread the gospel in
France and Germany by means of miracles that impressed the barbarians
and ensured his fame. Martin became for the French something of what
Patrick was to the Irish—a rural priest and miracle worker. A sanctuary
built in his honor became a focal point of French Christianity, a symbol
of religious devotion, a site of pilgrimage that lasted until it was destroyed in an act of Protestant iconoclasm in the sixteenth century. It was
sacked again by the revolutionaries of the French Republic, who sought
to make its destruction permanent by paving it over as a road. Such outrages, however, had to wait for the onset of post-Catholic civilization. In
his time Martin was, like St. Patrick, an apostle who trained learned missionary monks. In fact, St. Patrick is rightly seen as one of St. Martin's
heirs, studying as he did in the monasteries of western France.

But an even greater influence on the Church was St. Benedict, who was born the son of a noble Roman family in Ostrogoth-occupied Italy in 480. In his late teens, Benedict began a monastic life that was to find its culmination in the Rule of St. Benedict—the touchstone of Catholic monasticism and a reminder of the Church's Roman heritage. For more than anything else, Rome was the lawgiver to the world, and Benedict was the conscious lawgiver to the monasteries, establishing a regular, moderate, practical, ordered—in short, a classically Roman—mode of life. In contrast to the excesses of the East, Benedict argues that monasticism is "a school of divine service" in which "all things must be done in moderation for the sake of those who are less hardy" and which sternly avoids any form of self-flagellation. Even common prayer, Benedict says, is to be kept short. The rule is thus Aristotelian in spirit. It requires communal obedience to a routine of work, prayer, study, fasting, and self-denial. The only acceptable will is the will of the law, enforced by the abbot, who governs the monks as a father governs his family. An abbot gains his position by election and retains it for life. Like a good paterfamilias, the abbot is "not to be too suspicious, or he will never be at rest," and even in executing the law, justice comes second to mercy. The abbot should always remember that his role is to serve, and that he should govern by example rather than dictate.[22]

The abbot, Benedict writes in his Rule 64, should "keep his own frailty ever before his eyes, and remember that the bruised reed must not be broken. And by this we do not mean that he should suffer vices to grow up; but that prudently and with charity he should cut them off, in the way he shall see best for each . . . and let him study rather to be loved than feared. . . . In all his commands, whether spiritual or temporal, let him be prudent and considerate. In the works which he imposeth let him be discreet and moderate, bearing in mind the discretion of holy Jacob, when he said: 'If I cause my flocks to be overdriven, they will all perish in one day.' Taking, then, such testimonies as are borne by these and the like words to discretion, the mother of virtues, let him so temper all things, that the strong may have something to strive after, and the weak nothing at which to take alarm."[23]

The point of the Benedictine rule is to approximate as much as possible the life of Christ—a life of chastity, prayer, work, temperance, and obedience. The Benedictines established the classic medieval formula that to work is to pray. Unlike many monastic orders, the Benedictines take no vow of poverty. Instead, every monk is guaranteed his basic needs for clothing, food (though the monks eat no meat), wine, and sleep. All things are owned communally, but any wealth brought to the monastery through a monk's previous life or through donations is seen as a positive good—to support the order and to benefit the neighboring poor. Benedictines are meant to be self-supporting and generous. It is a life of service, teaching children, serving the sick, providing refuge and hospitality, doing whatever work needs to be done—corporal or spiritual—and, with typical moderation, avoiding the frenetic activity of the busybody, always remembering that to work is to pray.

Benedict comes down to us as an extremely winning personality. Humble, never wanting to inconvenience his fellow monks lest he give them "a just cause for grumbling,"[24] self-sacrificing, always looking after the least of charges, nature-loving—like St. Francis, he begged the crows to eat from his hand—studious, and dedicated to prayer. He is a consummate example of the best of the Church.

Benedict's great monument—aside from his rule; which was likely written there—was the monastery at Monte Cassino, formerly a temple dedicated to Apollo. Benedict consecrated it to Christ, and it became an ornate centerpiece of a priceless Christian heritage, beautiful in its art, from mosaic to painting, enlightened in its library full of carefully copied and illustrated scrolls, devoted to music and all forms of learning. Though built like a fortress, it did inevitably attract the attention of the barbarian; it was trashed by the Lombards toward the end of the sixth century, destroyed by the Saracens in the ninth, and finally bombed to rubble in the Second World War. It has now been rebuilt as the Abbey of St. Benedict, but it should also serve as a reminder that the barbarian is always with us.

He was certainly in the world of St. Benedict, but through his monasteries Benedict created cells of monks in every outpost of the West, bringing the barbarian to God and making Europe a Catholic civilization.

## CHAPTER SEVEN

# THE RESTORATION OF
# CATHOLIC EUROPE

⟹⟸

IN THE YEAR 518 old Rome struck back in new Constantinople. He was a soldier; a Latin, not a Greek; and a Catholic. The new Caesar of the East ended the religious schism with Rome. Under the guidance of Emperor Justin, the bishops of the East signed the "formula" of Pope Hormisdas, which affirmed the "first means of safety is to guard the rule of strict faith and to deviate in no way from those things that have been laid down by the Fathers. And indeed the words of Our Lord Jesus Christ: 'Thou art Peter; and upon this rock I will build my church,' cannot be disregarded; these things which were spoken are demonstrated by the results, for the Catholic religion has been preserved ever immaculate in the Apostolic See."[1] The Eastern and Western Churches were reunited, with certain exceptions—such as Egypt, which was now so chaotic with red-eyed zealots that it was felt prudent to let the province go to the dogs rather than attempt to enforce the imperial and papal will. Remarkable as this reunification was, in some ways it was more symbolic than real. For beneath the surface, the East continued to be a cauldron of bubbling sectarians. But for Justin, an old man and a practical soldier with no grand theological scheme beyond official imperial Catholic unity, it was enough.

Succeeding Justin was the dynamic Justinian, his nephew and chief adviser who had negotiated the end to the East-West schism. Justinian would rule the Eastern Empire for nearly forty years, from 527 to 565.

Like his uncle, he was a Catholic. Unlike his uncle he was interested in theology and required more from his subjects than symbolic unity. He wanted to create a truly Catholic Eastern Empire that would restore the imperial unity of the East and heal all theological rifts. Unfortunately, his wife, the empress Theodora, a reformed dancing girl with a presumed harlot's past, actively encouraged the rifts by patronizing the Monophysites, whose extreme monastic orders attracted her apparently repentant heart.

But what really attracted Justinian was Roman glory. He aspired to be the great sixth-century *Restitutor Orbis,* restorer of the world; and he was, in fact, a much more successful, much more profound restorer of Roman glory—even if it, too, was ultimately fleeting—than was Julian the Apostate. For where Julian had tried to recreate an idiosyncratic daydream of Rome's past grandeur, Justinian marched as true Rome marched—with the legions, the law, and a practical, orderly ambition to civilize the world.

He began by smiting the circus mob at home, which had grown so belligerent in a sixth-century form of soccer hooliganism that it had divided into two enormous armed gangs. Justinian obliterated them—his backbone stiffened by his wife—killing 40,000 of his subjects. Then, under the command of his gifted general Belisarius, Byzantium's legions struck to subdue Africa, completely annihilating the Vandal kingdom, as his predecessors centuries before had crushed Carthage. Roman troops marched to all points of the empire, rebuffing the Persians, taming the Arabs, reconquering Sicily, returning to the empire lost provinces in the Balkans and along the Black Sea, and in their greatest triumph they replanted the Roman eagle in Italy. They even recaptured parts of Spain.

In addition to his conquests, Justinian codified Roman law in a codex that is the basis for all systems of Western law and for the Catholic Church's canon law. Like Constantine, he used the treasury of the state to benefit the people. He dispensed not only charity, but tremendous construction projects that included one of the greatest churches ever built—now a museum—Hagia Sophia in Constantinople. Byzantine art and architecture had Justinian as its patron. Like many an imperial patron of the arts, he left the state treasury a wreck.

In religious matters, Justinian was much like Constantine—a defender of the Catholic faith, but with political compromises. He treated

Catholic bishops and the pope as advisers to the imperial throne—where rested the authority of both Caesar and Christ. In the East, of course, this was the established model of Church-state relations, and, given the febrile, hate-filled, fissiparous tendencies of the Eastern Church, it was possible to argue that Eastern clerics did indeed require the whip hand of the emperor to keep them in line. But the Western Church and the pope would not accept servility to the emperor, even so great an emperor as Justinian.

If pope and emperor were thus uneasy allies, they were allies of a sort nonetheless. Before Justinian's accession to the throne, the papacy had been torn in its relations with the Eastern emperor. A strong faction in the Church yearned for reunion with Caesar. Others wanted to make sure the emperor knew his place. Pope Gelasius (492–496) had made Rome's position clear when he wrote that there were two powers governing the world, the Church and the emperor, of which the Church was the superior. But the emperor was just as eager to assert his own rights. As the Eastern emperor Anastasius told Pope Hormisdas (514–523), "You may thwart me, reverend sir, you may insult me: but you may not command me."[2]

Before the empire was restored under Justinian, the Catholic Church had reached an accommodation with the Ostrogothic king Theodoric, who, though an Arian, gave the Church freedom to pursue its mission. During one contested papal election at the close of the fifth century, he was even called upon—as the authoritative political power in Rome—to decide the victor. If this was a bizarre honor to grant an Arian king, he nevertheless handled it with the grace of a Solomon, and it is striking testimony to the Church's confidence in the Romanized barbarian monarchy. Theodoric considered himself the Augustus of the Western Empire. His conception of government, however, might be seen as a precursor of the Catholic political ideal of subsidiarity. Theodoric saw himself at the head of a confederation of tribes and of Romans, each subsidiary nation having substantial independence and freedom under the imperial banner. Unity within the confederation was encouraged by marriage between barbarian royal families.

Relations between Theodoric and the Church broke down when the king compelled another pope, Pope John I (523–526), to petition the emperor Justin, for an end to anti-Arian persecutions. This, obviously, was a humiliating assignment. Reunification with Byzantium suddenly appeared much more attractive, especially when Pope John, who had resolved to limit his pleadings to a general call for toleration, was greeted in Constantinople by the emperor prostrating himself before him, the acclamation of crowds, and a place of honor set above of the patriarch of New Rome.

Justinian, like his uncle, recognized the pope's primacy in the Church. The first pope with whom he dealt—Pope Agapitus I (535–536)—forcibly reminded him of this, rebuking the new emperor for appointing an heretical bishop in Constantinople, something Justinian had done as a favor to his empress. Stunned by the pope's angry eloquence, he, too, prostrated himself before the Holy Father. He recanted the appointment and allowed the pope to choose the bishop's successor.

Justinian paid Rome its due, but as an Eastern emperor, he was also keen to keep ultimate authority for himself. The next pope but one, Vigilius, gained the papacy not by the clergy's approval—which he won after the fact—but by imperial authority, which allowed the new pope to send his predecessor, Pope Silverius (536–537), into exile. Once in the See of St. Peter, however, Vigilius proved less pliable than the imperial household wished. Justinian had the pope taken into custody for nearly a decade to win his compliance with imperial policy. So interested was Justinian in controlling the Church that Vigilius's political submission was more important to him than relieving Rome from besieging Goths—a troublesome little matter of state protection for imperial citizens that the pope tried, and failed, to get him to address.

Still, for all his Caesaropapist ambitions, Justinian was committed to restoring Catholic supremacy in the East and in Africa. He enacted harsh laws against heretics, encouraged Catholic missionaries, and resurrected the idea of the unity of Roman civilization—of one emperor, one law, one faith. In this, of course, he ultimately failed, in large part because his machinations to bend the papacy to his will only succeeded in bringing suspicion upon the inheritors of the Roman See. For example, when Vigilius succumbed to imperial pressure, the bishops of North Africa condemned him. When his successor, Pope Pelagius, bowed to the Byzantine court, northern Italy protested by putting itself in schism with Rome. The West simply would not accept as legitimate the supremacy of Caesar over the papacy.

More to the West's taste was Clovis I, king of the Franks until his death in 511. Like Constantine, he had a battlefield conversion to Catholicism and was its prime defender against the Western barbarian tribes. Unlike Constantine and Justinian, he left ecclesial matters to the ecclesiastics and accepted the faith with the simple humility that was typical of believers in the West. In the Frankish kingdom, Roman and barbarian were united in the Catholic Church.

After Justinian's death, the papacy required a reformer, someone who could re-establish the people's faith in the Petrine authority of the papal office as disinterested, legitimate, compelling, and independent from Byzantium's court. Luckily, such a man was waiting. His name was Gregory.

## GREGORY THE GREAT

GREGORY CAME FROM a wealthy Roman family with a long tradition of both civil and clerical service. Gregory himself had served as a Roman prefect before he became a monk and, eventually, by popular acclamation, pope.

The Italy in which he was raised was a land of chaos—of unending war, famine, and disaster stemming from Justinian's conquests, and their reversals. But amidst this worldly turmoil, he managed to acquire a patrician's liberal and legal education. Equally influential on him were his religious studies, which by his early thirties had inspired him to endow a handful of monasteries and devote himself to God's service. It was in the monastery that he claimed to have spent the happiest years of his life, but such was his reputation for learning and administration—and such was the crisis facing the Church—that Pope Benedict I (575–579) compelled him to accept ordination as a deacon of Rome. The next pope, Pelagius II (579–590), dispatched him as a papal emissary to Constantinople, to warn the Eastern Empire that yet another Germanic tribe, this time the Lombards, was threatening the Eternal City. Constantinople, at this point, didn't much care, and after six years, Gregory, to his relief, was recalled from Byzantium and allowed to return to his monastery, though he was still called out for other duty, apparently serving for a time as Pope Pelagius II's secretary. His popular standing is attested by the fact that when he tried to embark on a missionary journey to England, a popular uprising demanded his return.

In 590, on Pope Pelagius II's death, Gregory's popularity thrust him into the papacy. He went unwillingly. He even appealed the decision to the Byzantine emperor Maurice and, when that failed, attempted to flee Rome. The monastic Gregory did not want to be pope, and the exercise of his holy office and its power and perquisites never changed that fact. His entire papal life—most of which was plagued by ill health—was spent yearning to resume the cowl of his monastery. He nevertheless became one of the most active, important, and influential popes in history.

What St. Benedict did for the monasteries, St. Gregory did for the bishops and ultimately the papacy. He defined the episcopal office as one that ministers to heal the spiritual ills of the people, with every bishop on perpetual guard to serve them, not his own ego. It is from Gregory that the popes take the title "servant of the servants of God."

But even if the pope were to renounce ego, he could not renounce the extraordinary powers that had fallen to him. For in the collapse of civil authority since the invasion of the Lombards, it was the pope who looked after the physical welfare of the people—in the city and in papal dominions that exceeded a thousand square miles. Pope Gregory's elaborate relief efforts not only included providing food for every poor family known to the Holy See—their names were kept on a roster—but extended to his own table, where he dined with a dozen poor people, on simple fare, every night.

In addition, Pope Gregory directed the military and diplomatic affairs of Rome, as well as, of course, shepherding the church of the city, performing priestly and bishopric duties; praying for God's blessing on His people suffering from disease, famine, and war; and acting as leader of the universal Church. All the administrative qualities that had recommended him to earlier popes grew even more profound under a regimen of tireless work.

In Church government, he insisted on clerical celibacy. As the first monk to become pope, he showed a marked preference for appointing fellow monks—marked by self-discipline and an appetite for hard work—to administrative posts. Though personally humble, he emphasized the absolute supremacy of the Roman pontiff—pointedly noting that even the bishop of Constantinople accepted Rome's primacy—while encouraging Church-state cooperation in building and maintaining a Catholic empire. Gregory firmly believed in the divine right of Catholic kings to govern in secular affairs and saw these kings, from the perspective of an Italy rent by barbarians, as an essential support for the faith.

But, of necessity, Gregory assumed de facto imperial powers himself in Italy, appointing regional governors, giving orders to Roman generals, and negotiating a peace with the Lombards absent any action on the part of Constantinople. It was only after Gregory asserted himself that the representative of the Byzantine Empire finally marched from his provincial capital of Ravenna and dealt a blow against the barbarians. Such imperial relief proved short-lived, and the pope again had to lead the defense of the city. At one point, like Pope St. Leo and Attila, Gregory met the Lombard warlord Agilulf outside the gates of Rome and convinced him—apparently through promising a subsidy, a centuries-long standby of Roman diplomacy—to lift his siege.

Gregory, as a gifted administrator, was proud of the fact that papal diplomacy was paid for out of the papal treasury, putting no new tax burdens on the people. He was, among other things, a patriot and justified his independent actions to the Byzantine emperor as necessary for the defense of his country, his patria. He would not accept criticism from those who did not "suffer in this place among the swords of the Lombards" and he would not watch helplessly while Romans were "tied by the neck like dogs, to be taken to Gaul for sale."[3] This was the proud Roman Gregory who, even as a papal ambassador in Constantinople, refused to learn Greek and disapproved of any Westerner who mastered the language or adopted Eastern manners or theology. As an ardent Roman, he wrote, "How anyone can be seduced by Constantinople, and how anyone can forget Rome, I do not know."[4]

Missionary work was another recipient of Gregory's ardent support. The frustration of his own ambition to do such work in England prompted him to send a team of forty monks led by Prior Augustine, who became St. Augustine of Canterbury. In a celebrated story, Gregory was inspired to convert the English by seeing some of the islanders in a slave market.

"What nation are they?"

"Angles."

"Not Angles, but angels," Gregory was said to reply, with further puns to follow, but also a commitment to raise the Anglo-Saxons from worshiping rocks to worshiping God.[5] Gregory later reinforced Augustine and his men with additional missionaries. It was his hope to establish archbishops in York and London, which had been the seats of the old Roman administration. In addition, he encouraged the Church in southern France to buy British adolescent males from the local slave markets and train them as monks, whether to return them to the island as missionaries or simply devote them to God has been a matter of historical dispute.

What is not disputed is that Britain was regarded as extremely dangerous, having reverted to the most primitive forms of barbarism in the nearly two hundred years since the collapse of Roman authority. Bearing this in mind—and bearing in mind, as always, that Gregory was a practical Roman—the pope directed his missionaries not to worry unduly about perfection in their new charges, but to make use of local customs and ways, turning them to the advantage of the Church and gently leading the newly baptized to the light. He knew the value of religious art, especially in a time of mass illiteracy: "Pictures are the books of lay people."[6] He attempted to shore up the Church in Africa, newly Catholic Spain, and France; he used a Catholic Bavarian princess in the Lombard court to gain religious influence against the major military threat to Rome; and he even hoped someday to convert the Lombards, whom he called "that abominable people."[7]

It is amazing that a man who achieved so much—including, perhaps, the creation of Gregorian chant—was bedridden for so much of his pontificate, and wracked by such pain that he prayed for death, which finally came to him in 604.

With his death came a reassertion of Byzantine control over the Church, with the Eastern emperor affirming papal appointments. Yet Constantinople itself was now under threat. From the North came a Slavic tribe known as the Avars. To the South, the Persians, Rome's ancient Eastern enemy, came sweeping in an arc of conquest. Jerusalem—and the relic of the True Cross—fell to the Persians in 614, the worst symbolic geopolitical disaster for Christianity since the fall of Rome. Only twelve years later, the Persians besieged Constantinople before being driven back by the Byzantine armies.

An even more dangerous challenge was just beginning to emerge from the deserts of Arabia: Islam. The religion's prophet, Mohammed, died in 632, but Arabs fueled with his passion made it a religion-in-arms, seizing the historic Christian city of Antioch in 637, spreading like a flame that by the end of the seventh century had laid waste to Christianity along the entire southern rim of the Mediterranean. Beneath Islam's scimitar lay smoldering ruins, and a rival religious empire that would meet Christianity in Holy War and occupy its military energies for a millennium.

But first things first—Christians had scores to settle among themselves. From the East came a new doctrine meant to end the lingering Monophysite controversies by rallying every Christian to the idea that Jesus had two natures that acted as one. As communicated to Pope Honorius I (625–638)— who modeled himself on Gregory, encouraging missionaries, especially to Britain, and exercising sweeping secular authority in Italy—this doctrine appeared to be an affirmation of Rome's belief in the human and divine unity of Christ, and the pope accepted the compromise as such. Unfortunately, that's not what was meant at all, as later became clear when the doctrine defined Jesus' will as being purely divine, without a human element.

After Honorius's death, the emperor proclaimed the new doctrine as law. But now that the doctrine's meaning was clear, the papacy condemned what would become known as Monothelitisim, which was a mere variation of the Monophysite heresy. In retaliation, Byzantine troops raided and looted the Lateran Palace, and the pope's ambassador in Constantinople was imprisoned. A virtual state of war existed between the emperor and the papacy.

Joining the war in 649 was a new pope, who would be martyred for the orthodox Catholic faith. When Martin I (649–653) took the papal throne, he bravely did so without waiting for the emperor's consent, and then called a synod of more than a hundred Western bishops, who definitively refuted the Monothelite heresy. Martin presented the decision to the emperor Constans II, not as an act of *lèse-majesté,* but as correcting a mistake made by the emperor's patriarchs. Such diplomacy did him no good. The emperor wanted the pope's submission or his death. What he got was his arrest. The emperor's henchmen dragged the pope in chains through the streets of Constantinople, beating him, flogging him, and finally convicting him of treason. Pope Martin was exiled rather than executed—but to the Crimea, which was suffering from famine, only ensuring that his death was more prolonged and painful.

The irony of the situation was that the Roman pontiff wanted no break with the Eastern Empire—he was, in fact, Greek—but Byzantium's demands were impossible. No pope could endorse heresy or willingly surrender the authority of St. Peter to the Byzantine emperor. Constans II later made a triumphal entry into Rome, where the people cheered him as a conquering hero and the new pope, Vitalian (657–672), kept a polite silence about the martyrdom of Martin. In thanks for this deferential reception, the emperor's Byzantine troops stripped the city of everything they could possibly transfer to Constantinople.

Justice was soon at hand. Not in the murder in his bathtub of Constans II, whose death was not mourned by even his own retinue, but in the rise of his son Constantine IV. Constantine wanted reconciliation with Rome, and in 681 he got it at the Sixth General Council of the Church in Constantinople. The process began with Pope Agatho (678–681), who worked with the emperor to again definitively reject Monothelitism and return the empire to Catholic orthodoxy. The pope and his successor, Leo II (682–683), succeeded, but at a cost. Monothelitism was officially anathematized, Rome's primacy reaffirmed, and the emperor credited with restoring unity. But the East wanted an additional sop; it wanted Pope Honorius I condemned as a Monothelite for his hasty, ill-judged, apparent approval of the doctrine. The accusation was unjust and struck at the heart of what even the Eastern Church conceded was the proper pride of Rome. While patriarchs and councils had wavered and contradicted themselves, no pope had ever budged from the universal faith or endorsed heresy. Rome was the very definition of theological stability and constancy. But there are always many—especially the envious—who like to see virtue humbled, and condemning Honorius I had the diplomatic advantage of spreading blame so that everyone had a share, not just Constantinople. For the sake of Catholic unity, and because Rome had triumphed on every other issue, Pope Leo II reluctantly complied, though he made it clear, publicly, that he believed Honorius I's crime was not committing heresy, but failing to stamp it out.

As always, the parchment of diplomacy withered over time. In 692, the emperor Justinian II convened the so-called Quinisext Council. Eastern bishops were the only participants—the pope was neither invited nor summoned to attend—and some of the more than one hundred disciplinary canons adopted by the council could be seen as direct attacks on Rome. In the West, celibacy was the discipline of the clergy; in the East, it was not. The Eastern practice was proclaimed mandatory. In the West, it was the practice to fast on Saturday; in the East, there was no fast. The Eastern practice was upheld. Devotion to Jesus as the Lamb of God was popular in the West; in the East, it was not. So conflating Jesus with the Lamb of God was outlawed. Constantinople again asserted its right to be second in precedence to Rome. And so on. The Council's decrees were sent to Pope Sergius I (687–701) to approve. He not only refused, but publicly encouraged devotion to the symbolic Lamb of God. When the emperor ordered his arrest, the pope had a surprise for him. The imperial troops in Rome rallied to the pope's defense, and their commander—who tried to enforce the emperor's order—was forced to go into hiding. He chose as his hiding spot the floor beneath the pope's bed, from which position he watched as the pope pleaded with the imperial troops to spare their commander's life. Not long after, a palace coup did away with Justinian II. But of Eastern rumblings there were no end; and the next would, in retrospect, be one of the strangest of all.

## SMASHING THE ICONS

ALONG WITH BEING the hotbed of heresy, the East was now increasingly threatened, as well as influenced, by the culture of Islam. In 726, the Eastern emperor Leo III proclaimed an end to the traditional Christian veneration of icons, which was especially strong in the East. The Muslims were iconoclasts and had at one point targeted Leo for conversion. He was also influenced by the Monophysites and other Eastern heretics who disapproved of images. Muslims succeeded on the battlefield, he apparently believed, because the Christian Church had fallen into idolatry forbidden by the First Commandment—a commandment better kept by the Jews and the followers of Islam. Leo felt entitled to make such a theological volte-face in traditional Christian practice because, as this warrior king declared, "I am priest no less than emperor"[8]—the typical Byzantine formulation, and Leo had the additional motive of invigilating religious and political uniformity in the East through his imperial office.

Enforcing the edict required violence. When troops tried to remove a famous picture of Christ from the gates of Constantinople, there were popular riots. The patriarch of the city was executed for his opposition, and equally opposed monasteries in the East were put to the torch—shrines, relics, and the monks themselves.

While the Byzantines were at each other's throats—a not unusual position for them—the West rose as one against this latest heretical and tyrannical ukase from Constantinople. In 731 Pope Gregory III formally declared that anyone who defiled a sacred image was immediately excommunicated from the Church. When the pope tried to get this message to the emperor, the emperor merely imprisoned the messengers and responded by embarking his war fleet for Italy. Unfortunately for him, the fleet was destroyed in a storm.

The destruction of the fleet was more than a military setback for the Byzantine emperor. It underlined a profound division, at least in the Western mind. East of the Adriatic was a kind of malarial theological swamp of madness. From the Italian peninsula and points west from the Tyrrhenian Sea was a rather more inspiring apostolic mission in the spirit of St. Paul. Between iconic violence, sunken sailors, and commanders hiding beneath the pope's bed, the great Byzantine Empire appeared more and more an annoying irrelevance to Rome and the Western world. Rome had once thought its division from the East was unfortunate. Now it was self-consciously severed by the East's *Kulturkampf;* its Orientalized intrigue, pretensions, and despotism; and the hothouse, politically driven theological speculations of the Byzantine court. The bluff, hardy, straightforward, and theologically stable Roman-Catholic-Germanic culture of the West had little in common with Byzantium.

It was not clear yet, however, who would win the culture war. If the emperor appeared unable to enforce his will on the pope, he nevertheless had an imperial army—albeit one that was also fighting Muslims, Slavs, and others—while Western kings who might be called to the pope's defense were dispersed in the developing feudalism of early medieval Western Europe.

There was an abortive attempt to reverse the policy of iconoclasm after Leo's death, when his son-in-law seized the throne. But he was deposed in a coup and ritually blinded by Leo's own son Constantine V (741–775), a noted coprophiliac. Constantine V redoubled the destruction of holy images, as coprophiliacs are wont to do, and had the patriarch of Constantinople publicly blinded—evidently a favorite punishment of Constantine V—and flogged in the street until he agreed to support the emperor. As did all villains of the time, the emperor called an ecclesiastical Council to approve his course of action, which of course the lickspittle bishops did. The emperor ensured episcopal agreement by including no representatives from the West, from Rome, or from the ancient sees of

Alexandria, Antioch, and Jerusalem—these last three surviving uneasily under the hand of Islam.

One ridiculous consequence of the iconoclastic persecution was the replacement of religious art in churches by non-offending secular images. Jesus was out. A still life of an apple—as long as it could not be construed as symbolic of, say, the Garden of Eden—was in. Also in was state-sponsored torture and murder of those who refused to go along. Constantine V's prime target was the monasteries, which he hoped to utterly destroy, ordering the seizure of the buildings, the exile or execution of the monks, and the beheading of a patriarch who was insufficiently compliant in his reign of terror.

The terror abated somewhat under Emperor Leo IV (775–780). It is a pattern of early Byzantine history that after an emperor or two go to war against the pope, another comes hoping to heal the rift. Leo was a healer not so much because of himself, but because of his wife, the empress Irene, who wielded the influence of the bedchamber, where she kept her own stash of sacred images. The Church has never been too proud to applaud such influence when it defends Catholic orthodoxy. Leo, however, could not be kept from persecuting forever. He was, after all, a Byzantine monarch. But before he could exile the empress and really get to work destroying things, he died, and the Catholic world cheered as the Empress Irene became the regent for her nine-year-old son, Constantine VI.

Under Irene, religious art was restored, monks returned to the monasteries, and her husband's puppet patriarch took up the cowl, publicly confessing that he was exiling himself as penance for his sins. An ambassador was sent to Rome, which led to a Council of bishops in 787 that finally refuted for the universal Church the heresy of iconoclasm. But Rome won other ground as well. The Council declared that bishops were to be appointed solely by other bishops, not by the state—a firm slap at the "priest-emperor" model of Constantinople that had reaped so much disaster.

Unbelievably, just over a quarter of a century later, Constantinople insisted on replaying the entire scenario again with a second iconoclastic war. The sole redeeming quality from this second sorry mess of heretical patriarchs and submissive synods rushing to confirm whatever the emperor demanded is the heroism of the monk St. Theodore, who saw the only hope for Eastern Catholicism in the intercession of the pope.

Theodore eloquently defended not only religious art and icons, but the universal Church of Rome: "Whatever novelty is brought into the Church by those who wander from the truth must certainly be referred to Peter or his successor. . . . Save us, chief pastor of the Church under heaven." Those who would protect traditional Christianity against imperial edicts and wayward councils, he wrote, must "[a]rrange that a decision be received from old Rome as the custom had been handed down from the beginning by the tradition of our fathers."[9]

As before, the court at Constantinople was sullied by murder—among others, the murder of Emperor Leo V, whose corpse was dumped in favor of Michael the Stammerer. There was also conspiracy, torture unto death, and the brutal whipping and branding on the face of St. Theodore, who was but one of many to perish. If Constantinople pretended to be the New Rome, it seemed to specialize in producing new Neros.

Relief came in 842, nearly three decades after the second persecution began, when the empress Theodora became regent for the future emperor Michael the Drunkard. Theodora, like Irene, restored the icons to the churches, an event that is commemorated in the schismatic Eastern Orthodox faith as symbolizing the triumph over all heresies, which is interesting, at the very least, in that it was a Catholic triumph. Theodora's action was affirmed by a synod that again approved the place of icons in Christian devotion. After the incredible damage inflicted by two enormous persecutions, all appeared to be well. The appearance, inevitably, was deceiving, because things are never well for long. In the boy Michael III, or Michael the Drunkard, was the cause of a great irreparable tear in the fabric of Christianity.

It wasn't entirely Michael's fault. The trouble was that Theodora tried to pass the regency to her brother Bardas. The patriarch, Ignatius, denied Bardas the regent's crown because of a pesky little problem Bardas had with incest. Bardas did what a Byzantine emperor always did when confronted by this problem. He deposed and exiled the patriarch and had him replaced, in this case by a suddenly elevated young layman—albeit one of extraordinary scholarship (though he had no Latin, a sign of the East-West *Kulturkampf*)—named Photius, who was already well connected at court. The pope's legates, who were later convicted of taking bribes from the Byzantine emperor, advised the pontiff to recognize the new patriarch. The pope not only refused, but excommunicated Photius—or, actually, by canon law, Photius had excommunicated himself by, among other things, accepting consecration from an excommunicated bishop for a See that was technically, and certainly in the pope's view, rightfully held by Ignatius, whom the emperor had illegally deposed. So began the so-called Photian Schism.

Photius and the emperor acknowledged that winning the pope's approval was necessary for the upstart patriarch's legitimacy. But Rome would not budge. After a decade of futile negotiations, Photius retaliated by calling a synod at Constantinople in 867, at which he declared he was excommunicating the pope and the Western church. He cited the tired old grounds of the West's fasting on Saturday, dating Lent differently, encouraging a celibate priesthood, reserving the power of confirmation to bishops rather than priests, and for holding to the idea that the Holy Spirit was transmitted by both the Father and the Son.

This last point would be known as the *filioque* controversy and was to provide the most important theological split between East and West. What is particularly odd about the *filioque* is the nature of the dispute. That the Holy Spirit came from both the Father and the Son was traditional Christian belief, a part of Trinitarian orthodoxy upheld against every Eastern variation of the heretical Monophysites. What made it controversial was its insertion by the Roman Church into the Nicene Creed in order to make this point clear to the newly converted tribes of the West, some of whom had been Arians and unsteady in their own understanding of the Trinity. Even in Rome, this insertion was controversial, as it meant a change in the established formula. It was accepted, however, because it *clarified* Church doctrine, rather than altered it.

But Photius used the insertion of the *filioque* as an unlikely stick with which to beat an unlikely source, Rome and the Western church, with an unlikely crime: heresy. Rousing Byzantine nationalism against Rome suddenly made the *filioque* a national and imperial cause in the East. Eastern bishops had been trained for centuries in affirming heretical innovations. This time they condemned Rome for changing the Creed, but on grounds that shaded Eastern theology to Monophysitical and Arian views of Jesus—heresies, of course, that many Eastern clerics had eagerly embraced before. Bizarrely, it is this issue—as well as the denial of papal supremacy and other minor addenda—propounded by Photius, an illegally appointed patriarch defending an incestuous emperor, that divides the Eastern Orthodox and Roman Catholic churches to this day.[10]

What makes it even more odd is that Photius lost his position that very same year, with a change of emperors and the restoration of the Catholic Ignatius to the See of Constantinople. Photius, from exile, worked to ingratiate himself with the emperor and eventually succeeded in becoming tutor to his son. He did so remarkable a job of rehabilitating himself that when the See of Constantinople fell vacant, the emperor recommended him for the post, and Pope John VIII (872–882) lifted the excommunication from Photius and confirmed his selection in 878.

Photius's subsequent behavior offers a variation of an old saw—beware of Greeks accepting gifts. For the new patriarch immediately set about returning the East to schism. He arranged for a council to deny the addition of the *filioque* to the Creed and approve aggrandizements of Constantinople's ecclesiastical power, and then sent the edicts to the pope for his approval—a rather backhanded and cheeky, but important, affirmation of papal supremacy. The pope responded as he had to, excommunicating Photius. The second Photian Schism lasted seven years, until a new emperor brought a new broom, and Photius was banished on grounds of treason. The schism didn't end immediately. But before the close of the ninth century, Rome and Constantinople were restored to communion until the near final break in 1054. By this time, while conceding the tragedy of a Christianity rent in two by Eastern heresy and bloody-mindedness, any self-respecting Westerner might be forgiven for thinking, "Away with them, then, and good riddance." For in the orthodox Catholic West the lineaments of a new geopolitical, cultural, and religious entity were taking shape. It would be called "Christendom."

## CHAPTER EIGHT

# THE RISE—AND NEAR FALL—

# OF CHRISTENDOM

⎯⎯⎯⎯⎯•⎯⎯⎯⎯⎯

IN THE WEST, three factors gave strength to the making of Europe. One was the simple acceptance of the universal, apostolic Church based in Rome. Another was the Roman tradition of liberty under law for Roman citizens and of the civic virtue of patrician landowners. The third was the Germanic ideal of liberty—an equality of warriors, respectful of tribe, with loyalty based on the personal authority of the warrior-king. These strands came together in the creation of feudalism. Feudalism dispersed political power yet kept Christendom united under the Church. It created a society based on reciprocal obligation to one's fellows, even between classes, as in the tradition of noblesse oblige. Because authority was based on personal allegiance, it encouraged the ideal—if not always the reality—that a king, prince, nobleman, any man in authority, should be characterized by *virtue.*

The kings of the early Middle Ages might not have been philosopher-kings like Marcus Aurelius. Many of them, like Charlemagne, were not even literate. By the standards of the Church they could be seen, accurately, as bloodstained fornicators. But their hearts were in the right place. One can usefully think of them as rather like the motorcyclists who descend on Washington, D.C., every Memorial Day waving American and MIA flags. Only the "Bikers for the Bishop of Rome" would be waving the papal flag or the white flag with the crimson cross of the Crusades. The best of them would be staffing monasteries, designing cathedrals, and creating the cultural tapestry of the Middle Ages. To put it as a cynic might, the newly converted barbarians of the West exhibited a nobler, humbler, less refined savagery than the Oriental despots of Byzantium. They were also commendably loyal to Rome.

As with the early Church, missionaries made converts largely through the spoken rather than the written word. There was, however, a book that helped explain Christianity to the warrior Saxon tribes. It was not the Bible per se; it was *The Heliand.* It retold how "the Chieftain of mankind is born in David's hill-fort"; how "Christ the Chieftain is immersed in the Jordan by his loyal thane John"; and how "Christ, the mighty Chieftain, chooses His first warrior-companions." It does not neglect how the warrior-companions gathered for the "last mead-hall feast," how "Christ the Chieftain is captured" and "Peter, the mighty swordsman, defends him boldly," and so on.[1] It was a New Testament that emphasized the one redeeming bond of the Dark Ages—feudal loyalty. Whatever their personal failings, the warriors of the West were unceasingly, even belligerently, loyal to the Church. It was this mixture of Germanic warrior vigor and pious, if imperfect, Catholic fidelity that gave birth to the medieval ideal of chivalry.

The heroes of this story are the noble Franks, a Germano-Belgic tribe. It was from their blood that sprang Clovis, founder of the alliance between the Franks and the Church at the end of the fifth century with his crowning in Reims Cathedral, which would be the holy site of consecration for French monarchs for nearly thirteen hundred years. It was Frankish knights under their warrior-kings who fought the early battles against the Moors, thwarting the rising tide of Islam that came sweeping up the Iberian Peninsula in 710.

Clovis was of the Merovingian line, but the royal mantle would eventually be borne by the Carolingians, who descended from Charles Martel, the hammer that halted the Moors at the battle of Poitiers in 732. That victory preserved the Franks' Catholic kingdom from what had befallen the Visigoths in what was now Saracen Spain. Charles's son Pepin III— also known as Pepin the Short—was the first king in the Carolingian dynasty, crowned by the pope's representative, a British monk, St. Boniface. Pope Stephen II (752–757) strengthened the bond between the Franks and the Church by affirming Pepin's line as the only royal house of the Franks. He consecrated them as the pope's defenders against the barbarian Lombards and tyrannical Byzantines. Pepin drove the Lombards from northern and central Italy in two campaigns, in 754 and 756, making a gift of his latter conquests to the pope, thus creating the Papal States: a swath of territory that would be ruled directly from the Vatican for eleven hundred years.

# CHARLEMAGNE

BUT THE GREATEST OF Carolingian kings was Pepin's son, Charlemagne, who in 774 not only conquered the Lombards—adding them to the Frankish kingdom—but deftly captured every rival claimant to the Frankish throne. A strong, handsome, and vigorous military prince, he had all the barbarian virtues, an army and imperial policy unmatched since the days of the Roman legions, and a sword consecrated to the Church. It is estimated that he fought more than fifty campaigns from one end of Western Europe to the other, often with the express goal of defeating and converting heathen tribes who would as soon burn a missionary as listen to the gospel. Charlemagne waged campaigns to the east against the Avars, to the north against the Saxons and the Vikings, and to the south across the Pyrenees against the Moors, a campaign that would later be immortalized in *The Song of Roland*. His Frankish armies fought throughout Italy, southern Germany, and the islands of the Mediterranean. His goal was that of all warrior-kings—conquest—but also conversion of the conquered to the Catholic faith.

Papal elections were going through a turbulent period, and Charlemagne brought his sword to bear here as well. The constant trouble was that factions formed around potential candidates and elections could be disrupted, or reversed, as mobs and troops intervened on behalf of their favorite. Even after a pope was elected unanimously by the clerics of Rome—as in the case of Pope Leo III (795–816)—he could find himself under physical attack by his enemies. Leo was dragged from his horse and beaten nearly to death by partisan thugs who attempted to tear out his eyes and his tongue, though both his sight and his speech recovered— miraculously, it is said—from the damage of their brutal fingers. Leo turned to Charlemagne for protection, and he got it. In return, Pope Leo III crowned Charlemagne emperor of the West on Christmas Day 800 and became the only pope in history to kneel before a king. It was Pope

Leo III who also—against his better judgment—allowed Charlemagne to install the *filioque* in the creed, affirming that the Holy Spirit came from the Father *and from the Son*. Theologically it was sound, but the pope objected not to its theology, but to *any* change on principle, as he was bound to do by Rome's traditional conservatism, especially change recommended by a layman. But Charlemagne, who took the Christian aspects of his empire seriously—his crowning marks the beginning of the Holy Roman Empire—thought from his own experience in the provinces that the *filioque* was essential to explaining the true faith to the Western tribes, and the pope reluctantly complied.

Charlemagne also encouraged the pope as a secular ruler. It was at Charlemagne's insistence that the pope maintained his own war fleet to protect himself from Saracen raiding parties. The Moors had by this time transformed much of the Mediterranean into an Islamic lake. The pope thus became, in defense, not only the Vicar of Christ and Lord Temporal of the Papal States but First Sea Lord of the Vatican.

It should also be mentioned that the Church assisted in the secular rule of Charlemagne's dominions. Beneath the emperor was a feudal network of nobles, as well as an occasional parliament made up of both lords and bishops, who governed in tandem. In Charlemagne's kingdom, the crozier of Christ's shepherds and the scepter of the king were united in governing a Christian people of many tribes and languages, but one Catholic faith.

Though illiterate, Charlemagne was nevertheless an educated man within an oral tradition, being able to understand Greek and Latin (which he could also speak), as well as his own Germanic tongue. As a sort of retirement hobby, he even tried to teach himself to write. He was consumed by a desire to learn and was interested in every academic subject. He eagerly followed theological debates and listened to readings from the Church fathers, his preference being for St. Augustine's *City of God,* which, in his position, had obvious practical applications. He was a great patron of learning, the arts, and religion, founding schools that became the foundations of Western Europe's first universities. He established institutes for church music, required the Church to provide a classical education for its clergy, and protected clerical privileges while insisting on clerical discipline. In addition, he promoted scholarship and encouraged writers to record Frankish legends, history, and law. Charlemagne's devotion to the work of monks and scholars in copying classical manuscripts ensured that these books survived beyond the Dark Ages. Among the scholars advanced by Charlemagne were Einhard, who became his biographer, and Alcuin of York, who revised St. Jerome's Vulgate Bible.

Charlemagne was a political and military genius, the savior of learning in the West, and the founder of the ideal and the reality of Western Europe as an entity united by Frankish swords and Catholic dogma. His Catholic empire stretched from France in the west to his military outposts on the borderlands of the Slavs and Byzantines. Given that so many missionaries came from Britain during this period—fulfilling Pope St. Gregory the Great's dream—one can even include the British Isles as a cultural and religious ally of Charlemagne. To the north, Frankish dominion extended over Germany, which he shielded from the Vikings. To the south it went all the way to the Pyrenees, where his knights confronted the rival Islamic empire.

Charlemagne as a man was as big as his domains, a towering six-foot-four Aryan hero, popular, intelligent in his tastes, moderate at his table, and of dynamic energy. He had four wives (in succession), numerous mistresses, eighteen children (eight of whom were legitimate), and a love of home life so strong that he forbade his daughters to marry. Rather than be deprived of their company, he winked at their illicit affairs, just as the Church agreed to wink at his own royal liaisons. Time, unfortunately, advances, and those of us separated from Charlemagne by more than a millennium can only sigh for those days when one could be both a Catholic warrior and a Frankish barbarian without contradiction.

Progress away from Charlemagne's model began with one of his sons, Louis the Pious, who would soon rise to inherit his father's crown. Louis embodied the fullness of the Catholic faith, a true *parfait, gentile* knight. He was as chaste as he was devoted to helping the poor, as handsome as he was valiant, as forgiving as he was brave, as worthy of his crown as he was devoted to ensuring that monks and priests remained worthy of their vows. Charlemagne lived to see this fulfillment and proclaimed, "Blessed be Thou, O Lord God, Who hast granted me the grace to see with my own eyes my son seated on my throne!"[2]

But Charlemagne's successors lacked the great man's gift for defeating calamities. His Carolingian successors fell into dynastic wars and disputes—especially after the death of Louis the Pious, whose sons were Adams of rebellion and who himself died while campaigning to settle such a war. It was the Church, then, that proved the most effective and reliable administrator of the West, and it was the Church that began to overshadow the crown, or, rather, the numerous crowns, as the West divided itself into a series of smaller kingdoms. The West was the Church. The various kings represented the Church—in arms, and arms the Church needed in plenty.

Churchmen were now the prime targets of the greatest outlaw tribe of the West, the Vikings, whose vast and frequent raiding parties were a source of terror from Ireland to Russia. They were an especial terror to the Church, because the Vikings saw churches and monasteries as easily plunderable treasure chests of golden goblets and jewel-encrusted crucifixes. To unfortunate cities like Tours, Viking invasions represented unpredictable, but periodic, plagues of fire, sword, rape, and pillage.

While Viking raids were unleashed like lightning from the north, Islamic scimitars surged like flames from the south, attacking Rome, capturing the islands of the Mediterranean, and seizing the Moor-facing coast of France. If the Vikings represented sheer brigandage, the Saracens of the Sahara were something else—not only a military but a religious challenge that intended to turn the Western world east to the God of the Prophet Mohammed.

In these wars, it was, again, bishops and abbots who defended the battlements of the Western world, directing armies and often living and falling by the sword. Catholic belief brings the assurance that disasters, too, will pass; and they do. For what was the fate of the fierce Norsemen? Those who eventually settled in Normandy mockingly paid homage to the king of France. Perhaps just as scoffingly they accepted baptism into the Catholic Church. But the faith took hold. The Normans would become another army supporting the Catholic civilization of Europe against the Saracens and the Byzantines.

In the short term, though, things looked bleak. Western Europe was in a perpetual state of warfare and the Church in a perpetual state of siege, with appended monasteries and churches lopped off here and there, sacked and destroyed, their priests, monks, and nuns murdered by any variety of villains. In *la belle France* recovery began with a new royal house—the house that would govern France for eight hundred years—when the Archbishop of Reims chose Hugh Capet as king in 987.

In Germany—seat of the Holy Roman Empire—restoration began with Otto the Great, German king from 936 to 973. In this time of violent upheaval, Otto insisted on reunifying as much of the Holy Roman Empire as possible, leading to warfare against dissident noblemen and conflict with the rival Franks, who were now, to all practical purposes, French in their allegiance rather than German. Otto proved his bravery by trying to restore order in Italy, which had fallen into a state of moral and political chaos from which it has never fully recovered.

Though France would go its own way, and Italy could not be saved, Otto made two crucial contributions to Europe. He defeated the Magyars—shutting them up into Hungary—and he restored Charlemagne's dream of an empire where Church and state were united in providing stability and justice. While Otto's relationship with the papacy was one of eventual conqueror—for its own good, it must be added—he was an enormous benefactor to the Catholic Church in Germany. He defended it from the Magyar hordes, granting it huge territories as ecclesiastical property. Under his sword, missionaries were free to go east, commerce could be conducted, and civilization could be restored. Otto also brought a semblance of order to Rome that would help rescue the See of St. Peter from some of its most inglorious days.

## THE DARK AGES OF THE PAPACY

BEING A POPE between the waning days of the ninth century and the opening of the eleventh was a hazardous occupation. The chances of being murdered in office were about one in three; survivors could be exiled or deposed. The pope's office could be bought, sold, traded, or seized by troops or the mob. Good men still made it to St. Peter's throne, but some of them were products of their time, churchmen with mistresses and ambition, and men who needed cold steel to defend themselves. Still, it is hard to condemn them too harshly when we consider that, whatever their personal failings, they struggled to preserve the light of faith when the entire Western world was convulsed in a tumult of incessant barbarian and Islamic invasions and internal dynastic warfare. It was a period in which the faith could easily have been crushed under foot, its vandalized cathedrals left as empty symbols, its memory fading with the ruins of Rome.

One of the heroes was Pope St. Leo IV (847–855), who, like so many of the great men of the Church, did not seek the power and glory of high position but had it thrust upon him. In 846, during the pontificate of Sergius II (844–847), the Saracens sacked Rome, plundering the churches of Saints Peter and Paul. Sergius died soon thereafter. With no reliable secular defender in sight, the new pope, Leo IV, built fortifications to protect the Vatican: a forty-foot-high, twelve-foot-thick military barricade that became known as the Leonine Wall. He helped other Italian cities with money and workers to build similar defenses, and he took the battle to the Moors, organizing a fleet of Italian warships that defeated the Saracens off the coast of Ostia. It is said that he anointed the boy-prince Alfred, who would become King Alfred the Great, the Charlemagne of England. It is certainly true that Alfred and his father came to Rome during the subsequent pontificate of Pope Benedict III (855–858). Benedict's successor, Pope Nicholas I (858–867), has gone into history as Nicholas the Great, a vigorous defender of papal supremacy, a benefactor to missionaries, and an enemy of the usurping and schismatic Photius.

While the Italian peninsula—and Rome—appeared to be in a state of perpetual danger and unrest, it was not until near the end of the ninth century that popes were customarily murdered by their opponents. By the tenth century, the papacy had become mired in a medieval equivalent of a Mafia gang war between powerful families contesting for the throne. One of the most notorious early scandals involved Pope Formosus (891–896), who, on his own merits, was a good pope; a particular friend of the English church; and of exemplary morals, scholarship, and practical intelligence. But nine months after his death, he was exhumed and put on trial by his enemy Pope Stephen VI (896–897). The only positive upshot of this macabre event was that prosecutor Stephen was then himself imprisoned and murdered by those outraged at his behavior. Between these, in the spring of 896, there was another scandal, involving another pope, Boniface VI. He was elected, not by the clergy, but by the mobbing populace of Rome, who in their democratic wisdom elected a former clergyman who had been defrocked for immorality. It was a blessing that this people's scandal was short-lived; Boniface reigned for only two weeks before he died of gout.

In these violent circumstances, the popes continued to be military as well as religious leaders. Pope John X (914–928) was called upon to raze Islam's crescent flag from central Italy, which the Mussulmen were laying desolate. Organizing a military task force that included armies of Italian noblemen and Byzantine naval support, he drove the Moor from Italy—a feat he was fond of remembering.

When Otto I—that is, Otto the Great—was anointed as restorer of the Holy Roman Empire and defender of the papacy, it was by Pope John XII (955–963), the illegitimate son of a Roman prince, whose elevation was made exclusively on the basis of political pressure. Pope John XII would, in due course, be effectively deposed by Otto and is supposed to have died while committing adultery. Otto, however, made a proper distinction between the man and his office. It was Otto who granted to the papacy, while John XII still sat on St. Peter's throne, dominion over two-thirds of Italy. He pledged his imperial defense to the pope and his territories and promised free papal elections subject to imperial approval. This condition was a necessary check on the powerful Roman families who had turned the religious politics of the Eternal City into a cockpit of violence and degradation. In the seesaw struggles for control of the papacy through the reigns of Otto II and Otto III—covering the final half of the tenth century—the Germans stood for order, and the Italians for a return to violence and degradation.

This left the Church in a conundrum. It applauded German order, while fearing German domination; the Holy Roman Emperor could guard, but could not legitimately rule, the Church. Even in this rough-hewn time, there was always a large body of men who knew that the Church had seen better days, that reform was necessary, and that the Church must be freed from the Mafiosi families who dominated and corrupted papal elections. The question was how such reform could be accomplished. Save by the protection of legions of angels with flaming swords and direct papal appointment by God, there appeared no easy answer. The world was a horribly fallen and chaotic place, and the popes as both secular and religious rulers had to make their way in it, through mobs governed by violence and in the halls of aristocrats behind whose curtains lay men with knives.

## HILDEBRAND, REFORMER OF ROME

THE SEEDS OF REFORM came whence they had come in the past—from stalwart monasteries, like the famous establishment at Cluny, in

France. It provided the scholarly training ground for four great popes—Gregory VII, Urban II, Paschal II, and Urban V—and inspired and governed more than a thousand well-disciplined monasteries across Europe, all of which maintained a feudal loyalty to the magnificent French church and its abbot. The fealty paid to Cluny and its devotion to reforming the Church led to a restoration of Catholic discipline, devotion, and learning. Reform was also found in the work of dedicated missionaries, like the brother monks Methodius and Cyril, who took the gospel to the Slavs and invented the Cyrillic alphabet.

Most of all, a great man, Cardinal Hildebrand, would be elected to St. Peter's throne as Pope Gregory VII (1073–1085) and take up rhetorical arms against every enemy of the Church, internal and external. Hildebrand was in a line—occasionally broken—of reforming popes that began near the turn of the millennium with Benedict VIII (1012–1024). Though elected the old-fashioned way—by armed force—Benedict was a warriorpope whose armies recovered the papal lands, again defeated the Muslims on the Italian peninsula, freed Sardinia from the Moors, and employed Norman and German troops to fight the Byzantines in southern Italy. He was a great reformer who stamped out clerical marriage and mistresses, threatening that the bastards of such liaisons would become serfs. Other popes picked up the banner of reform, enforcing the discipline of celibacy, working to abolish bribery in papal elections—a tactic used by the Mafiosi families—prohibiting simony, and refusing to recognize appointments to holy offices made by laymen.

Hildebrand's brand of reform was powerfully felt even before he became pope. As a reformist cardinal, he was a leading advocate of the popes being elected by the College of Cardinals, the highest-ranking bishops. He wanted the papacy to be independent of the Italian families who thought it was theirs by right; independent of the Holy Roman Emperor; and independent of the mob that felt that the people united can never be defeated, though of course they generally should have been.

It was Pope Nicholas II (1058–1061) who approved Hildebrand's plan and decreed that the College of Cardinals would henceforth elect the bishop of Rome. The election by the cardinals of Pope Alexander II (1061–1073), a friend of Hildebrand, was the first great test of the system. On principle, none of the other powers that traditionally interfered in papal elections wanted to accept the result. The Germans and the

Mafiosi families declared their own pope, Honorius II. But the Germans soon abandoned Honorius in favor of Alexander; and with Norman troops on hand in case the Mafiosi families decided to act, Alexander ascended the throne. He moved immediately to tighten Church discipline and consecrate Christian warlords who would keep the borders of Catholic Christianity moving outward in Spain and Sicily. He also blessed the military enterprise of William, Duke of Normandy, who would conquer England. As a consequence of William's fierce way with dissenters, the English church would be forcibly reformed of every corruption that afflicted the Church of the Dark Ages.

Hildebrand was the mind and spirit behind much of this reform. Trained as a Benedictine monk, he had among other appointments served as prior of St. Peter's monastery, which had been in a shocking state of decrepitude. He changed that, just as he changed everything he touched— including the papal treasury—with a mastery of administrative skills, an unending energy, and an unstoppable commitment to cleanse and reorganize the numerous Augean stables of the Church.

He had avoided being elected pope—a job he did not want, despite clerical and popular acclamation in his favor—after the death of Pope Leo IX (1049–1054), another reformer and friend whom Hildebrand had served as an adviser. As a papal ambassador to Germany, he succeeded in having Victor II (1055–1057) named as the next Holy Father. He played a key part in the election of every pope until his own election in 1073 by the College of Cardinals, affirmed by the clergy and greeted with overwhelming displays of popular approval. Again, Hildebrand tried to avoid the office, but as he had been raised by the very system of election he had worked so hard to achieve, he was in no position to do anything but accept and pray for God's guidance.

As Pope Gregory VII, he was a man of universally recognized virtue, a profound scholar, a proven administrator, and the epitome of a Christian gentleman, combining the stoic virtues and dignity long lost in Rome's antiquity with the Christian understanding and devotion of a monastic. He was the last pope to seek the approval of the Holy Roman Emperor, and he did so openly proclaiming that the emperor had no authority to determine who reigned as pontiff. The emperor, Henry IV, offered his assent nonetheless.

The principle of papal supremacy wasn't all Gregory hoped to reestablish. In a letter written in January 1075 to the abbot at Cluny, Gregory comments, "The Eastern Church has fallen away from the Faith and is now assailed on every side by infidels. Wherever I turn my eyes—to the west, to the north, or to the south—I find everywhere bishops who have obtained their office in an irregular way, whose lives and conversation are strangely at variance with their sacred calling; who go through their duties not for the love of Christ but from motives of worldly gain. There are no longer princes who set God's honour before their own selfish ends, or who allow justice to stand in the way of their ambition. . . . And those among whom I live—Romans, Lombards, and Normans—are, as I have often told them, worse than Jews or Pagans."[3]

Gregory had fought these evils as a papal adviser; now, as pope himself, he plunged deep into controversy by saying that he would brook no dissent from the discipline of clerical celibacy. He would abolish the sale and purchase of Church offices. These reforms were not popular. The clerical and political response was often one of condemnation, violence, and contumacy. Would-be protestants threatened to rent the Church on the grounds that it should lower its divine standards, allow priests to marry, and leave Church positions open for purchase—purchases that enriched the state in which the sales were held. Among the protesters was the Holy Roman Emperor, who gathered his churchmen together to denounce the pope, order him deposed, and most of all deny his right to govern all clerics, especially those who had honorably purchased their offices from the state. Gregory replied by excommunicating the emperor and his ecclesiastical supporters, telling the emperor's subjects that, as a logical consequence, they no longer owed fealty to Henry IV.

It was a showdown that would dramatically determine whether Church reform was possible and enforceable. It is testimony to both the continuing honor afforded the papacy, even after a century of darkness, and to the man Gregory VII that the emperor found himself abandoned by his lords, facing a Saxon rebellion, and compelled to seek an accommodation with the bishop of Rome. He did so in one of the most memorable incidents in history, trudging barefoot in the snow, approaching the pope at a castle in Canossa, seeking the pope's forgiveness. He was left waiting in the sleet and ice for three full days, without food, shelter, or adequate clothing, before the pope, on January 28, 1077, agreed to forgive him, in what proved to be—at least in terms of power politics—a mistake. For Henry IV's penitence was less than sincere, and the pope's

Christian forgiveness was rewarded with renewed assertions of state control over Church discipline and appointments.

Disgusted with Henry, the German princes elected Rudolf of Swabia as the true Holy Roman Emperor, loyal to the pope. Gregory, though, made no move against Henry until his hand was forced by Henry's threats to appoint an antipope. Gregory again excommunicated the unholy emperor and recognized the election of Rudolf. Henry was neither surprised nor appalled, but merely made good on his threat by elevating an excommunicated archbishop, who had purchased his previous office, as the imperial head of the universal Church—his authority stemming from Henry, the excommunicated emperor deposed by his own princes. But Henry had armies, and in 1080, after Rudolf perished in battle, Henry began a campaign to seize Rome, a military challenge that took him three years—from 1081 to 1084—to accomplish.

His conquest secure, the emperor showed the hand of imperial generosity. He assured Gregory that he would acknowledge him as the rightful pope, if the pope affirmed Henry as the rightful Holy Roman Emperor and as a symbol of papal approval crowned him with his own hands. There were plenty of *Realpolitik* reasons for Gregory to agree. But after a century of the papacy being disgraced and Church offices used for political and commercial appointments, Gregory drew his line in the sand—there would be no compromise of the dignity of Christ's Church. If the emperor wanted the crown, he would have to approach the pope as any other penitential sinner approached a priest. But because of Henry's position, there was an additional consideration. His request would have to be considered by an episcopal council, to assess whether he was worthy of the imperial throne.

As at Canossa, Henry pretended to agree to the pope's terms while acting to subvert them. The bishops gathered and boldly recommended that Gregory once more excommunicate Henry. Henry responded with force, seizing the Lateran Palace, putting his puppet on St. Peter's throne, and thus had himself crowned Holy Roman Emperor.

But the pope had allies. If Charlemagne had created the Holy Roman Empire, it was the Normans who now best embodied its idealistic spirit. The wild Norse settlers who had been civilized by the culture of *la belle France* and *l'église Catholique* had become the military hammer of the faith—hard, disciplined, well organized, and unforgiving of its enemies.

The duke of Normandy, Robert Guiscard, marched to the pope's defense, and the sound of Norman chain mail was enough to make Henry flee. The noisome Roman mob, however, remained, and rebelled against the Normans. The pope, in the name of peace, exiled himself to the Benedictine monastery at Monte Cassino. He had had enough. He yearned as so many of the Church's best men did, for a return to his monastic calling.

As death's cold hand strengthened its grip on the ailing pontiff, he forgave all who had sinned against the Church, except for Henry and his puppet antipope, who had led so many astray. His last words have gone into history as "I have loved righteousness and hated iniquity: therefore I die in exile,"[4] which is the ultimate pessimistic—and true—statement of Christian politics. It is one that Jesus would have understood; witness His own admonition to His apostles that "ye shall be hated of all men for my name's sake."[5]

But Gregory also knew of Jesus' promise—it is, of course, tied to the very honor given the papacy as the heir of St. Peter—that "upon this rock I will build my church; and the gates of hell shall not prevail against it."[6] Nor would the gates of Hell prevail, for with the rise of the later Middle Ages came a flowering not only of Catholic reform, but of the Church's triumph over the evils of the Dark Ages. The Church would take arms against its enemies. It would turn Europe's knights away from one another and unite them against the infidel. It was the age of the Crusader.

## CHAPTER NINE

# THE CRUSADES

---

IN 1071, THE SELJUK TURKS crushed the Byzantine army on the plains of Manzikert.

The scimitar of Islam—jagged as it was by ethnic and sectarian rivalries and divisions—extended from Spain through North Africa and the Middle and Near East. It swept by the very borderlands of Constantinople and stretched far eastward up the Central Asian steppes into the ancient civilizations of India and even China. Much more so than in the West, where the Franks, the Normans, and the Holy Roman Empire formed an impenetrable barrier to further Islamic expansion, the Byzantine empire felt the hot breath of the Muslim invader on its neck.

Islam threatened more than Byzantium. From the time of Jesus' death, Christians had made pilgrimages to the Holy Land—in particular to the tomb of Christ, the Holy Sepulchre. Even before Charlemagne—whom the Arabs recognized as the protecting lord of Christians in the Middle East—Frankish knights had defended Christian pilgrims on the dangerous journey. In the later chaos of the Dark Ages, the Arabs ravaged and destroyed the Holy Sepulchre and every Christian institution in Jerusalem. In 1027 the Byzantines intervened to guard Christian holy sites and pilgrims. It was a protectorate that lasted less than forty years, before Jerusalem was again submerged under Islam.

The creed of the Mohammedans would be the most dangerous religious movement to afflict Christianity until the time of Luther. Like the later Reformation Protestants, the Prophet Mohammed preached a simple, rational religion. It was a religion of the book—of the Koran. It was a religion of direct communication with God in set daily prayer. It dismissed the sacerdotal hierarchy of Catholic and Eastern Orthodox Christianity. In tune with many early heresies, it did away with the mystery of the Trinity, proclaiming that there was but one God, Allah. Moses, Jesus, and, most especially, Mohammed were his prophets. Islam's one nod to a priestly caste was to make religion and state a coherent body, with a single code of law, much as John Calvin would organize in Geneva; also like the Calvinists, the Moslems believe in predestination. Islam illustrates another important fact of religious life—that heresy builds on heresy just as protestant division begets protestant division. For the lands that fell to Islam—from North Africa, to Visigothic Spain, to the eastern possessions of Byzantium—were the areas most profoundly troubled by the earlier Arian heresy.

Aside from its simplicity, Islam appealed to the common man because it offered worldly as well as otherworldly benefits. A man was allowed as many as four wives at a time—with divorce available should any prove unsatisfactory—and any number of concubines (what would for the wealthy become harems). It had a creed of Holy War that attracted the nomadic tribes of the desert, who could now raid and pillage in the name of God and of divine conquest. Islam provided a creed of self-respecting ethics, and the dismissal of priests flattered the ego, with every man equal before God. The afterlife promised to the Mussulman was a Middle Eastern Trump Tower of luxury, with a virtually inexhaustible supply of houris to satisfy one's every sexual desire, even—despite the teetotal pledge of the Moslem during his terrestrial life—a heavenly overflowing of intoxicating liquors.

Islam spread by the sword, but it also found converts—which, given its promises and its simplicity, is not surprising. It is perhaps rather more surprising that the effeminate Byzantines did not as an empire willingly submit themselves to this Eastern creed, though to the Greek mind it is possible that its very simplicity argued against it. There is something to be said, indeed, for the idea that the ultimate mysteries and complexities of Catholicism, its affirmation of a tangible divine Incarnation in the created world, and its belief in free will provided the nurturing culture for Western Europe's eventual intellectual, scientific, industrial, and creative superiority over Islam.

In fact, this looming superiority was in some ways already in evidence. Byzantine civilization, though corrupt, was, like many corrupt civilizations, highly advanced. Certainly in its military organization it had a wealth of military scholarship that allowed the effete Greek-speaking emperors to recruit soldiers of hardier stock and to train and direct them with consummate skill. Upon this foundation of a relatively small, but highly professional, army the great civilization of Byzantium rested.

But it was the West that was the rising force of Europe. It was the mixture of Norseman, German, Saxon, Gaul, and Roman—the compounded spirit of the Celtic chieftain Vercingetorix, Caesar, Charlemagne, and the Church—that would soon change the world in one of the most extraordinary adventures in the history of mankind.

It started with a proclamation from Pope Urban II (1088–1099), a reformist in the tradition of Hildebrand. If the modern reader has any doubts about the papacy's undisputed leadership of Christendom, he need only look at the response of all Europe when Pope Urban II proclaimed a Crusade to regain the Holy Land and save the imperiled Byzantine Christians. "*Deus le volt!*" was the chant, "God wills it."[1]

The Crusades began, as did most things in the West where liberty and chaos freely intermingled, with disorganized false starts from a motley crew of unprepared, unarmed pilgrims—peasants, priests, and prostitutes—who followed the People's Crusade of Peter the Hermit,[2] which ended in disaster meted out by Turkish blades. Other civilian Crusaders fell to the Hun. There were also outrages, particularly against Jews in Germany, from villains who saw the proclaimed Crusade as an excuse for yobbism. But a rough skein of order developed as the Crusaders formed under the command of Frankish and Norman noblemen who became the field marshals of the First Crusade, bringing with them their private armies. Their goals: to serve Christ's Church and the pope's command; to help themselves with a remission of sins for completing their holy task; and—who can doubt it—for adventure, with the more enterprising hoping to carve out new feudal estates in the Near East.

When we think of these men from the West, we should see them as they might have appeared to the Moslems or the Byzantines. They were giant, lusty men fed on beef and beer; with heavy leather gauntlets and chain mail; mounted on armored horses of enormous size; violent, unforgiving, unretreating; and pious to a God whose chief ethical demands seemed to be feudal honor, noble independence, and stubbornness—the God of *The Heliand*.

As Robert Harrison notes in his introduction to *The Song of Roland,* the great *chanson de geste* written around this time, "To the medieval nobleman piety meant a familiar, almost intimate relationship to the human natures of Jesus, Mary, and the saints of the church, and included not only what we think of as religious devotion, but also an unswerving loyalty, national pride, chivalric honor, and a fierce sense of personal dignity. . . . Western Christianity had very little in common with the philosophical otherworldliness of the Eastern Church. . . . [T]he Frankish knight regarded his obligations to God in very much the same terms as his allegiance to his feudal overlord . . . wholly sincere and zealously militant."[3]

Central to militant, tangible, worldly Frankish Christianity was the sword. "[A]s a Christian symbol the sword acquired even more than ordinary significance. Its shape made it inevitably a makeshift crucifix in times of exigency on the battlefield, and it frequently was used in the last rites of men killed in action."[4]

In other words, Pope Urban II had brought together an international, Catholic, war-loving *Légion Étrangère* and shipped it east.

The Byzantine Emperor Alexius had begged Rome for help, but he was also acutely aware of how dangerous it was to have these French warlords on his doorstep. True, the Seljuk Turks—grim, wary archers on quick horses who were sweeping Mesopotamia, Asia Minor, and the Middle East—had already proven too much for Byzantine arms. But the Normans had also proven themselves against Byzantine soldiery, having evicted the Byzantines from southern Italy. As for the belligerent Franks—the men who centuries before had raised Charlemagne to be the Eastern emperor's imperial rival—never had Constantinople seen so many knights and men-under-arms as now made the march from the westernmost parts of France, and even England, to Byzantium. These Franks and Normans—the *Wehrmacht* of the Middle Ages—were a potential threat as they camped beneath the gates of the city. Vigorous fighting men with time on their hands, they were armies loyal to Rome, from which Constantinople was religiously divorced.

# LIBERATING THE BYZANTINES

THE EAST, BY ITS OWN ADMISSION, had been in wrongful schism many times in the past and had always resubmitted itself to Rome. Between the fourth and ninth centuries, by subsequent common agreement, Constantinople was in schism more than a third of the time. While the heresiarch Photius had diligently widened the Greek-Latin divide to secure his own paramountcy, he was not directly responsible for the near final break with the universal Church—for Photius died in exile around 892.

The Great Schism arrived more than a hundred years later, with the patriarch Michael Cerularius, who persecuted and shut down Latin-rite churches in the East. In response, the pope excommunicated him in 1054. The patriarch, in turn, excommunicated the Holy See and inflamed the nationalism of the Eastern churches, leading them into schism. The theological issues at stake were virtually nonexistent. A prime Eastern complaint was the Western Church's use of unleavened bread rather than leavened bread in the Mass.[5] Arianism's lingering influence played a part, too, providing a dim anti-Trinitarian memory that could be popularly tapped for the East's political opposition to the *filioque*.[6] The true issues in the schism were linguistic, cultural, and political: Greek versus Latin; Eastern nationalism versus Western Christendom; Constantinople's prideful ambition versus Rome's proud lineage; Caesaropapism versus the pope himself.

In 1054, Rome viewed the schism with the East as temporary—as it still does today—in line with so many other Eastern fits of pique and madness; and, indeed, over the centuries the schism has occasionally, if only momentarily, been healed. So Pope Urban II had no qualms about directing Catholic knights to rescue the schismatic emperor in Constantinople.

But Emperor Alexius, raised in an atmosphere of Byzantine intrigue, was taking no chances. He required an oath of fealty from the Frank and Norman leaders, all of whom but one—with varying degrees of enthusiasm—pledged their troth in order to get on with the business of slaughtering Muslims. As an added precaution, Alexius didn't allow the mighty warrior host to gather as one force in front of Constantinople, but hurriedly ferried them piecemeal across the Bosporus, where they could do no harm to anyone save the infidel.

The arrival of this army was itself a remarkable military feat if one looks at the distances involved. Equally amazing were its initial military successes. The Crusaders were never a unified body of men under a single command. Instead, they were an exceedingly loose alliance of nobles and their affiliated men-at-arms. The nobles even had competing interests in making their feudal claims. Another challenge they surmounted was the waterless desert—with every community of wells and provisions destroyed by the Turk. But the heavily armored men of the temperate lands of France, Germany, and Italy, crossed it, their only assistance coming from Armenian Christians who acted as a sort of World War II Free French resistance, helping the Crusaders with supplies. If the Crusaders had advantages, it was in the crush of their heavy cavalry—if they could bring it to bear at close quarters—and a fearlessness against the more numerous Oriental invader.

First to return to Christian hands was the historic city of Nicea, which had been held by the Turks for a decade and a half. The occupying forces capitulated to Byzantine diplomats, who could now invoke the threat of a Crusader invasion. The first great clash of arms was at Dorylaeum in Asia Minor in 1097, where the Turks fell back, as they continued to fall back under the crusading advance. Crusaders under the leadership of the Norman knight Tancred conquered Cilicia, in southern Asia Minor. A Frankish army under Baldwin crossed into Armenia, where he married a princess and established a settlement.

The main Crusader armies continued to Syria and the ancient city of Antioch. Here the day was won not only by the valor of the land-based Crusaders but by the Genoese fleet that provided the knights with provisions and supplies to lay siege to the Muslim-occupied city. The city fell, but the Crusaders were then themselves besieged for four weeks before they could beat back the Turks. Nearly a year was spent negotiating feudatory rights in Syria before the Crusaders marched down the Levant, seizing Tripoli and then attacking Jerusalem, which fell to the Crusaders on July 15, 1099, in a merciless killing spree that would have been recognized, and approved, by Titus Flavius who had reclaimed the city for Rome more than a thousand years before. But where Titus destroyed the Jewish Temple, the Christians, after their slaughter, came to pay homage to the Holy Sepulchre. Within a month, they were fighting again, as Muslims from Egypt tried to wrench the holy city back. The Egyptians failed, and with their failure Godfrey of Bouillon was reaffirmed by his fellow knights as feudatory lord of Jerusalem and "Defender of the Holy Sepulchre." Within four years of Pope Urban II's proclamation, the Crusades had succeeded in relieving Byzantium and recapturing Jerusalem.

But the Crusaders held only an isthmus in a Muslim sea, and they had an unworthy rearguard in the Byzantines, who immediately made claims to Crusader conquests. They were justifiable claims, given the Crusaders' oaths of loyalty, but ill-timed ones, nevertheless, that struck the hard-fought French knights as impertinent. With the grasping Byzantines came a return of the Turk, who wanted to renew his own claims to Antioch and eastern Byzantium. The pope sent reinforcements, but the Muslims slaughtered them as they marched across Asia Minor.

Tenuous as their grip on the Holy Land was, the Catholic knights held on to Antioch and Jerusalem and slowly pushed outward to expand their domains. Within twenty-five years, they had taken the principal ports of the Levant, in combined land-sea operations that involved French knights, Italian sailors, and even recently Christianized Norwegians under the command of their king, Sigurd Jorsalafare, whose exploits would be celebrated more than seven hundred years later in the music of Edvard Grieg. The Crusader holdings in the twelfth century incorporated, roughly speaking, contemporary Israel, Lebanon, Syria, and a hundred-mile-wide strip along the Turkish coast paralleling the island of Cyprus.

With these conquests came a greater sense of security and the reestablishment of Christian civilization. Pilgrims now received some protection, though the journey was still dangerous. They were often shaken down for funds by their fellow Christians or subject to Muslim brigandage on undefended stretches of road. Nevertheless, commerce, under Italian merchantmen from Venice, Pisa, and Genoa, returned and flourished. The whole Gallic panoply of French warlords, land-holding feudal bishops, and religious submission to Rome was recreated in the Near East, which blossomed with wealth. Frankish knights adopted what they thought were the most appealing aspects of Middle Eastern life—Arab clothes that suited the climate, baths with scented soaps—and intermarried with the native Christian population.

Indeed, the Catholic Levant developed something it has rarely been given credit for, a spirit of toleration. There was commerce and even friendship between Muslim, Jewish, and Christian communities when war did not intervene. The Franks learned Arabic while they continued to speak French and worship in Latin. But it also became apparent that if the Catholic Middle East of the Crusaders—known as Outremer—were to survive, it needed a class of men who would not grow enervated by the climate, which claimed many lives through malaria and other diseases, or grow soft by adopting the customs of Eastern opulence. It needed men who would be always ready for war; men who would be unstinting in their defense of Christian pilgrims to the Holy Land. To meet this need, new religious orders of monastic knights pledged themselves to defend the Catholic foothold in the Middle East against the Turk and the Saracen.

## THE MONKS OF BATTLE

JUST AS THE MONASTERIES had been the major source of intellectual, spiritual, and even political renewal in the first thousand years of Christendom, so now monastic orders bore the Cross of the Crusades. The monk who provided the intellectual support for these monks of war was the great St. Bernard of Clairvaux (1090–1153), another Frenchman of noble blood, like the knights who had reconquered Palestine. But where the knights were naturally men of war, Bernard was a man of scholarship and religious devotion, which led him to the monastery. As abbot of the monastery at Clairvaux, Bernard gained a great reputation, so that Clairvaux, like Cluny, became a seedbed for follow-on monasteries. More than that, Bernard became the patron of another blue-blooded Frenchman, Hugues de Payens, who had taken it upon himself to protect Christian pilgrims in the Holy Land, binding his handful of followers to his own monastic vows of poverty, chastity, and obedience. At first they were known as the "poor knights." The Frankish king of Jerusalem awarded them the title of "Knights of the Temple" and gave them free use, as living quarters, of what was thought to be the rebuilt remnant of Solomon's temple, now part of the royal palace. Bernard drew up a monastic rule for Hugues's men—the Rule of the Knights Templar, based on the rule of the Cistercians, who traced their own lineage to St. Benedict.

With a rule, a mission, and evidence of good works, the knights quickly won papal favor, which guaranteed their independence from outside authority. From poor knights, they became masters of estates, thanks to papal and noble donations. With such funds they built commanding castles in the Arabian desert from which to defend the faith.

Unlike most monks, they ate heartily—with meat and wine at every meal—mortifying the flesh, not through diet, but by military training and practice. Not being scholar-monks, their prayers and offices were kept simple and easily memorized. Their discipline was outstanding, their fearlessness renowned, and though their barracks never numbered more than a few hundred soldier-monks at one time, so willing were they to face death before dishonor and to put themselves at the center of every fight against the Saracens that their casualties have been estimated at 20,000 men over the two-hundred-year history of Outremer—or, to put it another way, every year the majority of enrolled Knights Templar died in battle.

Thus, by necessity, the Knights Templar became a forerunner of the French Foreign Legion. While officers were solely men of noble birth, the order accepted as recruits criminals-on-the-run, who would renounce all and swear complete and utter submission and loyalty to the order and, through the order, to the pope. The Templars were legionnaires with a difference, however, because they were also a forerunner of the Rothschilds. The Templars' probity, landed wealth, and international organization—necessary for recruiting and fund-raising—made them, over time, the bankers of Europe and royal financial consultants.

The nearest rivals of the Templars were the Knights Hospitallers, also known as the Knights of St. John, later as the Knights of Rhodes, and today as the Knights of Malta. The origins of the Hospitallers are obscure, save for this much: We know that the order began before the Crusades, around 1070, and was founded by Gerard de Martignes with the express purpose of providing shelter for Christian pilgrims in Jerusalem.

Once the Crusader kingdom was established, the Hospitallers and their mission grew, providing not only shelter but treatment for the sick, and enormous benefactions to the poor. As the order grew further, it established a military wing for the protection of pilgrims, and as this wing expanded it became an important part of the crusading armies. Like the Templars, the Hospitallers were favorites of the papacy and gained rapidly in wealth and prestige, eventually defending greater swaths of the Christian Holy Land than any other armed force; and also like the Templars, the Hospitallers were to be found in the hottest part of every battle between Crusader and Saracen. But unlike the Templars, the Hospitallers never ventured into banking and managing the national treasuries of jealous sovereigns—a dangerous business, as the Templars would discover. The Hospitallers' charitable services, and their distance from finance and politics, partially shielded them from the controversies that later engulfed the Templars, who were disbanded and partially amalgamated into the Hospitallers in 1312.

## RICHARD THE LIONHEARTED AND THE MONARCHS OF WAR

ASIDE FROM THE MONKS, the great military commanders of the later Crusades to the Holy Land were kings. At the time of the First Crusade (1095–1099), it was the noblemen of Europe, rather than their monarchs, who responded to the pope's call. But in 1146, St. Bernard of Clairvaux launched the Second Crusade. Enrolled in his host were the king of France, Louis VII, whose bride, Eleanor of Aquitaine, accompanied him on the Crusade, and the king of Germany, Conrad III, who was joined by the knight who would become known as Frederick Barbarossa. Setting out as they did, with nobles accompanied by their ladies, they were perhaps shocked by the realities of warfare in the desert, and certainly scandalized by the Byzantine Greeks who were keener on making money off the Westerners than they were on advancing the Crusade. The result was disaster. Conrad's German army took 90 percent casualties in Asia Minor; the French did less badly but were harried by Muslim raiding parties; and the entire operation ended in 1148 at the gates of Damascus, with the various Christian troopers retreating their separate national ways.

The result was not just a military catastrophe, but a crisis of faith for the West—how could God allow His Crusaders to be so humiliatingly defeated by the infidel? The answer was actually easily found, for those who dared to look. It was in the very nature of the West, in its contentious individualism, its spirit of unceasing striving for glory, fame, and accomplishment, which in the Crusades meant constant exposure to danger. The knightly love of honor led to a notorious jostling for position and supremacy among the feudal lords of Outremer. They were hard-drinking, infrequently raping, occasionally slaughtering, always fighting, perhaps even charming Errol Flynns bedecked with surcoats that bore Christ's cross—and always, of course, with a prayer, a sincere prayer, it might be

added, on their lips to the Virgin, to the martyrs, to the saints, or to the
Holy Trinity. When the Muslim was subdued, they turned on each other
or embarked on wild adventures—like that undertaken by a Frankish
knight named Renaud of Châtillon. Having already proven his mettle as
Crusader, romantic hero (he too married a princess), and all-around ruf-
fian, he decided to become a pirate. He sent buccaneering raiding parties
down the Red Sea—his boats ferried across the intervening desert on
camelback—with his ultimate jape being an attempt to destroy the tomb
of Mohammed. His command was ambushed and nearly wiped out by
the Mussulmen. Rather un-Islamically, the captured Franks were
butchered as a human sacrifice.

It was the very same swashbuckling Renaud of Châtillon who, in a
typical compound of arrogance, rapacity, and daring, invited the greatest
single opponent of the Crusades to battle. In the spirit of a highway rob-
ber, he seized a caravan and took captive the sister of a Moslem commander. That commander happened to be the Kurdish vizier of Egypt,
Syria, and Mesopotamia, and the most formidable Muslim general the
Christians faced. His name was Saladin, and in 1186 he responded to Renaud's bushwhacking with a call for Holy War, uniting the entirety of
Islam against the Catholic foothold in the Holy Land.

Renaud knew very well who Saladin was. The Frenchman's raids
along the Red Sea had sparked two Saladin-led attacks on Renaud's
mighty castle stronghold at Kerak. During one of these sieges, Renaud
was hosting a wedding party, which entailed typical, if bizarre, obse-
quies to chivalry amidst battle. Saladin the besieger received gifts of
food from the mother of the bridegroom in the castle. In return, the
generous Mussulman offered not to fire on the tower in which the hon-
eymooners were lodged—while busily attacking every other target of
Renaud's fortress.

This time, however, to avenge the kidnapping of his sister, Saladin
amassed a force of 100,000 men and marched toward Jerusalem. The
Crusaders could bring against him no more than 20,000 men—and that
meant a concentration of knights and attendant soldiers gathered from
the entirety of Outremer. Outnumbered five to one overall, ten to one in
cavalry, the Christians nevertheless attempted a daring offensive. It was
not a foolhardy misadventure, but a knowing throw of the dice on a desperate gamble. They hoped to save Jerusalem by bringing their crashing

heavy cavalry to bear in the open land outside the city of Tiberias, roughly three days' march to the east.

At a conference of Crusader commanders, Raymond of Tripoli advised his fellow knights not to go forward with the plan, but to hope that they might find a strong defensive position near the coast and draw the Muslims against them. "Though my wife is within those walls of Tiberias," Raymond pleaded, "and my children there and my goods, and though it is my own castle in my own land, yet I would rather all those were lost, my wealth there and those of my blood, rather than that the Kingdom itself should be thrown away; and surely if you march on Tiberias you will destroy the realm forever. I know the Turkish armies, I have seen them for a lifetime—and never was there gathered such an army as this."[7] But numbers never intimidated the Crusaders.

While Saladin waited near the Sea of Galilee, the Christians boldly marched across a burning expanse of desert to stop him. But Raymond was right, valor could not compensate against the heat, the thirst, and the impossible odds that weighed on the Frenchmen. Surrounded and pressed hard by Saladin's sheer numbers, penned in by fires set by burning Moslem arrows, any hopes of victory crumbled like ashes. Raymond's cavalry, however, burst through the Muslim line and escaped; their goal: to rally Christians on the coast. But the bulk of the Catholic army was destroyed on July 4, 1187, at the battle of Hattin. Among the captured knights was Renaud, who was personally executed by Saladin. He also ordered the death of every captured Hospitaller and Templar.

In one enormous blow, the Crusader kingdom had effectually been eliminated from Palestine. Saladin marched to the holy city of Jerusalem, which was still filled with Christian settlers and pilgrims, and claimed it for Islam. He showed tremendous mercy—the Christian chroniclers praise him highly—sending only 15,000 Christians into slavery.

Such generosity, however, was not long appreciated, for it was also part of the spirit of the West not to accept defeat. In 1187, Pope Gregory VIII announced the Third Crusade. He consciously viewed the Crusade as a means not only to recover Jerusalem but to reunify the feuding princes of Europe in a common cause. In this latter hope, though he did not live to see it, he had at least partial success. Frederick Barbarossa of the ill-fated Second Crusade, sixty-seven years old and at odds with the papacy, was now Holy Roman Emperor. But he joined the Crusade nevertheless and made his manners with the new pope, Clement III. The king of France, Philip Augustus, and Richard the Lionhearted, king of England, joined the Crusade. In these great imperial countries, in city-states, in backwater realms, and from Denmark and distant Viking kingdoms—yes, the Norsemen came again, Britons and Scandinavians striking at the Moors in Iberia, before continuing their journey to the Levant—animosity was buried as the sovereigns pledged themselves to the common cause of the Cross against the Crescent, of the Crusade against the jihad.

In 1189, Frederick Barbarossa's enormous Saxon host began its march to Constantinople and entered immediately into the Byzantine politics of Byzantium. He discovered that the Eastern emperor, Isaac Angelus, had actually entered into an alliance with Saladin, matching Islamic Arabs against Islamic Turks. He had also cut a deal with the Arabs to be in charge of Christian interests in the Holy Land. If this wasn't shocking enough to Western sensibilities, the Balkan states (through which Frederick's German army made its way) were in rebellion against the depredations of Constantinople. Frederick was further appalled when his emissaries to Byzantium, requesting transport across the Bosporus, were kidnapped and held hostage by the emperor, who suspected that Frederick sympathized with the Balkan rebels. He was right in that, but the Byzantine emperor's heavy-handed tactics only affirmed Frederick's belief that the Byzantines were corrupt and as much an enemy to Catholic Europe as the Moslems. Frederick sent word to Rome that he wanted a Crusade declared against the Greeks. The idealistic goals—and necessary military support—of the Crusades would never be satisfied, he argued, unless the West took over from Byzantium and held the straits that separated Europe from the Near East.

All, however, was patched up, through diplomacy. Frederick made his crossing, at Byzantine insistence, from Gallipoli, to the south of Constantinople, into the land of the Turks. Frederick had thoughtfully concluded a pact with the Turkish sultan affirming that Saladin's Arabs, not the Turks, were the target of his Crusade. But the Turks proved as untrustworthy as the Byzantines, sending noisome raiding parties against him. Still, battling the heat and the Seljuks, the massive German army marched on—to the fear of the Arabs. Then disaster struck. The great Frederick Barbarossa was drowned making a river crossing. With him sank the best hopes of the Third Crusade.

Because the Germans' loyalty was a personal bond to their king, many of the Teutonic princes and their soldiers returned to Deutschland. But others stayed true and continued the march to the walls of Muslim-held and heavily fortified Acre, on what is now the northern Israeli coast. This was the focal point of attack for the slowly assembling multinational Crusader army of Englishmen, including the archbishop of Canterbury, Scandinavians, Flemings, Frenchmen, and the Frankish remnant of Outremer.

The siege would last two horrible years, the besiegers suffering terribly from the wet winters and tropical disease. The battle was not won until the royals arrived. In 1191, the king of France entered the Holy Land. He was soon followed by Richard, Coeur de Lion, who, though king of England, spoke only French. Richard had been delayed because he was providentially shipwrecked, which allowed him to conquer Cyprus on his way to Palestine. Together, the monarchs of Western Europe—and the Italian navy, which sank the Egyptian fleet supplying the Muslims in Acre—completed the siege and took the city, massacring its inhabitants. This goal accomplished, the French king returned to *la belle France,* leaving Richard as the undisputed commander in chief of the Catholic forces.

Richard's mother was Eleanor of Aquitaine, who had her own experience as a damsel accompanying a Crusade. No crusading knight would ever rival the fame of her son. He became the very definition of a Crusader, simultaneously cruel and chivalrous. The duel between his armies and Saladin's, though largely meaningless in the greater context of history, became the preeminent legend of the conflict. Both men were merciless in butchering hostages to enforce bargains. Both men were chivalrous, as in the incident where Saladin sent a horse to Richard when he was unseated in the midst of battle. Adding to Richard's romantic legend was his military and political alliance with the fearsome Templars. In combat, Richard took pride in personally rivaling them for daring, leading from the front with his weapon of choice, a Danish axe. Inevitably, the Hospitallers found a patron in the French king, Philip II Augustus.

Richard pushed the Muslims back to Jerusalem, which, however, his own officers twice dissuaded him from attacking. As a consequence, he offered Saladin many proposals for peace—including a marriage pact between his sister and Saladin's brother, an offer that was later withdrawn. The final peace accord left Jerusalem in Saladin's care, but with a provision made for the safe passage of Christian pilgrims. The Christians retained possession of the Levant ports and promised equal freedom of movement to Muslims. Richard was in a hurry to reach this agreement because of political machinations against him at home. His passage to England was eventful. An Austrian duke and the Holy Roman Emperor kidnapped him, demanding an enormous ransom. He returned to England in time—as we all know—to reward Robin Hood for his loyalty against the villainous usurper, his own brother, Prince John. John later became Richard's successor and one of England's most unworthy kings, famous only for Magna Carta, which England's barons forced him to sign. Interestingly, he also ran afoul of the pope, who punished him for asserting secular control over the Church in England. King John was made to officially surrender the English kingdom to the papacy, receiving it back as a feudal trustee. That's interesting not only in itself, but in underlining the enormous power of the pope in Western Europe and contrasting it with the Eastern Church, which was a footstool for the Byzantine emperor.

## THE CRUSADE AGAINST BYZANTIUM

AFTER THE DUEL between Saladin and Richard the Lionhearted, the French and English knights returned home to settle scores amongst themselves and against each other. As a consequence, the Christian mission in the Holy Land became a German thing, and from the Germans sprang another extraordinary military order—the Teutonic Knights, who won the imprimatur of Pope Innocent III in 1199. Like the Hospitallers, the Teutonic Knights began with medical work, operating a military field hospital at Acre under the leadership of a German duke during the Crusaders' siege. But they were soon involved in protecting Christian pilgrims. The knights accepted monastic vows, consecrating themselves to the Virgin Mary, arming themselves for war, and adorning themselves in a habit that featured a black cross on a field of white.

Pope Innocent III, who held the chair of St. Peter from 1198 to 1216, wanted more men like the Teutonic Knights because he wanted another Crusade. Saladin died in 1193, and with his death the Islamic empire he had stitched together was unraveled by competing claimants. The West's crusading idealism, however, continued to suffer under the bane of calculated self-interest, sharp-eyed commerce, and knightly contention. Innocent

III was not so innocent of the world that he didn't have opinions on military strategy. He advised a new invasion route—through Egypt—that would give the Crusaders a wealthy base of supply and allow them to better take advantage of the naval support available from the Italian city-states of Venice, Genoa, and Pisa.

Where the pope might have suffered from innocence was in thinking that the Italian fleets would see this Crusade as their Christian duty rather than as a means to bilk money from both sides in the affair. The Italians demanded enormous sums for the transport of Catholic soldiers while secretly insuring the Egyptian sultan against a Catholic invasion, which, if it happened, could mean a loss of valuable trade for the Italians. The pope also tried, innocently, to end the Eastern schism, asking the emperor in Constantinople to reconcile with Rome and join the Crusade to retake the Holy Land. But that, of course, was asking too much of the Byzantine Church, which set so much stake on its vitally important theological differences with Rome, such as the Eastern requirement that priests have beards. Constantinople refused to fight for the Holy Land. The fighting would come to it anyway.

Frenchmen again dominated the Crusader army. With their Gallic pride and independence they quickly took the Crusade rollicking on a course of its own, a course that the pope kept trying to correct by pointing south to Egypt, while the Crusaders aimed at prizes in the north. First on the menu was the Adriatic port of Zara. Venice had once owned it; now the Hungarians did. The Venetian shippers said they would make good the shortfall of Crusader cash, necessary for their military transport to Egypt, if the Frenchmen would recapture Zara for Venice. The Crusaders obliged. But, victory in hand, the roving Frenchmen steered a course not at Egypt—but at Constantinople! The reason was named Alexius, son of the former Byzantine emperor Isaac Angelus, who had been deposed and blinded, in the traditional Byzantine fashion, by his usurping brother.

The Byzantines were not popular with the Crusaders, who regarded them, in the vernacular, as gay Greeks—effeminate, scheming, and bitchy. Alexius told the Frenchmen that if they restored him to the throne, he'd try to end all that, returning the Eastern Church to the full Catholic faith, paying the Crusaders a hefty sum of money, and pledging Byzantine soldiers for their war against the Moslems. The French responded with a

"*Formidable, bonne idée!*" and soon were off to restore Alexius to the purple, which they did, smashing into Constantinople, freeing papa Isaac Angelus from prison, and chasing his brother, also named Alexius, from the city. That was in July 1203. It was an action taken against the direct orders of the pope. By the winter of 1204, the Frenchmen began thinking that perhaps the pope had been right. They were getting angry about the continual delays in the Byzantines' making good on their promises. Any doubts about Byzantine treachery were erased when Alexius and his father were overthrown by yet another Alexius, this one openly hostile to the Crusaders. The Crusaders besieged Constantinople, conquered it, and sacked it as just and condign punishment. The Venetian shipping magnates, being partners in the enterprise, took half the spoils. The French Crusaders divided the remainder in the most honorable way—according to need, defined as one's feudal status. The higher one climbed the ranks of French nobility, the more one needed, bearing in mind all the retainers one had to support.

The biggest prize was the Byzantine Empire itself. A Crusader king—Baldwin, a knight of Flanders—was installed in Constantinople. The lands of New Rome were divided into feudal estates for noble Frenchmen, and the port cities were granted to the Venetian merchant shippers. A nod was made to France's traditional *mission civilisatrice* not only by seizing—and unfortunately sometimes smashing—Byzantine art for *la patrie,* but also in declaring French the language of the Byzantine Empire. Not forgetting religion, the conquerors appointed a Venetian prelate as bishop. Thus, with the flick of a sword blade, the Eastern schism was over.

These prodigious men then turned around and presented their accomplishment to the pope—who was simultaneously amazed, appalled, and finally accepting of what he could only regard, so stunning was the event, as God's will.

The original plan of reclaiming the Holy Land had to be put on hold, as the Crusaders tried to consolidate their conquests—which meant constant warfare—against both the rump of the Byzantines, now centered on Nicea, and the leaders of the Balkan states, who saw opportunities for themselves. But the Frenchmen held on, and much of Byzantium became an Eastern European version of Outremer. The French knights were outnumbered by hostile natives, precarious in their hold on power, but in power nonetheless. If they had not conquered the Holy Land, they had reunified the Christian world, so that every professed and abiding Christian—with the exception of the Byzantine rump, a handful of other small, scattered Eastern sects like the Nestorians, and the current crop of heretics—was again officially in full union with the Catholic Church.

The sacking of Byzantium is often regarded as a scandal, but viewed objectively, it is hard to see why this should be so. One rarely hears about the "scandal" of the English Civil War, or the American War for Independence, or the American War Between the States, though in each of these cases the combatants shared not only Christian belief of varying sorts, but the same language, the same culture, and, before the fighting, the same political allegiance. In the Crusaders' attack on Byzantium, nearly none of this held true. The Byzantines were notorious schismatics in religion. They no longer spoke the universal Latin tongue of the West. They were culturally and politically alien. They demanded the benefits but would not pay the martial costs of the Crusades and had in fact been a long-standing irritant to the Crusaders. Nor can it honestly—in terms of secular history and plain reality—be considered a "scandal" for there to be warfare between Christians, given that from the beginning of the faith Christians had been at either sword's point or sword's hilt. Especially in the East, warfare between competing sects was common. The scandal is not that the Crusaders sacked Byzantium; it is that the pope did not make every effort to reinforce the Crusaders and make the Crusaders' kingdom of Constantinople the necessarily heavily armored firewall against the Turks and the Mongols.

The pope, however, remained committed to his original intent of regaining the Holy Land, though he too was distracted. There were the Moors in Spain. There was the hippie disaster of the Children's Crusade—opposed by the Church—which hoped to retake the Holy Land with all the might of the Pied Piper. Instead, enterprising Italian merchants sold the children to the Muslims as slaves. There was a new outbreak of heresy—the Albigensians—in France. As the leader of Christendom, Innocent III took responsibility for settling Europe's sundry political disputes. His hope in the East was that if the French overlords of Byzantium could reconcile the Greek people to the universal Church, perhaps a unified Crusade to the Holy Land could be achieved after all.

The last great Crusade would begin just after his death.

# THE LAST CRUSADES

THE NEXT SOVEREIGN to take up the cross—at Charlemagne's grave—was Frederick II of Germany, the new Holy Roman Emperor. Frederick proved his bona fides by finding the merchants who sold the Children's Crusade into slavery. He had them executed. Unfortunately, he bollixed his reputation for military sanctity by failing to turn up when the Crusaders embarked for war.

Christian princes from across Europe continued to make independent crusading forays into the Holy Land. But what is known officially as the Fifth Crusade began in 1217, when the Crusaders returned to Innocent III's original plan of attacking the Holy Land via Egypt. They met with initial success, securing the city of Damietta from the Egyptians, and winning a peace overture from the sultan. After a bit more fighting, disputing over terms, and the nonappearance of Frederick's German army, the Christians were defeated outside Cairo in 1221 and had to settle for worse terms than they had been offered originally.

It wasn't until 1228 that Frederick finally bestirred himself to undertake the Sixth Crusade, though by this time his dilatoriness had earned him a papal excommunication. He nevertheless put on an astonishing performance. Trusting to his knowledge of Arabic, diplomacy, and intellectual fireworks rather than arms, he secured an agreement with the sultan that gave the Christians ownership of every site critical to them in the Holy Land, including Bethlehem, Nazareth, and virtually the entirety of Jerusalem, in the Treaty of Jaffa in 1229. As a crowning gesture, as it were, Frederick took advantage of being in Jerusalem to declare himself king of its Christian kingdom. He returned to Europe to find Pope Gregory IX still angry and actually in arms against him. But in 1230 pope and emperor were reconciled with the Treaties of San Germano and Ceprano, and the Treaty of Jaffa was approved.

Despite Frederick's crown, it was the French knights of the Levant who again took the chief Christian place in the government of Jerusalem. In the game of power politics, they tried to balance Arab Damascus, which became an ally, against the Egyptian sultanate. But the balance of power was crushed underfoot by another group of Turks, the Kharizim Turks, who seized Jerusalem in 1244. They themselves were fleeing a new terror, the Mongols, whose armed brutality had now charged to the gates of Christendom, having already enslaved Russia and defeated the Hungarians. Their leader was Genghis Khan.

Pope Innocent IV was as eager as every other pope to restore Christian fortunes in the Middle East, but the Crusading spirit was fading from the feudal lords and their people, who were tired of the endless, fruitless wars abroad and more concerned about the endless, contentious jostling for power at home. The exception was Louis IX of France, who reminds one of his own namesake, Charlemagne's son, Louis I. Louis I was known as Louis the Pious, and Louis IX would become St. Louis. Louis IX was a kind and decent ruler, noted in particular for his extreme generosity to the poor and as a devoted Crusader.

While both the pope and the French king sent religious ambassadors to the Mongols, seeing if they might be Catholic material and potential allies against the Mussulmen, Louis IX renewed the assault on Egypt. As in previous Crusades, he won his attack on the coastline but was defeated in the Egyptian interior, and the king himself was captured in 1250. In France, this news sparked a so-called Shepherd's Crusade of "the people" on behalf of their popular king. But, as with most peasant enthusiasms, it had to be put down as a threat to public order, and Louis was freed not by gnarled-handed commoners, but by surrendering his Egyptian conquests and providing a ransom from the royal treasury. A free man, he traveled not to France but spent four years in the Holy Land where he did what he could to secure the defenses of the remaining Christian cities on the coastal Levant. Twenty years later, the French king again sallied forth as a Crusader, landing at Tunis in North Africa, where he died, as he wished, on Crusade.

With the monarchs and noblemen of Christendom losing interest in the Crusades, the main support for Christians in the Levant came from Cyprus, which, like Crusader-occupied Byzantium and Outremer, was now a French island organized on a feudal model. The French, however, continued to be hampered by there being too few of them—a crying need that the world has not often recognized. But in the absence of complete French control of the eastern Mediterranean, the merchantmen of Venice and Genoa indulged their Italian genius for chaos. They turned the Christian cities of the Levant into arenas for Mafia turf battles that became a full-scale war of Venetian versus Genoese in the Holy Land. What was truly catastrophic was that the Genoese allied themselves with the rump of the Byzantines under the Eastern emperor Michael Paleologus—memorably described as a "selfish hypocrite . . . an inborn liar, vain, cruel, and rapacious."[8] Thanks to the Genoese, this flower of Byzantium recaptured Constantinople in 1261, effectively ending its Crusader kingdom, which thereafter survived only in Greece until Catalonian freebooters displaced the French adventurers near the beginning of the fourteenth century.

Meanwhile, the Egyptian Mamelukes—the former slave army of the Egyptian sultans, now ruling in their stead with a Mameluke dynasty— rolled up the coastline of the Levant, spilling rivers of Catholic blood and seizing half the great cities of the Catholic Middle East. It was this disaster that prompted Louis IX's final Crusade, the plan of which was to surprise the Egyptians with an attack from the west in North Africa. He actually hoped he could convert the Moslem Bey of Tunis to Catholicism and thus return the faith of St. Augustine to the land where the great bishop had once held sway. The plan foundered as Louis was felled by disease. But with him was Prince Edward of England, who continued the Crusade. He re-embarked his knights from the plague-ridden shores of Africa to the Holy Land, where he led skirmishes against the Moslems before returning to the isle of the Anglo-Saxons to be crowned King Edward I—the "Longshanks" recently made famous by the movie *Braveheart*.

The last hope of reconquering Palestine now rested with the Byzantines, with whom the papacy had been working assiduously to reunify the Christian world against the Muslim and Mongol hordes. The new pope, Gregory X, was actually a Crusader himself who had campaigned with England's Edward in the Holy Land and learned of his papal election in the city of Acre. Gregory held in check the snarling Franks—who of course distrusted the Byzantines—and at the ecumenical Council of Lyons in 1274 won the free submission of the Greek Church, through its delegates at the Council, to accepting the *filioque* and Roman primacy. In return, the Byzantine emperor expected the pope to keep the French on a choke-chain that would strangle any renewed Frankish Crusades against Constantinople. Christianity was again united. Pope Gregory's diplomatic triumph encouraged Christendom's kings to have another go at a Crusade. But that endeavor petered out after the pope's death in 1276. Worse, the Byzantine emperor failed to enforce the reunion of the churches. So the northeastern anchor of any expected Crusade—and, in the minds of the Crusaders, Constantinople would be an anchor only if it was unified with Rome—didn't exist.

The remnants of Outremer survived only because the Moslems were too busy fending off the Mongols. But in 1289, the Mamelukes took Tripoli, and in 1291 Acre was besieged by a Mameluke army more than four times the size of the city's Catholic population. The Catholics withstood the assault for more than forty days, in an incredible contest between Catholic soldiers led by the "monks of war" and the enormous and sophisticated Mameluke regiments. The Catholics tried to use the boats that kept Acre supplied from Cyprus to send away as many women and children as possible, but bad weather kept them from sailing. When the city finally fell, the Catholics fled for the few boats that might save them. The scene was ugly with disorder, fear, and—incredibly—extortion. Those who escaped risked drowning on overcrowded boats in the foaming, storm-tossed seas. Those left on the jetty were massacred.

While the city fell, the garrison of the Templars didn't. It held on for another ten days, as the knights hoped against hope to save the tens of thousands of Catholics who were still trapped in the city. When the Mamelukes began raping the inhabitants—both women and boys—the Catholic knights struck back, slashing down the Islamic flag and driving the Mamelukes from the gates. A Templar commander, called out to discuss surrender terms, courageously marched into the Mameluke camp, where he was summarily seized and beheaded. The Templars, Hospitallers, Teutonic knights—indeed every knight of every order that continued to serve in the city's defense—never surrendered but died in a blazing inferno of firebombs and mines that collapsed the walls of their garrison while the knights fought thousands of Mamelukes in hand-to-hand combat.

With Acre in rubble, the Mamelukes seized the remaining inhabitants and either martyred or enslaved them. The last outposts of the Catholic Middle East—small in comparison to Acre—were rapidly extinguished, and when they were gone, there was no one left to relight the Christian flame in the Holy Land.

## CHAPTER TEN

# CRUSADERS

# IN THE WEST

---

THE CRUSADES TO THE HOLY LAND were not the only wars—
real or rhetorical—of the Catholic Church between the eleventh and
thirteenth centuries. Popes directed Catholic knights to reconquer Spain.
The papacy waged a seemingly unending war to maintain the supremacy
of Christ's Church over every king and against every political power
aimed against it. And it was in this period that the Church nurtured some
of its great men to evangelize and articulate the deposit of faith.

## RECONQUISTA

SINCE THE EIGHTH CENTURY, the bulk of Catholic Spain, save for
the rallying points of the northern provinces, had been held captive by
Muslim invaders from North Africa. The mixture of Arab, Berber, and
Spaniard—the Spaniards themselves being of diverse Celtic, Iberian,
Phoenician, Carthaginian, Roman, Visigothic, and other stock—created a
highly advanced and cultured civilization, centered on the famously beautiful city of Córdoba. The ruling Islamic caliphs were, to start, relatively
lenient with the Catholics, though the list of Catholic martyrs during the
occupation was well under way by the ninth century, and accelerating in
numbers, so much so that the caliphs, like the Roman emperors, were
baffled by such Catholic ardor that welcomed—even actively sought
out—martyrdom.

Islamic Spain was no liberal state. The caliphs' persecutions eventually eliminated the so-called Mozarabic culture of the Moorish-Spanish Christians. Islamic raids against what remained of Catholic Spain climaxed at the beginning of the eleventh century with the battle of Calatanazor in 1002, where the Catholics hit the Spanish Moors so hard that Islamic rule slowly crumbled. After that defeat, the Muslims were increasingly preoccupied by internal petty wars amongst the more than twenty competing caliphs who divided Islamic Spain among themselves. Still, even with these divisions, the Muslims were not easily overthrown. The entire reconquest of the Iberian peninsula—a fight in which the Catholic monarchs would face two additional Moorish jihads from North Africa, one by the Almoravids near the end of the eleventh century and another by the Almohads in the middle of the twelfth century—would not be completed until 1492, the same year that Spain sent Christopher Columbus on his adventurous course that would launch a huge Spanish empire spanning oceans and continents.

The beginnings of the reconquest can be found in the pontificate of two popes. The first was Gregory VII, Hildebrand, who was a prime mover behind King Alfonso I of Aragon, known as "the battler," who began the great Spanish countermarch. The other was the pope who had called the First Crusade, Urban II, who waved his field marshal's baton over Spain, appointed bishops, and implanted Catholic feudalism behind every acre of land recovered by Alfonso I of Aragon and Alfonso VI, king of León.

Alfonso VI's greatest conquest was the recovery of the ancient Visigothic capital of Toledo in central Spain in 1085, which Pope Urban II established as the home of the Spanish archbishop. The conquest of Toledo was made possible in part by the work of Spain's greatest military hero of the Middle Ages, Rodrigo Díaz de Vivar, better know as El Cid, the Lord.

Conflicting feudal obligations had once put El Cid and King Alfonso VI at odds. As commander of the Castilian army, at the age of twenty-two, El Cid had pledged himself to King Sancho of Castile, one of Alfonso's rivals for dominance in Christian Spain. Only after Sancho's death did El Cid's lance move to Alfonso's side. But, given his earlier loyalties, the valiant knight never won the trust of King Alfonso and was eventually exiled.

With no king as his feudal lord, El Cid sought employment as a soldier of fortune, first for other Christian sovereigns, then as a commander for the Moors, in whose service he spent a decade as an ever victorious general. After more squabbling with Alfonso—which included El Cid's reemployment and re-banishment—the king finally decided that he needed the great Cid to retake the city of Valencia from the Moors. Thus began a siege of nearly two years in which El Cid—his own army largely populated by Moors—fought not only the defenders of the city, but the enormous Moorish armies that came to the city's relief. When Valencia fell, El Cid became its ruler, restorer of its Catholic churches, and military defender. Three years later, El Cid's badly outnumbered troops stymied a Moorish attempt to retake his prize. Valencia was safe as long as El Cid lived, but only three years after his death in 1099, the city fell again to the Moors who then held it for more than a century.

Filling the void after El Cid's burial was a new breed of religious military orders—the Knights of Santiago (St. James), the Knights of Calatrava, and the Knights of Alcántra. These knights were the direct inheritors of the Templars and the Hospitallers to whom the military-minded Alfonso I had willed his kingdom of Aragon and who were spread like Green Beret A-teams throughout Christian Spain.

The Knights of Calatrava were organized to defend the southern approaches to Toledo. Their order, based on the Cistercian model, was pledged to the king of Castile and, though created for a specific military purpose, was, if anything, stricter in its religious than in its military discipline. In that, the Knights of Calatrava reflected the native character of the Spaniard, his zealous Catholicism forged by centuries of Islamic oppression and war. The Knights of Calatrava were also the incubator for the Knights of Alcántra.

The Knights of Santiago developed as protectors of pilgrims on the road to the church of Santiago de Compostella—a pilgrimage undertaken to this day. The Knights, while technically an order of military monks like any other, were in other ways more of a lay movement, for they allowed the enrollment of married knights, whose families became members and whose property was absorbed by the order. The fact that married men— with wives and children—were among them does not seem to have made the Knights of Santiago any less fearsome. Their motto was *Rubet ensis sanguine Arabum* or "May the sword be red with Arab blood."[1]

As in the Middle East, the Knights generally faced an enemy of far greater number. The Moorish commanders sometimes used their numerical advantage by roping together their black African infantry as giant human cushions, impenetrably absorbing Spanish cavalry charges. Stuck in these flailing pockets of roped slave-soldiers, the Spaniards had to shield themselves from Moorish archers and slingers, and from flank attacks by masses of Berber horsemen—who, like later caballeros, used lassos to yank Catholic knights from their horses.

After the horrific Catholic defeat at Alcaros in 1195, in which 25,000 Castilian knights were killed or captured, the hard-fought battles of the *reconquista* began tilting in favor of the Spaniards. Magnificent Córdoba returned to Spanish hands in 1236. Two years later, El Cid's Valencia was retaken. Ten years later there was Seville, then Cádiz, and by the end of the thirteenth century, the Moors were penned into Granada on Spain's southern Mediterranean coast. With the Moors trapped, the Spanish kings, rather than uniting to provide the coup de grâce, turned, as the Muslim caliphs had turned before them in similar circumstances, against each other in warfare that would keep Iberia's knights sanguinely occupied for two hundred years.

But fighting, in the Middle Ages, did not forbid scholarship, for while kings perpetually jostled for kingdoms and knights continually sought action, scholar-monks always busied themselves with recording and adding to the knowledge of the centuries. The mailed fist and the monk's cowl traveled together. Spain, however, was somewhat unique, being both distant from the sources of Catholic renewal and having been subjected to half a millennium of Moorish domination.

In the thirteenth century, four hundred years after Charlemagne, Spain enjoyed its own Carolingian rebirth of Catholic culture under Alfonso X, also known as Alfonso the Wise, who was Spain's first great Christian patron of learning since the general success of the *reconquista*. Alfonso employed Christian scholars as well as Jewish and Islamic ones. In Spain, as in Outremer, religious tolerance and religious war coexisted, depending on circumstances. Alfonso codified Castilian law and developed special interests in astronomy, music, history, and literature, though his desire for knowledge was, like Charlemagne's, catholic in scope.

While culpably weak in his failure to secure Spanish unity, Alfonso X left as a consolation a legacy of contentious, but free, Hispano-Catholic city-states, underlining that in the Middle Ages, one would not say that eternal vigilance was the price of liberty, but rather that liberty was the result of constant fighting and feudalistic divisions that broke up—but did not entirely eliminate—centralized authority. Such liberty could survive only as long as independent Catholic warlords could amass sufficient allies to defeat common dangers. With the Moors no longer able to bolt out of Granada, there was no common danger, and the Spanish were free—free to fight amongst themselves as much as they pleased, and for this Spain's Catholic kings were truly grateful.

## THE VICAR OF EUROPE

WITH SPAIN RESTORED to Christendom and Outremer perched precariously on the coastline of the Levant, the popes had encouraged the expansion of Catholic and European civilization to its apparent, if temporary, western and eastern limits. But in the heart of Europe and in the courts of Christendom's kings, things were never quiet. The pope was involved in every dynastic dispute and many arguments of law, in every exercise of military power, in every question of religious authority, and directly or indirectly in encouraging the patronage of scholarship, culture, and the arts. The bishopric of Rome was the essential office, the pope the essential man, of the Middle Ages.

The pope, too, was central to Western ideas of liberty. He was the check on arbitrary power—against bishops, dukes, or kings. The pope was the court of ultimate appeal. It was the canon law of the Church that was the arbiter and basis—the touchstone—for common European ideals of justice. And if it is knowledge that makes us free, it was the monasteries and universities of the Church that were the havens, laboratories, and expositors of every intellectual endeavor.

As the central authority of Christendom, the pope was more than the ultimate monarch; he held the keys to the kingdom of Heaven in a time when Catholic belief was nearly universal, and unquestioned, in Western Europe. But there were still disputes, especially with the Holy Roman emperor, who wrestled with the pope the way that Jacob wrestled with God in the Old Testament. In essence, the issues had remained unchanged for hundreds of years. The German king wanted the same authority over the Western Church that the Byzantine emperor had over the Eastern Church. But it was the kings who were losing ground. While Pope Paschal II, pontiff from 1099 to 1118, had to fend off four challenges by antipopes—only one of whom, though, was appointed by Henry IV of Germany—the

German kings no longer even claimed the right to appoint a pope; they had narrowed their demand to control over the Church in Germany.

Pope Paschal refused to compromise where no legitimate compromise was possible. The Church was universal, not national, and beholden to no king for its authority or offices. In defending the supremacy of the Church, the pope played power politics and supported Henry V of Germany in his successful rebellion against his father. The new king and the pope then reached an agreement that Church offices would be appointed, as the pope demanded, by free clerical election. In the spirit of Hildebrandian reform, servants of the Church would be supported exclusively by Church revenues and stripped of properties that belonged to the crown, thereby removing claims of state control. The king and the pope agreed on these points, but the secular and religious leaders of Germany did not. In the chaotic protests that followed, the king surrendered to the popular will and Pope Paschal II was taken by imperial troops and imprisoned until he submitted that no clerical election was valid without royal consent. In 1111, after two months in prison, Paschal succumbed rather than run the risk of having the emperor install an antipope in the Holy See.

If this seems like a triumph of the crown over the crozier, that would be misleading, because not only did the pope win this argument with the kings of England and France, he eventually won it in Germany as well. The *reconquista* of papal rights began almost immediately, in 1112, when the Vatican declared that the agreement forced out of the pope was invalid, based as it was on violent coercion; and in the following years, the papacy continued to assert its rights to independence from the Holy Roman Emperor. In 1122 the diplomatic war was resolved with the Concordat of Worms, which reached the definitive compromise between Church and crown. Under the concordat, the Church reaffirmed that it had sole authority to appoint its own officials, but it allowed that it was perfectly acceptable for churchmen to pledge their secular loyalty to the king in whose realms they labored; priests and bishops thus held two feudal bonds—to the king, as his loyal subject, and to the pope, as Christ's loyal servant.

The pope's monarchical authority survived every conceivable assault and embarrassment, including the chaos of the contested papal election of 1130. That dispute dragged on for eight years, with three papal candidates—though only two at a time—claiming the holy office.

Anacletus II brought a Norman army as a surety and with it held the city of Rome. Innocent II, one of the negotiators of the Concordat of Worms, won the support of Bernard of Clairvaux—at a time when it was a public relations coup to be endorsed by an esteemed monk—and through Bernard of the kings of England, France, and Germany. Victor IV had no great claim at all except as Anacletus II's successor on the latter's death in 1138; in light of this, Bernard convinced him to resign. There were real issues at stake. Innocent II had been hastily—and secretly—elected by a minority of cardinals who had called a snap election on the death of the previous pope. The cardinals who had thus been excluded from the election, refused to ratify it and named Anacletus as their candidate, enlisting Roger II, Norman king of Sicily, as the secular power behind his claim. The cardinals were of different reformist camps, and their candidates supported by rival Roman families.

The eventual winner of this conflict was Pope Innocent II, and it is interesting to note that while Innocent II had to find security behind royal arms, he did not succumb to pressure from the German king, Lothar III, who repeatedly demanded royal rights over the Church in return for his support. The two remained allies nevertheless. Just as important, Innocent II's authority as pope was untarnished by the controversy. This was how politics was done in the Middle Ages. Roman emperors, barbarian chieftains, Catholic kings, and, yes, occasionally even popes ascended their various thrones on steps of swords held by soldiers, a process that in no way diminished the majesty and authority of the victors.

This was true even in cases where the victor—Innocent II, as with Paschal II—was taken hostage. Innocent II was captured, after battle, by the Norman warlord Roger II. Roger demanded that the true pope reaffirm the validity of the Sicilian crown—with attendant territories of southern Italy—handed him by the antipope Anacletus. Pope Innocent II agreed, the Normans being always worthy allies to have on hand—if one could keep them as allies.

The German kings, even crusading ones, remained a problem because of their unending attempts to overthrow the Concordat of Worms and become judge and jury of the papacy. The method of establishing German influence was, again, the offer of armed protection. In 1153, Frederick I (Barbarossa) and Pope Eugenius III (a former cloistered monk whom Bernard of Clairvaux thought was too innocent for the task of ruling

Christendom) signed the Treaty of Constance, which reestablished the Holy Roman Emperor's Charlemagnic role of acting as the papacy's military protector. In return, the pope guaranteed his support for the German crown. The pope needed military protection because Rome was so violent that the work of the papal court often had to be conducted elsewhere.

The trouble was that Rome was held by communards who had taken over the government of the city in 1143. The papacy, which has never had any time for communists, proto or otherwise, was continually being threatened by the city's radicals and street thugs. In 1144, Pope Lucius II was actually killed leading armed resistance against the revolutionary government. The sole English pope, at least so far, Hadrian IV (1154–1159)[2] took dramatic action. He denied the sacraments to the people of Rome until he could seize the leading revolutionary, Arnold of Brescia (like Luther, a disgruntled monk), and turn him over to Frederick to be executed. Frederick obliged, though the communards tried desperately to play the German emperor against the pope.

Disputes between emperor and pope about who owed what to whom remained, and Pope Hadrian IV—a son of the Norman Conquest and a former papal legate to the ancient realms of the Norsemen in Norway and Sweden—again adopted the Normans, his neighbors in southern Italy, as the pope's marines. He also gave his permission to the Norman king of England, Henry II, to incorporate Ireland into England's realm, a necessary project of civilization that remains uncompleted even a thousand years later.

Henry II's failure to win the perpetual allegiance of the Irish to St. George's cross was not the only blot on his copybook. More serious was his own Church-state conflict with the archbishop of Canterbury, his old friend, Thomas Becket, a man the historian Christopher Tyerman—no friend of Becket—calls flat-out "the most famous Englishman of the Middle Ages."[3]

Becket was one of those extraordinarily gifted medieval churchmen who were simultaneously soldier, diplomat, lawyer, financier, prelate, and in his case eventual martyr, counseling kings and countries. Indeed, Becket led troops in battle, served as the king's principal adviser, and was educated primarily as a lawyer. He was also able to balance a rollicking demeanor—he and the king have been described as being "like two schoolboys at play"[4]—as well as a taste for the high life and regal splendor with a serious religious devotion.⁵ Still, when the king nominated him archbishop of Canterbury—a position he had never sought—he had not completed his studies to become a priest. He had, however, been archdeacon to the previous archbishop, and this was judged good enough. He was quickly ordained and installed. As chancellor to the king, Becket had been an ardent defender of the monarchy's claims, so much so that Henry hoped to have him serve in both positions, just as Frederick Barbarossa, a contemporary, had appointed his own trusted chancellor as archbishop of Cologne. But Becket not only resigned the position of chancellor; he became yet more serious in his religious devotions and in his practice of personal mortification. He was no longer a boy at play; he was the pope's man in England.

As archbishop he insisted—as he had warned the king, before his appointment, that he would—on the Church's independence, its right to try its clerics in its own Church courts, and its right to make its own clerical appointments. As the once close friends became political enemies on these and other issues, Becket was compelled to flee the kingdom, going first to France and then to the court of Pope Alexander III. Becket remained in exile for six years before a vague reconciliation was reached and he returned as archbishop. But the disputes again became so heated that in December 1170, the very month and very year that he returned, Henry screamed, "Will no one rid me of this turbulent priest!" Four knights took this as an invitation to execute the king's will and murdered Becket in his cathedral. In even so violent a period as the Middle Ages, this was a notorious and shocking crime. The king was compelled to do public penance, and Becket was made a saint within three years of his death.

The pope who had sheltered Becket, Alexander III (1159–1181), was the pope who also had to face a showdown with Frederick Barbarossa. Alexander III was the legitimate successor to the English pope, Hadrian IV. He had in fact been Hadrian's chief counsel and intended to continue the Englishman's policy of favoring the Normans over the Germans. But Frederick's allies supplied the emperor with an antipope, and a diplomatic battle began to establish the legitimate heir. Alexander won the support of every church and crown west of Frederick's dominions. But nothing would budge Frederick, whose string of antipopes would lead one to another from 1160 to 1178.

The papacy and the Holy Roman Emperor were essentially at war. The pope found new allies with the Lombards of northern Italy, who were chafing under Barbarossa. They inflicted a defeat on the German imperial armies in 1176, a defeat that led to Frederick's eventual reconciliation with the pope. The war with Frederick was over, and the pope publicly forgave him.

The last great pope of the twelfth century was Pope Innocent III, who held the chair of St. Peter from 1198 to 1216. He was one of the most prominent defenders of papal supremacy in the Middle Ages, articulating that the pope was "set midway between God and man,"[6] with sovereignty extending universally over both Church and state. But while claiming immense powers himself, he was the very reverse of a man corrupted by the world or by zealotry; he was scholarly, personable, even-tempered, humorous, and hardworking and had written extensively on the *Misery of the Human Condition,* targeting in particular the problems of pride and vanity. Blue-blooded, thoroughly educated in theology and canon law, a cardinal who had actually supported another candidate in the papal election, he had no Napoleonic chip on his shoulder, nothing to prove by wielding power. The key to understanding Innocent III is the pilgrimage he made, while a student, to the shrine of St. Thomas Becket. His chief political goal was to keep the secular powers in check. His chief religious goal was to execute the responsibilities of the Vicar of Christ, a title he made famous.

While Innocent III was accepted as the arbiter of European politics—and had proven his political acumen by restoring peace in Rome and expanding papal territories within Italy—his political judgments were not infallible. The two claimants to the throne of the Holy Roman Empire—Philip of Swabia and Otto of Brunswick[7]—came to him to settle who was the rightful heir. Innocent chose Otto as the prince best pledged to defend the Church; he even allowed himself to predict that "If we two stand together, 'the crooked shall be made straight and the rough places smooth,' for the pontifical authority and the royal power (both of them supremely invested in us) fully suffice for this purpose, if each helps the other."[8] But this holy matrimony between the leading religious and secular powers of Europe foundered, yet again, on the Holy Roman Emperor's ambitions. In this case, Otto proved distressingly eager to defend territories that weren't his and threatened the papacy with German expansion in areas where the papacy had interests of its own: Sicily—whose king, Frederick II, another German, had been a papal ward—and southern Italy.

Quickly recognizing that Otto—he was officially Otto IV—would not help him make the rough places smooth, Innocent III declared Frederick II of Sicily the rightful Holy Roman Emperor.[9] In 1211, the German princes gathered at Nuremberg and officially elected Frederick king over Otto, an election that was confirmed by the king of France as well as by the pope, as a symbol of European unity. Otto tried to raise a rebellion but was defeated, and, for the remainder of his pontificate, Innocent III was free from German threats.

Apart from his dealings with the Holy Roman Empire, Innocent III achieved a peace between England and France; reconciled the French king to his wife; launched a Crusade against the Albigensian heresy, which was strongest in France; won a victory over King John of England on the issue of clerical appointments; received Aragon as a papal fief; encouraged the *reconquista* of Spain; launched a Crusade at Egypt (and inadvertently received Byzantium as a prize); chose the kings of Norway and Sweden; sent missionaries to convert the Prussians; strengthened the Church in Poland; resolved political disputes in the dangerous eastern realms of Hungary and Bulgaria; and accomplished much else besides.

Pope Innocent III also encouraged religious reform and revival—in particular through one of the Church's greatest saints, Francis of Assisi.

## THE HEART OF ASSISI

FRANCIS HAD THE WIT and ardor of a swashbuckler and yearned for knightly adventure. He found it at the age of twenty, but only briefly, in a battle between rival Italian cities. Captured, he was held prisoner for a year. After his release he still intended to become a knight, but bouts of ill health and dreams that told him to stay in Assisi kept him from following his martial desires. There was something else: a growing interest in religion and a developing sense that Christ had called him to poverty, to care for the uncared for, to use his martial discipline to overcome his worldliness, to give up fine clothes, to surrender himself to the company of the smelly and degraded, the lepers and beggars of the streets. He gave action to this divine voice, giving away everything he owned—including the clothes he was wearing. His father, a wealthy merchant in the cloth trade, and the people of Assisi thought he had gone mad. He certainly failed to impress a gang of muggers he met shortly thereafter. They recognized an easy mark and left him beaten and naked in the snow.

He became a sort of freelance apprentice monk, working to restore chapels and help the sick. By 1208, he had acquired a group of followers who joined him in preaching the gospel and practicing the most complete and utter charity to the poor. Giving his men a simple monastic rule, Francis led them to Rome, seeking papal sanction for their work. It is said that Innocent III had a dream in which he saw St. Francis bearing the entire weight of the Lateran Palace on his shoulders—an impoverished monk, yet an Atlas of the Church. Perhaps that explains why so patrician a pope as Innocent III should approve such a poor figure as St. Francis: pope and mendicant friar were merely hood and hem of the same seamless garment.

This new, officially sanctioned monastic order returned to Assisi, but had to avail itself of Benedictine charity to find a place to live and work. With the gift of a chapel, the Franciscans began to build their monastery. From it, they sang—literally—the praises of God to whomever would listen. Francis had been a carefree youth; now he led a band of men who sought to be carefree preachers of the gospel. Their high spirits, religious devotion, and willingness to toil alongside any peasant won them the admiration of the people. Soon the Franciscans had a female auxiliary—the Poor Clares, founded by another child of privilege in Assisi, Clare, who warmed to Francis's call and yearned to follow it herself. The Franciscan movement was growing.

The heart of a soldier still beat in Francis, and for two years he tried to join the Crusades. But again, as when he wanted to be a knight, circumstances—whether in the form of a shipwreck or bad health—kept him from the battlefield. Instead of converting Muslims, as he had intended, he was turned to relighting the lamp of faith in Europe. His disciples carried the gospel from Italy to Spain, France, Germany, and England. Entire congregations flocked to the Franciscans and their message of charity and forgiveness, of loving the unloved, of finding integrity in the imitation of Christ, of renouncing sins and welcoming God.

It was not until 1219 that Francis finally made it to the Holy Land, where he preached the gospel to the Crusaders—and passed straight into a Muslim encampment and preached it there as well. If he found no converts from Islam, it is extraordinary enough that he escaped unharmed, being only captured and released.

He returned to Italy the next year. There he worked with the future Pope Gregory IX to develop a more comprehensive rule for the Franciscan order. The order's numbers were exploding, but his mendicant friars, not being under firm government, were inevitably headed in disparate directions. He wanted them focused on a devotion to poverty, manual labor, and preaching the gospel by example.

St. Francis's example was the most beloved of the Middle Ages. He is remembered in our own time—eight hundred years after his death—for his love of flowers, animals, and nature; for preaching to the sparrows and Brother Wolf; and for his love of Christmas, symbolically welcoming the Christ child. It was St. Francis who invented the celebration of the Christmas manger, or crèche. For Francis—who referred to his own body, always pushed to its ultimate limits, as "Brother Ass"—and for Franciscans living as humbly as beasts in the field, the birth in the stable had special meaning.

St. Francis had hoped to die equally humbly, but his fame—combined with the fact that he had received the stigmata, the wounds of Christ, on his body[10]—made that impossible. His tomb became a site of miracles, and he was made a saint only two years after his death.

## ABELARD AND AQUINAS

WHILE ST. FRANCIS WON HEARTS by his winsomeness, transparent honesty, and devotion—indeed the Franciscans quickly became the largest religious order in Christendom—other great Catholics devoted themselves to the life of the mind.

A focal point of intellectual debate in the twelfth century was the work of the philosopher Peter Abelard (1079–1142), whose prime intellectual opponent was Bernard of Clairvaux. Some of Abelard's works would be condemned, but important parts of his studies would change the course of Catholic philosophy, cutting a road for St. Thomas Aquinas. Abelard's fame was abetted by his life encompassing that great medieval trinity of burning romantic passion, fierce confrontation, and dramatic religious vows.

Abelard was a contentious soul—his autobiography was titled *A History of My Calamities*—and as a student and a teacher he thrived on harsh debate, certain in his cocksure, handsome, egotistical way that he could never be bettered. He also prided himself on being an unrejectable ladies' man, though at the same time remaining chaste, for he was considering a priestly vocation. Still, comparing himself to a wolf lusting after a lamb, he boasted of how easily he had convinced the uncle of an attractive sixteen-year-old girl to let him be her tutor. In this ardent romance, the wolf, whose passionate love spilled over into poetry and song, lost control of himself, and the girl, Héloïse, became pregnant. Despite her stern arguments against their marrying—she wanted to be Abelard's mistress, rather than his wife, for wives, she argued, were a bane to philosophers and an impossibility for a priest—they were joined in holy matrimony, a matrimony they hoped to keep reasonably secret.

But Abelard's life was shattered when his uncle-in-law, Canon Fulbert, not only betrayed their secret but led his relations in attacking Abelard while he slept, summarily castrating him. The attackers were punished—Canon Fulbert by the Church—but the lovers were disgraced, and Héloïse and Abelard now took the only honorable alternative open to them: she retired to a nunnery and he assumed a monk's cowl.

Abelard proved no peaceful monk. Few monks, after all, considered themselves the greatest, if not the only true, philosopher on the face of the earth—an attitude that did not win him friends. While remaining a loyal churchman, who saw Christianity as the logical culmination of Mosaic Law and philosophical reason, who regarded the pope as the ultimate arbiter of Church disputes, and who railed like an orthodox Catholic reformer against priests who failed to uphold their vows, he tested the boundaries of Church tolerance. He wrote that the Bible had to be interpreted by reason and could not be taken literally; he was skeptical of traditions of saintly miracles; and he noted that the Church fathers openly contradicted each other, so unless their positions withstood rational scrutiny, they were superfluous. These positions could be provocative, yet they were not heretical. But his speculations on the Trinity as three metaphorical representations of God could be construed as Arianism. His belief that no one sinned unless he violated his own conscience could be regarded as Pelagianism, a denial of the doctrine of Original Sin. These and other positions strayed too far for Bernard of Clairvaux, who had always suspected that logicians who did away with the mystery of the faith would eventually do away with the faith altogether. If one wanted an example of the logicians' pernicious influence, one had only to look, after all, at Arnold of Brescia—a former student of Abelard's—who led the revolutionary communards in Rome.

Bernard of Clairvaux questioned Abelard's orthodoxy and his right to teach, a dispute that led to several of Abelard's works being officially condemned, and Abelard himself ordered to silence. But the abbot of Cluny intervened on Abelard's behalf, had Rome lift the condemnation, and not only reconciled the two monks but installed Abelard as a teacher at the venerable monastery that had been one of the fonts of Catholic reform. Abelard died soon after, at peace with the Church and at peace with Héloïse, who would be buried beside him.

The intellectual import of Abelard was his leadership of the scholastics, whose antecedent philosophers can be summarized by the letter A. There is Aristotle, providing the rationalist model of philosophical discourse; St. Augustine, whose encyclopedic treasury of philosophical wisdom was mined by St. Thomas Aquinas; and Averroës, the Islamic Spaniard whose works transmitted a modern Aristotelian approach to Western philosophers.

Following from these thinkers were the great scholastics themselves: St. Anselm, archbishop of Canterbury from 1093 to 1109, whose credo, "I believe so that I may understand," provided the religious cornerstone; Abelard, whose devotion to reason St. Thomas Aquinas accepts while carefully anchoring reason within the a priori fact of Christian revelation; and ultimately St. Thomas Aquinas (1225–1274) himself, "the angelic doctor" of the Church, whose massive *Summa Theologica* grounds the faith firmly in objective reason and logic.

St. Thomas Aquinas attended the University of Naples.[11] Excelling in his studies, and with fond memories of his pre-university academic work at Monte Cassino, he decided to enter a monastery—to the horror of his aristocratic family through whom he was related to Frederick Barbarossa and the royal house of Norman Sicily. Rather than see him throw away his temporal advantages, they imprisoned him for two years. But Thomas remained adamant—and studious—and was finally freed to join the Dominican order, where this large, blond, unassuming man earned the nickname "the dumb ox," which proved ironical by more than half. Aside from his monastic vows, he was ordained a priest, and by his mid-twenties had begun his life's work as a teacher in Paris, though his fame as a philosopher soon had him touring the great cities of Europe. So renowned was he as an elucidator of Christian doctrine that Pope Clement IV accepted that this was Aquinas's calling and allowed him to decline a papal appointment as archbishop of Naples.

We shouldn't think of Aquinas as a deracinated academic or a mere transcribing monk. As a man of the Middle Ages, he was a man of passion, and his passion expressed itself in an overwhelming desire to explain the mysteries of God to the logic of man. This passion could take charming turns. Once while at dinner with the king of France, he lost himself in preoccupied silence, then suddenly burst out: "That is the decisive argument against the Manicheans!"[12]

While he believed that reason and logic made the best arguments for the mind of man, Aquinas was also devoted to prayer. He never shirked the execution of his monastic and priestly duties. Pious exclamations dot the margins of his work, and he was transported by heavenly visions. When he set down his pen on December 6, 1273, after receiving such a vision, it was with words that should strike at the heart of any who dare scribble on a sheet of paper and think it good: "I can do no more. Such secrets have been revealed to me that all I have written now appears to be of little value."[13] Some might consider it a tragedy that his *Summa Theologica* was never completed. Slackers might cheer that there's not yet another hefty volume to get through—surely twenty-one of them is enough. But the simple reality is that Aquinas came to recognize the vanity of all intellectual accomplishment, no matter how great. All that matters, ultimately, is the beatific vision. His last words were a simple prayer. He had lived and worked, he said, in obedience to the Catholic Church, and if he had ever erred by ignorance, he trusted to that same Catholic Church to correct and forgive him.

The Church did more than forgive him; it declared him a saint and its patron of learning. Today, as Professor Ralph McInerny of the University of Notre Dame points out in a pithy overview of the history of philosophy, Aquinas is the lodestar of intellectual sanity. Nearly eight hundred years after his death, it is to the dumb ox that modern man—in a world that denies objective reason as well as faith—needs to repair to rediscover reason and find what it teaches.[14]

## CHAPTER ELEVEN

# INQUISITION

⟶⟵

THE PROBLEM WITH AQUINAS'S rational approach, of course, is that few men are reachable by reason; fewer still have the capacity for logical argument and proofs. St. Francis, with his simple piety, his preaching to the birds of the field, is better remembered, better loved, and won more devotion by far than St. Thomas, whose canonization took considerably longer to achieve—nearly fifty years.

Still, the two men illustrate an important point, which is the genius of Rome—its ability to adapt and sanctify new ideas and social conditions. Some churchmen were suspicious of Aristotle as a pagan philosopher transmitted by the Muslim Averroës. But Rome took Aristotelian reason and made it its own. Some feared ascetic movements that followed a path of poverty, like the Franciscans, seeing them as a challenge to the Church. But Rome did not. It saw their virtue, and also saw them as a counterbalance to other movements of poverty and ascetic purity—such as the Waldenses, followers of a Lyons merchant, often styled Peter Waldo,[1] who, unlike St. Francis, followed an inner voice of personal inspiration, rather than Catholic dogma and loyalty to the pope, and lapsed into heresy.

This genius for assimilation made the Church powerful. It reached men's hearts through mendicants like St. Francis, their minds through scholastics like St. Thomas Aquinas, their aesthetic sense through art, and their everyday lives through the inherited practices of the sacramental Church. The Church was confident and universal, and its orthodoxy virtually unchallenged in the West. This could lead, of course, to a certain laxness. In the diurnal practice of a parish priest, there was little or no attempt at the religious education of the people—and the priest himself might not have been terribly well educated.

The Church proceeded by custom and tradition, as part of the natural order of life. Such complacency and conservatism meant the Church did not feel terribly threatened by small, scattered outbreaks of religious eccentricity. These, as a rule, either collapsed without a papal push or were met with swift, vigilante justice before they came to the Church's attention. When local priests and bishops did see violent mobs converging on known or suspected heretics, the men of the cloth almost always tried to intervene on the side of peace, tolerance, and prayers for the conversion of the wayward. This was an extremely unpopular position—something the mob regarded as akin to intervening on the side of child molesters—but the Church believed in peaceable restraint.

There was, however, a singular exception—an internal Crusade within Christendom—during the reign of Pope Innocent III. The fighting began in 1209 and did not end until 1229 under the pontificate of Gregory IX. The Crusade was against what came to be called the Albigensian heresy, named after a region in southern France where it developed into a significant rival of the Church. The roots of the heresy lay in the East. Its pedigree included, historically, the Arians and especially the Manicheans. More immediately, it was influenced by the iconoclastic Paulicians, exiled from Byzantium; the violent Bogomils of Bulgaria (from which we get the useful word "bugger"); the Waldenses; a variety of church desecrators; and finally the Cathars, the Greek-named rationalist, Biblical-literalist, anti-clerical, anti-materialist movement of which the Albigensians were a part. Their combined thrust was against the world, the flesh, and the Catholic Church.

The poet and controversialist Hilaire Belloc once wrote:

Wherever the Catholic sun doth shine
There's always laughter and good red wine;
At least I've always found it so
*Benedicamus Domino.*[2]

The Cathars and the Albigensians represent the reverse. The Albigensians were a sort of Pro-Death League, opposed to marriage, children, and pregnancy (a calamity for which abortion was recommended); and if one could not follow a Pauline path of celibacy, the next best thing was fornication that did not perpetuate the species. Because matter was sinful—only the spirit was pure—death was to be hurried along. Suicide was accepted. The preferred Albigensian method was self-starvation supervised by helpful Albigensian hospice workers to make sure the loved one didn't slip out for some bread and wine.

Obvious in the Albigensian heresy and its heretical cousins are the developing outlines of Reformation Protestantism. The Albigensians were puritanical, opposed to the world, the flesh, and the devil—whose satanic stand-in was the wealthy and powerful pope in Rome. The Albigensians denied the sacraments of the Catholic Church but came up with one of their own, the *Consolamentum,* which offered a final absolution of sins and was available only once. The Albigensians also denied the hierarchy of the Catholic Church but divided their own ranks between the Perfect— or perhaps, in Calvinist terms, the Elect—and the Believers. The Perfect kept the cult's rigid strictures of self-denial, including celibacy, non-dairy vegetarianism (though fish was allowed), poverty, no swearing (not just profanity, but any oath, including an oath of feudal allegiance), pacifism, and so on. The mere Believers were given somewhat looser strictures, which allowed sodomy and fornication without conception.[3] More subtly, the Albigensian division between the Perfect and the Believers was an early outline of how Puritanism and Secularism could and did march together against their common enemy in the Church.

The Albigensians were a direct challenge to the Church, because they were evangelical, spreading across southern France preaching purity to Puritans, license to libertines, and reason to rationalists; and the vigilante violence that normally snuffed out heretics did not happen. The feudal lords of southern France prevented it, because they saw in the Albigensian heresy a way to gain money, power, and independence at the expense of the Church—which was a major regional landowner—and the French king, who was the Church's ally.

For the southern nobles, the issues involved were not doctrinal. They could not have cared less that the Albigensians denied the Trinity or the Virgin Birth or that they dismissed the whole panoply of Church custom as superstition. Nor, for that matter, did the nobles care that the Albigensians were economic communists. For the southern nobles, the Albigensians were merely a lever to separate Mediterranean France from the ambitious, martial-minded knights of northern France and from the powerful landed bishops of the Catholic Church. The real issue was who would rule and who would gain the wealth of the land.

Announcing their support for the Albigensians, the southern knights seized the feudal properties of abbots, bishops, and priests—representatives, or so the Albigensians said, of the Antichrist. Churches were sacked. Altars were desecrated. Crucifixes became try-your-luck targets for marksmen. The Vandal was back in Europe, preaching a liturgy of death.

The reaction of the Church was measured. By law, heresy was a capital crime. This, of course, had been true well before Christianity appeared. The Jewish penalty for heresy was death. The penalty for heresy in classical Greece was death; in pagan Rome, death. In fact, Christianity had distinguished itself, in the centuries before Constantine, by *not* making heresy a capital crime. After the empire and Christianity became one, the imperial penalty for heresy overruled Christian practice—though most of the leading members of the Catholic Church disapproved of such capital punishment. In the courts of medieval Europe, kings and emperors of even the most skeptical stripe, such as Frederick II, enforced the death penalty for heresy. As for the medieval Catholic Church, canon law on the punishment of heresy was lifted directly from the legal code of Emperor Justinian. The Church's process of discovering heresy—inquisition—was taken from judicial practice in pagan Rome and modified by the medieval royal courts of inquest that gathered evidence on matters of law and taxation.

Even though Pope Innocent III had already blessed a recourse to arms, if necessary, to extirpate the Albigensians, the Catholic archbishop of Gascony chose not to pursue a Crusade against his fellow Frenchmen of the Languedoc. At this point, the Church was less interested in enforcing the law per se—let alone waging war in France—than it was in promoting a popular revival of the faith. The Church wanted something that would make Albigensianism—which was obviously not going to *breed* new adherents; it could only recruit them—irrelevant. Monks like Dominic Guzman—who would become St. Dominic—were sent to southern France to win people back to the faith by rhetoric and public debate. They were to set a worthy example, walking humbly—like St. Francis—rather than with the feudal pride of the Catholic bishops, which was thought to fire puritanical resentment. They were to establish schools to educate Catholics about their faith. In all these things, Dominic and his men made progress. But it was not enough.

In 1208—ten years after the first monastic missions to reclaim southern France—a legate from the pope was murdered. The killer was a knight in the service of Count Raymond VI of Toulouse. Raymond, whose loyalty the Church was assiduously trying to regain, was a cynical patron of the Albigensians. With this murder he had overplayed his hand.

The Albigensians, the pope declared, were a greater threat to Christendom than were the Saracens. Here was a threat that was immediate, not far away. The Albigensians threatened the religious unity, health, and peace of Europe. Pope Innocent III declared a Crusade. Knights who pledged themselves to the cause received the same spiritual rewards as knights pledged to the Holy Land. Moreover, they had full legal right to seize the lands of the heretical nobles who waged war against them.

Sensing the shifting tide, Raymond of Toulouse re-enlisted in the divisions of the pope. He endured the obligatory penitential public scourging for his crimes and then joined with the Crusade, whose number included the king of France. Here was a war bitterer than the Crusade against the Muslim, bitterer than the Crusade against the Byzantines, as bitter as a civil war. For even though the men of north and south spoke different dialects, even given the predominance of separatist local loyalties, even given the horrible cult to which the heretics belonged, this was Frenchman versus Frenchman, and the bitterness led to dramatic effusions of blood.

The mighty host of loyal Catholics—Frenchmen, as well as knights from Germany and Belgium, representatives from the pope in Rome, and St. Dominic, who served as a chaplain—assembled in 1209. They laid siege to the fortresses of Beziers and Carcassonne, both of which were taken, the first, in particular, at fearful cost to the defenders. The quote often attributed to a papal legate—"Kill them all; God will know His own"—is apparently apocryphal, though one can see why it was invented, for it is a fair description of what actually happened during the slaughter at Beziers.

But amidst horror there are heroes, and the hero of this Crusade was Simon de Montfort—or Simon de Montfort the Elder, for his son held the same name and later contested for the throne of England. Born to a minor lordship, Simon had already distinguished himself as a Crusader in the Holy Land. He was devout, morally as well as physically courageous, and became the spearhead of the Crusade. For four years his army—which never numbered more than 4,500 men—won military victories and thousands upon thousands of sword-point conversions. The climax came in 1213 at the battle of Muret. Joining the heretics and their allies was an enormous army of Spaniards. Like the nobles of southern France, they cared not a whit for the doctrinal issues at stake—indeed, heretics in Spanish Aragon faced the death sentence, under secular law. They simply wanted to strike a blow against the mighty French monarchy. Simon de Montfort brought a thousand battle-tested knights to the field. Opposed to him was an armed rabble of perhaps 100,000 men.[4] St. Dominic celebrated a Mass for the Crusaders, who remained on their snorting, stamping horses throughout the service. Then, blessed by Dominic, with Simon de Montfort at their head, they charged. The disciplined French cavalry spread terror through the Spanish ranks, terror that rolled like a wave over tens of thousands of men, who sensed or imagined, no matter how far the danger, the slashing French blades at the tingling base of their Spanish skulls. Panic turned to tumult, tumult to rout, as the men of Aragon fled toward the Pyrenees and the ill-fated roads that had led them here. It was Simon de Montfort's greatest victory, and in 1215, he captured Toulouse and became the dominant feudal lord of southern France.

Still the war continued, and in 1218 Simon de Montfort was killed attempting to recapture his prize of Toulouse. The French king became the new military leader of the Crusade and eventually absorbed Simon's conquests. In 1229 the war was officially ended. Though the heresy persisted for another hundred years, it was, the pope decreed, the responsibility of the inquisition to root it out.

Pope Innocent III, who died in 1216, was dismayed that he could no more manage the Crusaders against the Albigensians than he could control the French knights who had given him the prize of Constantinople. He had been scandalized by how his Crusaders had become freebooters, massacring noncombatants and expropriating lands of southern French lords who were not listed as heretics. It was with this in mind that Pope Gregory IX entrusted the final excision of the Albigensian heresy to the scalpel of the inquisition rather than the sword of the Crusader. The surgery would be performed by a new order of monks, who understood the disease better than anyone, the Dominicans, named after their founder, who had ridden with the Crusaders, St. Dominic.

# LAYING DOWN THE LAW

PRIOR TO THE ALBIGENSIAN CRISIS, the Church had rarely done more than resort to its power of excommunication to punish heresy. In a society where nearly every man was a believer in the universal Church, exclusion from the sacraments and the salvation they offered was seen as punishment enough.

But the Albigensians fundamentally changed that in ways that deeply troubled the Church. Early in Innocent III's pontificate he wrote a letter to a French archbishop: "The little boat of St. Peter is beaten by many storms and tossed about on the sea. But it grieves me most of all that . . . there are now arising, more unrestrainedly and injuriously than ever before, ministers of diabolical error who are ensnaring the souls of the simple. With their superstitions and false inventions they are perverting the meaning of the Holy Scriptures and trying to destroy the unity of the Catholic Church."[5]

Christendom—that great creation of the Middle Ages, that great fulfillment of the Christian vision of a free society with the Church at its head, defended by former barbarians now Christianized as the knights of chivalry—was at risk. This new bacillus, this new *religious* opposition of the Albigensians, threatened to overturn every bit of progress and commonality the Church had so arduously preserved and built up—custom by custom, law by law, monastery by monastery, cathedral by cathedral, university by university—from the remnants of the Roman Empire.

Before the Albigensians, the Church had happily translated the Bible into every vernacular tongue.[6] But now the Church saw the authority of the Bible abused by cult leaders who preyed on the ignorance, or the latent extremism, of the people. In 1229, at the Council of Narbonne, in direct response to the abuses of the Albigensians and related heresies, the Bible was forbidden to all save priests, bishops, and others in religious vocations. The people would hear the Bible in Church. But mad-eyed fanatics would not be allowed to wave the Bible above their heads and claim some new revelation, some special reading—to common people who were mostly illiterate—that denied the Trinity or endorsed fornication, abortion, and suicide as positive deeds.

The Albigensians also convinced the Church that it could no longer expect heresies to shrivel by natural causes. Nor did the Church find it truly advisable to lay them waste by war. Rather than mob justice, and instead of holy war, Church and state joined their powers to enforce the long-established laws against heresy. The process by which they did so was inquisition.

In this process, the Church positioned itself as the more liberal partner. The giant, ecumenical Fourth Lateran Council convened by Pope Innocent III at the end of 1215, and attended by the leading kings of Europe, the patriarch of Constantinople, and more than twelve hundred bishops, abbots, leaders of the monastic military orders, and others, affirmed—along with the doctrine of transubstantiation, the requirement of annual private confession, papal primacy, and so on—that in all trials in which a cleric sat in judgment, the accused should have a full presentation of the facts and names of the witnesses against him so that he might adequately defend himself. The lightest penalties possible were to be enacted, though they were to escalate depending on the severity of the crime and the contumacy of the accused. While heretics were vehemently denounced and secular rulers—as well as bishops—charged with ridding their dominions of them, the penalties for heresy were exile, excommunication, and loss of property, not torture or death. Clerics, in particular, were to have nothing to do with bloodshed. Moreover, no Jew or Muslim was to be called before an inquisition into heresy, because they were people set apart—visibly so, as they were required to wear clothes that readily identified their religious professions.

One of the very reasons the Church involved itself in these matters of secular law was so that the secular authorities would not act arbitrarily or use laws of heresy merely to punish their enemies. Churchmen known for their scholarship—Dominican monks in particular—were charged to join such inquisitional courts so that heresy was judged on grounds of religion, not vendetta. Of course, even the Dominicans could be imperfect. One monk—with the ardor of a converted heretic, which he was—was found to have more blood-thirst than sense of justice. The Church responded, however, by clapping him in prison for life. More edifying were the Franciscans and Dominicans who protected Jews from mob violence.[7]

Torture, though initially proscribed, slipped into inquisitorial practice in 1252. It was inexcusable that it did so, if for no other reason than that the courts themselves discounted testimony gained through torture. There was no point to it. But instead of standing adamantly against torture, as it should have done, the Church limited itself to softening its blows, insisting that it was permissible only under the strictest constraints, only with the approval of the local bishop, only once, only in a manner that did not threaten the life of the accused, and only in cases where the weight of evidence offered a strong presumption of guilt. These constraints were gradually eroded in practice. Inevitably, abuses occurred by the principle that if you give a judge a yard, he will make it into a yardarm for a hanging—or for a burning at the stake. Because the Church refused to pass the sentence of death, those convicted of gross and impenitent heresy were given over to the state; and though the state did enforce the death penalty, the numbers who were executed appear to be a small minority of those convicted in the inquisitional courts.[8]

The inquisition of the thirteenth century did not strike fear into the people of Western Europe. Its scope was limited, its trials and punishments more lenient to the accused than its secular counterparts. Inquisitional punishment was often no more than the sort of penance—charity, pilgrimage, mortification—that one might be given by a priest in a confessional. If one were fortunate enough to live in England, northern France, Belgium, the Netherlands, Scandinavia, or, with the exception of Aragon, even Spain,[9] the risk that one might be called before an inquisitional trial was virtually zero. The focus of the inquisition was in the Albigensian districts of southern France; in Germany, where some of the worst abuses occurred; and in those parts of chaotic Italy rife with anticlerical heresy.[10] In all cases, inquisitional courts sat only where Church and state agreed that peace and security were threatened. Nevertheless, the courts were abused. The Church could not modify an ironclad rule of life, as true in the thirteenth century as it is today: Every recourse to law and the courts is a calamity. But the Church then, and people today, seem to assume it is better than vigilantes and war. There is no accounting for some tastes.

## STUPOR MUNDI

OF ALL THE KINGS encountered by the Church in the thirteenth century, none is more fantastical than that enthusiastic rooter-out of heretics—and near-heretic himself—Frederick II, Holy Roman Emperor, scholar, and scoundrel who grew up as a papal ward.

He was the son of Henry VI, poet and Holy Roman Emperor, whose domains—if one included his nominal vassals—included England, parts of France, Denmark, Germany, Hungary, Armenia, sections of Italy, Cyprus, and his great prize: the island of Sicily.

Given the centuries of turbulent relations between the popes and the emperors, it was papal policy to prevent the Holy Roman Empire from expanding. In particular, the popes wanted to avoid a German pincer movement, with Rome caught between a German-occupied northern Italy and a German-occupied Sicily and southern Italy.

For the Holy Roman Emperors Henry VI and Frederick II, however, the German throne was merely their natural right, not the fulfillment of any true German emperor's ambition. To their minds, it was Italy that was the vital stem of a German empire with the northern territories of Germany as the blossoms and the islands of the Mediterranean as the roots. But that German botanical development had been hacked away in the internal Teutonic wars of succession that came between the reigns of Henry VI, the poetic *Reich*-builder, and Frederick II—wars that resulted in Otto IV ascending to the German crown.

Frederick, on his father's early death (he died while preparing for a Crusade to the Holy Land) was raised under the care and protection of the papacy. As such, he is proof that the Jesuits were wrong when they later asserted that if they had the education of a boy until the age of seven, they would have him for life. Frederick was far from a forelock-tugging Catholic. It is true that his education under a papal guardianship had helped him develop a keen and penetrating mind, encouraged him to be extremely well read, and, along with geographical circumstances, had given him a cosmopolitan sense of the world. He was raised in Sicily, and his papal education was latitudinarian to the point of neglect—which is often a very good thing for a young boy—leaving him free to roam the streets of Palermo as Kipling's Kim roamed the streets of Lahore. The boy Frederick rubbed shoulders with Norman, German, Italian, and Muslim; he heard merchants striking deals in Arabic, Hebrew, and Greek. Over time, he came to value the raw power of Germanic man. Yet he considered himself Italian because Rome was still the center of the world, the seat of his guardian, Innocent III; while culturally, his ears never lost the faint echo of the muezzin's call to prayer, nor were his dreams ever shorn of the scholars, the bazaars, and the harems of the Mussulman.

Whereas his father had been both bookish and imperially ambitious while remaining a pale, weedy sort, Frederick combined his father's interest in literature with the more robust physical pursuits of his grandfather, Frederick Barbarossa. He wasn't tall, but he was muscular, and he lived to hunt. That is, he hunted when he was not waging war, holding court, governing his empire, founding his university, or pursuing his own studies in mathematics, literature, philosophy, magic, law, history, architecture, and everything else that might captivate the mind of man. But when it came time for him to write his own book, it was a treatise on falconry.

He was crowned king of Sicily at the age of four in 1198, with Pope Innocent III as his regent. He reached his legal maturity at fourteen; and he was thrust into real power politics early—at the age of fifteen—when the pope secured Frederick's control of the rebellious factions in Sicily. The pope did this by arranging Frederick's marriage to Constance of Aragon, who brought with her levies of troops to suppress insurgents against the boy-king. It was the pope who both shielded Frederick II from an invasion by Otto IV—by excommunicating the German king—and then worked with the German princes to depose Otto on Frederick's behalf. Frederick gave the pope firm promises that he would honor papal supremacy over the Church in Germany. He pledged to respect the papacy's Lebensraum by threatening neither the Papal States nor their buffer states—specifically he was not to unite the Norman kingdom of southern Italy with the Kingdom of Sicily. Finally, among other promises, he was to lead a Crusade. With these guarantees in hand, the pope made Frederick II Holy Roman Emperor in 1215.

Frederick ruled Germany with benign neglect, which worked its usual magic and gave the Germans years of peace and prosperity. Unfortunately, Frederick also neglected to join the Crusades. He had quietly decided that he would rather be a sultan than fight them, and his interests were turned, instead, to solidifying his hold on Sicily, its traditional southern Italian appendages, and northern Italy in a manner that successive popes regarded as increasingly ominous. But he reassured them with renewed insincere professions of an imminent Crusade and by taking harsh measures against heretics. He was an eager inquisitor, though on political (securing the peace of the realm) rather than religious grounds.

In religion, Frederick was unique: a freethinking nominal Catholic with pro-Muslim prejudices and even practices. But while he employed

Saracen mercenaries and slaves, and kept Jewish and Muslim scholars at his court and defended their freedom of religion, it was a crime, in Frederick's realm, for a Catholic to abandon the historic Roman faith and adopt another. At the University of Naples, which he established in 1224, only Catholics were legally entitled to teach. Frederick II, as an armed intellectual, a medieval version of Frederick the Great of Prussia, was known as the "wonder of the world" or *stupor mundi.* He allowed his own mind to roam, untrammeled; but as the emperor of a polyglot empire, he respected the restraining bonds of religion on the passions of men. In Frederick II, as in many of the Holy Roman Emperors, we see the titanic German passion for freedom from constraint, for dominion, and for the power of the *Übermensch.* In Frederick II this was combined with a desire to make himself a new Augustus of a new Roman Empire.

Pope and emperor did not come into serious conflict until 1227, when Pope Gregory IX excommunicated Frederick II for being more than a decade late in making good his vow to assist the Crusades. With this burr under his saddle, Frederick II embarked for the Holy Land, his Crusade now a necessity to lift his excommunication from the Church. He negotiated a peace with the Muslims, crowned himself—without benefit of clergy—king of Jerusalem, and was roundly abused by the Christian populace of the city as an excommunicate and insufficient Crusader. With Jerusalem's Christians, the pope agreed that Frederick was less than a worthy successor to Charlemagne, and given that excommunication meant that Frederick's subjects no longer—by Catholic law—owed fealty to him, the pope invaded southern Italy and Sicily to keep Frederick's dagger from the heart of Rome.

But Frederick returned, and with fire and sword he marched up the Italian peninsula, recovering cities that had transferred their secular loyalty from the emperor to the pope. With Frederick's armies piercing into central Italy, pope and emperor reached a peace with the Treaties of San Germano and Ceprano in 1230, and Frederick was restored to his lands and to the Church. It was an uneasy peace, because the pope still distrusted Frederick's ambitions, especially after the emperor put his illegitimate son on the throne of Sardinia. In 1238, the nonagenarian Pope Gregory IX constructed an allied army from his own Papal States, along with the Lombard League of northern Italy—even though this was a hotbed of republican anti-clericalism—and the merchant republics of

Venice and Genoa, to wage war against Frederick. With Italian republicans and capitalists under the papal banner in a united front against
expected aggression from Frederick's *Reich,* the pope again excommunicated the Holy Roman Emperor. The papal-imperial contest opened as a
miniaturized version of World War II. It was Catholics and economic
and political libertarians pitted against the *Führer*—albeit a *Führer,* in
this case, more inclined to renaissance ideas and Muslim dancing girls
than mass racial exterminations. At least initially, the emperor's troops,
as they marched from city to city, were greeted not with heavy resistance, but more often as the Austrians greeted the Germans in the
*Anschluss* of 1938. But when Frederick's navy captured a fleet of
Catholic bishops and other clergy and kept them hostage—under conditions that resulted in several deaths—he nearly lost the support of aristocratic Europe.

The controversy was diffused somewhat by the death of the pope in
1241 and by the fact that no successor would be named for two years, as
Rome lay under a fog of war. In 1244, a new pope, Innocent IV, agreed to
a peace with Frederick, but the treaty was sunk by the refusal of the Lombard League to go along. The only alternative now was total war to the
finish. Frederick and his supporters were excommunicated, and a Crusade
declared against him. Frederick struck back. He denounced the Catholic
Church in imperial declarations and had its partisans blinded, maimed, or
murdered by the sword—often a sword wielded by a Saracen. His own
realms in rebellion, he took civilian hostages and had them openly slaughtered *pour encourager les autres* to obedience.

Amidst this smoking blood of Italian war came a plea from the
French king, Louis IX (St. Louis)—a plea that epitomizes the mind and
culture of medieval Europe. This war of the papacy versus the emperor,
Louis IX told the pope, must stop because Frederick the heretic was
needed to help the French defeat the Saracens in Egypt. Before anything
could come of Louis IX's saintly plea for holy—as opposed to unholy—
war, Frederick's health faltered; and as he lay dying, he reconciled himself
with the Church, put on the robes, if not the vows, of a Cistercian monk,
and died in 1250. The papacy had won the gigantic struggle against the
Holy Roman Emperor by default, for while the papacy was an institution,
Frederick was a force of his own, and with his death came chaos rather
than a new *stupor mundi.*

The pope's winnings would be freedom from the shadow of an over-weening emperor. The downside, which was realized immediately, was a reversion to Italian anarchy and eventual rebellions from the northern Italian anti-clericals. Events shifted from organized war to unorganized war, with only the establishment of mercenary armies—led by *gli condot-tieri*—to compensate for it in the sphere of culture and the military arts. If one wants an example of the Italian psyche of this time, perhaps of all time, it is found in the battle of Montaperto in 1260 where the armies of Siena, allied to the inheritors of the Holy Roman Empire, defeated the armies of Florence, allied to the pope. Because the Sienese attributed their victory over the pope's allies to the Virgin Mary, they made Siena a feudal vassal of the Blessed Mother, and every adult in Siena renewed his feudal vow in a candlelit procession on the Feast of the Assumption.

## TILTING TOWARD *LA BELLE FRANCE*

WILD BANDS OF ITALIANS were running loose everywhere. There was even a mini-Frederick II, in the form of his illegitimate son Manfred, who had set up shop with troubadours, huntsmen, and imperial soldiers in southern Italy. The southern Italians rebelled against him in favor of the pope. Amid such strife, the papacy did the only rational thing and turned to the country that had been its greatest source of devoted knights—*la belle France,* now enjoying the reign of a king who would be made a saint, Louis IX. At the pope's request, Sicily and southern Italy became feudal properties of the French. The feudal lord was not Louis IX, who humbly declined the honor, but his brother, Charles, count of Anjou, who now became Charles I of Anjou, king of Naples and Sicily.

The prize was the pope's to give but could only be won by war, and war is what happened, with Charles defeating Manfred, who died a sol-dier's death. Manfred's half-brother Conradin tried to oust the French, but the young German king—still a teenager—had his army defeated, and was captured. He sacrificed his neck to the sword, and with it toppled the Hohenstaufen dynasty that had simultaneously been ally and enemy of the papacy for a hundred turbulent years.

In raising the loyal French to dominance in Europe, the popes ran the danger of having power corrupt their flower of chivalry, which was not difficult in any event. Charles I became not only king of Sicily and

Naples, but held substantial portions of northern Italy as well, and he, too, developed *le rêve impérial*. His brilliant strategy was to restore the French Crusaders' kingdom in Byzantium by returning Baldwin II to the throne of the Byzantine monarch, Michael Paleologus, who had recently deposed him. Under his command, French knights fought in Greece and Albania, seeking what Winston Churchill would later call the "soft underbelly of Europe." But the French were, again, overstretched.

In Sicily, Charles followed the French imperial model of the Crusaders, bringing with him an entirely French ruling class that was set over the people as priests and lords.

This was, of course, beneficent instruction in the way of civilization. But the Sicilians mistook it for arrogance, crushing taxation, and a looming danger of haughty Normans insisting on *le droit du seigneur*. As Charles innocently loaded his knights aboard ship to sail up the Aegean Sea and sack Constantinople, the Sicilians of Palermo erupted in a rebellion of such horrific genocidal violence as to shock even twenty-first-century sensibilities. Every Frenchman in the city—whether civilian, soldier, priest, or monk—was killed; French children in the wombs of Sicilian mothers were ripped out and stamped to death; and the terror spread over the island. These unspeakable acts, committed on Easter Monday at the hour of prayer, went into the history books as "the Sicilian Vespers" of 1282. What is even more outrageous is that this crime against God and man had been financed and planned by the Byzantines. The horrified Pope Martin IV (1281–1285) tried to help Charles recover the island by excommunicating the Sicilian rebels and declaring a Crusade against the murderers of Sicily, but the Sicilians found a champion of their own in Peter III of Aragon, who rebuffed Charles's arms and sank his fleet. With it sank the hope of reestablishing French Byzantium, let alone holding on to Sicily, which became Spanish.

If French Byzantium could not be reestablished, the great conciliator pope, Gregory X (1271–1276), who was an apostle of Christian unity in secular and religious affairs, had already—at least officially—reunified the Church. In 1274 he called the Second Council of Lyons, one of the largest Church councils yet held. It was there that the Eastern and Western Churches were again united—at least on paper—with the Eastern Church accepting the *filioque,* papal supremacy, and the Catholic position on every other issue that the fissiparous East had raised in controversy. But though the Eastern Church claimed to be a church of councils, this was yet another council whose decisions its prelates refused to uphold in practice. Thus the Eastern Church, and the culture and civilization to which it was attached, pursued a separate development from Christendom, a development captured, in acid, by Ambrose Bierce's famous aphorism: "All languages are spoken in Hell, but chiefly those of Southeastern Europe."[11]

Still, if the French could no longer dream of paddling their feet in the Black Sea as the masters of Byzantium, they were nevertheless turning up more often in the list of popes, as were other triumphant groups of the thirteenth century. In 1276, the first Dominican, Innocent V, became pope, followed in 1288 by the first Franciscan, Pope Nicholas IV, and in 1294, by the first eighty-five-year-old hermit, Pope Celestine V, who also became the first pope to resign the office.[12] He did this after only six months, his humility inspiring another religious order, the Celestines, and his imprisonment (so that he would not become a tool of any faction wanting to usurp his successor). These new bases of ecclesiastical power—though hermits and Celestines remained rare—were reflected in the College of Cardinals. The cardinals were called on to elect thirteen popes in the last fifty years of the century—a number that could easily have been larger, as there were periods when the throne of St. Peter was vacant. Once, when the cardinals took too long—in the opinion of the citizens of Viterbo, where they had gathered—they were imprisoned and deprived of food, and the roof was dismantled so that the cardinals were drenched by rain. The very fact that the cardinals were meeting outside Rome—or rather the fact that this was not unusual—says much about the times. Only twice in the thirteenth century was Rome considered safe and stable enough for the cardinals to gather there to elect a new pope.

The last pope of the thirteenth century was Boniface VIII (1294–1303). Succeeding the holy hermit Celestine V, Boniface was a return to the authoritative, legal-minded popes best captured in the pontificate of Innocent III, though Boniface proved a far lesser man. Like Innocent, Boniface had a brilliant legal mind that give him practical justification—on top of the authority of the papacy—to arbitrate political disputes over the entirety of Catholic Europe, from England to Denmark to Hungary, and all points in between. He was regrettably not a Frenchman but an

Italian and prone to the vices of the Italians, including hotheaded impetuousness and using his office to pursue family feuds and sodomy (or so he was accused by his French and Italian enemies). Nevertheless, at his papal consecration in Rome he was led on a white charger, its bridle held, in the traditional fashion of kingly obeisance to the pope, by the Angevin princes, descended from Charles I of Anjou. These were Charles II of Naples and his son Charles, who was the official French king of Hungary. Boniface would later have a falling-out with the king of France, Philip IV (also known as Philip the Fair), over whether the king could imprison papal legates and tax the clergy to pay for secular wars. The argument became so intense that the king even tried to excommunicate the pope; sent troops to kidnap him; and worked with the pope's enemies to manufacture charges of heresy, personal immorality, and financial corruption against the pontiff—rather ungrateful behavior, given that Boniface made Philip's grandfather, King Louis IX, a saint in 1297. But Boniface insisted on the independence and supremacy of the Church—something Philip IV found annoying and inconvenient.

Boniface was important for other reasons. He was a friend of education, scholarship, and art, reorganizing the papal archives and library, establishing a university in Rome, and employing artists like Giotto. He instituted the first Jubilee Year for the forgiveness of sins (1300) that brought hundreds of thousands of penitents to the Eternal City in flesh-and-blood confirmation of the pope as guardian and pilot of the Christian faith. Throughout his papacy, he did much to restore Rome as the working—and not merely symbolic—capital of the Catholic Church.

Boniface's problem was that grand pronouncements must come from a grand man, and Boniface, for all his pretensions and scholarship, was not grand. His many enemies included Dante, who cast him into Hell, upended, hanging like a bat. Most of the accusations of misconduct against him were untrue. He was, however, an abrasive and egocentric man who used—perhaps justifiably—papal armies to attack his enemies, one of whom was a rival Italian family that was, in contemporary jargon, "dissing" his papacy. He was, in fact, an extreme reaction to Celestine V's unworldly impracticality. The hermit pope had been elected because it was thought that a little unworldliness—and fewer excommunications and Crusades by a papal monarch trying to secularly right all the wrongs within Christendom—might do the Church good.

When Celestine sought advice on whether he could legally resign, his adviser was the man who succeeded and imprisoned him. This began the distrust (among his critics at least) that marked Boniface's ambitious papacy. His pontificate was epitomized in his blunt affirmation that every man's salvation depended on his being subject to the pope. This sentiment did not go down well coming from him, though there was nothing particularly new in it or anything shocking in his re-affirmations of papal supremacy over the crowns of Europe. It should also be noted in his defense that, when captured by mercenaries employed by his French and Italian enemies, he showed tremendous courage, saying that if they meant to kill him "here is my head, here is my neck. . . . I desire to die for Christ's faith and His Church."[13] And it was the people of Rome who rose up and rescued him. Though his belief in papal monarchy would have prevented such thoughts, Boniface might very well have benefited from a resurgent Holy Roman Empire to play against the French. It is from such calculations—frankly necessary at the time—that Machiavellians are born.

If Boniface had been elected in reaction to Celestine, the reaction against Boniface allowed the election of another unworldly monk, the Dominican Benedict XI (1303–1304). His reign was but a short interregnum. For the history of the Church in the fourteenth century would lie not with unworldly monks, but with the worldly French and their city of Avignon.

## CHAPTER TWELVE

# FLEUR-DE-LIS
# AND IRON CROSS

———⟫⟨———

WITH ITALY SUBDIVIDING into city-state republics, the Papal States slipping from Church control, and Rome itself hostage to the anarchy of the masses and the bold assertions of powerful families, the papal curia looked longingly across the Tyrrhenian Sea to France. True, the French king had proved a bit of a problem to Pope Boniface VIII, but the majority of the College of Cardinals was now French, as was the new Pope, Clement V (1305–1314).

France was the most important power on the continent. Aside from the Holy See, it was de facto the center of the Christian world. Pope Clement was eager to negotiate a peace between England and France so that these prize crowns of Christendom could unite for a Crusade. So in 1309, he moved the papacy to Avignon, in southern France, to assist in his negotiations—or at least that was the story. Avignon had other advantages. It offered the security of France but was independent of the French king, because in 1290 King Philip IV had given the city to Charles II of Naples. In 1348 the papacy purchased it outright, and Avignon remained a papal property until the end of the eighteenth century, when revolutionary France seized it.

The popes led the Church from Avignon rather than Rome for more than seventy years. The Italians refer to this period as the papacy's "Babylonian Captivity." But really, a more wistful attitude is called for. The popes had every human reason to be in France, just as their ultimate and

ineluctable duty was to be in Rome, on St. Peter's throne, no matter how
dangerous and chaotic the city might be. This duty became unmistakably
clear when the papacy's Avignon *vacances* ended in a smashup—the inevitable outcome for an unlucky holidaymaker who, needing a release
from the cares of the world, has a few too many tumblers of cognac.

The first problem, however, was not the move to Avignon, but recur-
rent rows with Pope Boniface VIII's nemesis, the French king Philip IV, a
not-so-merry monarch for the papacy.

## THE KNIGHTS TEMPLAR
## AND THE HATRED OF PHILIP THE FAIR

PHILIP IV, KNOWN AS Philip the Fair, was king of France from 1285
until 1314. Long reigns offer an opportunity for stability, visionary statesmanship, and the advancement of high ideals. In Philip's case, the reverse
happened. Like most people of his time, he was an intensely religious man
(in his own mind, the most orthodox of Catholics), but this did not stop
him from relentlessly engaging in unseemly disputes with the Church and
its agents.

The irritant was Pope Boniface VIII, whom he had denigrated and attempted to kidnap when alive, and whose memory he wanted defiled
when dead. Consumed with concerns about money to support his wars
against England and her allies the Flemish, the king did what all villains
do. He anathematized the kingdom's economic "elite," expropriating the
leading financiers in France. In succession these were the Jews (whom he
banished), the Knights Templar, and the Italian merchants whom the
French collectively lumped together as "Lombards."

The destruction of the Knights Templar is one of the most shameful
acts in medieval history. These glorious, extraordinary knights who had
achieved and sacrificed so much for Christendom, found themselves offered up—like Aztec human sacrifices—to the greed of Philip IV. The
thousands of Templar graves in the Holy Land counted as nothing—for
among the whispered insinuations of Philip's prosecutors was that the
Templars were to blame for the collapse of Outremer. They were accused
of having flaccid physical and pecuniary morals, of initiating new recruits
through satanic rituals, and of more eagerly contesting with their own

Christian rivals—chiefly the Knights Hospitaller—than defending against the Saracen. This last point, even if exaggerated, was the only one that bore some truth. In the past, the great King Louis IX of France and Pope Nicholas IV, a Franciscan, had both recommended, on separate occasions, that the two orders become one. The understandable regimental pride that prevented an amalgamation proved to be a pride the Templars could not afford.

In late 1307, the rumormongers having done their damage, King Philip IV ordered the arrest and inquisitional trial of every Templar in France. It was a procedure, complete with torture, inflicted without papal authority, permission, or cooperation—and indeed, was finally condemned by the pope. The Templar trials operated at the very same level of character assassination that had marked Philip's inquisition of Pope Boniface VIII. Among the tortured was the Knights' leader, Jacques de Molay, who had just submitted detailed plans to the pope for a new Crusade. The innocent Molay and many brave knights crumbled and broke to the torments of secular law, confessing to crimes they later recanted.

The confessions were the hook Philip needed to drag the Church into his scheme. If indeed the Templars were heretics, even internal enemies of the Church, surely it was the king's duty, in cooperation with the pope, to stamp them out. Pope Clement V was French and a good man, but he suffered terribly from cancer. The pain of his body made him weak in decision, and he did not see that by appointing a commission of cardinals to investigate the Templars—which seemed to him, simply, innocently, the middle road to finding the truth—he was playing into a conniving king's malicious hands.

The cardinals instituted one reform immediately—they ordered Philip's jailers to lock away their tools of torture. Molay told the cardinals the truth, retracting his confessions and denying the charges against the Templars. The Cardinals now faced a terrible dilemma. If they presented Molay's evidence to the royal court it would be judged perjury, and thus a relapse into heresy, punishable by burning at the stake. So they kept the evidence secret, as though it were told to them in a confessional, but hoped to use this knowledge to save him.

The trial, incredibly, continued until the spring of 1314 and spanned the globe; the entirety of the empire of the Poor Knights was investigated.

In virtually every case outside France, the Knights were cleared of wrong-doing. Even in France, in cases where the accused Templars had not with-drawn their confessions, the Church was able to pass sentences that amounted to penance, not death or imprisonment.

But, perversely, Knights who retracted their torture-extracted confessions and insisted on their innocence became subject to charges of perjury and heresy under secular law, and they were burned at the stake. A jury of churchmen tried to save Molay by recommending that he receive life imprisonment. Though he was once bent by torture, Molay now stood firm. He would not accept this or any other imputation of guilt. He had openly proclaimed the Templars' innocence for five years and would brook no compromise with injustice. As the cardinals feared, King Philip used these protests as evidence that the Templar Master had relapsed into heresy. The king overrode the churchmen and ordered Molay to be bound and burned at the stake. Both King Philip IV and Pope Clement V would die the same year; the common people thought they were being called to account for the destruction of the Templars.

Even before Molay's death, the Templars' cause had been lost. In 1312, Pope Clement V reluctantly agreed to dissolve, but not condemn, the order. The pope's decision came after the Council of Vienne, in which he charted a middle road on other issues as well. For example, Clement declared Boniface VIII a legitimate pope—which had been denied by Philip IV. But Clement also cleared the king of sinning against the Church in his attempt to kidnap and besmirch Boniface. Perhaps Clement rea-soned that a little roughhousing between kings and popes was to be ex-pected. In addition, Clement decreed that the Templars' properties were to go to the Hospitallers, except in Portugal and Spain, where military or-ders that had evolved from the Templars—the Order of the Knights of Christ and the Military Order of Montessa—were given possession. Of course, through royal legerdemain—a French word—the Templars' French properties became Philip's. Philip did, however, pledge himself, his sons, and the nobility of France to the Crusades, with the troops to be embarked within six years. Only Philip's death and war with England made it irrelevant. Philip was succeeded by Louis X, known as "the Quarrelsome," a sign perhaps that France would be less of a haven than Clement had initially hoped.

# THE FRENCH PAPACY

ACTUALLY, THE BAD SIGNS had started from the time Clement received his papal crown in Lyons in 1305. During the subsequent parade, a collapsing wall spooked his horse, which threw him; his brother and a cardinal were killed; the papal tiara lost a jewel; and the next day another of the pope's brothers was killed in a street fight. This was a city considered much safer than Rome.

From the supposed security of France, Pope Clement dispatched papal armies of Catalonian mercenaries to recover papal territory in Italy from the aggressive Venetian republic. But he was not a warrior by nature. He established universities and academic chairs, published decretals on law (he was a canon lawyer), excommunicated Robert the Bruce for murder, settled the succession in Hungary, and, among his other business, packed the College of Cardinals with members of his family, which in this rough age was not a sign of corruption but an act of necessary self-defense. Clement V was a weak pope only because the papacy was in a weak position; and as a practiced diplomat, he negotiated as best he could from the real-world circumstances in which he lived.

The next papal election illustrated the diaphanous weakness of papal security. The cardinals gathered near Avignon and were terrorized by a French mob that chanted death to the Italian cardinals and proved their bona fides by making an inferno of the building in which the cardinals had gathered, forcing the electors of the pope to break through a rear wall and escape. For two years, the Church was without a pope, and it was only with the protection of French knights that the cardinals were able to finally gather and choose the septuagenarian Pope John XXII (1316–1334)—a Frenchman, as were all the Avignon popes. Though elderly, he was known as a tough-minded administrator, such as was now required, and proved to be a vigorous pope, improving the finances and organization of the Church until he was ninety years old. Among his chores was disciplining wayward Franciscans. The Church saw religious poverty as a vow that nevertheless permitted private ownership and the necessary stockpiling of goods. Some Franciscans, however, were rigorists who took a far harsher line. They pronounced private ownership un-Biblical, and a few called the pope a heretic for teaching otherwise. Pope

John felt obliged to excommunicate these wilder voices, and reaffirmed that communism was heresy.[1]

The next pope, Benedict XII (1334–1342), was a baker's son, whose rise to the papacy proved—as had the pontificates of the English pope, Hadrian IV, a poor clerk's son, and Pope Urban IV, a cobbler's son—that the Church was the most meritocratic institution of its time. Among the popes were well-educated aristocrats, of course, and political placemen from important families, yes. But nowhere else in the medieval world were leaders chosen from a pool of candidates that included hermits, monks, bishops, scholars, lawyers, sons of the working class, and noblemen—with some candidates being all these things at once (well, nearly). The cardinals' choices—though sometimes prudently guided by the staves, torches, mobs, mercenaries, and armies that waited outside their conclave—were often free to the point of eccentricity.

The elevation of Benedict XII was a surprise, though he was French, which was the most important thing. He was also a Cistercian monk, scholar, expert theologian, and prosecutorially gifted—and judicially lenient—inquisitor. He took a broom to hangers-on and bribe-merchants in the papal court—eliminating both their economic drain and their corruption, which had fired Italian calumnies about the state of the exiled papacy. As an administrator, he was superb; as a diplomat, he failed. It was during the reign of Benedict that the one calamity the Church most hoped to prevent—war between England and France—burst into the open, with the onset of the Hundred Years War (1337–1453), which put paid to any hope for a renewal of the Crusades. In Italy, his reluctance to deploy armies led to the erosion of Church property, power, and influence. He gave peace a chance, and the result was retreat. But he wasn't foolish. It was under Benedict that the Palais Vieux was constructed in Avignon—a papal palace built like a fortified castle.

The next pontiff, Pope Clement VI (1342–1352), was well educated, of noble birth, and more attuned to *laissez les bons temps rouler* than Franciscan austerities. From his given name alone, Pierre Roger, one can surmise that he was regarded as a man who could put a more definitively French stamp on the papacy and pass the champagne of religious celebration more liberally. He declared, to wild support, that Jubilee Years would be held in Rome every half-century rather than every century so that all Catholics would have a better chance of enjoying one. Though a full-fledged Crusade was impossible, he gave rein to the Gallic spirit of adventure by bringing together the Knights of St. John with soldiers from Venice and Cyprus in two campaigns—limited in scope, but successful—against the Turks.

His free-flowing generosity to artists, the poor, and even the rich—all must have prizes; none must be disappointed—make him appear a sort of papal Santa Claus. But while Clement enjoyed laughter, wine, and, chastely, the company of women, he also showed the concomitant compassion, courage, and strength of private piety that often lie in such men. During the terrible Black Death (1348–1349), Clement proved a worthy leader for his beleaguered city of Avignon and offered sanctuary to Jews who were scapegoated as the cause of the plague. He was, on all accounts save financial ones, a good pope, but his spendthrift ways heightened resentments over papal taxation, especially as the papacy came to be seen not as a redoubt of sanity amidst the chaos of Italy, but as a tool of the French. The English—who were at war with France—and the Germans, whose imperial nationalism still smoldered, did not rush to funnel money to the Avignon papacy. For Avignon's critics, the papal flag and the royal fleur-de-lis had become synonymous.

The new pope, Innocent VI (1352–1362), swept away the confetti and wine bottles left behind by Clement VI. He, like Benedict XII, was a reformer intent on restoring discipline to every order of the Church and fiscal probity to all papal offices. Innocent, the fifth of the Avignon popes, knew—as they all did—that the papacy must eventually return to Rome. Pope Innocent VI, however, gave that knowledge force by employing a cardinal—Gil Álvarez Carrillo de Albornoz—who was also a trained soldier.

Gil de Albornoz was a blue blood related to the royal houses of Aragon and León. He believed in chivalry and condemned those—such as the Spanish king Pedro the Cruel—who failed the test. Innocent VI commissioned this fighting cardinal to regain the Papal States as the first step in making Rome safe for the papacy. The pope's commander quickly proved himself a flesh-and-blood medieval version of the twentieth-century high-tech machine gun known as the "street sweeper." By the end of 1354, the fighting cardinal had regained the papal territories surrounding Rome. By the end of 1356, virtually every other papal territorial claim had been made good; and the following year Gil de Albornoz bequeathed the Papal States their governing constitutions, which ensured their freedom under the pope into the nineteenth century.

Though eager to be rid of his diplomatic and military duties, Gil de Albornoz was the only man who could ensure the peace in Italy. With but a slight respite in Avignon, he was soon back among the condottieri and the dangerous, prideful, thrusting families of the Italian peninsula. The Cardinal's military service was so obviously necessary that he refused to be a candidate in the papal election of 1362, reluctantly acknowledging that his vocation was here, in Italy, among the mercenaries, ruffians, scheming merchants, and petty tyrants who needed to be tamed.

The cardinals elected Pope Urban V (1362–1370), a Benedictine monk. He retained the cowl of his order and was devoted to private study and prayer. While he continued the fiscal reforms and austerities of his predecessors, he had his own charitable weakness, which was supporting impoverished students and founding universities. He also pursued that great papal mirage of relaunching the Crusades. In Italy's condottieri he saw worthy allies for the knights of France. But the condottieri never joined up, their interests being parochial and monetary; and French victories, including the seizure of Alexandria, were evanescent. Pope Urban V suffered from another perpetual papal mirage: reunion with the Byzantine Church—a reunion that he was convinced could not be made from Avignon. The fact was, it could not be made from Rome either, but Urban was convinced he should try. In 1367, Urban landed in Italy, greeted by Cardinal Albornoz, cheering crowds, and submissive princes. The Lateran Palace had been destroyed by fire, so the pope moved to the Vatican, where restoration work had been under way for years. Peace Rome now had, but the city was still a burnt-out hulk of its former self—a depressing spectacle for the Frenchmen used to the beauties of southern France.

The papacy's return to Rome was popular throughout Christendom, and the pope did all he could to rebuild and restore the churches of the shattered city. But anyone who knew anything about the state of Rome knew that only duty kept the pope there. Even that erstwhile rival of the papacy, the Holy Roman Emperor, Charles IV, submitted himself to the pope and gave his imperial consent to papal conquests in Italy as a means to shore up the pope's security. The old enemy from the East, the Byzantine Emperor, also came to Rome, accepted the Catholic faith, and agreed to the dispatch of Catholic missionaries to his realm. Even so, with success greeting him at every turn in Italy—and with Avignon itself an increasingly unattractive sanctuary, as bored soldiers of fortune plied their craft nearby—Pope Urban V found a reason to return to France. He had, he said, to negotiate a peace between the French and the English. But the real reason for his return was to die on his native soil, which he did in 1370.

The last of the true Avignon popes was Urban's successor, Gregory XI, who, though French and resident in Avignon, was as convinced as any of the need to return the papacy permanently to Rome for the sake of Christian unity, the end of the East-West schism, and the remounting of the Crusades. His difficulty was at least two fold: the papacy's continuing interest in diplomatic intervention to end the Hundred Years War between England and France, and the continuing violent turmoil in northern Italy that threatened to spill down to Rome. More papal armies were dispatched to Italy, this time under the command of another cardinal and future antipope, Robert of Geneva, who presided over a notorious slaughter in the city of Cesena. But while the papacy preached diplomacy to the French and the English and fire and sword to the Italians, the pope listened to the appeals of a future saint, Catherine of Siena. She repeatedly implored him to restore the throne of St. Peter, to return to the seat of his apostolic forefathers, to lead the universal Church from the Eternal City. He agreed, and after a rough passage and many delays, Pope Gregory XI entered Rome, and found it an awful place. Still, though violence would eventually force him to live elsewhere in Italy, as it had forced so many previous popes, he stuck it out. It wasn't easy. Before death claimed him, this patriotic Frenchman yearned to leave pestilential Italy for *la belle France*. The French-dominated College of Cardinals was equally resigned to the fact that the pope must stay in Italy, never straying so far from Rome as to leave any doubt that he would return.

At least, that's what most of them thought; and their minds were concentrated on that conclusion by the furor after Gregory's death. The cardinals made their decision amidst riots, with mobs bursting into their deliberative councils. The men in red thought it wise to choose an Italian. They chose a Neapolitan canon lawyer and archbishop well-experienced in Italian politics. This was Pope Urban VI, a man with no weakness for Camembert, *le vin rouge,* or *les belles filles;* a tough, honest man prepared to cut a hard, straight path through the violent life of Italy.

But almost as soon as they had made their decision, the cardinals—at least the French among them—began to have second thoughts. A tough administrator they had wanted, but Urban VI, who relied on imperious threats and was an ungracious victor, seemed not so much tough as disagreeable. Among his threats was one to pack the College of Cardinals with Italians so as to teach the French, whom he considered morally lax, a lesson. The French cardinals struck back. They declared the election of Urban VI void, having been made under duress of mob violence. They elected in his stead Robert of Geneva, a warrior-cardinal who had shown himself bloodily handy at knowing how to deal with overly vibrant Italians. Robert of Geneva took the name of Pope Clement VII and moved into the papal palace at Avignon.

The universal Church now found itself with two popes, one in Rome and one in Avignon, both elected by a majority of the College of Cardinals, and both with powerful patrons, determined by geopolitics. Italians, of course, swarmed behind Urban VI, as did England, Germany, Portugal, and Central Europe. Clement VII had the support of France, Scotland, Spain, Denmark, and Norway. The cardinals had tied the papacy into a Gordian knot, known as the Great Schism. It was also a great tragedy, for it did much to discredit the Church as the two rival popes excommunicated each other, denounced each other's clergy as being in schism, and waged war upon one another with mercenary armies in Italy.

While Urban's election might have been canonically valid, it was a practical mistake. Even Italian cardinals who won appointment through his hand began to worry that he was unstable and perhaps needed to be deposed in favor of a regent. Urban ended such talk by torturing and executing alleged conspirators. Clement VII was by far the better man. He welcomed defecting cardinals from Urban's court. He refused to resign his pontificate, for he believed he was the rightful pope; and when Urban died in 1389, he hoped to have his position affirmed.

In fact, it should have been—save that Avignon and Rome each had a College of Cardinals. Rather than recognizing Clement VII, the Roman cardinals elected another Neapolitan, Boniface IX. Failing capitulation from Avignon (or Avignon's conquest of Rome) two lines of papal succession would permanently divide Christendom. Boniface undid much of the harm wrought by Urban VI, winning back several defecting cardinals with his charm and diplomacy. Full of the milder Christian virtues that were shockingly lacking in Urban VI, Boniface IX nevertheless wielded the sword of state with force, as he did in toppling the republicans in Rome and taking over the city's administration through appointed senators.

Pope Clement, in Avignon, desired peace with the worthy Boniface IX, publicly praying for the reunion of the papacy—under his own leadership, of course, for he felt bound to honor the cardinals who had made him pope. Boniface, for his part, would not resign, but offered to accept Clement's cardinals as valid, and to employ Clement himself as a papal representative to France and Spain. Neither olive branch was seized.

When Clement died, the cardinals in Avignon maintained their claim to the legitimate succession—despite the entreaties of the French king, Charles VI, who wanted negotiation with Rome. Instead, the cardinals elected a Spaniard as the inheritor of the French papacy. He took the name Benedict XIII. Like the first Avignon antipope, he had initially been a supporter of Urban, but now he was intransigent in believing that the antipope was in Rome, not in France. King Charles proposed that both popes resign to end the schism—and he was serious enough that he withdrew his support from Benedict when it became clear the Avignon pope would not cooperate. But Benedict was a supple politician and eventually won back the loyalty of the French with a renewed pledge to find an honorable solution to the dishonorable schism.

Not only was the schism dishonorable, but the papacy in Rome needed support. Both popes were hard up for cash, but the pope in Rome had the additional problem of the usual round of threatening familial armies and mob violence. In 1404, the Vatican was sacked—not by the Hun or by Vandals, but by the Roman mob itself, led by Giovanni Colonna, demagogue and head of one of Rome's turbulent, powerful families. The pope who endured this was the newly elected Innocent VII (1404–1406). Pope Gregory XII (1406–1415) succeeded him and, like his opposite number in Avignon, professed his desire for unity—but not at the cost of his own elevation.

In 1408, tired of Benedict's delays, the French again withdrew their support, and Benedict retreated to Spain. In 1409, the Council of Pisa resolved to finally end the schism. With a massive representation of cardinals, doctors of canon law, academics, bishops, archbishops, abbots, and others, including ambassadors from the leading crowns of Europe, the Council (in their absence) deposed both contending popes and elected a new pope, Alexander V, a Greek and an orphan who was adopted by a monk, educated by the Franciscans, and later went to Oxford and the University of Paris. But neither deposed pope accepted the verdict of the Council. Where once there were two, now there were three popes, with Alexander supported by France, England, the northern half of Italy, parts of Germany, and a few other holdings. But Alexander died within a year of his appointment, the divisions within Christendom hardened, and a new line of succession developed when cardinals loyal to Alexander elected John XXIII. So confused had the situation become that even today it is not clear whether Alexander was a pope or an antipope.

Of his successor, however, the Church is in no doubt. John XXIII was colorful, elected by a faction of cardinals who apparently thought that a man known more for his military skill than for his piety might rout and defeat his papal rivals. Yet, though colorful, John XXIII proved no Constantine and no pope. He could read the portents. The real power would lie not with him, but with a new council, the Council of Constance, which assembled in November 1414. It was the largest council in Christian history, with five thousand delegates, and John XXIII fled from its deliberations.

In 1415, the Council announced that it was superior to individual popes and had the full power of the Church: the only formulation that would allow it to resolve the schism. It deposed John XXIII, and the former warrior meekly accepted its judgment. Of the remaining two popes, Gregory XII cleverly offered to resign—on condition that he then officially reconvene the Council. That very act would, of course, acknowledge that he was de facto pope. The Council agreed. Those who had remained loyal to Gregory were held to be in good standing, and the elderly pope was pensioned off with a position as a regional governor. That left one pope standing—Benedict, who remained in Spain. Until his death in 1423, he proclaimed himself the one true pope, leading the loyal remnant of the Church, which apparently consisted of his followers in Castile. The Council officially deposed him, and he faded away into one of the quirkier corners of Church history, as Papa Luna of Peñiscola.[2]

With the three rivals dispatched, the Council finally elected the new pope, Martin V (1417–1431), who would restore Christendom. It took three years for the Council of Constance to complete its work, but when it did, it had put in St. Peter's chair a Colonna—that is, a member of the family that had led the sacking of Rome in 1404. Such familial responsibility did not lessen his shock at the violence, corruption, and devastation of the city, which he found impossible to enter—because of mercenary armies that held the roads—until 1420.

To be fair, the Colonna family had also provided many loyal servants to the Church—including nearly thirty cardinals, of which Martin was the only one to be made pope. Moreover, Martin did what duty required and not only refused to live in Germany or Avignon—both of which offered the pope shelter—but set about restoring Rome and defeating the condottieri, mobs, and petty tyrants who again dominated Italy. The papacy's French holiday was well and truly over.

# ALBION'S SEED

ACROSS THE ENGLISH CHANNEL, the blessed isle of England was, in the later Middle Ages, a model of Catholic dominion. There were no Albigensians here. No heretics. And while England fought France, the English people remained loyal to the Church and free from the tempests and turmoils that had smashed the Holy Roman Empire, left Italy a land of brigands, and had Frenchmen fighting everyone from the Mussulmen to the Byzantines to the Sicilians to the English to themselves. As with other states in Christendom, there were inevitable disputes between Church and state on taxation and sovereignty. In the grand scheme of things, though, the Church had no serious disputes with England.

But two English thinkers began untying the bonds that united Christendom. The first was William of Ockham (1285–1349). A Franciscan, educated at Oxford, Ockham was one of the most powerfully influential minds of the Middle Ages. In him, we see modern man. Like modern man, Ockham believed that God was beyond reason. Thus, Ockham was opposed to the entire scholastic experiment. He believed that the simplest explanation for any phenomenon is always the best[3] and that only tangible objects are real. Ockham's philosophy divided religion from the world. Religion was compartmentalized as the mystery of faith; it was not open to philosophical inquiry. So philosophy should focus on the empirical, the scientific, and the world that was subject to human manipulation. It is perhaps no surprise given these principles that Ockham believed in the political subordination of the Church (which dealt with mystery) to the state (which dealt with fact). To the modern or Protestant mind, such secularization seems natural. To the orthodox Catholic mind—which sees God present in the sacraments, creation, and reason—it does not.

Ockham was radical in another way not so appealing to modern man. For Ockham maintained that curious medieval balance between radical thought and Catholic devotion. He took his vows as a Franciscan seriously and was, in fact, one of the rigorist anti-materialists, opposed to the Church and churchmen owning anything.[4]

Ockham spent much of his life abroad and died in Germany. Another revolutionary English philosopher, John Wyclif (c. 1330–1384), stayed in England, though, ironically, his greatest influence would be felt in Bohemia. Like Ockham, Wyclif believed in state supremacy over the Church, which won him many powerful friends in government. Also like Ockham, he believed the Church should abjure goods and property. For both Ockham and Wyclif, religious poverty would purge the Church of corrupting political power.

It might be thought that this would allow the Church to focus entirely on the business of saving souls, but for Wyclif this was not true. For Wyclif believed in predestination—and if man was already predestined to Heaven or Hell, what need had he of clergy or sacraments? Under Wyclif's system, the Church could not excommunicate a king because the Church did not have such authority. But a king could expropriate the lands of a bishop, because seizing such land was within the rights of an earthly lord and sovereign.[5]

Like Ockham, Wyclif was trained as a scholastic but ended in rebellion. He was opposed to rational, Thomistic theology; opposed to the mystical idea of transubstantiation; and opposed to the Catholic understanding of tradition. Wyclif was "always an extremist." He believed that religious knowledge came from the Bible alone; that it was literally true even when that seemed impossible; that monasticism and churchly wealth were contrary to the Bible;[6] and that priests and bishops who committed sins should be deprived of their authority. Yet for all his protests against Catholic practice, Wyclif died while attending Mass.

Wyclif's ideas took root not because of their theological rigor or popularity. They were not popular at all in the pious England of the late Middle Ages. But they did strike at the Church's Achilles heel: its need for tax revenues and the undeniable wealth of many bishops. Taxes and lordly churchmen were unpopular, and in England, such discontent as there was with the Church was really a matter of money, money, who's got the money. Wyclif's faction had, at least initially, the tacit support of the warrior-nobles, eager to shunt episcopal wealth to the war against France. In 1381, three years before his death, Wyclif saw the Peasant Revolt led by Wat Tyler, in which the archbishop of Canterbury was murdered—for economic rather than religious "crimes." There had been a similar revolt, known as "the Jacquerie," in Paris in 1358—during the Avignon pontificate. In France as in England, the nobility closed ranks to destroy peasant radicalism with brute force.

The Black Death of the fourteenth century loomed over these anticlerical and radical economic movements. So many priests—who were responsible for dispensing the last rites—had perished in the Black Death that common people often had to shift for themselves in proclaiming final blessings.[7] Nobles, to maintain their standard of living in the postepidemic labor shortage, imposed starkly higher taxes and feudal exactions on the peasantry. In England the resulting peasant radicalism was also linked to heretical doctrines. In 1401, England began enforcing death penalty laws against heresy, which in fact were laws directed against the only heretics England had—the Lollards, who followed Wyclif's teachings, and were most easily defined as anti-clericals and deniers of the sacraments.

Wyclif had other followers—in fact, far more important ones—in Bohemia, led by Jan Hus (c. 1373–1415), a Czech nationalist and academic. He shared Wyclif's belief in state supremacy over the Church and in predestination. He opposed indulgences and the Catholic practice of private confession. Though excommunicated in 1411, he accepted a royal summons to appear at the Council of Constance in 1414, convinced that his famous eloquence would win him a reprieve. Instead, he was found guilty of heresy and executed in 1415, as was his friend Jerome of Prague in 1416, thus ensuring martyrs for Bohemian nationalism.

The key doctrine of the Bohemians who followed Hus and Jerome was that both priest and parishioner should partake of the Eucharist under the species of both bread and wine at communion, unlike the Catholic practice where the communicant received the Eucharist only under the species of bread, something the Church had adopted to guard against abuses of the chalice and underline the fact that the Body and Blood of Christ are inherent in every particle of the Eucharist. This democratizing of the chalice, however, proved less important than Bohemian nationalism in the bloody disaster that followed. Hundreds of noblemen rallied to their country's defense, denying that there were any heretics at all in the beautiful land of Bohemia, and promising armed protection to all patriotic Hussites.

As tensions mounted, so did violence, and priests who put doctrine above nationalism were ejected from their churches by the mobs. In 1418, the Holy Roman Emperor, King Wenceslaus of Germany and Bohemia, bowed to nationalist sentiment and declared that foreigners had no power over his subjects—essentially denying Rome's authority over the Church. But the next year, King Wenceslaus reversed himself, proclaiming that all churches must be restored to orthodox Catholic priests on pain of a Crusade against Bohemia. The result was the Hussite wars that would last until 1436.

King Wenceslaus died in 1419 and was succeeded by his brother Sigismund, the German king of Hungary. Sigismund saw in Bohemia fiery persecution against his German countrymen and orthodox Catholics—indeed, they were generally one and the same. Catholic Germans were his base of support against the Hussites, who were largely Czech and who fielded a peasant army whose farm tools had been transformed into weapons.

As the fighting became more severe, Hussite belief became more radical, finally preaching the complete abolition of the Church—the Hussites enforcing their will with fire and sword iconoclasm. In place of the Catholic Church—and Church buildings and priests—the Hussites propounded a new religious dispensation. Sole authority rested in the Bible. The only acceptable Christian practices were baptism, communion under both kinds, and the public confession of sin—with the sin to be published as a matter of secular law, given that, to the Hussite patriots, sin was an embarrassment to the state.

By 1420, the year Pope Martin V announced a Crusade against the Hussites, virtually the entire state of Bohemia had been wrested from the Holy Roman Emperor and the Catholic Church, whose priests and monks lay murdered. The more militant Hussites, known as Taborites, led mob destruction of churches and monasteries, altars and religious art. Communism was seen as the fulfillment of Christianity, which was meant, allegedly, to create a system of equality, abolishing individual possessions and human laws. Other splinter groups—who would soon be repressed by the Hussites themselves—desecrated the Eucharist (the veneration of which was considered idolatry), or advocated free love as a concomitant of Christian communism, or preached that the end of the world was nigh. Some even endorsed pacifism. But the reigning spirit was more that of the Taborite general Jan Zižka who willed that upon his death his skin be used for a war drum—and it was. Petty, provincial tyrants became the only source of, temporary, order.

As the factions grew, Bohemia descended into civil war, but even this calamity—and the repeated Crusades of King Sigismund's German knights—could not halt the Hussite advance. It began laying waste to Bohemia's neighbors—Hungary, Austria, and Germany—as it had laid waste to Bohemia itself. Every fear that Catholic Europe had of what an unraveling of Christendom might mean was proven in blood and anarchy by the Hussites.

Finally, in 1433, an alliance of moderate Hussites and orthodox Catholics agreed to a peace treaty, or what were called "compacts" between the contending parties. On matters of communion and state authority over the Church, the Catholics gave ground. In return, the Hussites proclaimed their allegiance to the pope, the universal Church, and the Catholic faith. But the Taborites—who behaved like Mongol peasants—refused the compact. In 1434, an allied Catholic and Hussite army at last crushed the Taborite hordes, and in 1436 Bohemia was sufficiently pacified for Sigismund to be welcomed to the Bohemian throne. Wars and rumors of war would follow, but nothing on this terrible scale.

Such was the butcher's bill of Wyclif and Hus in Bohemia. But in Wyclif's own England, things were different. The English had not yet adopted the belief that the "wogs begin at Calais" because at this point they were busy asserting that Calais was English. But they knew well enough that the wogs certainly did begin east of the Adriatic and were not only horrified at news from Bohemia, but certain that it would not happen in England.

True, King Henry V—the hero of Agincourt in 1415—did face his own heretical rebellion from Wyclif's children, the Lollards, in 1414. It was a rebellion, however, of only a few hundred people. After the Lollards' most visible leader, Sir John Oldcastle, was executed in 1417, the

sect faded slowly from sight until it was entirely extinguished by the sixteenth century when, unfortunately, a new and far more powerful rebellion would smash the unity of Catholic Christendom forever.

# THE TEUTONIC KNIGHTS
# OF THE BALTIC

AS LATE AS THE THIRTEENTH CENTURY, Christianity had yet to
penetrate into the thick forests of the Baltic states or even into Prussia.
But in that century, German colonists began forming settlements, and to
protect them came a new monastic military order, the Sword Brethren,
created specifically for the task, and an old order, the Teutonic Knights,
famed Crusaders who would eventually absorb the Sword Brethren. The
Teutonic Knights brought a Germanic exactitude and discipline to their
religious and military devotions. Unlike some military orders, they both
mortified the flesh and fasted. They were celibate, maintained occasional
vows of silence, performed prayers with the devotion of monks (which
they were), and read from the Bible whenever they sat for bread and
water or other fare. Devoted to the Catholic Church, ardent venerators of
the Virgin Mary, they were studiously and harshly drilled to defend the
faith by the sword.

In Prussia, they found a people cloaked in darkness, who practiced
human sacrifice, the ritual execution of widows, the judicial killing of
anyone unfit to lead their rough life in a haunted wood. Drunkenness,
tribal warfare, and the invention of creative tortures unto death for their
captives (such as roasting German knights in their armor) were the major
pleasures; the gods of the forest were the major fear. In 1230, the Teutonic Knights began the Catholic conquest of Prussia, and after Prussia
the Baltic states. The Knights, in white capes that matched the snow, on
heavy chargers and armed with heavy weaponry such as distinguished the
Crusaders in the Holy Land, hit the Prussian tribes with a force, vigor,
and determination that stunned these fearsome barbarians.

But the Prussians were not the only dangers. East of Prussia were the
Russians. It was only in the tenth century that Russia had become Christian, and before that it was only because of Viking conquerors in the
ninth century that Russia had become an organized state out of a bazaar
of Slavic, Oriental, Byzantine, and Middle Eastern peoples. According to

legend, the great grand duke of Kiev, Vladimir, declared Russia a Christian principality in 989 after inviting a representative of the Latin Church, the Byzantine Church, and Islam to his court. Duke Vladimir rejected Islam for his people because it prohibited alcohol, the greatest solace of the Russians. He rejected the Latin Church because of its habit of frequent fasting; the Duke valued his food. So the Russians embraced Byzantine Christianity and the Eastern Orthodox faith. Given the distrust with which experienced Crusaders regarded the Byzantines, the Russians were viewed as uncongenial neighbors. Worse, however, was what lay behind the Russians. In 1237, the Mongols burst forth anew, under the grandson of Genghis Khan. All of Russia that lay in his path was put to the torch. In 1241, having overridden Russia and Poland, the Mongols crashed into the Teutonic Knights. The Knights, as always, were grossly outnumbered, and the Mongols destroyed them.

Yet as swiftly as the Golden Horde had come, so swiftly did it depart, leaving the German Knights—who were nothing if not hardy—to reassemble for another war, to avenge the defeat of Catholic Sweden by the Russian Alexander Nevsky. But here, too, the brave and outrageously outnumbered Knights were defeated, maneuvered onto an ice floe that cracked and gave way, plunging them to an icy death or leaving them helpless before Russian knives.

After this litany of Catholic defeats, the Prussians and the tribes of the Baltic states saw their chance to throw off the yoke of civilization in a rebellion that killed tens of thousands of German settlers. If a new Baltic barbarian empire seemed in the offing, with Baltic armies marching against Catholic Slavs to the east, the Baltic warrior tribes counted the Germans out too quickly. The Czechs, who would later prove so troublesome in the Jan Hus affair, now allied with the Germans in a Crusade to restore the cross of Catholicism to Prussia and the Baltic states. By 1260, Prussia was restored to the faith and a former barbarian king was crowned as a Catholic one in Lithuania. The king's conversion proved temporary. Allied with the Russians and unrepentant Baltic barbarians, he put the Germans under siege. For very nearly the entire thirteenth century, the region was at war, with the Teutonic Knights becoming masters of guerilla warfare, deep penetration raids, and the sort of tactics—adapted to medieval weaponry—with which any Vietnam veteran with Special Forces training would be familiar. It also became a holy war where, because of Prussian and Baltic treachery, extermination was as much an objective as was conversion. But with the combination of heavy cavalry, special operations long-range patrols, and war-war taking precedence over jaw-jaw, the region was steadily tamed. In 1309, the headquarters of the Teutonic Knights was established in Prussia, at Marienburg, a tangible symbol that though scattered across the borders of Christendom, this was their unique Crusade; these hard-tamed regions were their land, Ordensland.

In the fourteenth century, Ordensland became a thriving colony, importing nobles as feudal lords (all of whom were themselves required to be feudatories of the Teutonic Knights), offering land for freehold farmers, bringing commerce and coinage, secure roads and river passage, grain and government, culture and Catholicism to the people of Prussia. Cistercian monks came to aid the order, reclaiming the land from swamp and the people from superstition. The entrepôts of Ordensland became part of the Hanseatic League of northern German cities, organized for mutual protection and free commerce. Out of one hundred years of savage war had come a prosperous peace that grew more prosperous as the Knights annexed portions of Poland, including the city of Danzig.

To the north, in the Baltic states, German settlers still clung to outposts protected by the Knights. It was wilder country; there was no peace here. The Knights were valued by the settlers, but were often at odds with the archbishop of Riga, who disliked and distrusted them and wanted them disbanded—a far cry from Ordensland, whose four bishops were members of the order. Though lacking the archbishops' support, pacifying the Baltic states was the major endeavor of the Teutonic Knights in the fourteenth century, plunging into trackless forests of a heathen empire that stretched from the Baltic Sea to Kiev in Russia. To fight the barbarian Lithuanians, the Teutonic Knights welcomed individual Crusaders from across Europe—daring men willing to join the battle against a foe who was cunning, cruel, and willing to kill himself and his colleagues—by mutual beheadings—rather than surrender. By the first decade of the fifteenth century, the Lithuanians were professed Christians and the Teutonic Knights dominated the Baltic Sea. The Knights' territory extended from the river Vistula in what is today northeastern Poland to the Gulf of Finland, incorporating the entirety of the Baltic states.

Now at its height, the Teutonic empire met its nemesis in the king of Poland and the king of Lithuania, cousins tied by blood and resentment of the Knights. They brought an army that included Jan Zizka, future general of the Hussite wars, and all the wildest tribes of Eastern Europe, the Huns, the Cossacks, the Mongol Tartars, and others, against the Knights at a place called Tannenberg in Prussia in 1410. The odds against the Knights and their allies were only two to one—good odds by the Knights' standards. But the Knights' honor and reckless courage demanded an open, frontal assault, and their heavy cavalry charges, while pummeling the wings, could not crack the center of the Polish line. In the fierce fighting that followed, the Knights were enveloped by the Tartar cavalry; and after a day of slaughter, it was the Poles—a motley crew of Catholics, Eastern Orthodox, and heathen—who emerged victorious.

For the rest of the fifteenth century, the Teutonic Knights in Prussia were fighting on the defensive and on the retreat. They sallied forth for occasional victories, but they could not prevent Ordensland from being invaded by the Poles, razed by the fanatical peasant armies of the Hussites, or rent by civil war. To the north, in Latvia and Estonia, the Knights fared better, routinely routing the Russians. But the northern crusade of the Teutonic Knights was over. They had made Prussia and the Baltic states safe for Christianity—if not for themselves—in one of the most extraordinary adventures of the later Middle Ages. To put it baldly, the last European peoples converted to the Catholic faith practiced human sacrifice and dwelt in forests so dark that they drove men mad; these barbarians were saved by monastic knights who created a country of their own, devoting it to Mary, commerce, and knighthood. Such were the borderlands of Christendom, and such were the men who defended them.

## CHAPTER THIRTEEN

# RENAISSANCE

———⟫●⟪———

THE RENAISSANCE POPES had three major objectives: to make the papacy an independent temporal power of its own, dependent on no sovereign king; to restore the grandeur of Rome, in what would become the greatest efflorescence of art and architecture in the history of the world; and to rouse the forces of Christendom to save the Byzantines and repel the Turk after the fall of Constantinople in 1453. To achieve these extraordinary feats, the popes of the fifteenth century were chosen less for their saintly qualities—none of them was canonized—than they were for their administrative, diplomatic, and military skill; their education and culture; and, as far as it could be discerned, their tenacity, a necessary talent to survive in ever turbulent Italy.

The picture of the Renaissance popes as luxury-loving orgiasts, languid and corrupt Borgias poisoning each other, followers of Pope Leo X's apocryphal advice—"Now that God has given us the papacy, let us enjoy it"—is unfortunately false. The Renaissance popes were, in fact, men of the normal religious piety of their times. No doubt they should have been better, but, if not prone to religious enthusiasm, they nevertheless faithfully executed their sacerdotal duties. In a time of increasing secularization, they upheld orthodox Catholic belief.

The myths surrounding the Renaissance popes stem from the propaganda wars waged against them by the powerful Mafiosi families of central Italy with whom they fought to secure the papal lands. Another

factor was the money necessary to finance Rome's reclamation and Renaissance. To fund this, the popes were quite willing to approve the sale
of indulgences—one of the major crimes held against them by later reforming Protestants. This sale of indulgences, however, was not new—except in scale. Nor, the modern reader needs to be reminded, were
indulgences a way to "buy" a plenary forgiveness of sins. An indulgence
only relieved a sinner who had already confessed his sins to a priest of the
burden of penance. In other words, an indulgence was the equivalent of
paying a fine rather than going on a pilgrimage in recompense for one's
sins. Granted, wherever there is money, there is plenty of room—and
plenty is on the factual record—for abuse. Yet if it was the sale of indulgences that paid for the work of Michelangelo and Raphael, it is hard to
think that it was money badly extorted.

The Renaissance popes were men who had to navigate the political
world captured in Machiavelli's *The Prince,* published in 1513. Though
the Church condemned *The Prince,* during his lifetime Machiavelli was
an adviser to two popes—Leo X (1513–1521) and Clement VII (1523–
1534). He based his model prince on Caesar Borgia, whose family itself
gave the Church two popes: Callistus III (1455–1458) and Alexander VI
(1492–1503). Actually, Caesar Borgia was the son of Pope Alexander VI.
But on matters of sex, one can say that some of the Renaissance popes
simply surrendered to their Mediterranean temperament or were prema-
ture Protestants.

There is certainly some truth in the Mediterranean argument if we remember that the Renaissance was a profoundly reactionary time: It identified with the high culture and aesthetic and intellectual standards of the
classical world. It was a true re-immersion in the achievements of historic
Rome, mixing Catholic and classical culture. Another important point is
that the Renaissance was not—as some scholars would have it, and as some
men of the Renaissance themselves believed—a radical break with the medieval world. On the contrary, it was the *fulfillment* of the Middle Ages. It
built on the work of monks who painstakingly transcribed Latin classics
and was bankrolled by a Church that spoke the same language as Caesar.
After the triumphant construction of Christendom, it was only natural that
Italy would rediscover its classical roots, adapting classical models of poetry, sculpture, and other arts to express Christian themes or simply, in
Machiavelli's case, to capture political reality. In addition to *The Prince* and

*The Art of War,* Machiavelli wrote a brilliant book of discourses on the Roman historian Livy—taking history and breaking it down into principles of statecraft. For the West, the classical world has always been the great tutor. In Catholic Rome, Aristotle, Caesar, and Christ became one.

In this rediscovery of the accomplishments of Greece and Rome, the popes themselves were leaders. It was they who amassed the great libraries in this time of the printing press. It was they who commissioned the great building projects, the great statuary, the great paintings of the Renaissance. It was they who were the leading advocates of this explosion of human creativity and genius, and not only in art—in its widest sense—but in science, navigation, and exploration, for this was the period of papal support for such as Leonardo da Vinci and Christopher Columbus. And for all this they would stand condemned by the Protestant reformers. In roughly the same period, the Teutonic Knights Christianized the Prussians and the Balts, only to be assaulted by them in a grand alliance of every wild tribe of northeastern Europe. So, too, the Renaissance popes nurtured the profoundest development of the Christian and classical aesthetic, only to be greeted by a Protestant revolution that insisted on denying the religious relevance of all books but the Bible, rejecting the humanistic culture of the classical world, and declaring irrelevant—or satanic—centuries of Christian doctrine and practice: smashing stained glass, defacing Madonnas, and taking battle-axes to altars, just like the iconoclastic heretics of old.

# THE RESTORATION OF ROME, THE LOSS OF CONSTANTINOPLE

THE BEGINNING of the military and civic rejuvenation of Rome began with Pope Martin V, the first of the post-Avignon popes. The previous papal schism, however, had left the authority of the pope vulnerable to challenge, and after Martin's death the College of Cardinals reached for the levers of power. They wanted a Church governed by councils—like the Council of Constance—that they could control. Martin V had no intention of handcuffing himself to conciliar government, but his successor, Pope Eugene IV (1431–1447), a pious Augustinian monk from a wealthy family, was elected precisely with the understanding that he would be obedient to the Council of Basle, which was already in session.

Eugene IV was a reformer who quickly proved that reform is often synonymous with "making worse." He struck a great blow at papal nepotism by disestablishing the Colonna family from all the papal lands it had been given under Martin V—thus ensuring the return of war and anarchy to central Italy. He dissolved the Council of Basle on the grounds that it did nothing; few members of the Church hierarchy even bothered to attend, and Eugene IV intended to convene a new Council in its place. All true, all irrelevant. The aggrieved cardinals forced Eugene to keep the Council of Basle in session.

Reaping the whirlwind of his war against the Colonna, three years into his pontificate, Eugene was forced to flee revolutionary Rome for Florence, where he was sheltered for nearly a decade. He was further humiliated when the Council of Basle decreed a drastic slashing in papal taxation and a shrinking of the papal court. It was only through the prestige Eugene won by arranging yet another temporary reunion with the Eastern Church in 1439—on terms that again had the Byzantines accepting papal supremacy, the *filioque,* et al.—that he was able to regain the full submission of most of the cardinals, who left Switzerland and the Council of Basle and rejoined him in Italy. A few stayed behind and declared themselves the true Church government, deposed Pope Eugene, and elected an antipope.

At first this seemed a piffling annoyance, until the pope found himself unsupported by the great continental crowns of France and Germany. Conciliar government would have made it easier for the monarchs to subordinate Church to state. So they remained neutral in the dispute, while enacting laws in accordance with the Council, limiting papal powers within their realms. This was especially the case in France, where Gallicanism, a French doctrine of limiting papal power, was in the ascendant.[1] But once Pope Eugene was back in Rome in 1443, the threatened schism passed. No crown endorsed the antipope.

Officially, the first of the Renaissance popes is Nicholas V (1447–1455). A better diplomat than Pope Eugene—who died wishing he had never been called from his monastic life—Pope Nicholas V brought order to Rome and its neighboring territories. He did so in ways Eugene would not have countenanced: cash payments, letting rivals fight amongst themselves, granting independence to unmanageable cities, governing through powerful intermediaries, and other tricks of the diplomatic trade. He swept like a miracle through the courts of Germany and France, restoring papal prerogatives in Germany, getting the French to cooperate in offering the Council of Basle's antipope an honorable retirement, and amenably dissolving the Council itself. At the end of his reign he even achieved a peace concordat between nearly all the major city-states of Italy and the Kingdom of the Two Sicilies. As a Renaissance pope and a man of learning, he refounded the Vatican library with his own massive collection of books and began commissioning Italy's century of unparalleled architectural achievement.

His great reign was darkened, in his own mind, by the fall of Constantinople to Mehmed II, whose nickname was "the Drinker of Blood."[2] The advance of the blood-drinker did not stiffen Byzantine resolve. In fact, nearly half of Constantinople's defenders were from the West. Fewer than 5,000 Byzantines—or just 5 percent of Constantinople's besieged population— were willing to take up arms to defend themselves against a Turkish army of 150,000 men. It was Western mercenaries—3,000 of them—who formed the backbone and leadership of Constantinople's defense.[3] They included the Italian condottiere Giovanni Giustiniani, whom the Byzantine emperor named his commander in chief; the German Johan Grant, who foiled the Turks' attempts to mine the city; and the Spanish knight Don Francis of Toledo who died with the Byzantine emperor, charging the Turks.

When Constantinople collapsed, Rome welcomed such exiles as could escape Turkish scimitars. These survivors brought horrifying tales of murder, mayhem, and the irretrievable loss of the cultural patrimony of Eastern Christianity. It could only depress a humane and scholarly pope like Nicholas V. A harder man, a pope like the future Julius II, would have steeled himself with memories of Frederick Barbarossa; of the Frenchmen who had briefly, gloriously, tried to make the Byzantines French (for their own good); and every other Crusader who had looked with contempt on the Greeks. The Turk had finally crushed enfeebled Byzantium. The Catholic West would prove hardier stock.

# THE BORGIAS AND THE RENAISSANCE POPES

THE NAME BORGIA[4] is the one most linked to the image of "the Renaissance popes," but the first pope from the Borgia family, Callistus III

(1455–1458), was a pious man, even if a lawyer. His noble desire was to retake Constantinople. For the sake of that Crusade he sacrificed gold and silver, art works, and money from the papal treasury. He delayed the rebuilding of Rome to achieve the recapture of Byzantium. Callistus was, if anything, an idealist, but his idealism was met largely with yawns—or financial complaints. Such Western knights as responded to his plea would bloody Turkish noses in Serbia and the Aegean, but there were not enough men for a full-out holy war.[5]

If the monarchs of France, Germany, and England were indifferent to a Crusade against the Turk and resentful of the pope's hectoring and taxing them on its behalf, Callistus was no more popular in Rome. Not only had he halted the brilliant projects of Nicholas V, but he put Spaniards— Catalans to be precise—in positions of authority and appointed two Borgias to the College of Cardinals. Such loyalty to family and country seems a minor vice—yet not to fifteenth-century Italians, who, after Avignon, were hostile to foreigners in the papal court.

More important than such xenophobia, it was Pope Callistus who declared illicit and retrospectively overturned the terrible and fatal conviction of heresy passed in 1431 by a corrupt French court on Joan of Arc. The Maid of Orleans was a devout, visionary, and sword-wielding heroine of France—she essentially won the Hundred Years War for her country. By rescinding her conviction, Pope Callistus undid one of the worst miscarriages of justice since the dissolution of the Templars.[6]

The brave Borgia Callistus was followed by another brave pope, Pius II (1458–1464), who came from that fruitful class—impoverished noblemen: men who know what cultivation and grandeur are; men of character and high calling; men who, however, have to suffer the fates and work the family fields themselves, toiling side by side with peasants to rebuild former greatness. Few upbringings can better prepare one to be a priest.

Pius was educated at the University of Siena, where he was an adept student but undecided whether he should pursue fame and flesh or a priestly and monastic vocation. He deferred that decision and moved to Florence. In this hub of Renaissance culture he read the classics and poetry before returning to Siena and studying law. He became secretary to a succession of bishops, and it appears their example had a salutary effect on him. During a mission to Scotland, Pius crossed seas so stormy that he expected to be drowned. He vowed that if he survived he would make a pilgrimage to a shrine of Mary. Landing on the snow-encased shores of Scotland, he walked barefoot ten miles to make good his pledge.

As a Renaissance pope, it is not surprising that Pius suffered from gout, but it was not acquired from overindulgence. Rather, it came from this pilgrimage redolent of the faith of the Middle Ages. This is not to say that he had finally chosen to become a priest, turning his back on the ways of the flesh. He had not. He had two illegitimate children and consistently refused, at this point, to pursue anything but a secular career within the Church. Indeed, seven years later, at the age of thirty-seven, he joined the court of Frederick III as poet and secretary in the service of the Holy Roman Empire. During this period he wrote a popular and highly risqué novel; an equally risqué dramatic comedy; and a wide variety of histories, essays, poems, and other works. Somewhat later he wrote a well-regarded history of Germany under its king. Later still, he wrote his memoirs.

At the age of forty, after a serious illness, his career moved back to the Church. He became a priest and then, a year later, a bishop. Though now a man of the cloth—and a pious and, finally, celibate one—he continued to serve the Holy Roman Emperor on a variety of diplomatic assignments. At the age of fifty-one, this (one must say it) Renaissance man—classically educated; poet, diplomat, and prelate; equally at home in Italy and Germany—became a cardinal. Within two years, he was pope. He continued to write, though his output was now pontifical.

As with Callistus III, Pope Pius II's attention was fixed on the Turkish threat in the East. To repel the Turk, he tried to create a new monastic military order. But the crowns of Europe—and their affiliated knights—remained unconcerned by the ravaging of the Eastern Christians. While it was impossible to rouse Christendom to fight Turks in the East, it was easy for Catholic princes to keep their swords sharp fighting each other. The focal point was, of course, Italy and the Kingdom of Naples, where the pope decided to support Spanish claims over French ones. It was a matter of balance of power. The result was war.

Actually, throughout Christendom, conflict was rife. Pope Pius II was intent on an unmistakable reaffirmation of papal supremacy over all men of the Church, over councils, over kings, and over compacts with such as the Hussites. This was his right and duty. It was also the only way he could achieve his ends, which were reformist. Indeed, he lived with marked frugality, patronizing artists and learning, but with an eye on saving money for his Crusade; and, though terribly ill throughout his reign, he was a model of generosity and charity, intelligence and devotion. But everywhere he met opposition. In sheer *Realpolitik,* which was the common coin of Renaissance foreign policy, the pope was regarded, respectfully, as a major power. But he was one whose claims kings, heretics, and comfortable clerics had a common interest in limiting or ignoring.

So it is no surprise that Pope Pius II found the straightforward threat of the Turk a more elevating subject than navigating the shoals of internal European affairs. He wrote a letter trying to convert to Catholicism the supposedly agnostic—or perhaps even secretly Christian, after the faith of his mother—sultan of the Islamic Turks. He promised the sultan the title of Eastern emperor and offered visions of a unified faith and another Augustan age. The pope received no response, perhaps because it appears that the letter was never sent. Undaunted, he beat every diplomatic and ecclesiastical drum he could find for a rebirth of the Crusades. When all else failed, he promised to lead the holy war himself. The pope, though sick in body, was the same man who tramped through the snows on his Scottish pilgrimage. He took a Crusader's pledge, journeyed from Rome to Ancona on Italy's Adriatic coast, where knights were to board Venetian ships. There he died, his Crusade dying with him.

The next pope was the handsome—and concomitantly vain (he was an Italian, after all)—Pope Paul II (1464–1471). Having been trained for a business career, he was perhaps shallow, but vanity appears his only serious fault. He, too, was a reformer, opposed to the abuse of indulgences. His reputation suffered, however, because he offended the cardinals who had elected him on a platform of yielding papal power. As pope he repudiated these promises as contrary to the historical—and therefore rightful—prerogatives of the papacy. His reputation also suffered among the humanists, because he cracked the whip on philosophers whose love affair with ancient Rome had spilled over into an advocacy of ancient Roman paganism as well.

If one sets aside disgruntled intellectuals and cardinals, he was the people's pope, with his movie star looks, his magnificent artistic endowments, and his proclaiming of quarterly holy years every century and numerous festivals. Diplomatically, he continued the failed policy of preaching Crusade against the Turks. But he proved innovative in other diplomatic maneuvers. He allied an anti-Turkish Iranian prince with Rome. He also nearly brought the schismatic Russian Orthodox Church to obedience. His method was to marry a princess from the Catholic royal house of Byzantium to Ivan III. Only the pope's death prevented him from achieving it, though we can perhaps shed sympathy for the poor girl who was spared this fate. An Eastern Orthodox Byzantine princess took her place. Ivan III proclaimed himself the inheritor of Byzantium, Caesar (or Czar), and declared Moscow the Third Rome, now that Christian Constantinople was no more. Somehow it did not occur to Ivan that there could only be one Rome and that is Rome. Thus Russia—even then renowned for its cruelty, a place where "terrible" meant "great"—became the seat of the Eastern schism, and Ivan a *refusenik* to papal entreaties to join a Crusade. The fact that Ivan III hired Italian architects to pretty up Moscow and died an alcoholic has never been enough to redeem him in Catholic eyes.

But while the Third Rome went the way of eye-gouging, tongue-ripping, and various other sports so enjoyed by the new leader of Byzantium, the successor to handsome Paul II was a Franciscan, a poor boy made good, Sixtus IV (1471–1484). With a previous reputation for scholarship, inspired preaching, and an unstained private life, as pope he seemed determined to prove that he was no unworldly monk, that he could be as Machiavellian as Italian politics required, that he was fit to lead the universal Church. In a time of growing nationalism and individual self-assertion, he meant to tame the combination of mobs and stiletto-wielding nobles who made chaos the natural condition of Italy. It is this aspect of his character that makes him the first of the Renaissance popes as advertised.

On the good side, this meant that he was a splendid patron of literature, music, architecture, painting, and sculpture. He dramatically accelerated the rebirth of Rome as a glorious and imposingly beautiful city of churches. He ordered the building of bridges, waterworks, roads, and the Sistine Chapel. He had workmen drain pestilential swamps and erect hospitals. He was also a great benefactor of the Franciscans, and a restrainer of zealotry in the Spanish Inquisition, which began in his pontificate.[7] On the flip side, his papacy was marked by ward politics, nepotism, and territorial and familial wars in Italy—with the pope ceremoniously blessing the artillery that served him. All this can be excused—if questioned—by the need to impose order on a disorderly people and secure safety for the bishop of Rome.

His massive expenditures meant selling indulgences on an ever greater scale, charging fees for Church appointments (as royal governments charged fees for state appointments), and other moneymaking schemes, including taking the papacy into the grain business. Even so, Pope Sixtus IV left a cavernous debt in the papal treasury—a situation not helped by his familial appointees who wenched, feasted, drank, and attired themselves in a manner fit to stun the proletariat and sober-minded papal accountants (if such there were).

What is truly amazing about all this is that the frenzied score-settling, vendettas, murders, raids, and wars that happily occupied all the leading families of the grand cities of Italy, including the pope in Rome, nonchalantly coexisted with this prodigious outpouring of painters, sculptors, and architects who were taking artistic creativity to empyrean heights, their work dedicated to religious themes.

The frenzy of chaos and culture, murder and majesty continued during the pontificate of Innocent VIII (1484–1492). At first it appeared that the mob now had the upper hand in the roaming street warfare. But the Roman nobility, with their private armies, took a break from fighting each other to restore order for the election of a new pope.

Innocent VIII, like Pius II, had been a father before he became a Father. Once a priest, he was true to his vows, though his past indiscretions were far from hidden. The pope surrounded himself with his children and grandchildren like any other proud Roman paterfamilias. Innocent VIII is a Renaissance pope easily imaginable with a cardigan, slippers, and pipe, content to delegate authority and trust to the laissez-faire of God's will. The Eternal City was crime-ridden, corrupt, violent, and spectacular. It was so before Pope Sixtus's wars; it was so after. So Pope Innocent VIII was content for his cardinals to employ guards and armies, secure themselves in homes built like fortresses, and carry on the basic functions of the Renaissance papacy. They opposed heresy, conducted the international diplomacy of the Church,[8] and raised vast sums of money to retire the papal debt and advance the art and splendor of Rome.

The poster boy of Renaissance popes is Pope Alexander VI (1492–1503), the Spanish-born Rodrigo Borgia, whose uncle was Pope Callistus

III. He took the name "of the invincible Alexander" for the very same reason that he named his son Caesar and that he was followed in St. Peter's throne by Pope Julius II. These were men who meant to be imperial conquerors: Alexanders and Caesars for Christ's Church.

Rodrigo Borgia was a cardinal before he became a priest, and avoided taking holy orders until he was thirty-seven years old. Unlike the popes before him, adding a cleric's collar did not change his life. He simply ignored his priestly vow of celibacy. But if Pope Alexander VI found Italy's romantic sensualism to his taste, it was a sensualism limited, for the suave and handsome pope, to women. To the excesses of food, drink, or riotous living, he was immune. He was a man of long hours spent executing his responsibilities. He was also, even notoriously, a man of familial bonds. If there is a loyalty among adulterers, he was loyal to the mistress who bore him his children. Early in his career, the Church had officially reproved him for the irregularities of his private life, but the Church also recognized him as an extremely gifted administrator. He could dispatch his duties with alacrity and skill; discoursed intelligently, pleasantly, and effectively with the elite; and had a flair for showmanship, treating the Roman mob, for example, to a Spanish bullfight when the Moors were finally driven from Spain in 1492.

His enthronement was one of the great spectacles of modern Roman history, with parades of priests, cardinals, and knights from across Europe, marching under *arcs de triomphe* laden with flowers, replicating the drama of massed imperial legions, captured beasts, and enshackled barbarians witnessing the installation of a new Augustus. Like a new Augustus, he proved himself a lawgiver, immediately striking out—via swift enforcement of the death penalty—against the lawless of Rome, a strategy that worked and was ascribed by the people to the power of God exercised through the Vicar of Christ.

He launched his own building projects, which had a more martial, castellated air than those of his predecessors—structures both magnificent and militarily defensible. His administrative skills were on display as he quickly balanced the Vatican's treasury, streamlined and regularized its operations, and presided over the spectacular Jubilee Celebration of 1500. Thousands upon thousands of pilgrims came to Rome to celebrate their loyalty to the Church, their trust that sins could be forgiven, and to mark a millennium and a half of Catholic history. Amid such strength and self-assurance, he was also a friend of the Jews, as well as of artists, dramatists, architects, scholars (the University of Rome was rebuilt at his command), and priestly missionaries. His tolerance of criticism fed—iron-ically—the mythmaking of his political enemies who made him notorious in history. "Rome is a free city," the pope said indulgently, "where every-one can say or write whatever he pleases. They say much evil of me, but I don't mind."[9]

As a statesman, he acted as a Solomon, dividing the new worlds of the East Indies and the Americas between the two great exploring nations of Iberia: Portugal and Spain. His children—to whom he was singularly devoted—were used as connubial diplomats. They became papal emis-saries for European peace, binding together alliances of blood in the man-ner of a noble family. Though his children were living embodiments of his peccadilloes, Pope Alexander VI upheld orthodox Catholic doctrine and theology;[10] he saw no reason why his own failings should lower the stan-dards and requirements of the Church.

The other aspect of Alexander VI that scandalizes the fainthearted is his practice of power politics in Italy. Using his golden-haired genius of a son Caesar as his general, he beat the noble families of central Italy—and their private armies—into submission, recovering the papal lands for the Church in military campaigns of stunning celerity and success. Of course, to fund the wars, retire papal debt, and pay for the restoration of Rome, Alexander reverted to the sale of indulgences and offices.

Such financial necessities brought critics. Critics also sprang from these ever-rebellious nobles, now crushed, who waged a propaganda war against the Borgias. Joining their chorus—though with completely differ-ent ends in mind—was the fanatic and puritanical Dominican monk Savonarola. Preaching apocalyptic warnings about the pagan culture of the Renaissance and the pope, he instituted a democratic republic in Flo-rence based on the principle of spying on one's neighbor and consigning vain adornments and pictures to the flames—"the bonfire of the vani-ties."[11] Pope Alexander, typically, tolerated Savonarola's ravings. But when Savonarola refused papal discipline, he was excommunicated. The mad monk expostulated: "Whoever excommunicates me excommunicates God,"[12] which unintentionally affirmed the wisdom of the excommunica-tion. The people of Florence soon had their fill of him and turned him over to the pope's men, who tortured and condemned him for preaching schism and heresy.[13] Before he was executed, Savonarola was offered, through the authority of the pope, a full remission of his sins and a restoration to communion, which he accepted.

Joining the propaganda war against the Borgia pope were increasing numbers of prickly Romans who saw him, in repetition of Callistus III, filling ecclesial offices with not only family members but—worse—Spaniards rather than Italians. Vile calumnies were circulated about all members of the family. Especially targeted, because of their high profiles, were Caesar Borgia and his sister Lucrezia. Caesar was a gifted hard man. Machiavelli called him "splendid and magnificent."[14] He was handsome and physically imposing, had a powerful practical intellect, and employed Leonardo da Vinci as his chief military engineer. Caesar Borgia specifically renounced a Church career to fight and politick in the manner of an Italian prince. His sister Lucrezia is a different matter. She is one of the most unjustly libeled and slandered figures in history, being in truth (and in contrast to the lurid imaginations of dramatists) a model of Renaissance Christian and feminine virtue: charming, educated, beautiful, pious.

The crowning public relations defeat for Alexander VI, however, came after his death, when Julius II, his long-standing enemy in the College of Cardinals, succeeded him.[15] Julius (1503–1513) was as much a Renaissance pope as Alexander. He, too, had illegitimate children. He, too, was devoted to the military and artistic glorification of the Church. Their differences were those of contestants for power; and in that pursuit, Julius schemed, complained, and willingly endorsed scandalous accounts against his enemy Alexander. Where Alexander laughed at his critics, never losing his equipoise, Julius was fearsome. He was happiest when camped on a battlefield with his papal troops, wearing armor and sleeping rough. His countenance often flashed anger. He had determined ideas. He was a man, in sum, perfectly suited for his time. He could fruitfully argue with the finest collection of artists ever employed by a statesman, and he happily led the pikes, swords, and cannons that were the only guarantor of order.

Unlike Alexander, Julius did not rely on his children for diplomatic, military, and political gain; he never sought to advance them within the Church. He relied on himself. He was simultaneously pope and his own Caesar Borgia, waging successful campaigns for papal territory against the local, petty tyrants who had supplanted the Church. With the tyrants tamed by the cannon's mouth, he turned against the Italian ambitions of the French. Though he had once conspired with the French against Alexander VI, he now formed a league—made up of Venice (which he had earlier fought and brought to submission), Spain, the England of King Henry VIII (whom Julius authorized to marry Catherine of Aragon), Germany, and Switzerland—against French interference in Italy. The Holy League was a success, and Julius II was the liberator of Italy, riveting the Papal States so firmly to the Church that they would not be unhinged again for another 360 years.

He was also the patron of Bramante, Michelangelo, and Raphael, among other builders and artists whose works have outlasted the territorial gains of the papal lands. To the modern reader, they are Julius's greatest and most awe-inspiring testament. Indeed, his martial and artistic triumphs overshadow the more strictly religious activities of his pontificate, though it was under Julius that bishoprics were established in the New World. He struck a blow against the memory of Alexander by abolishing simony, balanced the books despite his heavy expenditure on war and art, and necessarily continued the sale of indulgences to achieve his aims. He was one of the most intimidating popes in history—and popular for all that. It was his contemporary Machiavelli who wrote that it is better to be feared than to be loved. Such lessons came from the rough politics of the Italian Renaissance.

The last Renaissance pope before the explosion of the Reformation was Pope Leo X (1513–1521). Leo was from the Medici family and had been groomed since boyhood for the papacy. His talents were apparent, as he won election without bribery—a rare thing in the Renaissance.[16] Pope Leo X was not only educated in theology and canon law, but had traveled throughout Europe, and was a humanist, tutored in all the arts from literature to music to every other expression of man's creative calling. Such a humanistic training was itself religious. For the Renaissance had the artistic rendition of Biblical themes and papal history as it greatest accomplishment, however freely it employed classical forms and mythology, however devoted it was to a realistic depiction of the anatomy and physiognomy of Italian man, making man the centerpiece. In the Renaissance, the vines of the classical world and the Christian world, of Rome, were seen as intertwined. It was a historically minded culture where artists' representations of Cupid and the Madonna, of Hercules and St. Peter could exist side-by-side.

Leo did more than study and appreciate the finer things. He earned his spurs as an administrator. One of his assignments was with the papal army, an odd task for such a jovial and well-fed man, as Leo was known to be, though he was a keen hunter. As a temporal prince, he was a pragmatist. He granted ecclesiastical rights to the crown of France in exchange for French concessions in Italy. He left Florence in the hands of the Medici family. He maintained the papal call for a Crusade against the Turks, but knew perfectly well it would be ignored. He was content with that, because the real focus of his pontificate was the glorification of the Church through artistic and intellectual achievement. To that end he was a spendthrift. He was equally liberal in charity to monasteries, hospitals, and individuals. He endorsed huge expenses for civic improvements and celebrations in Rome. To pay for these massive benefactions, Leo X dramatically increased the sales of indulgences, required papal appointees to purchase their offices, and employed other financial measures that called forth the denunciations of an obscure German monk named Luther.

Leo paid little attention to Luther—and why should he, when he surrounded himself with Leonardo da Vinci, Michelangelo, Raphael (his favorite), Bramante, Ariosto, painters, sculptors, poets, architects, musicians, dramatists, wits, craftsmen, and scholars? At the University of Rome, he was an especial patron of studies in ancient languages; he venerated the classics. He wrote that "nothing more excellent or useful has been given by the Creator to mankind—if we except only knowledge and true worship of Himself—than these studies, which not only lead to the ornament and guidance of human life, but are applicable and useful to every particular situation, consoling in adversity, pleasing and honorable in prosperity; insomuch that without them we should be deprived of all the grace of life and all the polish of society."[17]

Pope Leo's interests went beyond classical literature to archaeological digs and the preservation of classical statuary, architecture, and art. His court, says the historian Will Durant, for sheer "quantity of culture" had never been equaled, "not even in Periclean Athens or Augustan Rome."[18] Leo X, however, did not understand—or did not think it was important—how much this learning and culture, and the papal fund-raising machine that had to pay for it, offended the looming Protestant sensibility. While the pope raised European civilization to its highest level, Protestants were, largely unnoticed, planting explosives beneath its foundation. They, like Savonarola, wanted to consign the works of the Renaissance to the bonfire of the vanities.

If Leo paid little heed to these guerilla voices, it was not only because Rome was a city beautiful to look at and full of sparkling conversation, but because it had become rich. Italian businessmen, investors, international merchants, and fortune-seekers followed the papal patronage that had rebuilt swampy, ruined, malarial, and murderous Rome and resurrected it as the capital of Christendom, where led all roads of scholarship, diplomacy, culture, commerce, and the Church. While morals were relaxed, virtue was still praised. If Renaissance Italians indulged the ways of the flesh, they did so while recognizing that others led better lives. Luther's mind could not understand this paradox. He was appalled by what he saw in Rome. Meanwhile a Catholic reformer of the most liberal stripe, Erasmus, found Leonine Rome a marvel of learning, beauty, and civilization.

It seems tragic that at this moment of triumph—of Rome restored— the very ideal of Christendom would be shattered. It would be the worst calamity in Western history since the fall of the Roman Empire. Again, the trouble came from a turbulent semi-barbarian from beyond the Danube.

# VIVA IBERIA

BEFORE WE MOVE on to the Reformation, let us stay awhile in the Renaissance, for Spain and Portugal had their own version. Through the simultaneous conquests of their shipmen, Catholicism stretched from Europe into the New World, Africa, and the Orient. Helmsmen with grand dreams and unlikely maps took ships where no European memory existed. They packed priests aboard with rough-hewn sailors, soldiers, and adventurers on voyages that could lead to death, disease, and destruction—or glory.

It began with Henry the Navigator of Portugal (1394–1460), who devoted himself to the exploration of western Africa. He sought Prester John, a mythical Christian king, and succeeded in making his country an imperial power. Portugal became a leader in the slave trade, muscling in on a business that was previously monopolized by Muslims from the desert and animists in black Africa. Portugal also became a leader in cartography and naval science. Henry himself encouraged the study of mathematics and medicine—things that would aid his explorers—and sent missionaries into West Africa, what would later be known as "the White Man's grave" because of malaria and other disabilities of its climate. Following in Henry's wake was Bartholomew Diaz, who found the Cape of Good Hope.

Then came Spain. In 1492, the last remnant of the Moors was driven from España. That same year, Christopher Columbus, an Italian captain, pledged himself to the service of Spain's King Ferdinand and Queen Isabella to find a new route to the riches of India. Instead, he found that the American continents were in the way, though he never confessed as much, insisting that these were, in fact, outcroppings of the Orient and that the natives were Indians. Another Italian, who sailed at different times for Portugal and Spain, Amerigo Vespucci, finally set the courts of Iberia straight on what they had discovered; and a Spaniard, Vasco Nuñez de Balboa, found that on the other side lay the Pacific.

The sea route to India, meanwhile, was actually found by another Portuguese, Vasco da Gama, who followed the route of Bartholomew Diaz around South Africa but then continued up Africa's east coast and across to India. Through the work of Columbus and da Gama, the Catholic Church gained a foothold on both the Indian subcontinent and in the New World. Catholic missionaries ranged from the Azores to the ports of West Africa, South Africa, East Africa, to Aden, Portuguese India, the islands of the Far East, and entrepôts in China.

With the explorers came conquerors, the new Crusaders, the Conquistadors. They were men like Juan Ponce de León, who put the Spanish ashore at Florida; Francisco Pizarro, who defeated the Incas and seized Peru; and Hernando Cortez, who toppled the Aztecs and conquered Mexico, bearing as his standard the motto of Constantine, *in hoc signo vinces*. Soldiering with Cortez was Bernal Díaz, whose remarkable account *The Conquest of New Spain* detailed how a relative handful of Spaniards— nearly all lacking guns, armor, or horses—routinely thrashed thousands of Indians at a time. Spanish victories were marked by a literal whitewashing of the bloodstained temples of Indian human sacrifice; the temples were then converted to Catholic churches or shrines to the Virgin Mary; the Indians were lectured that the days of ritual human sacrifice, cannibalism, and the feeding of human beings to wild beasts were over. The Conquistadors respected the Aztec chieftain Montezuma, as the Saladin of these New World Saracens; but it says something, too, that the Spaniards were able to enlist the other tribes of Mexico as allies against the Aztecs in a conquest that began in 1519 and was fully accomplished by 1521.

Spanish priests not only quickly established churches, but turned their hands and minds to constructing towns, aqueducts, hospitals, and schools for the Indians. They also taught themselves the Indian languages, and, in turn, taught the Indians Latin, among other subjects. But from the beginning in New Spain, the Church, while often working hand in glove with representatives of the Spanish crown, found itself battling for the rights of the Indians against the abuses of the Conquistador states. In 1537, for instance, at papal command, the Indians living in Spanish colonies were guaranteed equal rights as fellow communicants in the Catholic Church. Under unstinting pressure from the Mexican bishop Bartolome de Las Casas—who had arrived in the New World with Columbus and was supported by Queen Isabella—the use of Indians as slaves was officially forbidden by Spanish law. If Indian slavery was thus curtailed on the margins, the practice continued in fact, at a high cost of Indian life—though by far the higher cost came from the Indians' exposure to Western diseases, like smallpox. Indian labor shortfalls were made up with slaves imported from Africa. Churchmen admonished the soldier-conquerors that abuse of the native people—however primitive the Indians might seem—would endanger the salvation of the Spaniards themselves. Spanish friars in the New World continually warned the Conquistador-rulers that the Indians—even the non-Catholic Indians who seemed too dense to grasp the faith—were protected by Christ's admonition to treat one's neighbor as oneself.

In 1531 that truth was underlined in a shocking way. The Virgin Mother appeared as an Indian to a poor Indian, telling him she wanted a church built where she stood; as proof of her instruction and her identity she imprinted her image on a serape for the Indian to deliver to the skeptical local bishop. That serape now hangs in the church that was built on the spot.[19] Given the superiority the conquering Spaniards felt over their Indian subjects, it is surprising that the Spaniards themselves accepted the miracle and worshiped at a shrine to an Indian Mary, unless they honestly believed in the apparition. The Marian vision certainly had an enormous evangelical result: It is estimated that eight million Mexicans were baptized over the next seven years because of it.[20]

The monarchs behind Spain's expansion were Ferdinand and Isabella. She was a woman of the highest Christian character. He was another hard man, more feared than loved, and admired by Machiavelli. He had one obvious testimonial: He took a divided nation of separate kingdoms, partially occupied by the Moors, and unified it, making it a world power.

This process included the Spanish Inquisition. The Crown appointed the inquisitors, and the purpose of the Spanish Inquisition was quite blatantly to ferret out Quislings and internal enemies of the state. Their property, if they were found guilty, could be forfeited to King Ferdinand, or publicly auctioned, or transferred to the inquisitors. It paid for Ferdinand to have enemies, and Spain's unity advanced—it appeared—with his personal enrichment.

There were a few checks on the system. First, though appointed by the crown, the clerics were officially under Church discipline, and the Church did have a softening effect on the Inquisition, which would have been far harsher had it been a purely secular affair. Second, the courts had authority only over professed Christians—Jews and Moslems were exempt. The targets, in fact, were often converts, whose motives and behavior were held as suspect. Again, as with the earlier inquisitions, it is well to keep in mind that heresy was at this time, and would be in both Catholic and Protestant Europe, a capital crime, and the methods of the inquisition, even in Spain, were not much different from those of other courts. If anything the inquisition's courts were more lenient than those of the later Protestant witch-finders. The inquisition, for instance, treated witchcraft as a sign of insanity rather than heresy.[21]

The Spanish Inquisition began under Ferdinand and Isabella in 1478. As with the conquest of New Spain, the papacy quickly heard of abuses and tried, ineffectively, to stop them. The Church appointed Tomas Torquemada as the Inquisition's overseer. Torquemada's idea of reform was to expel all Jews—and later all Muslims—from Spain. King Ferdinand liked this approach and backed his inquisitor-general against papal attempts to limit his power. A contemporary Spanish historian called Torquemada "the hammer of heretics, the light of Spain, the savior of his country, the honor of his order,"[22] which puts in perspective the opinion of

Spaniards at the time. The clergy and religious in Spain were as subject to the Inquisition as anyone. Even future saints, like Teresa of Avila and Ignatius Loyola, were called to account for their orthodoxy. Spain was rejecting centuries of occupation and defining itself as a fully Catholic state.

The Spanish Inquisition remained a part of Spanish life for 350 years—that is, until the early nineteenth century. Modern scholarship has since established beyond doubt that the litany of abuses and crimes that have made the phrase "the Spanish Inquisition" notorious was dramatically overblown by a torrent of Protestant and secularist propaganda to which the Church—as in the case of the Renaissance popes—did not even bother to respond, especially as anti-Spanish Catholics in Italy and elsewhere eagerly joined the propaganda effort.[23] Though statistics are always open to dispute, it appears safe to say that far fewer people perished in 350 years' worth of the Spanish Inquisition (perhaps 4,000)[24] than were killed in a single day in the American Civil War. The comparison isn't flip, for the issues were similar—defining what it meant to be a Spaniard (or an American) and the limits of dissent (either in religion or in the right to self-determination, states' rights, secession, and slavery). In Spain, where centuries had been spent fighting the Moor, orthodoxy in religion became the very definition of a Spaniard, so much so that Spain, despite her empire, and her gold mines in the New World, never became a commercial power. The Spanish mind was consumed with visions of glory that demanded of its men careers as clerics or soldiers. If Christianity teaches humility, the Spaniard embraced the equally true, if reverse, Christian value of the dignity of every human being; and every Spaniard took up the gauntlet of honor. While chivalry expired as the Middle Ages developed into the Renaissance, in Spain, Cervantes would pen *Don Quixote,* a wonderful satire on how even the threadbare but prideful Spaniard envisioned himself as a knight, as a Conquistador.

Because of the Inquisition, Spain never suffered the internecine religious warfare unleashed by the Protestant Reformation (except in the Spanish Netherlands). Compared to the blood that would soon be shed between Protestant and Catholic, and between Protestant and rival Protestant sect, the blood on the hands of the Spanish inquisitors is but a thimbleful. Between 1551 and 1600, for example, the Spanish Inquisition claimed an average of four lives a year[25]—making Spain by far Christendom's safest haven in this time of religious strife. Nevertheless, tortures and judicial executions did occur, numbering in the thousands, and are repellant, no matter what the context, no matter how limited in comparison to what went on beyond the Pyrenees. But the context is important if for no other reason than to show that the Spanish Inquisition, in its rooting out of heresy or religious opposition, was far from unique—and to serve as a reminder of this somber fact: Far worse was to come.

## CHAPTER FOURTEEN

# TURKS AND PROTESTANTS

⟢⟐⟐⟐⟐

H ERE STOOD WESTERN EUROPE, united as Christendom, exploring new continents, reaching its cultural apogee in the Renaissance—and about to be blown to smithereens by a disgruntled monk.

There was, however, one man who exerted every sinew of his being to hold Christendom together—one man who simultaneously kept the Turks out of Europe, waylaid the Islamic corsairs who raided the Mediterranean, and more devotedly than anyone sought to defend the orthodox Catholic faith and keep Christianity from being smashed into a congeries of squabbling sects.

The Habsburg emperor Charles V is not well treated by historians, but he is this man. The papacy feared his strength, while it relied on his muscle. He was the perfect embodiment of Renaissance Catholic civilization outside Italy.

## THE KNIGHT OF THE GOLDEN FLEECE

HE CAME FROM THE HOUSE of Habsburg, a German-Swiss-Austrian family that now, through marriage, had brought the Netherlands, Spain, and Spain's New World possessions into one enormous empire on which "the sun never set"—a phrase the Habsburgs could claim before the British. The family was imperial and Catholic and had a familial sense of a shared European culture. Charles's primary language was French. His brother Ferdinand preferred Spanish. By blood they were German. Charles was raised in Burgundy. His childhood tutor was Adrian of Utrecht—a pious Dutch scholar who later became Pope Hadrian VI, and who, like his countryman Erasmus, supported reform of the Church.

When Charles defended the faith before Luther's assaults, he did so as one "born of the most Christian emperors of the noble German nation, of the Catholic Kings of Spain, the Archdukes of Austria, the Dukes of Burgundy, who were all to the death true sons of the Roman Church, defenders of the Catholic Faith, of the sacred customs, decrees and usages of worship, who have bequeathed all this to me as my heritage, according to whose example I have hitherto lived."[1]

Another inheritance of Charles was the Habsburgs' own order of chivalry, the Order of the Golden Fleece, which, in true Renaissance style, combined classical imagery with Catholic purpose. The Golden Fleece was transposed with the Lamb of God, the Argonauts with the Crusaders. When Charles fought Turks in North Africa, his victory was celebrated as a repeat of Rome triumphing over Carthage, complete with a triumphal parade in the Eternal City. His favorite book was Thucydides' *History of the Peloponnesian War.* In his retirement he translated French chivalric poetry into Spanish.

Charles was elected Holy Roman Emperor in 1519. Pope Leo X had opposed him, backing instead Francis I of France. The pope regarded the French as the traditional, necessary check on the power of the Holy Roman Empire. Under the Habsburgs, the empire would sweep across the entirety of Europe, from Spain to Austria, with Charles also heir to much of Italy through the Kingdom of Naples and the city of Milan, placing Rome directly between the jaws of the most powerful lion in Christendom.

But as emperor, Charles became Christendom's most ardent defender. In 1521, at the Diet of Worms, the twenty-year-old monarch condemned the rebellious monk Martin Luther by imperial right to punish heresy. He was Pope Leo X's ally in a war against France when the French became the greater threat to papal lands. He stayed loyal to the Church even when the vacillating Pope Clement VII turned against him out of fear, allying the papacy with France and the independent city-states of Italy.

But when the French were defeated and Francis I was captured in battle, Charles's imperial troops in Italy—many of whom were German Lutherans—grew so angry at their privations that they slipped from their officers' control and sacked Rome for eight days in 1527. They hanged one future pope—Julius III—by his hair, and raped, robbed, pillaged, and killed thousands of people.

Before this imperial sack of Rome, the papacy had viewed the Lutheran revolt as a distraction from fighting the Turk. Now the pope was finally confronted with the full, brutal reality of Protestantism-in-arms—something that Charles, as sovereign of Germany, knew all too well. Since Luther's break with the Church, the main Protestant contribution to civilization had been the bloodiest peasant uprising in the history of Europe (1524–1526), devastating Germany. Now Lutheran troops defaced the Vatican, dressed themselves as clerics, held mock—and sacrilegious—Catholic ceremonies, kidnapped the pope, and even threatened to eat him. After that experience, Pope Clement found it easier to accept Charles as an ally against the common enemy—the Turk—rather than contest with him for primacy on the Italian peninsula. The pope's priority remained the same: Repelling the Turks who had overrun Hungary was far more important than defeating the Protestants who had overrun Germany. The new schismatics could eventually be reconciled; the Turk had to be stopped.

The initial showdown between the Holy Roman Empire and the Turk was at Vienna, which was besieged in 1529. The odds were stiff against the defending Catholic army. The Turks, under Suleiman the Magnificent, brought 120,000 men and unmatched heavy artillery against not quite 17,000 Catholic soldiers. Even the disparity in numbers doesn't reflect the full odds against the Catholic forces.

Their emperor, Charles, was like the Dutch boy, trying to plug every hole in the dike of Christian civilization while mischievous troublemakers relentlessly poked him with cattle prods. Tickling Charles' back was a sword wielded by the French king, Francis I, secretly allied with the Turk, in Francis's ever mischievous attempts to upend the emperor who overshadowed the glory of France. In the emperor's own heartland, Germany, Protestant princes cheered the relentless Ottoman advance, for theirs was the shared goal of shattering Christendom like a glass. To the east, in Ottoman-occupied Hungary, where the Turks made slaves of thousands and left areas desolate of human life, collaborationist Hungarians assisted the Ottomans against the Catholic power that would liberate Austria and Hungary.

But Charles was a true *stupor mundi,* a Catholic inheritor of Frederick II, an Atlas who trusted that his armies, wherever they fought, against whatever numbers, would succeed in slapping away every threat to Christendom, to a Europe united by the Church. The Catholic commanders at Vienna were Count Nicholas von Salm, a military éminence grise, and Marshal Wilhelm von Rogendorf. Their troops: tough, German-speaking regulars—professionals, mercenaries, the fearsome *Landsknechts,* the *Doppelsöldners*—as well as seven hundred elite Spanish gunmen led by Luis de Avalos.

By the time the Catholic soldiers had taken their positions and built defensive works, the city was entirely surrounded. It was an island in an Ottoman sea, but an island from which the Austrian defenders made occasional daring sallies that threw the besiegers into a panic. Away from the cannon, bowmen, and sharpshooters, half the battle was fought underground in tunnels beneath the city and the encircling Ottoman camp. The Austrians stuffed explosives down Turkish mineshafts or met the Ottomans in claustrophobic hand-to-hand combat. For two weeks, the battle carried on—the Austrians, fiercely determined; the Turks, frustrated, exasperated, and finally beaten. On their retreat, the Turks slaughtered thousands of Christian hostages. The chivalric Catholic soldiers discovering this outrage mounted a pursuit and harried the Ottoman retreat into a full-fledged disaster of abandoned wagons, animals, and Moslems lying dead in the first deep Austrian snows.

As the ancient Romans held back the Parthians, so the Holy Roman Empire held back the Turk. Christendom was saved for the moment—at least from its external enemies—but the Turks were a continual call on the military forces of the Holy Roman Empire. Not only were troops engaged in Austria-Hungary. They were also engaged along the Mediterranean coastline. Here the Knights of the Golden Fleece found allies in the Knights Hospitaller who had patrolled the eastern Mediterranean for two centuries. During that time, the Hospitallers had been headquartered on the Isle of Rhodes, daringly close to the Turkish mainland—too close, in fact, to withstand the final great siege of Rhodes mounted by the Turks in 1522. So heroic was the Knights' defense that Charles V said of it, "nothing in the world was so well lost as Rhodes."[2] The chivalric emperor, at the request of Pope Clement VII, gave the Knights a new base on the Isle of Malta in 1530. Five years later, Charles himself led a brilliant and victorious campaign against Tunis, the capital of Islamic piracy.

But no victory is ever final, and Charles spent his entire reign defending against Turks in the east, the French in the west, and Protestants in the north. All the while, the French, the Turks, and even the mercantile city-states of Italy sometimes made overt common cause against him. The constant campaigning wore him down, and in 1555, he began transferring power to his brother Ferdinand and his son Philip II of Spain. Charles eased into a Spanish retirement to indulge his love of art and religion, rather than practice war and diplomacy. In 1558, feeling the cold hand of death, he kept before him a portrait of his late wife and the works of Titian, his favorite painter. After receiving extreme unction, he asked to attend a Mass. Though the priest told him it was unnecessary, Charles commented, "It may not be necessary, but it is good company for so long a journey."[3] He died clasping the same crucifix that his wife had held when she breathed her last.

Charles's greatest victories had been those of a Crusader against the Turks. With the Protestants, his subjects in northern Germany, he had long hoped for a rapprochement through an ecumenical council called by the pope. But there was little room for negotiation. The chief issue of the Protestant Reformation was never better expressed than by Charles himself when he said of Luther: "It is preposterous that a single monk should be right in his opinion and that the whole of Christianity should be in error a thousand years or more."[4] Preposterous, yes, but powerful forces supported it, and in the end they created a sort of "moronic inferno"[5] that left a chasm of fire between the historic faith of the Catholic Church and the endless varieties of Protestantism.

# MARTIN LUTHER,
## *ZERSTÖRER VON DIE CHRISTENHEIT*

IT WAS THE WORST CATACLYSM to befall the Western world since the sack of Rome in 410, and in some ways Rome was again the issue. It is no accident that when the dust settled upon the wars of the Reformation—a process that took more than a century—Catholic Europe had retrenched itself behind the old borders of the Roman Empire. True, North

Africa, the Middle East, and many of the provinces east of the Adriatic belonged to the Mussulman, and under the Mussulman's yoke could be found the Eastern Orthodox. But the heart of the empire of Augustus, Trajan, and Marcus Aurelius remained Catholic: Italy, France, Spain, Austria, what would become Belgium, and southern and western Germany. Joining the empire were parts of Hungary and Poland and most of Ireland. England, linked to Rome since its invasion by Julius Caesar in 55 B.C., was separated from the faith almost by accident. Its King Henry VIII was such a vocal opponent of Martin Luther that Pope Leo X awarded him the title "defender of the faith." Henry died thinking of himself as a Catholic. The Anglican settlement that was finally reached under Elizabeth I created a national church that claimed to be both Protestant and simultaneously part of the "one, holy, catholic, and apostolic Church." Beyond Hadrian's Wall, where Romans had feared to tread, there was no such ambivalence. The blue-painted Scots adopted the starker creed of John Calvin and John Knox.

Thus the Protestant revolt took power in what had been the barbarian provinces beyond the gates of Rome, in countries with fewer centuries of high civilization and Christianity: the Nordic countries, northern Germany, parts of old Helvetia (Switzerland), parts of what became the Netherlands, and Scotland. All the barbaric peoples who had gaped and mocked at the legions of Rome and later plundered Rome's empire now rose again in a new barbarian assault against Roman authority. Their objective was overturning the Roman power, not reconciling with it. If Charles V was the new Stilicho, a Roman of barbarian blood trying desperately to plug every hole in Rome's defense, the new Alaric was an ill-tempered, unbalanced, and unhappy monk, Martin Luther, who himself said that his monastery in Wittenberg, Saxony, was just one mile from the barbarians.[6]

Luther propounded a barbarian creed that had no need for priests or their sacraments—something suited to frontier peoples. As the barbarians saw Rome as decadent and unworthy of their support, so too did the Protestants see Roman Catholicism as decadent, its wayward clergy too corrupt to offer sacramental grace. While Catholics viewed the priesthood and the sacraments as a historical continuity of their incarnational faith—the expression of an entire Christian civilization—the Protestants saw a celibate priesthood and most of the sacraments as ir-

relevant: as irrelevant as Christian art, pagan philosophy, and an authoritative Church. With Luther, the people would themselves become "the
priesthood of all believers."

The founder and *primus inter pares* of this priesthood, Martin
Luther, was originally a servant of the Church, though not out of a sense
of fidelity or spiritual calling. He became a monk to escape and affront
his abusive parents—both of whom beat him severely. Luther's father was
not a Catholic, but an occultist who believed in darker Germanic witches,
hobgoblins, and demons. These would also haunt the imagination of
Martin Luther who had visions, which he believed to be actual physical
occurrences, of the devil hurling "shit" at him and his hurling it back. Indeed, in one of his many anal combats with the devil—in which Luther
would challenge the devil to "lick" his posterior—Luther thought the best
tactic might be to "throw him into my anus, where he belongs."[7] How
one wishes for an exegesis by Dr. Sigmund Freud of that passage.

Luther's mind and manner, needless to say, were not those of a noble,
polished Renaissance courtier, but those of a rough, gnarled, ham-fisted
working-class northern German. Being, in the words of the historian William Manchester, "the most anal of theologians,"[8] it is not surprising that,
like the American President Lyndon Baines Johnson, Luther conducted his
business while defecating. His "thunderbolt" idea that faith alone was sufficient for salvation came, in his own words, as "knowledge the Holy
Spirit gave me on the privy in the tower."[9]

But Luther had brains, was ordained a priest, and became a doctor
of theology. Initially, he was so thoroughly in favor of the papacy that he
professed his desire to be "the most brutal murderer" on the pope's behalf and "to kill all who even by syllable refused submission to the
pope."[10] Of course, this was while he was also disregarding the guidance
of his confessor, the rules of his monastery, and traditional Catholic
teaching in his excessive forms of penance and refusal to believe that he
had been absolved of sin. Luther was prone to panic attacks. He could
not look upon a crucifix. He tried to avoid performing a Mass or being
in the presence of the Blessed Sacrament. His life was one continual terror of damnation.

Then came his revelation on the privy, and he felt he had broken free
of his own sinfulness, not by the sacraments of the Church, but by faith
alone. As Luther says, rather arrestingly, "Be a sinner and sin on bravely,

but have stronger faith and rejoice in Christ, who is the victor of sin, death, and the world. Do not for a moment imagine that this life is the abiding place of justice: sin must be committed. To you it ought to be sufficient that you acknowledge the Lamb that takes away the sins of the world, the sin cannot tear you away from him, even though you commit adultery a hundred times a day and commit as many murders."[11]

It is often said—by Catholics as well as Protestants—that the Church of the Renaissance was crying out for reform with its abuse of indulgences, its sale of Church offices, the laughable mass market for false relics, the nepotism that appointed children as cardinals, the low standard of morality and education for much of the clergy, and so on. All that might be true, but it is also possible to exaggerate the Church's corruption and to neglect to mention its unchanging orthodoxy, its care for the sick and the poor, its leadership of Europe, its restraint on government power, and its patronage of the arts and learning. Most of all, as we see with Luther, we need to remember that it was not the Catholic Church of the Renaissance that freely forgave adultery and murder, let alone a hundred times, merely on the grounds that the sinner was a professed Christian. Whatever the shameful traffic in indulgences to raise money for the Church, at a minimum even the purchaser of an indulgence had to confess these crimes against man and God to a priest. The indulgence only relieved him of the otherwise obligatory penance.

Until Luther, all believers accepted the sacrament of penance—of making restitution: either by a fine with an indulgence, or by fasting and prayer, or by accepting service in the Crusades, or so on. It had been a keystone of Christendom, a discipline that had made even mighty monarchs perform pilgrimages on their knees. It had been one of the great motivating factors of the public piety of the Middle Ages, making it the Age of Faith. Its spirit was compellingly captured by Shakespeare in his play *Henry V,* when the king pleads with God to remember his works—not his faith alone—on behalf of the Church before the battle of Agincourt: "Not today, O Lord, / O, not today, think not upon the fault / My father made in compassing the crown! / I Richard's body have interred new, / And on it have bestow'd more contrite tears / Than from it issued forced drops of blood. / Five hundred poor I have in yearly pay, / Who twice a day their wither'd hands hold up / Toward heaven, to pardon blood; and I have built / Two chantries, where the sad and solemn priests / Sing still for

Richard's soul. More will I do; / Though all that I can do is nothing worth, / Since that my penitence comes after all, / Imploring pardon."[12]

But with Luther, a murderer could raise his bloodstained hands to heaven and say, "Thank God I'm a Christian." If the murderer was one of the "elect"—for Luther believed in predestination—he was assuredly saved. The murderer, in any event, was not responsible for his actions, because Luther, unlike the Catholic Church, denied that man had free will. These ideas of Luther were, as history would show, extremely dangerous.

As a reformer, Luther was not a voice crying in the wilderness. The Church knew that it had become worldly, and it could acknowledge the genius of some of its critics. The most celebrated Catholic intellectual of this time was Desiderius Erasmus who wrote virulent satires against the Church—the Church to which he nevertheless clung and which, at least while he was alive, praised his wit, wide reading, and humanistic attitude toward reform. He was even offered, but declined, a cardinal's hat. He had a ready stream of invitations to adorn the court of any Catholic king—or the pope, for that matter. But Luther, as Erasmus eventually saw, was not offering words to an educated elite, chiding them to reform. He was preaching a peasants' revolt against Renaissance civilization and learning. Where "Lutheranism flourishes the sciences perish," Erasmus wrote. Piercing beneath the motivations of Luther's followers, Erasmus saw that for them, the overthrow of the terrestrial power of the Church was motivated by a greed for Church property and a lust to break the bonds of celibacy. Lutheranism had "but two objects at heart," Erasmus said, "money and women."[13] It was also a movement of inevitable violence. As the duke of Saxony warned Luther, his doctrine of by faith alone "would only make the people presumptuous and mutinous."[14]

When Luther posted his ninety-five theses on the church door in Wittenberg in 1517, his immediate cause of protest was the sale of indulgences by a Dominican friar named John Tetzel whose mission was to raise money, in part, for the rebuilding of St. Peter's Cathedral. Tetzel was renowned for packing in the peasant faithful with his preaching. His commercial pitch, however, went far beyond the bounds of propriety and canon law, if not common practice. Ironically, it echoed, in an odd way, Luther's own doctrines of salvation by faith alone—Tetzel merely gave that saving faith a monetary value and material form. Anything could be forgiven, said Tetzel, if a punter paid his money and bought a papal indulgence. Luther struck at this inviting and disreputable target. While it was not an unusual occurrence for churchmen and academicians to publicly post theses and then debate them, this time a rhetorical firestorm erupted.

The tinder had been laid by the rising nationalism in Europe. That nationalism set out to subordinate the Church—in the eyes of some, an Italian Church (as it had been a French Church while in Avignon)—to the state. This would lead, two hundred years later, to the Protestant doctrine of separation of church and state, and two hundred years after that to the irrelevance of church to state. There was also the resentment of papal taxation, corruption, and luxury. Christendom's kings followed a low-tax regimen. No monarchy, from the Middle Ages until the democratic age, ever taxed its subjects by more than 10 percent. Often, as in Catholic England, it taxed them not at all. High taxes are an invention of democratic, republican, and socialist governments to pay for such services as schools, hospitals, and caring for the poor that under the Catholic monarchies had been the province of the Church, and to pay for things like armies, which had been paid for by the royal families and noblemen out of their own pockets. But the absence of royal taxes meant that the Catholic Church's demands for money to pay for its social services, or for the monasteries, or for cathedrals, or for rebuilding Rome, or for assembling Crusades, stood out as a burden imposed by a power centered in Italy—a burden that increasingly nationalist nobles and peoples resented.

There was also a new spirit of "primitivism" and "emancipation"[15] that recoiled from the complexity of civilization, history, and an authoritative Church. In part, this primitivism saw political power as corrupting the Church, so it wanted the Church stripped of such power. In part, it regarded the Renaissance as paganism and sought to separate—and degrade—pagan learning from the Bible alone as the source of authority. The result, over time, was that in Protestant countries, theology was no longer "the queen of the sciences" but only one source of knowledge, subject to individual interpretation, and was separated from secular inquiry. Because secular inquiry was seen as objective it eventually gained overweening predominance and prestige over doctrinally subjective Protestant religious thought—an intellectual development that has been *the* major factor in secularizing the Western world.

Just as damaging to Christianity was the primitivist Protestant desire to wrench Christianity from history—or what was seen as centuries of encrusted superstition. Salvation was now to be found in a single book, the Bible, and in the distant practice of an imagined unstained and primitive church. Almost immediately, but certainly by the eighteenth century, and rapidly increasing in the nineteenth and twentieth centuries, mainline Protestant scholars took a similarly critical attitude to the Bible, scraping at it until it appeared as full of errors and superstition as the Roman Catholic Church itself. Protestantism thus became one of the main solvents for scrubbing away any faith that went beyond a general social gospel of good intentions.

All this lay in the future, but it is the mark of a truly intelligent man—certainly a statesman or a responsible intellectual or, in Luther's case, a religious revolutionary—to foresee the outcome of his public tempests, controversies, positions, and actions. Luther did not—perhaps even could not—do this. He was a man of conflict rather than foresight.

Luther had not, at this point, entirely broken with Rome. While he dismissed Julius II and Alexander VI as inferior popes, he wrote to Pope Leo X in loyalty and submission to Church discipline. In this, however, Luther was less than honest. He swore he would accept his own death if the pope ordered it. But when Leo beckoned him to Rome, Luther shied away. Nor did Luther confide in the pope that in his private correspondence he was already linking the office of the papacy with the Antichrist.

While Erasmus had his own doubts about the power of the papacy, he trusted that reform would come from well-read, classically educated, humanist popes like Leo. Luther, on the other hand, was a violent rhetorician, pounding his cudgels wherever they would make the most resounding racket. The pope, inclined by temperament to listen to Erasmus and ignore Luther, regarded this noisy German as a mere distraction. The pope had more pressing business with the German princes, who had refused his demand to pay taxes and offer men for a Crusade against the Turks. Leo was committed to winning them over and enlisting the Scandinavian kingdoms for his Crusade as well. To dispense with Luther, Leo ordered that, instead of coming to Rome, the monk should face an inquiry at Augsburg, and if he repented of any unorthodox statements, he was to be forgiven and the whole business forgotten. Inevitably, Luther and the pope's emissary quarreled.

Still, Pope Leo took the initiative in reforming the Church precisely on the point Luther had attacked. In 1518, the pope clarified Catholic practice on indulgences, reminding the faithful that they could not buy their way to Heaven; indulgences were merely forms of penance, alms offered for forgiveness of temporal punishment, and certainly not a blank check for sins to be committed or to buy the freedom of a soul in Purgatory. A papal emissary ensured that Tetzel was disciplined, and Luther again affirmed his submission to the pope, while concealing his continuing doubts about "whether the Pope is the Antichrist or his apostle."[16]

The full break came when, in a public debate, Luther denied the primacy of the pope, held the Council of Constance in error, and even praised some of the doctrines of Jan Hus. He had now moved from being one of many vocal Church reformers—though easily the most politically powerful because of antipapal sentiment among the people and princes in Germany—to being a Hussite heretic. Even so, Leo made no move against Luther. The tolerant Renaissance pope still assumed that matters could be patched over. Christendom, he believed, faced a far more dangerous threat from the Turks, whose armies were separated from Italy only by the narrow Adriatic Sea to the east and hard-pressed Austria to the north. But it is the frequent misfortune of tolerant, high-minded, and far-seeing men to be attacked by petty, narrow, and ruthless ones, who generally have mobs at their sides. Such was the case with Pope Leo and Martin Luther.

By 1520, Luther was penning such reformist tracts as his *Epitome,* which openly declares "that the true Antichrist is sitting in the temple of God and is reigning in Rome—that empurpled Babylon—and that the Roman curia is the Synagogue of Satan. . . . [T]here will be no remedy left except that the emperors, kings, and princes, girt about with force of arms, should attack these pests of the world, and settle the matter no longer by words but by the sword. . . . [W]hy do we not attack in arms these masters of perdition, these cardinals, these popes, and all this sink of the Roman Sodom which has without end corrupted the Church of God, and wash our hands in their blood?"[17] There one has the voice of reformist Christianity, as preached by Luther.

Leo condemned Luther's writings but offered him another chance to recant. Luther responded by addressing himself to the German people, praising Germany's rulers (Germany was not yet a single state), just as Visigoths praised their virtuous warrior-chieftains against decadent Roman legates, while attacking the structure of the universal Church, especially the powers vested in the clergy and the pope. Luther declared that every man is his own priest. This doctrine—and its corollary, that every man should interpret the Bible for himself—not only made subjectivism and moral relativism Protestant doctrine, but—a crucial point—allowed Luther to blatantly subvert any sense of restraint that secular princes felt in attacking the clergy or the pope. In Luther's mind, the religious hierarchy of the Church deserved no special esteem and no independence under its own canon law from the state. Canon law, in Luther's view, was merely the law laid down by the Antichrist in Rome. The great medieval achievement of Christendom—of curbing and redirecting the martial spirit of barbarian Europe by transforming the Gothic warrior into the Frankish knight, subordinating him to unarmed priests, and making him kneel before the bearer of the cross—was undone. If Luther had been in New Spain, he would have told the Conquistadors to put the priests in their place, because the authority of the state was founded in Scripture while the authority of the pope and the clergy was not. Deference to the clergy was not a Lutheran virtue, because the established clergy served the Antichrist in Rome.

The real church, according to Luther, was an invisible institution, held only in the faith of men. The state—the German princes, the German *Reich*—was the only true, temporal reality, and it was to it, not to the Church in Rome, that men and laws should be subordinate. In Luther's words, "No one need think that the world can be ruled without blood. The civil sword shall and must be red and bloody."[18] In Luther we see the historic German view of blood and iron, of might making right, an inevitable conclusion from the supremacy of the nation-state over the Church. But more than that, we see in Luther a repeating current in German history—the desire of Germans to be free from outside constraints imposed by the Church; a barbarian yearning for radical moral freedom, recognizing the authority only of the state, or of the barbarian chieftain, or of the great man. It was true in the endless conflicts between the Holy Roman Empire and the papacy. It was true in the earthquake war between Frederick II, the "wonder of the world," and the pope. It was true now with Luther, as it would be true later with Bismarck and his *Kulturkampf* against the power of the Catholic Church in Germany; again with Nietzsche who proclaimed the death of God, the inversion of all values, and the birth of the superman freed from Christianity; yet again with Germany's "heathen heart," which Kipling saw putting its "trust in reeking tube and iron shard" in his 1897 poem "Recessional"; and with Hitler. Even Reformed Protestant historians have linked Luther's dismissal of moral law—on the basis of salvation by faith alone—with the eventual rise of the *Führer.*[19]

Luther was an avowed enemy of reason. He repudiated the Catholic tradition of natural law, the scholasticism of St. Thomas Aquinas, the philosophy of Aristotle—that "heathen . . . plague."[20] All the grand intellectual superstructure of Catholicism was un-Biblical and unnecessary. It, too, fell before Luther's assault on the Church's role in reconciling sinners to God. By Church teaching, no sin is merely personal. It is an affront to God and inevitably harms God's creation—one's family, friends, and neighbors. A priest acts in *persona Christi,* granting forgiveness in Christ's name and admonishing the sinner to sin no more, giving him penance as a means to expiate temporal punishment due to sin. Luther propounded a doctrine more in line with late-twentieth-century notions of "self-esteem"—and of lawlessness for the proud—to wit: "Christianity is nothing but a perpetual exercise in feeling that you have no sin, although you committed sin, but that your sins are attached to Christ."[21]

Just as it was wrong, in Luther's eyes, to be deferential to priests on matters of sin, behavior, and law, so, too, it was wrong to defer to Catholic teaching on the Bible. Interestingly, Luther was a Biblical literalist who simultaneously admitted that parts of the Bible remained a mystery. He felt that it was folly to even seek to understand them. Reason, he held, was insufficient to explain the Bible. Reason was even the enemy. It was what motivated men to think of Biblical narratives in terms of allegories—and that was nothing less than the atheism of the sophisticated. Luther's idea of such an atheist was Erasmus, but he could just as easily have named St. Ambrose or St. Augustine, the latter of whom nevertheless profoundly influenced Luther's ideas on predestination. Luther also exempted himself from a literal interpretation of the commandment against lying, for he publicly averred that it was perfectly acceptable to "tell a good thumping lie" if it benefited Christianity.[22]

When he did stick with a literalist interpretation of the Bible, Luther drew lessons from the Old Testament that the Catholic Church had rejected. For example, during the controversy over King Henry VIII of England's desire to divorce Catherine of Aragon, Luther advised that bigamy was preferable to divorce. In a similar spirit, he advised a venereal German prince that, given the example of the patriarchs in the Old Testament, bigamy was acceptable for a Christian, and the prince could pursue it, but Luther told the prince to keep his advice quiet.[23] He also advised, in writing, that, contrary to Catholic teaching, marriage was not a sacrament, and an impotent man could by rights allow another man to sleep with his wife.[24]

As interesting as this is, bigamy and wife-sharing were not a major part of Luther's reformist platform, though sexual liberation for clerics and national liberation for Germany was. Luther preached the necessity of having a German church for the German people. He struck another Protestant note by reshaping the Christian faith to bring it in line not only with nationalist but secularist and materialist "this world" sentiment. He declared that lust was invincible (his phrase was *concupiscentia invincibilis*).[25] As such, he opposed clerical celibacy as contrary to nature. He wanted to reduce the monasteries for the same reason. He wanted the state to abolish holy days—which were obviously an imposition by the Church in Rome—and to seize Church property. When German nobles became enthusiastic practitioners of this last proposition, Luther protested, vainly, that he preferred that such seizures be mere transfers to the German church. He wanted to keep German money in German hands, not see it frittered away by Italians. Luther's platform was earthy, populist, nationalist—and completely at odds with the ideals of Christendom, which were historical, hierarchical, and catholic, with all nations unified under Christ's Church, resting on the bones of St. Peter in Rome, with the pope, the Vicar of Christ, a monarch set over kings.

Astonishingly, the Church still hoped to reconcile with Luther—and Luther still addressed Pope Leo, in a letter, with respect for the pope's "blameless life."[26] But the Hitler in Luther soon won out. In retaliation for papal suppression of his works, Luther and his students made a bonfire of books of canon law, Catholic doctrine, and papal instruction. Luther declared that only Lutherans could be saved; that any who held fast to papal obedience were damned; and that God's will was not what the Church had taught for a millennium and more—it was what Luther now divined. Such were fighting words, and the words of any heretic in any century. The Church told Luther as much, reminding him that the

Bible was wax that could be twisted by demagogues to say anything; that beyond a universal Church that trusted to the unchanging and unquestionable deposit of faith lay chaos, irreligion, and war.

Still the Church held back from taking stern action against Luther. A new Holy Roman Emperor, Charles V, had been crowned, and at the Diet of Worms in April 1521 he and the representatives of the pope made one last attempt to keep Luther within the Church. But Luther refused to be appeased. Charles V's Edict of Worms said Luther's "teaching makes for rebellion, division, war, murder, robbery, arson, and the collapse of Christendom."[27] All this was true, yet the edict still gave him twenty-one days to recant.

Instead, Luther hid for a year in a castle in Wartburg, Germany, where he lost himself in massive bouts of eating and drinking, pausing occasionally to wrestle with the devil in a paroxysm of delusion, engaging him in battle by fart.[28] He also translated the Bible into German, rewriting passages so that they expounded Lutheran doctrine—for instance by adding the word "alone" after the word "faith" in Romans 3:28.[29] His daily prayers were rather unique as well. In Luther's words, "I am unable to pray without at the same time cursing. If I am prompted to say: 'hallowed be Thy name,' I must add: 'cursed, damned, outraged be the name of the papists.' If I am prompted to say: 'Thy Kingdom come,' I must perforce add: 'cursed, damned, destroyed be the papacy.'"[30]

While Luther swore, his adherents took more violent action, rioting against churches, libraries, and religious art and altars. Luther's invitation to the priesthood of all believers to interpret Scripture for themselves was eagerly taken up. Innovations began to pour forth from Luther-inspired leaders. Crucifixes were banned. Infant baptism was banned. The Latin Mass was banned. Music was banned. Books were repudiated as lures that led men away from simple, pure, peasant Christianity. An educated priesthood was unnecessary when God spoke directly to man. Monks and nuns were encouraged to break their vows. Priests were to marry. One of Luther's most eloquent religious disciples, Andreas Carlstadt, was among those throwing off his vow of celibacy. He was forty-one; his bride was fifteen. Luther applauded the marriage, though he later feuded with Carlstadt, as he feuded with Erasmus, and with everyone else who did not treat him as the *primus inter pares* of the priesthood of all believers.

Luther flew from his castle hideaway to regain the leadership of his revolution. He tried to restore things he liked, such as church music and religious art—he was a sentimentalist—and to give succor to Germans who retained a conservative, Catholic faith, to reassure them that they too were welcome in the new German church. But the manner in which he did so betrayed his incredible ego and arrogance. "I was the first whom God entrusted with this matter; I was the one to whom He first revealed how His Word should be preached to you. Therefore you have done wrong in starting such a piece of work without . . . having first consulted me," he told his Lutheran revolutionaries.[31] While some of his actions were those of a moderate, he still called for the blood of bishops to be shed: "All who contribute body, goods, and honor that the rule of the bishops may be destroyed are God's dear children and true Christians."[32] His ideas developed an increasingly leftward tilt. He openly warned the German princes—his putative allies—that they were next to be overthrown by the common people. And after them would be the rich and the merchants, for Luther was beginning to link his common man's Christianity with an economic reformation of rural communism.

Before the revolt of the peasants—Luther's Khmer Rouge—came a revolt of freebooting soldiers under the command of Franz von Sickingen, an old Luther ally, who would now be repudiated as he put Luther's words into action and waged war against the Catholic archbishop of Trier. His goal was to seize the wealth of the archbishop. But this being the Renaissance, he found that the archbishop was better armed and had better soldiers than he did. His attacks not only were rebuffed, but he was pursued all the way back to his own castle and fell to loyal papist swords.

Luther's revolution, however, had barely begun. The historical pattern was clear. In the fourteenth century, the "reformist" Lollards of John Wyclif had given birth to Wat Tyler's peasant revolt in England. Then Bohemia was convulsed with the horrible, nationalist, populist Hussite wars following the execution of the reformer Jan Hus. Now, in 1524, it was the turn of the peasants of Germany to respond to Luther's incendiary rhetoric with fire and revolution. He, of course, again repudiated his followers. But a firebrand named Thomas Munzer provided new leadership. The peasants' targets, he said, were clergymen and businessmen. The German nobility were invited to lead the peasants, as long as they accepted that communism would be the result of the revolution. The nobility didn't rally to the communist standard, but lower-middle-class Germans did, and the Church and its allies came under armed attack.

An "Evangelical Brotherhood" of peasants was formed under Ulrich Zwingli of Switzerland. Zwingli thought that he, not Luther, was *primus inter pares* among the priesthood of all believers, and took positions somewhat to the left of the German. The brotherhood's enemies were Church, state, and feudalism. Its goals were for a church of elected pastors, and for a relief of Church, state, and feudal taxes. The brotherhood promised to retract any demand inconsistent with Scripture. Luther wrote to the peasants and, while criticizing the bishops and the lords of Germany, bade the peasants remember that inequality and slavery were Scriptural, and that everyone should repent from violence and find a peaceful solution to the crisis.

Luther was dismissed as a coward, just as when Erasmus preached peace, Luther had dismissed him as a coward. Luther had told the people they were priests, as good as any man at understanding God's word, and in God's word they found a message of communism that would make all equal, humbling the mighty and raising the poor. Tens of thousands of peasants under a varied and disorganized command of unfrocked priests, discharged soldiers, and others, seized towns, proclaimed their religious and political independence, and indulged in the usual round of destruction that always focused on churches, monasteries, and bishops' palaces—defacing artwork, smashing altars, getting drunk on sacred wine. The peasants swept through town after town, executing nobles who had abused them, confiscating Church property in the name of the people, plundering the wealthy and loyal Catholics of whatever station, and reducing Germany to scenes of lawlessness and Sparticist revolution. Some bishops and lords surrendered to the new regime. Luther did not.

Having sparked a revolution, Luther now became a reactionary, penning his finest work—*Against the Murdering, Thieving Hordes of Peasants*—as well as other insightful books of social instruction. Luther commanded the noblemen who were gathering troops for a counterthrust to "brandish their swords, to free, save, help and pity the poor people forced to join the peasants—but the wicked, smite, stab and slay all you can." A prince, he wrote, can now "win heaven more easily by bloodshed than by prayer." Luther noted that one "cannot meet a rebel with reason: your best answer is to punch him in the face until he has a bloody nose"[33]—

advice that Pope Leo should, perhaps, have pursued with Luther when he posted his theses, though Luther was prepared to go much further than bloody noses. The peasants' ears, he wrote, "must be unbuttoned with bullets, till their heads jump off their shoulders. . . . He who will not hear God's Word when it is spoken with kindness must listen to the headsman when he comes with his axe."[34] Luther now firmly set his face against communism, condemning the "insane peasants in their raging" for economic equality. "I think there is not a devil left in hell; they have all gone into the peasants."[35] One can easily see from these remarks why Luther's translation of the Bible is a classic of German literature.

German noblemen, bishops, and right-wing mercenaries didn't really need Luther's advice as they rose to the task of defeating the devilish peasants with artillery, cavalry charges, and executions. More than 130,000 of the peasantry—let alone people of other classes—died in two years of civil war (1524 to 1526). That is sixty-five times the number of deaths the Spanish Inquisition claimed in its first ten—and by far its worst—years. According to the historian William Manchester, the number of German dead doubles to more than a quarter of a million if one includes the years 1523 and 1527.[36] Fifty thousand peasants were refugees. Tens of thousands of other Germans counted the costs in their ruined cities, towns, and countryside—or in those maimed, tortured, and wounded by the peasants and their subduers. True terror was to be found less in the inquisitional courts of Spain than wherever Protestant reformers did their work.

For Luther, the state, not the pope, was God's instrument, because "It is God," acting through the state, "not man, Who hangs, and breaks on the wheel, and decapitates, and flogs; it is God who wages war." The power of the princes he venerated. The power of the pope he condemned as evil—indeed satanic—and foolish: "The world cannot be ruled by a rosary."[37] He urged the Holy Roman Emperor to conquer the papal lands and recommended that the pope, cardinals, and others in the papal curia "have their tongues torn out by the backs of their necks, and nailed in rows on the gallows."[38]

As a respite from watching Germany devour itself, Luther married a former nun. His influence waned—the peasants turned against him as "Dr. Liar"—and, in married bliss, he worked with the German state to regularize Lutheran worship. His former colleague Andreas Carlstadt accused

Luther of acting like a "new pope," arrogating to himself all power of determining doctrine, some of which—such as "consubstantiation," Luther's reworking of the Catholic doctrine of transubstantiation—had, said Carlstadt, no Scriptural basis at all. The Lutherans banned Carlstadt's works. But the Swiss reformer Zwingli, who like Carlstadt believed the Eucharist was purely symbolic, came to Carlstadt's defense, and the Protestant sects turned their rhetoric against each other. Luther said, "I would rather drink blood with the papists than mere wine with the Zwinglians."[39] The Zwinglians, like the Calvinists—indeed, like all his enemies—Luther considered tools of the devil. As death closed in on him, twenty years after the peasant war in Germany, he believed the whole world was going to the devil because of the papists, the Jews, his evangelical enemies, and the rising tide of irreligion in his own Germany.

## CALVIN INVENTS THE CHRISTIAN POLICE STATE

LUTHER WAS RIGHT about one thing: His sundering of Christendom had opened Pandora's box, and out flew endless phantasmagoric Protestant sects—a process continuing today. If Protestants wanted primitive Christianity, they succeeded at least in reestablishing the chaos of the early centuries of the Church when innumerable heresies contested with Rome and the apostolic faith. In Protestant countries, the one brake against a repetition of Germany's peasants' war was the forceful intervention of the state. Princes who seized Church lands and the spoils of the monasteries designed the new Protestant settlement of state-controlled churches. Thus it happened in the Scandinavian countries, in the Protestant areas of Germany, and eventually in England.

But there was another model. To the raucous freedom of the Catholic Middle Ages and the Renaissance, to the subordination of Church to state under Luther, John Calvin responded with the invention of the first—and only—Christian police state.

The irony of John Calvin is that he was undoubtedly the finest theologian the Protestant churches ever had, and the most powerful in the devotion of his followers. Yet today Calvinism, as a doctrine, is moribund, if not dead, a casualty of the complete and inevitable collapse of Protestant theology into subjective rationalization.

Calvin had the advantage over Luther of being a Frenchman and middle class, and therefore of a more supple mind. He was also free of Luther's personal demons and paranoid fantasies. In fact, he was a man of secular reason and secular career—trained as a lawyer, not as a priest or a monk. Like the Catholic Church he believed in the application of universal moral laws—indeed, law was man's highest accomplishment. Also like the Church he believed that the truth was the truth, not a matter of opinion. Against the Catholic Church—which he held to be in error—he composed his own *Institutes of the Christian Religion,* which was meant to establish the one true faith. Where Luther's attack was—logically at least—weakened by its nationalism and irrationality, Calvin's was cool, precise, a duelist against the Church, matching reason against reason. The absurdity, as with Luther, was that against the infallible ancient Church was one man proclaiming his own presumptuously infallible critique.

Calvin, achieving manhood after Luther's revolt, came into a world in which Protestantism was already contesting against the Church and against itself. But Protestantism was far weaker in France than in Germany. The Catholic Church in France was as subject to the king as it was to the pope, so nationalism could be no rallying cry for the French Protestants. Heretics were extremely unpopular, and subject to execution. The French king Francis I was a patron of Renaissance art, a knight of the battlefield, a Don Juan of the boudoir, and a Machiavelli of diplomacy. Though he dallied with Protestant ideas, he felt compelled to persecute Protestants in his realm—not on doctrinal grounds, but because he wanted no repeat of Germany's peasant wars.

To understand Calvin's Europe, we need to go beyond the borders of his native France—from which he would exile himself in any event—and remember that the Reformation was essentially a fluctuating, European-wide war, and while there were religious fractures in France as throughout Europe, there were also occasional glimmers of hope that Christendom could be patched together. One paramount example was the Peace of Nuremberg in 1532, when the Holy Roman Emperor Charles V brought his German subjects—Protestant and Catholic—into a temporary alliance with each other and with imperial Spaniards and Italians against the resurgent Turks in Austria. But when the Turk was again defeated, the Lutherans refused to be bound by the rulings of any ecumenical council that might unite the faiths. Luther had tasted freedom and would countenance no deal with the devil in Rome. That was the religious argument.

But the rivalries of princes and kings, who now had the expedient of Protestantism to justify their plotting against one another, further shredded the unity of Christendom. Protestant German prince was set against Catholic German prince, though the religion they chose could be determined by whether they were upholding a claim or usurping it. The alliances were dizzying. Francis I of Catholic France was a frequent ally of the Lutherans in Germany, not to mention the Turks. Why? Because he was interested most of all in upsetting the power of the Holy Roman Emperor Charles V, whose territories surrounded him on all sides save the English Channel. Charles himself, though Catholic, and governing Catholic Spain, the Netherlands, Germany, parts of Italy, and points further east, was, of course, an occasional enemy of the papacy, in the long tradition of Holy Roman Emperor versus pope, most shockingly when his troops sacked Rome and kidnapped the French-allied pope in 1527. To the north, an ice curtain descended, sealing Scandinavia for state Lutheranism. The Teutonic Knights were among those who surrendered to the new dispensation, their monastic vows discarded, their arms maintained. England, too, was separated from the faith in its own inimitable way.

When Catholicism renewed itself in arms, in 1546, it was with Charles V, now allied with Pope Paul III, to restore the entirety of Germany to the faith, thus reuniting continental Christendom, minus, for now, the Scandinavian countries. Charles would have completely succeeded—were it not for the pope. As Charles's successes mounted, Pope Paul III withdrew his troops because of the recurring papal fear of an over-mighty Holy Roman Emperor. It was a fatal political mistake. As Charles's military supremacy foundered, the Catholic cause was again forced to seek an accommodation. The people of the various German principalities—it was agreed at the Diet of Augsburg in 1555—would follow the religion of their prince. *Cuius regio eius religio* was the Latin phrase on which would rest the uneasy peace of a religiously divided Germany.

Switzerland was also divided, with different cantons insisting on different orthodoxies. The Geneva in which Calvin established himself in

1536 was already Protestant in a manner that presaged the practice of the French reformer: Catholic priests were imprisoned; fines were levied against those who failed to attend Protestant services; a network of neighborhood spies was established to watch over the morals of the people. The Luther of Geneva was William Farel, a self-employed preacher of small stature but intimidating presence. He browbeat Calvin, who, like Farel, had never been ordained, to help him lead, shape, and govern the new, reformed church. Calvin reluctantly agreed. Soon laws governing Protestant practice flew off the Geneva printing presses—until he himself had to fly. Geneva's Catholics and libertarians, whom Calvin scorned as "libertines," successfully revolted against this attempt to ram Puritanism down their liberty-loving—as well as alcohol-, game-, theater-, and holy day–loving—hearts.

When Calvin returned to Geneva three years later, in 1541, it was under a different dispensation. As elsewhere, the Protestant church was subordinated to the civil authority, but that civil authority was dominated by burghers who had had enough of singing, dancing, fighting, and the general moral laxity that seemed to overtake the people when Catholicism was tolerated—and when the city lacked eloquent Puritan taskmasters like Calvin. Calvin was now authorized to exert the same oppressive Puritan rule as he had before, with the collusion of the city government, which saw it as both good for morals and good for business—it put workers on the straight and narrow. He worked tremendously hard in creating the foundation and structure of what would become the Reformed and Presbyterian churches that would spread from his desk in Switzerland to Scotland, parts of France, the Netherlands, a smattering of Eastern Europe, and eventually to the United States.

Gone in these Reformed churches was the "priesthood of all believers," which, if not explicitly repudiated by the various Protestant denominations, was now seen as impractical. In Calvin's system, clergy trained in his doctrine were to be the sole interpreters of Scripture. By 1552, such was Calvin's power that his *Institutes of the Christian Religion* was declared a "holy doctrine which no man might speak against."[40] Calvin, in fact, claimed more power than the pope, and his theocracy applied the death penalty to a far more sweeping definition of heresy than the Church ever had. Calvin found a code of law in the Bible, as the Muslims found

one in the Koran, and it was the job of Calvin's Reformed pastors to ensure that the Bible's laws became the civil law of the state. The authorities
obliged. Christians in Geneva did not confess their sins to a priest; they
confessed them to a magistrate in a court of law. A Lutheran who decided
to "sin on bravely" in Geneva, sure that Jesus would forgive him, would
not be forgiven by Calvin or the city council. In Geneva, the death
penalty could be invoked to cover adultery, pregnancy out of wedlock,
and striking a parent, not to mention blasphemy, heresy, and idolatry.[41]

In his *Institutes of the Christian Religion,* Calvin cited Scripture to justify his conclusion that the "Lord commands all those who are disobedient
to their parents to be put to death"—but judicially, only by a ruling from a
council of elders, of course.[42] The Catholic Church promised a sinner absolution through the sacrament of penance. The Calvinists looked to erase sin
by erasing the sinner. This made for hard law, and Calvin himself said that,
for most people, it would have been better had they never been born, and
more sensical had they "mourned and wept at the birth of their relations,
and solemnly rejoiced at their funerals."[43] Calvinist pastors regulated the
faithful to make sure they came to church—on time—as well as abstained
from feasts and did not break the Calvinist prohibitions on clothes color,
"dancing, singing, pictures, statues, relics, church bells, organs, altar candles; 'indecent or irreligious' songs, staging or attending theatrical plays;
wearing rouge, jewelry, lace, or 'immodest' dress; speaking disrespectfully
of your betters; extravagant entertainment; swearing, gambling, playing
cards, hunting, drunkenness; naming children after anyone but figures in
the Old Testament; reading 'immoral or irreligious' books," and so on, including ensuring that a woman's hair was not worn "at an 'immoral'
height."[44] Calvin was, of course, a democrat—each congregation elected its
pastor—proving the adage that if you want to be suffocated under a litany
of law, leave it to the people and their elected representatives.[45]

Calvin thought such laws were necessary because he—like Luther, but
far more articulately—saw man as thoroughly corrupted. So powerful
was sin that only those that God had predestined for Heaven could be
saved. They would be set apart and known by their faith—and, presumably, by abiding by the laws of Geneva. But their faith was not to be
found in a visible church, in the real presence of Christ in the Eucharist,
or in an apostolic priesthood. It was only to be found in Calvin's gloss of

Scripture. Outside of Calvin's invisible church of the predestined there was no salvation.

If Luther empowered his followers with feelings of nationalism and freedom from clerical vows and strictures, Calvin emboldened his by emphasizing the doctrine of election, of being God's chosen people. But since Luther shared this view of his own reformed church, and since neither church existed until the sixteenth century, one has to wonder if any previous Christians were saved, according to Lutheran and Calvinist doctrine, between the time of the Reformed churches and the invisible antecedents they assumed in primitive Christianity. Or had all the intervening Christians, going back a thousand, twelve hundred, or fifteen hundred years, been condemned—predestinedly condemned—as papists? Calvin's answer was that the "elect" always existed in their small numbers beneath the mistaken multitudes of the Catholic Church, though interestingly Calvin conceded that the Church had indeed been founded by God but had been corrupted by the time of the Renaissance.[46]

At bottom, though, questions like this were unimportant to Protestants. Their thought tended to spring from Biblical history to the present day—skipping over the intervening history of Catholic Europe, unless it was to highlight the decadence of a Renaissance pope. A signal example would be the iconoclastic Protestant attitude toward religious art. Despite its long history and its official confirmation by the Church after the iconoclastic wars, Calvin was as opposed as any modern ACLU lawyer to the public—or, for that matter, private—display of religious art, even of a crucifix, which, for him, was sheer idolatry, condemned in the Ten Commandments. To the Protestant, history—the historical experience of the Church—has no real meaning, because the Bible is the sole source of authority, though in the more liberal denominations today, secular opinion has that role. To the Catholic, this makes Protestantism seem disembodied, utopian, unrealistic, not to mention dull-minded, intellectually limited, and designed for people who have room on their bookshelves for only a single volume. From a Catholic perspective, Calvinism is blank walls, one book—or actually two, the Bible and Calvin's *Institutes of the Christian Religion*—and no fun; a religion in which Jesus turns water into castor oil rather than wine, tells parables about wedding wakes rather than wedding feasts, and instead of instructing the adulteress to go and sin no more, says "Well, we might as well stone her to death as she's pre-destined to go on sinning anyway."

After the peasant massacres of Luther's Reformation and the dutiful death-in-life-but-they-sure-do-make-wonderful-workers of Calvin's Geneva, it is with relief that one returns to Rome and the Whore of Babylon.

## CHAPTER FIFTEEN

# THRUST AND COUNTERTHRUST

⸺➤●◄⸺

WHAT WAS MOST AT STAKE in the Reformation was freedom. The Catholic Church was freedom's defender, and not merely by defending Europe against the Turks. It was the Church that nurtured the artistic freedom of the Renaissance and the Baroque. It was the Protestants who smashed religious art as idolatry and sensualism. It was the Church that sponsored the literary freedom of the humanists, and the Protestants who condemned it as paganism. It was the Church that affirmed man's free will, and the Protestants who insisted that every man's fate was determined before he was born. Most of all it was the Catholic Church that stood opposed to the absolute power of the state. It was the Church that claimed to be a universal, independent, and superior court of appeals to the edicts of kings, while the Protestants made religion a department of government to be controlled by princes (in Germany), or the city council (in Geneva), or the monarch (in England and Scandinavia). There is, in fact, a much underappreciated libertarian streak within the Catholic Church. It was seen in Pope Gregory IX's alliance with republicans and the capitalist city-states of Italy against the emperor Frederick II; it was seen in Renaissance Catholicism, to the scandal of the Protestants; and it was seen most especially in the conflict between the Church and the Tudor dynasty in England.

# THE KING'S GOOD SERVANT, BUT GOD'S FIRST

THE LEVER THAT separated England from the Catholic Church was a woman. She was popularly known as the "goggle-eyed whore," but her given name was Anne Boleyn.

King Henry VIII had been married to Catherine of Aragon—the daughter of Ferdinand and Isabella, the aunt of Charles V—for sixteen years before he became obsessed with the slim, long-haired, manipulative femme fatale who would cleave England from the Church. Her grounds were that she would not consent to be Henry's mistress. She insisted on being his wife, despite the complication that he was already married to a woman from the most powerful family in Europe, who had borne him six children (only one of whom survived), and who was piously Catholic and therefore unable to contemplate divorce. It was Anne who provided the remedy: Simply change England's religion.

To understand just how ferocious a spell Anne had cast upon the king, one needs to recall that Henry VIII was a deeply religious man. He was well educated, a dab hand at quoting the Bible, known to hear Masses three times a day, and the hope of such Catholic reformers as Sir Thomas More and Erasmus. He had also written a book condemning the heresies of Luther, which had won him the title of "Defender of the Faith" from Pope Leo X.

So breaking with Rome was no small thing. But there was another aspect to Henry—he was willful and tempestuous. As a young man, his grand physique and shining vitality had made him a renowned athlete: wrestler, horseman, soldier, hunter, and dancer. But with age, his volcanic temperament slid ever further into the exercise of sheer appetite. It can be seen in his portraits, as he degenerates from being "handsomer than any other sovereign in Christendom . . . his whole frame admirably proportioned"[1] into a gourmandizing behemoth who could not get up by his own strength. It is seen in his six wives (there were also mistresses). It is seen in the absence, sometimes through execution, of any but yes-men beside him. It is seen, as a historical circumstance, in there being no check on kingly power by the old nobility—the nobles having been shattered in the Wars of the Roses that brought Henry's family, the Tudors, to the throne. It is seen, finally, in a man who could deny himself nothing and so made himself head of his own national church.

But at the beginning of the struggle between king and Church, Henry tried to play by the rules. The legal point in question was whether Pope Julius II—Henry's old ally in a war against France—had erred in giving the king what he had wanted a decade and a half before: dispensation to marry his brother's widow, Catherine of Aragon. Now, of course, Henry wanted to undo his previous wish.

He was driven not only by his bullish lust for Anne Boleyn, but by an increasingly feverish conviction that he had committed a Levitical sin, which would explain why his marriage bed had been cursed without a single surviving legal male heir (bastards he sired were another matter). The original papal dispensation had been needed because canon law forbade such marriages. Henry argued that canon law was correct and no exception should have been granted. Pope Clement VII gave the king's arguments serious consideration—so serious that there exists in the Vatican archives a draft of a papal bull giving Henry what he wanted.[2]

But against Henry's case were insurmountable facts. For the noncynical the most important was that Catherine, whose character was unimpeachable, testified that her marriage to Henry's brother Arthur had never been consummated. They had been married at the age of fifteen, and Arthur had died soon thereafter. Every chivalrous instinct in the papal court rallied to Catherine's tearful plea to the king: "Sire, I beseech you for all the love that hath been between us and for the love of God let me have justice and right. Take of me some pity and compassion for I am a poor woman and a stranger born out of your dominion. I have no assured friend here. . . . When ye had me at the first, I take God to be my judge, I was a true maid without touch of man. And whether this be true or no, I put it to your conscience."[3]

The Biblical arguments were contradictory, as Old Testament passages were found that seemed to both condemn and require the practice of marrying a brother's widow. While theological opinion was split, the better part of it supported the fact that Henry and Catherine were legally and unbreakably married, and certainly there was no great enthusiasm in the papal curia for ruling that a papal dispensation had been in error.

There was also the argument of *Realpolitik*, though this cut two ways. Given that the pope had already endured one sacking of the Holy See at the hands of Charles V, he was undoubtedly loath to insult the emperor again by nullifying the marriage of his aunt to the English king. But weighed against this is that the papacy had no interest in alienating the most loyal king of England from the Church.

If this last political calculation, in the end, did not stop the pope from denying Henry's request, it is because England did not seem vulnerable to a Protestant revolt—and indeed, it was not, at least not until Anne Boleyn showed the king that he could both quench his lust and remain true to Christianity. She gave the king a book—*On the Obedience of Christian Man and How Christian Rulers Ought to Govern,* by William Tyndale. Tyndale was a Protestant and had translated the Bible into English. He argued in favor of the Protestant doctrine that kings in their separate kingdoms, not the pope in Rome, were God's instruments. Church and state, Tyndale argued, should be one, with the king supreme. It was now that the king's appetites—for power, as well as for Anne Boleyn—submerged his Catholic orthodoxy.

The king attached to himself an inner circle of lowborn, low-minded men. For theological succor he turned to Thomas Cranmer, a priest who had abandoned his vow of chastity to marry, and who was the master trimmer of his time, cutting a theological course as dictated by the king, holding to no firm principle save a general Protestant direction. Far worse, however, because far more powerful and diligent, was the newly elevated secretary to the king, Thomas Cromwell, whose predecessor as the king's fixer, Cardinal Wolsey, had been sacked and died in shame for failing to achieve the royal divorce. Cromwell was a man of no religious sentiment—indeed no sentiment whatever. He was a self-made man who saw life solely through a prism of money and power. For him, the religious issues at stake were a tissue of superstition and hypocrisy.

Cromwell's goal was to consolidate all power in the English state, allowing no foreign interference—which meant the international Church—and no domestic dissent. Cromwell's spy network was vast, his methods ruthless, and an Englishman's traditional right to free speech was ended. Cromwell's Reformation—and it really was *his* Reformation, engineered from his desk—marked the first victory of the nouveaux riches in alliance with the state. Indeed, Cromwell *made* a new class of nouveaux riches as he and the king shared with their toadies the plunder of the monasteries and the churches. Not understanding such a thing as principle, he took monks who refused to recognize the king as their religious head and had them disemboweled as a lesson to recusants. But it was easier, in the end, to simply hurl monks and nuns—at least 15,000 of them—into the street and tell them to get a real job, while Cromwell had his henchmen seize their monasteries, nunneries, hospitals, schools, churches, charitable houses, and land, dividing the booty among his fellow parvenu usurpers. Following behind, of course, was Cranmer, the timorous prelate with a golden pen, blessing every expropriation of the Church as advancing the true Protestant religion.

Henry VIII, as Winston Churchill noted in his *History of the English-Speaking People,* "chose as his advisers men for the most part of the meanest origin . . . [because] he distrusted the hereditary nobility, preferring the discreet counsel of men without a wide circle of friends."[4] One has only to compare the "small attorney" Cromwell and the "obscure lecturer in divinity"[5] Cranmer with their two most celebrated opponents to see how right Churchill was.

Bishop John Fisher and Sir Thomas More were exemplars of the high civilization of the Catholic humanists, men with an international reputation in the cosmopolitan world that was Christendom. More was famously learned, devout, humorous, satirical, a man of humane reason. Erasmus noted that More's "countenance is in harmony with his character, being always expressive of an amiable joyousness, and even an incipient laughter and, to speak candidly, it is better framed for gladness than for gravity or dignity, though without any approach to folly or buffoonery."[6] For all his geniality, events would prove another facet of his character: moral courage.

By profession he was a lawyer, but a lawyer who almost became a priest. He never forgot that man's first duty is to God. Though full of good cheer and banter, beneath his clothes he wore a hair shirt—the very model of a happy penitent. He cherished nothing more than his family, but he was also a man of enormous professional and administrative talent, integrity, and capacity for work. He was a rising star in Henry's realm. He had been a member of Parliament, written a mischievous book—*Utopia*—that was widely translated, and became chancellor of England after the death of Cardinal Wolsey. His friends included

Erasmus; John Colet, the English humanist and dean of St. Paul's; and the king himself, who delighted in More's wise and witty conversation while strolling with the pious lawyer, his royal arm draped behind More's neck.

When Henry broke with Rome, More resigned as chancellor. He remained silent on the great issue before the kingdom, but it was a silence that was damning to Henry's conscience. He did not attend the king's wedding to the already-pregnant Anne Boleyn. When he was finally pressed to accept Henry as supreme head of the Church, he refused, was charged with treason, and was sentenced to be hanged, drawn, and quartered, which the king commuted to simple beheading.

Some Protestants have seen this as fair play—and denounced More's reputation for tolerance as hypocrisy—for among More's duties had been sentencing heretics to death. But More was tolerant by the standards of his time, not ours. Like his fellow Catholic reformers, he believed it was permissible for educated men to have private doubts and debate these among themselves; it was quite another thing to allow heretical polemicists to sway people into a course not only of untruth—and this was a world that still believed in religious truth—but possible damnation. To a man like More, charged with executing the law, heretics were peddlers of hellfire. They were the sixteenth-century equivalent of crack dealers, offering a similar high—the intoxication of heretical opinion—and a similar low—a degrading life's end of torment. There was, for More, a yet larger issue. Heretics threatened the destruction of something we no longer have: Christendom, a Europe united by faith. More knew that Europe's Christian civilization was in the balance.

But we should also remember that More allowed his daughter Margaret to marry a young man named William Roper, who was a professed Lutheran. Roper had even been called before Cardinal Wolsey on a charge of heresy and been let off with a mild warning. More showed his son-in-law every hospitality, and when he could not convince him of his errors by dinner table debate, refrained from arguing with him at all. More restricted his hopes "to call him home" by private prayers for his "son Roper."[7] It worked. Roper returned to the Catholic Church and became his father-in-law's first biographer. More's way of dealing with familial dissent was rather more tolerant, loving, and gentle than either that of his sovereign, King Henry VIII, or of the government in Calvinist

Geneva, where the Reformer's own son-in-law and stepdaughter were executed for separate acts of adultery.[8]

More, the gentleman Catholic, met his death with admirable Christian calm, and his customary wit. When he ascended the rickety scaffold to his execution, More said: "I pray you, Mr. Lieutenant, see me safe up, and for my coming down let me shift for myself." He tied his own blindfold and told the crowd that he would die "in the faith and for the faith of the Catholic Church, being the King's good servant, but God's first."[9]

Erasmus, whose courage failed beyond his pen, was appalled that his friend had chosen martyrdom, but nevertheless commemorated him as a man "whose soul was more pure than any snow, whose genius was such that England never had and never will have its like again."[10] Charles V was blunt: "If I had been master of such a servant, of whose doing I myself have had many years no small experience, I would rather have lost the best city in my dominions than lose such a worthy councilor."[11]

Henry, however, was rather free about beheading the best and brightest in the kingdom. Bishop John Fisher had met the axe two weeks before Sir Thomas More. Likewise imprisoned for refusing to acknowledge Henry as head of the Church, he was executed because Pope Paul III had the temerity to raise the enshackled bishop to the rank of cardinal—something that enraged the king. Fisher had been one of England's brightest ecclesiastical lights, a reformer, and a man of high intellectual and personal character. He had taught at Cambridge, where he employed Erasmus. He was confessor to Catherine of Aragon. Like Sir Thomas More, he mortified the flesh, wearing a hair shirt beneath his clothes. He lived and dined simply and kept a skull on his table as a memento mori. Most of all, he was revered as a hardworking priest who had never been seen in "idle walk or wander"[12] and was devoted to caring for the people of Kent. If the king found him guilty of treason, the feeling was reciprocated, for Bishop Fisher openly lectured the king on his errors. He regarded the king as a traitor to his wife and to the Church and had—in a mixture of righteous indignation and diplomatic naïveté—even written to Charles V, asking for his intervention on behalf of the queen and the faith. Erasmus called Fisher and More "the wisest and most saintly men England had."[13] But wise and saintly men were not what King Henry wanted.

If Christendom was stunned by the executions, the king was also beyond religious rebuke. When Becket was murdered at Canterbury Cathedral,

King Henry II did penance, walking part of the road to Canterbury bare-
foot and being scourged by monks at the altar of the cathedral. But King
Henry VIII held himself liberated from papal discipline, and he would
certainly not lower himself to be scourged by monks. Cromwell even had
Becket's shrine destroyed and the saint condemned as a traitor. The
Church was the king's, not the pope's. Even the pope's allies—the duelists
Charles V and Francis I—ensured that Pope Paul III's draft excommunication of the English king was suppressed. Catholic monarchs saw no reason to quash the one Protestant principle of which they approved: the
divine right of kings.

The English Reformation, necessitated by lust, was enforced as a simple power grab. England had no Luther or Calvin. The Protestant revolt
was not even—at least in the king's mind—Protestant, for he continued to
uphold virtually the entirety of the Catholic faith. When the nobles of
northern England rebelled in defense of traditional religion and against
Cromwell's ransacking of the monasteries, Henry counterattacked with a
mixture of diplomacy, arms, and betrayal that defeated the rebellion, and
then ordered that "such dreadful execution . . . be done upon a good
number of the inhabitants of every town, village, and hamlet that have offended, as they may be a fearful spectacle to all others. . . . [Y]ou shall,
without pity or circumstance, cause all the monks and canons that be in
any wise faulty to be tied up without further delay or ceremony."[14] Yet,
when Henry settled on the Six Articles that defined the Church of England, he included among them, amazingly, an affirmation of monasticism, priestly celibacy, the real presence in the Eucharist, and the necessity
of private confession, among other Catholic doctrines. He tried liberalism—for a while allowing everyone to own a vernacular Bible—and then
retracted it when the usual chaos ensued, with men finding all sorts of exotic doctrines in the Bible's pages. If Henry beheaded and disemboweled
recusant Catholics, he did the same to vocal Protestants in a spirit of fair
play and frank equality before the law that was truly English.

Cromwell, however, sided with the Protestants—not out of religious
belief, for he had none, but because they were allies in centralizing power
under the king. For Cromwell, the destruction of shrines, the abolition of
holy days, the branding of Becket as a traitor, and the rest of the sledge-
hammer Protestant program were a way to deny rallying points for
Catholic resistance. When Cromwell himself finally fell victim to the royal

chopping block, it was because he betrothed the king to a Protestant princess, Anne of Cleeves. Her religion did not offend the king, but her looks certainly did. So Cromwell had to go, begging for his life. Faced with death, he made a sudden execution eve conversion to the Church that he had done so much to destroy in England.[15]

Cranmer proved more adept at dancing to his master's tune and repudiating his friends—including Cromwell—when necessary. But after Henry's death—and he died thinking himself a Catholic—his son, Edward VI, took the throne. The boy-king was only nine, and Cranmer at last had someone to whom he could speak as a near equal. Edward was to be the savior of the Protestant cause that had been fading from lack of royal support. So with Edward came another outburst of smashed altars, abolished saints, white-washed walls covering religious murals, proscribed rites, forbidden celebrations, denial of marriage as a sacrament, married priests, ecclesiastical sanction for divorce, and a purely symbolic communion of bread and wine. Edward, at the age of ten, proclaimed the pope "the true son of the Devil, an anti-Christ and an abominable tyrant."[16] The boy knew how to speak Cranmer's language. Edward died in his sixteenth year, but not before he and Cranmer, among others, had conspired to keep Henry VIII's daughter by Catherine of Aragon, the Catholic and rightful heir Mary Tudor, from the throne. It was a misbegotten conspiracy that made Lady Jane Grey queen for a fortnight and dead soon thereafter when she became the focal point of a revolt. Cranmer was arrested. He tried to prevent his execution by recanting his errors. When that didn't save him, he recanted his recantation. That didn't save him either. Therein lies a problem.

Mary Tudor could have gone into the history books as "Queen Mary, Restorer of the Faith," and with that, England might have remained a Catholic country. Instead, we know Mary as "Bloody Mary." In the battle between Catholics and Protestants over who could claim the most martyrs, Mary was an avid scorer of own goals.

When Mary entered London in triumph in 1553, it was with the support of the people, the nobility, and the arms-bearers of the kingdom. On St. Andrew's Day, England was officially, by royal decree, reunited in submission to Rome. The old religion was restored. The people's holidays, traditional forms of worship, and religious art were returned. Sensibly, Mary did not try to reclaim the monasteries for the Church, but let the expropriation stand as a sop to maintaining the peace of the realm.

Returning to England to advise her on reconstructing the Church was Cardinal Reginald Pole, who became archbishop of Canterbury. Pole had his own claim to throne—he was the son of Edward IV's niece—and during the reign of Edward VI had failed by a single vote to become pope. Previously, he had stood up to Henry VIII on behalf of Mary's mother and the Church, was renowned for his good character, and was regarded as a liberal Catholic eager to find common ground to reconcile Lutherans with the Church. By nature a peace-loving, studious man, he seems to have had little influence on Mary's domestic politics.

Her first misstep was her choice of husband, Philip of Spain. It was not, objectively, that Philip was a bad choice. In many ways, he was perfect, linking England, again, to the Habsburgs, the most powerful family in Europe, and he proved a wise counselor to the queen. What made him problematic was xenophobia, which, at this time, was the most popular legacy of the English Reformation. Because she was the daughter of Catherine of Aragon, and had now brought another Spaniard to the English court, Protestants bleated that England was being delivered to a foreign monarchy as well as to a foreign pope. In reality, Philip would give Englishmen little reason to fear. He would not force Englishmen to give up bear baiting in favor of bullfights. He would not import the Spanish Inquisition. He would not compel morris dancers to buy Spanish-made castanets and dance the flamenco. He was, in fact, very well aware of the mood of the people.

Oddly, it was his wife who misjudged her *Volk,* her mind perhaps already clouded by the cancer that is presumed to have killed her. It was she who was not content with reclaiming the throne and restoring the Church. She felt compelled to seek vengeance on those who had betrayed her mother, denied the Church, and remained a threat—in her own mind, at least—to her security. Between 1555 and 1558—against the advice of Philip and other Catholics close to the throne—Mary ordered executed nearly three hundred people. It was Mary who delivered to the Protestants of England their greatest propaganda weapon—a book, John Foxe's *Book of Martyrs*, which commemorated the burnings at the stake and forever linked in the English mind the Roman Church and persecution.

When Mary died in 1558, the Catholic cause in England was effectively ended. The new Queen, Elizabeth I, the daughter of Henry VIII and Anne Boleyn, issued an Act of Uniformity in 1559, which created England's unique Protestant-Catholic via media, with the queen reserving for herself all the powers her father had wrested from the Church. If she tilted the theology in a Protestant direction it was because she saw, as had Cromwell, Catholics beholden to a foreign pope backed by foreign princes. But she never tilted it too far, because Elizabeth was no more a Protestant than she was a Catholic. She had no sympathy with the Puritans, whose yearning for a democratic dictatorship, on the Calvinist model, would have threatened the crown and whose public strictures would have denied Merrie England its merriness and the English Renaissance the works of its playwrights, like Shakespeare, who, incidentally, was probably a Catholic.[17] She was simply a patriot who wanted a patriotic national religion and cared not a fig for theological dispute—and she won.

Elizabeth's huge advance over her father is that she made the Anglican Church popular. She did so by displacing the cult of the Virgin Mary with the cult of the Virgin Queen who was too devoted to her people to marry. Royal processions replaced religious ones. She became the embodiment of England. Her accession day became an immediate national holiday. She was the deliverer of battlefield victories, and the inaugurator of an English Renaissance of literary and worldly discovery, punctuated, in good Tudor style, by a chopping block for handsome members of the opposite sex, like the earl of Essex, who eventually offended the crown. If the queen—and her successor, James I, who executed Sir Walter Raleigh for mocking his Scotch antecedents—held the power to execute her handsomest and wittiest subjects, it was because she commanded a total state.

She had extremely powerful advisers—like William Cecil, Lord Burghley—but her bejeweled hand alone held the power of praise or condemnation, and she pursued a pragmatic course. She governed an English church whose trinity of God, Queen, and Country gave British sea dogs like Sir Francis Drake and Sir John Hawkins—the latter of whom took advantage of King Phillip II's moral qualms to elbow aside Spaniards in the slave trade—a banner of religious patriotism for raiding the Spanish Main. Where once Vikings had raided monasteries out of sheer rapine, now their English inheritors seized booty from Catholic Spain and her possessions, secure in the Protestant doctrine that they were justified by faith and were liberating gold from the allies of the whore of Babylon. Of course, it was also an awful lot of fun and personally enriching to boot.

Elizabeth's patriotism united the people. The swashbuckling exploits of her pirate heroes gave them pride. And she provided them with an enemy: Elizabeth did everything she could to distract the Catholic powers that might menace her. To hamstring Spain, she let sail her salty sea dogs, and she supported the Dutch Protestants in a bloody revolt against their Spanish overlords. She encouraged the Protestant Huguenots in a grim civil war in France that crippled any hope of reuniting the "auld alliance" of France and Scotland to place the Catholic Mary, Queen of Scots—and onetime queen of France, where she had been raised—on the English throne. Mary had, perhaps, a better claim to that throne than Elizabeth.[18] But the beautiful, troubled charmer, whose life was a Gothic melodrama, ended up fleeing to, rather than marching on, England. She reigned in Scotland for only six years, during which time she occasionally sparred in interviews with the Reformer John Knox. Her doom came when she was charged with being a murderous harlot. She was probably innocent of this once common Scottish practice, but her armies failed to resolve the matter in her favor. Elizabeth imprisoned her cousin for two decades, and then reluctantly ordered her executed as a potential Catholic usurper. As for Elizabeth's other Celtic problem, she sent a huge army to loyally Catholic and perpetually lawless Ireland under the earl of Essex. Essex had the impossible task of subduing that land of "happy wars and sad love songs," and if the reception and meting out of murder and slaughter do indeed cheer the Irish soul, this was a very happy time.

For those who were not united behind her Anglican church, Elizabeth had a simple remedy: she made Catholicism illegal and branded its adherents as traitors secretly in league with England's foreign enemies. While the people's patriotism shielded Elizabeth from charges that she was a Bloody Mary in reverse, the great British historian, and Protestant, Thomas Babington Macaulay wrote that Elizabeth's draconian measures against Catholics were "even more odious than the persecution with which her sister had harassed the Protestants. We say more odious. For Mary had at least the plea of fanaticism. She did nothing for her religion which she was not prepared to suffer for it. She had held to it firmly under persecution. She fully believed it to be essential to salvation. If she burned the bodies of her subjects, it was in order to rescue their souls. . . .

But what can be said in defence of a ruler who is at once indifferent and intolerant?"[19]

Elizabeth made that combination of indifference and intolerance the very law and spirit of England. While the majority of Englishmen remained at least nominal Catholics, their patriotism compelled nearly all of them to submit to the queen. Perversely, this was especially true after Pope Paul IV excommunicated her, presenting Catholic Englishmen with a choice they did not want to face. It is an irony of history that if the Church had retained its Renaissance spirit and not been thrown on the defensive by the Reformation, it might have employed subtler diplomacy with the English crown and recovered England for the Church. For the English Reformation was nothing if not worldly, done not on grounds of religion per se, but of maintaining peace and public order. On that score Elizabeth was, in domestic matters, as opposed to the Puritans on her left—she detested, for instance, John Knox, whose *First Blast of the Trumpet Against the Monstrous Regiment of Women* could not be much enjoyed by a queen—as she was to the Catholics on her right, despite their soundness on "the monstrous regiment of women" question.

Even as Catholics plotted against her—with the encouragement of the papacy—Pope Sixtus V readily confessed that "she is certainly a great Queen and were she only a Catholic she would be our dearly beloved. Just look at how well she governs! She is only a woman, only mistress of half an island, and yet she makes herself feared by Spain, by France, by the Empire, by all."[20] The one perhaps irreconcilable point of difference between a Renaissance pope and Elizabeth might have been authority over the appointment of bishops, but there were certainly precedents in France and elsewhere for an unhappy if necessary accommodation by the Church. As it was, the Church had no more interest in accommodation than Elizabeth did. The Church wanted victory.

And in the end, who can really blame Her? If continental Protestantism demanded that men believe, in Charles V's words, "that the whole of Christianity should be in error a thousand years or more," Anglicanism asked men to subordinate Church doctrine and practice to the discretion of the government. If this was an absurdity—and it was certainly not seen so by Protestants—it was an absurdity tied to patriotism, and an Englishman could grow fond of it over time, even as its inevitable outcome was to secularize society. As domestic *Realpolitik* it made sense, but it was an obvious denial of the importance—or even the existence—of religious truth, a denial that is perhaps the most important benefaction of Protestantism to the modern, secularized world. It is against that denial—and in defense of the historic faith—that Catholic martyrs went to their deaths in Elizabethan England.

With Catholicism proscribed by law, its priests hunted as though they were sacrament-bearing Robin Hoods, and with loyalist households creating that English gift to interior design, the priest hole, where outlaw clerics could be hidden from informers, a remarkable man and cardinal of the Church, William Allen, brought hope. He founded a seminary-in-exile at Douai, in what was then the Spanish Netherlands and is now part of France. Here he worked on an English translation of the Latin Vulgate Bible—the Douay-Rheims Bible, which was published shortly before the King James Bible—and trained priests who would be smuggled home.

By the end of the sixteenth century, more than three hundred priests were working in England's shadows, dodging the rack and the chopping block, offering the sacraments to believers. But an even greater number of loyal priests and laymen perished under the persecution. Among the most famous was the martyr—and later saint—Edmund Campion. Dashing, handsome, he had been a fellow at Oxford, where he had greatly impressed the queen with his oratory. His studies led him to Rome—or, rather, first to Douai. He became a Jesuit and returned to England as a priest to recusants. This was when to be a priest was to be a secret agent, comparable to a celibate and apostolically ordained James Bond, papal monogram on his cufflinks, smuggled into Soviet Russia. Campion was eventually captured and brought to trial. His words, spoken before the court that would sentence him to death, are unanswerable in their logic.

> The only thing that we have now to say is, that if our religion do make us traitors, we are worthy to be condemned; but otherwise are, and have been, as good subjects as ever the Queen had.
>
> In condemning us you condemn all your own ancestors—all the ancient priests, bishops and kings—all that was once the glory of England, the island of saints, and the most devoted child of the See of Peter.
>
> For what have we taught, however you may qualify it with the odious name of treason, that they did not uniformly teach?[21]

Campion was hanged and then butchered. The blood sprayed the coat of Henry Walpole, a young, easygoing, Cambridge-educated wit. That blood, and Campion's example, made a Jesuit and a martyr out of Walpole as well. And so the torch was passed.

The English historian C. R. N. Routh calls Campion "that noblest of all the Catholic martyrs. A scholar, a gentleman, a priest, a man of genuine holiness, he was also a lovable, courageous and honourable Englishman. . . . In the light of his pure religious faith, the natural and necessary political anxieties of his opponents appear almost mean and shabby."[22] But mean and shabby were the natural inheritors of the "goggle-eyed whore" and the flesh-flapping despot who had severed England from Rome. An accident of lust, consummated by state interest, ramified by strategic chess—with barely a theological word—made England the Protestant power par excellence, and the guarantor of religious division in Europe.

# THE HONORABLE COMPANY

IN 1559, THE YEAR ELIZABETH proclaimed her Act of Uniformity, the Venetian ambassador to Rome wrote, "In many countries, obedience to the pope has almost ceased, and matters are becoming so critical that, if God does not interfere, they will soon be desperate. . . . Germany . . . leaves little hope of being cured. Poland is in almost as hopeless a state. The disorders which have lately taken place in France and Spain are too well known for me to speak of them, and the Kingdom of England . . . after returning a short time to her old obedience, has again fallen into heresy. Thus the spiritual power of the pope is so straitened that the only remedy is a council summoned by the common consent of all princes. Unless this reduces the affairs of religion to order, a grave calamity is to be feared."[23] In fact, the Council of Trent had been in occasional session since 1537, but to little obvious effect. If the Council was of scant use, the papacy was not much better. From Leo X (1513–1521) through Julius III (1550–1555), the popes had been more adept at subsidizing art than subduing Protestants. Leo X thought Luther would go away. Pope Hadrian VI (1522–1523) was a reformer more worried about the Turks. Clement VII (1523–1534) showed that short of a papal army that could rival France and the Habsburgs, a pope was doomed to the vagaries of power politics, which Clement didn't play very well. After two ineffectual but upright popes, Paul III (1534–1549) was a throwback to the Renaissance. He commissioned Michelangelo, awarded cardinals' hats to relatives, and, unfortunately, like Clement, feared domination by the Habsburgs more than he feared the breaking up of Christendom. Julius III (1550–1555) kept the Renaissance spirit alive by making a handsome fifteen-year-old monkey-keeper a cardinal.

But beneath the view of the Venetian ambassador was a groundswell that would reinvigorate the sinews of the faith. The key man would be Ignatius Loyola; the key army, his creation, the Jesuits. He was born, fittingly, in a castle in 1491, and trained from boyhood to be a knight. Like St. Francis, his dreams were of chivalry and military action. After long service at court, where he led a boisterous and amorous life, he was transferred to the army barracks at Pamplona in 1517, and four years later he led the defense of the city against the French. He served gallantly, but when his right leg was broken by a cannon ball, the game was up, and the city surrendered. His French captors showed the beau geste spirit in gently bearing the wounded soldier back home to Loyola and his family. His recuperation was long and painful—his leg had to be rebroken and reset, then rebroken and reset again.

The young soldier, whose reading until now had consisted almost entirely of *Amadis of Gaul* and other tales of chivalry of the sort later satirized by Cervantes, had only two titles at his disposal: a life of Christ and a collection of lives of the saints. With nothing better to do, he read them—at first reluctantly and with boredom. Yet soon his imagination seized on the saints and the Holy Family. He saw them cast in a drama as stirring as knightly battles. In him was reborn the medieval dream of the Crusades. He would rival the saints in holiness and self-denial. He would single-handedly capture Jerusalem. But his ideas of ascetic competition and martial glory faded, replaced by a vision of peace. Holy Mary and the Christ Child appeared to him. Lust left his body and he was instilled with a commitment to celibacy and a mission, repeated throughout his life, to recall women to the example of the Virgin Mother.

He eagerly seized the sacrament of penance, taking three days to examine his conscience, list his sins, and confess them. He knelt in vigil before a statue of the Virgin and left his weapons at her altar. The former dandified officer gave his fine clothes to the poor and took on the garments of a pilgrim. He intended to march to Barcelona, and from there embark for Jerusalem. Along the way, he took shelter in a cave, where, in prayer and fasting, he underwent a dark night—actually, dark weeks—of the soul, mortifying his flesh for his terrible sense of sin, to the point that he almost killed himself.

He emerged from this bout battered but wiser—the experience of conquering his body became the basis for his famous *Spiritual Exercises*.

The two years that followed his vigil were a painful litany of sickness, hunger, and disappointment. After he had struggled so hard to reach the Holy Land, the Franciscans took one look at this madman Crusader, decided he would set "inter-faith dialogue"—as we would call it today—back by two centuries, and sent him packing. In 1524 he was back in Barcelona. With one medieval avenue cut off to him, he took up another: he became a student, spending more than a decade exercising his mind as he had exercised his body as a soldier. The former soldier who had once thought of nothing but honor, sat next to schoolboys, learning the Latin he had never learned before. After four years of cramming, he was ready for university studies. He moved restlessly and tumultuously from Alcala, to Salamanca, and finally to the University of Paris, obtaining a master's degree in 1535 but collecting along the way another roll call of trouble: twice imprisoned by the Inquisition, beaten senseless by young toughs for preaching chastity to women, mocked—and criticized—for his disciplined study and severe mortifications.

Still, in Paris he developed a following—a small company of men that he led, like a military officer, in spiritual exercises and hoped to lead to the Holy Land. Among them were two future saints: Pierre Favre, a former shepherd, and Francis Xavier, the future missionary to Asia, a man of birth, learning, wit, good looks, and good times, who had found himself won over by the piercing eyes—and piercing questions—of Ignatius.

They marched over the Alps to Venice, only to find the city at war with the Turks. There would be no passage to Jerusalem. Making the best of this, they had themselves ordained as priests and retired to Rome, where they offered themselves to Pope Paul III, to be deployed as he saw fit. Some were made professors, others assigned to hospitals or schools. Ignatius became a missionary to the prostitutes of Rome. He also drafted a rule for his new religious order. The rule would be expanded and perfected over the course of Ignatius's life. It emphasized immediate, unquestioning obedience to the "general" in charge of the order and to the pope. There was a two-year boot camp to drill candidates in executing orders, after which a member could, through advanced academic study, rise up a hierarchy of command. Interestingly, considering that Ignatius had done so much to mortify the flesh, the members of his company—the Society of Jesus—did not pledge themselves to any ascetic practices beyond the usual monastic vows of poverty, chastity, and obedience. Like the monastic military orders, Ignatius thought it more important for his men to be fit to fight, for they, too, would wage war for God and His Church. But they would go armed with intellect rather than swords. In 1540, the pope officially approved the initial rule of the new order, and in 1541 Ignatius was elected its first general.

The Jesuits became the spearhead of Catholic reform. Their incorruptibility, unshakable devotion, and intellectual prowess made them perfect foils to reclaim Protestants for the Church. They went to succor besieged Catholics in Britain. They stood athwart the Protestant advance in France. They recovered the loyalty of much of Mitteleuropa. Their spiritual ardor took them on adventurous missions to the New World, India, China, Japan, and elsewhere. No challenge was too great, for every Jesuit—a name given them by their Protestant enemies—wanted to prove himself in dangerous and difficult work. Jesuits won souls as missionaries, they cared for the sick, and many became educators. The Society created a network of free secondary schools and universities that had no equal. Their influence rose in society, and, just as the Templars became the bankers of Europe, so did the Jesuits become confessors to the aristocracy.

The Jesuits proved the dictum that the opposite of love is not hate, but power.[24] The Jesuits' love of Christ meant complete, unquestioning submission to the Church, Christ's corporate body. A Jesuit would no more think of criticizing Christ's body than a loving husband would think of criticizing his wife's. He would never say: "Your nose—it's too Roman. That carbuncle—that didn't used to be there. In fact, your neck is sagging, your eyes are lined, you drink too much—you're a wreck. I'm going to trade you in for a new model." Putting it that way is the way of Henry VIII, who would have added, "Damn me! What's the use of a brood mare who can't breed?" Luther would have been more graphic: "Be gone you stinking whore of corruption, whose pits of iniquity—like defecating weasels—despoil my bed linens." Or something like that. But, again, for a Catholic, *semper fidelis* is what matters.

When Ignatius Loyola punished his body, it was so that it would better serve God's will rather than his own. Such mortification seems positively perverse in our day, because we never think of training the body for God, only for athletic events or for personal power and prestige. In the world of modern psychobabble, if men are from Mars and women are from Venus, Ignatius Loyola was from Christendom and modern man is from commercial television. Loyola esteemed Christ and His Church. Modern man esteems himself. Like a Protestant, he finds his own individual salvation outside the corporate body of the Church. Like a Protestant, he believes in predestination, though in his case it does not involve damnation, but excuses—from biological determinism or psychology—for individual failings.

Loyola's goal was far different from that of modern education and commerce. It was to ensure that a Jesuit's mind was active and supple, but disciplined; while able to contest with any foe, its end was the love of God, and finding that love was the very purpose of his spiritual exercises. Though the Jesuits were the most talented religious leaders of their time, they preached no new creed; they set up no new Church. There was no will to power that characterized Protestant leaders like Luther and Calvin, who, in their intellectual pride, saw themselves as new prophets, new popes. For the Jesuits, the prophets remained in the Bible and there was only one pope, and he led Christ's apostolic Church.

# ROME RESURGENT

BY THE MIDDLE OF THE SIXTEENTH CENTURY, the real popes, in Rome, had finally become engines of lasting reform, but not before two engine backfires. The first couldn't be helped. Pope Marcellus II (1555), a reformer, died within a month of his elevation. The second proved that reform was not a simple matter. Pope Paul IV (1555–1559) was seventy-nine when he began his pontificate. The pent-up reformist fury of this septuagenarian ascetic led him to dismiss all other reformers as impediments (or worse) and to repeated political disasters. Because he hated Spanish domination of Italy, he went to war against the most orthodox

Catholic power in Europe. When the Spaniards defeated him, it was with humility—the conquering duke of Alva kissed his foot—and puzzled brows. The pope's ham-fisted demands on Queen Elizabeth—let alone his distrust of the Catholic Mary Tudor whose husband was that terrible thing, a Spaniard, and whose archbishop of Canterbury he suspected of too much liberalism—ensured that there would be no rapprochement with England. He gave teeth to the inquisition in Rome on the theory that the way to reform was to bite down hard on the lax and heretical. When the pope died, there was jubilation in the city and the inquisition's offices were ransacked.

Pope Paul IV's unfortunate idea of restoring a disordered house had been to break up all the furniture. His enmity not just for Spaniards, but for the Habsburgs—whom he saw as Lutheran appeasers—resulted in Ferdinand I being crowned Holy Roman Emperor in 1558 without the assistance of the pope; thus, on grounds of irreconcilable differences, the tumultuous seven-hundred-year marriage of emperor and pontiff was inadvertently dissolved. Subsequent popes, through the end of the sixteenth century, were more adroit and took a more rational, ordered, and measured line. Pope Pius IV (1559–1565) put brakes on the inquisition, informing its officers that they "would better please him were they to proceed with gentlemanly courtesy than with monkish harshness."[25]

Pius IV was equally diplomatic with Spain and Germany, repairing the damage done by Paul IV, and hoped—but was disappointed—that he might see a reunion with England. He renewed the papacy's role in subsidizing art and learning, which Pope Paul IV had angrily thrown overboard. Though, like a Renaissance pope, he had fathered children, he had the excuse of having pursued a secular career as a lawyer and administrator (he had also studied medicine) before being called to the Church. With him reform truly began. He closed the Council of Trent and put its words into action. The Council's most important work included reforming the Latin Mass as the liturgical standard for the next four hundred years, strengthening the intellectual standards of the Church through seminary requirements, restating Catholic doctrine and dogma in light of Protestant attacks, and reasserting papal supremacy.

His successor was a pope who became a saint, Pius V (1566–1572). If Pius IV eased the papacy into reform, Pius V cleansed it with austerity and purity. It was as if St. Francis had become pope. He shocked Rome with his personal care for the sick and the poor, his unstinting prayer and penance, the demanding moral standards he enforced on the clergy, and his reinvigoration of the Roman inquisition. Corruption was banished, but so, too, was the freedom of la dolce vita, so beloved of the Italians. The rulers courted by Pius IV found Pius V less accommodating. He excommunicated Elizabeth, admonished Catholics to depose the Virgin Queen in favor of Mary, Queen of Scots, and, unlike previous popes, urged the complete suppression of Protestants in France, the Netherlands, and the Holy Roman Empire. His great wish of defeating the Turk was granted in the tremendous naval battle at Lepanto on October 7, 1571, a victory still celebrated on the first Sunday in October as the Feast of the Rosary. Less pliant than Pius IV and not driven by vendettas like the vinegary Paul IV, Pius V brought a firm moral clarity to the papacy. Stringency goes down better when delivered by a saint.

Though not a saint—in fact, his pre-clerical life was more in tune with Renaissance mores—Gregory XIII (1572–1585) nevertheless proved a tremendous pope and diligent reformer. His keynote was education, endowing colleges to train clergy to win back Protestant England and Germany, convert Eastern Orthodox Greece, and embark on half a dozen other missionary endeavors, even to darkest Hungary and far-flung Japan. Like the Jesuits, with whom he worked on this project and for whom he built a college, he believed that the strength of the Counter Reformation would lie in a priesthood of superior education. One could say he took a special interest in Germany, so intent was he on educating German priests and keeping his fingers on the German pulse, but in fact his capacity for work gave him a special interest in everything. He sent priests as diplomats to Sweden, Russia, and Poland, and won at least the last back to full communion with the Church. He continued the rebuilding of Rome. He gave the world a new, more accurate, calendar—the one we use today—the Gregorian, thus highlighting that Catholicism was the religion of science, Protestantism the religion of ignorance. Protestants proved so difficult to teach that they actually prohibited the Gregorian calendar by law. It took many of them more than a century to understand. Britain, and by extension its colonies in North America, took a little longer, finally signing on in 1752. But if the Protestants were slow learners, they can take comfort that the Eastern Orthodox have proved slower still. Russia did not accept the new calendar until the czars fell to the communists in 1918, which was the wrong way to get it. Greece did not convert its calendar until 1923. Unhappy at this secular reunification with the West, the recalcitrant Eastern Orthodox churches have never accepted the Gregorian calendar. *Plus ça change* . . .

Gregory was a military pope as well. He organized an Irish invasion of England, which failed as a result of having an English soldier of fortune as commander in chief who diverted the troops to attack Morocco instead (it had a better climate). The pope famously celebrated a Mass of thanksgiving for the triumph of Catholicism over Protestant error in France—an event known to history as the St. Bartholomew's Day Massacre. Less well reported is that he wept when he learned of the bloody circumstances.

The one hindrance to his remarkable pontificate was money. For all the Protestant accusations about the scandalous material wealth of the papacy, the fact is, the papal treasury rarely had enough money to cover the enormous financial responsibilities of the Church—which covered everything from restoring and governing Rome and the Papal States, to establishing New World outposts, shutting the Turk out of Christendom, supporting schools and missionaries, caring for the poor, and a dozen other major commitments. Gregory's answer to this difficulty was to enforce the letter of the law on major landowners in the Papal States whose properties, by right, should have reverted to the papacy. It was a case, however, of Gregory being right by law, but wrong by practicality. The effect of enforcement was to turn these powerful Italian families into banditti chieftains who returned Bella Italia to its natural and ever recurring state of chaos and criminality. Under Gregory, the Church continued its process of self-purification, but Italy became more unmanageable.

In Pope Sixtus V (1585–1590), the man and the hour were met: the Church gained another towering pontiff and the Mafiosi found a pope who was bishop, judge, and executioner. If anyone doubts the Church's support for the death penalty, they should read the record of Sixtus V. If Judge Roy Bean was the law west of the Pecos in the American Wild West, Pope Sixtus V was the law of central Italy who proclaimed, "While I live, every criminal must die."[26] Every available noose was filled—*Noli me tangere* (Touch me not) became a papal inscription—and for once, Italy's roadways were safe from brigandage.

Along with laying down the law, he offered the disgruntled landowners a concession by allowing them to keep their property even if the deeds had officially lapsed. As a Franciscan—and therefore used to doing much with little—he proved an extraordinary administrator, balancing the papal books. At the same time, he continued the papacy's massive rebuilding and reclamation projects in Rome with waterworks, churches, hospitals, streets, a new Vatican library, and a restoration—and Christian appropriation—of pagan monuments; revised the Vulgate Bible; restructured the papal curia into a form that would last more than three hundred years; and played hardball diplomacy—successfully—to achieve a balance of power between Spain and France, the two great Catholic rivals in western Europe.

Because he had brought peace, prosperity, and good government to Rome, the people, being Italian, of course hated him. The next three popes—Urban VII, Gregory XIV, and Innocent IX—had combined reigns of little more than a year. The last pope of the sixteenth century was Clement VIII (1592–1605). Each of these last four popes suffered from malaria or other diseases, which perhaps illustrates how necessary was the rebuilding and sanitizing of Rome. Of them, Clement was the only one strong enough to survive and to advance the revitalizing of the faith. He was another man of tremendous personal piety and devotion—his confessor for three decades was a saint, Philip Neri. As pope, he revised Sixtus's revision of the Vulgate—which needed help—making it a standard Catholic Bible for three centuries. He recognized the former Protestant and formerly excommunicated Henry IV as the rightful Catholic king of France and, in doing so, accepted the Edict of Nantes, guaranteeing religious toleration to the Huguenots and putting the Church on the side of religious pluralism—at least where reality dictated its necessity. This was, interestingly enough, in liberal contradistinction to Protestant England and the Nordic countries. Such toleration did not mitigate missionary efforts. Under his pontificate, millions of Poles abandoned Eastern Orthodoxy for Catholicism. The Church reclaimed ground in Switzerland, and it continued its efforts to regain Protestant England and Scandinavia. Clement also continued the papacy's war against crime, but he balanced that unpopular policy with the Jubilee Year celebration of 1600 that brought three million faithful pilgrims to Rome.

It was a brilliant capstone to half a century of recovery and reform. But it could not disguise the fact that the great work of a millennium—the making of Christian Europe—had been undone. The Protestant revolt began the unraveling of Christianity. Over the next four centuries, many were those who would pull on the string.

## CHAPTER SIXTEEN

# A CENTURY OF WAR

⟫●⟪

FROM THE ACCESSION of Elizabeth I of England (1558) to the treaties of Westphalia (1648)—and actually spilling before and after—Europe was continually at war. Two of the greatest engagements were at sea. The first was a great Catholic triumph, the second a great Catholic failure.

The triumph came at Lepanto (now known as the Gulf of Corinth). There, in 1571, 66,000 men and more than 200 ships, not all of which could join the battle line, assembled from Spain, the city-states of Italy, and the Knights of Malta. This Holy League was organized by the pope and commanded by an Austrian, Don Juan, the bastard son of Charles V, which gave him good bloodlines as far as bastards go. Also enrolled in the Catholic battalions was Miguel de Cervantes, the future author of *Don Quixote*. Opposed to them was the equally large Turkish navy, which fully intended to dominate the Mediterranean. Don Juan would stop them.

Already that summer, the Turks had taken Cyprus—seizing the heroic Catholic commander, relieving him of his skin (while he was still alive), stuffing him, and returning him to the sultan as a hunting trophy. Don Juan's avenging fleet, attended by Jesuits, Dominicans, Franciscans, and Capuchin monks (who would join the fighting), unfurled its Catholic banners, consecrated by the pope. Sailing against them: the fleet of Islam, flying pennants with verses from the Koran, its spy ships painted entirely black and scouting the Catholic advance by night. When the two forces collided, it was the largest naval engagement in the history of Christendom. Galleys crashed into each other, grappling hooks secured them, and armed men leapt at each other's throats, arrow against harquebus, scimitar versus sword, blasting muskets meeting charging pikes. According to an eyewitness account, a marmoset belonging to Don Juan picked up a Turkish grenade and hurled it back at the enemy.

When the smoke cleared, and the timber-wrecked ships sank away, more than 30,000 Turks had perished, compared to 7,500 Catholics, though many of these were knights and noblemen. Their deaths, however, had freed 12,000 Christian slaves who had been chained as rowers for the Turkish ships. Bad weather, exhaustion, and pillaging prevented the Holy League from further pursuit of the devastated Turks. St. Pius V—who had insisted on prayer and holiness as an armor for his Crusaders—attributed the smashing victory to the intercession of the Blessed Virgin Mother, and Catholic churches rang out praises to God in celebration.

The next great Catholic sea battle was in 1588, when Philip II of Spain massed his Armada against England. Spain had long been ravaged by English piracy. Just the year before, Sir Francis Drake had led a rollicking series of raids on the Spanish coast, "singeing the king of Spain's beard" and leaving the Spaniards, like the pope, wishing that these daring Englishmen and their queen could be restored to the faith, for what marvels might they achieve on the side of the cross. But the exasperated Spanish king concluded that only swords and gunpowder would restore the English crown to the Church. The Spanish Armada was to propel a Spanish invasion of England. The Armada numbered 130 ships—far less than Philip's naval commanders requested for such an awesome task—and a force of nearly 30,000 men. Included among them were hundreds of religious men— monks and priests—blessing this western Crusade and ready to reconsecrate England for the Church. Another 30,000 men were in the Spanish Netherlands, ready to be transported to England once the Spanish forces had established a foothold on the island. In July 1588, the Armada appeared in the English Channel, and the English ships came out to meet it.

As at Lepanto, the Spaniards intended to ram the enemy fleet, dragging the ships in with grappling hooks, while Spanish swords and guns drenched the enemy decks with blood. But the English sea dogs had reinvented naval warfare. Their low-slung ships—making them hard to hit with cannon fire—favored the hit-and-run, blasting Spanish ships from a safe distance, and maneuvering speedily around them. The engagement lasted for several days—every one of them a disaster for the Spanish, who were peppered, hounded, and sideswiped by English ships, which they could not escape and which deftly avoided Spanish gunnery. After eight days of action, thousands of Spanish casualties, and every Spanish ship crippled, the Spaniards fled, swept by stormy seas, around Scotland, and then around Ireland, trying to arc back to Spain. Ships sank, drowning thousands, and shipwrecked men who had sailed with God in their hearts and priestly blessings on their heads were murdered in their hundreds by the Irish who regarded them as sheep to be slaughtered. Perhaps 5,000 men died on the trip around Ireland. Only 54 ships and 10,000 sick and wounded sailors and soldiers returned to Spain.

One of the commanders of the Spanish fleet, Juan Martinez de Recalde, had actually predicted the outcome. "It's very simple. It is well known that we fight in God's cause. So when we meet the English, God will surely arrange matters so that we can grapple and board them. . . . Unless God helps us with [such] a miracle the English, who have faster and handier ships than ours, and many more long-range guns, and who know their advantage just as well as we do, will never close with us at all, but stand off and knock us to pieces."[1] There was no miracle. Perhaps Pope Sixtus V—who had promised to subsidize an *invasion* of England, but not a naval failure—had too little faith in the enterprise. Perhaps God is, indeed, on the side of the big battalions, faster ships, and more accurate guns. If nothing else, the failure of the Spanish Armada should remind augurers of God's will not to presume too much.

We should also remember that rushing to England's defense were not only Drake and Hawkins, and other Protestant sea dogs, but the near entirety of Catholic England—who despite this patriotic showing continued to be persecuted. It is a fact of history that nationalism has nearly always trumped religion as a primary source of loyalty, and it did so here. Even Catholic Englishmen took pride in their nation's naval skill and in the defense of the realm. Not a single English ship was lost in the contest. England had defeated an attempted invasion by the greatest empire of the sixteenth century.

# THE WAR IN THE NETHERLANDS

THE VAST DOMINIONS of Spain crossed the seas to the Americas, the Philippines, and all the way to back to Europe via the Netherlands. But the Spaniards, rich in priests, monks, mystics, noblemen, bullfighters, and musicians, held an empire of conquistadors and gold. What Spain lacked was a merchant class to turn that gold into wealth. Spaniards, as a rule, did not trouble themselves with commerce. They lived off pride rather than profits, and thus, the vast empire of Spain was continually in debt.

This put the Spanish at odds with the most practical men within their empire, the burghers of the Netherlands. The Netherlanders were a commercial people above all else. They knew how to balance books. They knew the value of trade. They regarded their Spanish overlords as arrogant and improvident, and their Spanish garrisons as an affront.

The people of the Netherlands were, like the people of Spain, Catholic, but their Catholicism echoed that of their liberal countryman Erasmus. Unlike in Spain, however, there was a developing Protestant segment of the population, especially among the commercial class, who preferred a religion they could design for themselves, in the same way that they made their business arrangements. Allied to them were members of the petty nobility, who, like their colleagues in Germany, England, and France, saw Church property ready to be plucked in the name of reforming religion.

Even though Protestants were by far the minority, Netherlanders were united in their opposition to the Spanish Inquisition, which King Philip II inflicted upon them. They regarded it as a simple injustice and sent petitions to Margaret of Parma, the Catholic regent of the Netherlands, asking that she lift the Inquisition. She passed the petitions on to King Philip. At first, he adamantly refused; Margaret, in turn, was met in the Netherlands with official protests and mass emigrations. Within a month Philip reconsidered, and two months later officially ended the Inquisition in the Netherlands. Philip now learned a hard lesson in statecraft. Rebellions occur not when people are being repressed, but when oppression lifts and liberation is in the air. In the absence of the inquisitors, the ranks of religious dissenters swelled. Protestantism and nationalism again proved to be fervent and fruitful allies.

It was no more than two weeks after Philip's concession—which he already regretted—when the orgies of destruction began. As prescribed by Protestant scripture, churches were desecrated, with every chalice, altar, artwork, and musical instrument broken and destroyed; monks and nuns were chased through the streets, their libraries burned; priestly vestments and the Eucharist were torn apart or used in satanic parodies of the Mass. Though he disassociated himself from such scenes—and continued to do so throughout decades of war—the nationalist Prince William of Orange knew that revolution was to come. If he could lead it, the Netherlands would be his. The prince was still a professed Catholic, but he well understood that Protestants were his most likely allies, and German mercenaries his most likely recruits.

Philip, meanwhile, who lived in a palace that doubled as a monastery, responded to these outrages with a mailed fist. His instrument was the duke of Alva, the most fearsome commander in Spain. Alva's action was swift and brutal. His so-called Council of Blood, created in 1567, amounted to his own inquisition. It sniffed out traitors and heretics and executed them with judicial celerity. His troops marched into the more rebellious cities and crushed their resistance. The Spaniards were victorious, but Alva needed to keep his men in the field to douse the embers upon which William of Orange cast his hopes. To pay his army, Alva—who was now regent, Margaret having resigned—raised taxes to levels that Protestant and Catholic Netherlanders found punitive. He seized property belonging to protesters, rebels, and the English. The English reacted by cutting off trade with the Netherlands. The rebels launched another offensive, martyred priests, and in their hatred of the Spanish brought new color to man's lengthy catalog of murderous barbarity. "Spaniards had ceased to be human in their eyes. On one occasion, a surgeon at Veer cut the heart from a Spanish prisoner, nailed it on the vessel's prow, and invited the townsmen to come and fasten their teeth in it, which many did with savage satisfaction."[2]

Alva's men charged back into the field and sent the rebels packing, but they also went on a murderous rampage against *everyone,* with a destructive mania against *everything*—including Catholic churches—in their sight. While the duke of Alva was a brilliant soldier who cultivated a reputation for ferocity—even tyranny, gladly appearing worse than he really was—as a means of psychological warfare,[3] in the Netherlands he inexcusably lost control of his men. The Spanish duke, who postured as the merciless hunter of heretics, became the commander of a mob of indiscriminate butchers. If warfare is the controlled use of violence for political means, this was no longer war. It was simply blood-fevered savagery. Cities were besieged and entire towns laid waste. Hundreds at a time were murdered in mass reprisals. Even Netherlanders loyal to the Spanish king, including churchmen, demanded the dictator's removal. Among Alva's critics was Pope Pius V, who had previously praised his military triumphs. Others responded by throwing their lot in with the rebels.

Philip, whose severity of demeanor concealed his pragmatism, agreed that Alva had to go. The duke was relieved and sent to conquer Portugal. His eventual replacement in the Netherlands was the dashing Don Juan, who had been at a loose end since his victory at Lepanto. The Spaniards were still at war but trying to stay on their best behavior. Prince William of Orange put them on the diplomatic defensive when, in 1576, he called on all Netherlanders to expel the hated Spaniards and be confident that, in a liberated Netherlands, each man would have freedom to practice his own religion. This was a clever proposal, more attractive to the majority, liberal Catholic Netherlanders than to the beady-eyed Calvinists. William, for political reasons, had by now proclaimed himself a member of the Reformed faith, but he also saw that his ultimate victory would reside in winning over the majority Catholics on a platform of tolerance. He trusted that the Calvinists were his inevitable allies, even if their more fervent adherents publicly suspected him of irreligion.

If William outmaneuvered the Spanish in the war of words, the Spanish had another, even more serious, public relations problem. Their unpaid lunatic soldiers went on another rampage, even worse than the first. It went into history as the "Spanish Fury" against Antwerp in November 1576. Don Juan finally arrived in the Netherlands in the wake of this massacre. He quickly agreed with William that peace required religious toleration. Even more quickly, he decided that the Netherlands bored him. Instead of focusing on his duties, he pined to effect a romantic rescue of Mary, Queen of Scots—who was, after all, said to be quite beautiful. In the meantime, he had no constant, predictable policy in the Netherlands. Distractedly, he dithered and dabbled and backtracked, while whole cities fell in coups d'état to radical Calvinists. Still, Don Juan did have one last taste of military glory in the Netherlands, defeating a Protestant army, before he succumbed to fever.

Spain's new hope was the duke of Parma—Margaret of Parma's son—whose army had joined Don Juan for his final victory. The duke appealed to war-weary Netherlanders chafing under the tightly bound legislative ropes of the Calvinists. What most Netherlanders wanted was a return to their old liberal Catholic dispensation—even under a Spanish king, if it could be done without Spanish violence and inquisitions. The result was a division of the country. In 1579, the seven northern provinces—"the United Provinces"—aligned themselves with the prince of Orange, and became the modern Netherlands. The other ten provinces pledged their loyalty to King Philip II and the old regime. These provinces—"the Spanish Netherlands"—were eventually recognized as the independent country of Belgium. Today, 75 percent of Belgians are Catholics, and Catholics even outnumber Protestants in the Netherlands, by a ratio of 34 percent to 25 percent, with more than a third of the Dutch professing no Christian belief at all.[4]

The duke of Parma proved again the quality of Spanish commanders. He recaptured every Protestant-held city in the loyalist provinces. But again, there were epic horrors. The battle of Maastricht—like the siege of Vienna—included vicious fighting in tunnels below the ground and a mass slaughter that left only 600 survivors of the original 30,000 inhabitants. King Philip declared the prince of Orange "an enemy of the human race" who was wanted "dead or alive," promising a pardon for assassination, and if the killer "be not noble we will ennoble him."[5] It was a particularly inept move by the Spanish king and should have been a reminder to the Church—which had for a thousand years tried to suppress dueling—that when one tries to prohibit an honorable vice (dueling), the most likely result is its replacement by a dishonorable vice (assassination). When Cardinal Richelieu in France tried to outlaw dueling among noblemen he did it the Solomonic way—by having both contestants executed. But Philip, the sincere churchman, employed the means of his time.

The real issue, which King Philip completely misunderstood, was that Prince William had as much to fear from Calvinist extremists in his own ranks (who thought his promotion of religious tolerance amounted to atheism) as he did from Spanish threats. Moreover, the majority of the United Provinces were already drifting from loyalty to him. Philip's call to rid the Netherlands of "the said pest" only allowed the prince of Orange to cloak himself once again in the flag of a patriot—and to accuse Philip of a variety of unsavory crimes of his own.

Men need little incentive to violence, and Philip's words found their executioner, who put a bullet through William's head. William survived, but the stress of caring for him weakened his wife, who was carried off by a fever. In 1584, more than two years and several foiled attempts later, an assassin found his mark, killing William, prince of Orange. The people called for the killer's canonization, but the Church—not being a democracy—ignored them.

With William in his grave, it was the English who kept the United Provinces supplied and encouraged against Spain, and it was Philip who inadvertently guaranteed the United Provinces' survival. Instead of letting the duke of Parma finish the job in the Netherlands, Philip sidetracked him with plots against England and assignments in France, the last of which led to his death in 1592. All the while, William's son Maurice was proving himself a military genius in shoring up the Protestant strongholds of the north.

In 1598, the year of his own death, King Philip II deeded the Netherlands to Archduke Albert of Austria, a former cardinal of the Church now married to the king's daughter Isabella. Under the reign of Albert and Isabella, the southern provinces—the Spanish Netherlands, or Belgium—found peace, prosperity, a religious and educational restoration, an artistic renaissance, and, at last, good government. In 1609, Spain's King Philip III reached over the pacific southern provinces and negotiated a treaty with the United Provinces that, despite the objections of the hotheaded Maurice, temporarily ended the war. The peace lasted a dozen years and would have lasted longer were it not for the Calvinists of the United Provinces, who, then as now, were a minority among the Dutch. What they lacked in numbers, they made up for in political and religious zealotry over their more lackadaisical Catholic neighbors. The Calvinists prohibited, by law, the majority of the population from practicing their Catholic religion in the northern provinces. They denounced, and eventually enacted laws against, the liberals—who could be numbered among northern Catholics, burghers, nobles, and others—who believed in religious tolerance. Maurice rallied to the Calvinists, seeing them, as his father had done, as the foot soldiers of his path to power.

The new war began as a series of coups within the United Provinces. In 1617, the Calvinists quickly deposed the liberal burghers (many of whom fled to England) and outlawed all religious dissent. Two years later, Spain and the United Provinces were at war. The Dutch found a new ally in Spain's rival, Catholic France. Putting matters of state before matters of religion, the devious French cardinal Richelieu funded the Dutch Protestants to fight the occupying Spaniards. Dutch captains proved their mettle by imitating the English sea dogs in naval battles, raids, and piracy against the Spanish. In 1639, another Spanish Armada, this one directed at the United Provinces, met an equally disastrous end, losing seventy of seventy-seven ships, and more than 15,000 soldiers and sailors. Spain was no less unlucky on land. The French army under the young Prince de Condé destroyed the previously feared Spanish infantry at the battle of Rocroi in 1643. With that victory, the balance of power fell heavily on the side of the fleur-de-lis. In 1648, under the terms of the treaties of Westphalia, Spain capitulated, surrendering all claim to the United Provinces and terminating all hostilities, anywhere in the world, against the Dutch, whose merchants roamed the seas. Spain, as a great power, was finished. The Dutch, who ignored the Calvinists' laws and remained predominantly Catholic, prospered.

## THE WAR IN FRANCE

BY 1559, JOHN CALVIN ESTIMATED that 10 percent of the French population supported his doctrines. Calvinism's popularity was not static, but growing, and growing most dangerously among the Bourbons, a noble family with a claim to the French crown now held by the family Valois. The Valois were suffering from youthful mortality and weakening blood. In this they were not alone. The last half of the sixteenth century was a bad one for royal families. In England it marked the extinguishing of the line of the Tudors and the accession of the decadent Stuart king James I. In Spain, Philip II's violently unstable son, Carlos, died in prison (William of Orange accused Philip of murdering him). And France witnessed the guttering out of the Valois line with the physically, mentally, and emotionally deficient Charles IX and Henry III.

In 1559, the Valois king Henry II suffered a fatal wound while jousting. His fifteen-year-old son Francis II died after only a year on the throne. Both wanted to reestablish the death penalty for heresy, by which they meant Protestantism, in order to prevent religious chaos and war in their realm. Francis II had the additional motivation of having discovered a Protestant conspiracy of which he was the target. If this was the half-century of decaying royal families, it was also the half-century of political assassination as an accepted form of conduct. The old medieval restraints on the pursuit of power had been dashed along with the uniform Catholic faith of Christendom. The resulting clash of daggers recognized no restraint on the use of force. Hearkening to a nobler past, however, was Francis II's mother, Catherine de Medici, who persuaded him to follow a course of conciliation. It was a path seconded by the Church, which is not surprising, given that Catherine de Medici was related by blood to both Pope Leo X and Pope Clement VII.

Tolerance proved a difficult course to follow. The rival Bourbon family saw, as the prince of Orange had, that Protestantism could be a lever to achieve power. The Bourbons put themselves at the head of the Huguenots—the Calvinist party in France—and preached rebellion. Catherine de Medici hoped to avoid war by mollifying the rebels. On her son Francis II's death, she became regent for her next son in the line of succession, ten-year-old Charles IX. As regent, she made toleration the law of France and even won concessions from the pope—limiting the display of religious art and ensuring that the chalice was offered to the laity in the Mass—to appease the Huguenots' dislike and suspicion of Catholic practices. These extraordinary accommodations from an overwhelmingly Catholic state were not what the Huguenots desired. They conducted their services in public—specifically to affront Catholics. Wherever they came to local political power, Catholicism was outlawed. They vandalized and scorched Catholic churches, in the usual Protestant style, murdered priests, attacked faithful worshipers, ransacked monasteries and nunneries, and condemned more liberal-minded Huguenots who believed in religious toleration.

Catholics struck back, but Catherine de Medici was not among them. Her Italian blood saw instantly that the Huguenots were a marvelous excuse to extort protection money from the Church into the royal treasury—which she did. And while she condemned Huguenot violence and provocation, she also continued to seek grounds for religious compromise. But it was not to be. Tensions were epidemic, yet it was a minor incident that set off the big bang. The duke of Guise, attending a Catholic service, asked a neighboring congregation of Huguenots to defer their psalms—sung to drown out Catholic worship—until the Mass was ended. The Huguenots refused, a riot ensued, a hurled rock cut into the Duke, and the Duke's men cut into the mob. Hence, the first of an incessant string of wars—known in France as its "Wars of Religion"—began. Huguenots rallied to the standard of Louis de Bourbon, enthused that their hour of battle at last had come. The duke of Guise, knowing that Catherine de Medici was no woman to settle this score effectively, deposed her and became the reigning power of Catholic France in what was, in essence, a temporary military government. The contest was entered. The Huguenots called for assistance from England and the Lutheran princes of northern Germany. The Catholic French even countenanced help from Spain. Soon the land was divided.

The Protestants scored early victories in the south—where the Albigensian heresy had roots—and in the west, where English troops had landed. Guise, successful on the battlefield, died victim of a sniper. His son Henry assumed his mantle, and Catherine de Medici resumed her negotiations for peace. She succeeded in 1563 by granting further concessions to the Huguenots, including freedom of religion to all noble families. There were, however, precautions to limit friction, such as declaring Paris an exclusively Catholic city.

Catherine's peace ensured her son Charles IX's accession to the throne, at the age of fourteen. But the peace was short-lived. The people in their towns and counties never stopped bickering and hanging each other. Such petty strife was beneath the Protestant rival to the throne, Louis de Bourbon. He operated on a higher plane. First he tried to kidnap the royal family, and when that failed, he imported German mercenaries for another war. Catherine hired her own foreign troops: Swiss mercenaries, such as protected the pope, and Spaniards from the duke of Alva. Peace was restored in less than a year, but it was merely a lull in combat. For more than half a dozen years, such stop-and-go fighting ravaged France. The Huguenot armies were repeatedly defeated, but the Catholic armies lacked staying power—partly due to the ever looming problem of financing them, partly because Catherine de Medici kept hoping for a lasting, negotiated peace.

Events climaxed in 1572 in the notorious St. Bartholomew's Day Massacre, a popular eruption with complex antecedents in rivalries at the royal court. It is a tribute to Catherine de Medici's policy of tolerance that Protestants such as Gaspard de Coligny and the Bourbon prince, Henry of Navarre, were welcomed into the royal fold. Indeed, the latter had married into the royal family. But there remained enormous differences between them. Catherine maintained her policy of peace with all Christian powers, while Coligny, who was displacing Catherine as King Charles IX's chief adviser, wanted to go to war against Spain in the Netherlands. These were not mere verbal disputes. Each camp—Coligny and his Huguenots, as well as Catherine and her Catholics—was backed by its respective armed forces, which had but recently left the field against each other. Catherine had had enough of Coligny. With Philip II advising her to crush the Huguenots, she plotted Coligny's death. The resulting assassination attempt merely wounded him, leaving the king torn between loyalty to his mother and to the Protestant adviser whose plans for a Spanish war he approved.

All of France was now in turmoil—Huguenots marching on Paris seeking vengeance; Catholics girding themselves for another outbreak of civil war. The Huguenots targeted the Guise family—long the leaders of the Catholic armies—and in doing so had the angry approval of Charles IX, who suspected Guise complicity in the attempted murder of Coligny. Catherine approached the king, telling him that the Huguenots would not stop after murdering Guise. They were intent on revolution. They would kill her and kidnap the king—as they had attempted to do twice before during the Wars of Religion. There was only one alternative, she said. He must strike at the Huguenot leaders now in Paris. Kill them, the Huguenots would disperse, and peace would be assured. The unstable king protested. He wanted justice for Coligny. At the very worst, he finally conceded, he would consent to arrest the Huguenot leaders and put them on trial. Catherine and her allies responded that it was too late for trials—trials could not stave off a revolution. His mother threatened to leave France for her own safety if he would not act. The high-strung Charles snapped. He left the room cursing and spat as his final words that if she demanded it, he would consent to Coligny's death; but then they must kill every Huguenot—every one—so that they could not attack him for it.

Swords were sharpened. Catherine prudently ensured that her Protestant favorites—including Henry of Navarre—received royal protection. On August 24, St. Bartholomew's Day, 1572, the ringing of church bells was to be the signal for an all-out attack on every Huguenot in the city of Paris. Political assassination became mass slaughter. The people of Paris hated the Huguenots for their pride, their zealotry, and the terrible wars they had inflicted on France. They were seen as a pestilential, persecuting minority. Now, by royal sanction, they could be eliminated. The popular fury was without mercy; the violence exploded in intensity, like a fire feeding on itself. In a perfect example of the extraordinary madness of crowds, once the authorities had almost restored order, innocently tolling church bells were mistaken for a signal that the joyous slaughter should be renewed. It leaped from Paris and sparked massacres in city after city.

The pope praised the defeat of the Huguenots, having been told that a Protestant plot to overthrow the crown of France had been foiled in arms by loyal Catholics. He imagined it as a domestic Lepanto. With it, he thought, Europe had moved closer to restoring the unity of Christendom, a solid phalanx of Catholic Crusaders against the Turk. The Holy See's dreams remained in the Middle Ages, when France was steadfast and its king was St. Louis. But the pope had been misinformed. This convulsion of violence was no Lepanto. At least seven thousand Huguenots perished throughout France. Their deaths did not end the Wars of Religion, but merely ignited another, until the king once more granted the Huguenots religious freedom.

King Charles IX praised the massacres when he saw that they were popular but at other moments was driven madder by his screaming conscience. He died, sickly, like so many of the Valois, at the age of twenty-three, less than two years after the massacre. The last Valois king was his brother, Henry III, a fluttering transvestite who added sexual perversity to the family repertoire of decrepitude. It was clearly time for the Valois to go, though Henry proved the longest-lived remnant of this failing breed, reigning—like a queen—from 1574 to 1589.

He followed his mother's, Catherine de Medici's, pacific route with the Huguenots. In 1576, to end yet another religious war, he granted them more political and religious freedom than ever before—even dominance in certain cities. By this example he encouraged further wars, because though the Huguenots never emerged victorious, they always won more concessions from the crown. The wars continued, with the sturdy Guise family again taking the lead that had dropped from royal hands. Though the Guise could fight for the king, they could not reproduce for him, and in 1584, mincing Henry III announced that the Protestant, and manly, Henry of Navarre would succeed him. Manliness the French could use, but his Protestantism was another matter. The Huguenots were no more popular than they had been during the great killing spree a decade before. Catholics protested, and Henry of Navarre took up arms to ensure his right. He brilliantly routed Catholic armies with his own smaller force, which numbered both Catholics, who had had enough of the Valois, and Protestants.

Soon there were three parties—with armies at their backs—contesting for the throne: Henry III, who still held it; the Catholic Holy League, which supported the Guises as worthier representatives of France; and Henry of Navarre. Henry III, who took a pervert's delight in murder, in an act of treachery, had the duke of Guise assassinated and his fellows either imprisoned or killed. Catherine de Medici, horrified that her son had eliminated France's most stalwart Catholic nobles, died in her sorrow. Catholics, including the pope, became Henry III's leading opponents. In response, the pervert accepted the protection of the Protestant Henry of Navarre. Together, their armies defeated the Holy League. France, which remained 90 percent Catholic, now faced the prospect of a pervert-Protestant alliance that would rule over them. A murderous monk did away with the pervert, but that left the Protestant and his largely Catholic army.

In 1589, Henry of Navarre stood victorious outside the gates of Paris, defeating every force sent against him. Yet so unpopular was his religion that it appeared the crown—or at least the demotic legitimacy that all monarchs required—would nevertheless elude his grasp. "Paris," he famously said, at least in legend, "is well worth a Mass," and it was this concession that finally ensured his triumph.

Still, it would be wrong to assert—as most do—that Henry of Navarre's conversion to Catholicism was merely for reasons of state. For one thing, it did not happen immediately. Henry of Navarre, now Henry IV, was king of France for four years before he was received into the

Catholic Church. He took instruction, in part, from a former Protestant who had converted and become a priest—presumably because such a man could better address the questions of a doubter. It is likely that Henry IV's motives were similar to those of many princes of his time, a mixture of personal conviction, convenience, and calculation. Protestantism, especially when adopted by the nobility, was largely a negative creed, full of critiques of the historical Church admixed with aristocratic assertions of personal right. It was the first step toward skepticism—a skepticism that nearly two centuries later would bathe France in blood during the French Revolution. Henry IV frankly told the priests who were instructing him that he would not countenance "rubbish which he was quite sure that the majority of them did not believe."[6] Many Jesuits, certainly, doubted his sincerity—and as the Jesuits were seen as a serious, physical threat to the king, they were, as a body, banished from the kingdom, with but a couple of exceptions.

In 1598, the now officially Catholic Henry IV enacted the Edict of Nantes, guaranteeing civil and political liberties to the Huguenots. He was the first monarch strong enough to enforce an effective policy of toleration.[7] As far as the Catholic Church was concerned, he was anything but a purifying reformer. Instead, he treated the Church as though he were a domestic Renaissance pope, installing his bastard children in Church offices as it pleased him to do so. The Church was reinvigorated nevertheless by a religious revival at the turn of the century led by such priests as St. Francis de Sales, St. Vincent de Paul,[8] and others, who simultaneously raised intellectual standards for priests in the seminary classroom and exhibited a selfless dedication to the poor and suffering in cities and towns across France.

In the court at Paris, cynicism was by now an established tradition in French foreign policy. Henry IV continued it, doing everything he could to weaken France's rival powers—powers that happened to be Catholic: Spain to the south, the Spanish Netherlands to the north, and the empire of Habsburg Austria and southern Germany to the east. He supported the United Provinces in their rebellion, preferred Turks to Austrians in the Holy Roman Empire, and would gladly have smuggled Moors back into Spain.

Though he knew their foreign policy was different from his own, in 1603 he allowed the Jesuits to return to France and even made one of them, Pierre Coton, his confessor. But Henry IV's plethora of Huguenot advisers and his bellicose foreign policy against the other Catholic powers of Europe guaranteed him many enemies in this age of assassination. Henry IV had bravely withstood many threats and attempts before, but in 1610, a recently released prisoner who thought he was doing God's work stabbed and killed the mighty king.

Power in France fell at first to Marie de Medici, regent to the future king Louis XIII, who had yet to flower into his full degeneracy. But in 1624 Cardinal Richelieu became prime minister and chief adviser to the king. From that moment until his death in 1642, it was Richelieu who would determine the fate of France and, ultimately, the fate of the Counter Reformation in Europe.

In religion narrowly defined, the cardinal was strictly orthodox. He was incorruptible; a skillful Catholic writer and apologist; spotted and re-warded clerical talent; and as a Church administrator seconded the Counter Reformation emphasis on improving the education of the clergy. But he was a statesman more than he was a cleric, and as such endorsed the Protestant doctrine of subordinating Church to state, agreeing that rosary beads could not determine matters of war, peace, and the national interest (though he did consecrate France to the Virgin Mary). Above all, he was a patriot, whose primary aim was increasing the security and power of France.

His first challenge was subduing the Huguenots, who under the Edict of Nantes operated, in their city-strongholds, as a nation within a nation. The cardinal besieged their seaport city of La Rochelle. By military victory and a surprising—to the vanquished—magnanimous peace, Richelieu di-verted the Huguenots from their separatist power politics that weakened the state into commerce that strengthened it and the royal treasury. After the Huguenots, he went after the nobles, whose feudal estates were an-other potential challenge to the unity of France. He outlawed their inde-pendent fortresses and executed nobles who thought they were a law unto themselves. In every domestic issue, Richelieu centralized power. In every foreign issue, he sought to break it up. So the cardinal—who thought the Reformation had been a disaster—nevertheless recognized that it had hap-pened and played it to what he saw as France's benefit in foreign affairs. This meant supporting the Protestants in the Netherlands. When it looked as though Catholic armies might restore the entirety of Germany to papal obedience—and thus solidify Habsburg power in central Europe—it was

Richelieu who discovered and subsidized the military genius of the Protestant Swedish general, and king, Gustavus Adolphus, whose military victories ensured the religious division of Germany.

Richelieu was brilliant at achieving his every political measure. He was a great architect of modern France. But along with all the hosannas with which he is sometimes garlanded for his tough-minded and successful statecraft, we should recognize something he apparently did not. The Habsburg Empire—which the French saw as a *cordon strangulaire*— could never in fact have posed a mortal threat to France. Spain and the Holy Roman Empire were united by royal blood, but little else. The Austrian Habsburgs ruled over an empire that was the converse of Richelieu's centralized state, being a loosely held imperial band of diverse principalities, duchies, and kingdoms. In any event, the Spanish and the Austrians had foreign policy distractions enough: Spain with her empire, Austria with the Turks. France would have been just as secure had she cleaved to her medieval role of international defender of the faith—as in the grand old days of the Crusades and French Byzantium—than she was as an agent provocateur sabotaging the Habsburgs via the Protestants. Few historians prefer Christendom to the secularizing march of history, so few, if any, mention this quite obvious fact—obvious, at least, to one who, in his study, is not surrounded by Habsburg armies.

## THE WAR IN GERMANY

RICHELIEU ENDED THE WARS OF RELIGION in France, but he perpetuated the horrific Thirty Years' War in Germany, which forever ended hopes for the restoration of Christendom. Yet such restoration came close to happening. In central Europe, the Jesuits had won millions back to the faith, Austria and Poland especially ardently. The Polish king Stephen Bathory even planned to conquer all Russia for the Church, but died before he could make the attempt. Another Polish king, Sigismund III, plotted his claim to the Swedish crown in order to return Sweden to papal obedience. Austria, for its part, was the leader of Catholic Germany and the bulwark against the Turk. Interestingly, Poland and Austria were also the most religiously tolerant great powers in Europe.

But tolerance, reform, and the resurrection of the Church were put to the test of blood, beginning in 1618, when the Protestants in Hungary,

Bohemia, parts of Austria, and, of course, Transylvania, revolted against the Catholic Ferdinand II—a Habsburg—who had been named king first of Bohemia, then of Hungary, and in 1619 Holy Roman Emperor. Though the Protestant rebels—under their chosen King Frederick—had threatened to take Vienna, they were routed by the redoubtable Bavarian army led by one of the great marshals of the Thirty Years' War, Johann, Graf von Tilly, at the battle of White Mountain, near Prague. Catholic armies also seized the Lower Palatinate—in west-central Germany—whence Frederick had sprung, and restored it to the faith. Ferdinand II now dreamed of stretching a Catholic empire—and he was sincerely religious—from Austria to the Baltic. His dreams were, perversely, Richelieu's and the papacy's nightmare of an overwhelmingly powerful emperor.

Central Europe, but most especially Germany and what are now the Czech and Slovak republics, became the battleground of Protestant Europe—abetted by Richelieu, and sometimes Venice and other anti-imperial Catholics—against the Habsburgs. The Habsburgs had two great advantages: Graf von Tilly and another great commander, the fabulously wealthy (he raised and paid for his own army), Jesuit-educated, Bohemian nobleman Albrecht von Wallenstein. From 1625, when Wallenstein joined Tilly (though they operated separately), until 1627, the Habsburg forces rolled back the opposition throughout Germany. They even conquered the bulk of the Danish mainland from King Christian IV, who had invaded Germany on the Protestants' behalf and at the request of the Dutch and the English.

In 1629, Ferdinand issued the Edict of Restitution, which sought to recover all Church lands illegally appropriated by Protestants since 1552, the date of the last treaty governing such appropriations. It was a measure as just as it was undiplomatic. The obvious practical difficulties generally proved tractable when troops from Wallenstein, Tilly, or the Bavarian duke Maximilian appeared. Wallenstein's army was by many times the largest. Like many, if not all, of the armies involved in the Thirty Years' War, it showed that men would willingly kill for pay regardless of religious profession. Wallenstein's army enrolled Protestants as well as Catholics in its ranks and had a Lutheran as one of its leading generals. Wallenstein became a diplomatic and military power of his own. The same year as the emperor Ferdinand's Edict of Restitution, Wallenstein signed the Peace of Lübeck with King Christian IV, generously restoring to the king his territories in return for his staying out of the war. Some Catholic German princes were so fearful that the Ferdinand-Wallenstein juggernaut would override their independence that they, like Richelieu, sided with the Protestants. Ferdinand, confident that the war was won, took precautions himself against Wallenstein becoming overmighty. Despite the great general's warnings that Gustavus Adolphus threatened from the north, a series of imperial commands diverted some of Wallenstein's troops to other duties and put the remainder under the command of Duke Maximilian, leaving Wallenstein without an army.

But Wallenstein's warnings were, of course, right. Despite the Peace of Lübeck, Gustavus Adolphus proclaimed that Sweden could either wait to be conquered by the Holy Roman Emperor or could attack and seize parts of northern Germany for itself. Sweden, though sparsely populated, was a major northern power. It held Finland and the Baltic states against Russia and regarded the Danes and Poles as additional threats or hindrances to Swedish ambitions.

In 1630, Adolphus landed his troops in German Pomerania and gathered mercenaries from throughout Europe, for this was indeed a world war, with every European power taking part in some capacity. Like Wallenstein, the Swedish king included Catholic soldiers of fortune as well as Protestants among his officers; and Adolphus tried to keep his troops reasonably pure with required evangelical prayer meetings. Cardinal Richelieu sent Adolphus an enormous subsidy, including five tubs of gold for the king himself. The Swede responded by guaranteeing Catholics freedom of worship in any territory he conquered.

With Wallenstein not yet restored to command, Tilly and Adolphus marched toward each other, leveling any unhelpful garrisons that stood between them. Initial victory went to Tilly and his lieutenant Gottfried, Graf zu Pappenheim, who subdued the Protestant powerhouse of Magdeburg after an extraordinarily difficult—for the besiegers—six-month siege. When the imperial army broke through, the seventy-one-year-old Tilly lost control of his men. The resulting slaughter left the general distraught. He knew it was both a moral crime and a propaganda defeat that would be lodged against the empire.

Adolphus won his first German ally—the duke of Brandenburg—by compulsion but finally found a volunteer in the Duke of Saxony. Thus reinforced, he was prepared to meet Tilly, who engaged him, against his better judgment, at the battle of Breitenfeld, near Leipzig. The battle was hard fought. The superior Swedish artillery pounded the imperialist lines until the impetuous Pappenheim could stand it no longer and threw his cavalry at the enemy in repeated failed attacks, leaving the imperial left flank shattered. But on the right flank, the imperial cavalry of the Graf von Furstenberg had the Saxons running. Tilly seized his advantage, brushing past the fleeing Saxons to crush Adolphus's center. Had not the Swedish army been so mobile and well trained, it would have been swept from the field. Instead, Tilly's lunge for victory crashed into a regimental wall of Swedish-serving Scotchmen. Adolphus's counterattack on Tilly's opposite flank, which Pappenheim was too bloodied to hold, overturned the imperial army and destroyed it. Not only had the Protestants won the battle, but central Germany was now cleared for a Protestant offensive. Adolphus snatched Würzburg, Frankfurt, and Mainz, and collected avid allies among the Protestant princes. French troops joined in, snipping off western portions of the Holy Roman Empire for *la gloire de France*.

Wallenstein was returned to command but saw no action before Tilly was killed in Bavaria. While Adolphus continued his sweep through Germany, the Swedish advance was deceptive, for Adolphus's army, though excellent, was comparatively small, and his German allies unreliable. They did not intend to exchange an Austrian emperor for a Swedish one, and too many victories by Adolphus—not to mention pressure from Wallenstein—might swing them hesitantly in the direction of Ferdinand.

Wallenstein and Adolphus drew their full strength against each other at the battle of Lützen in 1632 on a misty morning soon shrouded in gunsmoke. Adolphus, charging on horseback with his men, was brought down by gunfire and killed by the sword. In retaliation, the Swedish army exploded with a furious onslaught from which Wallenstein thought it best to retreat and which left the great imperial commander Pappenheim with mortal wounds. It was an impressive tactical victory for Sweden, tarnished only by the loss of its "Lion of the North," whose iron jaw had successfully—and irretrievably—snatched northern Germany away from Catholic control.

If this result of the Thirty Years' War was now inevitable, the end of the fighting was not. Indeed, it seemed as though the war would never end. Its cost was ghastly, at least a third of the population of greater Germany; some estimates go as high as two-thirds. The famous were not spared, even if they survived the battlefield. After Lützen, Wallenstein seemed reluctant to fight, even scheming against his emperor. Wallenstein was again stripped of command. A handful of his own soldiers killed him, expecting an emperor's reward—and rewarded they were.

Wallenstein proved dispensable. The imperial armies recovered under the command of the emperor's son, who soundly defeated the Protestants at Nördlingen in 1635. The emperor followed this military coup with a diplomatic one, allowing a forty-year grace period before the Edict of Restitution would become law. Protestant princes now proclaimed their loyalty, and the Saxons turned to fight against the Swedes. In the west, Germans fought the annexing French, who held fast. Whether by firm occupation or tenuous grasp, no party willingly surrendered anything. All hoped to make gains. Sweden wanted conquest in the north. The returning Danes wanted to usurp the conquests of the Swedes. The French wanted Alsace-Lorraine, if not half or more of Germany (at one point they invaded Bavaria). The emperor—by 1637, it was Ferdinand III—wanted to reclaim the empire's pre-Reformation unity. The imperial princes wanted to ensure their freedom. Spain tried to defend its Habsburg ally. The Dutch fought Spain. Bohemia was Bohemian. And through it all, millions died beneath the swords and gunpowder of increasingly vicious mercenaries who acted as land-based pirates, leaving in their wake starvation and disease.

Peace finally came through the treaties of Westphalia in 1648, the treaties themselves a decisive defeat for the exhausted empire, which could no longer endure the ravaging of its people, cities, and farms. To achieve peace, it resigned itself to being a more regional power focused on Austria and Hungary. Sweden extended her occupation of Baltic shores and surrendered only her queen, Gustavus Adolphus's daughter, Christina, who gave up her crown to become a Catholic and pursue la dolce vita in Rome. France expanded at Germany's expense. Northern Germany remained Protestant, and the Reformation achieved its greatest negative goal: the Catholic-based civilization of Europe was in cinders.

Protestants dislodged the pope as a serious force in European politics, established the irrelevance of religion to power, ushered in four centuries of skepticism, and marginalized Christianity to an increasingly narrow and personalized sphere. The Age of Faith was over.

## AN ENGLISH CODA

THE WARS WROUGHT BY PROTESTANTISM were not quite finished. England was to experience Protestantism's two political strands—royal absolutism, unrestrained by the power of the Church, and totalitarian Calvinism—in the battle between the house of Stuart and Oliver Cromwell's Parliamentarians. After executing the academic instruction to "compare and contrast"—albeit, through the medium of civil war—the English people opted for neither of the above.

The first Stuart king, succeeding Elizabeth, was James I of England (James VI of Scotland), who reigned from 1603 to 1625. James I was a decadent, which in those days did not necessarily mean anti-Catholic. But though he personally held no great antipathy to the old religion—and indeed in some ways seemed to admire it (his mother, after all, was Mary, Queen of Scots)—he persecuted the faith on good Tudor grounds of solidifying the power of the state. No Catholic in England could, by law, either educate his children at home or send them abroad to be instructed in the ancient religion. Catholic priests and missionaries were prohibited, and any Catholic who failed to attend Anglican services was fined. If there was any solace for English Catholics, it was that the king was more interested in collecting Catholic fines than Catholic heads and was completely unsympathetic to the Calvinist parties, who, if they came to power, would likely make things even worse.

The Gunpowder Plot of 1605 was the Catholic highlight of James I's reign. A small, desperate handful of distraught Catholic noblemen, each with a frisson of caution-be-damned aristocratic hellfire within him, planned to blow up Parliament, with king, commons, and lords assembled. This rather draconian means of government reform suffered from a crisis of conscience among the conspirators—a crisis encouraged by Jesuit priests who tried to dissuade them. A plotter slipped a warning to Lord Monteagle, who alerted the authorities, and the arrests began. The only explosions were a propaganda coup for the king and a popular presumption that Catholics were traitors unless proved otherwise. Inevitably, there were new, even more restrictive laws. Catholics were prohibited from practicing law or medicine and traveling within the realm. Among those executed for their role in the Gunpowder Plot was a Yorkshireman named Guy Fawkes who lent to his name to the eponymous English bonfire holiday in which anti-popery sentiment could be annually renewed.

Under Charles I (1625–1649), air was blown on the embers of English Catholicism. The king left punitive laws against Catholics unenforced. Married to a French Catholic, he was a High Church Anglican, a Renaissance patron of the arts, and an opponent of the Calvinists. In other words, he was everything that Puritans hated, and they plunged the country into civil war over that and over the king's assertion that he ruled by divine right. Swords were drawn in two civil wars, the first lasting from 1642 to 1646, and the second recommencing in 1648 and dragging on until 1660. It was parliament versus the crown, Puritan Roundhead versus Anglican Cavalier. Catholics surged to the banner of the king, and as such unmistakably put themselves on the side of right, but again on the side that was destined to lose. Their king was executed—a thing that shocked Europe. His dignity before the chopping block made him an Anglican martyr.

Anglicans as well as Catholics were persecuted by the new Puritan dictatorship of Oliver Cromwell, for whom even Presbyterians were too High Church. Christmas was banned—as it would be prohibited in Puritan-dominated areas of the New World—as a pagan excuse for a saturnalia. Theatres were closed. Bear baiting was ended by the Protestant expedient of killing all the bears. And Merrie England was encouraged to be dour. But in 1660 relief came in the restoration of the monarchy with Charles II (1660–1685), who returned the celebration of Christmas, reopened the theatres, re-instituted horseracing (though over six feet tall, he rode a racehorse to victory in his fifties), and encouraged the Renaissance arts. Charles II renewed the concourses of civilization in the general Catholic manner because he was a crypto-Catholic. He thought Catholicism true, but believed that if he said so publicly he might end up like his father. His tolerance was deep and personal enough to include his mistresses. The most famous was perhaps "Nell" Gwynne, who won the hearts of all by declaring, "Pray, good people, be civil; I am the Protestant whore."⁹ Charles's deathbed conversion to Catholicism still left him fond

of "the Protestant whore." He instructed his brother, the future King
James II, "Let not poor Nelly starve." Charles left, by some accounts,
fourteen illegitimate children, but none to his actual wife, Catherine of
Braganza, who was a Catholic.

His entire reign—at least on the issue of Catholicism in England—
was spent working subtly against the legislative prejudices and murderous inclinations of the mob against Catholics. Among the mob was Titus
Oates who invented the tale of a "Popish Plot" against England. The tale
gained him fame as a patriot and led to the conviction and execution of
at least thirty-five innocent men, including the archbishop of Armagh
and Viscount Stafford. Oates even tried to implicate the queen. But he
was eventually proven a liar and a conspiratorial fantasist and was convicted of perjury.

Charles's success can be measured by the fact that he navigated such
nasty hysteria and died a popular monarch with a Catholic inheritor, his
brother, James, Duke of York, now James II, who reigned but three
years, from 1685 to 1688. The English historian C. P. Hill remarks of
James II that his "mistresses were numerous, if fewer than those of
Charles; they were also uglier, and Charles, whose taste was more dis-
criminating, once said he believed his brother had his mistresses given
him by his priests for penance." Though the historian notes, as well, that
"conversion [to Catholicism] made James more moral, in quantitative
terms; he was content with a single mistress thereafter. It also made him
even more reactionary in outlook."[10] So it seems as though it was a good
thing all around.

James not only lifted persecution against Catholics; he appointed
them to high places and openly showed favor to England's old religion.
This was not popular, but he might have gotten away with such dangerous toleration had he not also scared the fainthearted by simultaneously
creating a royal standing army (he had a military and naval background)
and undercutting the Anglican church in favor of the Catholic (something
he had pledged on his accession not to do).

English Catholics repeatedly warned the king that he was being unwise. So did the pope, Innocent XI, who additionally disliked James II's
friendship with King Louis XIV of France, whose royal absolutism over
the Church the pope was contesting. While Englishmen were catechized
into thinking that Catholicism meant tyranny, Innocent XI should have

been a reminder that it was the pope in Rome who, throughout history, was the most consistent opponent of the absolute power of the state.

James II's fatal decision was to take the advice of William Penn—of later Pennsylvania fame—and try to effect an alliance between Catholics and Protestant Dissenters. As in most attempts to forge cross-party unity he succeeded only in alienating his core of supporters. These were not Catholics (there were not enough of them) but Royalist Anglicans. They remembered wielding saber blows and gunfire against the Dissenters who had executed James's father. These loyalists—the Tories—felt betrayed. James had trusted that the Anglican divines would remain true to their doormat doctrine of never resisting royal power—*his* power—but they turned on him, telling the Dissenters that edicts of tolerance should come from Parliament, not from the king, and that the Anglican church was a surer source of tolerance than the pope. The Dissenters agreed. They would have no truck with a papist. Now that James II had compounded his missteps by siring a legitimate son, establishing a Catholic royal line of succession, a real plot—an anti-Popish, Protestant Glorious Revolution Gunpowder Plot—appeared in the form of William III of Orange, a former friend of the king, now seeking the British throne at the invitation of James II's enemies.

William had majority support among the Anglican church, but not entire support, for there were Anglican churchmen—whom King William would later dismiss—who stayed loyal to the Stuart king and held that the Anglican church's paramount doctrine was non-resistance to the crown. They had precedent on their side. After the duke of Monmouth's failed rebellion against James II in 1685, the duke said as he faced execution, "I die a Protestant of the Church of England." The Anglican prelates rebuked him, saying, "If you be of the Church of England, my lord, you must acknowledge the doctrine of non-resistance to be true." Sir Winston Churchill comments: "To this point had the Anglicans carried their abject theory."[11] In fact, the theory proved even more abject than that, because in their rebellion against James II, the Anglican divines put non-resistance to the prevailing political winds—an even more supine position—ahead of non-resistance to royal supremacy.

The king, hoping to win back the support of the Anglican church and the nobles, back-peddled furiously. He withdrew almost everything he had done to establish Catholicism—and religious tolerance—in England.

But it was too late. The English saw James II as a tool of an expansionist, repressive France and the barbaric Irish. Naturally, they turned to a Dutchman to keep the crown English, on the grounds that the Dutchman's wife—Mary, daughter of James II, raised a Protestant by royal command of Charles II— was heir to the English throne. In 1701, when that line exhausted itself, they were compelled to turn to a German. James II, abandoned by all, fled to the Continent, where he and his family harbored futile, but romantic, Jacobite plots to restore Catholicism to England from the Celtic peripheries—including the battle of the Boyne in Ireland (1690) and Bonnie Prince Charlie's Scotch adventure of 1745. Alas, it was not to be. Samuel Johnson said of the Jacobites, to whom he was sympathetic: "A Jacobite, Sir, believes in the divine right of Kings. He that believes in the divine right of Kings believes in a Divinity. A Jacobite believes in the divine right of Bishops. He that believes in the divine right of Bishops believes in the divine authority of the Christian religion. Therefore, Sir, a Jacobite is neither an Atheist nor a Deist. That cannot be said of a Whig; for *Whiggism is a negation of all principle.*"[12] For Whiggism we would read Liberalism, and Liberalism was the ideology that rode to supremacy on the wave of the Protestant Reformation.

James II was the last king of England to wash the feet of the poor in imitation of Christ on Holy Thursday (Maundy Thursday). He was, in essence, the last king connected to the medieval, Catholic "Age of Faith." The Protestant Glorious Revolution dispensed with such subservience to ancient ritual. With it went an entire civilization.

## CHAPTER SEVENTEEN

# RELIGION'S RETREAT

F OR THE FIRST TIME, Western Christianity was riven without
hope of restoring a united Catholic Europe. Never, since Constantine
made Catholicism the religion of the empire, had Christianity suffered a
greater repudiation—though this denial was disguised to the many and
the true believers by their new churches. But it is obvious to the historian,
just as it was obvious to the cynics and the skeptics whose numbers grew
after the demolition of the old faith. It is well to remember what a negative creed Protestantism was. It viciously attacked, of course, the pope in
Rome—who had been, in the West, the universally held cynosure of the
faith for more than a thousand years. Depending on denomination,
Protestantism held in contempt what had been bedrock concepts of the
faith, including apostolic succession; the communion of saints (which is
in the Apostles' Creed); Marian devotions (Marian art dates from the
Apostolic Age); the Trinity (denied by the Unitarians); and so on. To assault so violently the practice of Christianity as it had been known by
every personal, familial, and historical memory could have nothing but a
corrosive effect on the very idea of religious truth.

Among intellectuals, this led to an explosion of skepticism. Among
the ruling class, it meant that leaders no longer bowed before religion,
but used it as a means of domestic order and control. Among the literate
middle class, it led to design-it-yourself religious belief with the multiply-
ing Protestant sects. Among the Protestant proletariat, it made the very

bearers of historic Christianity—the pope, priests, monks, the faithful in their prayers and processions, churches with traditional art—targets for calumny, ridicule, abuse, and even destruction. Protestants were very keen on the Old Testament, but they somehow missed that they had turned Christianity into a Tower of Babel.

There were six main Christian camps. If one were to use the imagery of the later French parliament, the Catholic Church would be seated on the right and would still have by far the majority of the seats. The Anglicans would be the Center party. To their Left would be the Lutherans. The Anglicans and Lutherans could be described as Reformed Catholic denominations that placed their faith in state supremacy (rather than papal supremacy), nationalism, a secularization of the sacraments, and a wider circulation of authorized vernacular translations of the Bible. To their Left would be the Calvinists. These were the hard-core revolutionaries of Puritan morals, *sola scriptura* (along with Calvin's *Institutes of Religion*), and a movement away from the divine right of princes to a law-based theocracy with (totalitarian) democratic elements. They were the Islamic fundamentalists of the Christian world. It might surprise contemporary Southern Baptists to know that the Baptists and a grab bag of other dissenters would make up the Far Left of a seventeenth- and eighteenth-century Christian parliament: people who believed in inspiration, enthusiasm, and private revelation in addition to Scripture. Hard to place, except perhaps with the Anglicans, would be the new, rising force: the rational religion of the Deists. They offered a "prime mover" instigating Creation—something that reason could accept—but more or less left it at that, with a few curlicues provided by the state to ensure a modicum of religious conformity and peace. The Deists sought to create a mere Christianity, if it was Christianity, which all reasonable Protestants could accept.

There was no single Protestantism, no absolute definition, and this, along with the armies of northern Europe, guaranteed its survival. It could never be definitively refuted because it was never definitive. It kept dividing and subdividing. In the name of reason, or the Bible, the ultimate trend of Protestantism over the centuries was to disallow any final Christian authority outside the autonomous individual. Thus, the Reformation, to state the obvious, made for a Christian house divided. Where once, in the West, Christianity spoke in a single historic language—Latin—and held to an unchanging apostolic belief, now it spoke in the vernacular, with differences of belief innumerable. Indeed, if one accepted Protestants on their own terms—not as heretics, but as Christians—one could no longer speak of Christianity (singular), but only of Christianities (plural).

This made religion a subjective experience and therefore put it at a grave intellectual disadvantage in a fast secularizing world that increasingly looked to reason and science as objective arbiters of truth. This distinction between subjective religion and objective science did not exist before the Reformation. In fact, the Catholic Church—as a sponsor of the arts and learning—was the chief patron of scientific investigation.

But after the Reformation—after, that is, the breakup of the total Christian society of Christendom—things started to go wrong, and Protestants were all too willing to push in the same direction as secularists against the Church. Both agreed that the Catholic Church, which had given the world Aquinas, da Vinci, and Copernicus, was the vanguard of superstition and the enemy of reason.

## THE ASTRONOMER'S CHURCH

NICOLAUS COPERNICUS (1473–1543) was trained in canon law, studied and practiced medicine, and pursued the disciplines of mathematics and astronomy. His most famous asseveration was that the earth must revolve around the sun. His book proclaiming this theory was dedicated to the pope, and there is speculation that Copernicus himself might have been in holy orders; it is certain that he was once considered for nomination to a bishopric, was a loyal Catholic, and had been a diocesan administrator. His theory—the heliocentric theory—was published during the Reformation and was condemned by Luther and his followers as anti-Biblical. The Catholic authorities—at least initially—had no such problems with his work, which made the subsequent Galileo affair so interesting.

The popes supported astronomical research. Pope Gregory XIII (1572–1585), who straightened out the calendar, also built the Vatican's observatory, and Galileo Galilei (1564–1642) himself had Pope Urban VIII as a benefactor, friend, and even poetic champion—at least until the sharp-tongued Galileo made ridicule of the pope part of his elaboration on the Copernican system. There was nothing in Galileo's science that was at odds with the Church—the issue was his manner, and his manner was an issue because the Church had finally realized that the Reformation would not peter out on its own, but intended to be a full-out assault on the faith. The Church felt on the defensive. Where the Renaissance popes might have shrugged off Galileo's invective against the hand that fed him, Pope Urban VIII felt that he could not. It was a matter of Church discipline. Galileo had already been once called before the inquisition and put under explicit instructions from the Church that while he was free to continue his astronomical investigations, he could not *teach* the heliocentric system to students. The Church feared the Christian world was not quite ready for this idea now that the Reformation had temporarily narrowed—to the Church's disadvantage—European intellectual life.

The Church was trying to shore up its reputation where Protestants had attacked it, and one of the major attacks was on whether the Church adhered to the Bible, and the Bible implied—see, for instance, Joshua 10:12–14—that the sun revolved around the earth. In the words of historian Jacques Barzun, "One could say that in roundabout fashion, it was these [Protestant] Bible-ridden revolutionists who got Galileo condemned for his astronomy. If the literalism of the word had not been adopted at Trent to show that Catholics too revered Scripture, there would have been no need to make science confirm Genesis."[1] There had certainly been no such need before, and indeed Catholic interpretations of the Bible—such as had come from the Church fathers, like St. Ambrose and St. Augustine—had never been literal. St. Augustine's conversion had even depended on the Bible not having to be taken literally, a point made to him by St. Ambrose. Yet after the Reformation, even the late Copernicus fell under suspicion, albeit in modified form. The Church would not reject its scientists, but it required that the Copernican system be treated as theory, not fact. The new Catholic standard, set by Robert Cardinal Bellarmine, was that the literal interpretation of a Biblical narrative must take precedence over a scientific *probability*. Only in cases of scientific *certainty* would a Biblical passage be open to reinterpretation. So though the Church had not gone all the way to fundamentalist Biblical literalism, it had gone too far for Galileo, who now portrayed his patron pope as wearing a dunce cap.

Galileo's ridicule of the pope and his continuing to teach that the earth revolved around the sun led to his second inquisitional trial, which found him "suspected of heresy." The heresy could not be defined save that his astronomical system—in the words of his first trial, wherein he had been instructed not to teach—"appears to contradict Scripture."[2] He was sentenced to a rather leniently enforced house arrest and was allowed to write and even teach. His daughter, who was a nun, helped him perform his penance, reciting seven psalms a day for three years, as dictated by the sentence of the inquisitional court, a sentence to which the pope never gave his imprimatur.

As for the Church being opposed to science, it might be worth mentioning that the Jesuits—not to mention the Vatican—still operate their own observatory, and the Catholic Church remains by far the most prominent Christian spokesman regarding the ethical implications of modern science. The Church has also produced a fair number of clerical scientists throughout its modern history, including, perhaps most famously, the monk Gregor Mendel (1822–1894), a botanist, who made a major contribution to the science of genetics. More controversially there is Pierre Teilhard de Chardin (1881–1955), Jesuit priest, philosopher, and paleontologist, who did indeed run afoul of the Vatican for his mystical attempt to conflate evolution and Christianity. Among devout laymen one finds such as Louis Pasteur (1822–1895), who is perhaps the most important scientist in the microbiological battle against disease.

Actually, far more important than the presumed hostility between science and the Church was the very real hostility between Church and state, and between Catholicism and secularism, particularly in the growing superpower of Catholic France.

## THE SUN KING

IN THE SEVENTEENTH AND EIGHTEENTH CENTURIES, France was the battleground for every philosophical and political conflict between the Catholic Church and the world. Within France, on the Catholic side were vibrant religious orders; powerful prelates; and missionaries who dared death, hardship, and every conceivable challenge to bring Christianity to the Indians of North America. The Church was popular. It was the heart of France. On the secularist side were French philosophers like Descartes who drove a spike between faith and reason. There were polemicists like Voltaire, Diderot, and a host of skeptics who extended the Protestant mockery of Catholicism to include all Christianity (except perhaps Deism and its blind watchmaker God who set Creation in motion and then left it alone). The debate spilled into the royal court—and into the arguments of the king's opponents.

The first king in question was Louis XIV, who reigned from 1643— he took the crown at age four and a half; his mother, Anne of Austria acting as regent—to 1715. Until the War of the Spanish Succession at the end of his reign, he brought France every glory—martial, territorial, artistic, and intellectual—through generals, artists, and writers who operated beneath the glow of the "Sun King." He was also a sincere Catholic, though just as eager as previous kings to limit and control the power of Rome within his realms.

The early power behind the French throne was Cardinal Mazarin, a Jesuit-educated Italian. He had served as a papal soldier and diplomat, won the regard of Richelieu, and succeeded him as the red-robed guide of France's destiny. He continued Richelieu's program of religious toleration (both men made government appointments on the basis of talent rather than religion), centralized power, and high taxes—the last being necessary to support France's martial and diplomatic adventures. Heavy taxation had the downside of spawning two armed revolts that directly threatened Anne and the boy-king. The prince de Condé, whose armies had broken the Spanish, now turned his sword against French rebels: "the people," *Parlement* (a body of lawyers and the instigators of the rebellion), and his fellow nobles who rushed to lead the popular uprising. The incipient revolution folded almost immediately, as the lawyers decided they never wanted their arguments about taxes to lead to actual blows anyway—especially not against them.

The lawyers—before they were cowed—had put a price on Mazarin's head. This popular insurrection convinced the cardinal—as it had convinced the boy-king—that the only safe place for power was in himself, the queen-regent, and the young monarch. When the prince de Condé tried to muscle his way into royal influence, the cardinal had him imprisoned, causing another rebellion among the martial-minded nobles. This time they aimed solely at Mazarin. But they faced an equally martially minded cardinal, who rode onto the field himself. He was defeated—not on the battlefield, but by nerves. He released de Condé and accepted exile. De Condé, free, but with his dignity besmirched, declared a republican revolution.

The king was now a handsome thirteen-year-old. He claimed his throne, recalled Mazarin (who came with an army and then left again as a concession to ending de Condé's uprising), and watched his foes self-destruct. The rebels were as Catholic as the family royal, but were disadvantaged because the proletariat was on their side. What de Condé won by conquest, the mob threw away by rioting. Once again, the nobles and the middle class recognized that the great unwashed might spoil everything in a republic, and so the rebellion collapsed upon itself. The king was praised—even after he bade Mazarin return.

Mazarin was charming, but not demotically charismatic. If unpopular with the nobles and the people, he retained his influence over the royal family. They thought him the wisest counselor they had. In his foreign policy, Mazarin proved just as impervious to religious considerations as had Richelieu. He was, however, equally successful at defeating presumed enemies and enlarging France's domains, this time at Spanish expense with the Peace of the Pyrenees in 1659. He had one grave flaw that Richelieu had not—personal greed. He amassed what was perhaps the biggest fortune in France, though there were two compensations: first, in matters of the arts he was gifted with good taste; second, his wealth was majestically appropriated by the king after the cardinal's death, and thus enriched the beauty and financial power of *l'état c'est moi*.

But Mazarin was more than an aesthetic, financial, and diplomatic tutor and benefactor to the king. Mazarin's own attitude toward the papacy—especially Innocent X, with whom he feuded—was virtually the same as it was to rival monarchs. What was good for the power of France was paramount; political submission to the Church was not (though Mazarin did leave a financial bequest to the pope in order to finance resistance against the Turks).

Broadly speaking, Mazarin, like Richelieu, remained orthodox in belief. Along with the Jesuits, the king, and the papacy, he opposed—as had Richelieu—a Catholic movement called Jansenism. Jansenism responded to Calvinist jibes by co-opting two parts of the Calvinist program: predestination and moral Puritanism. The royal reaction was, as often, a bit extreme, and among the works that were condemned as Jansenist was a

Catholic classic: *The Provincial Letters* by Blaise Pascal. Pascal's sister was a nun at the convent of Port-Royal, a center of Jansenist philosophy, and in *The Provincial Letters* Pascal agreed with the Port-Royal position that the Jesuits were too lenient in their handling of confessions and too latitudinarian in converting pagans. On this particular point, Pascal was wrong, but time would show that in its totality *The Provincial Letters* was a great Catholic rejoinder to the swelling chorus of religious skepticism.

Pascal was a brilliant mathematician and scientist, an avocation shared with his father, and another refutation of the claim that Catholicism was opposed to scientific inquiry, for the entire family was devout. After a taste of worldly life, Pascal felt the lash of conscience and imposed severe personal mortifications, which were redoubled by perpetual ill health. He indulged in the sort of over-scrupulousness that the Church has always regarded with suspicion—as carrying dangers of its own.

But Pascal's mind remained clear and loyal to the Church, if not blindly so. He thought the inquisition had erred in punishing Galileo and he refused to accept criticism of the Jansenists as valid. He is most often remembered for his famous "wager," arguing that a savvy gambler would bet that Christianity is true and live accordingly. If he loses, he loses nothing more than he would have lost as a skeptic—his life. If he wins, he wins something the skeptic has no chance to acquire—Heaven. Famous it might be, but calculating one's faith on the basis of odds seems a trifle uninspiring. It also showed the Protestant, rationalist elements of Jansenism: the "it makes sense, it's practical, it's a good deal, a good contract, and you'll benefit" faith that came to typify the so-called Protestant spirit of capitalism. Pascal spoke to men of his time in this contemporary spirit—but it really wasn't the basis of his belief.

Rather better, and closer to his own faith, is Pascal's famous line "The heart has its reasons of which reason knows nothing."[3] The core of Pascal's thinking is that reason—and this comes from a mathematician and scientist—cannot apprehend the fullness of man, which is a mystery that can only be unraveled by a religion that is a flesh-and-blood experience, and that accepts the Incarnation. Pascal's God is not the God of the philosophers "of mathematical truths and the order of elements. . . . But the God of Abraham, the God of Isaac, the God of Jacob, the God of the Christians."[4] Pascal understood that for all Aquinas's logical proofs and all the Jesuits' clever arguments, no one truly reasons himself into Christianity. Because it is a revealed religion, one must *accept* the Revelation. Faith comes by the grace of God. Joseph Cardinal Ratzinger wrote in the twentieth century something that could have been written in any century of Catholic belief: "Meaning that is self-made is in the last analysis no meaning. Meaning, that is, the ground on which our existence as a totality can stand and live, cannot be made but only received."[5] This is completely antithetical to modern man; it is nevertheless true, and it is Pascal's point.

For Pascal, the road to faith is found in the Catholic Church, which embodies the Revelation and whose rituals wear away skepticism: "Bless yourself with holy water, have Masses said, and so on; by a simple and natural process this will make you believe, and will dull" your doubts.[6] It is in the living Church—not the Bible, which can be misinterpreted, or reason, which can be fooled or misled—that true religion exists. Pascal urged rationalists and dissenters to acknowledge the wisdom of submission to the ancient Church: "Philosophers and all the religions and sects of the world have taken natural reason for their guide. Christians alone have been obliged to take their rules from outside themselves and to acquaint themselves with those which Christ left for us with those of old, to be handed down again to the faithful. Such constraint irks these good Fathers ["dissenting" theologians]. They want to be as free as other people to follow the imaginations of their hearts. In vain we cry out to them as the prophets of old said to the Jews. 'Go in the midst of the Church, ask for the old paths and walk therein.' They have answered like the Jews: 'We will not walk therein, but will walk after the devices of our own hearts.' And they said: 'We also shall be like all the nations.'"[7] For Pascal, subjective religion and secularized religion were folly, and he became the rallying point for faithful Catholics in an increasingly skeptical world. Skeptics at least had to give Pascal his due as a thinker, prose stylist, and scientific mind, even if, in the end, they dismissed him as sounding the last trumpet of the old and passing faith.

The debate over Pascal highlighted that the intellectual division in France was not only between Protestant and Catholic, but between skepticism and faith as first principles. Some Frenchmen, like Mazarin and Richelieu, embodied these divisions within themselves, making a personal, mental separation of the principles of Church and state. In some ways more interesting than the cardinals—who, because of their calling, were a special case—was the king, a man who, though ruling by divine right, was a man of affairs, like his subjects. Unlike them, of course, he had access to more numerous affairs. But even here—in the royal amours—there was a Catholic gilding. One of his early mistresses later became a nun. The last, who became his secret, unadulterated wife, was a woman of humane and religious sentiment. She had worked at lowly jobs in a convent, then as a nurse and, later as a royal nursemaid. The king proved himself taken by her character as much as by beauty. For all his earlier infidelities—and his kingly passion for glory and war—Louis XIV felt the call to faith and admired it in others. Even in his wars, the idea of restoring Catholicism was not absent—he supported, for instance, James II's attempt to regain the English crown—even if it was secondary to enlarging the borders of France.

Similarly, while he defended the faith and refused to go into schism, he also jealously guarded the so-called Gallican liberties of France, which made the king head of the French Catholic Church. This was obviously—and had been—a source of conflict with the papacy and its French allies known as the "Ultramontanes." But the various particular arguments over authority always, eventually, even if at the point of rhetorical daggers, threats, and near divorce, resolved themselves short of any permanent or serious breach. Louis relied not only on his legal power to crack down on the Jansenists and break up their convent at Port-Royal, but appealed to Pope Alexander VII and later to Pope Clement XI to help him maintain orthodoxy and discipline within the Church, which the pontiffs willingly did. He also sought papal assistance—which came grudgingly this time—to oppose a movement known as "Quietism," which, up to a point, unplugged Catholic belief from the tangible sacraments and made it a mystical bathing of the spirit. As Jansenism was a Catholic form of Calvinism, so Quietism—at least in France—was a Catholic response to the Quakers and other Protestant movements that sought to find God in quiet contemplation.

Against the Protestants themselves, Louis XIV took more vigorous measures than had any king since the religious wars. The Church encouraged the king's initiatives and greeted them with clerical hurrahs for the triumph of truth. At the same time, priests, bishops, and the papacy warned against the overzealous use of force as a legal modus operandi. As a young king, Louis agreed with the clergy that the Edict of Nantes went too far and began limiting its scope. By 1679, the Edict of Nantes was essentially, de facto, abrogated. Ever increasing penalties fell on French Protestants, the Huguenots, who lost their right to public office, whose homes could be quartered with French troops, and who endured other civil disabilities. In 1685, the edict was officially repealed on the grounds that virtually every Frenchman was now a Catholic, and over the next three decades, compulsion accelerated against those who were not. Protestant schools and churches were forfeit. Protestant ministers were ordered into exile. Protestant children were to be baptized by the Church. Stubborn Huguenots were subject to every imaginable abuse, depending on the whim of local law and the local commander of troops in each city and province. In Paris, Huguenots were reasonably free. In other areas, while they could not be killed, they could be beaten, robbed, tortured, and humiliated. Louis XIV thought he would be applauded for crushing religious dissent. Instead, Pope Innocent XI—who despised Gallicanism—denounced the French king for the anti-Huguenot terror and persecutions. Though it was illegal for Protestants to emigrate, hundreds of thousands fled to Switzerland, Germany, the Netherlands, or England. Catholics in these countries sometimes welcomed the Huguenots as refugees from the hated French. Protestants saw them as martyrs for the reformed faith.

In reality, centralizing power was the issue. Though the Machiavellian cardinals Richelieu and Mazarin had been religiously tolerant, employing men by virtue of ability rather than religious persuasion, the king saw orthodoxy as a matter of state. As the feudal power of the nobility had been reduced to vest all power in the king, so now, too, whatever remained of Protestant dissent could be abolished, with all religious authority consolidated in the king's Catholic Church, a process that French prelates generally supported. There were isolated Huguenot uprisings, which angered the king—who was busy, as ever, with foreign wars—but they were of little real consequence, except that their crushing by French troops made for another Protestant propaganda victory. By law, to be French was to be Catholic, just as across the pond to be English was to be Protestant. By 1715, any unconverted French Protestant was made subject to the old laws on heresy. The French church had conquered all. But the grandsons of the victorious Catholic laity would live to see the debacle.

That they did was no fault of Bishop Jacques Bossuet (1627–1704), Louis XIV's ecclesiastical head of the French church. Bossuet was renowned for his sermons and as an orator has been called "the greatest, perhaps, who has ever appeared in the Christian pulpit—greater than Chrysostom and greater than Augustine; the only man whose name can be compared in eloquence with those of Cicero and of Demosthenes."[8] His sermons, like the works of Pascal, are landmarks of French prose.

He was an outstanding scholar whose training was both classical— Homer and Virgil were early favorites—and, preeminently, Biblical. His academic brilliance was matched by captivating speech, holy demeanor, and a devotion to work—whether that work entailed the normal duties of a priest and bishop, the instruction of the dauphin by royal appointment, or putting into words the fighting faith. He was a fair-minded man and, as such, took up the best Catholic position: right wing in principle, moderate in conduct. When the king abrogated the Edict of Nantes, Bossuet argued that force was justifiable to restore religious truth and political order. But in practice the bishop prescribed leniency and would not allow any of the outrages that were perpetuated in other districts. While a stunning controversialist, he remained friends with his philosophical opponents. He gave no ground in principle, but among his principles was behaving with humility and generosity. His paramount ambition was restoring Christendom by the power of his pen.

He was a difficult foil for Protestants because of his knowledge of Scripture—indeed, it was from Scripture that, as a Gallican, he was able to define and support the divine right of kings as embodied by Louis XIV, defended by St. Paul, and described throughout the Old Testament. His vision of history was providential, grounded in his reading of the Bible, and he was wary of the newly developing school of Biblical criticism, even when practiced by an orthodox Catholic priest. A case in point was the very interesting Father Richard Simon, a blacksmith's son and one of the first great modern Biblical scholars. His aim was to refute skeptical dismissals of the Bible. But working with rabbis, he also pointed out numerous apparent anomalies in the Old Testament and concluded, as had Pascal, that the only safe approach to Christianity was through the corporate Church. There was nothing unorthodox about this, and as scholarship, it was an impressive, if uneven, piece of work. But Bossuet condemned such scholarship because of his own veneration for the Bible and his belief that Simon had erred, especially in his later translation of the New Testament, an opinion that Simon perhaps agreed with, as he burned his own papers.

Bossuet wanted to make it easy for Protestants to return to the Catholic faith. He conceded Catholic faults but showed how minor they were when compared to the theological chaos of Protestantism. In fact, he wrote a four-volume treatise—*History of the Variations of Protestant Churches*—that brought scholarly objectivity and rhetorical demolition to the various Protestant sects. He readily admired the religious sincerity of the Reformers, just as readily shot to pieces their arguments, and illustrated how they had ruined Europe with war and set loose an intellectual virus that led to atheism. He also wanted to illustrate how Protestants could in good conscience reconcile themselves to the Church—the one Church whose teachings had remained unaltered for sixteen hundred years. By restoring her unity, they would restore Christian strength. It was a tour de force, which could not be gainsaid, though many Protestants tried. All it lacked was what the Reformers had—pikes and guns and leaders who could direct them in a personally enriching nationalist cause. Instead, the pikes and guns would soon be in the hands of the enemy Bossuet predicted. The French Catholic Church would face atheism-in-arms.

# THE WAR OF THE SPANISH SUCCESSION

FIRST, OF COURSE, Catholics faced off against themselves in the war that capped the Sun King's reign. It brought new bloodshed to the politics that linked France, the Holy Roman Empire, Spain, and the pope—and for the Holy See, it brutally underscored the degree to which political power had slipped away from the Vicars of Christ.

The scene was Spain and its idiot king, Charles II: huge of tongue, lantern jaw, mentally retarded—his mind, body, and visage a calamity of inbreeding. Europe waited for him to die, which he did in 1700 at the age of thirty-nine. Now the race was on to succeed him.

He had no heirs, but Louis XIV naturally thought that a Frenchman, the Bourbon duke of Anjou, his grandson, would make a splendid king for Spain, while the Austrian Habsburgs thought the Spanish crown was theirs by right of blood. In fact, both royal houses had claims to the throne though various bloodlines. The matter was further confused by several agreements negotiated by the European powers that, looking ahead to Charles II's death, had presumptuously divided the Spanish empire. None of these agreements, however, had been universally accepted, and none was binding.

With Charles II drooling his last, Pope Innocent XII (1691–1700) intervened to counsel the cretin king. Though the Gallican dispute had brought the papacy and Louis XIV to the very brink of schism, the pope reverted to the Vatican's traditional policy of using France as a counterweight to the Holy Roman Empire. In his initial will, Charles had made a Bavarian prince, Joseph Ferdinand, the grandson of the Holy Roman Emperor Leopold I, his inheritor. But the Bavarian prince had died. The one thought in Charles's troubled mind was to find a successor who would keep his empire intact. The pope advised him that Philip, duke of Anjou, if he abjured any claims to the French throne, was that man. Charles complied. The result was war.

The Spaniards greeted their new king, Philip V, as by divine right appointed; he was the popular choice among a people who felt more Latin than Teutonic. But the fighting began almost immediately. Louis XIV knew that neither the empire, nor the Netherlands, nor England (ruled by the Dutch king, William III) would accept a France whose power crossed the Pyrenees. Indeed, France's enemies formed the Second Grand Alliance—which was joined by Denmark, many of the German states, and eventually Portugal and Savoy (which had first sided with the French)—to contain the power of Louis XIV. They declared war on him, with the empire striking first, snipping off Spanish territories in Italy. France allied itself with Spain, Bavaria, and Cologne. The war also spilled over into North America between the French and the British. Here it was known as Queen Anne's War, Queen Anne having succeeded William III to the English crown in 1702.

The French had nearly half a million men under arms. In Europe the war became a display of military genius from two Alliance generals: John Churchill, duke of Marlborough, and Eugene of Savoy. Marlborough's string of victories—from Blenheim (1704) to Malplaquet (1709)—had the French everywhere in retreat. Louis XIV was so hard-pressed that he tried to surrender in 1706 and again in 1709, but the Alliance demanded too much. It was not until 1713 that the war finally ended against an exhausted and debilitated France.

For Pope Clement XI (1700–1721), who had tried to maintain papal neutrality, the war was another ominous sign of the Church's dwindling political influence. First, his attempt to mediate between the Catholic powers had been rebuffed. Then, in 1709, the Holy Roman Emperor's troops stormed through Italy and compelled the pope to back the new Habsburg aspirant to the Spanish throne: Archduke Charles of Austria, the future Holy Roman Emperor Charles VI. If this were not humiliation enough, the pope's territorial rights at the Treaty of Utrecht (1713) were blithely disregarded—so much so that Duke Victor Amadeus II of Savoy was given not only political but ecclesiastical control of Sicily. The pope condemned the usurping duke, who responded by ordering clergy loyal to the papacy into exile. In post-Reformation Europe, the prince of arms was universally regarded as more to the point than the Prince of Peace.

# THE VIEW FROM ROME—
# AND FROM PHILOSOPHY

THE POPES OF THE SEVENTEENTH CENTURY were by and large good men trying to make the best of their shrinking influence. Pope Paul V (1605–1621) had tried to act as a medieval pope—determining the fates of cities and kings by interdicts and excommunications—only to find that the world, even the Catholic world, no longer listened to the political prescriptions of the Holy See. He fought Gallicanism and lost. When the English Parliament demanded that Catholics take an oath denying papal power over kings, they did, despite the pope's protests. He even lost a political struggle with Venice. His glories came elsewhere— particularly in advancing missionary work in China and the arts in Rome. His successor, Gregory XV (1621–1623) tried to reinvigorate papal power by promoting the political advance of the Counter-Reformation. Urban VIII (1623–1644) had the task of keeping the warring Catholic parties together. He preferred the French to the Spanish—winked at Richelieu's machinations—but tried not to antagonize the Habsburgs, who were bearing the brunt of the Thirty Years' War. Papal Francophilia was understandable, but papal fear of the Holy Roman Empire was devastating to the Catholic cause in northern Europe. The Habsburgs are surely one of the most idealistic families in history, and their constant reward has been assaults by their enemies and undermining by their friends. Instead of subsidizing Habsburg arms, Pope Urban VIII subsidized Italian art—not to mention his relatives. Still, he was a great supporter of missionary activity and issued a papal bull prohibiting slavery—though it continued regardless—in the Catholic New World.

Pope Innocent X (1644–1655) was another great supporter of missionaries. Alexander VII (1655–1667) was a deeply spiritual pope, with literary tastes. He is perhaps best remembered for welcoming the queen of Sweden (now minus her crown) to the faith and for employing Giovanni Bernini to finish the piazza at St. Peter's. Pope Clement IX (1667–1669), an able administrator, tried, incredibly, to launch another naval Crusade, this time to drive the Turks from the island of Crete. He succeeded in mounting the operation, but it failed because of squabbling among the French, Germans, Spaniards, and Venetians who were taking part. His greatest contribution to civilization was inventing the comic opera. To the Romans, he was beloved for treating them like a kindly village priest— convivial, honest, and willing to bend a sympathetic ear.

Clement X (1670–1676) so assiduously warned King James II of England not to antagonize his Protestant people, and so strongly condemned Louis XIV's persecution of the Huguenots—"they must be led into the temple, not dragged into it"—that he has been called "a Protestant Pope."[9] Even so, no Protestant countries were converted. He continued the papal war to defend Western Europe from the Turks, with the battleground shifting to Poland. Here the pope funneled money to the strapping Jan Sobieski, who would become the Poles' King John III. Sobieski drove the Turks from the Ukraine, and as king devoted himself as a true Crusader to defending Europe from the Ottomans. Cooperation with Sobieski was continued under Innocent XI (1676–1689), who was so holy he was nominated for sainthood in 1714, and so opposed by the French that he was not made a saint until 1956. The pope helped ally the Poles and the Austrians—the French refused to help—in lifting another Turkish siege of Vienna. The pope's diplomacy later included forming a Holy League with Sobieski, Venice, and even Orthodox Russia, to defend Central and Eastern Europe from the Turks. But to the French, Pope Innocent

XI was the most ardent foe of Louis XIV's Gallicanism, and, of course, the French had long supported the Turks against the Habsburgs.

Popes Alexander VIII (1689–1691) and Innocent XII (1691–1700) also spent their pontificates battling Gallicanism on the one hand and Turks on the other. Clement XI (1700–1721) saw out the reign of Louis XIV. Aside from his efforts to end the War of the Spanish Succession, he once more organized the defense of Christendom against the Turks. He was less successful with encouraging Catholicism in China. The Jesuits had, controversially, allowed Chinese converts to bring their Confucian rituals with them, arguing that they were civil, not religious, ceremonies. Other popes had doubted this, and Pope Clement firmly prohibited the Jesuits from showing such leniency. The result was that the Chinese authorities ordered the destruction of the Church as a subversive institution. If he was wrong about how the Jesuits should proceed in China, even Protestants agreed that Pope Clement XI was an honest man of intellect, character, and faith—the kind you could really like while you ignored him with impunity.

As the papacy entered the eighteenth century, it had no hope of restoring by arms or by a military champion its medieval glories. War there would be in perpetuity—but it would no longer be in defense of the faith. What Catholicism needed now was a resurgence of its intellectual life to meet the challenge of an increasingly literate and secular society. Even if the vast majority of Europeans still clung to some form of Christianity, the tide was unmistakably moving against the Church. In part, this was the movement of reason—inaugurated in the English-speaking world by such as Francis Bacon—which wanted to sweep away all accumulated prejudice and tradition and build new, scientific, rational foundations for knowledge and learning. This, of course, presupposed religious skepticism.

Catholics, however, did not believe in sweeping aside tradition. They did not believe that a skeptic starting from a tabula rasa was more likely to find truth than was the Church building on the tradition of the Gospels, St. Augustine, St. Thomas Aquinas, and all the rest. But if skeptics thought the Church rested mostly on superstition or custom without reasonable foundations, they found a religious ally in the Protestants. In fact, Protestants agreed so wholeheartedly that they favored special disabilities against Catholics, because those who followed the ancient Christian traditions of more than a millennium were held to be uniquely, dangerously, and most blamably wrong. Protestants often classed Catholics with Unitarians—that is, barely, if at all, Christian—perhaps unaware that it was the Catholic Church that had defeated Arianism, a distant cousin of the Unitarian movement, more than a thousand years before Luther was born. Moreover, the Church did so on grounds of Catholic tradition over *sola scriptura,* because the word "Trinity" never appears in the New Testament—a rather interesting problem for *sola scriptura* Protestants who unthinkingly claim to be Trinitarians merely because the Church won that battle.

Even Protestant writers who were champions of tolerance—men like John Milton and John Locke, professed Christians, but each of a self-styled, minimalist creed—exempted Catholics as beneficiaries, for the papists were beholden to a foreign power, as if this were a religious issue. Where patriotism did not trump religion, reason and religious minimalism did. John Locke's *Reasonableness of Christianity* argues along similar lines as Pascal's wager. But unlike Pascal, who held to the sacramental Church, Locke adheres to the idea that faith alone in the divinity of Christ suffices. No more could be demanded than "what our Savior and his apostles proposed to, and required in, those whom they converted to the faith." Locke skipped over more elaborate theology as an irrelevance and not part of reasonable religion. Go beyond such Biblical minimalism "and you amaze the greater part of mankind and may as well talk Arabic to a poor day-laborer as the notions and language that the books and disputes of religion are filled with."[10]

There is, of course, some truth in this, but it is also an obvious "dumbing-down" of religion. The Catholic peasantry had never been known for its lack of faith, however sophisticated was Catholic theology. The two could coexist. But in Protestant eyes, superstition and idolatrous art were the contaminated source of popular Catholic devotion. Instead of that, Protestant peasants—and even Protestant intellectuals like Locke—were to subsist on religious minimalism. If Locke, as George W. Ewing writes in his edition of *The Reasonableness of Christianity,* "found himself neither Calvinist nor an Athanasian, if he refused to discuss the Trinity, or repudiated orthodox notions of atonement, predestination, or original sin, he appealed to the Scripture as the source of his ideas."[11] To a Catholic mind, this pointed out the pitfalls of the bizarre Protestant marriage of reason and *sola scriptura*. A Lockean Christian could skate from Anglicanism to Arianism without acknowledging or thinking the differences important.

This became the downfall of rationalist Protestant theology. For the logical conclusion of the Protestant rationalists, as reason gained the upper hand over Scripture, was Deism, and Deism was as far as many intellectuals—such as Thomas Hobbes—could, in private, bring themselves. A God who was a prime mover was reasonable, but the rest of the old Catholic program was not. Religion, for some of them, and for their philosophical followers, became a prudential sham: untrue for an enlightened mind, but necessary for the masses and social cohesion. A state-subordinated Protestantism of minimal dogma that encouraged good behavior was exactly the ticket—at least by the lights of rationalist political philosophers.

All of this was anathema to Catholicism, which saw these trends as heresy—as stripping the Church of its power, burning its library of theology (which, to the Church, was truth, even if too complex for Protestants to follow), and stupefying whatever apostolic doctrines remained in the ashes. The problem in reconciling faith and reason was not, as the rationalist philosophers liked to allege, Catholic theological obscurantism versus observable fact. The real problem was the Bible. It was the trap that well-meaning Protestants had laid for Christianity. Though philosophy had now declared its independence from religion and attempted to approach the world by reason alone, in the seventeenth century and through part of the eighteenth century, big minds still had to confront the Bible, in a way they did not have to—they could just dismiss it—in the nineteenth and twentieth centuries. But every non-clerical philosopher discovered what Father Richard Simon had. If the Bible was *literally* true, then God believed that the world was flat. Moses was writing books of the Pentateuch after he was dead. The sun revolved around the earth. God liked creation so much that he left two different stories of it in Genesis. Even the divinity of Jesus was problematic. The list of textual problems—at least for a literalist reading—was endless and in the end impossible to reconcile with reason. The Protestants, having wrenched religion from the Church and vested it solely in Scripture, had left Christianity defenseless against such inevitable textual criticism.

The answer for Protestant rationalists was the minimalism of Locke. To the purely philosophical intelligentsia, the Bible became a fairy tale for the common people. Some—like Baron Gottfried Wilhelm von Leibniz, a philosophical Deist of Catholic shadings and Lutheran profession—tried to devise a sufficiently deracinated Christian creed to suit all Europe. Bishop Bossuet shared Leibniz's goal of religious unity and corresponded with him. But the philosopher's purpose was one of social utility rather than the Catholic goal of religious truth. Others—for instance, Baruch Spinoza, raised a Jew, but also a philosophical Deist—could not read the Bible as any sort of literal truth but could confess an admiration for the ethical code of Jesus as something worth following.

Protestants undercut the Christian cause in another way. Catholics had never denied bloody history. They argued that it would have been far bloodier without Christianity, but they never saw the Church solely in terms of moral reform. Protestant attacks on immoral Rome now became skeptical attacks on the entirety of Christianity. How can Christianity be true or moral, the philosophers asked, if Christians themselves cannot agree on what it means, and indeed murder each other over their differences? How can Christianity be good when Christians behave so badly? Greed, crime, lust, war—the whole violent and wayward tale of European history—was this something Christianity was proud to have achieved? On what possible moral grounds could it be excused? Was not the Old Testament itself a litany of bloodshed, tribal war, and murder? How could Protestants possibly embrace—as God had—a lustful, vengeful Old Testament king like David, when David bore such a striking resemblance to a Renaissance pope?

If reason and philosophy were the standards of measurement, Bible-based Protestantism was nonsensical. Its defense, as with Locke, became one of prudence—of encouraging good behavior. Protestantism became less of a doctrine, a dogma, or an intellectual philosophy than a set of useful character traits to be embodied—such as honesty, hard work, and sobriety—and social morality took the place of sacramental religion. Thus, in Protestant countries, secularization was so natural a development as to be hardly noticed. But Catholics did not sink or swim on the raft of the Bible—literally or subjectively interpreted—as their sole support; and they did not rely on minimal theology as a means to achieve agreement. Catholics had the Bible, yes, but they also had doctrine, dogma, history, seventeen hundred years of religious practice, the inheritance of Rome and the classical world, and a deep philosophical heritage—in fact, from the Middle Ages through the Renaissance to the Reformation they were the philosophers of Europe. The result was that when secularization came to Catholic countries, it did not come painlessly and naturally; it came in convulsions and conflict, it came in civil war between radicals—who wanted to strike at the root of Christian civilization and plant new seeds of reason—and the Old Guard of Catholic conservatism. Again, the focal point was France.

## CHAPTER EIGHTEEN

# REVOLUTION

D URING THE REIGN OF LOUIS XIV, for every playwright inclined to skepticism, like Molière, there was a Catholic counterpoint, such as Racine; and even skeptics, like the essayist Montaigne,
could reconcile themselves to Catholic ritual and practice. Still, it was obvious that the thinking minds of Europe were unbinding themselves from
religion to pursue a new adolescence of questioning, mockery, and self-
discovery. The rhetorical violence of Luther would be given a Gallic flair
and then arrayed to blast religion *tout à fait*—always excepting Deism
and a theologically indefinable creed of good deeds.

The key figure in this transition to skeptical predominance was an unlikely candidate, Pierre Bayle (1647–1706)—unlikely unless one believes in
the romantic image of the ink-stained wretch in his garret, whose epistles
change the world. Bayle's did. He was, by profession, a Calvinist and the
son of a minister, but, like any other rationalist of his generation, he found
the Bible shot through with passages that made a literalist reading impossible. As for Christian practice, he thought hypocrisy was its operative
mode, religious tolerance the only solution. He wrote essays on these and
other intellectual subjects for his supper, and gained an appreciative audience in literary circles. But what really made his mark was his huge *Historical and Critical Dictionary*, which brought a skeptic's point of
view—though he continued to masquerade as a Calvinist—to the history,
literature, religion, and philosophy of the Western world. His *Dictionary*

became the Bible for the great skeptics who followed, including Voltaire, who wrote his own *Dictionnaire Philosophique;* Denis Diderot, who compiled the hugely influential *L'Encyclopédie,* which provided essay space for a battery of leading philosophes; and every freethinker looking to overthrow the established intellectual order. It was the most popular book among literate Frenchmen.

It was also a book that might have joined the library of a Renaissance pope—and that is the nub of the tragedy of this growing intellectual revolt. Bayle had been partly educated by Jesuits, who convinced him of Catholic truth. Bayle's father quickly tried to undo the Jesuits' work by dispatching him to a Calvinist university. There, Bayle surrendered to skepticism while pretending to be a Huguenot. Had he—and, defensively, the Catholic Church—not been subject to the intellectual constrictions of Protestantism, Bayle's rebellion might have been Erasmian—satirical, but in favor of a tolerant, intellectually capacious, cosmopolitan Catholicism. The very culture that Protestants reacted against—the Renaissance—was the culture that could have absorbed minds like Bayle's and kept them, however attenuatedly, on the side of the Church. When one leaves religion per se, one finds in Bayle a mind perfectly at home with Catholic modes of thought. For all his apparent radicalism, he was politically conservative, preferring monarchy to democracy; he was disdainful of the idea of human progress; he acknowledged that human reason is more likely to destroy than to build. Like Montaigne, perhaps, he could have remained a skeptical but sacramental Catholic. But the triumph of the Reformation was, albeit inadvertently, to leave the skeptic with no need for religion at all. When a skeptic saw Protestants taking hammers to break down altars, smash crucifixes, obliterate statues of the Virgin Mary, stamp on the Eucharist, and shatter stained glass, he could ask: Why stop there? Why not tear down the whole thing? If man is saved by faith alone, why not leave every man's religion to his conscience rather than to institutional religion and all its attendant dangers of intolerance, censorship, and coercion? If Christian culture and classical culture are entirely separate—as Protestants argued, in contrast to the Catholic fusion of the two in the Renaissance—what elevated mind could prefer the pottage of Christian superstition to the noble operation of classical reason? For post-Reformation rationalists, choosing agnosticism became the logical conclusion of Luther's doctrine of every man his own priest.

One critical tactic used by Bayle that became very popular in the eighteenth century was to criticize the West by comparing it with non-Christian cultures. Skeptics with pens no longer thought, as the Conquistadors and the Jesuits did, of taking the faith to savages. Instead, they pondered whether the savages might not be noble, untrammeled as they were by the superstitions of Catholic theology. If the West was not truly civilized (and in its apparent hypocrisy, brutality, and ignorance, how could it be) it was because since the Christian era, Western civilization was built on the Catholic Church. Here was the ultimate prize for the skeptics. Finding textual problems in the Bible was easy sport. No intellectual need long be detained with that or with Protestants who held to Biblical literalism. In any event, the Protestant denominations were subordinate to the state—an institution that skeptics preferred. But the Catholic Church was a different matter. Here was the citadel. If it could be taken, the entire philosophical and cultural inheritance of the West could be reduced to its foundations and rebuilt on reason.

In this battle the Catholic Church was matched against "the most brilliant writer that ever lived."[1] His name was Voltaire. His posthumous victory against the Church would come in blood, with the revolution of madame guillotine—which was not at all what he had in mind. In fact, Voltaire was another intellectual who, if Erasmian, Renaissance Catholicism had continued unchallenged, might very well have remained within the Church.

He was indeed the product of a Jesuit school. Of that experience he wrote, with telling sincerity:

> I was educated for seven years by men who took unrewarded and indefatigable pains to form the minds and morals of youth. . . . They inspired in me a taste for literature, and sentiments which will be a consolation to me to the end of my life. Nothing will ever efface from my heart the memory of Father Porée, who is equally dear to all who have studied under him. Never did a man make study and virtue so pleasant. . . . I had the good fortune to be formed by more than one Jesuit of the character of Father Porée. What did I see during the seven years that I was with the Jesuits? The most industrious, frugal, regulated life; all their hours divided between the care they took of us and the exercises of their austere profession. I call to witness the

thousands educated by them, as I was; there is not one who would belie my words.[2]

Voltaire made the philosopher's distinction between allowing "the people" to exercise their consoling Catholic religious myths—even praising, as here, the admirably selfless and intellectually sharp Catholic inculcators of such myths—and excoriating the Church among the literati. The Jesuits had given Voltaire three priceless educational gifts that he, unfortunately, turned against the Church: a righteous sense of justice and morality; a firm grounding in the Bible; and a keen wit. Voltaire's case against the Church was not a case against God—in the Deistic sense—and it was not an argument for debauchery. On the contrary, Voltaire was outraged at Christian intolerance that lent itself to wars and judicial murders; he was appalled at what he considered the stupidity of Christian censorship that blocked the free flow of ideas in the name of preventing heresy; he thought it ridiculous and repugnant that Christians would try to read God's will into such disasters as the Lisbon earthquake of 1755, which struck on a holy day and killed 15,000 largely Church-going people (Protestants saw this as divine retribution for Catholic error; Catholics saw it as a call to repentance). Voltaire raised the question we know as "the problem of evil"—how could a just, all-loving, and all-powerful God who was active in history allow the violent death of thousands of women and children? To Voltaire, it was merely proof that evil stalked the world and that God was completely unknowable.

Having been schooled by the Jesuits, Voltaire was probably a better Biblical scholar than most educated Christians today. His sense of justice and humanity ruled out worship of the blood-and-thunder God of the Old Testament. A literal reading of the Old Testament and such stories as Noah's Ark was patently absurd to him, and it called into question the sanity of anyone who believed it. His New Testament criticism is as modern as that of any twenty-first-century Bible scholar. He asked where Christianity came from—given that Jesus was a Jew who lived as a Jew, followed Jewish law, and preached to Jews. Who was Paul to decide to do away with the Jewish law Jesus had followed? Why had not Jesus come back to inaugurate the Kingdom of Heaven within the lives of the Apostles, as He apparently promised? By what authority had the Church taken it upon itself to determine that Mark, Matthew, Luke, and John were the canonical gospels, when there were so many other versions to choose from?

If this last point sounds vaguely Protestant, it is, in the sense that Voltaire saw his attack on Christianity as building on the work of the Reformers, whom he called "our fathers": "Have not our fathers taken from the people their transubstantiation, auricular confession, indulgences, exorcisms, false miracles, and ridiculous statues? Are not our people now accustomed to doing without these superstitions? We must have courage to go a few steps further. The people are not so weak in mind as is supposed; they will easily admit a wise and simple cult of one God."[3] Voltaire thought the supreme stupidity of Christianity was in attempting to define any theology beyond Deism. So he took Locke's minimalist creed to the next step.

He acknowledged that he could live under a state religion such as he had seen in England—one that was entirely toothless. As for the Lutherans and Calvinists, they had started the revolution against the Church, and were to be thanked for putting the churches under state control. But the triumph of reason, of the philosophes, Voltaire saw, meant the Reformers' terrible creed of predestination and of damnation for most of mankind would speedily be left on the rubbish tip of history. The Reformers had no more to offer for the triumph of truth, reason, and virtue. The real battle now was between the philosophes and the Church. Voltaire had an obsessive battle cry—which he lifted from Frederick the Great of Prussia—*écrasez l'infâme,* crush the infamy. The infamy was the Church.

Like Bayle, he hearkened to what we would call multiculturalism, citing virtuous American Indians, Brahmins, and others against the follies of Christianity. But for him the cult of the noble savage only went as far as attacking Christendom; he had no interest in the febrile, naturalistic, vaguely New Age religion of Jean Jacques Rousseau, as shown in Voltaire's famous dismissal of Rousseau's *Social Contract:* "I have received your new book against the human race, and thank you for it. Never was such a cleverness used in the design of making us all stupid. One longs, in reading your book, to walk on all fours. But as I have lost that habit for more than sixty years, I feel unhappily the impossibility of resuming it. Nor can I embark in search of the savages of Canada, because the maladies to which I am condemned render a European surgeon necessary to me; because war is going on in those regions; and because the example of our actions has made the savages nearly as bad as ourselves."[4]

By preference, Voltaire opted for the superiority of the classical world to the superstitions of the Church and its Dark Ages. He took Catholic vessels and filled them with secular wine: "I embrace my brethren in Confucius, . . . in Lucretius, in Cicero, in Socrates, in Marcus Aurelius, in Julian, and in the communion of our patriarchs."[5]

Voltaire turned out such a vast number of pamphlets, articles, sermons, books, and plays that he was for polemical literature what Napoleon would be for military science. When he was not laying siege to the Church himself, he waved others forward. This was his crusade: to extirpate "this infamous superstition." But, like Bayle, he did offer a note of caution. He meant to liberate the thinking classes, not "the rabble, who are not worthy of being enlightened, and who are apt for every yoke. . . ."[6] He feared that if mass man were liberated from the ideas of immortality and hell, he would be even more criminally inclined. For similar reasons he distrusted democracy, saying, "Independent of my love for freedom, I still would prefer to live under a lion's paw than under the teeth of a thousand rats who are my fellow citizens."[7]

Voltaire is not only the most striking and powerful of all the skeptics in the Age of Reason; he is the proof that a Renaissance Church—had there been no Reformation—would have kept vibrant minds such as his within the Catholic faith. Indeed, in some ways, it is not clear that he actually ever left. For all his rhetorical bombardment, he lived a quite different life. He built a Catholic chapel on his property and attended Mass. He sent his workers to Mass and had their children taught the Catholic catechism. He accompanied his solitary meals with sermon readings. He was an active member of a Catholic lay order. He put in writing that he wanted a Catholic burial. One could, of course, chalk this all up to Voltaire's stated desire to carry on the fight against *l'infâme,* not only from the barricades of literature, but from within the institution. But that seems no more than a partial—and perhaps even minority—truth.

Voltaire went so far as to ask the pope for sacred relics with which to sanctify his chapel; and the pope, in the spirit of Pope Leo X lauding the papal critic Erasmus, responded by sending him a hair shirt reputedly worn by St. Francis of Assisi. It seems more likely that Voltaire's Jesuit education bit deeper than perhaps even he himself realized. His war against *l'infâme* was, to him, a matter of simple justice, truth, and morality. But all the same, just as he acknowledged the virtues of the Jesuits, he found others to admire in the Church, not just in men of wit and learning, but in the nuns, the Sisters of Charity, of whom he wrote: "There is not, on all the earth, anything to equal the sacrifice of beauty, youth, and often high birth, which the gentle sex offers gladly in order to solace, in the hospitals, the welter of human suffering. . . . The nations separated from the Roman faith have but imperfectly copied so noble a charity."[8] The Roman Church, though it was *l'infâme*, at least spoke to the poet, at least offered examples of tremendous devotion to humanity along with its tremendous mythmaking and wars, and at least offered minds worth refuting. Perhaps it might be well to hedge one's bets just in case those bright Jesuits of his youth had in fact been right.

His sense of caution grew, and by the end of his life, he saw very clearly that the scales had perhaps tipped too far to the left; he turned his rhetoric against the *ennemis à gauche*. By that time, however, to be a deist—as he was—was to be a centrist. The torches, the passion for blood, the surge of history seemed to be with the atheists.

It is impossible to deny the horrendous destructive force of Voltaire, just as it is equally impossible to overstate his influence on shaping the modern mind—in short, he won; the Church lost. But his saber blows against the Church at least freed Catholic defenders from trying to out-dumb the Protestants. Instead they grabbed the sword of reason to fight the skeptics. Catholics abandoned their recently adopted Biblical literalism and returned to a sophisticated counterattack that exposed where the skeptics had been narrow, extreme, and inaccurate. More than one lunged for the *touché*: "Is not the fanaticism of your irreligion more absurd and dangerous than the fanaticism of superstition? Begin by tolerating the faith of your fathers. You talk of nothing but tolerance, and never was a sect more intolerant"[9]—a fact that would be proved when Reason became the state religion of France.

In this rhetorical battle of the mid–eighteenth century, the Jesuits were the most prominent defenders of Catholic orthodoxy. But just when the Church needed them most, they were disbanded, in perhaps the most shameful act of Catholic hara-kiri since the dissolution of the Knights Templar.

# THE SUPPRESSION OF THE JESUITS

THE JESUITS, OF COURSE, were targets of many rhetorical assassins. To Protestants they were the very symbol of the Counter-Reformation. To the Freemasons, they were the one immovable enemy of Deism. To the skeptics, they were the intellectual palace guard of the papacy that had to be defeated if reason was to triumph over *l'infâme*. And like the Knights Templar, they were targeted because they were powerful. As wielders of power, they risked having powerful enemies, among them King Louis XV. Royal confessors had refused to absolve the king's mistress, Mademoiselle de Pompadour, of the sin of adultery because they considered her impenitent. If this was an annoyance, the Jesuits' loyalty to the papacy raised other suspicions about their loyalty to the crown and their possible embroilment in subversion against the Gallican king.

Again, like the Templars, the Jesuits had become involved, very successfully, in business to finance the order, its schools, and other activities. With Jesuit outposts stretching from Europe to the Americas to Asia, they were well placed for international trade. In the late 1750s, the Jesuits had been suppressed in Portugal and Portugal's overseas dominions so that the state could suction Jesuit land and lucre. The Jesuits themselves were imprisoned or even executed by the Portuguese civil authorities, and Portugal fell into schism with Rome. In 1761, there was another business problem when the Paris *Parlement* ordered the Jesuits to pay the debts of a priest-entrepreneur. Father Antoine de La Valette had been forced into bankruptcy after English sea dogs had sailed away with several fortunes' worth of his exports.

This huge financial blow to the order was nothing compared to what came after. The *Parlement de Paris*—France's highest law court—used this case as a lever to investigate all aspects of Jesuit activity. The Jesuits were declared a subversive organization. Heaps of their writings were to be burned and their schools shut. The Jesuits' crime was that they were an international organization loyal to the pope in a time of centralizing state authority. The state would replace the Church as censor. The state would replace the Church as educator. It was a program around which Protestants, Jansenists, and skeptics could unite.

The king offered Pope Clement XIII a deal. If the Jesuits were Gallicanized—that is, made subordinate to the French state—he would allow them to work in France. The pope said, "Let them be as they are, or cease to be."[10] Several regional *parlements* expelled the order. Like the Jansenists, they argued that the Jesuits were morally corrupt. Like the skeptics, they argued that education was the province of the state, not the Church. The religious order that had trained Voltaire, Diderot, Molière, and Descartes, among others—which illustrated that they not only trained genius, but intellectual freedom—was held to be old-fashioned, impractical, and irrelevant: words that are always used to modernize—that is, worsen—education. In 1764, two years after *Parlement* formally declared the suppression of the Jesuits, the king agreed to enforce the law. Jesuit property was absorbed by the state. In 1767, even *former* Jesuits were, by order of *Parlement*, to be expelled, because there was no telling when Catholic wit might seep out of them and interfere with the plans of Puritans, bureaucrats, and skeptics.

That same year, the Bourbon king across the Pyrenees joined with Louis XV in frog-marching the Jesuits out of Spain, its Italian possessions, and its New World colonies, where the Jesuits were often infuriatingly idealistic—putting the needs of native peoples ahead of Spanish profits. Pope Clement XIV (1769–1774) was under pressure from the leading Catholic powers of Europe—France, Spain, even Austria—to completely disband the Society of Jesus. In 1773, Pope Clement—in groveling submission to the secular powers—disbanded the greatest force there had ever been of Catholic missionary and educational work. It was an infamous decision, and one that, in due course, would be overturned.

If Jansenist revenge, statist greed, the royal mistress, and papal weakness had precipitated the Jesuits' fall, it was the skeptics who were the great beneficiary—at least in France. Their deadliest rhetorical critics were gone. The skeptics granted that Jansenism triumphant would be worse than the Jesuits, because the Jansenists believed in Calvinism-by-law, while the Jesuits believed in "let us sit and reason awhile."[11] But bereft of the Jesuits—the Church's intellectual sword arm—Catholicism would be defenseless, the skeptics thought, in the new Age of Reason inaugurated by the philosophes. Voltaire said: "When we have destroyed the Jesuits we shall have easy work with the Infamy."[12]

The other great gainers from the suppression of the Jesuits were Protestant Prussia and Eastern Orthodox Russia. The extraordinary—and skeptical—Prussian musician, poet, general, and philosopher-king Frederick the

Great welcomed the Jesuits into his realm, as did the Russian empress Catherine the Great, both of whom had Catholic subjects. "Why," Frederick asked, "destroy those repositories of Greek and Roman civilization, those excellent professors of the humanities? Education will be the loser but as my brothers the very faithful, very Christian and apostolic kings have thrown them out I am collecting as many as I can. I preserve the breed and presently I'll sell them back again. I tell them so—I will easily get 300 *thalers* for you, my Father, and 600 for the Father Provincial."[13] Frederick was a much wiser man than the French Jansenists, statists, and skeptics. In fact, in his correspondence with Voltaire, it is the man-on-horseback Frederick who shines more often than the man-of-the-study Voltaire.

The generous warrior Frederick was a reminder of why a *feldmarschall* should sometimes be pope. A Julius II was what the papacy needed now—even Voltaire admired this aggressive Renaissance pope—but in the eighteenth century, the papacy had fallen into its worst trough since the tenth century. Again, the cause was a loss of independence. The popes were not morally bad men, but they were utterly at the will of the Catholic powers that surrounded them, and *every* Catholic power sought to subordinate Church to state on the Protestant model. The rise of the nation-state; the untamed fact of military might no longer mediated or subordinated to the pope as the leader of Christendom; and a new force, *liberalism*—the political manifestation of the philosophes, who sought to apply reason and order to the affairs of Europe—all worked against the papacy. The result would eventually prove, as so often in history, ironic.

The papacy is a monarchical institution; it was the sanctifier of monarchies and grew up amongst them; but the monarchies that appeared all-powerful in the middle of the eighteenth century would shortly be destroyed. The papacy would survive. Another irony: It would find its greatest freedom and opportunity, not on the continent where it had been the dominant power for more than a thousand years, not among the conservative states of Europe, but in the New World, in a liberal republic, the United States of America. This was partly a matter of how bad things had become for the Church in Europe. As Father Philip Hughes writes, "by 1790, outside the States of the Church and the new United States of America, there was not a single country in the world where the Catholic religion was free to live fully its own life, and not a single Catholic country where there seemed any prospect but of further enslavement and gradual emasculation."[14] The Church faced what at first blush seemed a factual impossibility, but was in fact a necessity: Constitutional liberalism was its hope for the future.

It was a hard lesson to accept, and the papacy had every reason to suspect republican liberalism. It was embodied not so much by the Jesuit-educated Voltaire—who, like most intellectuals, disdained democracy because it gave no electoral weight to reason and to men of reflection—but by Rousseau. Jean Jacques Rousseau was quite obviously insane. His life and works are those of a hypocritical, intellectually perfervid, and emotionally unstable actor. He is a precursor of New Age religion, and a smoother of that yellow brick road that leads from giving every man the vote to having every man's national and emotional aspirations embodied in a *Führer*. His idea that man was born good but made bad by society was the revolutionists' charter. There were far more reasonable republicans, like Montesquieu, whom today we would rank as conservatives. But in his own time, Montesquieu's naturalism, relativism, and Gallicanism ensured papal condemnation for his *Spirit of the Laws*. In France, where the cataclysm would hit, moderates upheld *The Spirit of the Laws* as Reason's model of a Deistic republican alternative to the crumbling remnants of France as a medieval Catholic state. In the English-speaking world, where overthrowing a medieval Catholicism was not on the agenda, Montesquieu was actually a buttress to conservative republicanism.

The pontiffs in Rome often responded ineptly to such dangerous political currents. Pope Innocent XIII (1721–1724), for instance, was an early anti-Jesuit, suspicious that the order was still tolerating Chinese rites, when his time might have been more profitably spent establishing Jesuit colleges in Europe. Pope Benedict XIII (1724–1730), a sincere Dominican monk (and the son of a duke), was that familiar but unheralded figure in the papacy, the unworldly man of faith thrust into power he doesn't want and, to a large extent, doesn't use. If as pope he could not be a full-fledged monk, his next preference was for acting as the parish priest of Rome. But the papacy needed a man who could be simultaneously holy and worldly. Pope Clement XII (1730–1740), another well-educated nobleman, had to undo the bollixing up of the papal finances that Benedict XIII's inexpert attempts at financial reform had inflicted. He failed, just as he failed in every aspect of foreign affairs, merely sanctifying—he felt there was nothing else to do—what power politics decided, and further harassing the Jesuits, opening an inquiry into their affairs in China. Clement did have two minor successes—one was in strengthening the Catholic loyalties of the Marionite Christians in the Lebanon, and the other was in continuing the artistic and cultural refurbishment of Rome.

Benedict XIV (1740–1758) was by far the best of the pre-Revolutionary eighteenth-century popes, but all that meant was that he was better at managing decline. A scholar, earning doctorates in theology and law, he was marginally more politically astute than his predecessors and was noted for his wit, capacity for work, and inspirational piety. He accepted royal supremacy as an unalterable fact, won state concessions for admitting it, and saw his role as protecting the rights of Catholic laypeople. In this he was remarkably successful, even with Protestant (which could mean agnostic or atheistic) kings, such as Frederick II (the Great) of Prussia. With the Catholic king of Spain, the pope sanctioned the diversion of Church monies to a government fund for fighting African pirates—always a worthy endeavor. Such clever diplomacy, however, did not protect papal Italy from invasion, as it was invaded throughout this century by assertive European monarchs. Though he was a notable reformer, Pope Benedict XIV confessed that the "pope orders, the cardinals do not obey, and the people do as they please."[15] Frustrating, yes, but that in a nutshell is the spirit of Catholic liberty: anarchy beneath a carapace of accepted theological truth; as opposed to the Protestant version of liberty: freedom protected, directed, and delimited by secular law. Benedict XIV was a great patron of both scientific and liberal learning—Voltaire even dedicated his play *Mahomet* to the pope—and was an important papal legislator. He set into place, among other reforms, the Catholic position on religiously mixed marriages—an issue of particular contemporary importance in Holland and Poland. The pope took a more lenient position than had the Council of Trent and made the chief concern of the Church that children of such marriages be raised in the faith.

Clement XIII (1758–1769) was, like his fellows, a scholar, but he lacked Benedict's wit, which had so enhanced the prestige of the papacy. His defense of the Jesuits against the crowns of Europe ended in failure; Germany was infected with a Teutonic form of Gallicanism (known as Febronianism) that he fought with mixed results; and he disconcerted Catholic artists with his Calvinistic prudery in ordering fig leafs for statues and paintings. Clement XIV (1769–1774) disemboweled the faith by suppressing the Jesuits. He felt it was this or face schism with every Catholic monarch in Europe. Pius VI (1775–1799) would witness de facto schisms and worse. In Austria, the Holy Roman Emperor Joseph II began a thorough, Enlightenment, Germanic reform of the Church within his realms. The spirit of Henry VIII was reborn, as many monasteries and nunneries were closed and others had their governing authority transferred from the pope to local bishops. Seminaries, ecclesiastical promotions, and every detail of worship were dictated by the state. The state managed Church finances. The emperor even laid out a grid so that there would be one parish church—and only one parish church—within an hour's distance from every parishioner. Such ideas, which marched under the name of liberalism and included toleration for Protestants, Eastern Orthodox Christians, and Jews, gained princely strength for Febronianism in Germany, northern Italy, and the Austrian Netherlands (Belgium). They were also coupled with the state's purging and suppressing of what were considered superstitious Catholic practices—such as reverence for saints and relics—unsuited to the Age of Reason. Such liberalism, however, proved unpopular and impossible to enforce. European Catholics remained a reactionary lot, especially after the French Revolution.

# REASON'S BLOODY TERROR

BEFORE THE REVOLUTION IN FRANCE came the American Revolution, in which the Catholic interest was not immediately apparent. While Catholic Spaniards had been tramping around North America—from Florida to New Mexico and beyond—since the early sixteenth century only one of the thirteen colonies that would become the United States had an appreciable Catholic population: Maryland, named after the Virgin Mary. The Stuart king Charles I had given the colony to Sir George Calvert, Lord Baltimore, in 1632. Lord Baltimore was a Catholic convert, and he intended Maryland as a haven for Catholics who could not practice their religion in the Old Country. But Catholics are, by nature, conservative, and few were inclined to abandon England merely because their religion was persecuted. So while Catholic landowners dominated Maryland—as Anglican aristocrats dominated Virginia—they remained a minority. Still, because Catholics controlled the Maryland Assembly, they were able to secure freedom for their religion—and freedom for all professed Christians—with a 1639 declaration of religious toleration and the Toleration Act of 1649, which would stand until undone by a series of Puritan rebellions and the democratic power of king numbers, which put the Protestants in control. The English crown took over the colony from 1691 until 1715, when power reverted to the Protestant colonials. Once Catholics lost their political predominance, they also lost their right to publicly celebrate their faith—as well as their right to vote or serve in public office; and they suffered other penalties. Only in Quaker Pennsylvania—where William Penn's dream of a Dissenter-Catholic alliance was realized—were Catholics completely free.

So Catholics, frankly, did not have a big investment in colonial America. The issues that drove the American colonists to rebellion were a hodge-podge of financial hedonism, political principle, and religious intolerance—against Catholics. The British had conquered the Canadian territories of "New France" in the French and Indian War of 1754–1763, and, in the words of Rudyard Kipling:

> Our American colonies, having no French to fear any longer, wanted to be free from our control altogether. They utterly refused to pay a penny of the two hundred million pounds that the war had cost us; and they equally refused to maintain a garrison of British soldiers. They intended to shake off all our restrictions on their trade, and to buy and sell in whatever market they could find. When our Parliament proposed in 1764 to make them pay a small fraction of the cost of the late war, they called it "oppression," and prepared to rebel.[16]

The colonists' rallying cry became the famous "No taxation without representation!" But along with money and politics, there was a religious issue as well. The Quebec Act of 1774 electrified Puritan New England against the crown, because the act granted French Canadian Catholics—who were now English subjects—freedom to practice their religion. The Continental Congress demanded that the act be repealed, as it was a religious threat to the colonies. Firebrand Samuel Adams proclaimed that King George III would soon fall prey to that dread temptation of all English sovereigns and take up the popish religion as his own. Adams thus inaugurated the paranoid strand of American politics. But his anti-Catholic views were widely held and frequently voiced by New England ministers. "To Gallic slavery, to Romish persecution and spiritual bondage, (blessed be God) we are utter strangers," sermonized Noah Welles in 1764.[17] The American Daniel Barber recorded in his *History of My Own Time,* published in 1827, that colonial anti-Catholicism was "so strong through the early part of the Revolution that the President of Princeton University [John Witherspoon] believed that common hatred of Popery, caused by the Quebec Act, the only thing that cemented the divergent religious groups in the colonies together sufficiently to allow them to make war, an opinion which was shared by British observers." These Puritan colonists were men who had come to America's shores to escape the Church of England. Popery was far worse than that. The pope was, in the words of the American poet John Trumbull, "Babel's scarlet whore."[18]

In 1776, the American colonists sent a delegation to Canada to win the French Canadians to the side of revolution. The Canadians naturally declined, preferring freedom of religion under the English crown to an alliance with American Puritans who disallowed the celebration of Christmas. But among the American delegates was Father John Carroll of Maryland, who would become the first Catholic bishop of the United States. His cousin Charles Carroll signed the Declaration of Independence and his brother Daniel Carroll participated in the Constitutional Convention. Father Carroll trusted that the liberal elite among the Founders—such as the Deist Benjamin Franklin from tolerant Pennsylvania, and, later, the Deistic Anglican George Washington—would work to lift the penal laws against Catholics. It turned out he was right, with the first states to do so being Pennsylvania, Maryland, Virginia (which nevertheless maintained its established Anglican Church until 1785), and Delaware, states where Carroll's influence could be directly felt. Carroll had been a Jesuit, before the order was suppressed, and he maintained a Jesuit's confidence that the faith could win any free argument of ideas—whether against rationalists or Protestants.

If the Canadians were unsympathetic, French Catholics in the territories of the Upper Midwest, and French and Spanish Catholics along the Gulf Coast, proved more eager to support the American colonists, especially as Spain declared war on England in 1779 and France had become America's chief ally in 1778—forging the fateful alliance without which America would not have won its independence in 1783. The participation of the French—with the marquis de Lafayette, the comte de Grasse, the comte de Rochambeau, and others[19]—as American allies eased anti-Catholic prejudice, and with the disestablishment of the various state churches in the colonies, now states, Catholicism was, by and large, free. The political outcome of the war had been oddly conservative, in some respects even reactionary. When the Constitution was ratified in 1787, it enshrined the traditional rights of Englishmen as the unalienable rights of every American citizen, and it went further, breaking up government power in a federal system, which was at odds with the centralizing trends of the eighteenth century. But it was, in fact, an organic development of the American experience of a century and a half and was, especially in the South, a somewhat feudalistic arrangement of dispersed power. On both grounds it fit in comfortably with the medieval heritage of Catholicism, even if there were precious few Catholics in the United States to experience it, probably only around 25,000.

Still, within fifty years of George Washington's inauguration as the first American president, Alexis de Tocqueville wrote, "America is the most democratic country in the world, and at the same time, according to reliable reports, it is the country in which the Roman Catholic religion is making the most progress." Indeed, he predicted "our grandchildren . . . will tend more and more to be divided clearly between those who have completely abandoned Christianity and those who have returned to the Church of Rome." Non-Catholics, he thought, would easily fall prey to "pantheism"—New Age religion—which was the philosophical system "most fitted to seduce the mind in democratic ages."[20] This process has been slowed only by the infinite divisibility of Protestant belief to the customer's satisfaction, as suits a democratic and commercial people.

But the immediate point was that in the aftermath of the American War of Independence, there was no religious animosity, and no hostility to men of property and social standing. The Americans remained a religious people, whatever the Deism of several prominent Founding Fathers. They were a commercially minded people, eager to get ahead, even though taxes were now higher than they had ever been under the British.[21] A home-grown aristocracy of businessmen in the North (men like John Adams) and landed proprietors in the South (men like Jefferson, Washington, Madison, and Monroe), along with the Constitution's hierarchical, republican political institutions, tempered the people's democratic spirit.

In France, things would not be so simple. Here the revolutionaries sought to smash any vestiges of feudalism. The French revolutionists did not seek an organic political development of Gallic traditions. Rather, they sought to wrench the country from tradition's soil and replant it in the vineyards of reason. The result was a harvest of blood and terror.

In comparing the two revolutions, we should not ignore the injustices inflicted on the American loyalists, who were subject to tar-and-feathering and other manifestations of mob violence. It is a shocking fact, but as the historian J. M. Roberts points out, "A much larger proportion of Americans felt too intimidated or disgusted with their Revolution to live in the United States after independence than the proportion of Frenchmen who could not live in France after the Terror."[22] Nevertheless, the French Terror was of a wholly different—and worse—character.

It is true that events in France began with echoes of the war in America. Money, again, was at the root of it. France had so bankrupted itself by its constant world wars that the king was compelled to find a way to shake down the nobility. But here the king was forcibly reminded of how interwoven European society was. "The paradox of eighteenth-century government could be seen at its most evident in France; a theoretically absolute monarchy could not infringe the mass of liberties and rights which made up the essentially medieval constitution of the country without threatening its own foundations."[23] Indeed, the liberal, centralizing monarchs of Europe had also failed to realize how much their authority rested on the Church they had been so keen to subordinate to the state. Subordination meant secularization, which, in turn, meant, in the minds of the people, a weakening of the religious prop for royalty.

King Louis XVI was himself of liberal inclinations and convoked the Estates-General, France's closest equivalent to a national parliament, so that he could solicit taxation with representation—a bad idea, as it turned out. The Estates-General, which had not met since 1614, was divided in three parts, representing the three constituent interests of medieval France: the clergy, the nobles, and the commoners. The parish priests made the terrible mistake of thinking that reform would be a good thing. They joined the commoners to form a national assembly, which took upon itself to write a new constitution for France—with most delegates thinking, initially, in terms of a monarchical republic. Every idea that

Frenchmen had of the new United States, all the intellectual ferment of
Voltaire, Montesquieu, Rousseau, and a dozen others, including the Marquis de Sade[24]—all this came to bear in the deliberations of the new national assembly, which was joined by the left-leaning nobles.

The simple churchmen did what they thought was their patriotic duty
and surrendered all Church lands to the state, to help the king retire the
national debt. Feudalism, the medieval inheritance of the Church and the
nobles, was abolished in the name of equality, and new administrative
districts replaced traditional boundaries. But the reforms went further.
The assembly voted a more thorough Gallican program. Priests and bishops were to become state employees and subject to election, with even
non-Catholics taking part in the voting. Monasteries and nunneries were
closed. Freedom of religion for Protestants and Jews was established.

And there was one final law that required the king's signature. Every
clergyman was to swear an oath of state supremacy. The king, who had already suffered mob violence, cautiously endorsed the law in December
1790. It was another three months before the politically feeble Pope Pius
VI roused himself and ordered Catholic priests and bishops not to take the
oath. The vast majority obeyed, even though it meant state prosecution.

The battle lines of the Revolution became clear. On the right—which
was where they sat in the assembly—were the Church, the monarchists, the
defenders of tradition. On the left were the radicals who wanted to recon-
struct France on the basis of reason. The rightists spoke for the dispersed
authority of the medieval regime—king, nobility, Church, and commons.
The Left spoke for centralized power that embodied the will of the people.

The clergy themselves were divided between the constitutionalists,
who took the oath of state supremacy, and the "nonjuring" priests and
bishops—the vast majority—who stayed loyal to Rome. The assembly
levied ever more serious legal threats against loyal Catholics, but the king
vetoed them. He would be bullied no further. He would stand as a
Catholic sovereign—which meant, in fact, that the mob would storm his
palace at Versailles; the Assembly would strip him of all his rights (in
1792) and imprison him; his son, the dauphin, would become a ward of
the state; and the king and his queen, Marie Antoinette, would be guillotined before a jeering mob in 1793. Tens of thousands of priests would
be exiled and threatened with death if they returned. Thousands of others
were killed for staying.

Here was the Age of Reason in power. Despite the violence and the terror that spread throughout the country—the Parisian mob, for instance, raided the city's prisons to murder priests and other reactionaries—the clergy remained firm. Regions—most famously, the Vendée, in the west of France—erected barricades, drew sabers, and loaded guns to protect the faith, and in the war that followed suffered the deaths of perhaps a quarter of a million people.[25]

The state had its own church. It began with priests whose vestments included the tricolor of the Revolution. It moved on to a cult of Reason, and Reason's altar replaced Christ's at the cathedral at Notre Dame. The state also endorsed a cult of Nature—Nature's god—and of course a cult of the State. Heroes of the Revolution replaced the saints of the Church. In all this, the French Revolution presaged the state religions of Nazism and Communism, and, indeed, in its mass murders, nationalist uniformity, militarism, and lootings in the name of the state and of equality, it embodied the same principles. But the Revolution also hearkened back to the Reformation. The revolutionaries congratulated themselves as if they were Protestant reformers, "wiping out eighteen centuries of error" by abolishing the Catholic Church. Constitutionalist priests were ordered to marry in order to propagate workers and soldiers for the state. Churches were stripped and religious art desecrated in the Protestant fashion. As Martin Luther altered the Lord's Prayer to condemn the pope, so now it was altered to praise the State and condemn enemies of the regime.

Eliminating Catholicism was a stated objective. The Gregorian calendar was junked in favor of a revolutionary one. Church bells and vessels were to be melted down and turned to "practical" uses. Priests and parishioners were hunted unto death. The metric system was imposed—because it was rational—and every tenth day became the reasonable man's day of rest, which the law compelled him to keep. Because it was a war against the Church, outrages of rape and murderous debauchery that especially offended Catholic sensibilities were de rigueur to show the democratic liberation of the mob-in-arms.

One of the most famous of the revolutionaries, Maximilien de Robespierre, had second thoughts about this carnival of terror. He became a moderate and argued in favor of Deism. Like Locke, he wanted a minimal creed around which Catholics, Protestants, and rationalists could find unanimity. He himself officiated at the cult of the Supreme Being, which joined the cult of Reason on France's state-sanctioned religious parade. But Robespierre suffered the fate of all moderates and was beheaded. The spirit of the Revolution was proclaimed by François-Joseph Westermann in his account of slaughtering Catholic loyalists: "I have trampled the children to death with our horses, I have massacred the women, and they are no longer going to give birth to any brigands. I am not guilty of taking a single prisoner, I have exterminated them all. . . . The roads are covered with corpses. There are so many of them at several places they form pyramids. The firing squads work incessantly. . . . [B]rigands arrive who pretend that they will surrender as prisoners . . . but we are not taking any. One would be forced to feed them with the bread of liberty, but compassion is not a revolutionary virtue."[26] Fittingly, Westermann was himself guillotined in 1794.

The Revolution made frequent references to killing women and children. Catholic women were targets not just for sexual mayhem and mutilation, of which the annals are sickeningly full, but because they had to be eliminated as breeders of "brigands." The Republicans also murdered the wounded, the sick, and the helpless as class enemies—and so that they would not have to feed them. There is, in the French Revolution, a horrible vein of murderous utilitarianism, of ideology trumping humanity, of the needs of the state being paramount, of hatred and depravity unleashed in the name of a higher purpose, which remains an uncomfortably common streak in modern man.

While the Revolution in France was consuming its own (and thousands of others), its victorious armies carried the torch of a new French empire abroad. For the Revolution had put the people in arms—the *levée en masse*—and the armies of the Republic where intent on evangelizing the new France by force, seizing territories to reclaim what were the announced, and ever expanding, natural boundaries of the French Revolution. Here, in the officer corps of that Revolutionary army, would come an unlikely restorer of the Church. His name was Napoleon Bonaparte.

## CHAPTER NINETEEN

# REVIVAL AND THE
# SYLLABUS OF ERRORS

⟶⬦⟵

THE MAN ON THE WHITE HORSE had been educated as a soldier and served the Republic as a gifted, young artillery officer. Nearly falling prey himself to one of the Revolution's periodic political purges, he was recalled to fire grapeshot into counterrevolutionaries and then emerged as an officer of genius when he was assigned abroad to conquer for the Revolutionary Republic, first in Italy and then on adventures farther afield. Killing French Catholics, though a convenient stepping stone to command, was unworthy of him; killing France's foreign enemies and expanding her glory—this he could do with relish.

He embodied that profound Western accomplishment—the man of action who is also a man of intellect: an integral prowess fast disappearing under the anti-intellectual, anti-historical, and anti-integral aftershocks of the Reformation. The Corsican lawgiver who gave the continent the Napoleonic Code "was Cesare Borgia with twice the brains, and Machiavelli with half the caution and a hundred times the will. He was an Italian made skeptical by Voltaire . . . [and] sharp by the daily duel of French intellects. All the qualities of Renaissance Italy appeared in him."[1] In other words, he was the product of a Catholic culture.

When Napoleon led his armies into Egypt in 1798, it was to conquer as an Alexander, but it was also with memories of the French-led Crusades, and with a vast retinue of scholars who came to catalogue, study, and appreciate the Orient. Napoleon invented Egyptology. He himself studied Islam to appreciate the religion of those he expected to be his subjects. It is a keynote of Catholic conquerors in history—whether Roman, French, or Spanish—that they respect and absorb native beliefs and customs. Their flexible, philosophical minds do not—in the Protestant evangelical way—completely reject or seek to obliterate foreign cultures, but attempt to understand them and redirect them.

The campaign in Egypt proved, ultimately, a military failure—thanks to Horatio Nelson and the British navy—but when Napoleon was recalled to France, he brought the same intellectual capacity, curiosity, vigor, and spark. Like Charlemagne, he rose above the bloody anarchy of his time. When "earth's foundations fled," as they did in the Revolution, he seized power and restored them. Not "for pay," as in A. E. Housman's *Epitaph on an Army of Mercenaries,* but for *la gloire.* He became, in the Roman phrase, *Restitutor Orbis*: the restorer of the world. A Deist in intellect, he nevertheless was a Catholic by blood, by *Realpolitik*, and, perhaps, on his deathbed, like that other conquering thunderer, Frederick II, even by final conviction, for he took the sacraments.

Like George Washington, he thought that religion was fundamental to society. This did not necessarily mean that rulers had to believe in Christianity, of course, but it was stupidity—such as Napoleon saw in the French Revolution—to think that *the people* could do without the consolations and restraint of their established religious faith. All of history argued against that. Neither was it wise—nor could it result in anything but terror if one tried, as the Revolution had—to uproot more than a thousand years of Catholic Christianity in France. Religion was the friend of law, and of order; irreligion was the gateway to crime and disorder. Religion was especially important to women: "What we ask of education is not that girls should think, but that they should believe. The weakness of women's brains, the instability of their ideas, . . . their need for perpetual resignation . . . all this can be met only by religion. . . . I want the place to produce not women of charm but women of virtue; they must be attractive because they have high principles and warm hearts, not because they are witty or amusing."[2] He sounds like a father of the Church.

Napoleon would have agreed with the modern historian Jacques Barzun: "Monarchy and monotheism go together."[3] It is ironic that Napoleon—viewed in his own time as a radical—was in fact a monarchist who believed in one God, one Church, one pope, one emperor, and a subsidiarity of subordinate kings and princes. He *was* a radical in the sense that he swept away the ancient Holy Roman Empire and reorganized French-conquered Europe on an orderly, rationalist, Enlightenment scheme that was impatient with all the petty duchies and idiosyncrasies of Europe's ancient, feudal, organic constitutions; and that he preached some of the ideals of the Revolution. But he was too clear-eyed about "the people" to think in terms of republics or democracies, after his initial ardor for the former as an officer of the Revolution. His vision became, in fact, very Catholic and very papal: monarchy was necessary to preserve order, but the highest commands were open to any man of talent, regardless of class. Napoleon was no egalitarian. Aristocrats rose easily under his command, because he recognized that they, as a rule, were more gifted with talent than common men. Indeed, he admired the model of the aristocratic gentleman. Yet every corporal could have a marshal's baton in his knapsack. Every man blessed with determination, talent, and luck could succeed.

In 1796, Napoleon—not yet emperor, still an officer of the Republic—began the French conquest of Italy. While these victories brought with them the Republic's dismissal of papal and priestly prerogatives—replacing religious law with civil law, subordinating Church to state, and appropriating churchly wealth—Napoleon distinguished himself as more moderate than the revolutionaries at home. He did not send bishops to the guillotine; he saw them as legates of civil order. He did not, however, hold supreme authority himself. The radicals were still in charge, and they believed that "The Roman religion will always be the irreconcilable enemy of the Republic."[4] The occupying French declared Rome a Republic in 1798, and the aged Pope Pius VI was taken prisoner. He died in 1799 in Revolutionary France, where the constitutional clerics treated him as an unimportant old man, a heretic from the Enlightenment's new religion of Reason, Nature, and the State.

His death opened a question: with revolutionary France holding Rome, would there any longer be a pope? Would Catholicism, at its historic capital, be abolished? Would the radical vision of the last king being strangled by the guts of the last priest now happen?

The papacy survived for three reasons. The first was that Italian Catholic loyalists rose up against the French. The second was that the Austrians provided a militarily defensible haven for the election of the next pope, Pius VII, in Venice. The third was that the French now recognized Napoleon as their First Consul—and the First Consul had no interest in ridding the world of Catholicism or deposing the pope; he merely wanted, at least for starters, to recover his Italian conquests from the Austrians. When he defeated them at Marengo, Northern Italy was again his. This time, he would govern it in cooperation with the faith: "I am sure," he said, "that the Catholic religion is the only religion that can make a stable community happy, and establish the foundations of good government. I undertake to defend it always. . . . I intend that the Roman Catholic religion shall be practiced openly and in all its fullness. . . . France has had her eyes opened through suffering, and has seen that the Catholic religion is the single anchor amid storm." He went further: "Tell the Pope that I want to make him a present of 30,000,000 Frenchmen."[5]

The new pope, Pius VII (1800–1823), who would be Napoleon's dueling partner for more than a decade, thought he could strike an accord with the First Consul. Pius VII had been a monk, and maintained a monk's humility and piety. He also proved politically astute, and recognized that the papacy must and could swim in the new political waters of Europe. Though vastly different men, Pius VII and Napoleon I would cooperate—albeit, after tempestuous rows—to restore the religious, if not the temporal, peace of France. A concordat was reached in 1801, and the pope's power to depose bishops was recognized—a necessity, in order to heal the breach between clerics who had given their allegiance to the Republic and those who remained loyal to Rome. To restrict this reassertion of papal power, Napoleon published a list of "Organic Articles" to the concordat the following year—the same year he became Consul for life.

The articles reaffirmed Gallicanism, the superiority of civil to religious law, and the legality of the state's seizure of Church property. It recognized Catholicism as the majority religion in France, but not the only religion, and made Catholic clerics state employees. Still, given the furnace of atheism, anarchy, and state-enforced New Agery through which the French Church had passed, this was a remarkable victory for the pope, the faith of the Apostles, and the Catholic foundations of Europe. The Left in France recognized this and was appalled. If France must have a religion, they wanted a Protestant France with married priests, minimal doctrine, and little authority. Instead, the old religion had triumphantly returned—returned by its popularity with the people and its attraction to the First Consul of France, the supposed field marshal of the Revolution.

Napoleon restored religious education for children, allotted seminaries to the Church, and went beyond the terms of the concordat to maintain Church-state amity. In 1804, he became emperor, and the pope agreed to crown him, but only after Cardinal Fesch—Napoleon's uncle—sanctified the union of Napoleon and his wife Josephine, which had before existed only in civil law. The crowning took place at the Cathedral of Notre Dame, with Napoleon crowning himself and his queen in the presence of the pope. Because of the popular acclamations that greeted the pontiff, the emperor had begun to regard him as something of a rival. Pius VII had hoped to win concessions from the emperor but achieved little more than imperial acquiescence to the restoration of the Gregorian—and therefore a Christian—calendar. But this allowed the emperor, in turn, to insist that the Church create the Feast of St. Napoleon on his birthday, August 15, citing in its defense an obscure Egyptian martyr whose name was somewhat similar to the emperor's own. The Church, with the good nature that is the mark of a sage, agreed.

The emperor, however, did not seem so good-natured. His rule became despotism—sometimes enlightened, often not. Instead of revolutionary terror, he relied on secret police. He asserted imperial authority over Church appointments, teaching, and other matters, and he imprisoned priests, bishops, and cardinals who annoyed him. Against the nations of Europe he was on perpetual campaign defeating every continental army. Only at sea, which belonged to Nelson and the British navy, and in Spain, where an Anglo-Irish general named Wellington was directing a small British army to assist Spanish guerillas, was Napoleon unable to completely enforce his will. Among his conquests, he added the crown of Italy to the crown of France and seized, as it suited him, territories that were the pope's. Napoleon wanted hostile powers—in particular Anglican England and Eastern Orthodox Russia—barred from papal ports, and foreigners banned from the Papal States and Rome. The pope refused in terms both imperial and liberal: The Church was to be a light of peace to all nations; it would have no enemies chosen for it by an emperor. The emperor was, he reminded, a nouveau creation compared to the ancient authority of the papacy.

Napoleon responded as frustrated emperors always did. He sent his troops to occupy Rome and the Papal States. For the second time in a decade, the pope was a prisoner of the French, and this time he would remain so for six years, from 1808 to 1814. There was a Pimpernel-like offer to rescue the pope, care of the British navy, but the pope knew it would be better for him to endure captivity and shame the emperor of France than to seem a political tool of England and the Allies. To openly side with England could lead to another French war against the Church in the name of patriotism. In captivity, the pope calmly reverted to his monkish habits and training. Politically, he offered Napoleon no compromise and refused to institute bishops, condone the emperor's divorce and remarriage, or conduct other papal business on behalf of the emperor.

By 1812, Napoleon's political position was beginning to weaken. He had ruined the *grande armée* on the retreat from Russia. Spain was a vicious nightmare. Yet he still dreamt of power and conquest. If he could only upset England, he would dispense with the Roman pope, reducing him to bishop with no extraordinary authority, and create a new papacy in Paris, from which France would direct Europe's religious and secular affairs. Events soon shattered that dream. His genius on the field continued, but he found that he could not keep allies. All of Europe was rising in arms against him. In 1814, Napoleon had the pope freed—which was an Allied demand—and returned to Italy. That same year, the Allied armies marched into Paris, and Napoleon was exiled to the island of Elba. His escape and return to France in 1815—where the country rallied to him again, deposed the restored Bourbon monarchy in favor of *l'empereur*, and lifted the colors to march to Waterloo—is one of the most remarkable stories in history. It is a period known as "the Hundred Days," and it ends with defeat for Napoleon and victory for the duke of Wellington and his German ally Gebhard Leberecht von Blücher.

Napoleon was exiled again, this time to the escape-proof island of St. Helena. It was here that Napoleon asked leave of the pope for a chaplain, which he was granted. "I was born in the Catholic religion. I wish to fulfill the duties it imposes, and receive the succor it administers." It is said, however, that Napoleon liked to amuse himself by playing the Devil's advocate, holding any form of religion—or irreligion—as higher than Catholicism. Once in the course of such a harangue one of his former generals stopped him and said: "I know your majesty does not believe one word of what you have just been saying."

"Yes," Napoleon confessed, "you are right. At any rate it helps to pass an hour."[6]

Napoleon died in exile in 1821; according to at least one recent historian's account he was poisoned—not by one of his captors but by a French colleague, the very general who doubted the emperor's sincerity when he criticized the Church.[7] Napoleon had risen to power on the back of an atheistical revolution, conquered Europe, and tried to extinguish the power of the papacy, even imprisoning the pope. Yet in the end, it was the defeated emperor who saw the pope restored as a prince of the concert of Europe. The pope's allies now included not only Catholic Spain and Austria, but Protestant England and Orthodox Russia. Napoleon had left Europe transformed—and in the hands of conservatives united against any further revolutionary troublemakers like himself; united, also, in defense of religion. The pope had regained the papal lands of Italy, and the honor of the papacy gleamed after a century of submersion.

Napoleon's wars had lifted the eighteenth-century's statist and then revolutionary stranglehold on Catholicism, but her neck still bore the bruises. The Church's vast institutional structure had been vandalized and left in ruins. In 1814, Pope Pius VII re-founded the Jesuits for the task of re-Christianizing Europe. He, and subsequent popes, negotiated a series of concordats guaranteeing Catholic rights on the continent, though the concordats almost invariably had the pope ratifying the election of bishops by the state, where rulers now considered bishops their vanguard to squash revolutionary ideas.

In England, in yet another irony, the enactor of the Catholic Emancipation Act of 1829 was the Iron Duke, Lord Wellington, the Irish Protestant victor over Napoleon at Waterloo and the quondam leader of the "ultras" in the adamant-against-all-change conservative party. He acted out of no love for the Catholic religion, but out of a sense that Ireland could not be kept in the empire unless Catholics elected to parliament were allowed to take their seats, which they could not under the 1688 Protestant settlement of William and Mary. In 1780, the enacting of even mild reform—as undertaken by the Catholic Relief Act of 1778, which allowed Catholics to pledge their allegiance to the crown without renouncing their faith—had led to the anti-Catholic Gordon Riots, which required 12,000 troops to suppress. Since then, anti-Catholicism had been tempered by what Britons had seen during the French Revolution. Tyranny, superstition, and Irish sedition were not necessarily the sole qualities of Roman Catholicism. On the continent, obviously, it could be a conservative force. Even though the Catholic Emancipation Act amended England's constitution, religious toleration that avoided civil war in Ireland, Wellington argued, was conservative statesmanship. After fractious politicking and debate, Wellington carried the day.

Intellectually, Catholicism fulfilled its role of affirming established authority. One of its most eloquent expositors was Joseph de Maistre, who loathed the Revolution and despised the Enlightenment thinkers who had breathed life into it. Nations and constitutions, de Maistre wrote, are divine creations that develop organically over time; and in fact the best laws and constitutions are those that are not written down. It is the unspoken laws of a country that are written on people's hearts, expressed in their habits, and part of their natural development and understanding that are the most vital. Abstract, rationalist attempts to recreate nations, or write-on-paper and enforce-by-law transformative constitutions, are therefore wrong—we would call them "social engineering"—and necessarily violent. Order depends on hereditary monarchs who rule like fathers (they can be good or bad, but their authority is necessary); on the Catholic Church, the only Church that can withstand the rationalists; and on the infallible pope, set above kings and countries. Oh yes, and on capital punishment as ordered by legitimate authority, so that the likes of the marquis de Sade, rather than Marie Antoinette, go to the guillotine. With de Maistre, the medieval vision of society was reborn, and it became the touchstone for every modern Catholic conservative movement on the Continent.[8]

The friendliness of the Church with conservative regimes did not keep Her from using liberalism to Her advantage, especially in the New World. After early support for Spain against the revolutions in South America, both Pius VII and his successor popes Leo XII (1823–1829) and Gregory XVI (1831–1846) treated with the new regimes. In the words of the politically wise Cardinal Consalvi, unless the Church responded to the political reality that these countries had won their independence, they might be "filled with Methodists, Presbyterians and new Sun-worshippers."[9] That disaster was prevented.

Such nimble statesmanship did not come naturally. The Church struggled to find its way in post-Revolutionary Europe. Pope Leo XII proved his shortcomings by thinking that, in reaction to the Revolution, the Church should impose Calvinistic social controls on Rome and the Papal States, with un-Italian restrictions on drinking, flirting, and anarchy. Jews, who had been beneficiaries of the Enlightenment and Napoleon's armies, were locked into ghettoes—or sought more profitable climes. Pope Leo was demonstrably fighting the last war with the wrong tools. Leo's blue laws were no solution to Italian nationalism—to which the Papal States were a geographic barrier—or the latest Protestant heresy, which he himself condemned: "indifferentism," a working out of Deist, Lockean minimal theology to its endpoint, which was that religion didn't really matter anyway. What really counted was science and materialism—that was reality; theology was mere guesswork. This would be the spirit of post-Enlightenment man. Leo's restrictions on freedom only helped ruin the papal economy and make him deeply unpopular. Pope Pius VIII (1829–1830), who followed him, worked to undo the damage.

A similarly misguided reaction occurred in the government of France, where the Bourbon king Charles X had attempted to crush dissent by limiting freedoms and asserting his divine right. He succeeded only in forcing his own abdication, to be replaced by the liberal duc d'Orléans as "King of the French," though he would prove almost equally hapless, if in a more republican direction. It was a direction that some clerics—notably Félicité Robert de Lamennais—thought the Church should endorse. He believed that the Church's real freedom and future lay not in the union of Church and crown, but in the separation of Church from state. Lamennais's argument was eventually undone by his behavior. He moved across the political spectrum from right to left and ultimately renounced his faith in God in favor of left-wing political nostrums, a path that would be well trod by future preachers of the "social gospel."

Rather more helpful was Vicomte François-René de Chateaubriand, who declared, "I am Bourbon as a matter of honor, royalist according to reason and conviction, and a republican by taste and character," and who provided an aesthetic—and therefore typically Catholic—defense of the faith: "Christianity is perfect; men are imperfect. . . . Christianity, therefore, is not the work of men."[10] While both Lamennais and Chateaubriand had the misfortune of being influenced by Rousseau, in Chateaubriand's case it resulted in his book *The Genius of Christianity*, which helped restore the link between Catholicism and the arts that had been broken by the French Revolution. Catholicism to this day retains a special appeal to artists and others moved by an aesthetic sense. In the nineteenth century that aesthetic sense was known as Romanticism. Romanticism had, at first, reveled in Napoleon as a classical hero. But later, after the post-Revolutionary disillusion, Chateaubriand—and, for that matter, the Romantic poets in England—made romanticism a reactionary religious counterpoint to rationalist reductionism. The romantic sensibility later turned medievalist—as in the English school of painters known as the Pre-Raphaelites—and was a major source of attraction for converts.

The Church's approach to reasserting its place in the world was less intellectual than it was based on experience, experience that was guided by statecraft. The great Austrian diplomatist Prince Klemens von Metternich was, with Wellington and his political colleague Lord Castlereagh, chiefly responsible for the "world restored"[11] after the fall of Napoleon. As an Austrian, a Catholic, and a guardian of the conservative postwar settlement, Metternich took great interest in the election of popes. During the conclave of 1830, he was influential in ensuring the election of Pope Gregory XVI, a monk who had distinguished himself by his literary defense of papal infallibility and supremacy.

The new pope had many good ideas—banning trains, forbidding democracy, and opposing political activity in the Papal States—but this required, or led to, armed intervention from Austria and France to defend him. Liberal republicans and simple brigands were rife in Italy, pillaging in the name of Italian nationalism. The French and Austrians were necessary to keep Italy at peace—and, of course, to balance each other's influence. Abroad, Gregory XVI asserted papal supremacy, sought reforms to relieve oppressed Catholics, and—such was his ingrained hatred of revolution—opposed clergy involving themselves in politics. He even denounced the Catholic people of Poland for their revolt against Russian tyranny—which included Eastern Orthodox religious tyranny—because the czar, too, was part of the Concert of Europe, and, though a brute, he at least was not a liberal. Catholic Poles, Belgians (who in 1830 threw off the rule of the Dutch, to whom they had been handed at the Congress of Vienna), and the Irish were, politically at least, liberal Catholics because liberalism offered them freedom from Russian, Dutch, or English constraints.

If the pope was resolutely on the side of the existing order, he did, nevertheless, assert Catholic prerogatives in Prussia, demanding that children of mixed Protestant-Catholic marriages be brought up as Catholics, and not, as the civil law had it, with sons taking the religion of their fathers, daughters the religion of their mothers. The dispute lasted nearly a decade, but with a Catholic victory. Marriages were made chiefly a religious rather than a civil matter, and the new Prussian king, Friedrich Wilhelm IV—a medievalist, as are all good men—undid some of the Enlightenment restrictions on the faith enacted by his predecessor, the Holy Roman Emperor Joseph II.

Pope Gregory XVI also took an interest in the New World, recognizing Baltimore as the episcopal see of the United States. He repudiated slavery and encouraged, in missionary settlements, the creation of native clergy. The Catholic Church, claiming universal dominion, has never known color barriers, and with Gregory its dominion over palm and pine grew. It followed European colonialism, as it had followed the Roman legions, but it also developed independent missions. In addition, Gregory busied himself with all the usual theological, artistic, and scholarly affairs—especially in archeology—that are a pope's prerogative, but he is remembered in the history of Europe as a very Metternichian pontiff, standing athwart progress, or the very idea of progress, in favor of the established order.

The wisdom of that course was proved by his successor, Pope Pius IX (1846–1878). Pius was an Italian patriot who, to Metternich's horror, looked kindly on republicans, enacted liberal reforms in the Papal States, and even seemed to embrace progress, approving the construction of railroads and the installation of other new-fangled gadgets like gas street lamps. These were all, needless to say, bad signs. Metternich thought a liberal pope was a logical impossibility, and, as usual, he was proved right. Pius IX quickly found that liberal reforms did not appease republican agitators but incited them to riot and escalating demands. They wanted Rome and the Papal States under secular control, and they wanted papal sanctification of an Italian rebellion against Austria. When the pope refused, the mobs turned to murder and assassination and drove him into exile. In February 1849, Rome was declared an anti-clerical democratic republic. In July, it was declared a papal city. What a difference five months and the French army can make. Pius IX learned that inviting liberal republicans to dinner meant bayonets at his throat. Having come to power as a political liberal, he now found it axiomatic that the Church must be allied with conservative monarchs. Live and learn.

His next lesson was that Italian patriotism (or more properly, nationalism), such as his own, would lead to the obliteration of the papacy as a temporal power. The movement to unify Italy was known as the Risorgimento. Its four most important leaders, all of whom had fought against the power of the Church and in favor of secularization, were

- Giuseppe Mazzini, who had helped establish the Roman Republic, but who was eventually pushed aside as too radical
- Giuseppe Garibaldi, the sword arm of the Risorgimento, allied to Mazzini, when Mazzini had power, but then to the more conservative Piedmontese
- King Victor Emanuel II of Piedmont and his prime minister
- Count Cavour, who could trust on the support of the French against the Austrian occupation of northern and central Italy

By 1861, Italy was united under its new king, Victor Emanuel II, and over the dead bodies of an international brigade of devout Catholics—many of them Irish or Canadian—who had tried to defend the Papal States. The pope's holdings were reduced to a citadel—the immediate environs of Rome—guarded by French troops. In 1870, the French withdrew to fight the Franco-Prussian war. The pope's own volunteers were no match for the Italian army—a phrase not often heard in history—which seized Rome for the king and for Italy, whose capital it now became. The pope, in his own words, became a prisoner of the Vatican. He refused any formal acknowledgment that the princely realms of the Vicar of Christ had been reduced to a few—albeit magnificent—buildings, and demanded that Italian Catholics refrain from politics and voting, which was a self-defeating ordinance indeed. What was truly remarkable, however, was not this secular, political defeat, but the fact that it was matched and exceeded by rising admiration for the papacy and by a Catholic revival. Freed from the necessities of politics and the dueling of princes, the pope became, ironically, a more religiously powerful pontiff. As states adopted the "indifferentism" the papacy condemned, they left a vacuum of religious authority. The pope filled this vacuum, reasserting his primacy to the huzzahs of the faithful.

Pius IX reigned longer than any other pope, and his religious achievements were enormous. In the administration of the Church, he vastly expanded its missionary branches and its organization in the New World; he created colleges for foreign seminarians in Rome, including the American College in 1859; he reestablished the Catholic episcopal hierarchy in England, Wales, and the Netherlands; and he negotiated numerous concordats with the states of Europe. He was active in defining dogma, as well. It was Pope Pius IX who affirmed as dogmatic belief the Immaculate Conception of the Virgin Mary (1854) and the Infallibility of the Pope when speaking ex cathedra on matters of faith and morals (1870, at the First Vatican Council, the very year that Rome would be taken from the Church). He also consecrated Catholic Christendom to the Sacred Heart of Jesus (1875). But his most memorable contribution was *The Syllabus of Errors* (1864), which targeted liberalism—and its spin-offs communism and socialism—in a list of eighty mistaken ideas. In an immortal phrase, lifted from a document in 1861, the *Syllabus* condemned the idea that "the Roman Pontiff can and ought to reconcile himself with progress, with liberalism, and with modern civilization." It is with regret that one notes that in the context of its original document, this was directed at the liberal Piedmontese and was defined thus: "if by the word 'civilization' must be understood a system invented on purpose to weaken, and perhaps to overthrow, the Church."[12] More interesting than its denial of liberal shibboleths, *The Syllabus of Errors* is a consistent attack on the power of the state and on the idea, which is explicitly condemned, that might makes right. In the context of twentieth-century politics, these are the striking passages.

Much as he disapproved of the political and religious temper of modern life, the pope did reconcile himself to creating dioceses in the most modern of all countries, the United States. The new dioceses stretched from coast to coast, including Buffalo, Cleveland, Peoria, and Grass Valley, California—all of which must have seemed a far cry from Rome, Vienna, and Paris. In all, he instituted nearly fifty dioceses in the United States, including, to add a bit of poetry, "the Vicariates Apostolic of the Indian Territory." He also continued his interest in new technology and even commissioned a modern English ship, which he dubbed, somewhat oddly, *The Immaculate Conception*.

What he could not do was reconcile himself to the likes of Otto von Bismarck in Germany. The showdown between the pope and the Iron Chancellor became known as the *Kulturkampf*, or, in more modern terms, the culture wars.

## KULTURKAMPF

IN 1848, THERE WERE liberal revolutions across the continent—including in Austria, Hungary, Italy, Germany, and France—that were put down, but that left liberalism with the taste of royal blood on its lips. The liberals stood for nationalism—such as uniting Italy—and therefore centralization. Liberalism was impatient with differences. It preached tolerance but was intolerant of the organic history of Europe. Liberals venerated not tradition but reason, and as there could be no legitimate argument against reason, opponents of liberalism were ipso facto superstitious, repressive, and reactionary: in other words, Catholics. Liberalism was secular Protestantism, with written constitutions as its *sola scriptura* and the saving grace and salvific purpose of nationalism and progress its *sola fide*. What impeded nationalism and progress were ancient crowns and traditions, the remnants of feudalism, its legacy of dispersed power, and Catholicism untamed by secular government.

The Germany of 1815 was made up of thirty-eight German-speaking states. Protestant Prussia was the dominant German-speaking power of the north, as Catholic Austria was in the south. But Germany remained as it had been since the beginning of time—even under the Holy Roman Empire (or the First Reich)—a confederation of independent states. The Prussian Otto von Bismarck wanted to change that. He wanted a powerful, centralized, unified Germany, and in 1866 he went to war with Austria to get it. He won most of what he wanted. The result was a northern German confederation that in 1871, after Prussia's victory in the Franco-Prussian War, grew to become the Second Reich—which included Catholic Bavaria—under a Prussian king.

While Germany's political parties were enthusiastic for unity, liberals and Protestants saw the Catholics of Bavaria and the Rhineland as a threat that had to be dealt with. Catholics were regarded as ignorant hindrances to progress. They were seen as not fully German—at least not in the Prussian sense—given their religious loyalty to the pope. Not only that, but Roman Catholicism was the religion of France, Poland, and Austria: countries Prussia regarded as potential belligerents. The Prussian platform was for Protestant religion—which kept out of politics and served the state—and secular schools, which were specifically designed to inculcate secular thinking. Like most German inventions, these secular schools were extremely well crafted. Germany gained a reputation for producing the best-educated people in Europe, and the Prussian education system for grade school and higher education became the model for public schools in the United States.[13]

Prussia stood for a disciplined, orderly, Germanic, and Protestant version of the Napoleonic spirit. Southern German Catholics were opposed to this program on nearly every contestable point. *The Syllabus of Errors* might have embarrassed liberal Catholic intellectuals, but it provided lay Catholics with a distinct political philosophy, later immortalized by Quincy Wagstaff (Groucho Marx) in the film *Horsefeathers:* "Whatever it is, I'm against it." Bismarck was not amused. The result was a massive propaganda war between faithful German Catholics and the Prussian state, which wanted to engineer socially useful workers, soldiers, and bureaucrats. If anything is anathema to the messy, organic, anarchic, anti-utopian, tradition-minded Catholic spirit, it is social engineering.

The culture war began in 1871 with the state insisting on the secular or state-Protestant supervision of Catholic schools. It was followed in 1872 by the expulsion of the Jesuits and other Catholic religious orders. The state passed laws favoring the so-called Old Catholics, who accepted state supremacy somewhat on the model of Gallicanism or Febronianism and were to be found in small numbers in Germany, the Netherlands, and elsewhere. In Germany there were also "State Catholics," who accepted the expanded liberal program that included state control of seminary education, clerical appointments, and the applicability (or non-applicability) of papal discipline. But the "Old" and "State" Catholics were few, and the overwhelmingly loyal and orthodox Catholics supported their bishops in peaceably refusing to acknowledge state supremacy. Fines were levied. When they weren't paid, the Prussian state began imprisoning Catholic priests. It enacted a variety of punitive measures against Catholic societies under the pretext that they were subversive organizations. Catholics refused to budge—in fact, support for the Catholic cause grew among the laity, who cast votes for Catholic candidates and supported a proliferation of pro-Catholic newspapers. The state increased its imprisonments, banished bishops, and closed seminaries. Yet the people listened to Rome. In 1875, Pope Pius IX declared that no Catholic in Germany was obliged to obey anti-Catholic laws. In the Middle Ages, such a declaration might have led noblemen to gather their knights under the banner of the cross and the Virgin Mary, perhaps even in a Crusade, against a renegade king. While the pope no longer commanded swords—at least not enough of them to matter—he did command the consciences and loyalty of faithful Catholics in their millions. These faithful refused to bow to Prussian tyranny, and more than a thousand Catholic priests paid the price in imprisonment or exile.

The tyranny increased via what amounted to another Reformation: monasteries were closed; Church land was expropriated; Catholic priests and bishops were denied their state-controlled salaries; and, as in the Napoleonic code, civil—rather than religious—marriage was made mandatory. Bismarck encouraged a *Kulturkampf* without borders, so that Switzerland, too, took up the cause of fighting the Church. Bismarck's successes in law and diplomacy came at a troubling cost, which he recognized. If his goal was unifying and strengthening Germany, the Sturm und Drang of the *Kulturkampf* debates in parliament indicated that it was a singular failure. Not only were Catholics increasing their electoral representation; so were conservatives—including conservative Protestants—who opposed the irreligious tone of the government. Beginning in 1879, the anti-Catholic laws, while not repealed, were less vigorously enforced, and exceptions to the laws were granted. There was a new pope in Rome—Leo XIII (1878–1903)—and Bismarck wanted an accommodation. Throughout this entire period the German constitution, which guaranteed the independent rights of the Catholic Church, had been forfeit. The papacy negotiated to restore these rights. The eventual compromises came in 1886 and 1887; and while constitutional guarantees, which had proven fruitless anyway, were not regained, the result was a victory for the Church. The Church conceded state approval of clerical appointments, state control of public education, and state supremacy in law. But the Church won back its seminaries, control over most of its own affairs, and its free and public practice of religion. The state granted further concessions in 1890 and 1891, lifting criminal sanctions against priests who had protested the punitive laws and restoring clerical salaries. In 1917, at the height of World War I, restrictions against the Jesuits were lifted. But in the decades to follow there would be trouble again.

# THE ENGLISH-SPEAKING REVIVAL

IN NINETEENTH-CENTURY ENGLAND would be found one of the greatest of all Catholic minds, John Henry Newman. He was born an Anglican of evangelical training, became a priest, and through sheer study and piercing logic found himself in middle age a Catholic. There were three initial prods. The first was history. Newman wanted to see the Anglican church as apostolically ordained from the primitive church of the Early Fathers. The second prod was a related issue. He recoiled from the idea that the Anglican church was a mere creation of the state—that its doctrine, practice, and administration could be determined by acts of Parliament, diplomatic alliances, and political convenience. No, he proclaimed, the Anglican church was historical and apostolic; it represented the true Catholic tradition without Rome's unscriptural elaborations of primitive church practice. Finally, he saw that liberalism was the enemy of religion. "If liberalism," he said, "once got a footing within her [the Anglican church], it was sure of the victory in the event. I saw that Reformation principles were powerless to rescue her."[14]

Newman and like-minded Oxonians led "the Oxford Movement," which sought to shore up the Catholic portions of Anglicanism. Newman was also the most important of the "Tractarians," who propounded in a series of *Tracts for the Times* an apologia for the Anglo-Catholic tradition. In the process, Newman discovered that the Anglican church was not a legitimate via media between Calvin's Zurich and papal Rome, any more than the ancient heresies of the Arians or the Monophysites had been appropriate via media for the faith of the Apostles. In fact, it was a matter of undeniable history that there was only one legitimate Church. It was the Church of Rome. It was from profound study and experience that Newman was forced to conclude—and indeed proclaim—that "one thing at least is certain; whatever history teaches, whatever it omits, whatever it exaggerates or extenuates, whatever it says or unsays, at least the Christianity of history is not Protestantism. . . . And Protestantism has ever felt it so." For why else, Newman asks, would Protestantism be so willing to dispense "with historical Christianity altogether" and form a new "Christianity from the Bible alone"? Protestants would never have put the Christianity of history "aside, unless they had despaired of it. . . . To be deep in history is to cease to be a Protestant."[15]

Newman's conversion came slowly, reluctantly, and at great personal cost and pain. It resulted in an extraordinary literary efflorescence that shines most famously in his *Apologia Pro Vita Sua* (1864), an immediately acknowledged classic of English prose. A searching philosophical and spiritual autobiography and a crushing historical and theological polemic against a Protestant antagonist—Charles Kingsley—it is a nineteenth-century equivalent of St. Augustine's *Confessions*. Its rhetorical power greatly improved the public estimation of Catholicism in England. It also contains its own syllabus of errors in Newman's "Note A" on "Liberalism" in which he lays out eighteen religious and philosophical propositions held by Oxford liberals that he considers manifestly untrue. They are instructive reading, because today probably most Christians and nearly all secularists share these liberal assumptions.

Newman's frontal assault on liberalism makes it all the more ironic that though he became a cardinal of the Church he was forever tagged as a liberal by his Catholic rivals and enemies. The fact that he could be is attributable to one overriding factor. In its fight for survival against the successive assaults of the Reformation, the statism of kings and the Enlightenment, and the Napoleonic and nationalistic revolutions, the intellectual brilliance of the Church had slowly, but progressively, been hidden. It was regarded as a jewel that could not be exposed, especially as the Church's schools, seminaries, and religious orders were vandalized, destroyed, banished, or seized by Protestants, liberals, or revolutionaries. Just as John Adams had said that he must study politics so that his children could study philosophy and his grandchildren porcelain,[16] so the Church had set itself foremost to opposing the erosive tides of violent history rather than nurturing its own intellect, scholarship, and the arts. These were far from extinguished, but they were no longer at the forefront of the Catholic religion, which now expressed itself more vigorously in popular devotions to Mary, the Miraculous Medal, the Sacred Heart of Jesus, and other demotic expressions of the meeting of physical and mystical truths.

Newman himself was a mystic, but he was also an intellectual, with an Englishman's variation of Renaissance learning that incorporated the classical and the Christian: "I understood . . . that the exterior world, physical and historical, was but the manifestation to our senses of realities greater than itself. Nature was a parable, Scripture was an allegory; pagan literature, philosophy, and mythology, properly understood, were but a preparation of the Gospel. The Greek poets and sages were in a sense prophets."[17] Newman wrote with a grace, refinement, and subtlety that men of equal refinement and subtlety could appreciate, but that in the hands of the devious and the dull could become, in Kipling's phrase, "twisted by knaves to make a trap for fools."[18]

One of his enemies was another colleague from Oxford, a fellow convert from Anglicanism and also a cardinal of the Church, Henry Edward Manning. But where Newman's gifts were literary and intellectual, Manning was a formidable politician. He became archbishop of Westminster—thereby head of the Catholic Church in England—and was a leader of the ultramontanes—that growing party that saw in a defiant, infallible pope the only rock that could withstand the storms of liberalism. To this vision, Newman assented, but with his perennial subtlety that Manning mistook for watery moderation. Manning distrusted Newman because he saw him, not as a wholehearted Romanist, but as representing an admittedly lofty, but parochial "English Catholicism. . . . It is the old Anglican, patristic, literary Oxford tone transplanted into the church."[19]

Before religion came between them, Manning was also a friend of the English prime minister William Gladstone, and it is Gladstone whom he more resembles: vigorous, confident, commanding, and assertive. In Manning's own words, "To be in the world and yet dead to it is the highest reach of faith."[20] He was very much in the world. He was a practical campaigner against poverty, set up Catholic schools for poor Irish immigrants, intervened in labor strikes, and was a leader of Victorian moral renewal. It was not just gin and Methodism that kept England's poor manageable, it was gin, Methodism, and Manning. Manning was an important influence on Pope Leo XIII's famous 1891 encyclical *Rerum Novarum* that sought to uphold human dignity in the new capitalistic (and socialistic) age by reiterating the Church's belief in private property and the right of the laborer to a living wage. On his death, it was workingmen from the slums who turned out in their thousands for the funeral of this Oxford-educated cleric from England's ruling class.

Newman and Manning successfully reasserted Catholicism as a public force in English life. They and others of the Oxford Movement embarrassed the Church of England, because, as the mocking skeptic Lytton Strachey put it, they "took the Christian religion *au pied de la lettre*. This had not been done in England for centuries. When they declared every Sunday that they believed in the Holy Catholic Church, they meant it. When they repeated the Athanasian Creed, they meant it. Even when they subscribed to the Thirty-Nine Articles [of the Anglican creed], they meant it—or at least they thought they did."[21] And by taking Anglicanism seriously, some of the church's finest minds had gone to the "superstitious" and "authoritarian" Church of Rome.

Another who subscribed to the Catholic Church and meant it—or thought he did—was Lord Acton. He himself was not a convert, though he came from a family that was Anglican on his father's side and Catholic on his mother's. Shunned by Cambridge—apparently because of his religion—he received his higher education in Germany and there imbibed that tempestuous idealism that is part of the German character. His learning was of monumental proportions—and was recognized as such—though his literary output was limited to scholarly journalism and lectures, for the price of genius was a continual dissatisfaction with his research materials. He never had enough to proceed with his planned *History of Liberty*.

Acton considered himself unique—and therefore without intellectual allies—in his stand as a "Liberal Catholic": "I find that people disagree with me either because they hold that Liberalism is not true, or that Catholicism is not true, or that both cannot be true together. If I could discover anyone who is not included in these categories, I fancy we should get on very well together."[22] In fact, it was unlikely that Acton would get along well intellectually with anyone. For the truth was that his thought was so complex as to confuse even himself. Acton was a moral absolutist known by his immortal epigram "Power tends to corrupt and absolute power corrupts absolutely." Within his moral absolutism, murder was the highest crime—murder ordained by power, the greatest sin, and from there the greatest sin of all was the inquisition, in which the Church, which should hold itself to a higher standard still, condoned, or, in Acton's view, manufactured, judicial—but unjustifiable—killing. Acton would not be swayed by arguments of circumstance or historical legal and moral standards. Absolute values were absolute through all history. He was not, however, a papal absolutist. Unlike Newman and Manning, he thought papal infallibility was flat out wrong, with no legitimate basis in the history of the Church. He remained in the Church not because he accepted this doctrine in obedience but because he felt it his duty to fight it from within, and trusted that the Church could not remain in error forever.

Acton was under the misapprehension that political liberty was a moral absolute handed down by God. As Acton once confessed in a letter: "Politics come nearer religion with me, a party is more like a church, error more like heresy, prejudice more like sin, than I find it to be with better men."[23] That last phrase is a saving grace, but his comments about politics as religion presage the twentieth century, where politics would indeed replace religion in the minds of many.

It is important not to underestimate Acton before we attack him. As a young man he admired Edmund Burke, the great political philosopher who, though a Whig and a Protestant, is beloved by Tories and Catholics for his brilliant dissection and repudiation of the French Revolution, and for his conservatism that, like his continental counterpart de Maistre, believed in organic constitutions. Burke counseled prudence, prescription, and the wisdom of prejudice. Acton couched his support for the Southern Confederacy in America's War Between the States in Burkean terms, as well as in terms of providing a necessary libertarian check on the power of the federal government.

But in the end, Acton denounced Burke as a political philosopher. Burke was not, in Acton's sense, a moral absolutist, nor was he an absolutist for liberty. Burke was, in essence, a conservative. Acton, who had once shared Burke's suspicions of abstract principles, eventually indulged the intellectual's pride of raising political principle above all. This is where he began to confuse himself. The man who condemned the inquisition for its killing in the name of God, venerated the American War for Independence and conceded the necessity of killing in the name of liberty. Indeed, he found it hard to assess the French Revolutionaries, for they, too, had embraced absolute ideas—liberty, equality, fraternity—and therefore were to be praised, even as these came at the price of blood. So moral absolutism ended in confusion. The man who denied killing to kings and popes granted it to liberal revolutionaries. The man who had a thoroughly pessimistic understanding of human nature and a profound grounding in the political implications of the doctrine of Original Sin, found himself endorsing liberty, excusing its crimes, and seeing that it must inevitably be checked by other power. His mind ended up checkmating itself.

If Acton was inadequate as a Catholic political philosopher, he, Newman, and Manning nevertheless proved Catholicism's intellectual bona fides to Englishmen. Just as important, they proved that the faith was not foreign to England, as had been drummed into Englishmen's heads for three centuries, but a historic and living, if submerged, truth that could claim the loyalty of three well-bred, well-educated men of the realm.

The English cardinal who welcomed Manning and Newman into the faith, Nicholas Wiseman, suffered the uproar that attended the reinstitution of the Catholic hierarchy in England. Prime Minister Lord John Russell had denounced it as an act of "papal aggression," referring especially to the territorial title of "Archbishop of Westminster." Parliament supported the prime minister's legislation forbidding territorial titles for Catholic bishops, but it was never enforced and anti-Catholic riots did not explode over England. What did occur was a dramatic resurgence in the number of priests and congregants. At the beginning of the nineteenth century, English Catholics had worshiped in chapels that "were purposely placed in quarters where they were unlikely to attract observation. It was common to locate them in mews, and in their exterior they were hardly distinguishable from the adjoining stables."[24] The faith was returning—and trusting to the tolerance of England.

So, too, in the British Empire, which in this century rose to its greatest and most glorious height. One quarter of the enlisted men in the British army were Irish, and the vast majority of those Irishmen were Catholic.[25] In England, Protestant divines commended themselves on their "muscular Christianity" and derided the celibate Catholic priesthood as unmanly. That opinion did not hold in the field. As the great modern historian of Queen Victoria's army has written, when it came to manly fighting "padres," "it was the Roman Catholics who won the respect of the troops, whatever their religious affiliation."[26] Rudyard Kipling shows a similar bias in his novel *Kim*. And one of the greatest of all muscular Christian heroes of the Victorian British army was Major-General Charles George "Chinese" Gordon, the martyr of Khartoum, who, though raised a Scotch Calvinist and noted as a Bible-toting evangelical, was favorably disposed to Catholicism, attended Roman Catholic

Masses, and might have been on the road to Rome before his death in the Sudan.[27] There were, of course, native conversions wherever nineteenth-century European empires planted their flags, from French Indochina to British and French Africa.

In the White Dominions of the British Empire, the faith was carried not by soldiers, but by settlers. Australia, of course, had a large Irish Catholic population, thanks to its use as a penal colony. Anti-Catholic persecution in Australia that lasted until the mid-nineteenth century—and the sparsity of convicted Irish clerics—led to a severe shortage of priests. But the Church grew rapidly after Australia became a country of free men with a free Church. Today, slightly more than a quarter of the country is Catholic, slightly less than a quarter is Anglican, and the rest is divided among Protestants, Jews, Eastern religions, and secularists.

In Canada, the Church was French and had been since the sixteenth century when French missionaries arrived to convert the Indians in a religious adventure that required physical hardiness, spiritual resourcefulness, and sheer courage. In the seventeenth and eighteenth centuries missionaries accompanied the *voyageurs* not only across the breadth of Canada, but across the Great Lakes into the upper Midwest of the United States, founding cities like Detroit. They navigated the Mississippi River, leaving a trail of Francophone cities from the Canadian border to St. Louis and New Orleans. In 1763, Britain won Canada, and the British Crown took responsibility for its own settlers and for the Québecois and the rest of the French Canadian Catholics, their priests, and their religious. Britain's first intention was to repress the faith in favor of an official Anglican settlement. But this plan began falling apart as early as the Quebec Act of 1774, which so frightened New England Puritans by granting religious liberty to French Catholics. Anglican resolve weakened further during the French Revolution, when Canada became a haven for French priests. In 1791, by act of the British Parliament, Catholics were guaranteed freedom of religion. Catholic loyalty to British Canada in the War of 1812 won the Church further freedom to establish territorial bishoprics and to control Catholic schools. By 1851, Catholic religious liberty was firmly established by royal edict. By that time—indeed from the beginning of the nineteenth century—the Church was no longer exclusively French, as Scotch and Irish Catholics emigrated to Canada and rose in the Church hierarchy.

To the south, in Lord Acton's beloved United States, as the Catholic population exploded from its small beginnings, Protestants continued to paint the faithful as foreign—which, as immigrants, they were—and beholden to a religion that was superstitious, corrupt, and flagrantly . . . well, perhaps "French" would be a good word. A bestseller in the 1830s— it also spawned a sequel and imitators—was *Maria Monk's Awful Disclosures of the Hotel Dieu in Montreal*. This book and others linked convents to illicit sex and child murder, all supervised by wicked authoritarian priests. Maria Monk was, in fact, not a nun, but a prostitute. Prostitute stories are always popular with "the people" and early democratic capitalism richly rewarded her with sales and anti-Catholic riots. She was the Harriet Beecher Stowe of anti-Catholicism, though she only gave voice to already existing mythology. In 1834, two years before the publication of her book, an Ursuline convent was burned down in Boston. Because the arson was popular, the perpetrators went unpunished. The idea of devoting oneself completely to God was, to Protestant eyes, the work of Satan, totalitarian priests, and perverted sex. Such early American Protestant attitudes have never really gone away.[28]

The initial waves of Catholic immigrants were Irish, who came in large numbers even before the horrible potato famines of the 1840s. German immigrants were the next largest group of Catholics, and after the War Between the States, Catholic Italians, Poles, and others came to America. Throughout the first two-thirds of the nineteenth century, issues in America tended to be divided by North and South. Because of the North's big cities—which attracted the Irish—and the Germans' preference for settling in the upper Midwest, the mass of Catholic communicants were in the North. But the Catholic mind was in the South. Baltimore was the organizational and intellectual focus of Catholic life, for it held the country's oldest archdiocese. Baltimore, as the War Between the States would prove, was in many ways a Southern city; geographically it was, in fact, south of the Mason-Dixon line. Moreover, the most important American bishop after John Carroll was the first bishop of Charleston, South Carolina, John England, a renowned orator—he was even invited to speak before Congress—who left his thumbprints all over the organization of the American Catholic Church. He founded the first Catholic weekly newspaper. He had served on diplomatic missions to Haiti. He founded Catholic schools for free blacks, slaves, and white women who could serve as nurses. He had great piety, tremendous energy and exemplified holy poverty in his lack of care for himself. He also reassured his congregation that the Bible mandated slavery.

His congregation was more reassured to hear it than one might first imagine. Not only did Charleston have slave-owners; it had survivors from the terror in Haiti, where a slave revolution had created a black republic—and a replay of the Sicilian Vespers, with every Frenchman, or every man, woman, and child with white skin, hunted down to be tortured, raped, and murdered. The defense of slavery was not an abstract issue to refugees from the massacres in Haiti.

Such experience no doubt weighed on Catholic minds, but the Church took no official position. When Protestant denominations tried to do so, they often split on regional grounds, and even on grounds of Biblical literalism. Northern abolitionist strength was with Protestants who had adopted the social gospel. What Scripture actually said was far less important—or, to New England Unitarians and Transcendentalists, practically irrelevant—than the immediate task of reforming society in a liberal direction. The social gospel was still alien to Catholicism. When the Church had acted in the past to denounce the slave trade and attempted to forbid slavery in Latin America, it did so purely on the grounds that slavery was degrading to the human person. But slavery in America was an established institution. It had legal standing of more than two centuries. Protestants who held to *sola scriptura* could point out that the Bible took slavery for granted. The book of Exodus even gives detailed laws for the treatment of slaves, including a master's right, under certain circumstances, over the offspring and even the wife of a slave (21:4). It offers the prescribed punishment for a slave who refuses freedom when it is offered: "he shall bring him to the door or doorpost; and his master shall bore his ear with an awl; and he shall serve him for life" (21:6). There is even this: "When a man strikes his slave, male or female, with a rod and the slave dies under his hand, he shall be punished. But if the slave survives a day or two, he is not to be punished; for the slave is his money" (21:20).

For Catholics the Biblical arguments, while clear, were not definitive. It was nevertheless the argument from Scripture that ensured that the Catholic Church waited until slavery's legal abolition in Brazil in 1888 before finally and forever condemning it, with Pope Leo XIII announcing that the Church was now "wholly opposed to that which was originally ordained by God and nature,"[29] a formulation that deftly managed to reconcile the Bible, Aristotle, and modern Catholic social doctrine all at once, and that put the Church on the side of countries that had abolished slavery without recourse to war.

A less flattering reality that shaped Catholic attitudes to slavery was an ethnic one. The Irish dominated the American Church, and Irish immigrants were notorious for hating blacks, whom they regarded as driving down Irish laborers' wages. In 1861, Archbishop John Hughes of New York informed the War Department that Irish Catholics were "willing to fight to the death for the support of the constitution, the government, and the laws of the country," but they would not fight "for the abolition of slavery."[30] In 1863, after the Emancipation Proclamation was declared law, Irishmen facing a military draft in New York rioted. The violence raged for four days and pitted Irish mobs against Irish-dominated police and Federal troops (perhaps also largely Irish). The riots, wrote the historian Samuel Eliot Morison, were "equivalent to a Confederate victory" for the pacification of the riots required troops that could have been used elsewhere, and the riots themselves inflicted a million dollars' worth of property damage.[31]

The Irish didn't just hate blacks; they were willing to have a row or a ruction with anyone—and so gravitated well to life in the army, the police, and politics. Germans brewed beer, the Irish drank it, and the subsequent Irish donnybrooks gave strength to nativist, anti-Catholic parties and organizations like the "Know-Nothings" who could point not only to scandalous convents but to the poverty and violent crime of Irish neighborhoods. In the biggest scrap to be had yet—the American War Between the States—the fighting Irish, and Catholics in general, readily took up arms for both sides: from the Confederacy's Louisiana Tigers to the Union's Irish Brigade of New York. Again, from sheer force of immigrant numbers in the big cities, more Catholics undoubtedly wore Union blue than Confederate gray, but it seems equally likely that much Catholic sympathy—not merely Lord Acton's—lay with the South. As the twentieth-century Southern poet—and eventual Catholic convert—Allen Tate wrote in his biography of Jefferson Davis: "In a sense, all European history since the Reformation was concentrated in the war between the

North and the South. For in the South the most conservative of the European orders had, with great power, come back to life, while in the North, opposing Southern feudalism, had grown to be a powerful industrial state which epitomized in spirit all those middle-class, urban impulses directed against the agrarian aristocracies of Europe after the Reformation."[32] In a battle between feudalism and modernism, the romantic heart of Catholicism had to be engaged on the side of the former.

Literature would certainly incline one to think so. The leading family in the archetypal—and historically accurate—Pulitzer Prize–winning novel of the War, *Gone with the Wind*, it is worth remembering, is the Catholic O'Haras. In that book, the difference between Southern Catholics and Northern ones are that the Southerners are rooted in the red soil of the South, while the Northerners are just off the boat. Confederate officer Ashley Wilkes exclaims that immigrants—mainly Catholic—are flooding into the Union army: "Why, Scarlett, the Yankees are buying soldiers from Europe by the thousands! Most of the prisoners we've taken recently can't even speak English. They're Germans and Poles and wild Irishmen who speak Gaelic. But when we lose a man he can't be replaced."[33]

Consider also F. Scott Fitzgerald's romantic Catholic attitude to the South, expressed in this dialogue between Amory Blaine and Monsignor Darcy in *This Side of Paradise:*

"I was for Bonnie Prince Charlie," announced Amory.

"Of course you were—and for Hannibal—"

"Yes, and for the Southern Confederacy." He was rather skeptical about being an Irish patriot—he suspected that being Irish was being somewhat common—but Monsignor assured him that Ireland was a romantic lost cause and Irish people quite charming, and that it should, by all means, be one of his principal biases.[34]

Pope Pius IX appeared to share this romantic view of the conflict. He sent Jefferson Davis a crown of thorns after the Confederate president was captured and held as a prisoner by the Federals at Fort Monroe. A year earlier, British diplomat Odo Russell had reported that the pope "would not conceal from me the fact that all his sympathies were with the Southern Confederacy and he wished them all success."[35] In late 1863, the official papal newspaper, *Osservatore Romano*, offered a series of stories giving a pro-Southern view of the struggle. The author was an American bishop, Martin J. Spalding, whom the pontiff rewarded by naming him Archbishop of Baltimore.

The war did not divide the American Catholic Church. There was no schism. Catholic Americans in the nineteenth century were united by their faith—and because they were happy to be here. The Germans became successful businessmen and farmers. The Irish had only to look back to the harsh poverty of the old country, and the memories of anti-Catholic repression, to welcome the freedom of the United States. If they remained poor, they nevertheless welcomed the opportunity to take over political machines, find secure government jobs, or occasionally even discover other avenues to success—and their faith was strong.

By the outbreak of the War Between the States, 10 percent of the American population was Catholic—making Catholics the largest single denomination in the United States, because American Protestantism was even more fissiparous than the European variety. Catholics maintained a distinct identity through parochial schools, which were made mandatory for every parish and for every Catholic parent. Catholic hospitals and Catholic relief organizations were created. As Americans moved West, they moved into lands that already had Catholic names from the Spaniards and the Mexicans who had been there before them. The west might have been wild, but it was dotted with missions. And, as illustrated by one of the great novels of the American West—Willa Cather's *Death Comes for the Archbishop*—it was still blessed by priests as devoted to their holy task as the daring French Jesuits had been in Canada, and the humble Spanish padres had been in California, in a faith that did not, like Protestantism, relentlessly divide, but that united Mexicans, Indians, and Europeans, old cultures and new lands. Cather captured this spirit in the novel's final paragraph: "When the Cathedral bell tolled just after dark, the Mexican population of Santa Fe fell upon their knees, and all American Catholics as well. Many others who did not kneel prayed in their hearts. Eusabio and the Tesuque boys went quietly away to tell their people; and the next morning the old Archbishop lay before the high altar in the church he had built."[36] Catholics, like the old archbishop, would contribute much to the building of America.

## CHAPTER TWENTY

# THE CENTURY
# OF MARTYRS

I T SHOCKS EVEN THOSE who lived through decades of it to acknowledge that the twentieth century was the most murderous in history, especially targeting Jews and Catholics. If it does shock us, it is only because we have all come to assume one of the main prejudices of liberalism—that it represents beneficial progress. But the Church that gave the world *The Syllabus of Errors* never believed this. If any institution warned that the working out of the Reformation, the Enlightenment, secularism, and liberalism would be a century scarred by the likes of Nazism and Communism, it was the Catholic Church, which had already endured, since the sixteenth century, armed assaults from each of these "progressive" forces. Each was intent on submerging, strangling, or abolishing the Church and its doctrines and replacing the Church's authority with that of the State and its own socially useful, progressive, legally required reforms.

The pope who propounded *The Syllabus of Errors*, Pius IX, could be both imperious—"The tradition? I am the tradition!" he once said—and winsome. He was universally known as "Pio Nono," the Italian form of his papal name, and was beloved by the faithful for his good humor, kindness, and piety. His was the longest papal reign in history—nearly thirty-two years—and one of the most popular. Nevertheless, his funeral procession was attacked by an anti-clerical mob. The new secular government of Italy not only failed to restrain the traditional disorders of Rome; it exacerbated them by celebrating irreligion with monuments, holidays, and tributes to "the red flag of revolution, the green flag of the masons, and the black flag of Satan."[1] It would take a dictator to restrain the mob—and a dictator is what Rome would eventually get. In the meantime, Italy would have to make do with a democratic dictatorship that passed laws abolishing religion in the schools and public life, closing monasteries and religious orders, conscripting priests into military service, attempting to seize Church missionary and other funds, and hindering, where it could, the free functioning of the Church.

The next pope to be elevated in these hostile surroundings was Leo XIII (1878–1903). He was well educated—both academically and in the real world of papal diplomacy, where his duties included disarming Italian brigands, enacting economic reform that favored small businessmen and farmers, whom he regarded as allies against the radical left, and working to improve education. With this background, some believed that Leo would mark a return to the early liberalism of Pio Nono, and in some ways this was true. Leo recognized that an accord would have to be reached with liberalism, which seemed everywhere ascendant. He was equally certain that reaching such an accord would not be easy. But Leo took the Jesuits' view that, whatever the political situation, the intellectual battle could be won and the faith would, in the end, be triumphant. He prescribed a return to the study of St. Thomas Aquinas. He encouraged Biblical research. He promoted Catholic scholarship in science (he was particularly fond of astronomy). The Vatican archives were opened to all scholars—not merely Catholic ones—as a sign that the Church of St. Peter was prepared to discuss its intellectual and historical merits with anyone.

As a diplomat he had mixed success. Germany was his triumph. He won Bismarck's respect—and the termination of the *Kulturkampf* on Catholic terms. The anti-clericals in Italy were a lost cause, but in France, he hoped to achieve a rapprochement with the new regime. After France's defeat in the Franco-Prussian War, a single vote turned the country from a monarchy into the "Third Republic." The monarchists were the traditional Catholic party, but as an opposition they were bitterly divided and—the pope saw—a force that was spent and would continue to shrink.

Popes had often looked to France, as "the first daughter of the Church," to offset the turbulence of Italy or the overwhelming power of the Holy Roman Empire. Faced with the "Triple Alliance" of Germany, Austria, and Italy—with the Church especially focused on the virulent anti-clericalism of Italy—the pope sought to strengthen this old Franco-papal bond, by establishing cordial relations with the new republican government. The effort failed. He succeeded only in angering his French allies, the monarchists. The republicans took the papal olive branch, broke it, and enacted an escalating series of legal, political, and financial restrictions on the Church.

Indeed, the liberals of the Republic enforced their own *Kulturkampf*. Primary schooling was made mandatory and secular. Priests who were open monarchists—and virtually all priests and bishops were royalists—found their salaries withheld. Church officials were forbidden to serve on the boards of charitable institutions. Nuns were barred from serving in hospitals. Then the convents and monasteries were closed—throwing more than 100,000 religious into the streets. Soldiers were denied the right to join Catholic clubs. Military officers could be dismissed on grounds that they were loyal Catholics who might not execute orders against the Church. Marriage, divorce, and burial were to be civil affairs, and Sunday trading permitted. By law of the Republic, no religious congregation had a legal right to exist unless it was given explicit approval by the French government.

Two thousand lawyers argued that these coercive laws were illegal; several hundred magistrates resigned in protest at their imposition. But the liberal juggernaut rolled on. As ever, liberalism was forcing a showdown with the Church. Two years after Pope Leo XIII's death, it came, with the French government forcibly seizing all Church property and transferring it to secular ownership. Churches were declared, in legal terms, public buildings, though private "cultural associations" of laypeople could acquire them, as well as seminaries and other Church property. In return for these outrages, the Republic offered one concession: The state would henceforth consider itself utterly divorced from the Church and would not interfere with clerical appointments. The state could, however, forbid any public act of worship, just as it could forbid any other public activity, if some expedient reason could be found.

But in the Janus-faced spirit of French politics, these measures against the Church were enforced only at home. France was an imperial power. Abroad, in its colonies and elsewhere, French foreign policy—designed by more conservatively inclined military and naval officers and imperialists—supported the Church. This was especially true in the Near and

Middle East, where French bayonets and French priests protected Christians from Moslem violence, in a conscious and continuing legacy from the Crusades. Throughout France's colonies, missionary activity was vibrant. But the fact that the government could enact such draconian laws against the Church at home illustrated that the government's electors—the French people—had accepted the Protestant view of state supremacy while simultaneously holding fast to their traditional Catholic liturgy and devotions.

Through the many previous changes of government since Napoleon Bonaparte—from the restored Bourbons, to the Orléans princes, to the empire of Napoleon III—the French Church had not always been treated well, but it had been a great force of Catholic devotion and renewal, of vigorous religious orders and worthy priests. Now, at the *fin de siècle*, the unceasing assaults of French liberalism made the very existence of the Church problematic. Its lack of property and the enforcement of secular education made it difficult to recruit and train priests. What the Revolution could not maintain by terror, liberalism looked to achieve through democracy and law. The one bright spot was that lay Catholic organizations remained active and eager despite—or perhaps even because of—the persecution. When liberal, anti-clerical regimes in Germany, Italy, or France punished the Church through legislation and law, popes talked over the heads of governments to the laypeople—the papacy was the beacon of the faith.

Yet if Pope Leo could not stave off this Gallic *guerre de religion*, if he perhaps made a tactical mistake by not working to unify the opposition and encourage a counterrevolution (hardly unprecedented in France's turbulent politics), it was because he hoped to achieve exactly the opposite effect. If the future of the Western world was democratic, he wanted to set a precedent that established that Catholics could be good democrats and that such political designations should not interfere with the faith. French liberals, unfortunately, took a different line. They did not want the Church interfering, as it were, in French life at all. They did not want it to impede "progress," and as such the liberals had as allies capitalists and, as in the Reformation, "people on the make."

Liberals wanted simply to deny history, a history as concrete as the cathedrals seized by the state, if it did not serve profits, convenience, or technical advance. It is fitting, then, that the French Church's strongest ally was the aristocracy—a class that did not need money, a class whose position and interests were tied to the history of France, and who were therefore more likely to be on the side of tradition than of innovation. Pope Leo could have played the class warfare card, but he did not. He hoped, with his usual confidence in the Church, that Catholics could win a democratic debate. Indeed, he believed that if Catholics unified and committed themselves to winning parliamentary seats in the Republic they could become the majority and thereby restore the monarchy through a free vote. He wanted to put the Church on the side of ballots rather than bullets, and through elections establish a conservative, anti-socialist, parliamentary Catholic monarchy. One of his admirers in this endeavor was the Eastern Orthodox czar of Russia, Nicholas II, who would find, however, that liberalism could still be a deadly creed.

If the situation in France was depressing, Pope Leo took comfort from the Catholic revival in England, fueled both by intellectuals like Newman, whom he made a cardinal, and by Irish immigration. He happily restored a Catholic hierarchy to Scotland. And he welcomed the rapid growth of the Church in the United States, even if he disapproved of its liberalism, though the American Church was liberal only in comparison to Europe's. In the context of the United States, the Church was theologically (and even in many ways politically) conservative. The hierarchy was on far better terms with Republican presidents like Theodore Roosevelt—who was virile enough not to be put off by a little "rum, Romanism, and rebellion"—than it was with the austere Presbyterian Democrat Woodrow Wilson. The Church championed immigrants, the poor, and the workingman but held socialism as anathema. The Irish had their political machines full of patronage, but their Catholic spirit kept them opposed to state-sponsored social engineering—especially in education, where they fought against the American Protestant idea of universal mandatory public schooling; agitated in defense of parochial schools; and worked to create religious colleges and universities at a time when American universities were rapidly secularizing themselves.

Catholics were also patriots and always over-represented in the American military. Even in World War I, when Irish and German Catholics saw little reason to intervene on the side of the Allies, Catholics again formed a far higher percentage of the armed services than their percentage of the general population. Of the nearly 4,000 Americans who registered as conscientious objectors in World War I, precisely four were Catholics; and not a single priest or bishop opposed the war.[2] The idea that Catholics weren't true Americans, and that they suffered dual loyalties, was disproved every time the country's bugle sounded reveille.

American Catholic priests and bishops thought they had turned American liberalism to their advantage quite successfully and had their own doubts about the Holy Father's Italy. The southern Italian immigrants coming into the United States seemed to them the most religiously ignorant and morally depraved people they had ever had the misfortune to shepherd. Rather than look quizzically at the bishop of Rome, however, they might have spared him sympathy, now that they had a better understanding of the mobs the popes had to endure for centuries. Still, as Italian-Americans, these immigrants were quickly scrubbed clean by the Irish and re-evangelized into the buoyant American Church.

In all these respects, the American Catholic Church seemed lively. When Pope Leo looked at his own continent, he saw nothing but political defeats in France and in anti-clerical Italy. He also saw continuing troubles in Ireland, Eastern Europe, and Latin America. At least there were consolations. As with his predecessor, he found a growing spiritual authority and popularity with laypeople. He witnessed a resurgence of Catholic scholarship. His own writings—not just *Rerum Novarum*, his most famous, on the labor question—won wide respect and covered every subject from the rosary to the Catholic view of liberty to the need to restore the separated Christian churches to the Body of Christ in the Church universal. His encyclicals are classics of the application of Catholic principles and philosophy to practical questions, setting a new standard of intellectual engagement with the modern world.

Pope Pius X (1903–1914) was another throwback of the type the Church perennially chooses for a change of perspective. Unlike his immediate predecessors, he had humble antecedents and spent his entire career occupied with the concerns of a parish priest. As pope he maintained these concerns to the point of regularly teaching children in Sunday school. He encouraged priests and laypeople to give precedence to prayer. He busied himself with revising the liturgy, the Church calendar, and the priests' breviaries. He let it be known that children who understood the rudiments of the faith should receive communion, and that all should receive communion more frequently. He raised the standards of catechetical instruction. He improved teaching in the seminaries. He streamlined canon law—and papal government—so that it was more easily understood and applied, essentially by centralizing power in the papacy. All these actions suited his presence: handsome, white-haired, easily approachable, and commonsensical. He was not insistently regal like Leo XIII, who once reminded his colleagues, "I am Peter." But he took just as strongly the claims of infallibility that had been propounded by Pius IX, whom he consciously emulated.

He could not ignore politics, for the Church has always engaged the world, and he brought to political discussion his sacramental vision. He abhorred the leading creeds of the twentieth century—socialism, liberalism, materialism, and utilitarianism—because they denied the primacy and the truth of the Catholic Church. It was the Church, and ultimately the pope, who was the doctor to the sacred soul of every individual. Before the Reformation, this would not have been an exceptional statement. At the opening of the twentieth century, there was not a government in the world that bothered to acknowledge that the Catholic faith was a primary fact of society. The only fact that modern governments recognized was the state. It is not surprising then, that when Pope Pius X issued his own *Syllabus of Errors,* it was in a decree known as *Lamentabili* and an encyclical entitled *Pascendi* wherein he lumped all contemporary doctrinal falsehoods under the name of "modernism."

Pius was unyielding to theological or political liberals. He believed that these men—we might call them accommodationists—showed a lack of faith, which was the very sum of modernism. The Church's role was "to restore all things in Christ,"[3] which was the motto he wanted as the keystone of his pontificate. Separation of Church and state on the liberal model was the denial of Christ's and the Church's primacy and was "a grave insult to God, the Creator of man and the Founder of human society."[4] These words might shock modern ears, but they did not shock Catholics, whose imaginations held fast to royal crowns consecrated to the Church and to the memory of Christendom. The Church remembered Pius X by canonizing him in 1954, another shock to "moderns," who don't believe in saints.

Benedict XV (1914–1922) had to deal with one of the first fruits of modernism—the "Great War," that catastrophic seismic shock that announced the arrival of the twentieth century. Catholic interests narrowly defined were not at issue. But Catholicism—as a universal religion; as a source of philosophical, moral, and cultural truths; as the heartbeat of the Western World; as a charitable and diplomatic institution—was involved, as it is involved in everything Europe touches. The pope devoted himself to attempting to restore peace and to succor, through immense outlays from his own pocket and the papal treasury, the suffering, regardless of their nation. His reward was to be both brushed aside by the warring states as irrelevant to their contest of blood and iron and to be reviled by the combatants for not proclaiming the Church's cause as the cause of Italy, France, or Germany.

The Church believes in nations but not in nationalism; and in this it has proven wiser than liberal statesmen. The fuse of the First World War was lit by Balkan nationalism, fanned by the Russians, whose armies, in turn, were being invited closer to central Europe by French railroads—designed to put Cossacks on the eastern doorstep of Germany. This Balkan nationalism was then and is now a source of war. Nationalism had been, since the Reformation, the enemy of Catholicism—putting the tribalism of nation, and the manufacturing of tribal religions, ahead of the universal claim of Christendom under the pope. Eastern Orthodox Christianity had always been nationalistic. It had put Byzantium first and devolved into autocephalous churches based on nationality. Now an Orthodox people, the Serbs, or at least the radicals among them, and an Orthodox empire, the Russians, sought an opportunity to break their fellow Slavs free again from a foreign—and Catholic—master, Austria-Hungary.

Rather than nationalism, Catholic philosophy was at home with a ramshackle, but well-governed, empire of several nations such as Austria-Hungary, this rump of the Holy Roman Empire, the home of Habsburgs—where Austrians, Magyars, Serbs, Croats, Czechs, Slovaks, Slovenes, Romanians, Poles, Italians, and others were united under "the Dual Monarchies," with diversity kept peaceful by shared loyalty to the Habsburg emperor. Such empires require tolerance. Nationalism does not. Though all nationalities jostled for position within the empire, none, at least in their majorities, saw any advantage in the empire's overthrow. All knew that they were freer under the Habsburgs than they would be under the czar or the German Reich, or, perhaps worse still, if they were at the mercy of some unknown division of national borders.[5] Among those who flourished in the empire were Jews. If the empire lagged behind Western

Europe economically, it was a leader in the arts: a cynic could say it was a model Catholic empire, not wealthy but baroque. It would take four years of the most devastating war Europe had seen to destroy it and scorch the earth for an even worse calamity.

More than eight million people died in the First World War. Twenty-one million were wounded. Bombs and blockades had devastated cities and civilian populations, who now fell prey to hunger and disease. A deadly postwar epidemic of flu claimed even more lives than had the war. As Winston Churchill wrote, "after years of struggle not armies but nations broke and ran. When all was over, Torture and Cannibalism were the only two expedients that the civilized, scientific, Christian States had been able to deny themselves: and they were of doubtful utility."[6]

Against these horrors the Catholic Church had warned; against violations of international law it had expostulated—in vain. The twentieth century trusted, not in the pope, but in massive force, machine technology, and money. When in 1917, Pope Benedict XV argued for a peace without reparations, he was accused of pro-German sympathies—a "*Boche* pope"—and he was shut out of the 1919 negotiations at Versailles that gave Europe a chaos of new borders and a disastrous lack of political order. It was a political hash that the liberals called peace.

To the east, there was another disaster. In 1917, the czar was overthrown in Russia, replaced first by the short-lived liberal government of Alexander Kerensky and then by the Bolsheviks, who were devoted to an official policy of atheism and an all-out war against religion. Though Russia had been Orthodox, it had a large Catholic minority in the west among ethnic Poles, Lithuanians, Germans, Ukrainians, and others. The Communists liquidated them and their churches. According to an American priest serving in Russia—indeed, he was one of only two Catholic priests left in the country—within seventeen years of the Russian Revolution, 5,300 Catholic churches and chapels had been destroyed. Two were kept standing for the benefit of tourists—and for the benefit of Communists to dismiss Catholic accusations of persecution.[7] In the first eight years of Bolshevik Russia, 200,000 Catholics simply vanished, as did every Catholic bishop—the sort of "missing persons" one came to expect in communist regimes.[8]

In the Ukraine, the Bolsheviks were unable to gain control of the entire country—it was partially absorbed by Poland and later occupied by the Nazis—until after World War II. But when the Soviets did take control, the four-million-member Ukrainian Catholic Church was denied any existence at all: clergy were imprisoned, churches destroyed or occupied, laypeople deprived of the sacraments. Pope Pius XI (1922–1939), who saw Bolshevik violence first-hand in Poland, made it Catholic practice that every Mass, every day, ended with a prayer for the conversion of Russia from Communism to Christianity. At least one-half of this prayer was granted, when the Soviet state began unraveling in 1989; dedicated missionaries are today working to achieve the second half.

## The Age of the Dictators

After the armistice ending the First World War in November 1918, Pope Benedict XV confronted a Europe crippled, charred, and threatened by communist uprisings. The crowned heads of Germany, Russia, and Austria-Hungary were gone. Woodrow Wilson—who as a student of Edmund Burke should have known better—trusted to phrases like "self-determination" and "democracy," which provided fertile ground for nationalist wars of violence. These were wars of "peoples" against "peoples" as multinational states dissolved. If a people were caught on the wrong side of a national border, or were a disliked minority, they were suspected as traitors or as belonging to a different nation—a de facto foreign invader. Here then came the infamous and still contentious massacres of Armenians by Turks: the Armenians protesting genocide, the Turks asserting self-defense against an ethnic, wartime enemy within the Ottoman Empire. "Nationalism," "self-determination," and "democracy" were words that in the chaotic aftermath of war served, in the more dangerous parts of Eastern Europe, as an argument for what today goes by the terrible name of "ethnic cleansing."

There was also every reason to believe that the new democratic regimes of Europe—which looked to be heavily socialist—would continue liberalism's war against the Church. But with the exception of Russia, this proved not to be the case, at least not at first. The pope quickly expanded the Church's diplomatic activity with the new states of Europe, planting seeds that would be reaped by his successor, and did the same overseas by encouraging missionaries to recruit native priests in colonial settlements. He even hoped that the calamity in Russia would lead to the fulfillment of every pontiff's dream—the reunification of the Eastern Orthodox with the Catholic Church, the two most ancient Christian entities standing together against the new atheism-in-arms. But the Eastern Orthodox remained stubborn to the last.

Benedict's successor, Pius XI, carried through Benedict's diplomatic overtures and over the next decade and a half concluded a dozen concordats establishing Catholic rights in the states of Europe. Though these pieces of paper had been easily torn up in the past, the Church had to trust to law, not having access to a million-man army of Swiss guards, an air force, and armored units.

In France, the crucible of war brought an end to the state's aggressive anti-clericalism, and by 1924 the Church had regained some say in the use of its property. In Italy, the Church achieved its biggest breakthrough. In 1929, after three years of negotiations, the Church regained a temporal status with the creation of Vatican City, all 108 acres of it, along with the Lateran Palace, Castel Gondolfo, and a few other holdings. In addition, Italy paid the Church a substantial sum in cash and government bonds to compensate it for the loss of the Papal States. Equally important was that the Church was restored to Italian life. Crucifixes returned to public schools, as did the teaching of Catholic doctrine. Catholic priests could conduct religious marriages. The war of Italian liberals against the Church was over, thanks to the Church's newfound ally—Benito Mussolini.

This was an unlikely alliance. Mussolini's father was an atheistic socialist. He named his son after Benito Juarez, the Mexican revolutionary, and taught him to admire Garibaldi. Mussolini's mother was a devout Catholic, but her influence didn't seem to take much hold. Young Benito was a juvenile delinquent, a self-proclaimed atheist and socialist like his father, a violent whoremonger, and a draft-dodger. He found his niche as a radical leftist orator, raging against God and aristocrats, monarchs and the military. When he owned nothing else, the one thing he saved was a medallion of Karl Marx.

After years as a ne'er-do-well, he became a socialist newspaper editor and agitator, whose extremism in mocking the Church shocked even the anti-clerical socialists. Another shock for his comrades came with the First World War, when he screamed for the socialists—who had proclaimed pacifism—to plunge Italy into the struggle. War, he said, would bring the revolution home. For socialists, this was treason. For Mussolini, it was the path to power. The former draft-dodger, who had later done his peacetime service, joined the army. He returned to a postwar Italy where veterans were abused, socialists were in the ascendant, and the liberal monarchy was seen as ripe for toppling as had been done to the czar. Communists marched in the streets and hurled their banners from churches. Workers sabotaged their works. Strikes crippled industries and services. Seeing all this, Mussolini changed sides.

He remained a socialist, but a socialist loyal to his former military comrades, a socialist who wanted Italy to be a great military power, a socialist who saw the radical left—from which he himself had sprung—as destructive of his own country. He founded a new socialist party—the Fascists—who were wedded to the idea of Italian greatness. He came to power not like Napoleon, through military conquest, but by means more suitable to this democratic age—street fighting, and black-shirted gang wars. Mussolini's Fascists provided the ugly brutes with truncheons behind which many more civilized Italians began to rally—seeing the Fascists as the only hope to save Italy from chaos and civil war. Policemen, soldiers, businessmen, and, yes, priests—all of whom had been targets of the socialists and communists—offered their support. As their ranks swelled, as they seized cities and railway stations, as they marched on Rome, the apparent hope for a functioning Italy and the apparent solution to the threat of civil war, King Victor Emmanuel bowed to the inevitable and recognized the Fascists as the party that should take the reins of government by forming a cabinet. Having thus seized power in 1922, parliamentary elections affirmed it, and that being done Mussolini promptly abolished opposition parties.

Political parties could be abolished, but, like Napoleon, Mussolini now realized that the faith could not be abolished—hence the Lateran Treaty that recognized the rights of the papacy in exchange for the pope recognizing, as no pope had before, the legitimacy of the unified kingdom of Italy. Mussolini, again like Napoleon, transformed his country from anti-clerical violence and chaos into an enormously successful reclamation project, raising living standards and slashing crime and disease. All Europe—even the archbishop of Canterbury—hailed his genius. So did Winston Churchill, George Bernard Shaw, Thomas Edison, Mahatma Gandhi, and countless others. Pius XI praised him as "a man sent by Providence."[9]

If Mussolini saved Italy as Napoleon had saved France—and restored the fortunes of the Church in the bargain—he ran into similar difficulties with the Church over his view of the total state versus the Church's insistence on freedom for intermediary institutions. In Italy's case, the issue was Catholic youth groups, which Mussolini wanted submerged within Fascist organizations. The Church's refusal to submit led to the first antifascist encyclical, *Non Abbiamo Bisogno*. Issued in 1931, it broadened the dispute to include fascism's "pagan worship of the state"[10] and convinced the Fascists to allow Catholics more freedom to organize. In Italy, the Church succeeded in acting as a minor brake on Fascist power.

The situation in Germany was more difficult. In 1933, when the Church reached a concordat with the German government—an accord that disbanded the Catholic Center Party in exchange for a guarantee of Catholic religious freedom—Adolf Hitler was the new chancellor of Germany. He immediately violated the terms of the agreement, just as he would ignore the terms of every other agreement that didn't suit his purposes.

Hitler had been baptized a Catholic and in childhood had taken an interest in the Church. But the death of his brother, among other childhood traumas, helped crush the ten-year-old Hitler's faith. His boyhood interest in religion was replaced by a hatred for authority—especially the authority of the Church, his teachers, and, later, Jews, capitalists, and the Habsburgs. All that remained of Hitler's early Catholicism was a love of art, architecture, music, and, perhaps, ceremony and an idealization of women.

Hitler's own life was far from ceremonious. It had many parallels to Mussolini's life, though, as befitted a man who titled his political autobiography *Mein Kampf* (My Struggle), his road to power was much harder. Like Mussolini, Hitler was a juvenile delinquent—only not as violent. His school days ended; he tried to live as an artist and ended up as a beggar, living in flophouses. He, too, was a draft-dodger and declared himself a socialist and was a rhetorically violent pacifist. As with Mussolini, the First World War changed everything. Hitler would not fight for the reactionary Habsburgs, but he would fight for progressive Germany. He was enrolled in the army and served for four years until he was temporarily blinded by poison gas. He returned to a Germany in the grip of revolutionary fever. The Kaiser was gone, and what had replaced him was a nightmare—even for a socialist like Hitler. There were mutinies, Communist red guards in the streets, a socialist republic declared in Bavaria.

Hitler's beloved Germany was in turmoil. At the head of every leftist faction that was ripping the country apart, that had stabbed it in the back while he and his colleagues had fought in the trenches, was a Jew, or so he thought. To fight the Jews, capitalists, and communists, Hitler took over the leadership of the National Socialist Workers' Party in 1921.

The National Socialists made little headway. The Weimar Republic, though perpetually shaky, and holding within it private armies of right and left who battled in the streets, was able to function as a modern democracy from 1919 until Hitler became chancellor in 1933. Until the 1930s, the Nazis had scant support, and even in the midst of tremendous economic and political strife, Germany maintained enough of its traditional sense of order—just as Italy after the war had reverted to its traditional anarchy—to keep the worst of the political extremists from seizing power. The Great Depression was the one blow too many for Weimar. By the elections of 1932, the Nazis had become Germany's largest political party, with more than a third of the national vote. In 1933, in the last free elections of the Weimar Republic, the Nazis—who made pioneering use of modern mass propaganda and "spin"—polled 44 percent of the vote, or roughly the same percentage won by William Jefferson Clinton against George Herbert Walker Bush in the 1992 elections in America, to provide a point of popular comparison.

Even then, in certain areas—such as Catholic Bavaria and the Catholic Rhineland—the Nazis had few supporters at all. A party that seemed to promise a new *Kulturkampf* was not attractive to Catholic voters who remembered the last one. The Nazis' electoral coalition was a grab bag of the disaffected: embittered nationalists, angry workers, and even Protestant ministers who thought the Nazis might cure Weimar decadence. But Hitler's philosophy was actually part of that decadence. Rarely, if ever, in the history of the world, had there been a more concentrated collection of psychopaths, sexual deviants, and petulant failures seething with conspiracies and virulent plans. Not one of the National Socialist leaders embodied the Aryan archetype they idolized. Not one was a "blond beast." They were dark and drug-addicted, bloated, mouse-like, or slick with ideology and slogans. Indeed, they were Social Darwinists whose position as the "elect"—as the *Führer* and the *Führer's* advisers— was based purely on the democratic success that gave them power, not on the doctrine of blood that they promulgated.

While they occasionally made overtures to Christians—praising Luther as a German patriot and quoting approvingly his anti-Semitic outbursts—privately the Nazi leadership had no time for the Christian religion, whether Catholic or Protestant. Both were seen as craven off-shoots from the original sin of Judaism. Both were slave religions that neglected the animal in man, the will to power, and the right of the strong to subdue the weak. No, the "scientific" doctrines of the National Socialist Workers' Party took the Nazis into the occult, pagan mythology, and the application of science to such projects as human breeding and extermination. As a transitional step for the German people away from Christianity, the Nazis created the "German Evangelical Church," which was meant to offer a state religion that delivered Nazism from the pulpit. It was this act of the Nazis that drove the great Protestant pastor Martin Niemöller from supporting the National Socialists to being imprisoned by them. When Germany went to war, Niemöller, from his concentration camp—he was eventually sent to Dachau—offered to serve (he had been a U-boat commander in World War I). His request was denied, and after the war he became an outspoken pacifist, pledged to Western disarmament.

It is certain that the German people as a whole—paralleling Pastor Niemöller as an individual—did not intend the full horrors of the Nazi regime. Few people—even in an educated country like Weimar Germany—pay much attention to politics or consider it rationally, though they still cast their ballots. Few Germans could have fully understood—or believed—what the Nazis planned to execute. Even at the height of the war, it is likely that most Germans kept their eyes focused on their immediate circumstances and duties, their personal affairs; perhaps even forced themselves to do so, for fear of what they might see otherwise. But Hitler also had no difficulty finding his willing executioners—both in Germany and among collaborators in Eastern Europe. His demagogic speeches inspired true believers and provided a rationale for murder.[11]

The Catholic Church's concordat with Germany in 1933 was no endorsement of the Nazis, any more than the Church's attempt at a concordat with Soviet Russia—which the Communists dismissed—would have been an endorsement of Bolshevism. Both regimes were utterly opposed to the Catholic religion, Catholic social teaching, and Catholic philosophy. In fact, if that reputed scandal of the Catholic Church, the inquisition, had been in force in a papally submissive Germany, the Nazi Party would never have come to power; the Holocaust would never have happened.

If ever there was proof that ideas rule history, it can be seen in Nazi Germany, for the Nazis inherited the most educated country in the world. But many of the ideas on offer happened to be bad ones.

It was in Germany that Friedrich Nietzsche, a towering intellectual figure (who also happened to go mad), proclaimed the death of God, the inversion of values—which were subjective—and praised the Superman who created and enforced his own morality, his own values. Nietzsche's philosophy had obvious roots in the historic German psyche and its frustration with moral constraints; and it had sweeping, lyrical, romantic, and intellectually brilliant paeans to the heroism of the Superman (this spirit perfectly captured in Caspar David Friedrich's painting *The Wanderer*). In the way that intellectual ideas filter down into society, these ideas had filtered down (indeed they are still popular today). So had the materialism of Karl Marx. Socialism was the operative ideology of both the Nazis and the Communists. So had the ideas of social and biological competition adopted from Charles Darwin—a "natural law" that would displace Catholic natural law. The experience of the First World War had further underlined material force as a determinant of history and also led, throughout Europe, to occultism, as people who felt they had outgrown Christianity sought to cope with their losses—or communicate with them around séance tables.

The Nazis offered a replacement religion, a mysticism of the *volk*, a worship of state and party, and promulgated laws that dispensed with traditional Catholic morality. Almost immediately after signing the concordat, the Nazis fell afoul of the Catholic Church by legalizing abortion and sterilization (for non-Aryans)—surgical procedures that are now known in the Western world as constitutional rights, but to the Catholic Church were a sign of the barbarism of the new regime.

The dehumanization inherent in Nazi genetic engineering was abhorrent to Catholics—but not, it must be said, to Protestants. In the 1930s, every Protestant country in the West adopted eugenics laws, except for Britain (where they were actually enacted and then repealed as a violation of civil liberty) and Holland. By contrast, not a single Catholic country even seriously considered eugenics laws.[12] Both the Nazis and the Soviet Communists had chosen a non-Catholic—to put it mildly—political path.

But the Nazis were sufficiently Western that, unlike the Communists, they took pains to disguise their actions behind a carapace of law.

When the Church negotiated its concordats, it negotiated to protect the faith, country-by-country, whatever regime was in power, self-consciously aware that it had few friends in liberal states and none in totalitarian ones. In Germany, the Church had denounced the Nazis before the concordat and continued to do so afterward. Within three years of the concordat's signing, the pope had issued nearly forty notes of formal protest to the Nazi regime. On Palm Sunday 1937 came the most dramatic papal denunciation of Hitler's Germany. It was an encyclical that had been slipped into the country by stealth and was read from every Catholic pulpit in the land. Entitled *Mit Brennender Sorge* (With Burning Anxiety), it catalogued the Nazis' violations of the concordat, pointedly affirmed Christianity's roots in Judaism, underlined the universality of the Catholic faith that treated all men of whatever nation and race as the children of God, and condemned the neo-paganism of the Nazis and their "mad prophet" Adolf Hitler. Against this, the pope wrote, "There is but one alternative left, that of heroism."[13]

The Nazis responded with repression and explicit threats against the Church. In his May Day address, Hitler declared that when Church leaders "attempt by any other means—writings, encyclicals, etc.—to assume rights which belong only to the state, we will push them back into their proper spiritual activity."[14] The Nazis circulated editorial cartoons and screeds that linked the pope to the hated Jews. Pope Pius XI happily affirmed the connection, saying that "anti-Semitism is inadmissible; spiritually we are all Semites."[15] The Nazi propaganda machine, meanwhile, whipped up a frenzied media assault on the "immoral" Catholic clergy, who were accused of widespread sexual perversion—with the alleged sex crimes serving as an excuse to close religious houses and imprison their members.[16] A Swiss paper quoted Hitler making an open declaration of war on the Church: "The Third Reich does not desire a *modus vivendi* with the Catholic Church, but rather its destruction with lies and dishonor, in order to make room for a German Church in which the German race will be glorified."[17]

Elsewhere in the world, the battle between atheist and Catholic was well under way. Within days of condemning the Nazis, the pope issued another encyclical, *Divini Redemptoris*, which denounced Bolshevism even more harshly. He specifically accused three communist regimes of conspiring to eradicate Christianity: Soviet Russia, Republican Spain, and another revolutionary republic—one that shared a border with the United States.

# THE CRUCIFIXION OF THE CHURCH IN MEXICO AND SPAIN

THE UNITED STATES has not always been a good example for its neighbors—not through any particular *fault* of its own, but through its nearly unique virtues. In almost the entirety of the world and its history, words and phrases like "independence" and "liberal constitutionalism" have been the starting part of a nation's decline. The exceptions to this rule have been the United States, Canada, and Australia—all sprung from the same taproot, each deriving its independent constitutional government on the basis of enshrining traditional rights, the rights of Englishmen, rights that came down organically from the Mother Country, developed out of common law that reached back even before the Magna Carta of 1215. This experience of the English-speaking peoples found few parallels elsewhere.

Other countries too, of course, inevitably had their own organic institutions. But in these states, liberal constitutionalism, or independence in the name of nationalism, was generally invoked as an attempt to break sharply with the past. In these countries, laws and constitutions did not seek to enshrine traditional rights enjoyed by the people, but rather to *create* a new people, to dispense with the old and the backward, to embrace a liberal idea of progress. Imposed by governments, these laws were inherently unstable, changing according to the whims and the aims of the parties in power. The state, by its self-made law, could mandate or abolish *anything*.

Every liberal constitutional regime bears within it this danger—of the law striking down traditional rights and erecting new, mandatory, coercive legislation. It can be done in many ways: by majority vote, by representatives of the vanguard of the workers, by *Il Duce*. The regimes can take a variety of forms, but all claim a democratic, nationalist source, invoking the will of the people. All are devoted to progress and uniformity and target those who will not conform or who represent alternative sources of power and value, especially aristocrats and the Church. But if a country loses its educated elite and suppresses the Church that gives society its *cult*, the basis of its culture, then its civilization inevitably declines.

This is what happened in Mexico. Until it gained its independence from Spain, in 1821, it had a more advanced, older, better-educated, and more devout civilization than the United States. As Evelyn Waugh notes in his book *Robbery Under Law:*

> By 1575, a century before the first printing press was set up in British America, books were being printed in Mexico City, not only in Spanish, but in twelve different languages. There were three universities in Spanish America nearly a century before the foundation of Harvard. There was a Medical School at the Royal and Pontifical University of Mexico two hundred years before Harvard's, and anatomy and surgery were taught with dissection eighty-six years before William Hunter opened the first school of dissection in England.[18]

The Jesuits with their Indian schools had done well—as did the nuns who provided schooling for Mexican girls. Learning was such a pronounced part of Mexican life under the Spaniards that Mexico was considered, when it came to education in both science and the arts, as on a European standard.[19]

Independence and the severance of the tie to Europe—a battle led, ironically, by two renegade priests—spun Mexico into decline. Because of its wealth and its leading role in society, the Church came under repeated threat from the country's various revolutionary and bandit leaders, including Benito Juarez, the hero of Mussolini's father. Independent Mexico did not enjoy a single period of good government until the French seized Mexico City in 1863 and held it for four years, an experience that gave the French Foreign Legion its annual celebration of the battle of Camarón;[20] and as every good political scientist knows, where the French Foreign Legion is, there is good government, as can be seen today in Tahiti and poor but proud Djibouti.[21]

Mexico did not experience another respite from decline until the benign dictatorship of Porfirio Díaz from 1884 to 1910. After that, the country plummeted once more, and in 1917 it became the first explicitly socialist, anti-religious, and constitutional revolutionary republic in the world. Even in 1938, when dictatorship was a common thing and Mexico was laxer in applying its anti-Catholic laws, Evelyn Waugh noted that the legal position of the Church in Mexico "has no parallel in any country except [Soviet] Russia."[22]

Nevertheless, throughout the century of turmoil that began with its independence from Spain, the Mexican people remained unhesitatingly and overwhelmingly loyal to the Church. But the revolutionaries who led the country regarded the Church as they came to regard foreign business investment: as an independent source of power and wealth that rightly belonged to the state. Mexican socialism led to the nationalization of foreign business. That was as nothing to its war against the Church. The Church's assets and property too were nationalized.

Today, in Europe, churches are routinely made redundant by lack of use and converted into private buildings. In Mexico, this was the law, even with congregations overflowing, and it was applied by force. "Between November 11th 1931, and April 28th 1936, four hundred and eighty Catholic churches, schools, orphanages, and hospitals were closed by the Government or converted to other uses."[23] They became cinemas, offices, garages, shops, libraries, and anything else one can imagine. The Mexican governments of the 1920s and 1930s were not content with nationalization. Under Mexico's socialist dictators, the Church suffered, in the words of Graham Greene, "the fiercest persecution of religion anywhere since the reign of Elizabeth."[24]

The Catholic Church was outlawed—its priests forced to act like secret agents to deliver the sacraments to the faithful, while the common desecrations of anti-Catholic history were repeated: every crucifix, chalice, and work of religious art profaned; the vestments and rituals of the religion mocked; the sacred vandalized—with the approval of the law. The beliefs of the Church's enemies were in the open. Governor Canabal of Tabasco province bragged that he had destroyed every church in his jurisdiction; he proclaimed that every priest who would not marry, and few did, would be exiled; and he named his own children Lenin, Lucifer, and Satan—true heirs of the twentieth century.[25] He even ordered that the shrine of the Virgin of Guadaloupe be destroyed. In this, he failed. The Indians guarded the shrine, then smuggled the sacred image of the Virgin to Costa Rica, until it was safe to return it.

The most famous of the Catholic martyrs in Mexico was Father Miguel Pro, who for his daring, winning personality, and faith Graham Greene compared to another Jesuit: St. Edmund Campion. After repeatedly delivering the Eucharist to loyal Catholics—more than a thousand at a time—and slipping away from the authorities like the Scarlet Pimpernel, he was finally captured. He was shot by a firing squad in 1927. The government caught the moment in a photograph and film footage that it distributed to broadcast the message of death to priests. The state would execute its laws—*and* those who broke them. But soon ownership of the photograph was itself an offense, because Father Pro, the martyr, became a rallying cry for the resistance. He had been shot, not groveling, as the authorities had hoped, but with arms outstretched in prayer. In the form of the crucified Christ he served, he solemnly repeated the basis of his faith as the bullets struck him down: *Viva Cristo Rey.*

Viva Cristo Rey. *Viva Cristo Rey!* This was the phrase of the faithful now. When Mexican Catholics, who were the overwhelming majority in the country, tried to rise in defense of the faith, they were called the *Cristeros*. But it was the Mexican Catholic bishops who told the *Cristeros* to disband, to go home, to shed no blood themselves, to suffer quietly and offer only passive resistance. As one bishop said, "We cannot be responsible before God and man for bloodshed. It is better that we should die and that out of the blood of martyrs should come a new growth—as it is sure to come."[26] Such forbearance, as the Mexican bishops preached, was heroic. More wonderful still, however, would have been a Constantine to lead the *Cristeros*. It has been argued that, even without one, if the United States had not supported the Mexican government in suppressing the uprising, in the name of stability, the *Cristeros* rebellion might have destroyed the revolutionary state.[27] In any event, it was only the fear of a second *Cristeros* revolt that provided a check on the government's depredations and won meager concessions to the existence of the Church.

The destruction of churches, the execution of priests, the seizure of all Church property, and the outlawing of the faith in Mexico proceeded with little international outcry. To liberal, or Protestant, eyes, the war waged by Mexican radicals against the Church was, after all, a Latin American issue. Turbulence was common in that part of the world, and undoubtedly modernization required that the illiberal, rapacious, corrupt, and backward Catholic Church be dismantled and the people freed from its superstitions. This attitude of Western, liberal, secular opinion, rooted in materialist assumptions, was something that Catholicism obviously did not share, and which allowed the faith to understand the truth at the heart of statist threats—like Communism and Nazism—sooner and more deeply than any other institution in the West; sooner certainly than Protestants, who, as Paul Johnson noted with regard to the German Protestant churches of the 1930s, "had no anti-state tradition. . . . Since Luther's day they had always been in the service of the State, and indeed in many ways had come to see themselves as civil servants."[28] Catholics, on the other hand, were regularly martyred by statist and communist regimes, perhaps most famously in the twentieth century in republican Spain.

There, in the 1930s, the sky was lit with the fire of burning churches; the soil bleached with the bones of the slaughtered faithful. For decades, politics in Spain had been bitterly divided between left and right, with each side occasionally claiming the government. Such exchanges of power did not lead to moderation, or stability, or an attitude of "better luck next time," but to hardening ideologies and extremism. On the left, anti-clericalism had alienated the center parties, as on the right it was accusations that the pro-Catholic, pro-monarchy, pro-military forces were edging into fascism. In 1936, with the country almost evenly divided, but the left claiming a narrow electoral victory, the arguments degenerated into blows. Increasing leftist disorders—from strikes to attacks on churches—were the justification for an attempted military coup. The coup was disorganized. Rather than suddenly seizing power, the country divided itself into warring factions. The military—the Nationalists—tried to shelter the Church, while the leftists—the Republicans—unleashed a blitzkrieg of anti-Catholic violence. Nearly seven thousand Catholic priests and religious were murdered—and most of these in the first months of the war, before the Nationalists could provide safe havens.[29]

Nuns were raped, monks were shot, and priests were tortured and humiliated unless they repudiated their vows. Instead, the phrase came again as they went to their deaths: *Viva Cristo Rey*. But martyrdom was not for the clergy alone. Catholic persons and property were at the mercy of leftist mobs. The British historian Hugh Thomas wrote: "At no time in the history of Europe, or even perhaps of the world, had so passionate a hatred of religion and all its works been shown."[30]

Maybe. But if Spanish radicals crucified the Church in a bout of extreme ferocity, it is equally true that the rapes, murders, and desecrations had been seen so many times before—in every major outbreak of anti-Catholic revolution—that it seems not only horrible, but tedious, to recapitulate them. Luther's partisans had done this, mocking the sacraments when they occupied Rome as soldiers of the Holy Roman Empire. The French Revolutionaries had done their best to ridicule the faith, destroy it by violence, and de-Christianize France by law, coercion, armed mobs, and the substitution of a secular creed. The Soviets were the most effective persecutors, having no mercy at all for religion—let alone a *foreign* religion.

Through all these and other persecutions, the Church never wavered, never even showed fear. It placed an endless trust in its regenerative powers. Never would the gates of Hell prevail against it. Always there would be a Father Pro, the next apostolic secret agent, returning with the sacraments of the real, tangible, and true faith. Graham Greene captured this spirit in his novel *The Power and the Glory*.

> The stranger said, "I have only just landed. I came up the river tonight. . . . I have an introduction for the señora from a great friend of hers. . . . If you would let me come in," the man said with an odd frightened smile, and suddenly lowering his voice he said to the boy, "I am a priest."
>
> "You?" the boy exclaimed.
>
> "Yes," he said gently. "My name is Father—" But the boy had already swung the door open and put his lips to his hand before the other could give himself a name.[31]

That was the Catholic faith as it was practiced in so much of the bullet-ridden 1930s. To be a Catholic priest in the interwar decades of bloody terror often seemed to be a very dangerous vocation, indeed—especially in socialist Mexico, Spain, or Russia. And yet, in 1939 the Church stood on the precipice of an even more dangerous time, confronting the most genocidal regimes in history.

## CHAPTER TWENTY-ONE

# THE GLOBAL STRUGGLE

———— ⟫•⟪ ————

T HE YEAR 1939 saw the elevation of a longtime papal diplomat, Cardinal Pacelli, to the throne of St. Peter. No candidate for the holy office was better prepared to deal with the inevitable crisis in Europe. He had been the chief negotiator of the concordats during the interwar years. He had seen Communist violence in postwar Bavaria—in a very personal way. Communists splashed his house with machine-gun fire in the hope of assassinating him. In another instance, he faced down Communist armed robbers with the words: "I have neither money nor food. For as you know, I have given all I had to the poor of the city. . . . This is a house of peace, not a den of murderers!"[1]

Though he had experienced Communist violence first-hand in Bavaria, it did not color his feelings about Germany. Communism he loathed, but Germany—her people, civilization, language, and literature—he loved. This combination did not, as his detractors claim, make him sympathetic to Hitler. Rather, he saw Hitler for what he was—a threat to German civilization. He first criticized the Nazis in 1921 in just these terms:

> The Bavarian people are peace-loving. But, just as they were seduced during the revolution by alien elements—above all, Russians—into the extremes of Bolshevism, so now other non-Bavarian elements of an entirely opposite persuasion have likewise thought to make Bavaria their base of operation.[2]

As Professor Ronald Rychlak points out, "Of the forty-four public speeches that Nuncio Pacelli made on German soil between 1917 and 1929, at least forty contained attacks on National Socialism or Hitler's doctrines."[3] As pope, he took the name Pius XII (1939–1958), a signal to the Nazis, among others, that he intended to continue the policies of his predecessor, the man who had issued *Mit Brennender Sorge*, a document that Cardinal Pacelli himself had drafted. It was Cardinal Pacelli, too, under Pope Pius XI's leadership, who had called on Catholic archbishops to lobby their governments to accept Jewish immigrants from Nazi tyranny.[4] The Nazis certainly understood that the new pope was their enemy. Shortly after Pacelli's election in 1939, a secret Nazi security report noted, "Pacelli has already made himself prominent by his attacks on National Socialism during his tenure as Cardinal Secretary of State. . . . In adopting his name [Pius], will he not also resume the work of that man whose collaborator as Secretary of State he has been in recent years?"[5] Indeed, Pius XI thought the Western democracies were not hard enough against Hitler, and couldn't be, because the true anti-Nazi and anti-Communist critique came out of Catholic philosophy.[6]

Pope Pius XII made desperate overtures to achieve peace, declaring, "Nothing is lost by peace: everything may be lost by war."[7] Surely even he, though a diplomat and prince of peace, must have known that it was impossible. He understood the Nazis and the Communists all too well. When the Hitler-Stalin pact was signed in August 1939, uniting the two most murderous regimes in history, the pope must have felt very much like Guy Crouchback, the hero of Evelyn Waugh's *The Sword of Honour* trilogy, when he hears the news: "The enemy at last was plain in view, huge and hateful, all disguise cast off. It was the Modern Age in arms."[8]

For the next six years, the pope devoted himself, as Pope Benedict XV had in the First World War, to bringing relief to the suffering. But Pope Pius XII had an additional mission. The Nazis openly persecuted the Jews in Germany and in every country into which they marched. Secretly, they were killing Jews by the millions. The pope—the commander in chief of the Swiss guards of Vatican City, surrounded by Fascist Italy, which, by 1940, was the ally of Nazi Germany—intended to bring as many Jews as he could to freedom. Thousands of Jews were housed, literally, in Church buildings in Rome—even after the Nazis occupied the city in 1943. But these were only a few of the hundreds of thousands of Jews that the

Church saved from the Nazi executioners. In 1967, Israeli diplomat Pinchas Lapide estimated that Pope Pius XII "was instrumental in saving at least 700,000, but probably as many as 860,000 Jews from certain death at Nazi hands."[9] In other words, no institution, outside the Allied armies, did more during World War II to save Jewish lives from the Holocaust than the pope and the Catholic Church. To put those numbers in even clearer perspective, consider that the Nazis had within their grasp 8,300,000 Jews. Six million of these were killed, leaving only 2,300,000 survivors.[10] If we take Lapide's lowest estimate of the Jewish lives that Pope Pius XII was "instrumental" in saving—700,000—it amounts to 30 percent of the Jews who survived Hitler's "final solution."

In recent years, Pope Pius XII has been accused of being "Hitler's pope" and of not having done nearly enough to protect the Jews of Europe. It might be noted, first of all, that Catholics themselves were targets of the Nazi extermination machine. At Auschwitz concentration camp alone, three million Polish Catholics were systematically murdered—including thousands of priests, 20 percent of Poland's entire clerical class (or "priest swine," as the Nazis called them).[11] It might be noted further that papal diplomacy and underground assistance were more effective at saving Jewish lives from the Nazis than they were at saving Catholic lives from the Communists in Soviet Russia. It was the Soviet Communists, in fact—no mean anti-Semites themselves—who began the "disinformation," after the Second World War, that Pope Pius XII had been a Nazi collaborator. The reason was simple: The pope was the leading religious anti-Communist crusader in the world. It is not surprising that atheistic Communists should hate the pope—it was as much a part of their ideology as anti-Semitism was a part of National Socialism. But, as Rabbi David G. Dalin noted in his authoritative article "Pope Pius XII and the Jews" in *The Weekly Standard*, this Communist big lie has been appropriated by "lapsed or angry" Catholic writers[12] as "simply the biggest club available for liberal Catholics to use against traditionalists." He continues:

> But Jews, whatever their feelings about the Catholic Church, have a duty to reject any attempt to usurp the Holocaust and use it for partisan purposes in such a debate—particularly when the attempt disparages the testimony of Holocaust survivors and spreads to inappropriate figures the condemnation that belongs to Hitler and

the Nazis. . . . The Talmud teaches that "whosoever preserves one life, it is accounted to him by Scripture as if he had preserved the whole world." More than any other twentieth-century leader, Pius fulfilled this Talmudic dictum, when the fate of European Jewry was at stake. No other pope had been so widely praised by Jews—and they were not mistaken. Their gratitude, as well as that of the entire generation of Holocaust survivors, testifies that Pius XII was genuinely and profoundly a righteous gentile.[13]

If the accusations against Pius XII are despicable, they are also ludicrous coming from liberals or secularists, who for hundreds of years pressed for the destruction of the Catholic Church as a temporal power—until it exists on a mere postage stamp of real estate—and the stripping of all conceivable authority from the institution. It is, however, perhaps a backhanded compliment to the papacy and the Catholic Church that no one asks why the Free Church of Scotland, the United Methodist Church, the Southern Baptists, the Anglican Church, or any other of the innumerable Protestant churches or the Eastern Orthodox churches did not do more to help the Jews. In such enormous world crises, there really is only one Christian voice and one Christian institution that matters; the rest—whatever great and heroic individual efforts are made—are so fractured, politically unimportant, or compromised as to be irrelevant.

The Nazis were sufficiently intent on silencing the alleged "Hitler's pope" that Hitler in 1943—the very year the Nazis occupied Rome—planned to seize the Vatican and kidnap Pius XII, which might have been tit-for-tat, as the pope had collaborated with aristocratic German officers plotting against Hitler. Another plan was developed for execution by SS cavalry units in 1944 to "massacre Pius XII with the entire Vatican," because of "the papal protest in favor of the Jews."[14] These plans, obviously, did not come off. But if the Nazis decided that they could not risk kidnapping or killing the pope, they did send Catholic priests to the death camps for "treason" against the Nazis. Moreover, they punished Jews even more severely whenever the Church condemned Jewish deportations. The Church delivered such condemnations repeatedly in 1942, with regard to Dutch Jews and Jews being deported from Vichy France—to no positive effect. In sheer fact, the Church—and this shouldn't be surprising—was most effective as a silent rescuer, by *doing* rather than merely talking. Our own age tends to prefer the latter, because it offers painless self-affirmation. But in World War II, public condemnations were no more than a lit candle in a window—a symbolic gesture—and, unfortunately, an incitement to those who would kill.

One uniquely telling proof of Pope Pius XII's work on behalf of the Jews—aside from the argument of numbers and the praise of such as Albert Einstein and Golda Meir—was that the chief rabbi of Rome, after the war, when there was no secular reason for doing so, converted to Catholicism and took Pius XII's Christian name, Eugenio. Granted, conversion rests not merely on admiration of a good man, but on an intellectual submission and a theological development. Yet it is surely a testament to Pius XII's moral stature and authority that this step should be taken by the Jewish leader closest to him and best able to observe him.

The Holocaust was one especially horrible aspect of a titanically horrible war. World War II claimed 50 million lives—more than six times the number of deaths in the First World War, the Great War, that was already more terrible than anything Europe could previously have imagined. Hitler's war aims included not only territorial conquest; he sought the extermination of European Jewry, the enslavement of the Slavs, and the dissolution of the Catholic Church. Heinrich Himmler, head of the SS, fumed that "We should not forget that in the long run, the pope in Rome is a greater enemy of National Socialism than Churchill or Roosevelt."[15] Luckily, the Nazis didn't have a long run. In the short run, the war was ended and Hitler's evil extinguished by the armies of Churchill and Roosevelt, two agnostic Anglicans (something of a tautology). Unfortunately, they also had an Eastern associate: a bloodstained mass murderer of even greater proportions than Hitler, his former colleague, the atheist-Communist "Uncle Joe" Stalin. The marriage of Hitler and Stalin—"the modern age in arms"—could not endure. Hitler's ugly Russian bride became a temporary ally of the West, and the ally who bore the brunt of the most vicious fighting. The alliance between the Anglo-Americans and the Soviets didn't last either. But for some participants, like Evelyn Waugh, the entry of the Soviets on the Allied side stripped the Western crusade of any meaning. Waugh was a Catholic, but Churchill, the agnostic Anglican, had a better grasp of the necessary, inevitable, difficult, and muddy moral choices required of statesmen. The historian John Lukacs, in his book *Five Days in London: May 1940*, makes a provocative asseveration that puts this in perspective:

> The greatest threat to Western civilization was not Communism. It was National Socialism. The greatest and most dynamic power in the world was not Soviet Russia. It was the Third Reich of Germany. The greatest revolutionary of the twentieth century was not Lenin or Stalin. It was Hitler. Hitler not only succeeded in merging nationalism and socialism into one tremendous force; he was a new kind of ruler, representing a new kind of populist nationalism. . . . His greatest reactionary opponent, Churchill, was like King Canute, attempting to withstand and sweep back that wave. And—yes, *mirabile dictu*—this King Canute succeeded: because of his resolution and—allow me to say this—because of God's will, of which, like every human being, he was but an instrument. He was surely no saint, he was not a religious man, and he had many faults. Yet so it happened.[16]

Churchill understood that Nazism was socialist tyranny that *might work*, while Soviet Communism—if more tyrannical and bloodthirsty—was doomed to collapse of its own brutal inefficiency. Churchill even predicted, with extraordinary prescience, from the vantage point of New Year's Day 1953, that Eastern European Communism would be consigned to history's rubbish bin by the 1980s.[17]

In addition, it was Churchill, as every schoolboy knows, who, in a speech at Fulton, Missouri, in 1946, announced, "From Stettin in the Baltic to Trieste in the Adriatic, an iron curtain has descended across the continent. Behind that line lie all the capitals of the ancient states of Central and Eastern Europe. Warsaw, Berlin, Prague, Vienna, Budapest, Belgrade, Bucharest and Sofia."[18] Vienna and West Berlin would be free, but the rest of these cities were now under the fist of Stalin and the Soviet Communists, their Catholic populations held captive. In this new war, the Cold War, it was the Catholic Church that became England's and America's most vocal ally in defense of freedom and against Communism.

Communism was no abstract ideology to the Vatican. Postwar Italy was rife with Communists. They were responsible for murdering more than fifty priests in the Emilia region of north-central Italy alone.[19] In defense against the Red menace, the papacy, which had tried to remain aloof from Italian politics ever since the Risorgimento, now took the lead to save Italy for the West. The moderate-conservative Christian-Democratic party became the Catholic political bulwark against the Italian Communists. Pius XII was also eagerly pro-American, an early believer that peace and the defense of freedom against Communism required close ties between the United States, Italy, and the rest of Western Europe.

In the East, behind the Iron Curtain, the tolling bell of martyrdom marked what would be nearly a half-century of postwar anti-Catholic terror. Every Communist regime in Eastern Europe repressed the Church, stripped its property, and abolished its rights; imprisoned, beat, and murdered monks and priests; and waged an unceasing torture and propaganda war against the Church's beliefs, practices, and people. Every Eastern bloc country has its own tragic, bloodstained story of totalitarian tyranny: East Germany, Yugoslavia, Romania, Bulgaria, the Baltic states, and all the rest. But the story, of course, transcends Europe. Wherever Communism came to power, priests, bishops, and laypeople proved in their unfortunate thousands upon thousands that they would die for the faith of Christ and His Church. The bloody footsteps of the Catholic martyrs to atheistic Communism can be traced in Asia—from Red China, North Korea, and especially, of course, in what had been the French colonies of Vietnam, Cambodia, and Laos. They can be followed, in fact, in virtually every repressive regime in the world. If one were to make a list of countries where the Catholic Church did *not* suffer martyrs in the twentieth century, it would number only a handful.

The mind numbs at the extent of the terror. In some countries, like Albania, the Communists attempted to scorch the Catholic Church from their borders. In others, like Poland, the government, while maintaining a tight secret police cordon on the Church, was obliged by force of popular sentiment to keep the churches open. In Czechoslovakia, more than 60 percent of Catholics in religious or priestly orders were incarcerated in specifically Catholic prison camps. Priests were harassed and licensed by the state, known Catholics were discriminated against in education and hiring, public gatherings of Catholics were broken up, and there were martyrs, like Cardinal Stefan Trochta, who died under police torture, as did several Franciscan Fathers and numerous others who faithfully served the Church and its people. In Hungary, in the late 1940s, the torture and subsequent show trial of Cardinal Mindszenty made Hungarian

Communism notorious. In 1956, after Soviet tanks rolled into Budapest, Pope Pius XII responded with three separate encyclicals condemning the Communists. After years in a Hungarian prison, Cardinal Mindszenty was released, but lived in proximate-exile—that is, in the American embassy in Budapest—for two decades, as a living protest to the regime that imprisoned hundreds of priests, closed the monasteries and nunneries, and tried to smother the voice of the Church. Even in brave and defiant Poland, which had suffered so much, torn between the murderous Nazis and the bloodthirsty Soviets in 1939, thousands of priests, survivors of the previous holocausts, would be arrested. All Catholic activity outside Church doors was prohibited—though this became unenforceable. A collaborationist church was created—and failed. The Catholic Church was not only vibrant in the soul of the Polish people; it was the rallying point of resistance to the Communist state. It was the heart of Solidarity, the anti-Communist trade union that became the fire-point for the collapse of Polish Communism.

Solidarity's chaplain was Father Jerzy Popieluszko. To his proud, noble, and chivalrous countrymen, Father Popieluszko preached hard but true words:

> Do not struggle with violence. Violence is a sign of weakness. All those who cannot win through the heart try to conquer through violence. The most wonderful and durable struggles in history have been carried on by human thought. The most ignoble fights and most ephemeral successes are those of violence. An idea that needs rifles to survive dies of its own accord. An idea which is imposed by violence collapses under it. An idea capable of life wins without effort and is then followed by millions of people.[20]

There is the true voice of the 2,000-year-old Church, whose message began with the Word, which was transmitted to the Apostles and that has survived while every earthly kingdom passes away to be replaced by another. We should remember, however, "the cost of discipleship."[21] Father Popieluszko was repeatedly arrested and beaten by the police, until finally they murdered him in 1984. When the Polish people in their sorrow looked to Rome, they took heart from another man who lived through the Nazi and the Communist repression, the first Polish pope, John Paul II.

# RESTORATION

IF CATHOLICISM HAD BEEN DRAINED from European politics in the first half of the twentieth century, the chief European architects of Western Europe's political reconstruction after two disastrous world wars were Catholics who saw their religion as essential to the continent's revival. In a world teeming with determinist ideologies—with the fate of nations and individuals supposedly determined by race, economics, history, psychology, genetics, or even, insofar as Protestants had any doctrinal beliefs, predestination—the Catholic Church alone stood radically in defense of man's free will, and therefore of man's God-given right to freedom.

In Germany, the outstanding and essential postwar chancellor was Konrad Adenauer, founder of the Christian Democratic Union. In Italy, the most important postwar politician of the twentieth century was Prime Minister Alcide de Gasperi of the Christian Democratic Party. In France, there were Robert Schuman of the Catholic *Mouvement Républicain Populaire*, who served in the immediate postwar years as finance minister, foreign minister, and premier, and the obstreperous and obnoxious but nevertheless giant figure of Charles de Gaulle, a man whose very name has been transformed into *Gaullism* to describe the major artery of postwar French conservatism, and who single-handedly restored that wounded nation's pride and stability.

De Gasperi had been the great anti-Mussolini of Italian politics; he was a politician who despised nationalism, arguing that in the name of liberty, Italians must be Catholics before they were anything else. It was only through the political acceptance of Catholic Natural Law, he contended, that man has any legitimate, defensible, absolute, God-given rights. Without that, with only the pagan worship of the state, men's rights were completely dependent on the whim of the *duces* or others who claimed to embody the popular will. To de Gasperi—a man who attended daily Mass—Fascism and Bolshevism were essentially the same. Against the Fascists and the Communists, de Gasperi proclaimed Catholic anti-statism—of Church and family being the fundamental institutions of society. The state, if an administrative necessity, was to be kept to a minimum. The Fascists jailed de Gasperi in 1927. Two years later, Pope Pius XI arranged for him to be freed and employed him in the

Vatican library, where he stayed for the next decade and a half. After the war, de Gasperi was the Church's political voice. He was Italy's first postwar prime minister, the man who was able to keep the Communists and the Socialists at bay, and the politician who was able to lock Italy into the Western alliance of the United States and the free states of Europe.

Adenauer shared much of de Gasperi's platform, adapted to German politics. He too thought that Christianity, family, and individual enterprise must be the foundation of society. He had opposed Prussian, bureaucratic statism—and Hitler—all his political life. He shared with other German Catholics a sense that a powerful state—whether Bismarckian, National Socialist, or Communist (as in East Germany)—meant persecution of the faith. The Catholic sensibility in both de Gasperi and Adenauer was supranational, familial, and anti-statist. Adenauer also had a profound sense of man's propensity for evil. Hitler, Hitler's democratic popularity, and the Holocaust had underscored this sense, which gave Adenauer two preeminent political principles: tying the West German people to a legal system that was based in Christianity and breaking up the power of the state.

Where Bismarck had sought to make Germany powerful by centralizing it, Adenauer stood for a federal Germany within a European Union, with political power diffused between various levels of authority to prevent both nationalism and the dangerous concentration of state power. These ideas came directly from the Catholic political principle of subsidiarity, of support for intermediary institutions. This anti-statist mentality also made him a friend of free-market economics, and under his leadership West Germany achieved its remarkable, postwar economic recovery, its *Wirtschaftwunder*. In addition, he was strongly anti-Communist—as were all Catholics, who risked excommunication if they joined a Communist party—seeing the Soviets as a horrible red maw, chomping on the bones of Germans and Christians.

In France, Robert Schuman was a fellow cosmopolitan Catholic, born in Luxembourg, whose first language was German and who in the First World War had served in the German army. After the war he became a French citizen, and during the Second World War he served in the French resistance. In the immediate postwar world, he collaborated with Adenauer to link France and Germany in an anti-nationalistic alliance bound together by trade and law. As such, Schuman and Adenauer were looking to take Europe backward in history, back to the idea of the Holy

Roman Empire. In the words of one contemporary observer: "The past is not dead, but survives in the German cultural world of Adenauer, Schuman and de Gasperi."[22]

Charles de Gaulle would eventually overshadow Schuman and would give France, in 1958, a new constitution, the constitution of the Fifth Republic, which is the law of France today, and a new president—himself. By nature and ego a monarch, he nevertheless accepted democratic politics even while believing, with Louis XIV, that "*l'état c'est moi.*" As such, he was much friendlier to the state as an institution than were the other great postwar Catholic politicians of Europe. Gaullism saw the state as the patriotic embodiment of France, the guardian of its culture, and the vehicle by which France would achieve its destiny, which was to lead democratic, Western Europe as the captain of the European Union. If Adenauer, Schuman, and de Gasperi formed the constituent parts of a new Holy Roman Empire, de Gaulle saw himself as Charlemagne, uniting Gaul and Teuton, creating an independent European power bloc, midway between the United States across the Atlantic and the Communists behind the Iron Curtain.

Thus, in the West, under the financial and military umbrella of the United States, Catholic politicians restored Europe from the worst aspects of what Wilhelm Röpke called "the ultimate source of our civilization's disease . . . the desperate attempt to get along without God."[23] But this was in the sphere of philosophy, politics, and economics. What of the faith itself?

In a century of Nazi paganism, Communist atheism, and hostile liberalism, the popes were called on to deliver vigorous reassertions and definitions of Catholic philosophical, political, and economic beliefs. Pope Pius XII, for instance, not only repudiated the Nazis and the Communists, but also theories of collective guilt against the Germans, the accommodation of theology to popular opinion and modern philosophies, and artificial insemination. The Church would not condone race-guilt, or any deviations from theological truth to make it palatable to liberalism and secularism, or a *Brave New World* future of artificially bred humans.

The Church also continued to deliver the sacraments, sponsor Biblical and other scholarship, and reform and define its practices, putting dogmatic fidelity before thoughts of ecumenical compromise or diplomacy. As Pope Pius XI said, "Can we endure [in the name ecumenism] . . . that the truth revealed by God be made the object of negotiations?"[24] The answer, of course, was no. When in 1950, Pope Pius XII invoked papal infallibility to define the Assumption of the Virgin Mary as a dogma of the Catholic faith, it was done purely on what he regarded as its theological and historical merits.[25] The Catholic Church and the Eastern Orthodox churches had celebrated the Feast of the Assumption from unknown beginnings, but probably for at least a millennium and a half. That it was a Catholic tradition, long held as true in ecumenical councils, was not in doubt. The real issue was the same as that over papal infallibility: whether it was prudent to proclaim as a dogma of the faith something that would offend Protestants and the Eastern Orthodox. Protestants regard Marian devotions and theology with a gimlet eye as un-Biblical. The Orthodox share Catholic belief in the Assumption but deny the pope's right to define it. The pope, properly, cared not a fig for their protests. When the Church felt that it should define a truth, it defined it: The Church was the Church, *c'est tout*.

This sense of historic certainty was what had attracted Cardinals Manning and Newman and the poet and Jesuit Gerard Manley Hopkins to the Church in the nineteenth century. In the twentieth century, it drew so many English-speaking writers and Anglican bishops' sons to the Church that the Catholic Church in England became the Church Literary to Rome's Church Militant. The trend began early, at the turn of the century, with the aesthetes who reformed and found moral regeneration: men like Oscar Wilde; the marquess of Queensbury, whose accusations of homosexual indecency prompted the libel action that sent Wilde to prison; poet and later priest John Gray (after whom Dorian Gray was named); the artist Aubrey Beardsley; and the poet Lionel Johnson.[26] Following them into the faith were G. K. Chesterton, the journalist Maurice Baring, Father Robert Hugh Benson, Father Ronald Knox, the historian Christopher Dawson, the artist Eric Gill, poet Alfred Noyes, Graham Greene, Evelyn Waugh, novelist Compton MacKenzie, poet Edith Sitwell, poet and novelist Siegfried Sassoon, novelist Muriel Spark, journalist Malcolm Muggeridge, and many others. Allied with them were cradle or near-cradle Catholics like Hilaire Belloc and J.R.R. Tolkien. Then there were American converts like the Trappist monk Thomas Merton who wrote the best-selling memoir *The Seven Storey Mountain*, poet Allen Tate, novelist Walker Percy, and Cardinal Avery Dulles (son of the American secretary of state John Foster Dulles), as well as cradle Catholics like

Flannery O'Connor and the journalist William F. Buckley Jr. Similar conversions, or literary eloquence from cradle Catholic writers, were also noted on the continent, particularly in France.

All of this stands as remarkable testimony to the intellectual and creative vibrancy of the Catholic faith. It is a great and lasting solace to fellow literary-minded Catholics. But what must, at the same time, be truly disturbing is that this massive literary expenditure on the faith made almost no lasting impression on the English-speaking people at all. The postwar revival of religion collapsed in the 1960s and has never stopped declining. In England, the Anglican church had as its twentieth-century literary spokesmen the like of Dorothy Sayers, T. S. Eliot, and C. S. Lewis. Yet weekly church attendance is around 8 percent and falling. Only a million Anglican communicants—out of a British population of roughly 60 million—attended Easter services in the year 2001. That is not even the worst of the story. While two-thirds of British retirees believe in the Resurrection, fewer than a third of Britons under the age of thirty-five do.[27] There is a striking change in other behavior as well. In 1950, 2 percent of British babies were illegitimate. In 1998, nearly 38 percent were.[28] Other indices of social pathology, including crime figures, have also skyrocketed. But the economy continues to work, which seems to be all that matters.

Catholicism is the last serious foothold of Christianity in Britain. In sheer numbers, more Catholics attend church on Sunday in England than do Anglicans, even though Catholics are only 13 percent of the population. Church attendance among Catholics is three times the Anglican rate, but that itself is a pitiful number; and it too is falling. Even the most powerful literary voices seem powerless against the march of secularism, the chief weapons of which are a quintet of -isms that pretty much define the modern Western world: materialism, individualism, solipsism, indifferentism, and relativism. The first is a distraction, though through its ubiquitous engine—advertising—a powerful and shaping one. The next four prevent adherence to dogma. The last three are what the late professor Allan Bloom diagnosed as *The Closing of the American Mind*—and they make any discussion of religion, philosophy, or, indeed, any rational intellectual discussion at all impossible. Literary Catholics can speak only to those few who still experience a life of the mind. For the rest, the Catholic Church must compete with both these secular forces and with Protestant denominations that actually cater to them by offering emotionalism, minimal dogma, and—the inevitable concomitant of these two qualities—a focus on self, or what is called "a personal relationship with God."

After the death of Pope Pius XII in 1958, the Church, already seeing these looming trends, bestirred itself to liberalize, to find a new way to carry on the apostolic mission. That would prove to be a mistake.

## VATICAN II AND *HUMANAE VITAE*

POPE JOHN XXIII (1958–1963) had, it must be admitted, a certain resemblance to Christ—and to St. Nicholas. The future pope, like the Christ child in the manger, slept among cows and grew up among farmers. He became in succession a doctor of theology, a hospital orderly, and a military chaplain, and then had a long career in the Vatican's diplomatic service, especially in the East. There, he developed an interest in the Eastern churches and in Islam, and during the Second World War, he was active spiriting Jews to safety from Nazi-occupied Greece. As pope, an openness to the world—including the Communist and secular worlds—became a trademark. He felt he had nothing to fear from meeting with sinners—including Soviet premier Nikita Khrushchev's son-in-law—and he saw his pontificate as an opportunity to go in Christ-like pursuit of his lost sheep, to address himself, in his own words, "to all men of goodwill." Like St. Nicholas, Pope John XXIII was fat, elderly, genial, approachable, outgoing, and extremely popular. He felt that by calling a Second Vatican Council he could make a Christmas-like gift to God's people—that is, to all people: a refurbished Catholic Church that no longer set up barricades against the modern world, but that threw open the doors of welcome. The dawning of the 1960s seemed to make everyone—popes, prime ministers, and pop stars—assume that, in Harold Macmillan's words, "the wind of change" was blowing. The pope, even though he was conservative enough to insist that priests still be taught in Latin, appeared to welcome these winds of change, which he took as a call for renewal through the Holy Spirit. In Italian the word used to capture this papal directive was *aggiornamento*.

President John F. Kennedy, the first Catholic president of the United States, was elected during the pontificate of John XXIII, and however different the two men were in personal morality and upbringing, their public utterances tracked a similar sort of conservative idealism. One remembers the Kennedy of "Ask not what your country can do for you"; of the idealistic founding of the Peace Corps and the Green Berets, *de oppresso liber*; of "we all breathe the same air." Then we think of the pope, who penned *Ad Cathedrum Petri*, on the nature of Christian service and cooperation between Catholics and other Christians; *Mater et Magistra,* on the obligation of the rich to help the poor; and *Pacem in Terris*, on reconciliation and peace through diplomacy that recognizes universal rights and aspirations. We can even remember the call for the Second Vatican Council, the aims of which were to be pastoral—directed to the service of the laity—rather than dogmatic, defining the truths of the faith. Together, in 1963, the satyr president and the saintly Pope John XXIII, a man who combined the best qualities of parish priest and papal diplomat, fell dead. Their optimism would prove misguided.

The pope's Vatican Council was already under way and would last for three years, from 1962 to 1965. Nearly 3,000 Catholic bishops attended, as did representatives from the Eastern Orthodox churches and from Protestant denominations. The task of the Council was to restate, in friendly, welcoming language that might prick modern ears, the ancient truths of the faith. Unfortunately, the actual documents of the Council often proved less important than did the fact that they were hijacked by invokers of the "spirit" of Vatican II to enact sweeping "reform" that the documents themselves did not necessarily call for. Thus, out went the Latin Mass in favor of a vernacular liturgy—in one stroke eliminating the historic and universal language of the Church that echoed from Rome to Mexico to India every Sunday. In came guitars and more lay participation in the Mass, including, in some dioceses, such illicit and unwelcome innovations as hand-holding during the Our Father and cupping one's hands in imitation of the priest— offenses that should have been dealt with under *sharia* law, adopting the Islamic punishment for thievery, as part of the Church's new openness to other religions. Out went *some* of the separation that distinguished priests and religious from laypeople. In came a demand for increased lay participation in the affairs of the Church, including, helpfully, a reminder that every Catholic should aspire to be a saint.

On other matters, Catholic triumphalism was erased at its borders so that the Eastern Orthodox churches and Protestant sects were recognized as containing important aspects of the truth. It was affirmed that the

Jewish people had a special relationship to Christians and were not
uniquely responsible for the crucifixion of Christ. The Church acknowledged a fundamental human right to religious freedom, including freedom for non-Christian religions. Missionary work was to be continued,
however, for the Catholic faith was the one fully true religion and offered
the surest salvation of mankind. The modern world was not condemned,
as in the past, but accepted as the world in which the Church and every
Catholic was on a pilgrimage.

The new pope who was to lead the Church on this pilgrimage was
Paul VI (1963–1978). He inherited an almost impossible situation. Vatican
II was drenched in worldly praise, which is always a bad sign, and its inar-
guably disastrous results came pouring in soon after. The number of seminarians collapsed. Thousands of priests and religious abandoned their
vows to more fully participate in the world—in a manner of a speaking.
Laypeople followed, becoming more like their Protestant and agnostic
brothers and sisters, divorcing, contracepting, and eventually aborting at
similar rates.[29] "Openness to the world" brought with it a spirit of indisci-
pline. Vatican II documents were broadly interpreted to justify experimen-
tation, beliefs, and practices that were unjustifiable. This should have been
no surprise—and to conservatives in the papal curia, it wasn't. It was ever
thus with liberal reforms—they do not easily end or define themselves. In
one horrible flush, the postwar Catholic recovery was lost as Catholics
looked to reconcile themselves with a decade memorably described by the
social scientist Robert Nisbet: "I think it would be difficult to find a single
decade in the history of Western culture when so much barbarism—so
much calculated onslaught against culture and convention in any form,
and so much sheer degradation of both culture and the individual—passed
into print, into music, into art and onto the American stage as the decade
of the Nineteen Sixties."[30]

Paul VI's first pontifical act was to sell his papal tiara to benefit the
poor—another bad sign for those who knew that the pomp and grandeur
of the Church is manna to the soul of the believer, just as the pomp and
circumstance of the military feeds the soul of the patriot. Paul VI was a
complex man—someone who saw himself, accurately and somewhat de-
spairingly, as a Hamlet figure, something that John XXIII and others had
noted about him. Seeing the good and the bad in all factions of the contesting Church, he weaved a difficult middle path. Well-traveled and a

bibliomaniac, he was committed to the ecumenical aims of John XXIII. He was avid to embrace the Anglicans, whom he called a "sister church," and the stubborn Eastern Orthodox, whom in 1967 he convinced to join him in a mutual lifting of excommunications. He shared Pope John XXIII's concern for social and political actions that benefited the poor. In like continuity, he worked to ease tensions with the belligerent Soviet Union—to the extent of annoying Western capitalist states, and even disciplining such a staunch anti-Communist as Cardinal Mindszenty for standing in the way of thawing East-West relations. If such ecumenism and economic and political teaching were seen as liberal, he held fast to the disciplines and dogmas of the Church. He upheld—in the face of the most explosive sexual upheaval since the French Revolution—clerical celibacy. He went even further in an action that would stun liberals and define his pontificate in the popular mind by issuing an encyclical entitled *Humanae Vitae*.

*Humanae Vitae* states simple facts that are denied by modern secular culture and even by many professedly religious people. First, it proclaims that life is a gift from God, sacred, and not to be aborted by man. Second, it affirms that a man's and a woman's reproductive organs are, in fact, just that, and to use them for other purposes or to artificially subvert their use is a morally disordered action; it is a violation of natural law. Third, biology provides a natural spacing of fertile and infertile periods, which a couple is allowed to observe and use intelligently.

*Humanae Vitae* pointed out what should be obvious but is not to most people. Artificial contraception is an invitation to promiscuity. It blurs the distinction between licit conjugal sexual activity and every other objectively deranged form, from the predictable fornication, to pornography, homosexuality, and other perversions: "perversions," in the sense of sexual "misusages," all of which, by being in contradiction to natural law, have, by definition, a harmful effect on the individual and society. It can be recognized immediately that linking sexual activity to reproduction, marital fidelity, and family, as it should be linked, connects the sex act to giving—the giving of life, which entails perpetually giving in the raising of children. Sexual activity that is indulged in *solely* as an act of pleasure, animalistic release, or whatever other form is inevitably selfish in intent, uncommitted in principle, and bereft of responsibility; it can thus, in the mind of man, turn people into objects to be used for gratification rather than as sacred individuals considered as fully human. This is no small thing to reaffirm in a century when Communists and Nazis denied the fact that every individual is sacred, or today, for that matter, when the natural result of sexual activity, a human life, is considered an abortable object of no inherent or sacred value.

It is interesting, too, that *Humanae Vitae* perceives that to grant legality to artificial contraception, means, de facto, to give such power not only to the individual, but to the state. The Church, in essence, predicted the one-child policy of Communist China and the state indoctrination of "sex education" that has become a commonplace in schools in the Western world. The invasive power of such sex education programs grows with every report of rising teen pregnancy—something noted by the writer Tom Wolfe, whose fictional character Pottho Mboti, an African anthropology student, observes that American schools pump their students' heads full of information on sex from the age of thirteen and yet "Americans are at the same time baffled that the number of pregnancies out of wedlock among schoolgirls rises continually. In this, the Americans are somewhat like the Kombanda tribesmen of our country, who, ignorant of the causal relation of activities separated by time, believe that pregnancy is caused by the sun shining on the bare midsections of females of a certain age."[31] The Church, however, is not as credulous as secular society— or the Kombanda tribe. The Church has always taught the virtue of chastity. Modern secular society teaches that chastity is impossible—and has propagandized to make it so.

*Humanae Vitae* is important for yet another reason. Just as the National Socialists used nationalism and racism, among other levers, to overthrow Christian morality, in modern, liberal society the levers have been sexual liberation and consumerism. These two "freedoms to choose" have replaced objective morality with the dogma of whatever the customer, or the individual, wants is right. In opposing this attitude, the Church is often accused of being "opposed to sex." Such an accusation reveals the incredible poverty of modern thought. Far from being opposed to sex, the Church affirms that sex is a definable thing: God made them man and woman. The Church affirms the twofold "unitive" and "procreative" purpose and virtue inherent in conjugal activity and cherishes the result: the bonding of man and wife and their commitment to raise their children. And as anyone remotely familiar with the paintings and sculptures in the Vatican can affirm, the Church celebrates the human body, celebrates the reality of sex and the erotic (in the same spirit as the Bible's *Song of Solomon*), and indeed celebrates marriage as a sacrament. It is modern, liberal secularists who are "opposed to sex" in that they attempt to blur the distinctions between male and female, ignore the objective meaning of sexual activity, and who think that its natural result should be freely and inconsequentially aborted if it cannot otherwise be prevented. To a logician of an Aristotelian or Thomistic kind—in other words, a Catholic theologian, one of the few defenders of logical, objective reason in modern society—this is simply ludicrous. It is also, needless to say, majority opinion in the Western world.

By putting his name to *Humanae Vitae*, by merely reaffirming the constant teaching of the Church about human life and sexuality, Pope Paul VI was repudiated by every liberal voice that had previously held him in such high esteem. The pope was certain that *Humanae Vitae* was objectively correct. He was equally aware that it did not change Catholic teaching, but only underlined it, and thus should not have been controversial. He was so shocked by the negative reaction generated by *Humanae Vitae* in 1968 that he never wrote another encyclical, though he reigned for a further decade. Feeling the weight of his papal office, he brooded over his turbulent flock, the sweeping chaos of the "sex, drugs, and rock and roll" society, and the new wave of terrorism that in 1978 claimed the life of one of his closest childhood friends, the Italian Christian Democrat politician Aldo Moro. That same year, the pope—who saw in his duty the loneliness of Jesus on the cross—died, perhaps mercifully.

Next to ascend St. Peter's throne was Pope John Paul I, though he refused to be crowned, one-upping Pope Paul VI's donation of the papal tiara. The new pope's name promised a continuation of his predecessors' initiatives. This might have been unwise given the sadness felt by Pope Paul VI at the state of the Church after the Second Vatican Council. The new pope had come from parents who were socialists, but over the decades his own politics had moved slowly to the right. Certainly on matters of dogma and doctrine, he was orthodox, defending, for instance, *Humanae Vitae*. He was a gifted writer and speaker. Great things were expected from him, but he died within a month of his elevation. The next pope, however, would be a giant, ushering in another great effort of Catholic restoration.

## THE ERA OF POPE JOHN PAUL II

IN OCTOBER 1978, the College of Cardinals chose a remarkable man. The newly elevated Pope John Paul II was the first non-Italian pope in more than 450 years. He was a Pole who had lived through World War II, witnessing both Nazi terror and Communist persecution. He was a scholar, philosopher, and linguist, but also a poet, playwright, and actor, as well as an athlete. Before becoming a priest he had had a girlfriend, considered a secular career, and worked as a manual laborer. It is to the great benefit of the Church that he felt called to a priestly vocation and pursued it—as was necessary—like a secret agent, studying surreptitiously and eluding Nazi death squads that marked every young Pole of military age for death. He served a suffering Church in Soviet-occupied Poland. When he was elevated to the papacy, Soviet KGB chief, and later head of the Soviet Union, Yuri Andropov immediately recognized a threat to the Soviet regime.

But the new pope was also a symbol to the West. Young, vibrant, brimming with élan vital, self-evident goodness, philosophical clarity, and strength, he could appeal to the media-drenched Western mind and its demand for charisma. He could also speak to it in terms of authority. When the pope issued challenges to respect human dignity, even the commercialized West had to pay attention to this man who spoke having personally stood witness to the greatest Hell-bent ideologies of the twentieth century, a man who had come through that inferno not only with the wisdom that comes from suffering and the confrontation with evil, but with a love of life and the joy of Christ manifest in his face and spirit.

He was the first pope to actually turn the Second Vatican Council to good use. The Council's documents became a means to sharpen St. Peter's sword against the Communists who occupied his country. He had participated in every one of the Council's sessions and had been keenly involved in the Council's declaration of religious freedom as a fundamental right. He saw that the old altar-and-throne model of Catholicism had died with the Habsburg Empire after World War I, though the Church had never conceded this. What was needed now was a new banner of religious freedom to challenge the primary threat to the faith—Communist totalitarianism. When the Council decided to put the liturgy into the vernacular, the future pope, who understands the primacy of culture, saw springs of popular renewal. When the Council called for greater lay participation, it is apparent that what John Paul II envisioned were movements like Opus Dei—which he ardently supports—a Catholic "personal prelature" that seeks to sanctify work and everyday life. Opus Dei adopts the medieval idea that to work is to pray. It is an idea that also motivated the Polish labor union Solidarity, which, with the Church, was the vanguard of Polish resistance to the Communists. Pope John Paul II's greatest triumph was in seeing the totalitarian menace collapse, seeing his fellow Poles chanting, "We want God!," seeing the red tide of Communism ebbing away, evaporating, a nightmare struck by daylight.

He was committed to being an active pope and is, indeed, the greatest globe-trotter in the papacy's 2,000-year history. He has also proved a prolific writer of encyclicals and other papal documents applying the deposit of faith to issues of the contemporary world. As a priest, he had taken a particular interest in advising married couples, and he strongly supported *Humanae Vitae*, which had drawn on his own book *Love and Responsibility*. He reaffirmed *Humanae Vitae* in his own *Veritatis Splendor* in 1993, and two years later condemned abortion in *Evangelium Vitae*, as one of the most terrible manifestations of a "culture of death" that kept the world in its talons.

In 1994, he ruled out further discussion of the priestly ordination of women, saying that such consideration was denied to the Church on the basis of Christ's clear example. That would seem an inarguable proposition, but this, too, proved controversial because it denied two great modern heresies: that sex is a form of class struggle, and that all principles and facts are soluble to modern ideas of equality, self-fulfillment, and human wishes.

Another, somewhat similar, heresy that the pope dispensed with was liberation theology, which viewed Third World Communist revolutions on behalf of the poor as the logical working out of the "social Gospel." In Nicaragua, Pope John Paul II stood on the runway and admonished Father Ernesto Cardenal, who served the Communist Sandinista regime, "Regularize your position with the Church." The picture snapped of the event gave the clear impression, from the pope's gestures, that he was delivering a papal rebuke to a wayward priest.[32] In any event, with the collapse of the Soviet Union, these revolutionary regimes lost their patron, and liberation theology became a footnote in Church history.[33]

The pope did not, however, neglect the Church's mission to the poor. His writings on economics underscored the Church's hostility, not only to Communism, but to economic liberalism if it considers man as a mere cog in a machine, or if it does not recognize the need to pay a man a living wage so that he can support his family, or if the rich neglect their obligation to help the poor. Equally condemned, in wealthy Western nations, is materialism that degrades the human mind and spirit—that can, in fact, in an age of mass marketing and communications, actually subvert the human mind and spirit.

At the level of ecumenism, the pope's greatest wish was to heal the rift with the Eastern Orthodox churches. Their departure, he said, had left the universal Church, in his words, breathing "through only one lung." But his hopes have been disappointed, if not crushed, by the East's lack of enthusiasm. With the Anglicans, the ordination of women widened the schism and also sent a small platoon of Anglican priests and worshipers into the Catholic Church.[34] There have been overtures to the Lutherans and cooperation with Evangelicals, who share the Church's opposition to abortion, but there seems little real hope of the separated Christian churches ever restoring themselves to Catholic unity.

The pope is interested in non-Christian religions, especially Judaism. It was under his pontificate that the Holy See finally extended formal recognition to the state of Israel; and as a Pole, he felt a special kinship with the sufferings of Jews in the Holocaust, though this has not shielded him from occasional verbal attacks when he has marked the graves of Catholic martyrs of the Second World War. He is the first pope to pray in a mosque. And if his repeated apologies for any conceivable Catholic historical offense grate on those of us who wish the Sack of Byzantium to be a feast day of the Church, it would seem churlish to deny the benign intent that motivates them—or the strength that lies behind the apologetic words, for the pope's billion-strong Church does not suffer from what Freud called "the narcissism of small differences" that afflicts the Eastern Orthodox or the hydra-headed schisms of the Protestants.

All the globe-trotting, all the encyclicals and papal letters, all the political activity should not for a moment obscure the deeply powerful personal faith of Pope John Paul II, a faith that makes him not a modern man—though his charm could make him seem that way—but a man whose faith is as old as St. Peter and linked to eternity. When he was struck by an assassin's bullet, he credited his recovery to the Blessed Virgin Mother and prayed at Her shrine in Fatima to express his devotion and gratitude. His hours of prayer are intense. His Catholic belief defines his every thought, utterance, and action, and he clearly seeks to follow the apostolic path of being a missionary for the faith. He has done as much as any man can possibly do. But, as with the early Apostles, there remains a world to be won.

# A FEW GOOD MEN

———⇒●⇐———

I T IS STUNNING, in a way, to think how far the Catholic Church has fallen. During the Crusades it could unite Europeans from the Mediterranean to Norway. Today, the proportion of Catholics in the Scandinavian countries, to take but one example, is no more than 1 percent of the population—a terrible figure unless one notes that even the number of observant Swedish Lutherans is only 3 percent.[1] More than four hundred years after the Swedish Reformation outlawed Catholicism, the faith claims a quarter of all believers in a land that Protestantism has lost.

Throughout Europe such depressing rates of Christian belief point to a gradual extinguishing of the faith. In America, the rates of church attendance are better—but with one serious caveat. In Europe—though this is changing the longer secularism remains dominant—people know what Christianity is and have turned their backs on it. In the United States, people believe what they want and call it Christianity, as a quick perusal of any phone book will show. A similar attitude is spreading to Latin America, where Protestant churches are making inroads on what were once Catholic countries. In Brazil, the rate of Mass attendance among putative Catholics is less than it is in England. In northern Europe, the faith is weak. In southern Europe, things are generally better, but not much. In America, there is room for hope—but it is hope that requires work.

Still, for all its flaws and downward trends, the Catholic Church remains the largest religion in the world,[2] numbering roughly a billion people. It is stretched—unlike any other—over every continent in substantial numbers. It claims to be universal, and is. It is also the most ancient institution in the Western World. Rome and its bishop date back two thousand years. As Paul Johnson has written, "The popes stand for continuity, and they stand for certitude. What they teach is in all essentials what they taught in the first century A.D., when they were hunted men living in the catacombs. That, to most believers, is the central attraction of the Catholic Church, and the chief virtue of the papacy which rules it."[3]

This is true, and the Church stands, above all else, for a defining historic truth that it has faithfully carried on, expounded, and evangelized. But it is equally true that in the third Christian millennium there are powerful new challenges that only the Church can overcome—namely the challenges of science to human integrity. Already there are humans created in test tubes. Human genes and animal genes have been mixed. Man is well on the road to redesigning what it means to be human. It might soon be possible to clone human beings, to create human duplicates that can be raided for body parts by their selfish masters, or even to create animalized humans for special commercial tasks. The object of Dr. Frankenstein might soon become reality—indeed, his dreams easily surpassed.

There is, however, one serious opponent to this future. The Catholic Church is the only substantial institution with a well-articulated philosophy opposed to such artificial genetic engineering of humans, and only if the Catholic Church and Catholic people have sufficient power and influence can it be stopped. If the world truly is ruled by ideas, Catholic ideas need to extend into universities, laboratories, and government councils to a far greater extent than they do now. To stop the *Brave New World* future that might otherwise be in store is an enormous—apparently Sisyphean—task. But it is the Church, and the Church alone, that has even the remotest chance of doing it.

In the late twentieth century, Graham Greene argued in favor of priestly celibacy, saying: "I think that for many people, especially the young, the priesthood must have the attraction of a crack unit. It's an organization which has to train for combat, one which demands self-sacrifice. . . . I'm convinced that the drop in vocations has to do with the fact that we don't put across clearly enough the attraction to be found in a difficult and dangerous calling."[4] Today the Church, more than ever, needs a few good men—or many good men—for such crack units that will win hearts and minds for Christ.

Predicting the future is impossible. Nothing—*pace* the Protestant doctrine of predestination—is preordained. Man can find his own future. We can only work and pray that he does so with the lamp of Christ held high. The triumph of the Catholic Church, from its beginnings with the Apostles filing out from the Holy Land, to its rising to be monarch over kings, to its continued survival and worldwide development against every conceivable persecution is the most extraordinary story in the world. The Church is a great force, and perhaps through it—indeed, only though it—Christendom will rise again.

# NOTES

## PROLOGUE

1. Edmund Burke, *Reflections on the Revolution in France* (Penguin, 1982), p. 170.
2. The validity and meaning of the different accounts of Constantine's vision—and whether he conquered under the sign of the cross, or under Christ's initials, the labarum, which would become Constantine's campaign banner—is usefully debated in D. G. Kousoulas, *The Life and Times of Constantine the Great: The First Christian Emperor* (Rutledge, 1997), pp. 239–244, and in Michael Grant, *Constantine the Great: The Man and His Times* (Scribner, 1993), pp. 131–149. For a terse account, see the entry for Constantine in Simon Hornblower and Anthony Spawforth, eds., *The Oxford Companion to Classical Civilization* (Oxford University Press, 1998). There are, of course, many others.
3. Eusebius, translated by G. A. Williamson and Andrew Louth, *The History of the Church from Christ to Constantine* (Penguin, 1989), pp. 322–324.

## CHAPTER ONE

1. The First of Book of Maccabees 1:1–4. This and all subsequent Biblical citations come, ironically, from the King James Version—a Protestant Bible—because I believe it to be the translation most likely to be found in any English-speaking home, Protestant or Catholic. Many Protestant Bibles, including King James editions, don't include Maccabees at all. A better edition will include it in the Apocrypha. One King James edition I can recommend for its unique design and brief helpful commentary by Catholic convert Lodowick Allison is *The Bible Designed to Be Read as Living Literature, The Old and The New Testament in the King James Version*, arranged and edited by Ernest Sutherland Bates, with updated scholarship and a new introduction by Lodowick Allison (Simon & Schuster, 1993). A good Catholic Bible is the Revised Standard Version published by Ignatius Press. Catholic Bibles include the "apocryphal" or "deuterocanonical" books because Catholic Bibles are based on the third-century-B.C. Greek translation of the Hebrew Bible known as the Septuagint. The Septuagint was the version quoted almost exclusively by the early Christians. On this point, see Bruce

M. Metzger and Michael D. Coogan, eds., *The Oxford Companion to the Bible*
(Oxford University Press, 1993), especially their entries for "Septuagint" and
"Bible." Protestant Bibles, which date more than a thousand years from the first
Christian Bibles, go back to the Hebrew Bible, edited a bit. Eastern Orthodox and
Ethiopian Christians accept the deuterocanonical books and have additional se-
lections of their own. Erwin Lutzer, an evangelical, in his book *Seven Reasons
You Can Trust the Bible* (Moody Press, 1998), p. 187, lists among reasons for rejecting the Apochrypha that they contain historical errors. He cites an argument
made by Norman Geisler and William E. Nix in their book *A General Introduction to the Bible* (Moody Press, 1986): "'It is claimed that Tobit was alive when
the Assyrians conquered Israel (722 B.C.) as well as when Jeroboam revolted
against Judah (931 B.C.),' which would make him at least 209 years old. Yet according to the account, he died when he was only 158 years old." Oh, well, that's
all right then. An evangelical who came to a Catholic interpretation of the Bible
can be found in two books by Mark Shea: *By What Authority?: An Evangelical
Discovers Catholic Tradition* (Our Sunday Visitor, 1996) and *Making Senses Out
of Scripture* (Basilica Press, 1999). High churchmen who find evangelical debates
callow can wisely skip the issue.

2. Rome had some respect for Judaism because it was ancient, and Rome trusted
   tradition and pragmatically doubted innovation. This is why the first Church historian, Eusebius, continually makes the point to his Roman readers that Christianity is the fulfillment of the Old Testament.

3. Matthew 3:2–5.

4. Matthew 3:14.

5. Philip Hughes, *A History of the Church: An Introductory Study*, Vol. One (Sheed
   & Ward, 1937), p. 39. Heresy, however, we have always with us and there is a
   Jesus for every taste; the meaning and the validity of every line of Scripture is disputed. For a liberal feminist view see Thomas Cahill, *Desire of the Everlasting
   Hills: The World Before and After Jesus* (Doubleday, 1999). For a view from a
   historian who believes "in the Bible but not in God"—which is the wrong way
   round, surely—see Robin Lane Fox, *The Unauthorized Version: Truth and Fiction
   in the Bible* (Knopf: 1992). There are also the continuing deliberations of the
   Jesus Seminar, which believes not in the Bible but in a God who is Himself an agnostic. The Seminar is redacting the Gospels to remove anything that is miraculous, a fulfillment of Old Testament prophecy, or would in any other way offend
   the sensibilities of a modern, anti-ecclesiastical skeptic—with predictable *reductio
   ad absurdum* results. There are, of course, many, many more exotic examples.

6. See the discussion of this passage in Ian Wilson, *Jesus: The Evidence* (Regnery,
   2000), pp. 43–44.

7. John 8:12.

8. John 14:6–7.

9. John 2:14–16.

10. Matthew 7:28–29.

11. Matthew 5:17.

12. Matthew 6:24.

13. Matthew 7:14.

14. Matthew 12:8.

15. Mark 14:3–9.

16. Mark 14:25.

17. See Matthew 21:33–46. And there are other examples as well—for instance, Mark, 8:31–33.

18. Matthew 22:21.

19. Luke 22:27.

20. Zechariah 9:9–10.

21. Matthew 16:18–19.

22. Eusebius, translated by G. A. Williamson and Andrew Louth, *The History of the Church from Christ to Constantine* (Penguin, 1989), p. 104.

23. Michael Grant, *Jesus: An Historian's Review of the Gospels* (Scribner, 1977), pp. 203–204. See also Ian Wilson's *Jesus: The Evidence*, especially p. 39; the discussion in William F. Buckley Jr., *Nearer, My God: An Autobiography of Faith* (Doubleday, 1997), chapter seven; Jeffrey L. Sheler, a journalist with *U.S. News and World Report* provides a roundup of modern scholarship in *Is the Bible True? How Modern Debates and Discoveries Affirm the Essence of the Scriptures* (HarperSanFrancisco/Zondervan, 1999); Will Durant is his usual wise and cogent self in *Caesar and Christ: A History of Roman Civilization and of Christianity from Their Beginnings to A.D. 325* (MJF Books, 1971), see especially p. 557. More titles offering a variety of perspectives are offered in the far-from-exhaustive Select, Critical Bibliography at the end of this book.

24. Paul Johnson, *A History of Christianity* (Atheneum, 1987), pp. 27–28.

25. Acts 26:10–11.

26. Acts 26:12–15.

27. Acts 26:16–18.

28. See Acts 7:58.

29. Acts 26:21.

30. II Corinthians 11:24–33.

31. I Corinthians 9:20–21; 10:33.

32. Romans 2:13–15.

33. Romans 8:35–39.

34. Acts 15:28–29.

35. I Corinthians 7:32–33.

36. I Corinthians 14:34–35.

37. I Corinthians 11:15 and 11:7.

38. I Corinthians 6:9–10.
39. II Corinthians 3:6.
40. I Corinthians 13.

## CHAPTER TWO

1. Acts 18:8–15.
2. Acts 2:10.
3. Luke 23:4.
4. Luke 23:22.
5. The phrase is Kipling's; see his poem *Recessional*.
6. Romans 13:1–3.
7. I Timothy 6:7.
8. I Timothy 6:10.
9. Ephesians 5:25.
10. Ephesians 6:5–9.
11. I Corinthians 7:20.
12. Quoted in Eusebius, translated by G. A. Williamson and Andrew Louth, *The History of the Church from Christ to Constantine* (Penguin, 1989), p. 39.
13. Ibid.
14. Gaius Tranquillus Suetonius, translated by Robert Graves, *The Twelve Caesars* (The Folio Society, 1994), p. 240.
15. Ibid., p. 232.
16. Ibid., pp. 227, 241.
17. Ibid., pp. 230–231.
18. Ibid., p. 225.
19. Tacitus, *Annals* 44:3–8, quoted in E. P. Sanders, *Paul* (Oxford University Press, 1991), p. 17.
20. Quoted in Eusebius, p. 36.
21. The classical historian Michael Grant, in his book *Saint Peter: A Biography* (Scribner, 1995), says that it is "probable" that Peter "was executed during Nero's persecutions, possibly, though not necessarily, dying when the persecution began in A.D. 64, or at any rate before Nero's death in 68." See p. 152. Moreover, there has "been a shrine of Peter in the Vatican area since at least A.D. 160–170." Considering that Christians were subject to persecution until the reign of Constantine, this was a significant statement of faith in the tradition. See p. 154.
22. Eusebius, p. 80.
23. Suetonius, p. 306.
24. Ibid., p. 318.
25. Ibid., pp. 308–309.
26. Ibid., p. 318.
27. Eusebius, p. 80.

28. Julian Bennett, *Trajan: Optimus Princeps, A Life and Times* (Indiana University Press, 1997), p. 123.

29. Ibid., pp. xvi–xvii.

30. Ibid., p. 124.

31. Paul Maier, *Pontius Pilate* (Kregel, 1990), pp. 349, 370.

32. Robin Lane Fox, *Pagans and Christians* (Knopf, 1989), p. 434.

33. Ibid., p. 420.

34. For a discussion of James and his relationship to Jesus, see the entry on "Brethren of the Lord" in *The Catholic Encyclopedia* (Encyclopedia Press, 1912).

35. Eusebius, p. 59.

36. Ibid., p. 68.

37. See the discussion in E. P. Sanders, *Paul* (Oxford, 1991), pp. 39–41.

38. Ephesians 4:5.

39. Matthew 16:18.

40. St. Irenaeus, *Adversus Hereses*, iv, 26, 2, quoted in Philip Hughes, *A History of the Church: An Introductory Study*, Volume One (Sheed & Ward, 1937), p. 117, note 1.

41. I Corinthians 15:3–8.

42. Hughes, p. 39.

43. Matthew 16:19.

44. Quoted in Hughes, p. 67. William A. Jurgens makes a good case that the letter could be dated earlier, circa A.D. 80, in his *The Faith of the Early Fathers*, Volume One (The Liturgical Press, 1970), p. 7.

45. Quoted in Philip Hughes, *A Popular History of the Catholic Church* (Macmillan, 1953), p. 8.

46. Quoted in Alan Schreck, *A Compact History of the Catholic Church* (Servant, 1987), p. 19.

47. Philip Hughes, *A Popular History of the Catholic Church*, p. 7.

48. Joseph Cardinal Ratzinger, *Introduction to Christianity* (Ignatius Press, 1990), p. 43.

49. Hebrews 11:1.

50. G. K. Chesterton, *Collected Works, Volume II* (Ignatius, 1986), *The Everlasting Man*, pp. 380–381.

## CHAPTER THREE

1. Matthew 19:12.

2. Matthew 10:16–34.

3. The source for this story is Eusebius, see the translation by G. A. Williamson and Andrew Louth, *The History of the Church from Christ to Constantine* (Penguin, 1989), pp. 206–267. The bishop would likely have been Pope Fabian, though Eusebius's editors doubt the story's truth (see p. 406).

4. This title generally goes to St. Hippolytus earlier in the third century, but there is now some doubt about this; see the interesting discussion in J.N.D. Kelly, *The Oxford Dictionary of the Popes* (Oxford University Press, 1996), p. 15.

5. This line was recently cited in a wonderful essay, "Chesterton at the *Fin de Siècle*: Orthodoxy and the Perception of Evil," by William Oddie, *The Chesterton Review*, volume xxv, number three, August 1999, pp. 329–43. The Wilde quote is on p. 343.

6. This is the estimate of Alan Schreck, in *The Compact History of the Catholic Church* (Servant, 1987), p. 22.

7. Quoted in D. G. Kousoulas, *The Life and Times of Constantine the Great: The First Christian Emperor* (Rutledge, 1997), p. 96.

8. Eusebius, p. 258.

9. Ibid., p. 264.

10. Ibid., p. 265.

11. Quoted in Will Durant, *Caesar and Christ: A History of Roman Civilization and of Christianity from Their Beginnings to A.D. 325*, (MJF Books, 1971), p. 597. A rather stiffer version is given by William A. Jurgens, in his *The Faith of the Early Fathers*, Volume One (The Liturgical Press, 1970), p. 116, though Tertullian's acidic line just above it is worth quoting: "But it is mainly the practice of such a love which leads some to put a brand upon us. 'See,' they say, 'how they love one another'; for they themselves hate each other. 'And how they are ready to die for one another,' they themselves being more inclined to kill each other."

12. Durant, p. 613.

13. Thomas Cahill quotes to good effect the classical historian Donald Kagan making a similar point: "To understand the ancient Greeks and Romans we must be alert to the great gap that separates their views, and those of most people throughout history, from the opinions of our own time. They knew nothing of ideas such as would later be spoken in the Sermon on the Mount, and they would have regarded them as absurd if they had. . . . Modern states, especially those who have triumphed in the Cold War . . . are quite different. . . . The most important of these [differences] is the Judeo-Christian tradition. . . . There are now barriers of conscience in the way of acquiring and maintaining power and using it to preserve the peace that would have been incomprehensible to the Greeks and Romans." See *Desire of the Everlasting Hills: The World Before and After Jesus* (Doubleday, 1999), pp. 308–309.

14. Durant, p. 612.

15. Ibid., p. 599.

16. The Church's opposition to contraception passed from tradition into Church law at the Council of Braga in 572.

17. Owen Chadwick, in his *A History of Christianity* (St. Martin's, 1996), dates its first use to Rome in 180 as a baptismal rite; see p. 286. For a full discussion of the

making of the Apostles' Creed, see the entry in *The Catholic Encyclopedia* (Encyclopedia Press, 1912).

18. There are some minor variants in the early written records, but it appears that the creed was regularized in this form by at least the latter half of the fifth century.

19. What remained was the Catholic doctrine on baptism: that is, it is the sacrament itself that matters, not the person delivering it (in this case repentant schismatic priests). As such, the Church affirmed St. Paul's teaching that no sincere Christian can be separated from the love of God.

## CHAPTER FOUR

1. Constantine's mother, Helena, went on pilgrimage in Palestine and is credited with having found the true Cross. The story is retold in Evelyn Waugh's novel *Helena*.

2. Quoted in D. G. Kousoulas, *The Life and Times of Constantine the Great: The First Christian Emperor* (Rutledge, 1997), p. 304.

3. Ibid., pp. 310–311.

4. The Trinitarian argument is too complex to go into here; suffice it to say that it was the tradition of the faith and can be seen in Matthew 28:19: "Go ye therefore, and teach all nations, baptizing them in the name of the Father, and of the Son, and of the Holy Ghost." Such Trinitarian formulations were used in baptismal rites of the apostolic Church, and the dogma of the Trinity was central to the historic faith.

5. Edward Gibbon, *The History of the Decline and Fall of the Roman Empire* (The Folio Society, 1985), vol. 3, *The Revival and Collapse of Paganism*, p. 43.

6. Quoted in Kousoulas, p. 353.

7. Or Victor, as *The Catholic Encyclopedia* (Encyclopedia Press, 1912) less romantically has it. The other was Vincentius. See the entry for "Nicea, the First Council." Vito is the name given in Kousoulas, p. 357.

8. Quoted in Kousoulas, p. 378.

9. Of course, in Imperial Russia under the czar—the Russian Caesar—Caesaropapism would continue into the early twentieth century, until Slavic Christianity too succumbed, first to secular democrats, then to Bolsheviks who brought with them a new age of anti-Christian terror.

10. Taxes were so high that even beggars and prostitutes allegedly felt the pinch of Constantine's internal revenue service.

11. Quoted in Kousoulas, p. 449.

## CHAPTER FIVE

1. Quoted in Michael P. Riccards, *A Republic, If You Can Keep It: The Foundation of the American Presidency, 1700–1800* (Greenwood Press, 1987), p. 41.

2. Quoted in William A. Jurgens, *The Faith of the Early Fathers*, Volume Two (The Liturgical Press, 1979), p. 190.

3. Quoted in William A. Jurgens, *The Faith of the Early Fathers*, Volume One (The Liturgical Press, 1970), p. 346. The letter dates from A.D. 341.

4. Will Durant, *Caesar and Christ: A History of Roman Civilization and of Christianity from Their Beginnings to A.D. 325* (MJF Books, 1971), p. 602.

5. Quoted in Edward Gibbon, *The History of the Decline and Fall of the Roman Empire* (The Folio Society, 1985), vol. 3, *The Revival and Collapse of Paganism*, p. 40.

6. Ibid., pp. 40–41.

7. Ibid., pp. 68–69.

8. Ibid., p. 70.

9. Quoted in ibid., p. 92.

10. Ibid., p. 88.

11. Ibid., pp. 98–99.

12. Ibid., pp. 166–167.

13. Quoted in Philip Hughes, *A History of the Church: An Introductory Study*, Volume One (Sheed & Ward, 1937), p. 224.

14. Ibid.

15. Lord Macaulay, *The Lays of Ancient Rome* (Regnery, 1997), p. 19.

16. Quoted in G. R. Watson, *The Roman Soldier* (Cornell University Press, 1969), p. 49.

17. See the entry for Ambrose in *The Catholic Encyclopedia* (Encyclopedia Press, 1912).

18. The great soldier-emperor Trajan was also a Spaniard.

19. Gibbon, p. 277. In a footnote, Gibbon remarks that the ancient historian "Pacatus prefers the rustic life of Theodosius to that of Cincinnatus; the one was the effect of choice, the other of poverty."

20. Pope Damasus I reigned from 366 to 384.

21. Quoted in Gibbon, p. 295. Gibbon's ironical commentary follows: "The faith of a soldier is commonly the fruit of instruction, rather than of inquiry; but as the emperor always fixed his eyes on the visible landmarks of orthodoxy which he had so prudently constituted, his religious opinions were never affected by the specious texts, the subtle arguments, and the ambiguous creeds of the Arian doctors."

22. Quoted in Gibbon, p. 323.

23. See the entry for St. Ambrose in *The Catholic Encyclopedia*.

24. Gibbon, p. 324.

25. In the East, things were different. Constantine's son, Constantius II, had established the Caesaropapist principle: "My will is canon law!" This was heresy, of course, and St. Hilary of Poitiers even wrote a book entitled *Against Constantius*, but it remained true for the East. Constantius's outburst—for which Athanasius is the source—is quoted in Hughes, p. 256.

26. The story is retold in *The Catholic Encyclopedia* entry for St. Ambrose. The source is Paulinus of Milan, Ambrose's contemporary and biographer.

27. Hughes, p. 267.

28. Quoted in ibid., p. 268.

29. Quoted in ibid., p. 269.

30. Quoted in the entry for St. Ambrose in *The Catholic Encyclopedia.*

31. Ibid.

32. Quoted in *The Catholic Encyclopedia* entry for Pope Liberius.

33. Ibid.

34. Gibbon, p. 60.

35. For a discussion of the controversy, see the entry under Liberius in *The Catholic Encyclopedia.*

36. Quoted in Will Durant, *The Age of Faith: A History of Medieval Civilization—Christian, Islamic, and Judaic—from Constantine to Dante: A.D. 325–1300* (MJF Books, 1950), p. 52.

## CHAPTER SIX

1. Quoted in Edward Gibbon, *The History of the Decline and Fall of the Roman Empire* (The Folio Society, 1985), vol. 3, *The Revival and Collapse of Paganism,* p. 333.

2. Ibid., p. 29.

3. All of which is *not* to say that Christians were not patriotic Romans. They were— a point that Christopher Dawson makes in his book *The Making of Europe: An Introduction to the History of European Unity* (Barnes & Noble Books, 1994), pp. 39–41; he notes Salvianus's critique in an endnote (see number 9, p. 246). A brief biographical entry for Salvianus can be found in *The Catholic Encyclopedia* (Encyclopedia Press, 1912). However bad things were in Rome, Gibbon cites Salvianus as describing Roman Carthage as worse. In Gibbon's paraphrase, it was the sink in which "the peculiar vices of each country were collected." Gibbon, footnote, p. 184. It was in Carthage, of course, that St. Augustine taught rhetoric.

4. St. Augustine, translated by Rex Warner, *The Confessions of St. Augustine* (New American Library, 1963), p. 116.

5. Ibid.

6. Ibid., pp. 182–183.

7. Though, to be fair, Greek inconstancy, even to heretical ideas, ensured that the heresy died out faster in the East than in the West.

8. Quoted in Eamon Duffy, *Saints and Sinners: A History of the Popes* (Yale University Press, 1997), p. 31.

9. This is the translation given in *The Catholic Encyclopedia* (Encyclopedia Press, 1912) of this famous line. See the entry for Pelagius and Pelagianism.

10. Ibid.

11. The phrase is Paul Johnson's; see chapter one of his *A History of the English People* (Weidenfeld & Nicolson, 1985).

12. See for instance the discussion in Will Durant, *The Age of Faith: A History of Medieval Civilization—Christian, Islamic, and Judaic—from Constantine to Dante: A.D. 325–1300* (MJF Books, 1950), pp. 71–73.

13. William A. Jurgens, *The Faith of the Early Fathers*, Volume Three (The Liturgical Press, 1979), p. 1.

14. Quoted in ibid., p. 38.

15. Philip Hughes, *A Popular History of the Catholic Church* (Macmillan, 1953), p. 60.

16. Quoted in Paul Johnson, *The Papacy* (Barnes & Noble Books, 1997), pp. 45–46.

17. Quoted in Thomas Bokenkotter, *A Concise History of the Catholic Church* (Image Books, 1990), p. 83.

18. This is the definition given in E.A. Livingstone (editor), *The Concise Oxford Dictionary of the Christian Church* (Oxford University Press, 2000), p. 397.

19. Bokenkotter, pp. 84–85.

20. The traditional hierarchy of churches was Rome, then Alexandria or Antioch—they were fierce rivals—followed by an unambitious Jerusalem.

21. This is the translation given in *The Catholic Encyclopedia*. See the entry for St. Patrick.

22. The quotes in this paragraph are as translated by Philip Hughes, *A History of the Church: An Introductory Study,* Volume Two (Sheed & Ward), pp. 88, 90.

23. This is *The Catholic Encyclopedia* translation. See the entry for St. Benedict of Nursia.

24. Quoted in ibid.

## Chapter Seven

1. As quoted in *The Catholic Encyclopedia* (Encyclopedia Press, 1912), under the entry for Pope St. Hormisdas.

2. Quoted in Eamon Duffy, *Saints and Sinners: A History of the Popes* (Yale University Press, 1997), p. 40.

3. Ibid., p. 50.

4. Ibid., p. 48.

5. The most famous telling of this story is found in Venerable Bede, *A History of the English Church and People* (Barnes & Noble Books, 1993), pp. 99–100. The *History* dates from 731.

6. Quoted in Alan Schreck, *The Compact History of the Catholic Church* (Servant, 1987), p. 38.

7. Quoted in Richard Fletcher, *The Barbarian Conversion: From Paganism to Christianity* (Henry Holt, 1997), p. 112.

8. Quoted in Philip Hughes, *A History of the Church: An Introductory Study*, Volume Two (Sheed & Ward), p. 147.

9. Quoted in *The Catholic Encyclopedia* entry for Iconoclasm.

10. It is also what prompted some Greek Orthodox clerics in the year 2001 to call Pope John Paul II the "arch-heretic" and "two-horned grotesque monster of Rome." See John Thavis, "Bold Moves: Upcoming Papal Trips Pose Major Ecumenical Test," *The Arlington Catholic Herald*, 5 April 2001, p. 23.

## CHAPTER EIGHT

1. See the excellent version by G. Murphy with S. J. Ronald (translator and commentator), *The Heliand: The Saxon Gospel* (Oxford University Press, 1992).
2. Quoted in Will Durant, *The Age of Faith: A History of Medieval Civilization—Christian, Islamic, and Judaic—from Constantine to Dante: A.D. 325–1300* (MJF Books, 1950), p. 471.
3. Quoted in *The Catholic Encyclopedia* (Encyclopedia Press, 1912). See the entry for Pope St. Gregory VII.
4. Quoted in Eamon Duffy, *Saints and Sinners: A History of the Popes* (Yale University Press, 1997), p. 98.
5. Mark 13:13; see also Luke 21:17 and Matthew 24:9.
6. Matthew 16:18.

## CHAPTER NINE

1. See the description of the Council of Clermont, where the pope called for the Crusade, in Steven Runciman, *A History of the Crusades* (The Folio Society, 1994), vol. 1, *The First Crusade and the Foundation of the Kingdom of Jerusalem*, pp. 88–91.
2. Actually, some of them followed a holy goose and a holy goat—others a holy donkey—"who were carried in the front, and to whom these worthy Christians ascribed an infusion of the divine spirit." See Edward Gibbon, *The History of the Decline and Fall of the Roman Empire* (The Folio Society, 1985), vol. 7, *The Normans in Italy and the Crusades,* pp. 265–266. See also the footnote on p. 266: "Had these peasants founded an empire, they might have introduced, as in Egypt, the worship of animals." The worship of animals would have to wait, however, for the arrival of childless, well-to-do, late-twentieth-century women.
3. Robert Harrison (translator and introducer), *The Song of Roland* (Mentor, 1970), pp. 19–20.
4. Ibid., p. 33.
5. The Western practice came from the Jewish Passover, such as Jesus would have known.
6. The *filioque* also did not translate easily or well into Greek and for that reason is not used in Catholic churches in Greece.
7. Quoted in Hilaire Belloc, *The Crusades: The World's Debate* (TAN Books, 1992), p. 238.
8. Quoted in Will Durant, *The Age of Faith: A History of Medieval Civilization—Christian, Islamic, and Judaic—from Constantine to Dante: A.D. 325–1300* (MJF Books, 1950), p. 652.

CHAPTER TEN

1.  The translation is from Desmond Seward, *The Monks of War: The Military Religious Orders* (Penguin, 1972), p. 152.

2.  His given name is the wonderfully evocative Nicholas Breakspear.

3.  Christopher Tyerman, *Who's Who in Early Medieval England* (Shepheard-Walwyn, 1996), p. 202.

4.  See the entry for St. Thomas Becket in *The Catholic Encyclopedia* (Encyclopedia Press, 1912).

5.  "His private life," writes Sir Winston Churchill of Thomas Becket, "had always been both pious and correct." See Sir Winston Churchill, *A History of the English-Speaking Peoples* (Dorset Press, 1956), vol. 1, *The Birth of Britain*, p. 206.

6.  Quoted in J.N.D. Kelly, *The Oxford Dictionary of Popes* (Oxford University Press, 1996), p. 186.

7.  Philip was of the Ghibelline party and Hohenstaufen family that stood for German imperial ambition. Otto was of the Welf family and Guelph party that posed as pro-papal.

8.  Quoted in Eamon Duffy, *Saints and Sinners: A History of the Popes* (Yale University Press, 1997), pp. 111–112.

9.  Otto's original rival, Philip of Swabia, was already dead at the hands of a murderer.

10. St. Francis was the first recorded case of the stigmata.

11. The University of Naples had been created in 1224 by the Holy Roman Emperor Frederick II, in whose court Thomas's father served. Its royal, secular foundation was rare, as universities were a medieval invention of the Church. Naples followed the establishment of the other great medieval universities: Salamanca in Spain; Oxford and Cambridge in England; and a half-century earlier, the universities of Paris and Bologna.

12. Quoted in Will Durant, *The Age of Faith: A History of Medieval Civilization—Christian, Islamic, and Judaic—from Constantine to Dante: A.D. 325–1300* (MJF Books, 1950), p. 963.

13. Quoted in the entry for Aquinas in *The Catholic Encyclopedia*.

14. See Ralph M. McInerny, *A Student's Guide to Philosophy* (ISI Books, 1999).

CHAPTER ELEVEN

1.  E. A. Livingstone (editor), *The Concise Oxford Dictionary of the Christian Church* (Oxford University Press, 2000), points out that the earliest sources refer not to Peter Waldo, but to a man named Valdes; see p. 615. Though many Waldenses subsequently returned to the Church, the anti-clerical Puritanism of the heretics set an example for pre-Reformation Protestantism.

2.  This little ditty is generally known as "The Catholic Sun." I stumbled across it in Robert J. Hutchison, *When in Rome: A Journal of Life in Vatican City* (Double-

day, 1998), p. 1—a delightful book. A variation is employed as a stanza in Belloc's poem "Heretics All," which can be found in Hilaire Belloc, *Sonnets and Verse* (Sheed & Ward, 1944), p. 128.

3. Not a Reformation Protestant ideal, but more of a mainline Protestant one since the 1930 Lambeth Council when the Anglican Church became the first Christian church to accept artificial contraception.

4. These numbers are taken from Hilaire Belloc, *The Great Heresies* (TAN Books, 1991), pp. 93–94; Philip Hughes, *A History of the Church: An Introductory Study* (Sheed & Ward, 1935), vol. 2, p. 393, gives the numbers as 700 versus 40,000. Belloc's numbers include camp followers and auxiliaries.

5. Quoted in Will Durant, *The Age of Faith: A History of Medieval Civilization—Christian, Islamic, and Judaic—from Constantine to Dante: A.D. 325–1300* (MJF Books, 1950), pp. 773–774.

6. See the discussion in Kevin Orlin Johnson, *Why Do Catholics Do That?* (Ballantine Books, 1994), pp. 24–26. Johnson's book is much better than its flippant title might suggest.

7. An example is given in Durant, p. 780.

8. See the discussion in ibid., pp. 782–783.

9. Spain did not employ the inquisition as tool of state until the fifteenth century.

10. These anti-papal Italians are probably best described as *gli bastardi*.

11. Ambrose Bierce, *The Shadow on the Dial and Other Essays* (A.M. Robertson, 1909), p. 108.

12. Celestine wrote one of the cardinals that the college's failure to elect a pope—it took more than two years—was a scandal inviting God's wrath. The cardinals assented, saying in essence, "*You* want the job; it's yours."

13. This is the version given in *The Catholic Encyclopedia* (Encyclopedia Press, 1912) entry for Pope Boniface VIII.

## Chapter Twelve

1. This is a very simplified version of a very complicated issue. For further reading in general sources see *The Catholic Encyclopedia* (Encyclopedia Press, 1912), entries for "Pope John XXII" and "Fraticelli."

2. After his death, his four cardinals suffered a schism of their own. Three of them elected Clement VIII to the schismatic crown. The fourth cardinal elected Benedict XIV. Clement and his antipapal court were reconciled with Rome in 1429, and the pope rather magnanimously made Clement bishop of Majorca. Benedict disappeared into complete obscurity, but we are told that "in 1467, in Armagnac, some fanatics were still awaiting the vindication of Benedict XIV." See J.N.D. Kelly, *Oxford Dictionary of Popes* (Oxford University Press, 1996), pp. 240–241. See also *The Catholic Encyclopedia* (Encyclopedia Press, 1912), entries for "Martin V" and "schism, western."

3. This is known as the doctrine of "Ockham's razor." See Bertrand Russell, *A History of Western Philosophy* (Simon & Schuster, 1972), p. 472, where he points out that while Ockham "is best known" for this maxim, it "is not to be found in his works." Perhaps the most famous analyst of Ockham's influence on the modern mind is Richard Weaver. In particular see p. 3 in his book *Ideas Have Consequences* (University of Chicago Press, 1984): "It was William of Occam who propounded the fateful doctrine of nominalism, which denies that universals have a real existence. His triumph tended to leave universal terms mere names serving our convenience. The issue ultimately involved whether there is a source of truth higher than, and independent of, man; and the answer to that question is decisive for one's view of the nature and destiny of mankind. The practical result of nominalist philosophy is to banish the reality which is perceived by the intellect and to posit as reality that which is perceived by the senses. With this change in the affirmation of what is real, the whole orientation of culture takes a turn, and we are on the road to modern empiricism."

4. It should perhaps be noted that neither orthodox Franciscans nor monastic orders who devote themselves to even greater austerity—such as the Capuchin Friars Minor—nor any other Catholic institution is communist; Communism is, in fact, a heresy.

5. A bishop should not, by Ockham's and Wyclif's lights, own land in the first place.

6. Monasticism was certainly contrary to Wyclif's self-interest. He lost an academic post when his college became a monastic institution. See the very interesting entry for Wyclif in Michael Hicks, *Who's Who in Late Medieval England* (Shepheard-Walwyn, 1991), pp. 146–147. "Always an extremist" is Hicks' phrase.

7. Where priests did not die, they sometimes fled. For a brief, interesting discussion of this point, see Simon Schama, *A History of England: At the Edge of the World? 3500 B.C.—1603 A.D.* (Talk Miramax Books, 2000), pp. 232, 238.

## CHAPTER THIRTEEN

1. Philip the Fair's battles with Pope Boniface VIII in the late thirteenth and early fourteenth century were another example of Gallicanism—at least of a sort.

2. Mehmed thought highly of his enemy Vlad III, known as "the Impaler," prince of Walachia (in Romania), ally of the Hungarians, Crusader against the Turks, and the historical inspiration for Dracula. When Vlad wasn't killing Turks, he liked to kill his own people, especially those of German heritage—tens of thousands of whom he sadistically executed or tortured to death. Vlad was applauded by Orthodox Russians of his time and is still a hero to Romanians, who obviously like the slap of firm, impaling government. Like Vlad III, Mehmed II enjoyed torture for its own sake; and among sadists, there must exist, one imagines, a certain bond—and gag.

3. These are the numbers given by Geoffrey Regan in his book *The Guinness Book of Decisive Battles* (Guinness Publishing, 1992), pp. 78–79.

4. The Borgias were not an Italian family; they were Spanish. "Borjas" became corrupted in Italian to Borgia.

5. Nevertheless, we shouldn't sell these valiant Crusaders short. In particular, the battle fought in Belgrade in 1456 was crucial in stemming the Turkish advance. One battlefield commander in that tremendous victory was a Franciscan friar and papal representative, John Capistrano, later made a saint. He is commemorated in the Spanish Mission of San Juan Capistrano in California, which, appropriately for a Franciscan, is famous for the annual return of its swallows.

6. Joan of Arc was made a saint in 1920. Mark Twain, of all people, was devoted to her memory, wrote a novel about her, and concluded: "Taking into account, as I have suggested before, all the circumstances . . . she is easily and by far the most extraordinary person the human race has ever produced." See Mark Twain, *Joan of Arc* (Ignatius Press, 1989), p. 452.

7. Unfortunately, his agent of restraint was Tomas de Torquemada, Dominican monk and Queen Isabella's confessor. He was a man unsuited to the task.

8. Innocent VIII affirmed Henry VII as king of England, thus establishing the Tudor dynasty.

9. Quoted in Will Durant, *The Renaissance: A History of Civilization in Italy from 1304–1576 A.D.* (MJF Books, 1981), p. 407.

10. Celibacy is a matter of Church discipline, which can be changed. It is not a matter of Church doctrine or dogma, which cannot.

11. Will Durant points out that such "bonfires were an old custom with mission friars." See Durant, p. 156.

12. Quoted in Philip Hughes, *A History of the Church: An Introductory Study* (Sheed & Ward, 1947), vol. 3, p. 493.

13. Preceding this, Savonarola had been challenged by a Franciscan to a "trial by fire." Sensing a trap, another Dominican stood in for Savonarola. At the appointed hour, the Franciscan disappointed everyone by not showing up.

14. Quoted in Durant, p. 422.

15. Between Alexander and Julius was the month-long pontificate of Pius III.

16. It is equally rare in our own time, when politicians attempt to buy voters with government programs.

17. Quoted in Durant, p. 488.

18. Ibid., p. 484.

19. The story—and its credibility and implications—is well discussed in Evelyn Waugh, *Robbery Under Law: The Mexican Object Lesson* (The Akadine Press, A Common Reader Edition, 1999), pp. 222–234; and Graham Greene, *The Lawless Roads* (Penguin, 1982), pp. 86–90.

20. These figures come from Alan Schreck, *The Compact History of the Catholic Church* (Servant, 1987), p. 151.

21. See Will Durant, *The Reformation: A History of European Civilization from Wyclif to Calvin: 1300–1564* (MJF Books, 1985), p. 216.

22. Quoted in the entry for Torquemada in *The Catholic Encyclopedia* (Encyclopedia Press, 1912).

23. See for instance Henry Kamen, *The Spanish Inquisition: A Historical Revision* (Yale University Press, 1998), surely the final word on the subject.

24. This is the figure given by historian H. C. Lea in his multivolume history of the Inquisition as cited in Will Durant, *The Reformation*, p. 215. Henry Kamen says Lea's history "remains still the definitive history of the tribunal. Though Lea had strong [pro-Catholic] prejudices that he expressed uncompromisingly, his work once and for all rescued the tribunal from the make-believe world of invented history, and placed it firmly in the arena of documented fact." Quoted in Kamen, p. 312.

25. See Durant, *The Reformation*, p. 641.

## CHAPTER FOURTEEN

1. Quoted in Andrew Wheatcroft, *The Habsburgs: Embodying Empire* (Viking, 1995), pp. 117–118.

2. Quoted in Desmond Seward, *The Monks of War: The Military Religious Orders* (Penguin, 1995), p. 265.

3. Quoted in Wheatcroft, p. 138.

4. Quoted in Bard Thompson, *Humanists and Reformers: A History of the Renaissance and Reformation* (Eerdmans, 1996), pp. 403–404.

5. The phrase comes from Martin Amis's (not recommended) book of essays on America.

6. See Will Durant, *The Reformation: A History of European Civilization from Wyclif to Calvin: 1300–1564* (MJF Books, 1985), p. 344.

7. Quoted in William Manchester, *A World Lit Only by Fire: The Medieval Mind and the Renaissance* (Little, Brown & Company, 1993), p. 140.

8. Ibid., p. 139.

9. Ibid.

10. Quoted in *The Catholic Encyclopedia* (Encyclopedia Press, 1912), entry for Martin Luther.

11. Ibid.

12. See William Shakespeare's *Henry V*, act IV, scene I.

13. Quoted in *The Catholic Encyclopedia* entry for Martin Luther.

14. Quoted in Durant, p. 345.

15. The words are Jacques Barzun's. See Barzun, *From Dawn to Decadence: 500 Years of Western Cultural Life, 1500 to the Present* (HarperCollins, 2000).

16. Quoted in Durant, p. 349.

17. Ibid., p. 351.

18. Quoted in Philip Hughes, *A History of the Church: An Introductory Study* (Sheed & Ward, 1947), vol. 3, p. 520.

19. See Bard Thompson, who mentions the celebrated Swiss theologian Karl Barth, in particular, p. 394.

20. Quoted in Hughes, p. 518.

21. Ibid., p. 513.

22. Quoted in *The Catholic Encyclopedia* entry for Martin Luther.

23. See Barzun, pp. 17–18.

24. See Durant, p. 355.

25. See Hughes, p. 509.

26. Quoted in Durant, p. 355.

27. Ibid., p. 363.

28. See Manchester, p. 175.

29. See Thompson, p. 404.

30. Quoted in *The Catholic Encyclopedia* entry for Martin Luther.

31. Quoted in Durant, p. 367.

32. Ibid., p. 377.

33. Quotes taken from Paul Johnson, *A History of Christianity* (Atheneum, 1987), p. 283.

34. Quoted in Durant, p. 393.

35. Ibid., p. 390.

36. Manchester, p. 178; the other statistics come from Durant, p. 392.

37. Both quotes are cited in Durant, p. 448.

38. Ibid., p. 450.

39. Quoted in Johnson, p. 286.

40. Quoted in *The Catholic Encyclopedia* entry for John Calvin.

41. See Manchester, p. 191, and Durant, p. 474.

42. Quoted in Will Durant and Ariel Durant, *The Age of Voltaire: A History of Civilization in Western Europe from 1715 to 1756, with Special Emphasis on the Conflict Between Religion and Philosophy* (MJF Books, 1992), p. 728.

43. Quoted in Durant, *The Reformation*, p. 466.

44. Manchester, p. 191; see also Durant, *The Reformation*, pp. 473–474.

45. The adage is the author's.

46. Noted by Durant, *The Reformation,* p. 471.

## CHAPTER FIFTEEN

1. Quoted in John Cannon and Ralph Griffiths, *The Oxford Illustrated History of the British Monarchy* (Oxford University Press, 1988), p. 318.

2. A picture of Henry's petition to the Vatican can be seen in Eamon Duffy, *Saints and Sinners: A History of the Popes* (Yale University Press), p. 160.

3. Quoted in Simon Schama, *A History of Britain: At the Edge of the World? 3500 B.C.—1603 A.D.* (Talk Miramax Books, 2000), p. 301.

4. Winston S. Churchill, *A History of the English-Speaking Peoples* (Dorset Press, 1956), volume ii, *The New World*, p. 31.

5. Ibid.

6. Quoted in the entry for St. Thomas More in *The Catholic Encyclopedia* (Encyclopedia Press, 1912).

7. The quoted phrases are cited in Peter Ackroyd, *The Life of Thomas More* (Doubleday, 1998), p. 231.

8. See William Manchester, *A World Lit Only by Fire* (Little, Brown & Company, 1993), p. 191.

9. Quoted in ibid., pp. 214–215.

10. Ibid., p. 215.

11. Quoted in Will Durant, *The Reformation: A History of European Civilization from Wyclif to Calvin: 1300–1564* (MJF Books, 1985), p. 558.

12. Quoted in Robert, Lacey, *The Life and Times of Henry VIII* (Weidenfeld and Nicolson, 1996), p. 139.

13. Quoted in C.R.N. Routh, *Who's Who in Tudor England* (Shepheard-Walwyn, 1990), p. 94.

14. Quoted in Durant, p. 567.

15. For the psychology behind Cromwell's conversion, see Hilaire Belloc, *Characters of the Reformation* (TAN Books, 1992), p. 58.

16. Quoted in Schama, p. 322.

17. On this last point, see, for instance, Ian Wilson, *Shakespeare the Evidence* (Headline, 1994).

18. For a discussion of this, see the chapter on Mary Stuart in Belloc, *Characters of the Reformation*.

19. Quoted in Owen Dudley Edwards, *Macaulay* (Weidenfeld and Nicolson, 1988), pp. 96–97.

20. Quoted in C.R.N. Routh, p. 205.

21. Quoted in Evelyn Waugh, *Edmund Campion* (Little, Brown & Company, 1952), pp. 221–222.

22. Routh, p. 342.

23. Quoted in *The Catholic Encyclopedia* entry for "The Counter-Reformation."

24. This dictum comes from the southern writer Andrew Nelson Lytle.

25. Quoted in Durant, p. 926.

26. Quoted in Will Durant and Ariel Durant, *The Age of Reason Begins: A History of European Civilization in the Period of Shakespeare, Bacon, Montaigne, Rembrandt, Galileo, and Descartes: 1558–1648* (MJF Books, 1961), p. 140.

## CHAPTER SIXTEEN

1. Quoted in Geoffrey Regan, *The Guinness Book of Decisive Battles* (Guinness Publishing, 1992), p. 100.
2. Quoted in Will and Ariel Durant, *The Age of Reason Begins* (MJF Books, 1961), p. 448. All Protestants can be grateful that at least these "savage" Dutchmen did not superstitiously venerate the sacred heart of Jesus and treat it as an icon.
3. Part of Alva's psychological warfare was to play "bad cop" to King Philip's "good cop"—a role Philip didn't play very well.
4. See the *Oxford Family Encyclopedia* (Oxford University Press, 1997), p. 475, for the Netherlands. Compare to *The Cambridge Encyclopedia* (Cambridge University Press, 1990), p. 843, to see how Dutch belief is rapidly shrinking. For the more stable Belgian statistics, see *Oxford*, p. 78, or *Cambridge*, p. 125.
5. Quoted in Durant, p. 455.
6. Quoted in ibid., p. 363.
7. The Edict was unpopular, and Pope Clement VIII condemned it as an unnecessary and unworthy surrender.
8. In his youth, rather like St. Patrick, Vincent de Paul had been captured by pirates and sold as a slave to the Muslims.
9. This is the version quoted in C. P. Hill, *Who's Who in Stuart Britain* (Shepheard-Walwyn, 1988), p. 234.
10. Ibid., pp. 325–326.
11. Quotes come from Winston S. Churchill, *A History of the English-Speaking Peoples*, volume ii, *The New World* (Dorset Press, 1956), p. 389.
12. Emphasis in the original. See James Boswell, *The Life of Johnson* (Penguin, 1984), pp. 109–110.

## CHAPTER SEVENTEEN

1. Jacques Barzun, *From Dawn to Decadence: 1500 to the Present, 500 Years of Western Cultural Life* (HarperCollins, 2000), p. 40.
2. These two quotes come from Galileo's entry in *The Catholic Encyclopedia* (Encyclopedia Press, 1912).
3. Quoted in Peter Kreeft, *Christianity for Modern Pagans: Pascal's Pensées Edited, Outlined and Explained* (Ignatius Press, 1993), p. 231.
4. Quoted in ibid., p. 285.
5. Joseph Cardinal Ratzinger, *Introduction to Christianity* (Ignatius Press, 1990), p. 43. This quote was cited in chapter two, but it bears repeating.
6. Quoted in Will Durant and Ariel Durant, *The Age of Louis XIV: A History of European Civilization in the Period of Pascal, Molière, Cromwell, Milton, Peter the Great, Newton, and Spinoza: 1648–1715* (MJF Books, 1991), p. 65.
7. Quoted in Kreeft, p. 241.
8. See the entry for Jacques-Benigne Bossuet in *The Catholic Encyclopedia*.

9. Both quotes taken from Durant and Durant, *The Age of Louis XIV,* p. 432. The latter comes from the English Catholic historian Lord Acton.

10. John Locke, *The Reasonableness of Christianity,* edited and introduced by George W. Ewing (Regnery Gateway, 1989), pp. 192–194.

11. Locke, p. xiv.

## CHAPTER EIGHTEEN

1. Will Durant and Ariel Durant, *The Age of Voltaire: A History of Civilization in Western Europe from 1715 to 1756, with Special Emphasis on the Conflict Between Religion and Philosophy* (MJF Books, 1992), p. 753.

2. Quoted in ibid., p. 4.

3. Quoted in ibid., p. 741.

4. Quoted in Bertrand Russell, *A History of Western Philosophy* (Touchstone, Simon and Schuster, 1972), p. 688.

5. Quoted in Durant, p. 739.

6. Quoted in ibid., p. 739.

7. Quoted in Erik von Kuehnelt-Leddihn, *Leftism Revisited: From de Sade and Marx to Hitler and Pol Pot* (Regnery Gateway, 1990), p. 67.

8. Quoted in Durant, p. 751.

9. Quoted in ibid., pp. 760–761.

10. This is the translation given in J.N.D. Kelly, *The Oxford Dictionary of the Popes* (Oxford University Press, 1996), p. 299.

11. It is of course open to debate whether the Jesuits' approach was the right one, *vide* the old Dominican joke: "Question: If the Dominicans were formed to combat the Albigensians and the Jesuits to combat Protestants, what's the difference? Answer: You don't see any Albigensians."

12. Quoted in Philip Hughes, *A Popular History of the Catholic Church* (Macmillan, 1953), p. 203.

13. Quoted in Nancy Mitford, *Frederick the Great* (E. P. Dutton, 1984), p. 278.

14. Hughes, p. 211.

15. Quoted in *The Catholic Encyclopedia* (Encyclopedia Press, 1912) entry for Pope Benedict XIV.

16. C.R.L. Fletcher and Rudyard Kipling, *Kipling's Pocket History of England* (Greenwich House, 1983) p. 240.

17. Franklin P. Cole, ed., *They Preached Liberty* (Liberty Press, no date), pp. 160–161.

18. Both quotes taken from Kuehnelt-Leddihn, pp. 50–51.

19. Not to mention Polish military adventurers of Catholic faith like Thaddeus Kosciusko and Count Casimir Pulaski, who served the Americans as officers of engineers and cavalry respectively.

20. Alexis de Tocqueville, *Democracy in America,* translated by George Lawrence, edited by J. P. Mayer (Doubleday/Anchor, 1969), pp. 450–452.

21. See Norman Gelb, *Less Than Glory: A Revisionist's View of the American Revolution* (G. P. Putnam's Sons, 1984), pp. 231–232. Gelb's view of the war is similar to the author's.

22. J. M. Roberts, *The Pelican History of the World* (Penguin, 1985), p. 693.

23. Ibid., p. 689.

24. For the marquis de Sade's influence, see Kuehnelt-Leddihn, chapter seven.

25. Stephen Tonsor, ed., *Reflections on the French Revolution: A Hillsdale Symposium* (Regnery Gateway, 1990). This is the figure given by John Willson in his essay "The Gods of Revolution," p. 28.

26. Quoted in Kuehnelt-Leddihn, p. 82.

## CHAPTER NINETEEN

1. Will Durant and Ariel Durant, *The Age of Napoleon: A History of European Civilization from 1789 to 1815* (MJF Books, 1975), p. 259.

2. Quoted in ibid., p. 256.

3. Jacques Barzun, *From Dawn to Decadence: 1500 to the Present, 500 Years of Western Cultural Life* (HarperCollins, 2000), p. 249.

4. Quoted in *The Catholic Encyclopedia* (Encyclopedia Press, 1912), entry for "Napoleon I (Bonaparte)."

5. Quoted in Eamon Duffy, *Saints and Sinners: A History of the Popes* (Yale University Press, 1997), p. 206.

6. Quotes come from *The Catholic Encyclopedia* entry for Napoleon; the historian Alan Schom, however, considers the source of this conversation, Charles Tristan de Montholon, a congenital liar, though not necessarily in this case. Schom's biography of *Napoleon Bonaparte* (HarperCollins, 1997) is hostile to its subject.

7. See Schom, p. 787.

8. A good entrée into his thought is Joseph de Maistre, *On God and Society,* edited by Elisha Greifer and translated with the assistance of Laurence M. Porter (Henry Regnery Company, Gateway Editions, 1959).

9. Quoted in Duffy, p. 215.

10. Quoted in the entry for François René de Chateaubriand in *The Catholic Encyclopedia.*

11. This is the title, in fact, of Henry Kissinger's doctoral thesis: Henry Kissinger, *A World Restored: Metternich, Castlereagh and the Problems of Peace, 1812–1822* (Orion, 2000).

12. Quoted in Thomas Bokenkotter, *A Concise History of the Catholic Church* (Image/Doubleday, 1990), pp. 281–282.

13. This might be worrying given Germany's later history were it not for the saving grace that so little education of any kind can break through the congenital stupidity of the average American student.

14. Quoted in the entry for the Oxford Movement in *The Catholic Encyclopedia.*

15. John Henry Cardinal Newman, *An Essay on the Development of Christine Doctrine* (University of Notre Dame Press, 1989), pp. 7–8.

16. The full quote is: "I have studied politics so that my children would have the liberty to study mathematics and philosophy, and in order that their children will have the right to study painting, poetry, music, architecture, statuary, tapestry, and porcelain." It is cited in Michael P. Richards, *A Republic, If You Can Keep It: The Foundation of the American Presidency, 1700–1800* (Greenwood Press, 1987). See the dedication and acknowledgments pages.

17. Quoted in *The Catholic Encyclopedia* entry for John Henry Newman.

18. The line is from Kipling's poem "If."

19. Quoted in Roger Ellis, *Who's Who in Victorian Britain* (Shepheard-Walwyn, 1997), p. 78.

20. Quoted in ibid., p. 423.

21. Lytton Strachey, *Eminent Victorians* (Harvest/HBJ, no date), p. 18.

22. Quoted in Gertrude Himmelfarb, *Victorian Minds: A Study of Intellectuals in Crisis and Ideologies in Transition* (Ivan R. Dee, 1995), p. 186.

23. Ibid., p. 187.

24. See entry in *The Catholic Encyclopedia* for "England (After 1558)."

25. See Byron Farwell, *Mr. Kipling's Army* (W. W. Norton & Company, 1981), p. 80.

26. Ibid., p. 219.

27. For a discussion of this, see Roy MacGregor-Hastie, *Never to Be Taken Alive* (Sidgwick & Jackson, 1985), p. 139.

28. They often now appear in the secular popular media.

29. Quoted in Paul Johnson, *A History of Christianity* (Atheneum, 1987), p. 464.

30. Quoted in Samuel Eliot Morison, *The Oxford History of the American People*, vol. 2, 1789–1877 (Mentor, 1972), p. 451.

31. Ibid.

32. Allen Tate, *Jefferson Davis: His Rise and Fall* (J. S. Sanders & Company, 1998), p. 287.

33. Margaret Mitchell, *Gone with the Wind* (Macmillan, Anniversary Edition, 1975), p. 250.

34. F. Scott Fitzgerald, *This Side of Paradise* (Scribner, 1920), p. 25.

35. Quoted in James Hennesey, S.J., *American Catholics: A History of the Roman Catholic Community in the United States* (Oxford University Press, 1981), p. 156.

36. Willa Cather, *Death Comes for the Archbishop* (Modern Library, 1993), p. 336.

## CHAPTER TWENTY

1. Philip Hughes, *A Popular History of the Catholic Church* (Macmillan, 1953), p. 254.

2. James Hennesey, S.J., *American Catholics: A History of the Roman Catholic Community in the United States* (Oxford University Press, 1981), p. 225.

3. Ephesians 1:10.

4. Quoted in Eamon Duffy, *Saints and Sinners: A History of the Popes* (Yale University Press, 1997), p. 252.

5. For a discussion of this see J.A.S. Grenville, *A World History of the Twentieth Century, Volume One 1900–45: Western Dominance* (Fontana, 1983), pp. 119–120.

6. Winston S. Churchill, *The World Crisis*, revised and abridged (Scribner, 1931), p. 4.

7. See Robert Royal, *The Catholic Martyrs of the Twentieth Century* (Crossroad, 2000), pp. 44 and 62. See also Hughes, p. 267.

8. Royal, p. 51.

9. Quoted in Duffy, p. 258.

10. Quoted in ibid.

11. For contrasting views of German attitudes see Johannes Steinhoff, Peter Pechel, and Dennis Showalter, *Voices from the Third Reich: An Oral History* (Regnery Gateway, 1989) and Daniel Jonah Goldhagen's controversial *Hitler's Willing Executioners: Ordinary Germans and the Holocaust* (Knopf, 1996). See also Jan Tomasz Gross, *Neighbors: The Destruction of the Jewish Community in Jedwabne* (Princeton University Press, 2001), for a truly terrifying account of how easily, willingly, and even joyfully collaborators would massacre their Jewish neighbors—to the astonishment of the Nazis.

12. See the fascinating article "Don't Blame Eugenics, Blame Politics," by Terence Kealey, in *The Spectator* (of London), 17 March 2001, pp. 10–11.

13. Quoted in Royal, p. 153.

14. Quoted in John Cornwell, *Hitler's Pope: The Secret History of Pius XII* (Viking, 1999), p. 183.

15. See, for instance, Ronald J. Rychlak, *Hitler, the War, and the Pope* (Our Sunday Visitor Books, 2000), p. 93, and the stunning article "Pius XII and the Jews," by Rabbi David G. Dalin, in *The Weekly Standard*, 26 February 2001, pp. 31–39 (see in particular pp. 35–36, where one of the cartoons is reprinted). Rabbi Dalin calls Rychlak's book "the best and most careful of the [many] recent works" on Pope Pius XII and the Second World War, "an elegant tome of serious, critical scholarship."

16. See Thomas Bokenkotter, *A Concise History of the Catholic Church* (Image/Doubleday, 1990), p. 350, and Rychlak, p. 94, for examples.

17. Quoted in Rychlak, p. 94.

18. Evelyn Waugh, *Robbery Under Law: The Mexican Object-Lesson* (A Common Reader Edition/Akadine Press, 1999), p. 122.

19. Ibid., pp. 121–124.

20. A good account of the war in Mexico can be found in Douglas Porch, *The French Foreign Legion: A Complete History of the Legendary Fighting Force* (HarperCollins, 1991), chapter seven. For younger readers, it's worth trying to find a used copy of the out-of-print classic by Wyatt Blassingame, *The French Foreign Legion* (Landmark/Random House, 1955).

21. A charming anecdote about Catholic life in the Legion is to be found in Christian Jenning's memoir *A Mouthful of Rocks: Modern Adventures in the Foreign Legion* (Atlantic Monthly Press, 1989), p. 22: "This was the padre assigned to our unit. He wore full combat kit and a large silver crucifix on a chain, which matched his parachute wings. . . . A Spanish recruit I had been playing poker against started making faces and gesturing behind the Padre's back, when suddenly, without taking his eyes off the Frenchmen to whom he had been talking, the priest jerked his elbow backwards into the Spaniard's face, slamming him against an oven."

22. Waugh, p. 238.

23. Graham Greene, *The Lawless Roads* (Penguin, 1982), p. 66.

24. Ibid., p. 19.

25. For more information see Royal, p. 16.

26. Ibid., p. 17.

27. Ibid., pp. 31–32.

28. Paul Johnson, *A History of Christianity* (Atheneum, 1987), p. 484. Johnson criticizes the Catholic Church for recognizing the Nazi threat but surrendering too easily to it in the 1930s. As the Church showed with the *Cristeros*, however, it was less inclined to raise a sword than previously.

29. Royal, pp. 108–109.

30. Hugh Thomas, *The Spanish Civil War* (Simon & Schuster, 1986), p. 271. The war became a focus of international attention when Hitler and Mussolini intervened on the side of the Nationalists led by Francisco Franco, and Stalin intervened on the side of the Republicans. For many Western idealists, the Republican cause was the cause of the hour. A famous account of the fighting—and the internal infighting on the Left—is George Orwell's *Homage to Catalonia*. Some, however, did intervene on the side of the Right, including the poet Roy Campbell, part of whose sojourn in Spain provides the conclusion to his autobiography, *Light on a Dark Horse*. The standard biography of the *caudillo* who led Spain after the war is *Franco*, by Paul Preston. It is a hostile portrait.

31. Graham Greene, *The Power and the Glory* (Penguin, 1977), pp. 221–222.

## CHAPTER TWENTY-ONE

1. Quoted in Ronald J. Rychlak, *Hitler, the War, and the Pope* (Our Sunday Visitor, 2000), pp. 14–15.

2. Quoted in ibid., p. 18.

3. Ibid.

4. Ibid., p. 105.

5. Quoted in ibid., p. 110.

6. Eamon Duffy makes this point in *Saints and Sinners: A History of the Popes* (Yale University Press, 1997), p. 261.

7. Quoted in ibid., p. 263.

8. Evelyn Waugh, *The Sword of Honour Trilogy, Men at Arms* (Penguin, 1984), p. 11.

9. Quoted in "Pius XII and the Jews," by Rabbi David G. Dalin, in *The Weekly Standard*, 26 February 2001, p. 31.

10. These figures are taken from Robert Leckie's superlative one-volume history of World War II, *Delivered from Evil: The Saga of World War II* (Perennial Library, 1987), p. 914.

11. See Robert Royal, *The Catholic Martyrs of the Twentieth Century: A Comprehensive World History* (Crossroad, 2000), p. 193.

12. Specifically, John Cornwell, author of *Hitler's Pope* (1999); Garry Wills, author of *Papal Sin* (2000); and James Carroll, author of *Constantine's Sword* (2001).

13. Rabbi David G. Dalin, "Pius XII and the Jews." The line about the "biggest club" is from p. 32, as is the first half of the longer quote, beginning, "But Jews . . ." The second half of the quote, beginning with "The Talmud," comes from p. 39.

14. Ibid., pp. 36–37.

15. Quoted in Alan Schreck, *The Compact History of the Catholic Church* (Servant, 1987), p. 110.

16. John Lukacs, *Five Days in London: May 1940* (Yale University Press, 1999), p. 218.

17. Ibid., p. 214.

18. Quoted in Martin Gilbert, *Never Despair: 1945–1965* (Houghton Mifflin, 1988), p. 200.

19. Duffy, p. 266.

20. Quoted in Royal, p. 217.

21. This is the title of a book by Dietrich Bonhoeffer, a Lutheran pastor martyred by the Nazis.

22. Quoted in Paul Johnson, *Modern Times: The World from the Twenties to the Eighties* (Harper & Row, 1983), p. 593.

23. Wilhelm Röpke, *A Humane Economy,* (ISI Books, 1998), p. 8.

24. Quoted in Duffy, p. 262.

25. Alan Schreck reminds us (see Schreck, p. 151) that, "There have been more appearances of Mary reported in the last one hundred and fifty years than at any other time in the Catholic Church's history." These appearances are important for the historian if for no other reason than that they illustrate the wellsprings of popular devotion. The appearance of Mary to Bernadette Soubirous at Lourdes in 1858 has made Lourdes a major and miraculous site of pilgrimage and healing. On a much smaller scale, the appearance of Mary at the little village of Pontmain, France, in 1871, led not only to the consecration of a barn into a chapel, but to the erection of a basilica to Our Lady of Hope in 1900—reminding us of the faith of the Middle Ages, and the fact that the Church is a living body of ever renewed faith.

26. For a fascinating article on this subject, see "Chesterton at the Fin de Siècle: Orthodoxy and the Perception of Evil," in *The Chesterton Review*, August 1999; see also chapter one of Joseph Pearce, *Literary Converts: Spiritual Inspiration in an Age of Unbelief* (Ignatius Press, 2000).

27. "Christianity: How We Lost Our Faith," *The Week* (British edition), 21 April 2001, p. 16.

28. "Statistics of the Week," *The Week* (British edition), 17 March 2001, p. 17. If there is any comfort to be found in these figures it is that in Sweden, the *majority* of children are born out of wedlock, and, of course, the economy is still perfectly sound.

29. Cardinal Ratzinger makes an interesting point on clerical celibacy and marriage. "People need to get straight in their minds that times of crisis for celibacy are always times of crisis for marriage as well. For, as a matter of fact, today we are experiencing not only violations of celibacy; marriage itself is becoming increasingly fragile as the basis of our society. . . . The candidate for the priesthood has to recognize the faith as a force in his life, and he must know that he can live celibacy only in faith. Then celibacy can also become a testimony that says something to people and that also gives them the courage to marry. The two institutions are interconnected. If fidelity in the one is no longer possible, the other no longer exists: one fidelity sustains the other." See Joseph Cardinal Ratzinger, *Salt of the Earth: The Church at the End of the Millennium, An Interview with Peter Seewald* (Ignatius Press, 1997), pp. 196–197.

30. Quoted in Kevin Phillips, *Post-Conservative America* (Random House, 1982), p. 18.

31. Tom Wolfe, *The Purple Decades* (Farrar Straus Giroux, 1982), p. 332.

32. See George Weigel, *Witness to Hope: The Biography of Pope John Paul II* (HarperCollins, 1999) p. 454, for an interesting discussion of this incident.

33. Save in some seminaries and academic theology departments.

34. Including this author.

## EPILOGUE

1. See George Weigel, *Witness to Hope* (HarperCollins, 1999), pp. 591–592.

2. In 2000, for the first time, Islam surpassed the Catholic Church as the world's largest religion, but only if one ignores schisms within the Muslim world.

3. Paul Johnson, *The Papacy* (Barnes & Noble Books, 1997), p. 219.

4. Quoted in Joseph Pearce, *Literary Converts: Spiritual Inspiration in an Age of Unbelief* (Ignatius Press, 2000), p. 418.

# SELECT, CRITICAL BIBLIOGRAPHY

Note: A few books are listed only in the endnotes, not here, and vice versa. I should also note that a wide variety of Catholic materials, from classics like St. Augustine's *City of God* to papal encyclicals to reference works like St. Thomas Aquinas's *Summa Theologica,* are now on the Internet.

Ackroyd, Peter. *The Life of Thomas More* (Doubleday, 1998).

Aquinas, Thomas (edited by Ralph McInerny). *Selected Writings* (Penguin, 1999).

St. Augustine (translated by Rex Warner). *The Confessions of St. Augustine* (New American Library, 1963).

———. (translated by J.H.S. Burleigh). *Of True Religion* (Henry Regnery Company, 1959).

———. (edited, with an introduction by Henry Paolucci, and an interpretive analysis by Dino Bigongiari). *The Political Writings of St. Augustine* (Gateway Editions, 1987).

Barone, Michael. *The New Americans: How the Melting Pot Can Work Again* (Regnery, 2001). Deft ethnic history with chapters on Irish, Italian, and Latino Catholic immigrants.

Barzun, Jacques. *From Dawn to Decadence: 500 Years of Western Cultural Life, 1500 to the Present* (HarperCollins, 2000). Rather annoyingly designed, but interesting nevertheless.

Bates, Ernest Sutherland, and Lodowick Allison (editors). *The Bible Designed to Be Read as Living Literature, The Old and The New Testament in the King James Version* (Simon & Schuster, 1993).

Bede. *A History of the English Church and People* (Barnes & Noble Books, 1993).

Belloc, Hilaire. *Characters of the Reformation* (TAN Books, 1992). Belloc is fast becoming one of the most neglected of great English writers of the last century. Though he wrote too much, and the padding can show, he deserves to be rediscovered.

———. *The Crusades: The World's Debate* (TAN Books, 1992).

———. *The Great Heresies* (TAN Books, 1991).

———. *The Path to Rome* (Gateway Editions, 1987).

———. *Sonnets and Verse* (Sheed & Ward, 1944).

Bennett, Julian. *Trajan: Optimus Princeps, A Life and Times* (Indiana University Press, 1997).

Bierce, Ambrose (edited by S.O. Howes). *The Shadow on the Dial and Other Essays* (A.M. Robertson, 1909).

Blassingame, Wyatt. *The French Foreign Legion* (Landmark/Random House, 1955). A good book for kids.

Bloom, Allan. The *Closing of the American Mind: How Higher Education Has Failed Democracy and Impoverished the Souls of Today's Students*, (Simon and Schuster, 1987).

Bogle, Joanna. *A Book of Feasts and Seasons* (Gracewing, 1998). A wonderful book for families looking to celebrate the Christian calendar—and a reminder of how our ancestors had Christianity deeply threaded through everyday life. The focus is on English—and English Catholic—Christianity.

Bokenkotter, Thomas. *A Concise History of the Catholic Church* (Image Books, 1990). A counterpoint book to this one, focused on liberal Catholicism; oddly dated by its fascination with the Sandinistas and "liberation theology."

Bonhoeffer, Dietrich. *The Cost of Discipleship* (Touchstone, 1995).

Boswell, James (edited and abridged by Christopher Hibbert). *The Life of Johnson* (Penguin, 1984).

Buckley, William F., Jr. *Nearer, My God: An Autobiography of Faith* (Doubleday, 1997). Not a celebrity's reminiscences, but a very useful and interesting discussion of the Catholic faith.

Burckhardt, Jacob (translated by S.G.C. Middlemore). *The Civilization of the Renaissance in Italy* (Harper & Brothers, published in two volumes, 1958. This edition is introduced by Benjamin Nelson and Charles Trinkaus). A classic study. Burckhardt prefers the pagan to the Catholic, but is forced to admit that the roots of modern science are in the Catholic Middle Ages and that the Catholic Renaissance was intellectually free. He notes: "Everybody had some cowled or frocked relative, some prospect of assistance or future gain from the Church. . . . Yet it must never be forgotten that all this did not hinder people from writing and speaking freely. The authors of the most scandalous satires were themselves mostly monks and beneficed priests."

Burke, Edmund (edited by Peter J. Stanlis). *The Best of Burke: Selected Writings and Speeches of Edmund Burke* (Regnery, Conservative Leadership Series, 1999). A superlative, handsomely produced collection of the essential works.

———. *Reflections on the Revolution in France* (Penguin, 1982).

Bury, J. B. *The Life of St. Patrick: And His Place in History* (Book-of-the-Month Club, 1999).

Cahill, Thomas. *Desire of the Everlasting Hills: The World Before and After Jesus* (Doubleday, 1999).

———. *How the Irish Saved Civilization: The Untold Story of Ireland's Heroic Role from the Fall of Rome to the Rise of Medieval Europe* (Anchor Books, 1995).

*Cambridge Biographical Dictionary* (Cambridge University Press, 1990).

*The Cambridge Encyclopedia* (Cambridge University Press, 1990).

Campbell, Roy. *Light on a Dark Horse* (Henry Regnery Company, 1952). The rollicking memoir of a South African lyric poet, Catholic convert, and man of action.

Cannon, John, and Ralph Griffiths. *The Oxford Illustrated History of the British Monarchy* (Oxford University Press, 1988).

Cantor, Norman F. (general editor). *The Encyclopedia of the Middle Ages* (Viking, 1999). A superb reference book.

Carpenter, Humphrey. *Jesus* (Oxford University Press, 1986). Another in Oxford's excellent "Past Masters" series.

*Catechism of the Catholic Church* (Image/Doubleday, 1995). It's all here, in the first official, updated summary of Catholic beliefs in four hundred years. There are several editions available, but I like this one for aesthetic reasons; it's the most compact.

Cather, Willa. *Death Comes for the Archbishop* (Modern Library, 1993).

*The Catholic Encyclopedia* (Encyclopedia Press, published in 16 volumes, 1912). A remarkable achievement and an essential reference. It is now also available on the Internet.

Cecil, Lord Robert, and H. J. Clayton. *Our National Church* (Frederick Warne & Co., 1913). Dated, obviously, but a good, patriotic account of the Anglican church.

Chadwick, Owen. *A History of Christianity* (St. Martin's, 1996).

*Chambers Dictionary of World History* (Chambers, 2000).

Chesterton, G. K. *Collected Works,* Volume One (Ignatius Press, 1986).

———. *Collected Works,* Volume Two (Ignatius Press, 1986). This volume contains *St. Francis of Assisi, St. Thomas Aquinas,* and *The Everlasting Man*—the last is particularly interesting because it puts the Incarnation at the heart of history, which makes Chesterton virtually unique. *The Everlasting Man* was meant as a rejoinder to H. G. Wells's *The Outline of History.*

———. *Collected Works,* Volume Three (Ignatius Press, 1990).

———. *Collected Works,* Volume Four (Ignatius Press, 1987).

Churchill, Sir Winston. *A History of the English-Speaking Peoples* (Dorset Press, published in four volumes, 1956).

———. *The World Crisis* (revised and abridged) (Scribner, 1931).

Clark, Kenneth. *Civilization: A Personal View* (Harper and Row, 1969). Clark was a great art historian and eventual Catholic convert.

Cole, Franklin P. (editor). *They Preached Liberty* (Liberty Press, no date).

Colley, Linda. *Britons: Forging the Nation, 1707–1837* (Yale University Press, 1992). Tells how Protestantism became one of the means to unify the United Kingdom— along with trade, empire, and the monarchy.

Collins, James (editor). *Philosophical Readings in Cardinal Newman* (Henry Regnery Company, 1961).

Cornwell, John. *Hitler's Pope: The Secret History of Pius XII* (Viking, 1999). A shameful book, exploitative and sensationalistic.

Craughwell, Thomas J. *The Wisdom of the Popes* (St. Martin's Press, 2000).

Cunningham, Lawrence S. *The Catholic Faith: An Introduction* (Paulist Press, 1987).

Dante (Dante Alighieri, edited and introduced by Paolo Milano). *The Portable Dante,* (Penguin, 1982).

Davis, Burke. *The Campaign that Won America: The Story of Yorktown.* (Eastern Acorn Press, 1997). Mesmerizing study of the Yorktown campaign; especially good at highlighting the role played in the American victory by the French at sea and on land with such as "the swaggering hussars of the Duke de Lauzun's Legion, with saddlecloths of tiger skin and tall fur hats. . . . Many of the Legion were Irish and German mercenaries; there were also Poles, men with huge mustaches who carried lances and curiously curved sabers. . . . led by a swarm of French noblemen—barons, counts and viscounts, and at least one prince . . ." thus adding Catholic color to the proceedings.

Davis, Kenneth C. *Don't Know Much About the Bible: Everything You Need to Know About the Good Book but Never Learned* (Eagle Brook/William Morrow, 1998). Don't look to this book for Catholic orthodoxy. It's the Bible broken down and analyzed for hip, modern, liberal suburbanites.

Dawson, Christopher. *The Making of Europe: An Introduction to the History of European Unity* (Barnes & Noble Books, 1994). Dawson is one of the classic Catholic historians.

Díaz, Bernal (translated and with an introduction by J. M. Cohen). *The Conquest of New Spain* (Penguin, 1963). The amazing story of how Cortez conquered Mexico, as told by one of his Conquistadors. Read it.

Duffy, Eamon. *Saints and Sinners: A History of the Popes* (Yale University Press, 1997). A very readable and attractive account of papal history.

———. *The Stripping of the Altars: Traditional Religion in England, 1400–1580* (Yale University Press, 1992).

Durant, Will. *The Age of Faith: A History of Medieval Civilization—Christian, Islamic, and Judaic—from Constantine to Dante:* A.D. *325–1300* (MJF Books, 1950). *The Story of Civilization* series, of which these are the most relevant volumes, is a brilliant work of integral history—evenhanded, wise, witty, and highly recommended. Especially not to be missed is the "Epilogue in Elysium"—an imagined dialogue between Voltaire and Pope Benedict XIV that closes the volume *The Age of Voltaire.*

———. *Caesar and Christ: A History of Roman Civilization and of Christianity from Their Beginnings to* A.D. *325* (MJF Books, 1971).

———. *The Reformation: A History of European Civilization from Wyclif to Calvin: 1300–1564* (MJF Books, 1985).

———. *The Renaissance: A History of Civilization in Italy from 1304–1576* A.D. (MJF Books, 1981).

———. *The Story of Philosophy: The Lives and Opinions of the Greater Philosophers* (Washington Square Press, 1961).

Durant, Will, and Ariel Durant. *The Age of Louis XIV: A History of European Civilization in the Period of Pascal, Molière, Cromwell, Milton, Peter the Great, Newton, and Spinoza: 1648–1715* (MJF Books, 1991).

———. *The Age of Napoleon: A History of European Civilization from 1789 to 1815* (MJF Books, 1975).

———. *The Age of Reason Begins: A History of European Civilization in the Period of Shakespeare, Bacon, Montaigne, Rembrandt, Galileo, and Descartes: 1558–1648* (MJF Books, 1961).

———. *The Age of Voltaire: A History of Civilization in Western Europe from 1715 to 1756, with Special Emphasis on the Conflict Between Religion and Philosophy* (MJF Books, 1992).

Edwards, Owen Dudley. *Macaulay* (Weidenfeld & Nicolson, 1988).

Ellis, Alice Thomas. *Serpent on the Rock: A Personal View of Christianity* (Hodder & Stoughton, 1994). A novelist's meditation on the decline of the faith in modern Britain and Ireland.

Ellis, Roger. *Who's Who in Victorian Britain* (Shepheard-Walwyn, 1997). This and the other volumes in the *Who's Who in British History* series, scattered throughout these listings, are wonderfully direct and full of character, contention, and authorial personality.

*The Essential Catholic Handbook: A Summary of Beliefs, Practices, and Prayers* (Ligouri, 1997). A good companion to the *Catechism*.

Eusebius (translated by G. A. Williamson and Andrew Louth). *The History of the Church from Christ to Constantine* (Penguin, 1989).

Faragher, John Mack (general editor). *The American Heritage Encyclopedia of American History* (Henry Holt, 1998). Politically correct history at your fingertips.

Farwell, Byron. *Mr. Kipling's Army* (W. W. Norton & Company, 1981).

Fitzgerald, F. Scott. *This Side of Paradise* (Scribner, 1920).

Fletcher, C.R.L., and Rudyard Kipling. *Kipling's Pocket History of England* (Greenwich House, 1983).

Fletcher, Richard. *The Barbarian Conversion: From Paganism to Christianity* (Henry Holt, 1997). Tries to answer the question of why the barbarians accepted the faith of Rome.

Fox, Robin Lane. *Pagans and Christians* (Knopf, 1989).

———. *The Unauthorized Version: Truth and Fiction in the Bible* (Knopf, 1992). Fox is a skeptic.

Fromkin, David. *The Way of the World: From the Dawn of Civilization to the Eve of the Twenty-First Century* (Vintage Books, 2000). A secular, not a religious, view of history.

Gardiner, Juliet, and Neil Wenborn (editors). *The History Today Companion to British History* (Collins & Brown, 1995). A very good reference book.

Gelb, Norman. *Less Than Glory: A Revisionist's View of the American Revolution* (G. P. Putnam's Sons, 1984).

Gibbon, Edward. *The History of the Decline and Fall of the Roman Empire* (The Folio Society, published in eight volumes, 1985).

Grant, Michael. *Constantine the Great: The Man and His Times* (Scribner, 1993).

———. *Jesus: An Historian's Review of the Gospels* (Scribner, 1977).

———. *Saint Peter: A Biography* (Scribner, 1995).

Greeley, Andrew. *The Catholic Imagination* (University of California Press, 2000). Greeley—priest, sociologist, novelist—builds on the work of David Tracy to explore the meaning of the unique qualities of the Catholic imagination. A key point, which touches the historian, is this: "Catholic theologians and artists tend to emphasize the presence of God in the world, while the classic works of Protestant theologians tend to emphasize the absence of God from the world. The Catholic writers stress the nearness of God to His creation, the Protestant writers the distance between God and His creation; the Protestants emphasize the risk of superstition and idolatry, the Catholics the dangers of a creation in which God is only marginally present. Or, to put the matter in different terms, Catholics tend to accentuate the immanence of God, Protestants the transcendence of God."

Greene, Graham. *The Lawless Roads* (Penguin, 1982). An extremely atmospheric account of Greene's journey into Mexico to witness the persecution of the Church.

———. *The Power and the Glory* (Penguin, 1977).

Grenville, J.A.S. *A World History of the Twentieth Century,* Volume One: *1900–45: Western Dominance* (Fontana, 1983). A handy history; well done.

Gross, Jan Tomasz. *Neighbors: The Destruction of the Jewish Community in Jedwabne* (Princeton University Press, 2001).

Harrison, Robert (translator and introducer). *The Song of Roland* (Mentor, 1970). Highly recommended to capture the spirit of the Middle Ages.

Haythornthwaite, Philip J. *Invincible Generals: Gustavus Adolphus, Marlborough, Frederick the Great, George Washington, Wellington* (Indiana University Press, 1992).

Hennesey, James, S.J. *American Catholics: A History of the Roman Catholic Community in the United States* (Oxford University Press, 1981). A well-balanced and reliable history.

Hibbert, Christopher. *Cavaliers and Roundheads: The English Civil War, 1642–1649* (Scribner, 1993).

Hicks, Michael. *Who's Who in Late Medieval England* (Shepheard-Walwyn, 1991).

Hill, C. P. *Who's Who in Stuart Britain* (Shepheard-Walwyn, 1988).

Himmelfarb, Gertrude. *The De-Moralization of Society: From Victorian Virtues to Modern Values* (Knopf, 1995).

———. *Victorian Minds: A Study of Intellectuals in Crisis and Ideologies in Transition* (Ivan R. Dee, 1995).

Hitti, Philip K. *Islam: A Way of Life.* (Gateway Editions, 1987).

———. *The Arabs: A Short History.* (Gateway Editions, 1990).

Hollis, Christopher. *Death of a Gentleman* (Burns Oates, 1944). Hollis was a Catholic convert and contemporary of Evelyn Waugh at Oxford. This is the first volume in the "Fossett Trilogy"—novels of ideas that are even more provocative now than they could possibly have been in the 1940s.

———. *Fossett's Memory* (Hollis and Carter, 1945).

———. *Letters to a Sister* (Hollis and Carter, 1947).

*The Holy Bible*, in the King James Version, and *The Holy Bible*, in the Revised Standard Version, Catholic Edition.

Hornblower, Simon, and Anthony Spawforth (editors). *The Oxford Companion to Classical Civilization* (Oxford University Press, 1998).

Housman, A. E. *The Collected Poems of A. E. Housman* (Henry Holt, 1966).

Howard, Michael, and William Roger Louis. *The Oxford History of the Twentieth Century* (Oxford University Press, 1998). Modern times made dull. Useful to highlight the poverty of contemporary thought.

Howarth, David. *1066: The Year of Conquest* (Barnes & Noble Books, 1993).

Hughes, Philip. *A History of the Church: An Introductory Study*, Volume One: *The World in Which the Church Was Founded* (Sheed & Ward, 1937). The Hughes histories are standards that, unfortunately, are part of the large corpus of Catholic literature that started to fall out of print with the collapse of Catholic publishing after Vatican II.

———. *A History of the Church: An Introductory Study,* Volume Two: *The Church and the World the Church Created* (Sheed & Ward, 1935).

———. *A History of the Church: An Introductory Study*, Volume Three: *The Revolt Against the Church: Aquinas to Luther* (Sheed & Ward, 1947).

———. *A Popular History of the Catholic Church* (Macmillan, 1953).

Hutchison, Robert J. *When in Rome: A Journal of Life in Vatican* City (Doubleday, 1998). A Catholic journalist offers an entertaining account of a yearlong sabbatical in Rome.

Jaki, Stanley L. *Newman's Challenge* (Eerdmans, 2000).

Jenning, Christian. *A Mouthful of Rocks: Modern Adventures in the Foreign Legion* (Atlantic Monthly Press, 1989). Jennings is a Catholic, and his book is easily classifiable as a quick and morally offensive read.

Jeremias, Joachim. *The Problem of the Historical Jesus* (Fortress Press, 1964).

Johnson, Kevin Orlin. *Why Do Catholics Do That?* (Ballantine Books, 1994). An art historian looks at the symbolism, traditions, and practices of the Church—and finds signs of ancient Rome, among other things. Highly recommended.

Johnson, Paul. *The Birth of the Modern: World Society, 1815–1830* (HarperCollins, 1991). All of Johnson's histories are idiosyncratic, tub-thumping, and well worth reading.

———. *A History of Christianity* (Atheneum, 1987).

———. *A History of the American People* (HarperCollins, 1997).

———. *A History of the English People* (Weidenfeld & Nicolson, 1985).

————. *Modern Times: The World from the Twenties to the Eighties* (Harper & Row, 1983).

————. *The Papacy* (Barnes & Noble Books, 1997). Johnson provides the introduction and afterword; the actual chapters are contributed by scholars. The overall effect is not the usual hash, but a very readable history.

Jones, A.H.M. *Constantine and the Conversion of Europe* (The English Universities Press, 1965).

Jurgens, William A. *The Faith of the Early Fathers*, Volume One (The Liturgical Press, 1970). One of a three-volume trove of extensively cross-referenced nuggets from the early Church Fathers.

————. *The Faith of the Early Fathers,* Volume Two (The Liturgical Press, 1979).

————. *The Faith of the Early Fathers,* Volume Three (The Liturgical Press, 1979).

Kamen, Henry. *The Spanish Inquisition: A Historical Revision* (Yale University Press, 1998).

Kee, Howard Clark. *Jesus in History: An Approach to the Study of the Gospels* (Harcourt Brace Jovanovich, 1977).

Kelly, J.N.D. *The Oxford Dictionary of the Popes* (Oxford University Press, 1996). An excellent resource. Like most Catholic histories the tone becomes more critical once one reaches John Paul II.

Ker, Ian. *John Henry Newman: A Biography* (Oxford University Press, 1990). An outstanding biography.

Kipling, Rudyard. *Rudyard Kipling's Verse: The Definitive Edition* (Doubleday, 1940).

Kirk, Russell. *The Conservative Mind* (Regnery, 1995). The entire Kirk oeuvre—almost uniformly excellent—remains, unfortunately, locked in a ghetto of conservative cognoscenti. Kirk was a Catholic convert.

————. *The Roots of American Order* (Regnery Gateway, 1991). One of Kirk's best.

Kissinger, Henry. *A World Restored: Metternich, Castlereagh and the Problems of Peace, 1812–1822* (Orion, 2000).

Kousoulas, D. G. *The Life and Times of Constantine the Great: The First Christian Emperor* (Rutledge, 1997). A sprightly biography backed by terrific scholarship.

Kreeft, Peter. *Christianity for Modern Pagans: Pascal's Pensées Edited, Outlined and Explained* (Ignatius Press, 1993).

Kreeft, Peter, and Ronald K. Tacelli. *Handbook of Christian Apologetics* (InterVarsity Press, 1994). Thomistic logic applied to modern questions about Christianity. Not many people are up for the rigors of logic these days; but if you are, here are the logical proofs of basic Christian doctrines.

Kuehnelt-Leddihn, Erik von. *Leftism Revisited: From de Sade and Marx to Hitler and Pol Pot* (Regnery Gateway, 1990).

Lacey, Robert. *The Life and Times of Henry VIII* (Weidenfeld & Nicolson, 1996).

Leckie, Robert. *Delivered from Evil: The Saga of World War II* (Perennial Library, 1987). A monumental, captivating one-volume history of the Second World War.

Lewin, Ronald. *Slim: The Standardbearer* (Leo Cooper, 1990). Field Marshal the Viscount Slim, leader of Britain's "forgotten army" in Burma during the Second World War, was a lapsed Catholic, though, as the author says, "he was *anima naturaliter Christiana.*" This is a good biography of the man.

Lewis, C. S. *Mere Christianity* (Macmillan, 1960).

*The Little Flowers of St. Francis of Assisi* (Book-of-the-Month Club, 1996).

Livingstone, E. A. (editor). *The Concise Oxford Dictionary of the Christian Church* (Oxford University Press, 2000). Useful reference.

Locke, John. *The Reasonableness of Christianity* (edited and introduced by George W. Ewing). (Regnery Gateway, 1989).

Long, Jeff. *Duel of Eagles: The Mexican and U.S. Fight for the Alamo* (William Morrow and Company, 1990). Good on the cultural atmosphere surrounding the collision in Texas.

Longford, Elizabeth. *Wellington, Pillar of State* (Weidenfeld & Nicolson, 1972).

López de Gómara, (translated and edited by Lesley Byrd Simpson). *Cortés: The Life of the Conquereror by His Secretary* (University of California Press, 1964). López de Gómara was proud that the Spanish conquered the Aztecs "with little bloodshed" and converted them to Catholicism, convincing the Aztecs to give up polygamy, sodomy, human sacrifice, and cannibalism. He exposes himself, therefore, as a very judgmental and politically incorrect fellow.

Lowry, Charles W. *The First Theologians* (Gateway Editions, 1986).

Luck, Hans von (introduction by Stephen E. Ambrose). *Panzer Commander: The Memoirs of Colonel Hans von Luck.* (Dell Publishing, 1991). In a very interesting exchange between Hans von Luck and Field Marshal Erwin Rommel in late 1942, Rommel insists the war is lost and that the Germans must seek an armistice with the western powers. "This assumes, of course," Rommel says, "that Hitler must be forced to abdicate; that we must give up the persecution of the Jews at once and make concessions to the Church." Interesting that the Church is included here. Rommel concludes: "The threat to Europe and to our civilized world will come from the East. If the peoples of Europe fail to join forces to meet that threat, western Europe will have lost. . . . I see only one 'warrior' prepared to champion a united Europe: Churchill!"

Lukacs, John. *Five Days in London: May 1940* (Yale University Press, 1999).

———. *Confessions of an Original Sinner.* (St. Augustine's Press, 2000). Memoirs of the Catholic historian, a Hungarian native, whose experiences of Nazism and Communism affirmed for him the truth of Original Sin and the necessity of reactionary values. He quotes this passage from Karl Stern's *Pillar of Fire* with approval: "The Nazi years taught us a lesson. It happened not infrequently that you met a friend whom you had known for years as a 'staunch liberal,' and he turned out to be eager for any compromise to save his skin. On the other hand, we saw people whom we had disclaimed as 'reactionaries' go to concentration camps and to the gallows. In the beginning it seemed confusing. But gradually the issue became clearer and it was obvious that the only thing that counts in this world is the strength of moral conviction."

Lutzer, Erwin. *Seven Reasons You Can Trust the Bible* (Moody Press, 1998).

Macaulay, Lord Thomas Babington (edited and abridged by Hugh Trevor-Roper). *The History of England* (Penguin, 1986).

———. *The Lays of Ancient Rome* (Regnery, 1997). Schoolboys used to memorize this book. They ought to do it again.

MacGregor-Hastie, Roy. *Never to Be Taken Alive: A Biography of General Gordon* (Sidgwick & Jackson, 1985).

Machiavelli, Niccolò. *The Discourses* (Pelican Classics, 1981).

———. *The Prince* (Penguin, 1982).

MacMullen, Ramsay. *Constantine* (The Dial Press, 1964).

Maier, Paul. *In the Fullness of Time: An Historian Looks at Christmas, Easter, and the Early Church* (HarperCollins, 1991). The author, a professional historian and professed Protestant, affirms the Biblical account.

———. *Pontius Pilate* (Kregel, 1990). A novel based on the historical record.

Maistre, Joseph de (edited by Elisha Greifer, and translated with the assistance of Laurence M. Porter). *On God and Society* (Henry Regnery Company, Gateway Editions, 1959).

Manchester, William. *A World Lit Only by Fire: The Medieval Mind and the Renaissance* (Little, Brown & Company, 1993). Manchester has a journalist's nose for retelling good stories and not letting scholarly debates and revisionism stand in his way.

Marcus Aurelius (translated and introduced by Maxwell Staniforth). *Meditations* (Penguin, 1964).

Marks, Richard Lee. *Cortés: The Great Adventurer and the Fate of Aztec Mexico* (Knopf, 1993).

Mauriac, François. *Holy Thursday: An Intimate Remembrance* (Sophia Press, 1991).

McInerny, Ralph M. *A Student's Guide to Philosophy* (ISI Books, 1999). A good gift for any college student, it is a guide to philosophical sanity, which McInerny finds in the systems of Aristotle and Aquinas.

Merton, Thomas. *The Seven Storey Mountain* (Harcourt Brace Jovanovich, 1976). A beautifully written, classic memoir by a twentieth-century American who became a monk.

Metzger, Bruce M., and Michael D. Coogan (editors). *The Oxford Companion to the Bible* (Oxford University Press, 1993).

Mitchell, Margaret. *Gone with the Wind* (Macmillan, Anniversary Edition, 1975). Not a Harlequin romance, but a real classic of literature, featuring the Catholic O'Haras.

Mitford, Nancy. *Frederick the Great* (E. P. Dutton, 1984).

Morison, Samuel Eliot. *The Oxford History of the American People* (Mentor, published in three volumes, 1972).

Muggeridge, Malcolm. *Jesus Rediscovered* (Doubleday-Galilee Book, 1969). A journalist roué rediscovers Christ. Long after this book was published, Muggeridge joined the Catholic Church.

Muggeridge, Malcolm, and Alec Vidler. *Paul: Envoy Extraordinary* (Harper & Row, 1972). A charming book, recreating Paul's travels in conjunction with a BBC film.

Murphy, G. Ronald, S.J. (translator and commentator). *The Heliand: The Saxon Gospel* (Oxford University Press, 1992). Christianity meets Beowulf.

Nash, George H. *The Conservative Intellectual Movement in America: Since 1945* (Basic Books, 1979). Nash notes that "One of the most remarkable features of this movement was that, in a country still substantially Protestant, its leadership was heavily Roman Catholic, Anglo-Catholic, or critical of Protestant Christianity."

Newman, John Henry Cardinal (edited by David J. DeLaura). *Apologia Pro Vita Sua* (Norton Critical Editions, 1968). This classic, densely argued autobiography of Newman's religious life will be hard going for many modern readers, but the lasting imprint on the mind is unshakable.

————. *An Essay on the Development of Christine Doctrine* (University of Notre Dame Press, 1989). A work of stunning intellectual power.

————. *The Idea of a University* (Gateway Editions, 1999).

Oman, Sir Charles. *Seven Roman Statesmen of the Later Republic* (Edward Arnold & Company, 1934).

Orwell, George. *Homage to Catalonia* (Harvest/HBJ, 1980).

————. *The Penguin Essays of George Orwell* (Penguin, 1984). Orwell often conflated—in the context of the politics of the 1930s—Catholicism and Communism as dual dictatorships, giving people something to believe in. In this, Orwell exhibited a John Bull tic of the liberal-minded Englishman. In his essay "Inside the Whale," he notes: "There had been a sort of false dawn a few years earlier when numbers of young intellectuals, including several quite gifted writers (Evelyn Waugh, Christopher Hollis and others), had fled into the Catholic Church. It is significant that these people went almost invariably to the Roman Church and not, for instance, to the C. of E., the Greek Church or the Protestant sects. They went, that is, to the Church with a world-wide organization, the one with rigid discipline, the one with power and prestige behind it." In a later essay, "The Prevention of Literature," he argues that, like Nazism and Communism, "Orthodox Catholicism, again, seems to have a crushing effect on certain literary forms, especially the novel"—which is surely one of the most ridiculous things Orwell ever wrote (and I speak as an Orwell admirer).

*Oxford Encyclopedia of World History* (Oxford University Press, 1998).

*Oxford Family Encyclopedia* (Oxford University Press, 1997).

Palanque, J. R., et al. *The Church in the Christian Roman Empire* (Macmillan, 1953).

Pearce, Joseph. *Literary Converts: Spiritual Inspiration in an Age of Unbelief* (Ignatius Press, 2000).

Peddie, John. *The Roman War Machine* (Grange Books, 1997).

Pelikan, Jaroslav. *Mary Through the Centuries: Her Place in the History of Culture* (Yale University Press, 1996).

Phillips, Kevin. *Post-Conservative America* (Random House, 1982).

*The Poem of the Cid* (translated by Rita Hamilton and Janet Perry, with an introduction and notes by Ian Michael). (Penguin, 1984).

Porch, Douglas. *The French Foreign Legion: A Complete History of the Legendary Fighting Force* (HarperCollins, 1991).

Power, Eileen. *Medieval People* (The Folio Society, 2000).

Preston, Paul. *Franco* (Basic Books, 1994). A hostile biography of the dictator who rescued the Church and defeated the Communists in Spain.

Procopius (translated by G. A. Williamson). *The Secret History* (The Folio Society, 1990).

Prümmer, Dominic M., O.P. *Handbook of Moral Theology* (Roman Catholic Books, 1957). This was the pre-Vatican II guide for priests to counsel their flocks.

Przywara, Erich, S.J. (editor). *The Heart of Newman* (Ignatius Press, 1997). Snippets from Newman, arranged by theme.

Ratzinger, Joseph Cardinal. *Introduction to Christianity* (Ignatius Press, 1990). Ratzinger has one of the subtlest, best-informed, and most articulate minds in the Church.

————. *The Ratzinger Report: An Exclusive Interview on the State of the Church* (Ignatius Press, 1985).

————. *Salt of the Earth: The Church at the End of the Millennium, An Interview with Peter Seewald* (Ignatius Press, 1997). Of Ratzinger's books, this one is especially recommended for its mixture of easy reading and profundity.

Regan, Geoffrey. *The Guinness Book of Decisive Battles* (Guinness Publishing, 1992).

Riccards, Michael P. *A Republic, If You Can Keep It: The Foundation of the American Presidency, 1700–1800* (Greenwood Press, 1987).

Richter, Melvin. *The Political Theory of Montesquieu* (Cambridge University Press, 1977). The best collection of Montesquieu's political writings.

Roberts, J. M. *The Pelican History of the World* (Penguin, 1985).

————. *The Triumph of the West: The Origins, Rise, and Legacy of Western Civilization* (Little, Brown & Company, 1985). A good account of how the West spread ideals of self-determination that helped, ironically, to undermine its paramountcy.

Röpke, Wilhelm. *A Humane Economy* (ISI Books, 1998).

————. *The Moral Foundations of Civil Society* (Transaction Publishers, 1996). Röpke was one of those great thinkers who was not a Catholic but should have been, as witness this excerpt: "This is not the place to value the immeasurable contribution of the Church as an institution which, during the darkest days of the Middle Ages, kept the spark of culture burning under the ashes and by so doing laid the foundation for everything else, a mission without which Europe would have become a mere peninsular of Asia."

Rosenblum, Mort. *Mission to Civilize: The French Way.* (Harcourt Brace Jovanovich, 1986).

Rousseau, Jean Jacques (translated and with an introduction by Willmoore Kendall). *The Social Contract* (Gateway Editions, 1982).

Routh, C.R.N. *Who's Who in Tudor England* (Shepheard-Walwyn, 1990).

Royal, Robert. *The Catholic Martyrs of the Twentieth Century* (Crossroad, 2000). A necessary book that covers a missing chapter in most histories.

Runciman, Steven. *A History of the Crusades* (The Folio Society, published in three volumes, 1994).

Russell, Bertrand. *A History of Western Philosophy* (Simon & Schuster, 1972). A pellucid and rather amusing guide to philosophy, by a religious skeptic.

Rychlak, Ronald J. *Hitler, the War, and the Pope* (Our Sunday Visitor Books, 2000).

Sanders, E. P. *The Historical Figure of Jesus* (Allen Lane, 1993).

————. *Paul* (Oxford University Press, 1991). Part of Oxford's "Past Masters" series, maintaining its usual high standard.

Schama, Simon. *A History of England: At the Edge of the World? 3500 B.C.–1603 A.D.* (Talk Miramax Books, 2000). Vibrant history.

Schmemann, Alexander. *The Historical Road of Eastern Orthodoxy* (Henry Regnery Company, 1966). A much more sympathetic account of the Eastern churches than is found in this book.

Schom, Alan. *Napoleon Bonaparte* (HarperCollins, 1997).

Schreck, Alan. *Basics of the Faith: A Catholic Catechism* (Servant, 1987).

———. *Catholic and Christian: An Explanation of Commonly Misunderstood Catholic Beliefs* (Servant, 1984).

———. *A Compact History of the Catholic Church* (Servant, 1987). The best of the pocket histories.

Schweitzer, Albert. *The Quest of the Historical Jesus: A Critical Study of Its Progress from Reimarus to Wrede* (Johns Hopkins University Press, 1998). Schweitzer was a great man and this is still one of the most important studies of its kind. His conclusions tried hard to avoid despair but really meant the death-knell for mainline Protestantism—of rational religion divorced from the sacraments. "There is nothing more negative than the result of the critical study of the Life of Jesus," wrote Schweitzer. ". . . The study of the Life of Jesus has had a curious history. It set out in a quest of the historical Jesus, believing that when it found Him, it could bring Him straight into our time as Teacher and Saviour. It loosed the bands by which He had been riveted for centuries to the stony rocks of ecclesiastical doctrine, and rejoiced to see life and movement coming into the figure once more, and the historical Jesus advancing, as it seemed, to meet it. But He does not stay; He passes by our time and returns to His own."

Seward, Desmond. *The Monks of War: The Military Religious Orders* (Penguin, 1972). The most important book of its kind. The Folio Society issued a handsome, revised edition in 2000.

Shakespeare, William (edited by David Bedington). *The Complete Works of Shakespeare* (third edition) (Scott, Foresman and Company, 1980).

Shea, Mark. *By What Authority? An Evangelical Discovers Catholic Tradition* (Our Sunday Visitor, 1996).

———. *Making Senses Out of Scripture* (Basilica Press, 1999).

Sheler, Jeffrey L. *Is the Bible True? How Modern Debates and Discoveries Affirm the Essence of the Scriptures* (HarperSanFrancisco/Zondervan, 1999).

Shulvass, Moses A. *The History of the Jewish People*, Volume One: *The Antiquity* (Regnery Gateway, 1982). A wonderfully terse, straightforward account.

Simpson, Howard. *The Paratroopers of the French Foreign Legion: From Vietnam to Bosnia.* (Brassey's, 1997). Here one finds the story of a chaplain in Bosnia, giving out medallions of the Blessed Virgin Mother, while admonishing his legionnaires that the medallion "does not replace good cover and it does not replace armor. I don't do voodoo here. So be careful"—spoken like a true Catholic realist.

Sobel, Dava. *Galileo's Daughter: A Historical Memoir of Science, Faith, and Love* (Walker & Company, 1999).

Steinhoff, Johannes, Peter Pechel, and Dennis Showalter. *Voices from the Third Reich: An Oral History* (Regnery Gateway, 1989). A very interesting book, with first person testimonies from Manfred Rommel and Helmut Kohl, among others.

Stokesbury, James L. *A Short History of the American Revolution* (William Morrow and Company, 1991).

Stott, John R.W. *Basic Christianity* (InterVarsity Press, 1971). A minor masterpiece by an Anglican clergyman.

Strachey, Lytton. *Eminent Victorians* (Harvest/HBJ, no date).

Suetonius, Gaius Tranquillus (translated by Robert Graves). *The Twelve Caesars* (The Folio Society, 1994).

Tate, Allen. *Jefferson Davis: His Rise and Fall* (J. S. Sanders & Company, 1998). Helps explain why so many Southern Catholics still whistle "Dixie."

Thomas, Hugh. *Conquest: Montezuma, Cortés, and the Fall of Old Mexico* (Simon & Schuster, 1993).

———. *The Spanish Civil War* (Simon & Schuster, 1986).

Thompson, Bard. *Humanists and Reformers: A History of the Renaissance and Reformation* (Eerdmans, 1996). A well-illustrated and thorough one-volume treatment.

Thompson, Neville. *Wellington After Waterloo* (Routledge & Kegan Paul, 1986).

Thornton, Francis Beauchesne. *Return to Tradition* (Roman Catholic Books, no date, originally published 1948). An anthology of the nineteenth- and twentieth-century Catholic literary revival, featuring English, Irish, French (in translation), and American authors.

Throckmorton, Burton H., Jr. (editor). *Gospel Parallels: A Synopsis of the First Three Gospels* (Thomas Nelson, fourth revised edition, 1979). An invaluable reference for checking the Gospel accounts side-by-side-by-side.

Tocqueville, Alexis de (translated by George Lawrence, edited by J. P. Mayer). *Democracy in America* (Doubleday/Anchor, 1969). A book that is ever enlightening.

———. *The Old Regime and the French Revolution* (Doubleday/Anchor, 1955). Especially good on the nature of revolution.

Tonsor, Stephen (editor). *Reflections on the French Revolution: A Hillsdale Symposium* (Regnery Gateway, 1990).

Twain, Mark. *Joan of Arc* (Ignatius Press, 1989).

Tyerman, Christopher. *Who's Who in Early Medieval England* (Shepheard-Walwyn, 1996).

Vos, Howard F. *Highlights of Church History* (Moody Press, 1960). This brief history is less interesting than the story of how it fell into my hands. It was given me by a church-going Catholic, who received it from a Catholic monk, and the book is inscribed by "Richard C. Halverson, U.S. Senate Chaplain." The last chapter, "The Present Situation," details the four great threats that evangelical Christianity must fight: Communism; nationalism with its pagan religion; cults; and Catholicism. With regard to the last, the author warns: "In city after city of the United States it [the Catholic Church] has been successful in filling public offices with its candidates. . . . In Holland, a traditionally Calvinistic country, the balance has been slowly swinging to the Catholics. . . . In Germany . . . the balance of power has swung to the Catholics." And so forth.

Warner, Rex (translator). *The War Commentaries of Caesar* (Meridian Classic, 1987).

Watson, G. R. *The Roman Soldier* (Cornell University Press, 1969).

Waugh, Evelyn. *Edmund Campion* (Little, Brown & Company, 1952).

———. *Helena* (Penguin, 1984).

———. *Robbery Under Law: The Mexican Object Lesson* (A Common Reader Edition, The Akadine Press, 1999). The Akadine Press deserves huzzahs for bringing this volume back into print.

———. *The Sword of Honour Trilogy, Men at Arms* (Penguin, 1984).

Weaver, Richard. *Ideas Have Consequences* (University of Chicago Press, 1984).

Weigel, George. *Witness to Hope: The Biography of Pope John Paul II* (HarperCollins, 1999). A magisterial biography.

Wheatcroft, Andrew. *The Habsburgs: Embodying Empire* (Viking, 1995).

Wills, Garry. *Papal Sin: Structures of Deceit* (Doubleday, 2000). Should have been titled, *What Embarrasses Me About Catholicism When I'm in the Faculty Lounge at Northwestern*.

Wilson, Ian. *The Bible Is History* (Regnery, 1999). Wilson is a self-described "liberal-minded convert to Roman Catholicism." He is also one of the leading students of the Shroud of Turin.

———. *Jesus: The Evidence* (Regnery, 2000). A quick and interesting read, lavishly illustrated.

———. *Shakespeare the Evidence* (Headline, 1994).

Wiltgen, Ralph M. *The Rhine Flows into the Tiber* (TAN Books, 1967).

Wolfe, Tom. *The Purple Decades* (Farrar Straus Giroux, 1982). An insightful portrait of recent American culture.

# INDEX

## PRAYER TO ST. MICHAEL THE ARCHANGEL

St. Michael the Archangel, defend us in Battle; Be our protection against the wickedness and snares of the Devil. May God rebuke Him, we humbly pray, and do Thou, O Prince of the Heavenly Host, by the power of God, thrust into Hell, Satan and all the other evil spirits, who prowl through the world, seeking the ruin of souls. Amen.